Business & Economics / Reference

THE ENCYCLOPEDIC DICTIONARY OF

ECONOMICS

FOURTH EDITION

THE
ENCYCLOPEDIC
DICTIONARY
OF
ECONOMICS
FOURTH EDITION

Don Cole, *Drew University,* served as Editorial Adviser for the *Encyclopedic Dictionary of Economics, Fourth Edition.* He reviewed entries for currentness and accuracy, provided updated information where it was necessary, and wrote new or revised entries for this edition.

The Dushkin Publishing Group, Inc.

Credits and Acknowledgments

Cover design; Meredith Scheld, DPG; p. 14 Talbot Lovering; p. 23 Chrysler Corporation; p. 29 Library of Congress; p. 35 DPG; p. 37 Frank Tarsitano—DPG; p. 54 Frank Tarsitano—DPG; p. 67 General Electric Company; p. 79 UN; p. 99 John Kenneth Galbraith; p. 102 Novosti Photo; p. 108 Pamela Carley Petersen; p. 150 Library of Congress; p. 155 Courtesy TVA Washington Office and Tom Sweeten; p. 157 Federal Reserve Bank of Boston; p. 161 U.S. Bureau of Printing and Engraving; p. 191 UN; p. 197 Cheryl Kinne; p. 203 U.S. Small Business Administration; p. 214 J.R. Eyerman; p. 219 Paul A. Samuelson; p. 228 National Cattlemen's Association; The Chase Manhattan Money Museum, photo by Larry Link; p. 234 New York Stock Exchange; p. 237 Bay Area Rapid Transit; p. 239 EPA Documerica; p. 245 General Motors; p. 246 IBM Corporation; p. 251 UN; Pamela Carley Petersen; p. 254 UN; p. 256 UAW Public Relations

Library of Congress Catalog Card Number: 90-81960

Manufactured in the United States of America

Fourth Edition, First Printing

ISBN: 0-87967-884-4

Preface

In order to understand a discipline—its development, accomplishments, contributions and problems, one must have an understanding of the language of that discipline. The social sciences in general, and economics in particular, use language with specific meaning to the practitioners of that discipline. The publication of this revised and updated edition of the *Encyclopedic Dictionary of Economics* is an undertaking designed to provide easy access to a substantial representation of the language, institutions, and practices unique to the study of economics.

AUTHORITY

Each of the more than 1400 entries and articles in the *Encyclopedic Dictionary of Economics* was prepared by an authority working in his or her area of specialization. The longer articles bear the signature of the author. The shorter, unsigned entries were prepared by the same authorities who authored the longer articles.

This revised edition is the result of the efforts of a large number of experts over a long period of time. In some instances we have retained articles that were prepared by contributors to previous editions. These entries have been reviewed for accuracy and currentness by our Senior Adviser for this volume, who also had the role of coordinator and reviewer. Susan Hunt, *University of Pennsylvania*, wrote new articles and made revisions to others in this updated edition of the *Encyclopedic Dictionary of Economics*. Our other advisers and contributors were: Khamis Abdul-Magid, Robert B. Archibald, Peter Asch, Frank J. Bonello, George E. Brandow, Robert L. Brite, Thomas O. Depperschmidt, Martin T. Farris, T. Aldrich Finegan, John P. Formby, Irving Goffman, Josef Hadar, Walter W. Haines, Clyde A. Haulman, Joseph M. Jadlow, Algin B. King, Allan B. Mandelstamm, John R. Matthews, Jr., Anne Mayhew, Charles W. Meyer, Carlisle E. Moody, Jr., Clarence C. Morrison, Walter C. Neale, Lawrence H. Officer, Francis W. Rushing, Leonard G. Schifrin, and Charles Staelin.

Preparing an encyclopedic dictionary of this nature presents a problem of what to leave out as much as what to include. Difficult decisions had to be made, especially in the areas of biographies. The advisers were involved in a process of assembling an enormous body of information, while at the same time, paring it down to the essentials. We have sought to create a reference tool of greatest use to the nonprofessional reader, and this goal guided our decisions concerning presentation of the information. Readers who find that there is no entry for their favorite economist can be sure that the omission was the result of careful consideration of the available space. Many of our contributors and advisers have made important contributions to the professional literature, but for this volume, they were asked to approach the material from the viewpoint of the needs of the nonprofessional.

It is not within the scope of a reference tool such as this to provide exhaustive information on particular subject matter. Rather, the goal of the *Encyclopedic Dictionary of Economics* is to answer specific questions quickly and easily and to demonstrate the nature of the interrelationships among the elements of economics in America. For maximum utility, the short-entry, alphabetical form was adopted. Where it is appropriate, simple definitions have been provided for specific terms, with cross-references for background information and further in-depth discussion. The major products and processes of economics, including allocation of resources, market operation, business cycles, and other areas, are given comprehensive treatment in lengthier articles. Several unique features have been provided to make these major subject areas easily accessible.

ORGANIZATION

This encyclopedic dictionary was constructed topically to ensure complete coverage and then arranged alphabetically for ease of access. This organization has allowed us to include a number of guidance features as an integral part of the volume.

Cross-References are of three kinds. *See* references, which appear as individual entries in the alphabetical sequence, take the place of an additional index and send you directly to the location of the information you want. *See also* references at the end of an article direct you to supplementary information. Some entries contain a "defining cross-reference" which gives you a simple definition and refers you to another article for more complete information.

Illustrations are used functionally in the encyclopedic dictionary. Maps, diagrams, organization charts, tables, and photographs are included as integral parts of the articles in which they appear.

Topic Guides point out specific relationships between individual articles in the book and lead in a meaningful sequence from one article to another. The pages on which these topic guides appear are listed on page XI.

Subject Maps show the detailed interrelationships among the various components of a particular major subject area. They demonstrate in graphic form the subareas that can be studied for further information. The pages on which these subject maps appear are listed on page XII.

Subject Directories follow this introduction. For selected major subject areas, we have provided an alphabetical directory of the articles pertaining to that subject. These areas are:

Biographical Entries
Topic Guides
Subject Maps

GUIDELINES FOR USING THIS ENCYCLOPEDIC DICTIONARY

The structure of this encyclopedic dictionary is designed to provide the information and background necessary to understand the institutions, people, decisions, trends, and movements that have defined economics. With this in mind, many narrow or specific entries have been treated under the broader headings of which they are a part. If an individual or event does not have an entry, that subject may be discussed in one of the many major articles contained in this encyclopedic dictionary.

We believe that this encyclopedic dictionary is a unique and indispensable resource for the study of economics. It will be updated and revised as necessary so that it will remain a source of current information. We welcome suggestions or comments that will assist us in continuing to make this encyclopedic dictionary as valuable as possible.

Biographies

Below are listed the biographies that appear in the encyclopedic dictionary.

Baumol, William Jack, 13
Becker, Gary, 13
Böhm-Bawerk, Eugen, 15
Boulding, Kenneth Ewart, 16
Burns, Arthur Frank, 18
Chenery, Hollis Burnley, 28
Commons, John, 35
Debs, Eugene Victor, 52
Fisher, Irving, 94
Fourier, François Marie, 95
Friedman, Milton, 96
Galbraith, John Kenneth, 99
Gompers, Samuel, 101
Hansen, Alvin Harvey, 105
Hayek, Friedrich Von, 105
Hicks, John R., 106
Jevons, William Stanley, 124
Keynes, John Maynard, 125
Kindleberger, Charles, 125
Kirkland, Lane, 125
Klein, Lawrence, 125
Koopmans, Tjalling, 126
Kuznets, Simon, 126
Lenin, Vladimir Ilich, 135

Leontiff, Wassily, 135
Lewis, John Llewellyn, 136
Machlup, Fritz, 139
Malthus, Thomas, 140
Mao Zedong, 141
Marshall, Alfred, 149
Marx, Karl, 150
Meany, George, 151
Menger, Carl, 152
Mill, John Stuart, 154
Mises, Ludwig Von, 155
Modiglianni, Franco, 156
Myrdal, Gunnar, 167
Okun, Arthur Melvin, 178
Owen, Robert, 181
Pareto, Vilfredo, 181
Pigou, Arthur Cecil, 187
Quesnay, François, 209
Reuther, Walter, 217
Ricardo, David, 217
Robinson, Joan, 218
Sahlins, Marshall, 218
Samuelson, Paul, 219

Schultz, Theodore, 221
Schumacher, Ernst Friedrich, 221
Schumpeter, Joseph, 221
Shultz, George, 224
Smith, Adam, 225
Sombart, Werner, 228
Sorel, George, 228
Stalin, Joseph, 232
Stigler, George, 233
Taussig, Frank, 241
Tinbergen, Jan, 250
Tobin, James, 250
Triffin, Robert, 252
Veblen, Thorstein, 262
Walras, Leon, 266
Webb, Sidney and Potter, Beatrice, 267
Weber, Max, 267
Wicksell, Knut, 268
Wicksteed, Phillip, 269
Wieser, Friedrich Von, 269
Woodcock, Leonard, 269

Topic Guides

The following topic guides are contained in the encyclopedic dictionary.

Allocation, 3
Balance of Payments, 9
Choice, 29
Cost Function, 47
Demand, 53
Equilibrium, 71
Equilibrium of the Firm, 72
Human Resources, 107
Incomes Policy, 110
Inflation, 113
Interest Rates, 117
Investment, 122

Labor Force, 127
Law of Supply and Demand, 134
Long Run, 137
Marginal Analysis, 141
Market Structure, 147
Model, Econometric, 155
Money, 160
Monopoly, 163
Multiplier, 166
National Income Measurement, 173

Oligopoly, 178
Opportunity Cost, 180
Perfect Competition, 184
Phillips Curve, 186
Poverty, 190
Profits, 201
Public Utilities, 206
Saving, 220
Scarcity, 221
Taxation, 242
Unemployment of Labor, 256

Subject Maps

Below are listed the subject maps that appear in the encyclopedic dictionary.

Antitrust Policy, 5
Banking System, 11-12
Business Cycles, 19
Capital, 23
Circular Flow, 30
Demand Theory, 56
Economic Systems, 65
Factor Markets, 82

International Trade, 120
International Trade Theory,
  120-21
Labor Market, 128
Labor Movement, 130
Market System, 148-49
Money and Monetary Policy,
  159

National Income, 169-70
Price Level, 194
Public Finance, 205
Regulation, 212
Supply and Costs of
  Production, 238
Theory of the Firm, 248-49
Wages, 264

A & P CASE. *See* United States v. New York Great A & P Company.

ABILITY TO PAY, a wage criterion that is an important consideration in union-labor negotiations: namely that justified increases in wages can be granted only if the management is in a position to be able to pay the higher wage rate. However, determination of whether management is able to pay is frequently a very controversial issue. It often involves undesirable exposure of company operations to unions, and often leaves unions in unfair bargaining positions.

See also Wage Criteria.

ABILITY-TO-PAY PRINCIPLE, a criterion for "fair" taxation that states that taxes should be based on a taxing unit's ability to pay the tax. This criterion divorces the incidence of the taxes paid from the incidence of the expenditures made by the government as a result of the taxes collected. The most common ability-to-pay base is income, implying that a "fair" tax should rise as income rises. An important issue that this principle does not answer is how fast tax burdens should rise as income increases.

See also Benefit Principle; Progressive Tax; Proportional Tax; Regressive Tax; Taxation.

ABSOLUTE ADVANTAGE. Adam Smith said trade between nations would increase real wealth via the division of labor. He assumed an absolute advantage necessary, in that an exporting industry must be able to produce, with given inputs, a larger output than any rival. Assume that two countries use the same composite input mix of land, labor, and capital with the result that country A produces twice as much of two commodities as country B. Country A has an absolute advantage with respect to both commodities; therefore, B cannot produce for export trade. Smith's analysis could not deal with the situation of B; this awaited the formulation by David Ricardo in terms of comparative advantage.

See also Comparative Advantage; International Trade Theory.

ABSOLUTE COST ADVANTAGE, the ability of a firm in an industry to produce an item at a lower cost than another firm in that same industry. When a firm has an absolute cost advantage, it can sell its product at a lower price than other firms in the industry, thus gathering a greater share of the market and possibly forcing out other firms. As a second alternative, it can sell its product at the same price as other firms but receive a larger profit, because its costs are lower.

ABUSE THEORY OF MERGERS, thesis, first developed in the United States Steel decision (1920), that one firm's domination of an industry, however obtained, did not violate the antimonopoly provisions of the Sherman Act unless specific abuses of power were proven. Allowing "intent" to be disregarded and ignoring the market influence which can result from mere possession of power, this interpretation severely limited antitrust enforcement until countermanded by the 1945 Alcoa case findings.

See also Antitrust Policy; Sherman Antitrust Act; United States v. Aluminum Company of America; United States v. U.S. Steel Corporation.

ACCELERATOR, the humped pattern of induced investment that causes larger variations in investment demand than the causal variations in demand. A firm or industry operating at or slightly below capacity will have a fairly constant investment demand for replacing worn-out capital goods and sold-out inventories. If demand rises above capacity or previous level of sales, there would be an induced demand for capital (or inventory) goods in order to increase capacity. But once this new capacity is installed, investment demand will fall to replacement level again.

When the capital goods have a longish life (several years), the fall will first be to the original replacement level of demand, followed later by a rise to a higher level of replacement demand as the new equipment wears out. When the increased investment is in inventory to service a higher level of wholesale or retail trade, the first hump of inventory investment will be followed immediately by the new, higher replacement demand. The importance of the accelerator is that it introduces into the level of investment an instability, which magnifies the changes in the demand for the products from which the investment demand derives.

ACCELERATOR THEORY OF BUSINESS CYCLES (Accelerator Principle) was first introduced in 1917 by John M. Clark to explain the larger variations in investment than in product output that occur during a business cycle. This principle states that small changes in demand induce disproportionately large changes in the amount of investment needed to meet that demand. In 1936, this principle was combined with Keynes' theory of consumption to generate a model of a business cycle.

The accelerator principle is used to assay future growth when the economy is close to full employment, but it erroneously assumes that gross investment can fall below zero and that industry is already operating at full capacity.

See also Business Cycles, Theories; Consumption Function.

ACCOUNTING PROFITS, profits that are equal to the difference between a firm's total revenue from sales and its total explicit costs. These explicit costs do not include the opportunity cost of capital but include all other costs of production, including such items as depreciation.

ACREAGE LIMITATIONS. *See* Crop Restrictions.

ACREAGE RESERVE. *See* Soil Bank.

ACT FOR INTERNATIONAL DEVELOPMENT OF 1950. *See* Point Four Program.

ACTUAL INVESTMENT, or REALIZED INVESTMENT. The amount of spending on currently produced capital goods that occurs during a year is equal to planned investment only when planned investment equals planned savings. When planned savings exceeds planned investment, actual investment is likely to be greater than planned investment because inventories will accumulate when households do not buy as much as expected, but actual investment could be less than planned investment, if induced investment falls more rapidly than inventories accumulate. When planned investment exceeds planned savings, actual investment is likely to fall short of planned investment, because households will buy more than expected and reduce inventories, but actual investment could be more than planned investment, if the higher incomes produce more investment than originally planned. The unexpected accumulation or reduction of inventories is called *unintended*, or involuntary, investment, or disinvestment.

    See also Disinvestment; Investment Schedule; Marginal Efficiency of Capital.

ACTUAL RESERVES. *See* Multiple Expansion of the Money Supply.

ADMINISTERED PRICES are the result of a type of pricing policy that is found mainly in oligopolistic industries. An administered price is a predetermined price that is derived after accounting for all costs of the industry and deciding upon a desired amount of profit. Administered prices must also take into consideration approximately how many items will be sold at the predetermined price. When an administered price has been selected, all items in the industry must adopt this price in order for it to be effective. It is for this reason that administered prices cannot be effective in purely competitive or monopolistically competitive markets.

    Because there are only a few firms in a given industry, oligopolistic market structures are able to carry out administered pricing policies effectively by the use of collusions or tacit agreements.

ADMINISTERED PRICING, a theory that there are some firms in the United States economy that are so large that they have much more discretion in setting prices than the competitive model indicates. One version of this theory states that some firms are afraid of increased government regulation, so they are very careful to increase prices only when they have an "excuse," such as an increase in taxes or in labor costs.

The theory states that when they increase their prices in the face of a tax increase, they increase prices by more than the tax increase so that their profits increase.

    In addition, the theory states that when demand drops in recession, these firms may hold prices relatively constant and adjust their output, employment, and inventories. When this pattern is combined with a willingness to raise prices in expansionary periods, the result is a ratchet effect, with prices rising during expansion but failing to decline in contractions. The result could be a creeping inflation that persists in recessions.

    See also Inflation.

AFFIRMATIVE ACTION. The Office of Federal Contract-Compliance Programs (OFCCP) requires that all federal contractors make a positive effort to bring the numbers of women and minorities employed up to the level of their availability in the labor force. Problems in enforcement and compliance have been encountered at every turn, but the most serious seem to involve the mechanics of the program and the possibility of reverse discrimination. There appear to be conflicts between Title VII of the Civil Rights Act and the OFCCP standards of affirmative action.

AFFLUENT SOCIETY, THE (1958) attacks what author John Kenneth Galbraith called the "conventional wisdoms" of production. Galbraith suggests that economics traditionally has been concerned with productivity, insecurity, and inequality. However, in American society (the affluent society) the emphasis has switched to productivity because insecurity could be cured if production were large enough, and inequality can be eliminated only when the rich have satisfied their demands and have enough left over for the poor.

    Galbraith feels that the key to America's economic problems is the emphasis upon private production which results from our society's belief that only the private sector produces wealth. This view, combined with a distaste for taxation, leads to a rejection of governmental expenditures. Galbraith, feeling that public-sector expenditures are many times the only means of correcting the problems of society, advocates increasing governmental participation in the economy.   —*Clyde A. Haulman*

    See also Galbraith, John Kenneth.

AGENCY SHOP exists when workers in a bargaining unit are not required to join the union that represents them but must make a payment to the union equal to the dues. This protects the workers' freedom to choose whether to join the union or not but does not permit "free riders" to benefit from union representation without helping to support it. Agency shops are particularly important to the unions in states with "right-to-work" laws, which outlaw compulsory union memberships.

AGGREGATE DEMAND. *See* National Income Determination.

AGGREGATE OF INCOME. *See* National Income.

AGGREGATE MEASURES OF ECONOMIC ACTIVITY. *See* National Income Measurement.

AGGREGATE SUPPLY-AGGREGATE DEMAND EQUALITY. *See* National Income Determination.

AGGREGATE SUPPLY CURVE. *See* 45° Line.

AGRARIAN ECONOMY. *See* Traditional Economy.

AGRICULTURAL ACTS OF 1965, 1970. *See* Price-Support Programs.

AID TO FAMILIES WITH DEPENDENT CHILDREN (AFDC), a large federally-subsidized public assistance program. The program provides direct cash grants and supporting services to families with dependent minor children present. Single parent, female-headed households constitute the majority of recipients.

AFDC is provided under an open-ended, matching grant formula that requires wealthier states to provide a relatively larger share of the aid dollars distributed. In spite of an aid formula that favors poorer states, recipients still tend to receive lower income assistance amounts in poorer states.

Other major issues surrounding the AFDC program have included the status of the working poor in terms of eligibility, the impact of the program on the integrity of the family unit, and the effect of AFDC on work effort.

The Family Support Act of 1988 treats welfare mothers as unemployed and in need of a job, or the education and training to get one. This reflects a new perception that mothers as well as fathers have bread-winning responsibility. The bill also contains new provisions for enforcing child-support orders for absent fathers by payroll withholding.

See also Negative Income Tax; Public Assistance; Social Insurance.

ALCOA CASE. *See* United States v. Aluminum Company of America.

ALLOCATION, decision as to what is to be produced in the economy and who is to receive what is produced. Because of the scarcity of resources used in production, these resources and the products they create have to be allocated efficiently and profitably.

Allocation of natural resources in a capitalistic econ-

ALLOCATION: TOPIC GUIDE

A definition of allocation in its economic usage is found in the adjacent article. For a consideration of the pervasive nature of the allocation question, see ECONOMIC SYSTEMS. The allocation process in our economy is explained in detail in MARKET SYSTEM. For a somewhat more specific analysis of how a market economy answers the three component questions—the production, technological, and distributional questions—of the larger allocation question, see the articles on FACTOR MARKETS and PRODUCTION. For the methods and criteria of evaluation of how well the allocation process is accomplished, see EFFICIENT RESOURCE ALLOCATION.

The student will also find it useful to consult the Subject Map accompanying the article MARKET SYSTEM for clarification of other relationships of the allocation process to the economy.

---

omy is usually done through the price system. Those products in the greatest demand and with the highest prices have priority in the allocation of resources. Allocation of the four factors of production is done in very much the same way as allocation of natural resources. Land, labor, capital, and entrepreneurship are usually channeled into the most profitable production areas. The price of labor is wages, for example, and wages are usually higher in high-demand areas.

In the allocation of resources price is the determining factor. Allocation is determined by who is willing to pay for the products and how much each person is willing to pay. Therefore, in a capitalistic economy, it can be said that the price system acts as the main allocator of both the inputs and the outputs of production.

—*Robert L. Brite*

ALTERNATIVE COST. *See* Opportunity Cost.

ALTERNATIVE INDICATORS are more realistic measures of economic progress than the traditional Gross National Product (GNP). GNP tells only how much a nation is producing, not whether it is using up nonrenewable resources, fouling the air, or increasing the risk of cancer in the process. GNP takes depreciation of capital equipment into account, but not soil exhaustion. From 1971 to 1983, for example, Indonesia's GNP grew at a rate of 7% per year. But it was selling irreplaceable mineral wealth, and soil depletion canceled out increased farm yields, so when alternative indicators were taken into account, sustainable growth was about half the GNP figure. More pollution can actually boost the GNP, since money spent cleaning up oil spills and installing scrubbers appears as growth on the national income accounts. For nations as well as individuals, growth can be just excess weight.

AMERICAN AGRICULTURAL MARKETING AS-SOCIATION. *See* Farm Bureau Federation, American.

AMERICAN CAPITALISM: THE CONCEPT OF COUNTERVAILING POWER (1956) by John Kenneth Galbraith, develops his theory of countervailing power that states: (1) the force which compels oligopolistic industries to meet consumer wants and maintain prices close to cost is not the traditional inter-firm competition that economic theory indicates, but powerful buyers exercising countervailing power and (2) this power on the buyers' side emerges systematically in response to power on the sellers' side.

Economists reacted strongly to this concept. The historical record was examined, and the prediction of strong unions and retail chains rising sooner in industries with powerful firms was not supported. Also, even if strong buyers can obtain price reductions, there is no guarantee that these will be passed along to consumers.

See also Countervailing Power; Galbraith, John Kenneth.

AMERICAN FEDERATION OF LABOR (AFL), labor organization conceived and established in 1886. It represented the skilled trades, whose members did not want to be associated with the Knights of Labor. The union was organized by Samuel Gompers and under his leadership reached a position of national prominence.

In 1955, the union combined with the Congress of Industrial Organizations to form the AFL-CIO. In 1956 the AFL-CIO reached its peak membership (as a percentage of labor) with 25.2%.

AMERICAN FEDERATION OF LABOR AND CONGRESS OF INDUSTRIAL ORGANIZATIONS (AFL-CIO), formed in 1955 by merger of the AFL and CIO. The AFL was founded in 1886 under the leadership of Samuel Gompers to represent the skilled trade unions who did not want to be affiliated with the Knights of Labor. It experienced mild success in its formative years but did not become a powerful group until the 1930s, with passage of the Norris-La Guardia Act in 1932 and the National Labor Relations Act in 1935.

It was also during the 1930s that the unskilled labor groups began to find fault with the AFL. Its refusal to grant charters to several industrial unions such as steel, automobile, and rubber workers led John L. Lewis, then vice president of the AFL, to help these workers organize. He was so successful that the AFL ordered these groups to disband. They refused and left the AFL to join the permanent Congress of Industrial Organizations in 1938.

Both the AFL and the CIO experienced individual success in the late 1930s and early 1940s. However, in 1947, with the passage of the Taft-Hartley Act, union power was curtailed. So, after much deliberation, the two organizations merged in 1955, thus forming the AFL-CIO. The organization presently has a total membership in excess of 14 million. The only major unions not affiliated with the AFL-CIO are the United Mine Workers and the National Education Association.
　　　　　　　　　　　　　　　—William D. Wagoner

See also Labor Movement.

ANALYSIS OF VARIANCE is a technique used to separate the variation of a variable into two components: systematic variation (caused by other variables) and random or chance variation. It is often used to test for significant differences among several sample means.

See also Significance.

ANALYTICAL SOCIALISM. *See* Pre-Marxian Socialism.

ANARCHISTIC COMMUNISM presumes that men are born good, reach fulfillment in voluntary and spontaneous cooperation with others, and thus instinctively seek communal life. Proponents feel that the state and the economic institutions it supports, especially private property, are artificial agencies of exploitation that restrict the individual. Therefore, the state should be abolished; free cooperation in ideal communities would eliminate oppression and make government superfluous. Leading figures in the movement have included W. Godwin, P.J. Proudhon, P.A. Kropotkin, and M. Bakunin.

See also Associationism; Cooperativism.

ANCILLARY AGREEMENT, one secondary or subsidiary to the main purpose of a business agreement, the ancillary agreement being a minimum condition necessary to effect the main legal purpose.

In common law, the sale of a business might be conditional on the seller agreeing not to compete with the buyer for a certain time or within a certain geographic area, the latter agreement being ancillary to the sale agreement. Common-law courts judged such agreements according to the limitation on competition they imposed. Agreements limiting competition in a whole market for an indefinite time were considered general or nonancillary restraints of trade, *per se* illegal; those with less comprehensive limitations were considered partial or ancillary restraints and judged on the "reasonableness" of the limitations.

Interpreting the Sherman Act prohibition on restraints of trade, the Supreme Court adopted a similar distinction until 1911 (*United States v. Standard Oil Company of New Jersey*). In this case, the test of reasonableness ostensibly was applied to nonancillary (price fixing, market sharing) as well as ancillary restraints. Since then, however, federal courts rather consistently have condemned nonacillary restraints *per se* illegal. — *Thomas O. Depperschmidt*

See also Antitrust Policy; Restraint of Trade.

ANTIMERGER ACT. *See* Celler-Kefauver Act.

ANTITRUST DIVISION, DEPARTMENT OF JUSTICE, one of two federal agencies (along with the Federal Trade Commission) charged with enforcing the Sherman and Clayton Antitrust Acts, and several other related statutes designed to maintain a competitive economic environment. Enforcement includes providing advisory and counseling services to businesses, along with prosecuting violators. Most suits brought by the antitrust division are settled by consent decrees. The direction and strength of the antitrust division have varied greatly over time, based partly on general public attitudes toward business, but mainly due to the fact that the key officials are appointed by the president.

See also Antitrust Policy; Consent Decree; Federal Trade Commission.

ANTITRUST POLICY. The central ingredient of antitrust policy as it has emerged through court interpretation of the three major antitrust laws (Sherman Antitrust Act of 1890, Clayton Act of 1914, and Federal Trade Commission Act of 1914) and amendments thereto, is the promotion of competition among business units and the prohibition of anticompetitive practices. Only secondarily and indirectly are consumer interests protected. That is, the consumer is thought to benefit from the lower prices, more efficient allocation of resources, and better quality products that the more competitive economy yields.

Method. The promotion of competition in major legislation is through blanket prohibitions on restraint of trade and monopolization (Sherman Act, Sections 1 and 2) and unfair trade practices (Section 5 of FTC Act). In addition, price discrimination, tying contracts and exclusive dealings, mergers, and interlocking directorates are prohibited where such practices may affect competition adversely (Clayton Act, Sections 2, 3, 7 and 9).

The vigor with which these practices have been checked in the 80-plus years of antitrust enforcement gives a truer picture of what antitrust policy is today than does legislative intent.

History. In the area of restraints of trade, courts have condemned flagrant price fixing, market sharing, and exclusion of competitors, but hard evidence of such overt practice is rarely available. Use of the doctrine of conscious parallelism as a substitute for such evidence increased the effectiveness of Section 1 through the mid-1950s (when a judicial reversal set in), but has yielded only occasional results consistent with the policy of competition. The reluctance of courts until 1945 to find untoward behavior in the dominant size of a firm severely limited enforcement of the prohibition on monopolization. Except for the

---

ANTITRUST POLICY

LAWS
COMMON LAW
CLAYTON ANTITRUST ACT (1914)
FAIR-TRADE LAWS
  McGuire-Keogh Act (1952)
  Miller-Tydings Act (1937)
NATIONAL INDUSTRIAL RECOVERY ACT
  (NIRA) (1933)
SHERMAN ANTITRUST ACT (1890)
WHEELER-LEA ACT (1938)

COURT CASES
SCHWEGMANN BROTHERS v. CALVERT
  CORP.
UNITED STATES v. ALUMINUM CO.
  OF AMERICA
  Alcoa case
UNITED STATES v. AMERICAN TELEPHONE
  AND TELEGRAPH
UNITED STATES v. AMERICAN TOBACCO
  CO.
  American Tobacco case
UNITED STATES v. E. I. DU PONT
  AND CO.
  Du Pont case
UNITED STATES v. INTERNATIONAL
  BUSINESS MACHINES
UNITED STATES v. NEW YORK GREAT A&P
  COMPANY
  A&P case
UNITED STATES v. STANDARD OIL CO.
  OF NEW JERSEY
  Standard Oil case
UNITED STATES v. U.S. STEEL CORPORATION

AGENCIES
ANTITRUST DIVISION, DEPARTMENT OF JUSTICE
ANTITRUST POLICY
FEDERAL TRADE COMMISSION (FTC)
  trade regulation rules

ECONOMIC AND LEGAL CONCEPTS
ABUSE THEORY OF MERGERS
CARTEL
  trade association
CONSENT DECREE
CONSPIRACY DOCTRINE
DISSOLUTION, DIVESTITURE, DIVORCE
ECONOMIES OF SCALE
  diseconomies of scale
MARKET CONCENTRATION
  concentration ratio
MERGER
CONGLOMERATE
  diversification
  horizontal merger
  vertical merger
MULTINATIONAL COMPANY
MULTI-PLANT FIRM
PATENT
TRIPLE DAMAGES

ILLEGAL ACTIONS
COLLUSION
  overt collusion
  tacit collusion
CONSCIOUS PARALLELISM
  parallelism
DECEPTIVE ADVERTISING
EXCLUSIVE DEALERSHIP
INTERLOCKING DIRECTORATE
MARKET SHARING
MONOPOLIZING or MONOPOLIZATION
PREDATORY PRACTICES
  cutthroat competition
PRICE DISCRIMINATION
PRICE FIXING
  resale price maintenance
  price maintenance
  retail price maintenance
RESTRAINT OF TRADE
SUBSTANTIAL LESSENING OF COMPETITION
TYING CONTRACT
UNFAIR AND DECEPTIVE PRACTICES
  deceptive practices
UNFAIR METHODS OF COMPETITION

ban on deceptive advertising, Section 5 of the Federal Trade Commission Act has been virtually useless, prohibition of "unfair trade practices" being vaguely worded and overlapped by the Sherman Act. The law on price discrimination has been clouded by judicial protection of competitors, not competition. Interpretation of the prohibition on tying contracts and exclusive dealings has bogged down over the definitions of what is a "substantial" lessening of competition.

The law on mergers has been effective when enforced, especially since the passage of the Celler-Kefauver Act in 1950, but the magnitude of the task, when mergers run in the thousands per year, has meant less-than-effective overall enforcement. The prohibition on interlocking directorates—limited to those in the same plane of commerce, where firms are direct competitors—is a dead issue.

Significance. Central to the problems of antitrust policy resolution and enforcement is the nature of competition. Economists tend to emphasize market structure as an indicator of illegality, while lawyers stress performance of firms. In addition, antitrust policy at any time is influenced by the will of an administration to enforce the laws, by the general economic climate (typically, there is less vigorous enforcement in recession), and by the preoccupation of the nation with other problems.

During the 1970s, antitrust law was applied vigorously in order to block conglomerate mergers. During the 1980s, the Reagan administration felt that the evolution of global markets made concentration at home less threatening, and that competition would weed out inefficient behavior without government intervention. Antitrust action under this doctrine was reserved for behavior that obviously encouraged collusion. This hands-off antitrust policy resulted in a dramatic decrease in both public and private antitrust suits and a wave of mergers and takeovers.

— *Thomas O. Depperschmidt*

See also Conscious Parallelism; Federal Trade Commission; Market Sharing; Monopolizing; Price Discrimination; Price Fixing; Restraint of Trade; Tying Contract; Unfair and Deceptive Practices.

APPRECIATION, CURRENCY. If the rate of exchange on the British pound were to rise in the United States from $1.18 to $1.30, the number of pounds required to buy dollars in London would drop from £.85 (= $1.00/1.18) to £.78 (= $1.00/1.30). The pound would appreciate relative to the dollar, and the British would then have more purchasing power in the dollar market. There can be no appreciation of a currency unless there is depreciation elsewhere.

See also Depreciation, Currency; Devaluation; Exchange Rates.

APPRENTICESHIP, a training period in which a trainee works with master workmen on the job in order to learn the necessary skills of a trade. Although apprenticeship programs have been in existence throughout history, in 1937 the United States established its apprenticeship policy with the National Apprenticeship Act (Fitzgerald Act). This act is administered by the Bureau of Apprenticeship and Training in the U.S. Department of Labor. Its main function has been to promote apprenticeship programs.

APPROPRIATE TECHNOLOGY for developing countries has been evaluated according to differing criteria over the four development decades since 1950. In the 1950s and 1960s, appropriateness depended on the ability of a technology to maximize growth or output. The output of developing countries grew rapidly at this time, but employment growth stagnated. So in the 1970s, the emphasis shifted to maximizing employment.

The Appropriate Technology (AT) movement traces its intellectual heritage to Mahatma Gandhi and E.F. Schumacher (*Small is Beautiful*, 1973). AT emphasizes low-energy, environmentally sound technologies and the use of locally available resources to produce for local markets rather than for export. AT promotes local self-reliance and the preservation of local community structures, and advocates sensitivity to differences in the tastes, preferences, and needs that emerge from local cultures. This last point distinguishes AT from most other development paradigms, which tend to view all humankind as proceeding along the same development trajectory toward some optimal civilized state (roughly resembling the twentieth-century United States). An appropriate technology is one developed by and for the people who will live by it.

See also Buddhist Economics; Gains from Trade; Gandhian Economics; Schumacher, E.F.

APPROPRIATIONS. See Federal Budget.

ARBITRAGE, the simultaneous buying and selling of two or more currencies in different markets for purposes of gain. The most prevalent forms are exchange and interest rate. *Exchange arbitrage* eliminates discrepancies in cross rates; *interest rate arbitrage* eliminates interest rate differentials. *Gold arbitrage* exists where there are free markets in the metal.

See also Capital Movement; Exchange Rates.

ARBITRATION, a process by which labor-management disputes may be resolved, utilizing a third party to render a decision. Arbitration may deal with controversies arising in the determination of a new contract (interest arbitration) or with disagreements over the interpretation of an existing contract's provisions (grievance arbitration).

Arbitration Characteristics. Grievance arbitration is common labor-management relations and is an extremely useful method of resolving disputes that otherwise might lead to work stoppage. For this reason, it is almost always "compulsory" in that the process is automatic and the decision binding. Interest arbitration, much less common, is usually strictly voluntary, that is, not automatic and perhaps not even binding. The best-known cases of compulsory interest arbitration are those disputes in the railroad industry in which Congress has intervened to resolve bargaining disputes and impose its decisions on the industry and the workers.

ARC ELASTICITY. When the coefficient of elasticity of demand is to be computed between two widely separated prices, the concept of arc elasticity should be used. Because elasticity measures the percentage change in quantity demanded, caused by a percentage change in price, the problem encountered in large price changes involves choosing the appropriate base upon which the percentages should be calculated. This problem is handled in the arc-elasticity format by using the arithmetic mean of the two quantities demanded as the base for percentage change in quantity and the arithmetic mean of the two prices as the base for percentage change in price.

ARITHMETIC MEAN. *See* Central Tendency.

ASSETS OF THE BANKING SYSTEM. *See* Balance Sheet, Bank.

ASSOCIATIONISM, the utopian socialist concept that the solution to social problems would be provided by voluntary association on the basis of some preconceived plan, predicated on natural harmony, with the identity of the individual preserved. Such association was deemed the only means of both suppressing competition leading to monopoly and preserving individual liberty and freedom of producers. The best-known representatives of associationism were Robert Owen and F.M.C. Fourier.

See also Cooperativism; Fourier, François Marie Charles; Owen, Robert.

ATTRACTION TO RISK. *See* Expected Utility.

AUTHORITARIAN SOCIALISM. *See* Command Economy; Socialism.

AUTOMATIC (BUILT-IN) STABILIZERS are automatic fiscal adjustments that reduce the national income multiplier and therefore cushion the effect of changes in autonomous spending on the level of income. The two groups of stabilizers are taxes, in particular income taxes, and government transfer payments, such as unemployment compensation and welfare benefits. These stabilizers moderate the fall in income when private spending declines and restrain the increase in income when private spending rises.

AUTONOMOUS INVESTMENT, investment—demand for new capital goods—that occurs independently of changes in aggregate demand—consumption, government, and foreign demand for goods and services. Autonomous investment occurs because there are opportunities to increase profits by investing even if aggregate demand does not rise. Examples would be new technologies that replace old ones and save on costs (cash registers with built-in calculators allowing supermarkets to hire fewer checkout clerks), or that produce new goods to replace older goods (the bus and the airline replacing the passenger train). In most elementary treatments of national income determination the investment considered is autonomous investment because limiting the examples to autonomous investment simplifies the arithmetic.

See also Induced Investment; Investment; Investment Schedule; Marginal Efficiency of Capital.

AVERAGE. *See* Central Tendency.

AVERAGE COST is obtained by dividing total cost by the number of units of output associated with that total cost. Average total cost is the sum of average variable and average fixed costs.

See also Marginal Cost; Total Cost.

AVERAGE FIXED COST OF PRODUCTION (AFC), the cost of all the fixed inputs (overhead) per unit of output. If TFC is total fixed cost, and X is output, then AFC = TFC/X.

See also Cost Function.

AVERAGE PROPENSITY TO CONSUME (APC), the ratio of consumption at a specific level of disposable income to that income.

AVERAGE PROPENSITY TO SAVE (APS), the ratio of saving at a specific level of disposable income to that income. Although it plays no role in national income analysis, in development economics the APS is useful in estimating a country's capacity to invest and, hence, to develop.

AVERAGE REVENUE is computed by dividing total revenue by the number of units produced and sold. Where all units are sold at the same price (in the absence of price discrimination), average revenue is simply the sales price of a unit of output, and the demand curve and average revenue curve are identical.

See also Marginal Revenue; Total Revenue.

AVERAGE TOTAL COST OF PRODUCTION (ATC), the cost of all the inputs used per unit of output. If TC is total cost, and X is output, then ATC = TC/X.

See also Cost Function.

AVERAGE VARIABLE COST OF PRODUCTION (AVC), the cost of all the variable inputs used per unit of output. If TVC is total variable cost, and X is output, then AVC = TVC/X.

See also Cost Function.

BACKWARD BENDING SUPPLY CURVE depicts the situation in which, after a certain wage level is reached, workers begin to leave the labor force. The supply of labor, under normal conditions, has been found to be a function of the wage level. As wages increase, the decision to enter the labor force becomes more attractive and the supply of labor increases. This is due to the fact that, as wages increase, the economic cost of leisure hours rises. Thus, there is a positive relationship between wage rates and the supply of labor. However, it has been found that after a certain wage level has been attained, workers again begin to leave the labor force. One explanation of this occurrence is that there is often no longer a need for the income of secondary workers in the household because of the higher income of the principal wage earner. Another possible explanation is that workers may feel they can work fewer hours at a higher wage rate and still maintain the standard of living they desire.

BAD, ECONOMIC. If an economic *good* is anything that adds to human happiness, an economic *bad* is anything that detracts from the enjoyment of life. Waste and pollution are examples of economic bads. A "good" is defined as a commodity for which more is preferred to less, and a "bad" is a commodity for which less is preferred to more. Everyone (presumably) prefers to have less nuclear waste, water pollution, air pollution, and ordinary household garbage.

Society tries to control the overproduction of irritating or dangerous economic bads through zoning, social regulation, and other legal sanctions. Economists classify the various methods available to society for controlling economic bads according to their degree of intervention in the market process. The least interventionist method is moral suasion, which carries no legal authority. Its goals are to persuade offenders to reduce voluntarily their offending practices and to sensitize people to a problem. Anti-littering campaigns are an example. Another method is to assign property rights or pollution rights. If property rights are assigned to protect you from being damaged by pollution, then you can sue harmful polluters. The second approach is for the public sector to sell individuals or firms licenses to discharge wastes.

Approaches that are more interventionist include structuring markets so that external pollution costs will be internalized. External costs are costs borne by the society at large, rather than by the polluter. Tax penalties or effluent charges are attempts to internalize these costs—make them felt by the polluter. Direct regulation requiring prohibition of the production of economic "bads" may be desirable in the case of extremely dangerous materials such as radioactive wastes. When totally eliminating a form of pollution is too costly relative to the benefit society gains from its removal, the government often tries to limit noxious wastes through regulations and standards. The rule of thumb is that marginal social cost must equal marginal social benefit. Reducing pollution beyond this point would mean that society would suffer a net loss of utility. According to this analysis, it is not optimal for society to completely eliminate economic bads without regard for cost.

BALANCED BUDGET, federal budget policy calling for annual equality between government revenues and government expenditures. Therefore, there will be no current deficit or accumulation of government debt. This is a very popular concept, with some parties calling for a constitutional amendment to require that the federal government annually balance its budget. Others have argued for a cyclically balanced budget, with a government surplus in years of inflation and boom, offset by government deficits during recession. The arguments in favor of a balanced budget include: (1) selling government debt to the private sector drives up the interest rate, causing fewer funds to be available for private investment activity ("crowding out"); (2) public officials have political pressures to spend more, but to tax less, leading to chronic deficits and an ever-expanding public sector; and (3) government deficits are a leading cause of inflation in the economy.

In spite of its popular appeal, several problems do arise in trying to implement an annually balanced budget, including: (1) the presence of many "entitlement" programs, which naturally increase expenditures when the economy experiences a downturn; (2) the growth in so-called off-line budget items, including activities of some public agencies and also long-term commitments of agencies that promise future expenditures; (3) political resistance to tax increases and/or cuts in federal programs necessary to bring the budget into balance; and (4) uncertainty over the macroeconomic implications of a balanced budget.

—*Michael S. Johnson*

BALANCED GROWTH, system by which a country creates and expands its industries in the same proportion and at the same pace as domestic demand, supplying almost all its needs from its own production and reducing the traditional reliance on imports and exports. The severe depression of the world market for the primary product exports of most less developed countries (LDCs) before and after World War II led many development economists to look unfavorably at the traditional pattern of growth through exports.

BALANCE OF PAYMENTS (B/P), for a country, a summary of all economic transactions between it and the rest of the world for a given period of time. B/P reflects all payments due and made to the country as well as all liabilities accrued and paid to other countries. All recorded transactions follow the accounting procedure of debits and credits, and the B/P, therefore, always balances. On the U.S. balance of payments, transactions that give rise to foreigners' money claims are debits; transactions giving rise to money claims by Americans on foreigners are credits. Important credits are merchandise exports, interest and dividends on investments abroad, investment by foreigners in America, and foreign travel in the United States. Important debits are merchandise imports, tourist expenditures abroad, shipping services, and investment abroad. The debit items give rise to the demand for foreign exchange; credits give the supply of exchange; the rate of exchange is determined by demand and supply. Whether or not a given rate is an equilibrium rate depends on what transactions are necessary to make B/P balance.

Accounts. Balance of payments generally include the current account, capital account, and gold account. The current account is the "real" side of B/P, comprising transactions in current goods and services, including services being currently rendered by capital but not capital movements themselves. Capital and gold accounts relate to the financial side of B/P. Gold moves to make B/P balance as do short-term capital movements in the capital account—they are balancing items and go "below the line." Long-term capital transactions are generally undertaken independently of other B/P transactions. The presence of balancing items indicates disequilibrium, which implies that there is some pressure on exchange rates.

Basic Equilibrium. Current-account exports of goods and services plus long-term capital imports equals current-account imports of goods and services plus long-term capital exports. Capital imports are credits, and capital exports are debits. The absence of gold and short-term capital items shows that B/P is

self-financing, not needing international reserves or pressure on the currency. If credits exceed debits, B/P is in surplus disequilibrium, and gold imports or short-term capital exports must finance the surplus. A deficit disequilibrium results from debits exceeding credits, and gold exports or short-term capital imports must finance the deficit.

Gold exports are credits, and gold imports are debits. Short-term capital movements relate to transactions to be completed or reversed within a year and take the following forms: (1) exports through increase in American-owned balances abroad or decrease in foreign balances in the United States, and (2) imports through decrease in United States balances abroad or increase in foreign balances in America. These balances are generally demand or time deposits or short-term debt instruments, such as Treasury bills.

America's Payments Deficit. To help in analyzing the United States B/P deficit, which has persisted since the late 1950s, the liquidity and official settlements bases have been developed. Both bases look at net changes in certain liabilities as they relate to net changes in the holdings of international monetary reserves (gold, convertible foreign currencies, and liquid reserves at IMF). The liquidity concept places change in total short-term liabilities to foreigners (public and private) below the line; the official settlements concept puts only changes in liabilities (both short- and long-term) to foreign official agencies below the line, as only they can command gold. When these changes are greater than changes in international reserves, the deficit has increased. Therefore, the size of the deficit depends on what goes below the line; all foreign liabilities to the United States go above the line, a treatment unique to the United States.

—John R. Matthews, Jr.

See also Balance of Trade; Capital Account; Devaluation; Exchange Rate; Foreign Investment.

BALANCE OF TRADE, the difference between merchandise exports and imports in a nation's balance of payments. If exports exceed imports the balance of trade is favorable, or in surplus; if imports exceed exports the balance of trade is unfavorable, or in deficit. Mercantilists of the sixteenth and seventeenth centuries had the acquisition of gold and, thus, a favorable balance of trade as a major tenet of commercial policy. David Hume, in his specie-flow analysis, proved that all nations cannot have a favorable balance of trade simultaneously; one nation's gain is another's loss. Hume showed that the income and price effects of gold movements would automatically reverse a favorable or unfavorable balance of trade, and gold would stop flowing when exports and imports were in balance.

Merchandise exports and imports are the two most important entries in the current account of the balance of payments. The difference between them may show an unfavorable balance, but there will be no disequilibrium in the balance of payments because of other items in the current account. Many countries, such as Great Britain, are noted for unfavorable balances of trade, with the deficit being financed in the current account by such items as shipping and financial services. For many years the United States had a favorable balance of trade, but many of the excess exports were carried in ships of foreign registry, somewhat mitigating the balance. It is the surplus or deficit relative to the current account, not the balance of trade, that has to be financed by capital movements and gold. In addition, when a country has reached a mature creditor stage, either the balance of trade or the entire current account must be unfavorable in order for capital to be repatriated.

—*John R. Matthews, Jr.*

See also Balance of Payments; Exchange Rate; Terms of Trade.

BALANCE SHEET. The main purpose of a balance sheet is to show the assets, liabilities, and net worth of a business concern. The balance sheet and the income statements are the two major financial statements of a firm. In practice, total assets should equal total liabilities plus net worth. For example, if a corporation sells $100 worth of stock, $100 would then be entered under cash on the asset side of the balance sheet, and $100 would be entered under issued stock on the liability plus net worth side. Thus, assets would equal liabilities plus net worth. Depending on the individual firm, a balance sheet is kept current on a monthly, quarterly, semiannual, or annual basis.

BALANCE SHEET, BANK. The balance sheet of a bank is identical in principle to any other corporate balance sheet, differing only in the type of items included. The two most obvious differences from, say, a manufacturing corporation, are that almost all of the bank's assets are financial rather than physical and that its liabilities, which greatly exceed its net worth, are almost entirely short-term obligations to depositors: demand deposits and time deposits. As an example, a *consolidated balance sheet*, adding together the figures for all 10,000 commercial banks in the United States in 1989, is shown.

Cash. Cash and due from banks (usually called simply cash) represent funds readily available to meet the demands of depositors. Currency and coin (vault cash) and deposits in the Federal Reserve bank are basic reserves. Deposits due from other banks are generally considered reserves for state banks that are not members of the Federal Reserve System. Cash items in process of collection represent checks that have been deposited but not yet collected from the banks on which they were drawn. They will become reserves as soon as they are collected, usually within a day or two. Cash is a liquid asset but produces no income.

Loans and Discounts. Lending is the primary function of commercial banks and represents both their major source of income (interest) and the way by which they provide multiple expansion of the money supply. Commercial loans are made to businessmen most frequently for carrying inventory and for periods of one to three months, though the loans may often be renewed rather than repaid at maturity. Industrial loans are for longer periods, though seldom for more than five years. Commercial and industrial loans represent about 40% of all loans made by commercial banks.

Mortgage loans are made both on private homes and on commercial property and normally run for 15 to 25 years. They represent another 25% of bank lending activity. Not far behind are other loans to individuals, consisting primarily of consumer installment loans of from one to three years, repaid by monthly payments.

Loans to banks include a small number of ordinary loans but consist mainly of federal funds, a form of overnight loan in which the lending bank gives the borrowing bank a check drawn on its account with the Federal Reserve bank of its district in exchange for repayment the following day. The borrowing bank increases its reserves in this way, while the lending bank earns interest on temporarily excess reserves.

Investments. United States government securities, particularly Treasury bills, are secondary reserves bearing a relatively low rate of interest but easily sellable if cash is needed. State and local government securities may bear an even lower interest rate, but this interest is not generally subject to corporate income taxes, so that net income is higher than it is on taxable issues. Other securities are almost exclusively corporate bonds. Banks may hold a small amount of corporate stocks, but normally this type of investment is considered too risky to suit the needs of commercial banks. About half of other assets consists of the bank building, furnishings, and supplies. The rest is quite miscellaneous.

Liabilities. By far the greatest part of a bank's liabilities consists of demand deposits and time deposits owed to its customers, primarily individuals and corporations. Banks borrow primarily from other banks, including the Federal Reserve banks, for periods up to 15 days. Banks may also borrow small amounts from the public on capital notes or, more rarely, bonds.

Net worth represents the equity provided by the stockholders of the bank and includes capital, surplus, and undivided profits. Net worth is only 7% of total assets, a very small figure by comparison with almost any other type of corporation.

—*Walter W. Haines*

BANK FAILURE occurs when a commercial bank or savings bank is unable to meet the demands of its

BALANCE SHEET: 1990

Assets and Liabilities of U.S. Commercial Banks (in billions of dollars)

Assets:			Liabilities:		
LOANS AND SECURITIES, excluding interbank	$2,601.1		DEPOSITS	$2,241.9	
Comerical and industrial loans		631.9	Demand		613.7
Other loans		1,374.5	Savings		542.7
U.S. Treasury securities		389.8	Time		1,085.5
Other securities		204.9			
			BORROWINGS	551.7	
CASH ASSETS, total	223.2		OTHER LIABILITIES	222.1	
Currency and coin		28.1	NET WORTH (assets less liabilities)	202.8	
Reserves and Fed. Res. banks		24.5			
Balances with depository institutions		30.6	TOTAL LIABILITIES AND NET WORTH	$3,218.5	
Cash items in process of collection		89.8			
Other cash assets		50.2			
OTHER ASSETS, including interbank loans	394.2				
TOTAL ASSETS	$3,218.5				

Source: *Federal Reserve Bulletin*

creditors. The primary creditors are depositors whose claims are payable on demand, so a bank fails when it is unable to pay cash to depositors who wish to withdraw funds. More than one-third (10,308) of the banks in operation in 1922 had failed within a decade. In response, bank supervision under the Federal Reserve System and the Comptroller of the Currency was tightened, and the Federal Deposit Insurance Corporation (FDIC) was set up to insure deposits. Until the 1980s, bank failures seldom exceeded 4 or 5 per year. In the 1980s, high interest costs, fraud, and a weak real estate market squeezed profit margins to the point where commercial banks were failing at a rate of more than 150 per year. Between 1980 and 1989, more than 1,000 savings and loans were closed or merged with sounder institutions. By 1989, 600 S&Ls, one-fifth of the total, were still thought to be insolvent, and losses to the FSLIC were expected to be at least $120 billion.

See also Federal Deposit Insurance Corporation; Resolution Trust Corporation.

BANKING SYSTEM, in a broad sense, all those institutions involved in the business of lending or borrowing money or of dealing in monetary instruments, such as stocks, bonds, mortgages, or other evidences of debt. In this sense, the banking system includes both commercial banks and financial intermediaries. Commercial banks can create money through the issue of demand deposits, an ability they share with no other institution except the federal government, which can create money through the issue of currency. All other financial institutions must obtain savings from individuals or other institutions and cannot lend money that does not exist, as can commercial banks.

Analysis. The banking system, in this broad sense, consists of a multitude of institutions of many types, some highly specialized, some operating with a wide diversity of situations.

Functions, if not institutions, can be classified in several ways, as by the type of lender, the type of borrower, the form of monetary instrument, or its

THE BANKING SYSTEM (continued)

RESERVES
- legal reserves
- reserve ratio
- secondary reserves
- correspondent balances

FRACTIONAL RESERVES
100% RESERVES
VAULT CASH

LOANS AND DISCOUNTS
CALL LOANS
- demand loans

STOCK

assets

PORTFOLIO

GOVERNMENT SECURITIES
- government bonds
- short-term government bonds
- long-term government bonds
- savings bonds
- Treasury bills
- certificates of indebtedness
- government notes

consolidated bank balance sheet
monopoly bank

BALANCE SHEET,
BANK

accounting

FINANCIAL INTERMEDIARIES
- Federal Savings and Loan Insurance Corp.
- savings and loan associations
- credit unions
- pension funds
- finance companies
- government credit agencies
FEDERAL DEPOSIT INSURANCE CORPORATION
TREASURER OF THE UNITED STATES
COMPTROLLER OF THE CURRENCY
RESOLUTION TRUST CORPORATION

FEDERAL RESERVE SYSTEM
- Board of Governors
- Open Market Committee
- float
FEDERAL RESERVE ACT
MONETARY CONTROL ACT OF 1980
BRANCH BANK
BANK FAILURE
CENTRAL BANK
MONETARY AUTHORITY, CENTRAL

BANKING SYSTEM

structure

liabilities — DEPOSITS — DEMAND DEPOSITS / TIME DEPOSITS

FEDERAL RESERVE
BANKS
- district banks
COMMERCIAL BANK
MEMBER BANK
- reserve city bank
- country bank
- central reserve city bank

NATIONAL BANK
STATE BANK

---

maturity. In terms of maturity two broad and important markets can be distinguished. The money market consists of institutions and facilities concerned with short-term financial obligations, whose maturities do not exceed one year: Treasury bills, commercial paper, federal funds, and so on. The basic operations of commercial banks fall in the money market. The capital market deals with securities with more than one year to run: most bonds, stocks (which are not strictly a credit instrument at all, because they connote ownership rather than loan), mortgages, and other long-term obligations.

The principal function of the banking system is to channel funds from areas with excess money to areas in need of money. The system provides, partly through the great number of institutions involved, a wide variety of terms, maturities, conditions, and interest rates, so that any lender or borrower can presumably find some institution or monetary instrument that closely meets his needs.

The Banking System and Deposits. In a stricter sense, the banking system is limited to those institutions that accept deposits repayable on demand or after a specified period of time. Only commercial banks accept demand deposits, but both commercial banks and savings banks accept time deposits. With rare and localized exceptions, no other institution accepts deposits from the general public in the normal course of business, and, hence, no other institution can properly be called a bank in the limited sense. There is a movement afoot to give savings and loan associations the powers of banks, but this alteration

would require a substantial change in the law.
— *Walter W. Haines*

BANK MULTIPLIER. *See* Multiple Expansion of the Money Supply.

BARGAINING. *See* Bargaining Unit; Bilateral Bargaining; Collective Bargaining; Industry-Wide Bargaining; Key Bargain; Multi-Employer Bargaining.

BARGAINING UNIT, the group of workers or jobs that the union represents in its bargaining with the employers and to which the contract terms apply. The unit may include all the production workers, such as the meatcutters or truckdrivers, in a large work force.

Since there is no standard definition of bargaining units, defining them is one of the highly controversial matters in labor law. When conflict over such definition exists, the National Labor Relations Board is frequently called upon to specify the appropriate scope of the unit.

BARRIERS TO ENTRY, term used to indicate the problems a firm must overcome in order to enter a particular market. The two main types of barriers to entry are natural and artificial.

Natural barriers are built into the nature of the firm. One type of natural barrier exists where the optimum scale of plant is so large compared to the size of the market that entry cannot be profitable. The best examples of this type of barrier occur in the utility and transportation markets, such as telephone and electric companies as well as railroad companies. Another natural barrier occurs in industries where the enormous capital needed to enter the market is almost impossible to obtain. A perfect example of this is the automotive industry.

Artificial barriers include restrictive laws, such as patent rights and licensing laws, such as those in the interstate public transportation field, that limit those who may enter the market.

Another artificial barrier is the price policy of established firms in the industry. For example, existing firms may threaten to undersell any new firms. Other barriers are established product differentiation that discourages the use of "offbrands," and control of strategic sources of raw materials.
— *William D. Wagoner*

See also Entry.

BARTER, direct exchange of goods or services without the use of money. A barter agreement between countries provides for the exchange of specified quantities of goods.

See also Balance of Trade; Terms of Trade.

BAUMOL, WILLIAM JACK (1922-   ), American educator and authoritative writer on economic theory.

He graduated from the City College of New York in 1942, and received his Ph.D. in economics from London University in 1949. He won nationwide attention for his coauthorship (with Princeton economist William G. Bowen) of *The Performing Arts — The Economic Dilemma* (1966), the first full-scale study of the financial plight of professional performing artistic activity in the United States. He is the former chairman of the Economic Policy Council of New Jersey and former vice president of the American Economic Association. He is the Joseph Douglas Green '95 Professor of Economics at Princeton and is also on the faculty at New York University. Baumol's other works include *The Theory of Environmental Policy: Externalities, Public Outlays, and the Quality of Life* (1974).

BAYESIAN APPROACH. *See* Probability.

BECKER, GARY (1930-   ), imaginative and innovative modern economist, who has contributed to many new and diverse areas of economics. His analysis of human capital—the concept that, in economic terms, an individual be considered in many ways to have the characteristics of capital (earning power over the individual's lifetime can be capitalized into a present value and this present value can be changed by investing in the individual through education, job training, better health care, and so on)—broadened the scope of economics. Becker's contributions to the economics of crime, his economic analysis of fertility behavior, his work on the economics of discrimination, and his analysis of time in economic theory have also broadened the scope of economics and challenged economists and other social scientists. Becker became professor of ecnomics at the University of Chicago in 1970. His works include *Economic Theory* (1971) and *The Economic Approach to Human Behavior* (1976).

BEGGAR-THY-NEIGHBOR POLICY, program of increasing exports or decreasing imports at the expense of other countries. Nations with unemployment have tried at times to increase exports to increase jobs at home. Raising tariffs is one way of creating an export surplus. This has the effect of exporting unemployment to the nation that buys more of a country's goods and has its exports reduced. It usually invites swift retaliation.

BENEFIT-COST ANALYSIS, a form of systematic economic analysis that is useful at all levels of decision-making, from households and firms to government. Benefit-cost analysis is related to cost-effectiveness studies, but is a more thorough process. While cost-effectiveness focuses on identifying, quantifying, and comparing the total costs incurred in alternative ways of accomplishing a specified objective, benefit-cost analysis identifies and weighs both the total benefits and total costs of each alternative, for a given project,

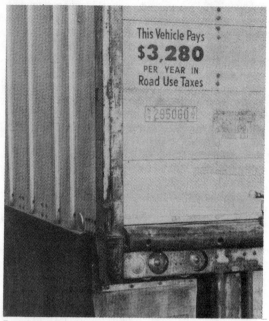

Benefit-Cost Analysis: Because trucking firms derive greatest benefit from highway use, they pay more heavily for it.

and results in a benefit/cost ratio for each proposal. Ratios greater than one are deemed favorable, the larger the ratio the more favorable.

Benefit-cost analysis is particularly important, and widely used, in public-sector decision-making. It involves identification of all impacts, consequence-positive (benefits) and negative (costs), direct and indirect (so-called externalities, or spillover effects), present and future. The quantification of these benefits and costs often requires the use of sophisticated economic theoretical and statistical techniques; and future values, both benefits and cost, are converted to present values through the "discounting" process. By summing the present values of all benefits, on the one hand, and of all costs, on the other, two aggregate figures are arrived at that determine the final benefit-cost ratio. Uncertainties in the data or choice of methods are taken into account in "sensitivity analyses" that allows for some flexibility in the final benefit/cost ratio. While such final ratios, even with sensitivity analyses, must be used advisedly, they often provide very useful information and guidelines for making more informed economic decisions in both the private and public sectors.

—Leonard G. Schifrin
See also Bad, Economic; Merit Goods.

BENEFIT PRINCIPLE, a taxation concept that rests on the belief that a taxing unit (household or firm) should pay taxes on the basis of the benefits received from the activities financed by the tax. This criterion ties the expenditure and the revenue sides of the budget together, as if the spending and taxing decisions are joint.

The benefit principle is most applicable in those cases where the beneficiaries of the government spending are easy to identify, where revenues can be varied on the basis of the amount of the activity provided to each taxing unit, and where such taxation is not contrary to the spirit of the public expenditure program. For example, the benefit principle can be applied to the use of a public golf course or for water service provided to a business, but a benefit tax is very hard to utilize for national defense expenditures and may be inappropriate for financing public assistance. This concept is also referred to as the benefits-received principle or the compensatory principle of taxation.

See also Ability-to-Pay Principle; Taxation; User Charge.

BENSON PLAN. Ezra Taft Benson, Secretary of Agriculture during the Eisenhower administration, opposed much of the farm legislation on the books when he took office. He attempted to move in the direction of free markets and away from rigid price supports and production controls. In particular, he favored flexible price supports, a device written into earlier legislation but given little opportunity to operate. Flexible supports provide a sliding scale of support prices—high when supplies are low, low when supplies are large. Since production was large and the government was accumulating surplus stocks, the prospects were that price supports would be low most of the time if supports were flexible. Congress did not put flexible supports into effect, but under the pressure of surplus production, accumulating stocks, and high program costs, price supports on most commodities were lower when Secretary Benson left office in 1961 than when he took office in 1953.

See also Price-Support Programs.

BEST FIT. The curve that best fits a set of data plotted on a scatter diagram is the one which minimizes the sum of squares or error (least squares), where "error" is the difference between the observed and the computed value of the dependent variable. The errors are the e's in the figure.

See also Curve Fitting; Scatter Diagram.

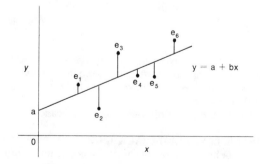

BILATERAL BARGAINING, a situation in which each side represents a monopoly power of sorts. The union representing the bargaining unit is viewed as the single seller (monopolist) of labor services, and the firm, if it accounts for all or most of the employment in the labor market, can be viewed as a single buyer (monopsonist). With this sort of market power on each side of the table, the process, strategies, and outcome may be different from those in other bargaining situations.

BILATERAL MONOPOLY, a market with both a pure monopoly and a pure monopsony, only one seller of the good and only one purchaser of the good. The typical bilateral monopoly occurs when a labor union is selling labor to a single company. The two monopoly powers tend to offset one another, in that the wage rate and compensations may be equal to the value of the output of the worker. In this situation the factor of production will not normally be exploited.

BLACK MARKET, an illegal market that emerges when price ceilings are imposed. A price ceiling is a maximum legal price. Price ceilings cause shortages (excess demand) because the market-clearing price (where supply equals demand) is higher than the legal price. Consumers demand more than they would at the market-clearing price, and producers supply less. Since producers are willing to supply more at a higher price, and consumers are willing to buy more, there is a strong incentive to ignore the price ceiling. In a black market, price controls are ignored, and agents buy and sell at prices higher than the legal maximum.

BLUE-COLLAR WORKER, a term used to distinguish between those workers who are employed on the administrative end of a firm and those workers who are not. The term originated at a time when factory floor workers wore blue collars and office personnel wore white collars. Blue collar does not imply a skill level. A skilled machinist and the janitor who sweeps the floor are both considered blue-collar workers.

BOARD OF GOVERNORS. *See* Federal Reserve System.

BÖHM-BAWERK, EUGEN (1851-1914), Austrian economist and several times minister of finance, his outstanding contribution to the field of economics is his theory of interest, marking a major advance in the understanding of why capital yields profit. Underlying this theory is a combination of the time-preference and marginal-productivity principles; it is derived from the marginal utility theory of value, of which Böhm-Bawerk gave the most comprehensive presentation.

His views were set forth in *Capital and Interest* (1884) and *The Positive Theory of Capital* (1889). The second of these, principally a presentation of Böhm-Bawerk's personal theories, gained much attention for his ideas and stimulated broad controversies still unsettled. The argument was constructed thus: (1) people tend to overestimate future resources and underestimate future wants; (2) goods available now will yield goods of higher value in the future; (3) people will then tend to place a higher value on present goods than on future ones of the same kind and quantity; and (4) therefore, to induce them to exchange present for future goods, people must be paid a premium which will make the value of the future good equal to that of the present. The premium is known as interest.

Böhm-Bawerk's critical analysis of the Marxian theorem of the declining rate of profit is also considered a classic. He maintained that socialism's criticism of capitalism was in reality a criticism of the problem of scarcity, which was in fact the central problem of the human condition and with which, therefore, even socialism would eventually have to cope.

Having demonstrated in his early work that interest is a basic component in any rational economic calculation, even noncapitalistic, Böhm-Bawerk developed later in his life a general theory of laws of economic rationality which applies to every type of social order. His work contributed significantly to the development of non-Marxist socialist theory after 1918.

—*Clyde A. Haulman*

BOLSHEVIKS, a term (Russian for "men of the majority") used by followers of Lenin in 1903 when they won a temporary majority in the executive committee of the Social Democratic Party. The majority was soon lost to Menshevik (minority) opponents, but the name was retained until 1952.

In 1917 the Bolsheviks provided such leadership that the second (November) revolution was named after them. The party accepted the Marxist revolutionary creed dogmatically, and was characterized by highly centralized leadership, tight regime of party discipline, absolutism of party line, intolerance of compromise or disagreement, and an attitude of manipulation relative to mass organization.

See also Lenin, Vladimir.

BOND MARKET. The bond market is not a place but a variety of brokers, dealers, and other institutions that facilitate the purchase and sale of bonds. These agencies are connected by telephone or direct wire so that information can be obtained and transactions completed almost instantaneously. New corporate bonds are usually issued through investment banks. New federal government securities are sold through the agency of the Federal Reserve Banks. Most transfers of already-issued bonds are handled by specialized dealers who buy and sell for their own account, thereby making a continuous market for the general public wishing to sell or buy. Banks and stock brokers will handle orders, or the dealers may trade directly with the public. A few bonds are sold on the stock exchanges.

See also Bond Prices; Open Market Operations.

BOND PRICES. A bond has two different prices. Its par value is the price printed on the face, usually $1,000 or multiples thereof. The bond is normally sold at this price when newly issued. More important, it is the price at which the bond will be redeemed at maturity. Market price is the price at which present bondholders can sell their bonds to prospective purchasers. Unlike par value, market value may fluctuate partly because of changes in the financial condition of the issuer from day to day, though not nearly as much as stock prices, but even more in consequence of a change in the general level of interest rates.

Bond yield is the annual dollar interest paid on a bond divided by its market price and adjusted for appreciation or depreciation to maturity. Every reduction in a bond's market price raises its yield; every increase in price reduces yield. Therefore, as interest rates rise, bond prices fall, and *vice versa*.

BONDS, in finance, interest-bearing certificates issued either by a business firm (corporate bonds) or by a government that promises to pay the bondholder a specified sum of money on a specified date. The main purpose of bond issuance is to raise capital.

Bonds can be divided into two basic categories according to the term to maturity of the bonds: *short-term bonds* have a term to maturity of less than one year; *long-term bonds* have a term to maturity of greater than one year. Short-term bonds generally do not have a stated interest rate but are usually sold at a discount. Thus, a one-year bond that can be redeemed for $1,000 in a year will sell today for something less than $1,000, such as $900. In this case the interest rate is equal to the return on the bond, $100, divided by the price of the bond, $900, or 11%. A long-term bond carries an interest rate and the holder of the bond sends in coupons periodically, usually once a year, to receive interest payments. These bonds are also called *coupon bonds*.

There are many different types of bonds. A popular bond issued and guaranteed by the United States government is the *savings bond*. Sold at a discount, it matures to face value after a designated period of time, usually 7 or 10 years.

A bond issued by a city, county, or district government is called a *municipal bond* while state government bonds are simply called *state bonds*. Some municipal bonds are referred to by the purpose for which they are sold, such as *construction bonds* or *bridge bonds*. All of these types are usually secured, or guaranteed, bonds. There are also unsecured bonds, called *debentures*, that are backed only by the credit

standing of the issuing agency.

Often, a bond is named for the terms of payment of the interest or the principal. For example, an *annuity bond* has no maturity date; thus the interest is continuing. A *callable bond* is one that must be presented for payment upon due notice to the bond holder. A *continued bond* is one that does not have to be turned in at maturity but may be held indefinitely at the same rate of interest. A *convertible bond* gives the holder the right to exchange his bond for a different type of security, such as stock. Other terms-of-payment bonds include gold bonds, income bonds, installment bonds, and extended and deferred bonds.

Bonds are also named for the way in which they are secured. For example, with an *assumed bond* the principal, or the interest, or both, are guaranteed by a corporation other than the one that issued the bond. These bonds are also known as *guaranteed* or *endorsed bonds*. Also, a *blanket bond* indicates a general mortgage pledged as security. Other bonds that fall into this category include a *bottomry bond,* which is secured by a mortgage on a ship, a *collateral trust bond,* a *division bond,* and a *sinking fund bond.*

—*William D. Wagoner*

BOOK COST. *See* Original Cost.

BORROWED RESERVES. *See* Free Reserves.

BORROWING. Governments may meet their financial obligations by raising funds through taxation, by creating new money (federal) and by borrowing. The act of borrowing requires that the government, usually through the Treasury Department, issue bonds which may then be offered for sale to private individuals and firms, commercial banks, or the central bank and other government agencies. Though the particular certificate will usually bear a stated face value and fixed amount of interest coupons until date of maturity, the actual price paid by the buyer may differ from the face value, depending upon the going rate of interest for low-risk investments. Thus, a $1,000 bond paying 5% interest for 10 years ($50 per year) will usually sell for something less than $1,000 if the buyer is able to earn, say 7%, on alternative investments of similarly low risk. The total of outstanding bonds of various maturities constitutes the gross public debt.

BOTTLENECK INFLATION. *See* Sectoral Inflation.

BOULDING, KENNETH EWART (1910-   ), a critic of many aspects of modern economics. Having made important contributions to microeconomics, Boulding attacked the failure of economics to be integrated with other social sciences in his *Reconstruction of Economics* (1950). This theme has dominated much of Boulding's work and has reached an eloquent peak in his *Economics As Science* (1970), a series of essays dealing with the larger scientific background of economics. Boulding's additional concern that economists have failed to explain distribution in a macroeconomic sense has led to his important work in considering various aspects of the grants' economy. Boulding became professor of economics at the University of Colorado at Boulder in 1968. His other works include *The Economy of Love and Fear* (1973) and *The Social System of the Planet Earth* (1977).

BOYCOTT, one of the most familiar weapons of labor used to exert pressure on employers. Strikes are not usually considered as coming within the meaning of "boycotts"; rather, the term is used almost exclusively to mean an organized refusal to deal with someone in order to induce him to do something. This is a primary boycott. It may take the form of refusing to patronize a product or refusal to handle certain goods. It may involve only one product, or it may involve a particular store or chain of stores.

Boycotts often become more complicated than strikes because they can involve pressure on a third party. When a third party becomes involved, there is a secondary boycott. In 1947, the Taft-Hartley Act deemed the secondary boycott an unfair labor practice and made it illegal. Unfortunately, in actual cases it is sometimes difficult to determine and prove a secondary boycott.

BRANCH BANK, a commercial bank or, sometimes, a savings bank that maintains at least one branch office in addition to the head office. Until the 1980s, branch banks were permitted only within the state where the head office was located. The Reagan administration reversed this prohibition, and by 1985, 20 states permitted branches run by out-of-state banks.

BRANNAN PLAN, a plan for supporting farm income proposed in 1949 by Secretary of Agriculture Charles F. Brannan. It differed from earlier policy principally in (1) making extensive use of direct payments to farmers to compensate them whenever market prices for livestock fell below target prices; (2) calculating target prices by a formula that differed from the parity price computation; (3) limiting payments that the larger farmers could receive; and (4) making it possible to require farmers to comply with production controls as a condition for receiving benefits if surpluses appeared. Price support for storable crops was to be continued as before, but for more crops. The plan generated much controversy and was not enacted by Congress.

See also Parity Prices.

BREAK-EVEN POINT, term used in business to designate the exact amount of income required and the number of items that must be sold in order for a firm to meet expenses exactly and be at the position

In this diagram, point a is considered the "break-even" point because any price higher than P_0 (like P_2) generates positive economic profits and any price lower than P_0 (like P_1) generates negative economic profits. At point a, economic profits are equal to zero, i.e., the firm breaks even. Point d is considered the "shut-down" point (see Shut-Down Point).

where neither a loss nor a profit is made. For example, if a firm has a fixed cost of $20 and an operating cost of $5 for every item it produces and if the item sells for $10, the break-even point will occur after the fourth item has been sold because the cost to produce the items, $40, equals the income of $40 generated by their sale. A firm must be able to reach the break-even point to justify remaining in business.

In national income analysis, the break-even point is the disposable income at which consumption is 100% of disposable income. It is a useful reference point to compute in solving national income problems.

BRETTON WOODS. In 1945 representatives from 40-odd nations assembled at Bretton Woods, New Hampshire, for the purpose of laying plans for an orderly approach to short-run currency and exchange problems and long-run problems of reconstruction and development. Out of this conference came the International Monetary Fund and International Bank for Reconstruction and Development (World Bank) to handle the short-run and long-run problems, respectively.

BRITISH LABOUR PARTY, formed in 1900, stemmed from late nineteenth-century labor unions, the Fabian Society, the Social Democratic Federation, and the Independent Labour Party. It advocates evolutionary socialism within a framework of political democracy.

Believing that private owners can neither meet the necessities of modernization nor bring about growth, steady employment, and a fair distribution of national income, the Labour Party has recurrently urged the nationalization of basic industries. When in power, it has imposed controls on finance and investment, furthered government planning on land utilization, put agriculture under national guidance, expanded construction in public housing, and created a system of socialized medicine.

The Labour Party adopted a socialist-orientated constitution in 1918 and won its first national election in 1924. It returned to power in 1929-1931. Since then it has won four elections, but it has been out of office since 1970.

See also Evolutionary Socialism; Fabian Society; Nationalism.

BUDDHIST ECONOMICS. The Buddhist perspective on economics was popularized by British economist E.F. Schumacher in his book, *Small is Beautiful*. According to his analysis, Buddhist economics is the systematic study of how to attain given ends with the least possible means. The aim of Buddhist economists is to maximize human well-being with a minimum of consumption, a very different view from Western capitalism's emphasis on maximizing consumption.

Buddhist economics favors local production from local resources and distinguishes between renewable and nonrenewable resources, favoring renewable resources and using nonrenewable materials sparingly. Work is also viewed differently by the Buddhist economist, who sees it as an occasion for humans to develop creativity in dignity and freedom. The emphasis is less on the nonhuman product than on the value of useful, disciplined work.

These considerations are combined in the Buddhist attitude toward technology. Technology that enhances the natural power and skills of the worker while consuming the minimum of resources is embodied in Schumacher's concept of appropriate technology.

See also Appropriate Technology; Schumacher, E.F.

BUDGET LINE, CONSUMER, a line in the commodity space representing all commodity bundles whose cost equals the consumer's income. The budget line's slope is negative, and its magnitude equals the ratio of the prices of the commodities in question.

BUDGET LINE, FIRM. If two inputs are plotted on the respective axes, then, for every possible money outlay by a firm, a budget line can be constructed. This line indicates, given factor prices, the locus of points that show varying combinations of inputs available to the firm for a given expenditure. A family of budget lines shows the total cost of every possible factor combination of the inputs in question. Budget lines will be linear and parallel, reflecting the assumption that a firm can purchase all it wishes of the inputs without affecting their prices. If prices do change, the slope of the budget lines will change correspondingly.

BURNS, ARTHUR FRANK (1904-   ), Austrian-born economist, educator, and expert on business cycles and macroeconomics. He received his A.B. (1925), A.M. (1925), and Ph.D. (1934) in economics from Columbia University. His numerous publications include *Measuring Business Cycles* (1946, with W. Mitchell), *Prosperity Without Inflation* (1957), *The Management of Prosperity* (1966, with Paul Samuelson), and *The Business Cycle in a Changing World* (1969). His public service is wide and varied, including positions as chairman of the President's Council of Economic Advisors (1953-1956), chairman of the Advisory Board on Economic Growth and Stability (1953-1956), president of the American Economic Association (1959), and chairman of the Board of Governors of the Federal Reserve System.

BUSINESS AGENT. In labor unionism, a full-time employee of the local labor union hired to manage the day-to-day affairs of the organization. Often an ex-officer of the union, he provides a variety of services and, while not officially a policy maker, may have a major impact on union policy.

BUSINESS CYCLES. Economies have proven themselves subject to regularly recurring periods of slump and recovery, particularly since the Industrial Revolution and in England, France, the United States, and other industrialized countries where the economies are not controlled centrally. Since the beginning of the nineteenth century, culminating in the Great Depression of the 1930s, the economies of these countries have been subjected to large changes in the levels of income or wealth. In 1815, 1837, 1873, 1893, and 1929 the United States experienced severe depressions, which were interspersed with periods of prosperity, and with milder depressions in 1847, 1857, 1867, 1883, and 1907. Since World War II there have been no real depressions in the United States or other advanced countries (although the recessions of 1974 and 1982 were more pronounced than those of 1949, 1954, 1961, and 1970. However, most modern governments now intervene in their economic systems, even in so-called free-market economies, distorting the behavior patterns of business cycles that have been established over the last century, so that traditional theories can no longer be expected to apply without considerable variation. President Nixon's New Economic Policy (Phases I and II) is such an example.

The costs of business fluctuations are considerable. Depression and recession result in irretrievable losses of real output and wealth, while creating great hardships for the unemployed, whose numbers are also increased. The costs associated with such fluctuations explain the interest of economists in the study of

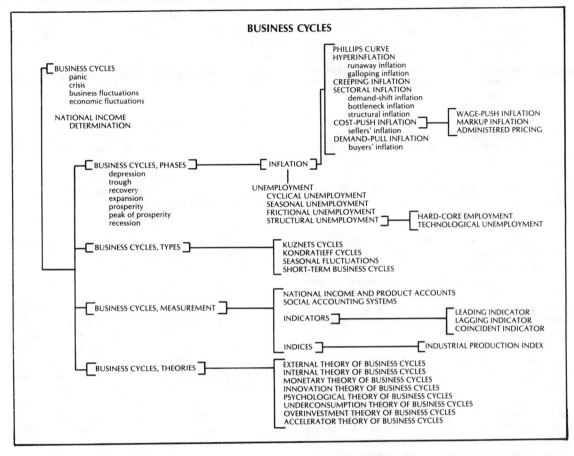

BUSINESS CYCLES

BUSINESS CYCLES
    panic
    crisis
    business fluctuations
    economic fluctuations

NATIONAL INCOME
DETERMINATION

BUSINESS CYCLES, PHASES
    depression
    trough
    recovery
    expansion
    prosperity
    peak of prosperity
    recession

INFLATION

PHILLIPS CURVE
HYPERINFLATION
    runaway inflation
    galloping inflation
CREEPING INFLATION
SECTORAL INFLATION
    demand-shift inflation
    bottleneck inflation
    structural inflation
COST-PUSH INFLATION
    sellers' inflation
DEMAND-PULL INFLATION
    buyers' inflation

WAGE-PUSH INFLATION
MARKUP INFLATION
ADMINISTERED PRICING

UNEMPLOYMENT
CYCLICAL UNEMPLOYMENT
SEASONAL UNEMPLOYMENT
FRICTIONAL UNEMPLOYMENT
STRUCTURAL UNEMPLOYMENT

HARD-CORE EMPLOYMENT
TECHNOLOGICAL UNEMPLOYMENT

BUSINESS CYCLES, TYPES

KUZNETS CYCLES
KONDRATIEFF CYCLES
SEASONAL FLUCTUATIONS
SHORT-TERM BUSINESS CYCLES

BUSINESS CYCLES, MEASUREMENT

NATIONAL INCOME AND PRODUCT ACCOUNTS
SOCIAL ACCOUNTING SYSTEMS

INDICATORS

LEADING INDICATOR
LAGGING INDICATOR
COINCIDENT INDICATOR

INDICES

INDUSTRIAL PRODUCTION INDEX

BUSINESS CYCLES, THEORIES

EXTERNAL THEORY OF BUSINESS CYCLES
INTERNAL THEORY OF BUSINESS CYCLES
MONETARY THEORY OF BUSINESS CYCLES
INNOVATION THEORY OF BUSINESS CYCLES
PSYCHOLOGICAL THEORY OF BUSINESS CYCLES
UNDERCONSUMPTION THEORY OF BUSINESS CYCLES
OVERINVESTMENT THEORY OF BUSINESS CYCLES
ACCELERATOR THEORY OF BUSINESS CYCLES

business cycles, as well as governmental involvement in moderating wide swings in cyclical activity.

Phases. Prior to World War II a typical business cycle passed through four phases: depression, recovery, prosperity, and recession. Prosperity culminated in a peak, or upper turning point, and depression, on the other hand, eventually reached a trough, or lower turning point.

In more recent years, the variation in economic activity has not been as great as before. Modern macroeconomic thought defines cyclical behavior in terms of an upswing, a peak, a recession, and a trough. Policies aimed at stabilization are intended to eliminate the typical business cycle extremes that were experienced throughout the 1800s and early 1900s.

The business cycle is enmeshed in other rhythms and patterns of economic activity. There are, for example, seasonal variations in sales, output, and employment; sales are always higher at Christmas and Easter than in nonholiday periods; construction employment is usually higher in the summer than in the winter. Economic activity also tends to expand from year to year. Per capita gross national product, for example, has grown at an average rate of over 2% per

annum since 1870. These regularly recurring events and natural expansions, therefore, indicate trends in business activity in addition to the cyclical or fluctuating patterns. The combination of natural expansion and business cycles results in peaks and troughs that are higher in subsequent time periods.

Alvin Hansen distinguishes between minor cycles associated with variations in inventory investment, lasting 2 to 6 years, and major cycles associated with investment in plant and equipment, averaging 7 to 10 years. In addition to such major and minor cycles, Simon Kuznets has identified and analyzed 25-year fluctuations in the rate of growth, associated with immigrations and natural rates of population growth, railroad building and capital imports, and the growth rate of the money supply. The Russian economist N.D. Kondratieff claims to have identified certain long waves in economic activity lasting 40 to 60 years, which he attributed to changes in technology, new markets, and war and revolution. Finally, certain industries or sectors of the economy have their own cycles, such as the well-documented 15- to 20-year cycle in the construction industry. Other individual cycles have been observed in shipbuilding, corn and hog production, and the like.

At any given time, various cycles can interact with one another, making clear identification or prediction difficult. If a downturn in a major cycle coincides with a downturn in an individual cycle, such as construction, and retardation in the rate of growth, the result could be a more severe recession than a major cycle would produce alone.

Business Cycle Theories. Throughout the nineteenth century, economists spent little time researching cycles, holding that Say's law of markets ensured that unemployment was a temporary phenomenon in spite of the recurrence of cyclical fluctuations in incomes and employment. Business and industry previously concentrated on the crises and panics that signaled the end of an expansionary phase rather than planning over the long term. The first study of the business cycle, as a whole, was by Clement Juglar in 1889, since which time many theories of the business cycle have been advanced. Internal theories tend to stress the cumulative, self-generating nature of business cycles, while external theories focus on exogenous factors, such as crop yields and random shocks. Some early endogenous theories emphasized psychological factors, underconsumption, overinvestment, and fluctuations in the supply of credit. For many years modern business cycle theory was based primarily on Keynesian macroeconomic analysis and the accelerator.

However, other explanations now exist. For example, Milton Friedman's "fooling model" is based upon the notion that workers' labor supply curve depends upon the wage rate adjusted by an expected price level, while the demand for labor is based upon the real wage rate. Also, the long-term characteristics of labor contracts is used to help explain what is called the non-market clearing model, a body of thought recently advanced by Don Patinkin, Robert Clower,

Robert J. Barro, and Hershel I. Grossman. These explanations of the business cycle examine the consequences of sticky wages and prices with respect to economic activity.

Is the Business Cycle Obsolete? Several institutional changes in the United States have contributed to increasing stability in economic activity. The growth of the service sector relative to manufacturing has tended to stabilize the economy. Workers in the service sector tend to be salaried employees rather than wage earners, and demand for services tends to be stable. The progressive income tax, unemployment insurance, and stable corporate dividend policies also tend to act countercyclically. Finally, the government has declared its intention to prevent widespread unemployment and galloping inflation. The combination of stabilizing institutional changes and progress in economic theory has resulted in an economy that is less apt to experience wide cyclical fluctuations than that which existed prior to 1929.

Although deep depressions and periods of severe inflation may be avoided through correct monetary and fiscal policy, there will in all probability be slight recessions and short periods of high inflation. In fact, the problem of stagflation—persistent high unemployment and inflation—caused many people to question the validity of existing business cycle theories. The newer explanations of the business cycle, along with the natural rate hypothesis and explanations of a vertical Phillips Curve, are outgrowths of the necessity to explain stagflation.   —*Carlisle E. Moody*

See also Accelerator Theory of Business Cycles; Inflation; Multiplier.

BUSINESS CYCLES, MEASUREMENT. Business and economic activity in the United States is measured by a wide range of statistical observations: National income and products accounts which include

BUSINESS CYCLES

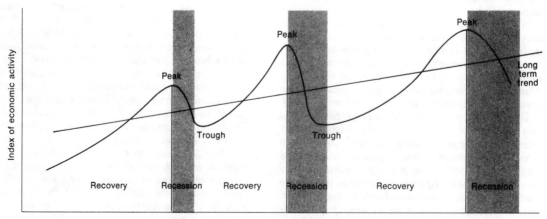

measures of GNP, NNP, National Income, and Personal Income; indices of industrial production; price indices, and labor force and employment data.

Recently, monetary growth rates have been viewed along with the index of leading economic indicators as gauges of expected changes in business activity. Also, surveys of government, consumers, and business intentions are used in an attempt to predict future trends in the level of business activity.

BUSINESS CYCLES, PHASES. Prior to the 1940s, most economists characterized the four stages of a business cycle as depression, recovery, prosperity, and recession.

Depression. The depression phase of the cycle experiences severe unemployment and excess capacity; that is, idle workers, plant, and equipment. Unemployment implies low aggregate demand and income, which, in turn, leads to low levels of production and output. Prices generally fall, and profits become abnormally low or negative. Excess capacity, falling or stagnant consumer demand, and uncertainty contribute to a low level of investment spending. Net investment may be negative as business fails to replace plant and equipment. The lowest ebb of business activity is the trough, or lower turning point. Eventually, through an external or internal force, some element acts to stimulate the economy, and the cycle enters the recovery phase, if the stimulus is strong enough. The stimulus could be an autonomous increase in consumer or government demand or an increase in investment demand.

Recovery. Increased demand leads to increased production and employment, and rising employment implies increasing income and demand through the multiplier, which leads to increases in investment spending for capital goods, and further increases in employment, output, and aggregate demand in a cumulative process. Business attitudes change from the pessimism of the trough to cautious optimism as the expansion gains momentum. As favorable expectations are confirmed, business attitudes become buoyant, and orders are placed for new plant and new equipment. Prices and wages begin to rise, although slowly, as previously idle capital and labor is rehired. As the expansion gathers force, the rising price of raw materials places pressure on firms to raise produce prices. The combination of rising prices and increasing demand reinforces business optimism and results in further increases until full-scale prosperity or a boom emerges.

Prosperity. As expansion continues, the economy approaches its full-employment output level, and the rate of growth in aggregate demand will begin to slow. Because of the action of the accelerator, there will be an absolute decline in fixed investment. Fixed investment may also fall because of shortages and bottlenecks in the capital goods industries. As the capital

goods sector approaches capacity output, its rate of growth of employment and output decline. The action of the accelerator will again ensure an absolute decrease in the level of investment.

Other forces are generated by the boom that can halt the investment boom and set the stage for a contraction. Wage rates will rise rapidly as firms bid against one another for qualified workers, and union wage demands will be resisted in the face of high profits and sales. Productivity, or output per capita, will decline due to fatigue, hasty work on rush orders, and employment of less qualified labor. The combination of rising wage and raw material costs with declining productivity causes profits to be squeezed. Also, rising interest rates and construction costs increase the costs of capital goods. Therefore, declining profits, rising capital costs, and decreasing consumer demand cause investment demand to fall, resulting in a downturn.

Recession. The recession phase is marked by a cumulative contraction in business activity. As investment spending decreases, there is a decline in production and employment in capital goods industries. Consumer demand falls as incomes decline and unemployment increases. Unless checked, the contraction will continue to gather force until the depression phase is reached, and the cycle begins again.

Currently, a recession is defined as any two successive quarters of declining real gross national product. Business cycle theories now focus on the pattern that has become typical, that is, movement from recession to a trough (or bottoming out) through a period of recovery and prosperity to a peak, and into another recession. Existing stabilization policies appear to be successful in eliminating the depression phase from the "typical" business cycle.

Considerations. It should be noted, however, that no two cycles are identical, and no cycle will follow the preceding course exactly. Many economists think that the four phases are structured too rigidly, preferring a two-phase scheme (expansion and contraction), or a simple discussion of the turning points. In any real business cycle, there is not a sharp transition from expansion to contraction; thus economists discuss turning zones rather than points. At the upper turning zone, or "peak," for example, the forces of contraction are building up faster than the forces of expansion, and the predominant force is downward.

However they are described, not all regions, sectors, or businesses will behave in the same way over the cycle. For example, as the economy reaches the peak of the boom, some firms are already experiencing declines in sales and profits. As the number of firms experiencing contractions begins to outweigh those experiencing gains, the cycle passes its peak and the recession begins. Similarly, even at the bottom of the depression, some firms can be enjoying gains in sales and profits. As this experience spreads in other firms and industries, the recovery phase begins. Thus, contraction begins while expansion is prevalent, and expansion begins while contraction is dominant. The term "cycle," however descriptive, should not lead one to believe that business fluctuations are regular and unvarying.   —Carlisle E. Moody

See also Accelerator Theory of Business Cycles; Investment; Multiplier.

BUSINESS CYCLES, THEORIES. Many economists have developed theories to explain cyclical fluctuations in income, productivity, investment, and employment. The first study or theory of business cycles, as a whole, was introduced by Clement Juglar in 1889. Many theories have been advanced since that time, and generally fall into one of two categories: external (exogenous) and internal (endogenous).

External Theories assume that fluctuations in economic activity or business cycles are caused by factors outside the economic system. They include, for example, sunspot cycles (an obsolete nineteenth-century theory), wars and revolutions, and political and social events. Other external factors which lead to fluctuations are the rates of immigration and population growth, discovery of new resources, and scientific and technological innovations. Most of these external elements, although plausible influences, are neither predictable nor controllable over the long run and suggest that business cycles are neither predictable nor controllable either.

Internal Theories acknowledge that certain external factors influence economic activity but contend that, on the whole, the major causes of business cycles are forces within the economic system. Among the endogenous theories are profit motive (psychological), monetary, overinvestment, and underconsumption. Some internal theories suggest that mechanisms within the system will naturally generate economic cycles so that, predictably, every expansion will be followed by recession, contraction, and renewed expansion. However, modern governments' interventions in the economy, even in so-called free-market economies, distort expected behavior patterns established over the last century, so that traditional theories can no longer apply without considerable modification.

BUSINESS CYCLES, TYPES, refers to specific cycles of fluctuation in economic activity, each lasting from over a year to upwards of 60 years. In the United States, business cycles last, on the average, about 4 years. There is also cyclical activity associated with specific industries, such as the well-documented 15- to 20-year cycle in the construction industry. Seasonal fluctuations over any given year and long-term trends are noncyclical and do not directly affect business cycles.

Some economists distinguish between minor, or short-term, business cycles associated with inventory investment and major cycles triggered by net real investment in plant and equipment. Inventory investment cycles can last from 2 to 10 years, depending upon whether one accepts the theories of Alvin Hansen or those of Joseph Kitchin. Major cycles average 7 to 10 years. On a broader scale, so-called Kuznets cycles, involving fluctuations in the supply trends of resources and the productivity and efficiency with which they are used, last about 25 years. The longest type of fluctuation is called the Kindratieff cycle, named for the Russian economist who identified long waves of price, production, and trade.

Distinction among the types of business cycles is useful for a variety of purposes. However, because they interact, identification and study of each are difficult. A minor downswing in one industry, for example, can coincide with a major downswing in capital formation, thus producing a greater recession than might otherwise be expected. At any given point it is hard to separate the influence of each component on the level of economic activity.

BUSINESS SAVINGS, which usually total more than half of total gross savings in the United States, come from undistributed profits (retained earnings) and depreciation reserves. Business savings constitute a leakage from the national income stream, since they reduce the economy's marginal propensity to consume. However, they serve a useful function, inasmuch as they are generally reinvested in the businesses themselves for expansion and long-term growth.

See also Personal Savings; Saving.

BUSINESS UNIONISM refers to one of the possible organizational philosophies in the labor movement, and, in contrast to other concepts, stresses the economic goals of the union. Thus, the proponents of business unionism would argue that the role of the union is to get better wages and protect members' jobs from competition, not to act as an agent for social or economic reform. Generally, U.S. unions, particularly the craft unions, have worked within the existing political structure, and have not organized a labor political party. Business unionism is sometimes called "bread-and-butter" unionism.

BUYERS' INFLATIONS. See Demand-Pull Inflation.

BUYERS' MONOPOLY. See Monopsony.

CALLABLE BONDS, bonds that must be presented for payment once the issuer has given due notice to the holder of the bond. A callable bond differs from most bonds, because it has no set maturity date but can be called at any time.

CALL LOANS, or demand loans, loans made in a

CAPITAL

DEMAND FOR CAPITAL

TECHNOLOGY
TECHNOLOGICAL CHANGE
NET PRODUCTIVITY OF CAPITAL
MARGINAL EFFICIENCY OF CAPITAL
DISCOUNTED VALUE
CAPITAL STOCK
CAPITAL EQUIPMENT
CAPITAL DEEPENING
   capital widening

CAPITALISM
CAPITALIST
ENTREPRENEUR
INNOVATOR

UNCERTAINTY
RISK
PROFIT SYSTEM

PROFITS
   EXCESS PROFITS
DIVIDENDS
   distributed earnings
   CORPORATE EARNINGS
   UNDISTRIBUTED PROFITS
MONOPOLY PROFITS
INTEREST
   INTEREST RATES
   INTEREST RATE STRUCTURE

period of one day automatically renewed unless the borrower repays or the lender demands repayment. They are, thus, the most liquid of all loans, because repayment can at any time be required within 24 hours. Demand loans are most often made by banks to security brokers against the deposit of stock certificates as collateral.

See also Liquid Assets; Portfolio Balancing.

CAPITAL. In the language of economics, capital has two meanings. The first, *physical capital,* refers to one of the three factors of production—land, labor, and capital. Physical capital refers to the durable and long-lasting inputs to the production process, such as machinery, buildings, and tools. The second meaning of capital is *financial capital,* which usually refers to the sources of the funds to purchase the physical capital. In the business world, there are two sources of financial capital—equity financing and debt financing. In equity financing, the owner or owners of the firm provide from their own wealth the funds necessary to purchase physical capital. For the corporate form of

The sprawling Chrysler headquarters and plant illustrate the large amount of capital and labor involved in a major corporate enterprise.

enterprise, this equity financing normally comes from the issue of new stock or from the use of retained earnings, which are profits of the firm that are held by the firm instead of being distributed to its owners, the stockholders. In debt financing, the source of the funds to purchase physical capital is from borrowing. This borrowing can take many different forms, such as bonds.

The price of capital is called the interest rate. The interest rate is the market price that firms must pay to purchase physical capital through borrowing, or debt financing. If firms use equity financing to purchase physical capital, the interest rate is the opportunity cost of that capital. If the firm did not buy the particular piece of physical capital with its financial capital, the firm could lend it to some other firm and receive the interest rate as a return. Therefore, if a company uses its own financial capital as a source of financing, it gives up an amount equal to the interest rate. The interest rate represents the cost, or price, of capital under both debt and equity financing.

— *Timothy P. Ryan*

See also Factors of Production.

CAPITAL ACCOUNT, in a balance of payments, records transactions involving paper claims and debts, rather than real commodities or services. Purchases and sales of stocks and bonds, lending and borrowing, and changes in bank balances make up the capital account. *Long-term capital movements* (loans and investments with maturities exceeding a year) can finance a new flow of goods and services from lending and investing countries to borrowers and recipients. *Short-term capital movements* primarily serve to finance gaps between payments and receipts relative to transactions in the current account. Unilateral transfers (for example, government grants and immigrant remittances) differ from ordinary capital transactions in that they involve no reciprocal obligations or claims. If the current account in the balance of payments does not balance, the discrepancy is financed by capital movements or transfers of gold.

See also Balance of Payments; Capital Movement.

CAPITAL CONSUMPTION ALLOWANCE (CCA), used in national income accounting, the amount deducted from gross national product (GNP) to obtain net national product, representing the portion of GNP resulting from the value of capital assets consumed or declining in value in the production process. CCA includes capital goods depreciation, accidental losses of capital assets, capital goods bought and consumed in the same period, and such expenditures incurred in finding new resources as oil and mineral exploration costs.

See also Gross National Product; Net National Product.

CAPITAL DEEPENING, a rise in the ratio of capital to both labor and output. Any factor that increases expected returns or lowers the cost of capital will increase investment demand. Growth of new technology and development of new products stimulate the production of new types of capital, and the amount per unit of output would likely increase, thus deepening capital by changing the ratios of it to other factors in the productive mix. A widening of capital results from growth in an economy demanding more capital goods of accustomed types with no change in the capital-output ratio; capital is accumulated in balance with labor.

See also Capital Equipment; Demand for Capital; Technological Change.

CAPITAL EQUIPMENT, the existing stock of machines, factories, plants, and other long-lasting inputs into the production process. In microeconomic theory capital equipment is fixed in the short run. In other words, firms can only increase or decrease the capital equipment over a reasonably long period of time. Capital equipment physically wears away over time; this is called depreciation. In order for firms to keep up their original productive capacity they must replace this equipment that has depreciated. Any investment in capital equipment over and above this replacement is called net investment, a very important part of macroeconomic activity.

CAPITAL GOODS. See Capital.

CAPITALISM, an economic system based on private ownership of the majority of the factors of production—such as capital, land and all the resources embodied in the land (oil, gas, metals, water, and the like). In addition, capitalism is characterized by private property rights, private ownership of personal items, such as homes, automobiles, and so forth. The basic premise of capitalism is that private owners of capital will take the necessary risks in order to produce the goods and services that the consumers demand. In return for this risk taking, the capitalists are allowed to retain the profits that might result from the sale of the goods and services. Under capitalism, individuals have the freedom to engage in economic activities of their choice with limited legal and governmental restrictions. In a capitalistic economy the consumer determines the allocation of scarce resources through the market mechanism of demand. Producers are free to shift resources to meet the demands of consumers expressed via the market mechanism.

Characteristics. Economists are not in agreement as to the exact economic and political characteristics of capitalism. Some of the important characteristics of capitalism are: (1) commercialization of economic life through a market-determined system of wages and prices, (2) the central role of profit in the decision-making process as to the allocation and use of economic resources, (3) technological innovation resulting from a high degree of competition, (4) a significant degree of risk taking and a spirit of entrepreneurship, and (5) a highly developed banking and credit system.

Government plays a relatively minor role in a capitalistic economy, serving primarily to make rules, protect welfare, and carry on activities avoided by private enterprises as unprofitable.

Origins. As a political-economic system, capitalism had its origin in Western European culture and by the eighteenth century had become the dominant system of economic thought in England and the United States. In countries where capitalism was the predominant economic system, societies have achieved high material standards of living for the greatest possible proportion of their citizens. Other terms sometimes used in economic literature as synonyms for capitalism are "private enterprise system," "market system," and "free price system."   —*Algin B. King*
See also Economic Systems; Free Enterprise.

CAPITALIST, a key figure in a market economy, is the private owner or controller of capital equipment and resources, who hires labor to conduct business enterprises; also anyone who provides capital funds through purchase of stocks and bonds.
See also Market Economy; Profit System.

CAPITALIZED VALUE OF AN ASSET. In some situations where it is important to evaluate the price or value of an existing asset, the evaluator does not always have enough information to determine the current market price of the asset. One way to accomplish the evaluation in these cases is to assume that the current value of the asset is equal to the discounted value of the future income or earnings stream that will result from the asset. This process is referred to as determining the capitalized value of the asset. An example of this process is the determination of the value of the "good will" of the firm's name when the firm is being sold. The value of this asset is equal to the discounted value of the extra profits that the firm makes because of good will.

CAPITAL MOVEMENT, liquidation of capital investment of one kind (or in one place) and the reinvestment of the realized funds in another kind of investment (or in another place). Assume that a foreign country sells bonds in the United States to get funds to purchase railroad equipment. Assume further that there is a delay in delivering the equipment and the proceeds of the flotation are invested in certificates of deposit (CDs) until needed. If three months later the equipment is exported and paid for by cashing the CDs, the U.S. balance of payments will have experienced movements in real capital, long-term capital, and short-term capital.
See also Balance of Payments.

CAPITAL OUTPUT RATIO (or Capital Productivity Ratio) is the ratio of marginal capital cost to marginal output, or, phrased differently, the ratio of net investment of the resulting increase in output or productivity. If the ratio is 3:1, then 3 units of additional capital will yield 1 additional unit of output.

CAPITAL SAVING, the effect of an innovation or invention that lowers the share of capital (inventory, property, or money) relative to the share of labor used in a business or industry. An example of a capital-saving device would be the use of leased equipment in a business. Although the total cost of leased equipment over a period of time may be greater than in the case of purchased equipment, the initial capital outlay will be much smaller. In addition, the manufacturer avoids the ever-increasing risk that his equipment will become obsolete before its initial cost can be written off against production.
See also Labor Saving.

CAPITAL STOCK, the actual amount of physical capital and inventories in existence at a given time, or, in terms of business organization, a source of funds used for capital. In the latter case capital stock is the common and preferred stock outstanding in the equity section of a firm's balance sheet.
See also Capital Equipment; Demand for Capital.

CAPITAL WIDENING. *See* Capital Deepening.

CARTEL, an agreement (and sometimes the organization) among independently operated business firms in an industry to eliminate price competition among themselves and thereby increase member firms' profits. The agreement typically sets production quotas and market shares so that by output limitation the agreed price can be maintained as if the firm were one entity (in effect, acting as a monopolist would act). The agreement is binding on member firms, with penalties assessed for violations. The cartel is thus a tighter arrangement than a trade association, which may engage in the same practices less formally. Cartels are illegal in the United States (Section 1 of the Sherman Antitrust Act) but legal in most other countries.
See also Antitrust Policy; Restraint of Trade; Trade Associations.

CASH DRAIN. *See* Multiple Expansion of the Money Supply.

CELLER-KEFAUVER ACT (1950), sometimes called the Antimerger Act, amends sections of the Clayton Act, which forbade business mergers through stock acquisition only. Celler-Kefauver closed a loophole by forbidding mergers effected through asset acquisition.
See also Conglomerate; Merger.

MEMBERS OF OPEC

- Algeria
- Ecuador
- Gabon
- Indonesia
- Iran
- Iraq
- Kuwait
- Libya
- Nigeria
- Qatar
- Saudi Arabia
- United Arab Emirates
- Venezuela

The Organization of Petroleum Exporting Countries (OPEC) is an example of a cartel in which there is a formal agreement among the members regarding pricing or dividing up the market.

CEMENT CASE. *See* Federal Trade Commission v. Cement Institute.

CENTRAL BANK, a bank of issue, that is, an institution, usually owned by the government, that controls the amount of currency created in the nation. Demand deposits having replaced currency as the most important part of the money supply, the central bank has become increasingly involved in control over commercial banks, the primary creators of demand deposits, in order to achieve a desired monetary policy. The structure, operations, and objectives of central banks differ from country to country. In the United States the Federal Reserve System acts as the central bank.

See also Monetary Authority, Central.

CENTRALIZATION, the centralized planning and control of economic activities. A basic element in a command economy, central planning also occurs in a capitalist economy in wartime. Whatever the system, centralization involves comprehensive and detailed planning of practically all phases of economic activity in response to planners' sovereignty. Also, resources are allocated primarily by administrative commands in real (physical) terms. Consumer sovereignty is not a major consideration, and markets and prices do not perform their usual roles.

The system's directors make important planning decisions, relay them to operational units by direct commands or directives, and establish a mechanism to assure fulfillment. This mechanism includes: (1) vertical coordination and control, (2) a system of material balances to achieve consistency among the various plans, and (3) "taut planning," to achieve the most rapid mobilization of available resources—maximizing outputs and minimizing inputs and inventory levels. Central planning usually aims at a high rate of economic growth, but planners seem to prefer centralization as such, even at the expense of growth.

—*John R. Mathews, Jr.*

See also Command Economy; Consumer Sovereignty; Economic Systems; Nationalism.

CENTRALIZED DECISION-MAKING. *See* Command Economy.

CENTRAL LIMIT. *See* Sampling Theory.

CENTRAL PLANNING, the methodology used by government in a controlled economy to determine what goods and services will be produced. Such political-economic systems as socialism, fascism, and communism employ central planning as the means of allocation of economic resources to the major components of gross national product—consumption goods, capital goods, and government purchases. Central planning results in an economic blueprint that details the quantities and sources of each type of goods and services to be produced during a given time period. Under most centrally planned economies the economy is government-directed, and economic decisions are typically based on predetermined national goals.

Problems. As an attempt to substitute bureaucratic planning and coordination for the market system in meeting economic goals and needs, central planning encounters many problems. The most significant are the problems of individual productivity, motivation, and overall coordination. Even with the use of complex input-output tables, central economic planners encounter problems of disallocation, failure to meet quota, and so on, due to complexities of interrelationship of the many economic decisions and events. For example, if a steel mill fails to meet its production quota and is unable to supply a tractor-producing factory with its assigned amount of materials, then the tractor factory is also unable to meet its goals.

Central planners attempt to overcome the problem of coordination by the use of such techniques as planning by negotiation (each major administrative unit in the plan has a chance to review in advance the central committee's master plan and propose changes), reserve stocks (to avoid stock-outs due to unforeseen contingencies), and a priority principle to shift resources from low-priority sectors to high-prior-

ity sectors of the economy after bottlenecks occur.
—Algin B. King

See also Command Economy; Communism; Fascism; Socialism.

CENTRAL RESERVE CITY BANK. *See* Member Bank.

CENTRAL TENDENCY. Given a set (distribution) of data, such as the heights of undergraduate males at a university, we might want to describe the data by using a single summary measure rather than reproducing the entire set. One method of describing a distribution is to find a number that expresses the central, or representative, value of the data set. Such summary statements are called measures of central tendency and serve to locate the distribution.

Suppose that the following set of numbers, the X_i's, are to be described by a single summary measure:
$[X_1, X_2, X_3, \ldots, X_9, X_{10}] = [1, 2, 2, 3, 4, 5, 8, 15, 20, 100]$

Arithmetic Mean. The most commonly used measure of central tendency is the arithmetic mean, or simple average, X.

$$\overline{X} = \frac{X_1 + \cdots + X_N}{N} = \frac{\sum\limits_{i=1}^{N} X_i}{N} \ where \ \sum\limits_{i=1}^{N}$$

means to sum all the numbers (X_i) from X_1 to XN. In our example N = 10, as we have 10 numbers.

$$\overline{X} = \frac{\sum\limits_{i=1}^{10} X_i}{10} = \frac{160}{10} = 16$$

So the arithmetic mean is simply the sum of the observations divided by the number of them that we have.

Median. The median is the middle value of a set of numbers arranged in order of magnitude. It is the value that splits a distribution of numbers in two. It has the property that there are as many observations with values above the median as there are observations with values below the median. Where we have an odd number of observations, the median is the middle value. With an even number of observations, the median is the average of the two middle values. In our example, we have 10 observations, so the median is midway between the 5th and the 6th observation and is equal to 4.5.

Unlike the mean, the median is not sensitive to extreme values, such as the value 100 in the example. It is therefore useful for describing income distributions, where a few large incomes could appreciably raise the mean and distort it as a central, or typical, value.

Fractile. A fractile is an observation below which lies a certain proportion of the data. The *median* splits a distribution into two parts. Correspondingly, there

MEASURES OF CENTRAL TENDENCY

Positively skewed

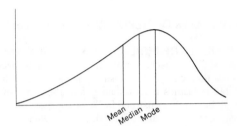

Negatively skewed

are 3 *quartiles*, which split the distribution in 4 equal parts; 25% of the observations lie below the first quartile, 50% lie below the second quartile, and so on. We can also divide the distribution into *deciles*, which split the distribution into 10 parts, and *percentiles*, which split the distribution into 100 parts.

Mode. The mode is the most frequently observed value in a given distribution. In our example, the modal value is 2, as we have observed that value twice. The relationship between the mean, median, and mode is shown in the figure. There are two other more rarely used measures of central tendency: geometric mean and harmonic mean.

Geometric Mean. Economic growth is a multiplicative or compound interest process, rather than an additive process. A description of the "average" rate of growth should take this into account. The appropriate mean for a multiplicative process is the geometric mean:

$$X_G = \sqrt[N]{X_1, X_2, \cdots, X_N}$$

The geometric mean is most easily computed using logarithms:
log XG = (log X_1 + log X_2 + . . . + log XN)/N.

The geometric mean rate of growth is the only rate that, when applied to each year, will yield the terminal value XN.

Harmonic Mean. The harmonic mean is the reciprocal of the arithmetic mean of the reciprocal values of our observations:

$$X_H = 1 \left/ \frac{1}{N} \sum\limits_{i=1}^{N} \frac{1}{X_i} \right.$$

The harmonic mean is most useful for averaging ratios.

Properties. Each of these measures of central tendency has specific properties that are advantageous. The mean, for example, is easy to compute and includes the influence of every observation in the sample. The median and the mode are not affected by extreme values. All these measures are loosely referred to as "averages" and anyone who wishes "to lie with statistics" can choose an average to fit his or her point.   —*Carlisle E. Moody*

See also Frequency Distribution; Probability Distribution.

CERTIFICATES OF DEPOSIT. *See* Time Deposits.

CERTIFICATE OF PUBLIC CONVENIENCE AND NECESSITY, a special permit from state or federal agencies that companies desiring to enter certain regulated industries must obtain before they can engage in business, construct facilities, or perform a service. Entry is restricted in this way when it is thought that monopolies will provide better service than competing companies.

See also Public Utilities; Public Utility Entry.

CERTIFICATES OF INDEBTEDNESS. *See* Government Securities.

CHANGES IN SUPPLY. Supply has been defined as a schedule of intentions; graphically, it depicts voluntary firm (or industry if that be the case) outputs for varying prices. Changes in supply must therefore, by definition, deal with changes in the schedule of intentions, or, graphically, with changes in curves.

Mathematically we are dealing with the problem of dimensions. For ease of exposition a two-dimensional relationship is portrayed; supply is delineated graphically as a curve showing different quantities supplied at differing prices, *other variables being held constant.* These "other variables" give the clue that the true supply relationship has more than two dimensions. Wage rates, technology, and so on also affect supply. When these so-called parameters change, then supply intentions (and therefore the supply curve) must also change. Thus for every possible wage rate and every possible technological change there exists a possible supply schedule. What is more, there are combinations and permutations for all these potentially important determinants of supply, and the possibilities are manifold.

If we are dealing with industry or market supply, then another possibility for a change in supply exists. Since industry supply is the horizontal summation of all the individual supply curves, an increase in the number of firms in the industry due to short-run excess profits or a decrease in the number of firms due to short-run losses will result in an increase or de-

crease in supply, respectively.

A change in supply implies that quantity supplied will be greater or lesser (depending on the circumstances) at every price than it was previously. Alternately, a change in supply implies that the new circumstances require that price be higher or lower before given outputs will voluntarily be produced and offered for sale.   —*Robert L. Brite*

See also Supply; Supply and Demand, Law of; Supply Curve; Supply Schedule.

CHECKING ACCOUNTS. *See* Demand Deposits.

CHENERY, HOLLIS BURNLEY (1918-   ), American economist noted for his contributions to the theory of growth in less developed economies, with emphasis on investment criteria. He received a B.S. from both the University of Arizona (1939) and the University of Oklahoma (1942), an M.A. from the University of Virginia (1946), and a Ph.D. in economics from Harvard (1950). His publications include *Arabian Oil* (1949, coauthor), *Interindustry Economics* (1959), *Studies in Development Planning* (1971), and *Redistribution with Growth* (1974). Professor of economics at Harvard from 1965 to 1970, he has been an economist for the Economic Cooperation Administration in Paris (1949-1950), and a consultant to the governments of Pakistan, Japan, and Israel (1955-1961). Since 1963, he has also been consultant to the Organization of American States, the Agency for International Development, and the World Bank.

CHILD LABOR. Before the twentieth century, no serious attempt had been made to limit or prohibit child labor in the United States. Children were wage earners in the same sense as their parents, and no special provisions were made in regard to the number of hours they worked or the amount they earned.

In the 1900s two cases involving child labor were brought to the Supreme Court. The first was *Hammer v. Dagenhart* (1918). The legislation under review denied transportation in interstate commerce to the products of establishments which employed children under a certain age. The court declared the legislation unconstitutional since it attempted to control the conditions of employment within the states.

In *Baily v. Drexel Furniture Co.* (1922), a federal tax on profits of establishments where children under a certain age were employed was likewise held invalid.

In 1938, Congress succeeded for the first time in getting a law passed to improve the working conditions of children. The Fair Labor Standards Act declared the employment of children under the age of 16 unlawful in establishments producing goods for interstate commerce. In 6 particularly hazardous occupations, the minimum age of employment became 18. In certain non-mining and non-manufacturing industries exception to the minimum age is made. In state laws

Children working in textile mills had to work the same hours and face the same hazards as adults prior to the advent of child labor legislation.

covering child labor, the minimum age varies anywhere from 14 to 18.   — *William D. Wagoner*

CHOICE: TOPIC GUIDE

Choice is at the heart of economic activity and economic analysis. Its central role in these regards is further explained in the articles on SCARCITY and RESOURCE ALLOCATION. The necessity of choice creates OPPORTUNITY COSTS. To see how choices are made in an economy such as in the United States, consult the major article on MARKET SYSTEM as well as the Subject Map accompanying that article.

CHOICE. In a free-market economy, choice is at the very heart of the system. The results of the choice process can be of fundamental importance for all economic activity. Consumers (households) must choose among a variety of goods and services—not all of which can be bought, given a limited budget—between spending now or saving for later, and between hours of work and hours of leisure. Business, in deciding what to produce and how to produce it, must choose among the available resources (land, labor, capital, and entrepreneurial ability). Competition will force each business to combine resources to achieve the highest profits. Government must determine how to best utilize the nation's resources. This must be done on two levels. Government must determine how many resources should be channeled into collective goods and services and national defense. It must also choose a mix of monetary and fiscal policies to control inflation and unemployment. Society as a whole must choose the goods and services that will most satisfy its wants. This choice is made through the aggregate of consumer spending decisions. The composition of spending, as registered through the price system, influences the composition of the nation's total economic output.

CHOICE UNDER UNCERTAINTY. *See* Expected Utility.

CHRONIC DEFICIT in a nation's balance of payments indicates that structural changes in the economy are in order and/or the exchange rate is overvalued. Overvaluation keeps import prices lower and export prices higher than balance-of-payments equilibrium justifies. The chronic situation also implies that the deficit is financed through use of international monetary reserves, a situation that cannot last forever. Chronic deficits cry out for solutions before all reserves are exhausted.

See also Balance of Payments.

CIRCULAR FLOW OF INCOME. The recognition by economists that all economic activity is interrelated has led to the development of numerous theories and hypotheses to explain economic activity and the behavior of various elements of the economic system. One of the most basic and yet most useful of these models of the economic system is the circular flow model.

The model begins with the concept that some relationship exists between the major flows in the economic system. The relationship is one of mutual interdependence. In order to produce goods and services, the producers in the economic system (usually businesses) must obtain the means of production, or resources, from the owners of the resources (usually households). In exchange for their resources, resource owners gain income. The income generated in such a

CIRCULAR FLOW OF INCOME

CIRCULAR FLOW
    OF INCOME
    flow of income
    expanded circular flow

INTERDEPENDENCE OF
    ECONOMIC BEHAVIOR

INPUT-OUTPUT
    MODELS

MODELS, ECONOMETRIC
    macroeconometric models
    microeconometric models

REAL FLOW
- GOODS — INTERMEDIATE GOODS / FINAL GOODS
- SERVICES
- FACTORS OF PRODUCTION — LAND / LABOR / CAPITAL

MONEY FLOW
- CONSUMPTION
- INJECTION — INVESTMENT / GOVERNMENT SPENDING
- FACTOR PAYMENTS
    FACTOR INCOMES
    functional distribution of income
- WITHDRAWALS — SAVING / TAXES

manner is then spent to purchase goods and services to satisfy the households' demands. The interesting aspect here is that the goods and services that households purchase were produced with the resources that they sold to the producers.

Assuming that households own all resources in the economic system and that businesses produce all goods and services, the major flows are: (1) the flow of resources from owners (households) to users (businesses), (2) the opposite flow of income that occurs when resources are exchanged, (3) the flow of goods and services from producers (businesses) to the con-

sumers (households), and (4) the opposite flow of consumer expenditures that arises from the purchasing of goods and services by consumers. The accompanying figure indicates these basic flows. The first and third are called real flows, because they involve the physical transfer of goods, services, or resources, and the second and fourth flows are considered money flows, because they involve the movement of funds in response to real flows.

Each of these flows depends upon the existence of all the others: if any one were stopped, all would be stopped. For example, if resource suppliers stopped

CIRCULAR FLOW OF INCOME

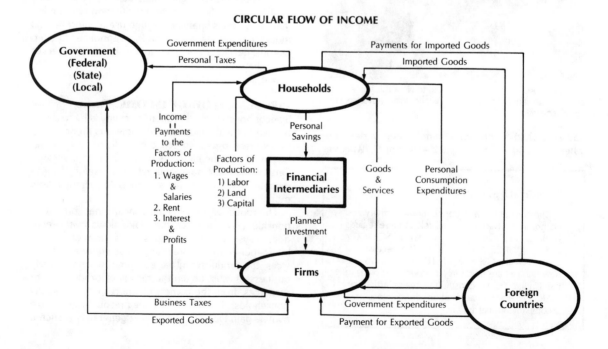

making factors of production available, the income stream would dry and producers would stop production, because they would have no resources available and because without the income stream there would be no effective demand.

The Expanded Circular Flow Model. Several additions to the simple model can provide important insights into macroeconomic relationships. The simple model indicated that all income automatically turns into consumer expenditures. However, many households save a part of their income, thus withdrawing some income from the circular flow, unbalancing the flows, by the amount of saving. At the same time households save, however, businesses spend to purchase capital goods (investment). Thus, an injection of spending exists. If the injection of investment equals the withdrawal of saving, the circular flow remains stable—as in the figure. If the withdrawal and the injection are not equal, changes will occur in the economic system. It is the role of macroeconomic theory to explain how saving and investment can be equal and what happens when they are not equal.

Saving and investment are important withdrawals and injections, but they are not the only ones to consider. When government is added to the basic circular flow model, a number of additional flows develop. The government generally taxes both households and businesses, who in turn receive the public services of government. In addition to these new flows, government spends to purchase both resources and goods and services, affecting the existing economic flows. The expanded circular flow figure indicates the impact of including government in the circular flow. If government taxes and expenditures are equal, the circular flow is unaffected. If, however, the government has a surplus or a deficit, the circular flow will be changed. Economic theory again must indicate the effects of unbalanced government budgets.

A final step in expanding the circular flow model is the consideration of the economy's interchange with other economies. The importing or exporting of goods and services, resources, and capital; government foreign-aid programs; and various other foreign transactions affect the circular flow in many, sometimes quite complex manners. The realization that such injections and withdrawals can be vital to an economy is easily demonstrated with a circular flow model.

Limitations. The circular flow model has several limitations. The most important is the lack of detail concerning the various mechanisms that allow the flows to occur in complex economies and the means by which the flows are regulated. The role of microeconomic theory is to explain this detail and to observe and analyze the behavior of individual units rather than the sector analysis of the circular flow model. In addition, the circular flow model ignores

intrasectoral flows, which are important elements of the economic system.   —*Clyde A. Haulman*

See also Money Flow; Real Flow.

CIVIL AERONAUTICS BOARD (CAB), a semi-independent regulatory body charged with the economic regulation of commercial air transportation. The CAB was created by Congress as part of the Civil Aeronautics Act of 1938 and was the first major federal regulatory body to be discontinued when it went out of business at the end of 1984.

In addition to the CAB, the Civil Aeronautics Act of 1938 also created the Civil Aeronautics Administration (CAA), which was responsible for controlling air traffic, enforcing safety rules, and investigating air accidents. In 1958, the CAA was replaced by the Federal Aviation Administration (FAA).

During its peak years of power, the CAB was able to limit entry by new firms into the airline industry, control fares, ensure service to smaller airports, and control mergers by air carriers. Through the leadership of its chairman during the Carter administration, economist Alfred Kahn, the CAB continually loosened its grip on the economic actions of air carriers and potential air carriers. This trend was made official by the Airline Deregulation Act of 1978, which led to the abolition of the CAB. The remaining regulatory rules (concerning overbooking and bumping, no-smoking regulations, and baggage complaints) are now handled by the Department of Transportation through the Federal Aviation Administration.

—*Michael S. Johnson*

See also Deregulation; Federal Aviation Administration.

CIVIL SERVICE REFORM ACT OF 1978, an act that gave statutory support to certain federal government employees and their unions following years of regulation through Executive Orders. In Title VII, the Federal Labor Relations Authority (FLRA), comparable to the NLRB, was established and bargaining rights granted. Employees covered by this act cannot bargain over wages and benefits and may not strike or picket if the picketing disrupts the agency. Unfair labor practices similar to those in Taft-Hartley are included. Not covered are postal workers and members of the Federal Bureau of Investigation, Central Intelligence Agency, General Accounting Office, and some other federal agencies.

CLASS ANTAGONISMS. See Class Conflict; Communism.

CLASS CONFLICT, in Marxian theory, occurs because worker proletariats can only sell their labor to the capitalist bourgeoisie for subsistence wages, while the products that they produce sell for more than this. The resulting surplus value provides for further accumulation of capital, with adverse effects on workers who find their plight unbearable. Revolution occurs, and the bourgeoisie is eliminated.

See also Marx, Karl; Proletariat.

CLASSICAL ECONOMICS. The period from the publication of Adam Smith's *Wealth of Nations* (1776) until the development of marginalism (the 1870s) is generally considered the classical period of economic thought. Some of the greatest economists were active during this period. Men such as Smith, Thomas Malthus, David Ricardo, John Stuart Mill, as well as Karl Marx, laid the foundation of modern economics and developed economics into a unified body of theory.

The most distinguishing characteristic of classical doctrine was its reliance upon economic individualism and a harmony of interest. It was generally felt that a free, competitive market would efficiently guide production and distribution in the best interest of society if each individual pursued his own self-interest. In addition, while the government had the responsibility of formulating the framework within which markets would operate, its role was considered one of laissez-faire. Under these conditions, classical economists felt that the economy would become a full-employment, self-adjusting system.

Another important contribution of classical economics was the development of the abstract, deductive method of analyzing the economic system. Applying this methodology, significant developments occurred in the theory of international trade, price theory, the theory of economic growth and development, and many other areas of economic theory.

— *Clyde A. Haulman*

See also Malthus, Thomas; Mill, John Stuart; Ricardo, David; Smith, Adam; Wealth of Nations, The.

CLAYTON ANTITRUST ACT (1914), a companion law to the Sherman Antitrust Act of 1890, with more explicit prohibitions on illegal business behavior, and concerned more with the effect of such behavior, less with intent.

The main provisions of the act prohibit four practices, specifically: price discrimination by a seller where the effect may be to injure his competitors (Section 2), amended by the Robinson-Patman Act of 1936 to prohibit injury to buyers; tying contracts and exclusive dealerships where the effect is to lessen competition among potential rivals who might otherwise sell to a buyer (Section 3); acquisition of the stock of a business rival where the effect is to lessen competition substantially (Section 7), amended by the Celler-Kefauver Act of 1950 to prohibit asset acquisition as well; and interlocking directorates among competing firms of a certain size (Section 8). Illegal activities under Sections 2, 3 and 7 require a showing of actual or potential injury to competition, while Section 8 requires evidence that an interlock between competitors would violate some provision of the antitrust laws.

Section 6 seemingly provides agricultural marketing and labor organizations with blanket exemption from antitrust prosecution, but its interpretation by the courts showed otherwise. Substantial exemption to both groups was provided, however, in subsequent legislation and court decisions.

The Clayton Act is enforced jointly by the Federal Trade Commission and the Antitrust Division, Department of Justice.   — *Thomas O. Depperschmidt*

See also Exclusive Dealership; Merger; Price Discrimination; Substantial Lessening of Competition; Tying Contracts.

CLOSED SHOP makes union membership a precondition to employment or requires preferential hiring of union members. The Taft-Hartley Act (1947) outlawed the closed shop. However, Taft-Hartley has not been interpreted in a way that forbids de facto closed shops. These are shops in which the matching of workers and jobs normally done through the union hiring hall (as in the building trades and longshoring) leads to the exclusive use of union members. Specific exemptions to the ban on the preferential hiring of union members was afforded the construction industry by the Landrum-Griffin Act in 1959.

See also Landrum-Griffin Act (1959); Open Shop; Taft-Hartley Act (1947).

COEFFICIENT OF ELASTICITY OF DEMAND, a measure of the responsiveness of quantity demanded to the impetus provided by a price change, computed by dividing the percentage change in quantity demanded by the causal percentage change in price. The algebraic sign of the coefficient of elasticity will be negative, reflecting the inverse relationship between price and quantity demanded for a typical demand curve. The absolute value of the coefficient provides insight into the behavior of quantity demanded and can range from 0 to infinity.

It can be inferred that a coefficient of elasticity of zero implies that the percentage change in quantity demanded has been 0, in response to a given price change. That is, consumers have not changed their purchases at all in response to a price change (completely inelastic demand). Coefficients of elasticity in absolute value 0-1 mean that the percentage change in quantity demanded is smaller than the percentage change in price (relatively inelastic demand). A coefficient of elasticity equal to 1 implies that a given percentage change in price has evoked the same percentage change in quantity demanded (unitary elasticity). Whenever the absolute value of the coefficient of elasticity is greater than 1, the result of a given percentage change in price has caused a percentage change in quantity demanded that exceeds the change in price (relatively elastic demand). The logical limit to elastic coefficients of demand is negative infinity, where a given percentage change in price has caused an infinite percentage change in quantity demanded. —*Robert L. Brite*

See also Elasticity of Demand.

COEFFICIENT OF ELASTICITY OF SUPPLY, the numerical result of dividing the percentage change in output by the percentage change in price. This number will normally be positive, since there is a direct relationship between price and quantity supplied: if price rises quantity supplied will normally rise; price reductions normally lead to decreases in quantity supplied. The responsiveness of quantity supplied to price changes can be gauged by the size of the coefficient of elasticity of supply. The larger the coefficient, the greater the output response to price change. Relatively small coefficients (fractions) imply that output response to price change is slight.

See also Elasticity of Supply.

COINCIDENT INDICATOR, an economic measurement or time series that experiences peaks and troughs at the same time as total economic activity. Coincident indicators include the Industrial Production Index, GNP in current dollars, and manufacturing and trade sales.

See also Business Cycles, Measurement; Lagging Indicator; Leading Indicator.

COINS, metal tokens accepted by tradition as part of the money supply. Present American coins are copper alloyed with some nickel or zinc. Coins formerly were pieces of metal whose intrinsic value was certified by the stamp on their faces, such as silver dollars or gold pieces.

See also Currency.

COLLECTIVE BARGAINING, a process by which decisions regarding the wages, hours, and conditions of employment are determined by the interaction of workers, acting through their unions, and employers. The term thus applies to the administration as well as the negotiation of contracts. This day-to-day relationship, while often less dramatic than the periodic contract-bargaining process with its publicity and tensions, has come to be recognized as the important "other half" of the labor-management relationship.

Contracts and Impact. There are well over 100,000 collectively bargained contracts in force. Since many of these are multi-year agreements, the number of contracts negotiated each year is nearer 50,000.

The impact of collective bargaining varies from industry to industry. In some of the major mass-production industries, from 80% to 100% of the production employees are covered by contracts, while in others the percentages range downward to quite low levels. For the entire manufacturing sector, an estimated two-thirds of production employees are included in recognized bargaining units.

Results and Effects. The results of collective bargaining are difficult to assess. Although approximately 20 million workers belong to unions, there is no conclusive evidence that unionism and collective bargaining have provided higher wages for these workers than they would have received otherwise. Furthermore, collective bargaining has many facets and dimensions that do not lend themselves to quantitative measurement and comparison or to generalization.

However, certain observations are warranted. Collective bargaining has made contributions to both labor and management in stabilizing and professionalizing the relationship between them. To labor it affords a large measure of job and income security, protection from arbitrary treatment, and a sense of self-determination. To management it affords a helpful method of resolving controversies, reducing frictions, and effecting better communications with labor.

Collective bargaining agreements are defined by law. Labor and management, if either so desires, must bargain over matters that the National Labor Relations Board has decided are within the definition of "the terms and conditions of employment." Beyond that, there are matters that are legally bargainable if both parties agree to bargain over them, but over which neither side is compelled to bargain. Last, there are certain matters that are not legally bargainable, usually because an agreement between labor and management in these areas would itself be in violation of the law. —*Leonard G. Schifrin*

See also Arbitration; Conciliation.

COLLECTIVIZATION. One of the critical tasks that the Soviet regime faced in the 1920s was to determine the best model for rapid industrialization. The problem was to design a set of institutions that would generate a large amount of investment funds, ensure food supply, and make agricultural labor available to the urban areas. Stalin decided in 1927-1928 that the only solution was to bring agriculture under the central control of the state.

Announced as voluntary, collectivization was in fact coercive. The poorer peasants and the urban workers forced the richer peasants (kulaks) from their lands, and many kulaks were killed in the process. The kulaks retaliated by destroying their crops and livestock. Collectivization was so rapid and so disruptive that in 1930 Stalin slowed its pace and reemphasized the voluntary nature of the program, but by the end of 1932 nearly two-thirds of the total sown area in the Soviet Union was collectivized.

COLLUSION, an agreement or conspiracy, usually secret, among nominal competitors to engage in anticompetitive practices in violation of antitrust laws. The essence of collusion is the avoidance of price competition to ensure that a competitor's price will not ruin a firm's profits.

Identical price policies are not themselves prima facie evidence of collusion. More revealing are the measures taken by the organization to ensure compliance of member firms with its price and output decisions. Thus, the term typically refers to tighter-knit agreements, such as cartels, involving pressure on member firms to comply. Collusion is evident in most price-fixing and market-sharing schemes, but it may refer to conscious parallelism of action in which competitors tacitly comply with the price policies of their rivals.

Collusion is prohibited under the Sherman Act, Section 1, which declares that any contract, combination, or conspiracy in restraint of trade is illegal. Where evidence of collusion exists, the practices undertaken by competitors to eliminate competition are *per se* illegal. These practices may include limiting production, engaging in price discrimination against nonparticipants in the agreements, suppressing technology that may lead to lower costs and prices, preventing entry of new firms into the industry, and abusing patent rights, such as in cross-licensing and restrictive licensing.   — *Thomas O. Depperschmidt*

See also Cartel; Conscious Parallelism; Conspiracy Doctrine; Price Fixing; Restraint of Trade.

COMMAND ECONOMY, an authoritarian socialist economy that has centralized economic decision-making as its chief characteristic. This term was originated to describe the Soviet Union's economic system. The economic plan permeates the entire system. Government decisions can be transmitted to the production units by directives that dictate the behavior of the economic units and permit only minimal flexibility at the enterprise level.

A command economy has an ability to generate high levels of investment funds. The Soviet experience has shown that investment levels of 20-30% of gross national product are possible if the center, through its taxation policies, imposes on the population its propensity to save. The center has the power to mobilize resources and to direct them toward such objectives as rapid industrialization. Although the command system has a record of high levels of investment and rapid growth during the early stages of industrialization, its performance is less exemplary when the complexity of the economy increases, and the efficiency becomes necessary for maintaining high rates of growth.   — *Francis W. Rushing*

COMMERCIAL BANK, a financial institution whose basic functions are the receipt, creation, and transfer of demand deposits (checking accounts) for the general public. Originally a commercial bank made short-

term (commercial) loans to merchants for the primary purpose of buying inventories that would soon be sold, the proceeds used to repay the loan. Today commercial banks also make substantial amounts of industrial, agricultural, personal, and real estate (mortgage) loans, accept time deposits, provide safe deposit facilities, manage trusts, act as brokers for securities, deal in foreign exchange, underwrite and sell municipal securities, engage in industrial research and security analysis, issue credit cards, and provide many other specialized services.

There are about 14,000 commercial banks in the United States, ranging in size from minor institutions in small towns to large city or statewide banks with deposits in excess of $10 billion. One-eighth of all deposits in the United States are held by 12 major New York City banks. In their primary capacity as creators of demand deposits, commercial banks provide the greater part of the money supply and are, therefore, the chief objects of monetary policy.

— *Walter W. Haines*

See also Banking System; Federal Reserve System; Financial Intermediaries; Multiple Expansion of the Money Supply.

COMMERCIAL PAPER refers either to the promissory notes of businessmen given to a commercial bank to obtain a loan or to large-scale issues of promissory notes sold by prominent corporations to commercial banks or others who have sizeable sums of money to lend for short periods. The latter, usually called open-market commercial paper, is similar to a corporate bond except for a maturity of six months or less. When such commercial paper is sold by personal finance companies or sales finance companies, it is called finance paper.

COMMODITY CREDIT CORPORATION (CCC), the agency within the U.S. Department of Agriculture that handles the money and makes financial arrangements for the department's farm-price and income-support programs and for several lesser activities. It makes or insures commodity loans, makes direct payments to farmers, stores products acquired for price-support purposes, disposes of them, pays export subsidies where authorized, and provides current financing for the P.L. 480 program. It may borrow up to $20 billion from the U.S. Treasury, and it is reimbursed for losses by Congressional appropriations.

See also Commodity Loans; Price-Support Programs; Public Law 480.

COMMODITY LOANS, in general, are loans secured by a commodity as collateral. If the loan is not repaid, the lender may take the collateral; and if the value of the commodity is less than the loan, the borrower remains liable for the difference.

Nonrecourse commodity loans are much used by

the U.S. government to support market price of crops. The level at which price is to be supported is the value at which farmers may borrow on stored crops used as collateral. If the market price of the commodity is less than the loan rate at repayment date, the farmer may still turn over the collateral in full as final settlement of the loan. No recourse is available against him for any deficiency between the amount of the loan and the market value of the collateral.

When such a price-support loan is available and the market price is below the loan rate, farmers eligible for the program will ordinarily store some or all of their crops under the loan rather than sell on the market. The reduced market supply raises the price to the vicinity of the loan rate. If the market price rises above the loan rate, farmers may repay their loans, redeem the collateral, and use it as they wish.

— *George E. Brandow*

See also Commodity Credit Corporation; Price-Support Programs.

COMMODITY MARKETS, large-scale, organized exchanges, similar to stock markets, where vast quantities of goods are exchanged. In these markets such goods as corn, wheat, cotton, sow bellies, frozen orange juice, cocoa, gold, silver, and the like are traded. The best-known commodity market is the Chicago Board of Trade. The existence of these markets makes the markets for the traded commodities much more efficient, since they provide excellent information about the prices of the traded commodities. Business people often try to manage their potential risks by buying or selling futures contracts for certain commodities.

See also Futures Markets.

COMMON LAW, in the United States, has come to mean the body of law developed in decisions of English and American courts involving private (non-governmental) litigants, as contrasted to statutory law or public legislation. Common law draws heavily on the traditional and universal principles developed in the courts, especially regarding property, crime, tort, and contract. Its development is particularly important in the areas of trade-union organization and antitrust policy.

COMMONS, JOHN R. (1862-1945), a much-admired American spokesman for economic and social reform. Born in Ohio, the son of active abolitionists, Commons attended Oberlin College while working part-time as a printer. It was during this time that he became interested in trade unionism. After graduate work at Johns Hopkins University, he taught for 10 years at Wesleyan, Oberlin, Indiana, and Syracuse before moving to the University of Wisconsin where his reputation as a student of American labor problems was to grow. It was at Wisconsin that he wrote *A*

Documentary History of American Industrial Society and *History of Labour in the United States.*

Commons believed that the trade union movement emerged out of the efforts of individual workmen to protect their job rights against less-expensive labor. He claimed that the effectiveness of unions depends on their ability to control conditions within the product market area in which they operate. As a policymaker, Commons helped to make Wisconson a leader in social and economic reform. He was involved with such issues as legislation for unemployment insurance, workmen's compensation, civil service, and public utility and railroad regulations. In 1915 he became a member of the Industrial Relations Committee under President Wilson.

Among Commons's most famous works are *The Distribution of Wealth* (1893), *Legal Foundations of Capitalism* (1924), and *Institutional Economics* (1934).

COMMON MARKET. *See* European Economic Community.

COMMON STOCK, a class of capital stock having certain rights and privileges. If no other type of stock is issued in a corporation, common stock enjoys exclusive claim to the net assets as well as to the profits of the corporation. Common stock is divided into shares usually transferable by endorsement. These shares of stock may or may not be assigned a par, or face, value. Common Stock is also called equity stock or ordinary stock.

See also Stock.

Many businesses are financed through the sale of stock, as in the sample certificate portrayed here.

COMMUNICATIONS INDUSTRY. *See* Regulated Industries.

COMMUNISM, according to Karl Marx, is the last stage of economic development. It is achieved only if and when all class antagonisms are eliminated, the workers have developed attitudes that make them want to perform their social functions, and the state has withered away. Under communism only the proletarian class would exist; socialist organizations would permit the system to produce in abundance, each worker contributing to society according to his ability and receiving according to his needs; and, with the necessity for government having ceased, individuals would enjoy true freedom. Neither Marx nor his ideological successors have described the specific path or the length of time necessary to achieve full communism.

Following World War II, the countries of Eastern Europe, China, Cuba, and the Soviet Union were referred to as "communist" countries. For more than 40 years after the war, the leadership of these countries were followers of the teachings of Marx, but the economies never progressed beyond the socialist stage of development before most of them began to shift toward free-market economies in 1989.

See also Anarchistic Communism; Marx, Karl; Planning (Centralized).

COMMUNIST MANIFESTO (1848), a political and economic tract by Karl Marx and Friedrich Engels written to arouse organized political action by the proletariat. The authors felt (1) that property, which is the basis of the bourgeois system, restrained production, and (2) that the system, which could no longer control itself, would be exposed to a constant stream of crises. The solution, according to the authors, lay in a structure involving abolition of property, nationalization of industry, universal education, and a progressive income tax.

COMPANY UNION, one organized by a company for its employees. The concept emerged during World War I with the hope of easing the problems of high labor turnover and labor unrest. Chiefly to dilute the appeal of trade unions, many industries began company unions. Most important of their many drawbacks was that, with the union owing its strength to the company, workers had little bargaining power. There are a number of unions limited to one employer that are not to be confused with the historical company union, however. These unions feel their interests are better served with this arrangement.

See also Labor Movement.

COMPARABLE PAY, the same pay for jobs requiring similar levels of skill. The Equal Pay Act of 1963, coupled with Title VII of the Civil Rights Act of 1964, made it illegal for employers to discriminate against any employee with respect to pay when males and females perform work requiring similar skills under similar work conditions. These laws as written did not touch on the situation in which a particular job is performed entirely, or almost entirely, by females. As long as all workers in the job were treated equally, no violation of the law occurred.

Comparable pay proponents hold that jobs of equal worth should be equally rewarded and that job descriptions and evaluation techniques can be used to measure the important characteristics of each job, the required abilities of the worker, and the relative values of different jobs. Thus, two different jobs performed under different conditions will be paid the same if they are of equal value. Opponents argue that comparable pay ignores market forces and that job evaluation is not a sufficiently accurate measuring tool. The issue has been tested in several court actions without conclusive results.   *—William D. Wagoner*

See also Equal Pay.

COMPARATIVE ADVANTAGE. Gains from international trade are maximized when each nation specializes in the production of those goods in which its comparative advantage is greatest (or comparative disadvantage least). Assume that with the same composite inputs, Country A provides twice as much of one commodity (X) and 3 times as much of another commodity (Y) as Country B. Country A has an absolute advantage in both; its productivity is twice that of B relative to X and three times B's relative to Y. Therefore, A will specialize in Y (comparative advantage greatest) and B in X (comparative disadvantage least). Mutually advantageous trade can develop with 1 of X exchanging for no less than 2 nor no more than 3 of Y.

See also Absolute Advantage; International Trade Theory; Specialization; Terms of Trade.

COMPENSATED PRICE EFFECT. *See* Consumer Equilibrium.

COMPETITION, usually referred to as perfect competition, the market structure that most economists claim is the most efficient method of organizing production. Competition exists in a market in which (1) there are many sellers or buyers, and no one individual or group can influence the market; (2) the sellers or buyers deal with a homogeneous product; and (3) there is unrestricted entry to or exit from the market. Each seller and buyer regards the price as given, and in the pursuit of their own self-interests—sellers seeking maximum profits and buyers seeking optimum consumer welfare—the competitive market is cleared (quantities demanded and supplied are equal), and market price is established. Nonprice competition does not apply in a competitive market model.

The marginal principle is important in all economic analysis. In the competitive model, buyers pay what the last unit is worth to them, and producers supply an amount so that the cost of the last unit is equal to the market price: marginal cost equals price. This result can be shown to be efficient.

See also Economic Systems; Invisible Hand; Marginal Analysis; Market Economy; Profit System.

The competitive market structure flourishes when there is unrestricted entry and a homogeneous product.

COMPLEMENTARY GOODS, in consumption, goods that are generally used together. If the price of one good fell, the demand curves for its complementary goods would shift outward, away from the origin, indicating an increase in the demand for the complementary goods. Formally, two goods are said to be complements if an increase (or decrease) in the price of one leads to a decrease (or increase) in the demand for the other.

See also Substitute Goods.

COMPTROLLER OF THE CURRENCY, a presidential appointee who acts as administrator of national banks and banks in the District of Columbia. The comptroller approves new national banks and branches, consolidations, and mergers, and, through a staff, examines each bank at least once a year.

COMPULSORY SAVING. *See* Forced Saving.

CONCENTRATION RATIO, a measure of the extent to which a market or industry is dominated by a few firms. The most widely-used concentration ratios are those published by the Commerce Department as part of the various censuses of business (manufacturing, mining, retailing, etc.). The Commerce Department's four-firm concentration ratio gives the domestic value of shipments by the four largest domestic firms as a

ratio of the total domestic shipments by domestic firms. The percentage of sales by the 8 and the 20 largest firms are also used. The closer the ratio is to 1 (or 100 if in percentage terms), the more concentrated the industry, while as the ratio approaches 0, the more competitive the business environment. Concentration ratios are often used to gather initial evidence of possible monopolistic behavior by firms and are often part of antitrust studies. Trends in the concentration ratio also give indications of major changes in economies of scale due to technological change or due to important shifts in the size of the market for a product.

These ratios must be interpreted with caution. For example, the four-firm concentration ratio in the newspaper industry is only 19, indicating a relatively competitive business environment; however, only a handful of newspapers have a nationwide circulation, and concentration would be more accurately measured by looking at sales in each metropolitan area, not for the nation as a whole. On the other hand, the concentration ratio of 93% for the automotive industry (motor vehicles and car bodies) overstates the true extent of market concentration, because foreign-made imports are not included in the calculations.

—*Michael S. Johnson*
See chart p. 38; *see also* Market Concentration.

CONCILIATION, a form of third-party intervention

SELECTED FOUR-FIRM CONCENTRATION RATIOS (1982)		
Industry	Number of Firms	Concentration Ratio (%)
Aircraft	139	64
Bread, cake, and related products	1,869	34
Bottled and canned soft drinks	1,236	14
Construction machinery	817	42
Motor vehicles and car bodies	284	92
Newspapers	7,520	22
Paper mills	135	22
Petroleum refining	282	28
Pharmaceutical preparations	584	26
Soaps and detergents	642	60

into collective bargaining over new contract terms when the bargaining has broken down or threatens to do so. The conciliator attempts to promote reconciliation and to restore constructive bargaining.

This narrow though often useful function has expanded somewhat through time, and there is now little difference between conciliation and mediation. Both seek to generate agreement between labor and management by skillful and tactful methods that cool tempers, save face, and encourage continued bargaining and compromise.

See also Collective Bargaining; Mediation.

CONFIDENCE INTERVAL, a probability statement concerning the value of an unknown population parameter, based on the sample mean and standard deviation. For example, a 95% confidence interval indicates that 95 times out of 100 a given set of parameter values will contain the true population value.

See also Sampling Distribution.

CONGLOMERATE, a business firm producing and selling products in more than one market or line of commerce, products usually (though not necessarily) dissimilar to, and therefore not competitive with, each other. The conglomerate typically is formed by multiple mergers of previously independent firms, although the same conglomerate structure could be achieved through diversification internally, without merger. It is the merging of firms producing dissimilar products that distinguishes the conglomerate merger from other types of mergers (vertical and horizontal).

An assessment of the legal and economic implications of conglomerates is pending. The question legally is whether the Clayton Act prohibition on mergers tending to lessen competition can "reach" conglomerates, particularly in their practice of reciprocal dealing among member units. Reciprocal dealing limits the access of outside competitive firms to conglomerate members to the extent that member units deal exclusively with each other for needed goods or materials. From an economic viewpoint, the conglomerate represents a business organization quite different in size and potential market power from the single-product independent producer portrayed in conven-

tional economic theory.

— *Thomas O. Depperschmidt*

See also Celler-Kefauver Act; Clayton Act; Diversification; Merger.

CONGRESS OF INDUSTRIAL ORGANIZATIONS (CIO). In 1935, a group of industrial union leaders led by John L. Lewis, vice president of the American Federation of Labor, met for the purpose of organizing workers within the AFL. They were successful with such unions as shipbuilding, automobile, rubber, and flatglass, which had had previous problems trying to get charters from the AFL. The AFL, alarmed by the developments of the CIO, ordered the organization to disband but Lewis refused and, instead, resigned his position as vice president. Two years later the CIO unions were expelled from the AFL.

The CIO, meanwhile, was in the process of organizing the steel industry and by 1937 the union was so powerful that it could close down Carnegie-Illinois, U.S. Steel's biggest subsidiary, if it decided to strike. For this reason, U.S. Steel agreed to recognize the CIO as a bargaining agent. The CIO also began to make gains in other major industries, namely rubber, automobiles. CIO membership began to grow rapidly, and in 1937 and 1938 surpassed the membership of the AFL. After establishing themselves in the mass production industries, the CIO received little opposition from the AFL.

In 1938, the CIO set themselves up as a permanent organization. During World War II membership continued to increase, and the years following the war saw drastic union gains and wage increases. However, post-war strikes soon got out of hand. Rising wages set off a spiral of rising prices, and the economic problem became one of inflation. Public opinion began to go against labor, and the result was the Taft-Hartley Act of 1947. This act curbed labor's rights and, in a sense, repealed much of labor's gains of the Wagner Act of 1932.

In 1955, after much deliberation, the AFL and the CIO merged. At this time the CIO was claiming the six largest unions—which accounted for one-third of all union membership. The Teamsters Union and the United Automobile Workers left the AFL-CIO but were reaffiliated in the 1980s, bringing two of the largest unions back to the organization.

See also Labor Movement.

CONSCIOUS PARALLELISM of action, a business practice wherein a firm refrains from price competition with competitors without their overt agreement, but knowing that they will do likewise. The resulting identical or parallel prices in the market are not unlike a conspiracy to fix prices. Conscious parallelism has been treated with ambiguity by the courts in this century. The current position is that some overt evidence of agreement is needed to constitute violation of Sherman Act prohibitions against restraint of trade.

See also Collusion; Conspiracy Doctrine; Price Fixing; Restraint of Trade; United States v. American Tobacco.

CONSENT DECREE, negotiated private settlement prior to final judgment in a civil antitrust suit between the prosecuting FTC or antitrust division, and a business-firm defendant. After agreement on the terms of the settlement, a district court almost always accepts the terms and issues the decree (court order) incorporating these terms. The decree may include penalties or agreements to take or stop certain actions by the defendant. Between 80% and 90% of all antitrust litigation is settled by consent decree in a typical year.

See also Antitrust Policy.

CONSERVATION RESERVE. *See* Soil Bank.

CONSPICUOUS CONSUMPTION, the practice of consuming far beyond one's needs, as a display of wealth, power, and success. Thorstein Veblen coined the phrase in his *Theory of the Leisure Class* (1899). He felt that to maintain status in the leisure class (that group which is involved in the predatory seizure of goods without actually working to obtain them), members must avoid productive pursuits and their consumption must be wasteful. Also, because the leisure class is dominant, its outlook is adopted by the other classes of society, so that even the poor indulge in some conspicuous consumption.

See also Veblen, Thorstein.

CONSPIRACY DOCTRINE, a common-law principle holding, in its most general form, that an agreement or combination by two or more parties to intend or do injury to a third party is a criminal act. Its use against labor unions in the United States in the late eighteenth and early nineteenth centuries reflected the philosophical orientation to the natural law of early capitalism. Unions, because they sought higher wages and better working conditions, were accused of upsetting the "natural" balance of a market-oriented economy, as well as the price-wage policies of a specific employer. The organization of workers itself was taken

as evidence of conspiracy. Subsequently, court decisions and federal legislation in the twentieth century removed unions from liability under the doctrine.

Conspiracy in restraint of trade is forbidden to business competitors in the Sherman Antitrust Act. Its use here is premised on the belief that competition is the most satisfactory regulator of activity in a market economy, and that collusive agreements to increase prices artificially by price-fixing or market-sharing agreements destroy the advantages to society of free competition.   —*Thomas O. Depperschmidt*

See also Clayton Act; Collusion; Market Sharing; Price Fixing; Restraint of Trade; Sherman Antitrust Act.

CONSTANT-COST INDUSTRY, one in which expanded resource use does not lead to increases in resource prices. The resources used by this industry are not specialized and represent only a small part of the aggregate used by all industries. We are dealing with the long run; therefore, we must consider exit and entry of firms. The short-run effects of an increase in demand for this product will include a price rise and increased output and excess profits for existing firms. New firms with identical cost curves will appear; price falls and the industry supply schedule will be parallel to the axis, at minimum average cost.

CONSTANT VALUE refers to a national income account adjusted for price changes: what remains is a dollar measure that changes only because of changes in the quantities of goods and services. If, for example, constant-value GNP increases, the quantity of goods and services produced by the economy has increased.

Simple Technique. One technique for calculating constant-value GNP is to use price indexes to deflate GNP: constant-value GNP is the ratio of current-value GNP to a price index for the year multiplied by 100. The constant-value GNP so calculated is denominated in terms of prices prevailing in the base year of the price index. Clearly, if prices are increasing, market-value GNP will be increasing, but so will the price index: both the numerator and the denominator used in the calculation of constant-value GNP will have risen and removed the effect of higher prices.

The difficulty with this approach is that the generality of the price index employed may be sharply limited in comparison to the generality of the goods and services included within GNP. For example, if the Consumer Price Index (CPI) is employed, CPI refers to or characterizes the changes in the prices for consumer goods and services; but GNP includes much more than just consumer goods and services, and the price behavior of these other goods and services may be quite unlike the price behavior of consumer output. The same objection arises if the Producer Price Index (PPI) is used instead of CPI.

Refined Technique. Because of these difficulties an

alternative technique is used in estimating constant-value GNP. This process involves the calculation of a price index for various components of GNP. Each component is measured in terms of current value and is then deflated by its appropriate price index. The constant-value components of GNP are then added together to obtain constant-value GNP. The value of the GNP deflator, the ratio of current-value GNP to constant-value GNP multiplied by 100, represents a price index that reflects a much broader picture of price change than either CPI or PPI.

—*Frank J. Bonello*

CONSUMER CHOICE exists within an economic system when individuals are free to purchase the goods and services that they desire and for which they have the money. This freedom is sometimes denied during economic and political crises, such as World War II and severe grain shortages. The alternative to consumer choice is rationing, either with coupons or direct allocation of goods.

CONSUMER CREDIT CONTROLS. *See* Installment Credit Controls.

CONSUMER DEMAND. It has long been observed that there is an inverse relation between price and quantity demanded of a good. Explanations of downward sloping demand curves have focused on the behavior of the individual consumer. How does a consumer decide how to allocate his or her income among various goods and services?

An initial explanation employs the psychological data that the more of a good or service that is consumed, the less is the satisfaction gained by increasing the consumption rate. The last unit of a good consumed will not add as much to a consumer's satisfaction as the previous unit. This is known as diminishing marginal utility. Given that a consumer attempts to maximize the satisfaction (utility) obtained from the goods and services consumed, it can be shown that diminishing marginal utility will lead the consumer to purchase more of a good when its price falls and less when its price rises.

While diminishing marginal utility is still used for exposition in introductory economic courses, it has been supplanted as an explanation of downward sloping demand curves by an ordinal theory of utility measurement.   —*Gerald A. Whitney*

See also Consumer Equilibrium; Demand Curve; Maximizing Behavior; Utility Function.

CONSUMER DETERMINISM. *See* Consumer Sovereignty.

CONSUMER EQUILIBRIUM, a situation in which the consumer allocates his income in the most desirable fashion, purchasing the most preferred bundle

CONSUMER EQUILIBRIUM

Fig. 1

Fig. 2

Fig. 3

Fig. 4

Fig. 5

Fig. 6

within his budget. Because the optimal bundle has the highest level of utility, an equilibrium position is represented by a point on the highest indifference curve within the feasible set.

The Basic Situation. If the consumer has an income of M dollars per period of time, and the prices of X and Y are P^x and P^y, respectively, then the maximum amount of good X that the consumer can purchase is M/P^x, and the maximum amount of Y is M/P^y. Points on the line joining M/P^x and M/P^y in Figure 1 represent bundles of X and Y that cost exactly M dollars. The line is called the *budget line*. Points in the shaded triangle in Figure 1 represent bundles whose cost is less than M dollars. The entire triangle, including its boundaries, is called the *feasible set*.

Given the conditions depicted in Figure 1, the highest indifference curve that the consumer can reach feasibly is the curve labeled I, and therefore, the bundle containing X_1 units of X and Y_1 units of Y represents an equilibrium position. Geometrically, an equilibrium position (except for some special cases) is a point of tangency between the budget line and an indifference curve. At that point, the slope of the indifference curve equals the slope of the budget line.

The Equilibrium Condition. To analyze the equilibrium condition further, it is instructive to examine the economic meaning attached to the slopes of the indifference curves and the budget line. Both slopes are negative. The magnitude of the indifference curve's slope is the ratio of the marginal utilities, U^x/U^y. This ratio shows how much Y a consumer must give up per unit of X gained in order to leave his level of utility unchanged; this ratio is called the marginal rate of substitution in consumption. $MRSC_{xy}$. The magnitude of the budget line's slope is the ratio of the prices, P^x/P^y. This shows the rate at which the consumer can substitue Y for X and leave his total expenditures unchanged. Since the slopes of the budget line and isoquant are equal at equilibrium, the equilibrium condition may be stated as $MRSC_{xy} = P^x/P^y$ ($U^x/U^y = P^x/P^y$) or equivalently as $U^x/P^x = U^y/P^y$. Hence, at equilibrium the utility gained from the last dollar spent on each good must be equal.

Income Effects. When their incomes change, consumers adjust their purchases and move to a new equilibrium position. Figure 2 illustrates an increase in income from M_1 to M_2. This increase causes the budget line to move to the right in a parallel fashion, thereby increasing the size of the feasible set. Following this change, the consumer moves from his initial equilibrium point E_1 to the new equilibrium at E_2.

When an increase (decrease) in income induces the consumer to purchase more (less) of a good, it is called a *superior* or *normal good*. When an increase (decrease) in income causes the consumer to purchase less (more) of a good, it is called an *inferior good*. In Figure 2 both X and Y are superior goods. In Figure 3, on the other hand, X is a superior good, and Y is an inferior good.

Price Effects. The effect of a change in a price is to change the price ratio P^x/P^y. For example, an increase in P^x increases the ratio, indicating that good X has become more expensive relative to good Y. Because the ratio is also equal to the slope of the budget line, an increase in P^x makes the budget line steeper. Figure 4 illustrates the effect of an increase in P^x from P^x_1 to P^x_2. This change causes the budget line to rotate clockwise around its intercept on the Y axis, thereby reducing the size of the feasible set, and inducing the consumer to move from the initial equilibrium E_1 to the new equilibrium E_2. In this particular example, the consumer reduces his purchase of X and increases his purchase of Y. When an increase (decrease) in the price of X causes the consumer to purchase more (less) of Y, then Y is said to be a *substitute* for X. When an increase (decrease) in the price of X causes the consumer to purchase less (more) of Y, then Y is said to be a *complement* for X. Thus, in Figure 4, good Y is a substitute for X.

The example illustrated in Figure 5 shows the effect of a decrease in P^y from P^y_1 to P^y_2. The budget line rotates around its X-intercept, bringing about an increase in the size of the feasible set, and inducing the consumer to move from E^1 to E^2. In this example, good X is a complement for good Y. An unusual feature of this example is the fact that the decrease in P^y makes the consumer purchase less of good Y. Such a phenomenon is referred to as the *Giffen paradox*, and the good in question (good Y in the present case) is called a *Giffen good*. It can be shown that Giffen goods are inferior goods.

Compensated price effects. When the price of a commodity increases, the budget line moves closer to the origin, reflecting the fact that a price increase reduces the consumer's purchasing power, or his *real income*. Thus, a price change affects the consumer's economic conditions in two ways: (1) it changes the relative prices confronting him, and (2) it changes his real income.

It is possible to separate the effects of these two changes by means of a compensated price change, by giving the consumer a compensation in nominal income to offset the loss in real income. If P^x increases from P^x_1 to P^x_2, the budget line rotates around its Y-intercept, as shown in Figure 6. To maintain the consumer's initial purchasing power, his nominal income is increased from M_1 to M_2, where the increase $M_2 - M_1$ is just enough to make the new budget line go through the initial bundle E_1. Thus, the new budget line represents the consumer's market opportunities following an increase in income designed to keep his real income constant. As a response to this compensated price change, the consumer moves from E_1 to E_2, and the changes in quantities demanded are referred to as *substitution effects*. The change in the quantity of X, $X_2 - X_1$, is referred to as the *own substitution effect,* being a change in the quantity of a commodity due to a change in its own price, and the change in the quantity of Y, $Y_2 - Y_1$, is called a *cross-substitution effect.* One conclusion of the theory of consumer behavior is that own substitution effects are always negative; that is, a compensated increase (decrease) in the price of a good always brings about a decrease (increase) in the quantity demanded of that good. This result is also known as the *law of demand.*

CONSUMER GOODS. *See* Goods; Goods and Services.

CONSUMERISM, a movement to extend and deepen the protections of the "rights" of consumers vis-à-vis sellers of goods and services that gained wide acceptance during the 1970s and has remained quite powerful since. The essence of consumerism is to afford government protection to consumers against poor quality and unsafe commodities, by setting standards for production and instigating product recalls and other corrective measures when these standards are not met, and by providing legal recourse to buyers to redress their complaints and seek compensation for damages. Consumer rights and protections have used the mechanism of class-action suits, which unite many small buyers against large sellers, with great success; occasionally, a state attorney-general may even press a class-action suit on behalf of the citizens of his state. Consumerism also has spread to the area of professional services: medical malpractice suits have become fairly common as, to a lesser extent, have legal, investment, and other personal services malpractice suits.

CONSUMER PRICE INDEX (CPI), the most frequently quoted price index, often used in discussing the aims and objectives desired for the price level. It is essentially a statistical measure of changes in the prices of items necessary to maintain a certain standard of living for an urban family. Each listed item is given a weight. This weight is usually determined by its importance in the family budget, noted from consumer spending patterns. Included in this list are certain types of foods, clothing, rent, and other items for daily living.

The prices of the items are compared to a base year to get an indication of the level and direction of price changes. CPI is compiled by the Bureau of Labor Statistics of the Department of Labor and is reported monthly. CPI is sometimes referred to as the cost-of-living index and is often used to compute pay increases in labor-management negotiations.

See also Price Indexes.

CONSUMER PRODUCT SAFETY COMMISSION (CPSC), a semi-independent federal agency created

CONSUMER PRICE INDEXES FOR URBAN WAGE EARNERS (1982-84 = 100)		
Year	CPI All items	Purchasing power of consumer dollar (1982-84 = $1.00)
1946	19.5	$5.13
1947	22.3	4.48
1948	24.1	4.15
1949	23.8	4.20
1950	24.1	4.15
1951	26.0	3.85
1952	26.5	3.77
1953	26.7	3.75
1954	26.9	3.72
1955	26.8	3.73
1956	27.2	3.68
1957	28.1	3.56
1958	28.9	3.46
1959	29.1	3.44
1960	29.6	3.38
1961	29.9	3.34
1962	30.2	3.31
1963	30.6	3.27
1964	31.0	3.27
1965	31.5	3.18
1966	32.4	3.09
1967	33.4	2.99
1968	34.8	2.87
1969	36.7	2.73
1970	38.8	2.58
1971	40.5	2.47
1972	41.8	2.39
1973	44.4	2.25
1974	49.3	2.03
1975	53.8	1.86
1976	56.9	1.76
1977	60.6	1.65
1978	65.2	1.53
1979	72.6	1.38
1980	82.4	1.21
1981	90.9	1.10
1982	96.5	1.04
1983	99.6	1.00
1984	103.9	.96
1985	107.6	.93
1986	109.6	.91
1987	113.6	.88
1988	118.3	.85
1989	124.0	.81

in 1972, whose members are appointed by the President. The CPSC has been given the task of enforcing several federal laws that relate to products and product safety problems, such as the Flammable Fabrics Act and the Federal Hazardous Substances Labeling Act. Among its most powerful regulatory weapons is the power to ban immediately the sale of products deemed to represent an imminent hazard. An example might be a new crib toy that is found to have a part that can be easily dislodged and swallowed by small children. The commission can also hold hearings and write industry standards regulating the design and content of products.

Two aspects of the CPSC stand out as regulatory successes: the development of a nationwide reporting system of accidental injuries and deaths, based on a computer link to hospital emergency rooms and doctors' offices, and also some early regulatory success with respect to products used by and for children. Two examples of the latter are fairly low-cost changes in crib design that prevent accidental strangulation of infants, and also changes in the design of children's slides that make them safer.

On the other hand, the CPSC has had its share of critics from both sides of the product safety debate. Some critics have argued that the CPSC is too slow to act, and is "captured" by the industries it is supposed to regulate. Others claim that the commission has been responsible for unnecessarily driving up the cost of goods and services, largely in an attempt to protect people from themselves. This reasoning suggests that consumers will choose safe products if they desire them, but that the marketplace can adequately make this determination. Still others wish to see the CPSC expand its role as a provider of information, but reduce its attempts to set standards for particular products. This view points out that informed consumers are necessary for the argument that a free marketplace aids consumer welfare and that often information is underprovided by the private market.

—*Michael S. Johnson*

See also Consumerism; Merit Good, Pure Public Good.

CONSUMER PROTECTION. In today's economy, the consumer needs a great deal of information concerning the quality and side-effects of the products that he or she buys. In many cases, the average consumer does not possess the knowledge or time to obtain this information. The consumer must therefore rely on the producer of the product to provide the information or to make sure that the consumer is always protected. There are many who believe that the producers have no incentive to do this; thus, the consumer is subject to great risks. Those who believe this argue that the government must protect the consumer through various means. Some of the most common areas of abuse against which consumers need protection are:

(1) emergence of monopoly, with its powers over pricing and the amount and quality of product offering;

(2) misleading or false advertising efforts;

(3) misleading or false personal selling practices, such as termite inspections resulting in unneeded home treatment;

(4) excessive interest rates and carrying charges, as when small loan companies or retail stores tack on very high carrying charges by concealing them in the total payback price;

(5) the marketing of harmful products, for example, cosmetics causing skin disorders, foods packed under unsanitary conditions, or automobiles with safety problems;

(6) deceptive labeling or packaging of products, such as the failure to inform the consumer of the limitations or potential dangers associated with using the product;

(7) environmental pollution by industries or consumers themselves.

Protecting the Consumer. Local, state and federal governments act as rule makers and policemen, regulating various aspects of business by passing such statutory laws as the Sherman and Clayton Antitrust Acts, the Pure Food and Drug Act, and the Truth in Lending Act. In addition, administrative laws and regulations are handed down by agencies such as the Federal Trade Commission and the Food and Drug Administration, which are charged specifically with regulating commercial activities.

Industry's own efforts to protect consumers from questionable business practices are exercised via trade associations, chambers of commerce, and better business bureaus, through the adoption of codes of conduct and product standards.

Consumer advocates may study industry practices and product performance to determine if there are abuses against which the consumer should be protected. Their chief weapon is carefully documented publicity that is adverse to a company or a product. Consumer movements are sometimes formalized: delegates meet and attempt to exert pressure for legislation to protect the consumer. —*Algin B. King*

CONSUMER SOVEREIGNTY, the theory that states that, in a free-market economy, the consumer determines which goods and services will be produced. Competing theories state that producers decide what they will produce, and use advertising to convince consumers to buy the goods and services produced. Under the consumer-sovereignty approach, consumers will not buy goods and services that they do not want. The profit motive of firms will then cause firms to produce those goods and services that the consumers want, since this is the only way that they will make profits. Under this theory, advertising is mostly informational; the purpose of advertising is to inform consumers about the quality and availability and price of products.

CONSUMER'S PREFERENCES, an individual's personal preference for one form of goods or services over all other alternatives offered, as revealed by his or her purchases in the markets. An economic system is said to be dominated by consumer preferences when it allocates resources to reflect these tastes.

CONSUMER SURPLUS, the difference between the total utility received from a product and the total market value of that product. The surplus is received by the consumer but not at the expense of the producer. According to the law of diminishing marginal utility, a consumer receives less and less utility from the purchase of identical items; a consumer will purchase items up to that point where he or she no longer receives any utility. Therefore, consumers will purchase items until they stop receiving a surplus. Consumer surplus is measured on a graph by the vertical distance between the price (which measures what a consumer must pay for a good) and the demand curve (which measures what a consumer is willing to pay for that quantity of the good).

The concept of consumer surplus is very often used in making decisions of a social nature. For example, the decision whether to build a bridge or to build a road may be based on the amount of consumer surplus of each. The item that allows for the most consumer surplus will very often be the one decided upon. If the decision calls for a public vote, each citizen will vote for the item that will give him or her the most surplus. Although in most cases consumer surplus is very difficult or impossible to measure, consumers are able to relatively price a surplus.

CONSUMER WELFARE, a term for the satisfaction or utility of the consumer. In economics, consumer theory is based on the assumption that consumers attempt to maximize their own welfare or utility. Individuals can maximize their utility by choosing those items that provide the greatest amount of marginal utility per dollar spent until the marginal utility per dollar spent on each good is equal to the marginal utility per dollar spent on every other good.

CONSUMPTION, the amount spent by households on currently produced goods and services. Consumption refers to *spending* by households, not to the acts of eating or using or wearing out, nor does it refer to the motives of the household in making a purchase. Thus if a household buys an old house or a used car, economists do not call this consumption but the exchange of one asset (money) for another asset (used car) in the "balance sheet" of the family. Similarly, the purchase of a bond or share of stock is not "spending" but the exchange of one asset for another.

Household as a Firm. When a household is both a consuming unit and producing unit—a farm family is an example, or a father-and-son house repair team working out of the basement—economics treats the business aspect of the family's life as a "firm." Thus the receipts of the house repair team would be called "revenues of the firm." Whatever they buy in order to

do business is classified as a business outlay (nails—current cost of production; a saw—investment, to be depreciated over the life of the saw). Only the purchases that are not used in production are called household consumption.

Motives for Consumption. Economists, and the theory of income determination, do not deal with motives for consumption other than in the most general way of saying a household chooses its level of consumption (and saving) to maximize its welfare (or utility).

Patterns of Consumption. The theory of income determination focuses on the empirical (statistical) relationship between a household's disposable income, wealth, expectations of future income and wealth, and access to credit, without regard to the individual motives or collective decision-making processes of the household. Consumption spending is closely correlated to (1) current income, (2) wealth, (3) expected future income, (4) expected future wealth, and (5) the availability of credit.

Significance in Income Determination. There are two reasons why the theory defines consumption as "spending by households on currently produced goods and services." First, the considerations and circumstances that cause households to spend and to save (not to consume) are different from the profit motive and opportunities that dominate investment decisions. Thus, household spending and saving intentions do not correspond with business investment intentions, or government's aims in public policy. Second, it is spending on currently produced goods and services that determines how much is produced (GNP), how many are employed and whether inflation occurs. The focus of the theory is on the *aggregate consumption demand* in money terms, which is the sum of all households' consumption spending.

—*Walter C. Neale*

CONSUMPTION, CROSS-SECTION. Studies of the relationship between personal disposable income and consumption (as given by household budget surveys) for households in different income brackets during the same period of time make it possible to draw cross-section consumption functions, which support the assumption that consumption is largely determined by the level of income, and that the marginal propensity to consume is less than 1. High-income households consume more than low-income households, but high-income households also save a larger proportion of income than do low-income households.

CONSUMPTION, TIME-SERIES, the method of examining the relationship between income and consumption by pairing consumption expenditures for previous years with personal disposable income for each of the years to produce a historical consumption function. Such consumption functions show a higher long-run marginal propensity to consume than the short-run MPC shown by cross-section studies.

CONSUMPTION FUNCTION, the relationship between disposable income and consumption, in which it is assumed that the level of disposable income determines the level of consumption, that is, that consumption spending depends on income. Expressed in a table, it is called the *consumption schedule,* and shows all possible incomes paired with the consumption spending which would occur at each income. It should be read as a set of "if . . . then . . ." propositions: "If disposable income is $Ya, then consumption will be $Ca; if disposable income is $Yb, then consumption will be $Cb," and so on.

When these values are plotted on a graph, the curve is called the *consumption function.* The consumption function can also be written as an algebraic equation; most simply in the form C = C of "Breakeven Point" + (MPC) × (disposable income − Break-even Point value of income). More complex equations result if one introduces wealth or other considerations as additional determiners of consumption.

The phrase "propensity to consume" expresses the idea that consumption depends on disposable income and, more broadly, on wealth and expectations about future income, wealth, and prices. When the propensity to consume is put in the form of a specific relationship between income and consumption, it is called a consumption function or consumption schedule. The propensity to consume is an empirical (statistical) relationship and is not a statement about consumers' motives, nor is it a statement about their rationality. — *Walter C. Neale*

See also Consumption; Consumption, Cross Section; Consumption, Time Series; Permanent Income Hypothesis; Pigou Effect.

CONSUMPTION POSSIBILITY. World production and consumption possibilities are maximized under free international trade. In the absence of trade a nation's welfare is limited by its production-possibilities frontier in the following manner: Country A can produce 10 units of commodity X or 20 units of Y. Country B can produce 10 units of X or 30 of Y. These are the rates at which X can be "transformed" into Y and vice versa in each country. Let trade commence: B reduces output of X by 10 and A increases X output by 10; the quantity of X remains same. Y output decreases by 20 in A but increases by 30 in B with a net gain of 10. Trade has resulted in no reduction in one commodity accompanied by an increase in the other. All products can increase via specialization and free trade and the world's consumption possibility and welfare increase.

See also Comparative Advantage; International Trade Theory; Specialization.

CONTESTABLE MARKETS are those in which competitive pressures from potential entrants exercise strong constraints on the behavior of incumbent suppliers. For a market to be contestable, there can be no significant entry barriers. In equilibrium, a contestable market offers no economic profit to a potential new entrant and is efficient in its pricing and in its allocation of production among incumbent suppliers. These conditions hold regardless of the number of firms in the industry, even if there is only one, because it is potential competition from potential entrants rather than competition among incumbent suppliers that constrains the equilibrium behavior of the firms already in the industry. A perfectly contestable market is characterized not only by an absence of barriers to entry, but also by an absence of exit costs (i.e., there are no sunk costs).

CONTRACT NEGOTIATION. *See* Collective Bargaining.

CONVENIENCE DEMAND. *See* Liquidity Preference.

CONVERGING EQUILIBRIUM, a true equilibrium. In converging equilibrium, the system will return to a point of equilibrium if any factor causes the original equilibrium to be disturbed. Converging equilibrium is contrasted with an *explosive equilibrium,* where any disturbance of the original equilibrium will not result in a return to a point of equilibrium.

See also Explosive Equilibrium.

CONVERTIBLE BONDS, bonds that give the holder the right or option to exchange his bond for a different type of security. Often, this security option is a common or preferred stock. Some convertible bonds can only be converted at maturity, although others can be converted at any time, upon due notice.

CONVERTIBLE CURRENCY, currency that can be exchanged for any other currency without loss to the holder and for whatever purpose the holder desires. Under a pure gold standard, currency is freely convertible into gold. Under the initial International Monetary Fund system it was envisaged that all currencies would be convertible into dollars and hence convertible into each other at a fixed rate via the dollar.

See also Exchange Rates; Fixed Exchange Rates; Gold Standard.

COOPERATIVISM, a form of economic organization characterized by the absence of any special capital-providing class. Workers put up the capital in producers' cooperatives. In consumers' cooperatives, historically more successful, the consumer, instead of the nonexistent capitalist, provides the capital and organizational control.

See also Associationism; Fourier, François Marie Charles; Owen, Robert.

CORPORATE BONDS, interest-bearing certificates issued by a corporation that promise to pay the bondholder a specified amount of money at a specified date. The main purpose of corporate bonds is to raise money for the corporation. Usually ownership of these bonds can be transferred by endorsement.

See also Bonds.

CORPORATE EARNINGS, corporate profits before taxes. In Gross National Product statistics they comprise about 10% of total earnings. Corporate income taxes are paid on corporate earnings, and what remains is paid out in dividends or kept in the corporation as retained earnings, which are important, because these funds can be combined with depreciation allowances in a given year to accommodate expansion without having to tap the capital markets or borrow from banks.

See also Dividends; Interest Rates; Undistributed Profits.

CORPORATE INCOME TAX, a levy on the net income of corporations. The federal corporation income tax was first collected in 1901. This tax became a major revenue source immediately after World War II, constituting 26% of federal revenues in 1948. Generous depreciation rules written into the 1981 tax act greatly reduced the corporate share of federal revenues (to roughly 6%). The 1986 Tax Reform Act (when fully implemented) is expected to increase this share to about 12%. A tax on corporate income is imposed by 45 states, in addition to the federal tax.

The incidence of this tax is a matter of some controversy. The tax is often perceived by the public as being paid by "business," but the economic question is whether the tax reduces after-tax corporate profits, reduces all profits both corporate and noncorporate, raises prices of products produced by the corporate sector, lowers wages of corporate employees, or some combination of the above. Another source of controversy is the fact that corporate earnings are effectively taxed twice: stockholders pay tax on the dividends received from the firm, yet the corporation pays a tax on its profits, without any allowable deduction for dividends paid to the stockholders.

CORPORATE STATE. *See* Fascism.

CORPORATION, the most common form of business ownership among large firms, although small firms sometimes use the corporate organization. The corporation is essentially a legal "person," with all the rights of a person. Upon application the state will grant a charter conferring these rights to a firm. Thus, the corporation separates its affairs from that of the owners. The owners are not personally responsible for the legal transactions of the corporation. This exemption is referred to as limited liability of stockholders; that is, stockholders' responsibilities are restricted to the amount invested in stock.

The corporation has the legal advantage of eternal life. Unless it is dissolved, by mutual consent of the owners, it does not die. Thus, it has the advantage of existing without major setbacks even upon the death of an owner.

In large corporations, control is by an elected board of directors. The board, in turn, selects the officers of the corporation and decides on the use of profits earned. Profits are usually divided into two categories: distributed profits, which are given to stockholders, and undistributed profits, which are usually reinvested.

See also Limited Liability; Partnership.

CORRELATION is a concept that refers to the degree of association between variables. We can obtain an exact measure of the relationship between the variables X and Y. We can use the coefficient of correlation, r_{xy}

$$r_{XY} = \frac{\sum_{i=1}^{N} (X_i - \overline{X})(Y_i - \overline{Y})}{\sqrt{\sum_{i=1}^{N} (X_i - \overline{X})^2 \sum_{i=1}^{N} (Y_i - \overline{Y})^2}}$$

We can shorten this formula by using deviations from the mean. Let $x_i = (X_i - \overline{X})$ and $y_i = (Y_1 - \overline{Y})$.

$$r_{XY} = \frac{\sum_{i=1}^{N} xy}{\sqrt{\sum_{i=1}^{N} x^2 \sum_{i=1}^{N} y^2}}$$

The coefficient of correlation lies in the range $[+1, -1]$. If Y increases as X increases, r_{xy} is positive and close to 1. If y decreases as x increases, r_{xy} is negative and close to -1. If there is no association between X and Y, $r = 0$. Standard tests exist to determine whether a coefficient is significantly different from 0.

Coefficient of Determination, a measure of the proportion of the variation of Y explained by the linear influence of X. It is the square of the correlation coefficient (r). Since r_{xy} lies in the range of $[-1,1]$, r_{xy} can only take values between 0 and 1: $r^2 = 0$ implies that none of the variation of Y is explained by X, and $r^2 = 1$ implies that all of the variation of Y is explained by X. One can test if a given r^2 is significantly different from 0.

Rank Correlation Coefficient can be computed from ranked data and has the same interpretation as r.

Partial Correlation, Multiple Determination. A

CORRELATION

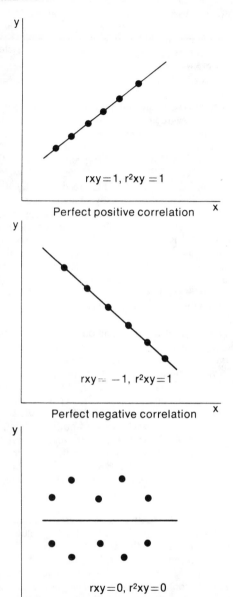

rxy = 1, r²xy = 1

Perfect positive correlation

rxy = −1, r²xy = 1

Perfect negative correlation

rxy = 0, r²xy = 0

Zero correlation

dependent variable can be a function of several independent variables. In $y = f(x_1, x_2)$, y will be associated with both x^1 and x^2. A measure of the association of y with x, holding z constant, is the partial correlation coefficient between y and x computed with the linear influence of z eliminated. The proportion of y explained by the combined effects of x and z is called the coefficient of multiple determination and is denoted R_2.   —*Carlisle E. Moody*

See also Curve Fitting; Significance.

CORRESPONDENT BALANCES. *See* Reserves.

COST EFFECTIVENESS. *See* Benefit-Cost Analysis.

COST FUNCTION: TOPIC GUIDE

The cost function of a business firm has many aspects. For the time dimension, see the articles SHORT RUN and LONG RUN. Some of the different cost concepts in the function are explored in the articles TOTAL COST OF PRODUCTION and MARGINAL COST OF PRODUCTION. For a view of the cost function as it bears on decision-making in the firm, see PROFIT MAXIMIZATION, EQUILIBRIUM OF THE FIRM, and FIRM SUPPLY CURVE.

The reader will also find it useful to consult the Subject Map accompanying the article SUPPLY for further coverage of the Cost Function.

COST FUNCTION. When producers vary the level of their outputs (over some fixed period of time), they do so by changing the amounts of the inputs used in the production process, and this causes a change in the cost of production. The relationship between various levels of output and the cost of production is called a cost function. When the planning period is relatively short, certain inputs, such as the physical plant, heavy machinery, and others, remain fixed even when output is changed; other inputs, such as labor and raw materials, vary with the level of output. Consequently, the total cost of production (TC) can be separated into two types of cost: total variable cost (TVC), including all the costs which depend on the level of output, and total fixed cost (TFC), which comprises the costs that are independent of the level of output. These 3 concepts are related by the basic cost equation TC = TVC + TFC.

The 3 types of total cost are illustrated by means of the cost schedules in Table 1 (p. 48), showing hypothetical cost figures for the output levels 0 through 10. Input prices are assumed to be fixed, that is, they are not affected by the amounts of the inputs purchased by the producer. It is to be noted that, while TFC remains constant, both TVC and TC increase with output. Furthermore, when the level of output is 0, then TC = TFC, indicating that when no production takes place, the producer still incurs the cost of the fixed inputs—so-called overhead cost.

If the output is capable of continuous variations, then the cost functions can be depicted as continuous curves as shown in Fig. 1 (p. 48) in which cost (in $$) is measured on the vertical axis, and product X on the horizontal axis. TFC is a horizontal line, since it is independent of the level of output. According to the diagram, TFC is equal to A dollars. TVC is an increasing function (that is, it has a positive slope), and it goes

COST FUNCTION

Units of output	TC in $	TVC in $	TFC in $
0	24	0	24
1	34	10	24
2	42	18	24
3	48	24	24
4	52	28	24
5	54	30	24
6	60	36	24
7	73	49	24
8	88	64	24
9	105	81	24
10	124	100	24

Table 1

COST FUNCTION

Units of output	TC in $	TVC in $	TFC in $	ATC in $	AFC in $	AVC in $	MC in $
0	24	0	24	—	—	—	—
1	34	10	24	34	24	10	10
2	42	18	24	21	12	9	8
3	48	24	24	16	8	8	6
4	52	28	24	13	6	7	4
5	54	30	24	$10^{4/5}$	$4^{4/5}$	6	2
6	60	36	24	10	4	6	6
7	73	49	24	$10^{3/7}$	$3^{3/7}$	7	13
8	88	64	24	11	3	8	15
9	105	81	24	$11^{2/3}$	$2^{2/3}$	9	17
10	124	100	24	$12^{2/5}$	$2^{2/5}$	10	19

Table 2

Figure 1

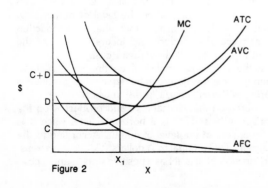

Figure 2

through the origin; this is so because when output is 0, TVC is also 0. The TC curve lies above the TVC curve, and the vertical distance between them is always equal to TFC, that is, A in the above example. In general, at relatively low levels of output TVC and TC increase at a decreasing rate, while at relatively high levels of output they increase at an increasing rate.

If total cost is divided by the level of output, one obtains an average cost, that is, cost per unit of output. There are 3 average costs: average total cost (ATC), where ATC = TC/X, average variable cost (AVC), where AVC = TVC/X, and average fixed cost (AFC), where AFC = TFC/X. If both sides of the basic cost equation TC = TVC + TFC are divided by X, one obtains ATC = AVC + AFC. Finally, marginal cost (MC) is defined as the increment in total cost due to a small increase in output. For a discrete increase in output, MC is defined as $\triangle TC/\triangle X$, where $\triangle$ denotes "change in." For an infinitesimal increase in output, that is, when cost is represented by a continuous curve, MC is defined as the slope of the TC curve (or slope of the TVC curve). All the 7 types of cost are illustrated in the hypothetical cost schedules shown in Table 2.

When output varies continuously, average costs and marginal cost can be represented by continuous curves as shown in Figure 2. These curves have the following general characteristics: (a) In general, ATC, AVC, and MC are U-shaped; (b) AFC has the form of a rectangular hyperbola; (c) ATC lies above AVC; (d) The vertical distance between ATC and AVC is equal to AFC at the respective level of output; (e) MC cuts AVC where AVC has its minimum; and MC cuts ATC where ATC has its minimum; (f) In the range in which MC > ATC (AVC), ATC(AVC) is falling; in the range in which MC < ATC(AVC), ATC(AVC) is rising.

—*Josef Hadar*

COST OF LIVING, a frequently used wage criterion in wage negotiations. The cost-of-living value is usually determined by the consumer price index. The union representatives use rising prices as the basis for justifying wage increases. Because wages are usually fixed from contract to contract, rising prices during the fixed periods reduce purchasing power or real wages. To avoid this, many contracts have automatic cost of living adjustments, called escalator clauses, which specify a precise relationship between changes in the cost of living and changes in the wage rates to be paid employees.

Another type of provision in many bargaining contracts states that the contract may be reopened for negotiations during the term of the contract given a specified increase in the cost of living.

Escalator clauses, the most popular cost of living provision, began in 1948 with a contract between General Motors and the United Automobile Workers.

COST-OF-LIVING INDEX. *See* Consumer Price Index.

COST OF PRODUCTION. *See* Cost Function.

COST-PLUS PRICING. *See* Full-Cost Pricing.

COST-PUSH INFLATION, or sellers' inflation, creeping inflation that continues even in periods of deficient aggregate demand. If unions push for wage increases beyond any increase in productivity, firms with a great deal of market power may be able to pass the resulting cost increases on to the consumer. For cost-push inflation to persist, it is necessary either that the firms in question face inelastic demand for their products or that the monetary authorities increase the money supply to prevent decreases in employment and output.

See also Administered Pricing; Markup Inflation; Wage-Push Inflation.

COUNTERCYCLICAL POLICY. *See* Monetary Policy.

COUNTERVAILING POWER, a concept developed by John Kenneth Galbraith which holds that economic organizations with original market power bring into being, and eventually are challenged by, organizations on the other side of the market who offset or countervail that original power. Whether buyers or sellers, the theory runs, these holders of original power are prevented by the countervailing sellers or buyers from abusing it.

CRAFT UNION, an organization of workers that have in common the knowledge of a particular skill. It is the aim of the craft union to create a monopoly for a skill in order to control the market by restricting supply and thus be able to bargain effectively over wages and other benefits.

Usually conservative in nature, the craft union is very much akin to the medieval guilds. An initiation as well as an apprenticeship is usually a prerequisite for membership. Though some unions are open to any person possessing the necessary skill, others limit enrollment considerably. Some unions limit their apprenticeships to, or give preference to, relatives of current members, thus effectively controlling membership. Such rules have generally been relaxed in recent years.

See also Labor Movement.

CRAWLING PEG. *See* Exchange Rate.

CREDIT [from the Latin verb "to trust"], the present acquisition of anything of value in exchange for the promise to return its equivalent at some time in the future. Usually credit means either buying goods with payment to be made later or borrowing money. Credit requires that the debtor pay when the debt falls due.

Individual credit is extended by private persons through occasional loans to friends, the purchase of securities, deposits in banks, or loans to other financial intermediaries. *Mercantile credit* is extended by business when it provides goods against a credit card or on open-book account to be paid at the end of the month or on the installment plan. *Finance credit* includes loans by institutions specializing in lending money: banks, finance companies, savings and loan associations, credit unions, life insurance companies, and so on.

Loans may be made to consumers, government, or business. Business loans may be short-term (commercial) or long-term (investment). Loans may be unsecured, or secured by mortgage or other property dependent entirely on the signature of the borrower. One of the most important forms of credit in the United States is the demand deposits of commercial banks, which form the largest part of the money supply.

Credit normally carries an interest charge to reimburse the lender for the costs of carrying on the credit business, the risk of nonpayment, and the reduction of liquidity inherent in holding the debt instead of liquid assets. In charge accounts, however, the interest cost is often hidden in the price of the merchandise. Interest rates tend to be higher for small loans, risky loans, and loans with long maturities. —*Walter W. Haines*

See also Commercial Bank; Demand Deposits; Financial Intermediaries; Liquid Assets; Money Supply.

CREDIT CONTROLS. *See* Installment Credit Controls.

CREDIT UNIONS. *See* Financial Intermediaries.

CREEPING INFLATION, a historical term used to describe the phenomenon of persistent price level increases at a relatively low rate (1% to 4% per year). Most advanced industrial countries experienced creeping inflation in the years following World War II. Although it may have increased profits and stimulated investment and growth, creeping inflation resulted in significant redistributions of income.

CROP RESTRICTIONS have been used in the United States since 1933 in the government's efforts to limit production for the purpose of keeping farm prices and incomes higher than they otherwise would be.

Early Restrictions were more commonly put on land devoted to crops than directly on the amounts of crops produced. Historically, acreage allotments for a restricted crop were assigned to farms on the basis of acreages of the crop grown in a prior base period. Efforts were made to get farmers not to exceed some selected percentage of their allotments. Marketing quotas were, in practice, compulsory acreage allotments—growers were permitted to market whatever they produced on permitted acreages. Controls were compulsory on all growers only when growers had first approved them in a referendum where the choice was between (a) price support and crop controls or (b) no price support or only nominal price support and no crop controls. Voluntary controls up to the mid-1950s usually did not attract much farmer participation because inducements for signing up were not attractive.

More Recent Controls. Beginning with the Soil Bank in 1956 and increasingly in the 1960s, government programs offered payments sufficiently high to attract enough participation in compulsory control programs. Variations in yields per acre make total production less controllable than acreage.

In the 1970s rice, peanut, and tobacco programs used compulsory acreage allotments (for some types of tobacco, poundage quotas were also in force). For feed grains (except oats), wheat, and cotton, producers were asked to hold idle certain proportions of their alloted or base acreages; but no additional limit was imposed on acreages of these crops actually grown. Payments were offered to attract participation and, especially for wheat and cotton, to supplement producers' incomes. No control programs were in effect for hay, soybeans, and oats, the other large-area crops.

In addition to programs annually idling some land on many farms, a few programs have aimed at retiring whole farms of low productivity for several years. The Conservation Reserve of the Soil Bank was the principal example. Later programs were given little or no funding by Congress.   —George E. Brandow

See also Price-Support Programs; Soil Bank.

CROSS SECTION. Observations on a variable taken at a particular point in time comprise cross-section data. Some examples are observations of consumption expenditures of different families, profits and dividends of different companies, or prices and wages of different cities. Cross-section data is available in official publications, such as the *Census of Population*, or from sample surveys.

CROSS-SUBSTITUTION EFFECT. *See* Consumer Equilibrium.

CURRENCY, that part of the money supply consisting of coins and paper bills issued by, or under the authority of, the government. In earlier days, currency included state bank notes, national bank notes, silver certificates and gold certificates. The only forms of American paper currency now being issued are federal reserve notes and United States notes.

CURRENCY CONTROLS, controls placed over the free exchange of currencies to ensure government supervision of foreign exchange transactions. Reasons may be to curb inflation, prevent speculative flows of capital, and deal with balance of payments problems. All foreign exchange is bought from and sold to an official government agency at prescribed rates. The rate system provides exchange to importers at low rates for those imports desired by the government, while those it wishes to discourage are charged higher rates. Exports the government wishes to promote command higher rates in payment for foreign exchange than those offered to exporters shipping goods the government wishes to discourage. Through this mechanism the balance of payments can be kept under control while domestic programs are promoted. Licensing and bilateral trade and payments agreements are other examples of currency controls. All imply inconvertibility of the currency.

See also Balance of Payments; Capital Movement; Exchange Rates.

CURRENT VALUE. GNP is normally defined in terms of current market value, or the quantities of various outputs—final goods and services—multiplied by their respective prices and summed together. Thus, GNP may change because of a change in prices, a change in the quantities of goods and services produced, or some combination of the two. This use of current market value is justified on the basis that it is perhaps the easiest and least expensive technique for the measurement of overall economic activity. Once GNP in current value is estimated, various techniques can be employed to remove the impact of price change. One reservation should be made: some items in GNP do not really have a price, for no actual market transaction that yields a price has taken place. Examples of this reservation include the rental value of owner-occupied housing, certain services provided by financial intermediaries, and income in kind.

See also Constant Value.

CURVE FITTING. In economics one postulates many functional relationships among variables; for example, the consumption function, and the demand and supply functions. In many cases even the form of the function is specified by the theory. The consumption function is usually assumed to be linear with a slope (marginal propensity to consume) between 0 and 1. If the assumptions concerning the relationships are true, one would expect that data gathered on income and consumption and plotted on a scatter diagram would lie approximately along a line $C = a + bY$. The process of estimating the parameters a and b in such a way as to approximate the points on the scatter diagram is called curve fitting.

The most common technique used to estimate a functional relationship is least-squares regression. The first step in regression is to transform the data if necessary so as to derive a linear relationship. Any polynomial and many exponential and logarithmic functions can be made linear for estimation purposes. The next step is to choose the estimates of a and b in such a way that the sum of the squared errors is at a minimum. A correlation coefficient will then measure the success of the regression and the validity of the theory. — *Carlisle E. Moody*

See also Best Fit; Correlation; Hypothesis; Significance.

CUSTOM DUTY. *See* Tariffs.

CUSTOMS UNIONS AND FREE-TRADE AREAS. Countries form a customs union if they remove all trade restrictions between one another and erect a common tariff against the rest of the world. If the countries retain their individual tariff structures against the outside world, then their grouping is called a free-trade area. The European Economic Community (EEC), also called the Common Market, was established in 1957, uniting France, Germany, Italy, Belgium, the Netherlands, Luxembourg, and later, Great Britain, in a customs union. Examples of a free-trade area are the European Free-Trade Association (EFTA) and the Latin American Free-Trade Area (LAFTA).

CUTTHROAT COMPETITION. *See* Predatory Practices.

CYCLICAL BALANCED BUDGET, budgetary principle advocating the balancing of the budget over the course of a complete business cycle rather than in particular fiscal or calendar years. Over the course of the cycle, tax receipts and expenditures would be equal. Under this principle, a surplus budget is called for during times of prosperity to restrain inflationary pressures and a deficit budget is called for under the condition of cyclical depression in order to stimulate the economy. Ideally, the surpluses and deficits would offset each other over the period of the cycle, thus providing budget balance. The absence of a built-in mechanism to assure a symmetrical cycle is a major obstacle confronting this type of policy.

See also Balanced Budget.

CYCLICAL DEFICIT, the difference between government expenditure and government revenues that results when the macroeconomy operates below the full-employment level. Cyclical deficits must be distinguished from structural deficits, which occur when the economy is operating at full capacity and which are the result of government taxation and spending programs. An economic slump reduces tax revenues. If government spending remains unchanged, a cyclical deficit will result.

CYCLICAL EXCESS CAPACITY. *See* Excess Capacity.

CYCLICAL UNEMPLOYMENT, the dominant form of unemployment in our modern economy. It is the result of recurrent fluctuations in business activity, which have been called the business cycle. While the business cycle has existed since American industrial development began, mass unemployment of a cyclical nature was not a problem until the Great Depression of the 1930s.

The basic concept of cyclical unemployment is that as business activities expand demand for labor increases and therefore unemployment falls. On the other hand, during "troughs" in the business cycle demand for labor falls and unemployment increases. The effect of cyclical unemployment was felt most severely during the 1930s (the decade of the Great Depression). Other business cycle troughs occurred in 1949, 1954, 1958, 1961, 1972, 1975, 1980, and 1982. Unemployment rates were in cycle lows in 1948, 1953, 1957, 1960, 1969, 1973, and for much of the period after 1983.

Although the economy seems less susceptible in recent years to the extreme boom-depression cycle of the 1920s and 1930s, cyclical unemployment is still a problem. — *William D. Wagoner*

See also Unemployment of Labor.

DAS KAPITAL represents the final development of Karl Marx's economics. The first volume was published by Marx in 1867 with the second and third volumes edited and published by Friedrich Engels after Marx's death.

Based upon the labor theory of value and Hegelian philosophy, Marx developed a criticism of classical economics. He felt that classical economists had become apologists for bourgeois interests, and that the profit of the capitalist was derived from the exploitation of labor. Accepting the widely held classical belief in the falling rate of profit, Marx felt that the capitalistic system would lead to a concentration of capital in the hands of a small group who would then be forced to increase the rate of exploitation of labor. As the standard of living of workers declines, they become more willing to revolt, and the basis for the end of the capitalistic system comes into being. "The knell of capitalist private property sounds. The expropriators are expropriated."

See also Labor Theory of Value; Revolutionary Socialism.

DEBENTURES are vouchers or certificates that acknowledge a debt owed by the issuer. In finance a debenture bond is an unsecured bond backed only by the general credit standing of the agency that issued it. Bonds that back direct obligations of the government are examples of debentures, because they are secured only by the taxing power of the government. These differ from revenue bonds of the government that are backed by revenue received from a certain project.

DEBS, EUGENE VICTOR (1855-1926), trade union leader, founder of the Socialist party. Debs was born of immigrant parents in Terre Haute, Indiana. A railroad worker at fourteen, he became an officer of his local in 1875, and by 1880 was secretary-treasurer of the National Brotherhood of Railway Firemen.

In 1893 Debs founded the American Railway Union, organized on industrial lines and open to all crafts. In the Pullman strike of 1894, which was broken by violence and the courts, he was jailed six months for violating an injunction. In jail Debs studied socialism, and upon release he worked with Victor L. Berger to consolidate radical factions to form the Socialist party. Debs ran as Socialist candidate for president in 5 elections, starting in 1900; in 1912 he received 6% of the popular vote.

Convicted in 1918 for speaking against participation in World War I, he was sentenced to 10 years' imprisonment. He campaigned from inside Atlanta Penitentiary and received 919,801 votes for president. In response to public pressure President Harding commuted Debs' sentence in 1921. After his release and the decline of his party, Debs wrote on prison conditions and edited the socialist weekly *American Appeal*.

Eugene Victor Debs

DEBT CEILING, a limit set by Congress on the amount of federal debt that may be outstanding during a time period. The debt has grown consistently and often approaches this ceiling. Because the debt ceiling is raised so often, it does not actually limit the federal debt but rather it serves to force periodic reviews of federal finances. Sometimes, when the debt approaches the ceiling, the Treasury uses financing methods which do not increase the debt but which actually cost more than borrowing. This is often cited as an argument against a debt ceiling.

DEBT MANAGEMENT. Management of the federal debt consists of interest payments on current issues of securities, sales of new securities, refunding of old securities when deficit budgets necessitate it, and staggering of maturity dates to avoid excess pressure for refunding.

DECEPTIVE ADVERTISING, that which misleads the consumer in some material respect about a product offered for sale. This current legal position, supplanting the earlier view that deceptive advertising is that which misleads the consumer in any particular, recognizes that while some exaggeration or "puffing" of claims for a product is inevitable, the consumer is entitled to protection against substantial misstatement or intent to deceive.

Deceptive advertising is prohibited in the Wheeler-Lea Act of 1938. It is generally recognized, however, that a less-than-successful enforcement record has resulted from the vastness of business' advertising effort, the limited staff and budget of the Federal Trade Commission (empowered to police interstate advertising), the time consumed in prosecuting one violation of the law, and the deficiency of penalties for deceptive advertising.

See also Antitrust Policy; Federal Trade Commission; Unfair and Deceptive Practices; Wheeler-Lea Act.

DECEPTIVE PRACTICES. *See* Unfair and Deceptive Practices.

DECILE. *See* Central Tendency.

DECREASE IN DEMAND, the shifting downward and to the left on the Cartesian plane of a demand function. This graphical shift indicates that a smaller quantity of a good is being purchased at every price. The position of a demand function depends upon the incomes, tastes and preferences, and expectations of buyers, as well as the prices of related goods. If one of these determinants of a demand function's position changes appropriately, it will result in a new demand function being defined. If the new function shows smaller quantites demanded at each price, demand is said to have decreased.

Decreases in income cause demand curves for normal goods to decrease. Adverse trends in consumer preference will result in decreased demand. Increases in complementary goods' prices and decreases in substitute goods' prices will decrease demand. If a depression in prices were expected by the economic community, it is likely that it would refrain from buying as much of any commodity as was purchased previous to the change in price expectations, causing a decrease in demand. —*Robert L. Brite*

DECREASE IN SUPPLY means that quantity supplied will be smaller at every price than it was previous to the change in circumstances. Graphically, the supply curve shifts backward to the left. If wage rates rise for a firm, technology (and therefore marginal product of labor) remain constant, then marginal cost will now be greater at any given output than it was previously. The marginal cost curve therefore rises; costs of production have been increased. Due to the increased marginal costs, the firm will require higher prices before it will produce given outputs voluntarily, otherwise profits will fall unnecessarily.

DECREASING-COST INDUSTRY. Since constant-cost industries have supply schedules with 0 slope (parallel to the horizontal axis) and increasing-cost industries have supply schedules that are positively sloped, one might expect negatively sloped supply schedules for decreasing-cost industries. However, this is not the case.

If the firm is producing where P = MC (selling price equals marginal cost of output), then it should be in equilibrium. But if this firm expands, its unit costs will fall, and further and further expansion will result. The first firm to expand will have competitive advantages. Persisting decreasing costs will inevitably lead to the breakdown of perfect competition; either oligopoly or outright monopoly will result.

DEFLATION, a decrease in the general level of prices or an increase in the value of money in terms of goods and services. In a deflationary period, falling prices are usually accompanied by declining levels of both output and employment caused by a deficiency in the amount of spending in the economy. The main problem with deflation is that as output decreases, people have less goods and services available, and individuals have a greater chance of losing their jobs than in a stable economy.

As with inflation, deflation has a redistribution impact on income in several ways. For example, those people that have fixed incomes, such as pensioners, benefit by a deflationary period, because it raises their real income or purchasing power. Deflation also benefits creditors at the expense of debtors, who pay back money that has more purchasing power than the money originally borrowed. A third distribution effect of deflation is that it increases the value of savings in the same way that it aids creditors.

—*William D. Wagoner*

See also Inflation.

DEFLATIONARY GAP. *See* Inflatory Gap.

DEMAND: TOPIC GUIDE

Demand is an essential concept in both macro-economic and microeconomic analysis. For its macro meaning and significance, consult the article on NATIONAL INCOME DETERMINATION. The components of total demand can be examined in the articles on CONSUMPTION, INVESTMENT, and GOVERNMENT SPENDING.

For the micro aspects of demand, begin with the articles on CONSUMER DEMAND and MARKET DEMAND. For the expression of demand, see DEMAND SCHEDULE and DEMAND CURVE; the conceptual basis for these expressions is explained in DEMAND THEORY.

The Subject maps accompanying the articles on DEMAND THEORY and NATIONAL INCOME help to clarify the concept of Demand in economic analysis.

DEMAND, the relationship between the quantity of a commodity that consumers desire to purchase and the various prices that can exist for the commodity. Individuals desire commodites to achieve progressively higher levels of satisfaction. If all desires were satiable and if resources were unlimited, then the concept of demand would be sterile and academic: to completely satiate himself an individual would merely go to some central distribution point and lay claim to all the goods and services that he could possibly consume. Given the virtual infinity of human desires and the finite nature of the world's resources, such utopian conditions will never be met.

Satisfaction-fulfilling goods being scarce, and human wants being unlimited, a system of individual and community priorities must be developed to allocate goods. In market societies the products are distributed to those persons who are willing and able to purchase them. The price determinant of quantity demanded becomes a rationing device for allocating the scarce goods among their many demanders. The concept of demand applies to all economic societies. Although it is much easier to understand the demand function's application in market societies, even the strictest command societies must heed the concept.

—*Robert L. Brite*

See also Demand Theory.

DEMAND CURVE, a graphic representation of the relationship between price and quantity demanded.

The demand for one product is influenced by the availability of others. These meats and sausages offer many substitute choices.

The construction of a demand curve is accomplished by plotting the number of units of a commodity demanded per unit of time along the horizontal axis (abscissa) of a Cartesian coordinate plane. The vertical axis (ordinate) of the Cartesian plane is used to identify price data. The empirical price and corresponding quantity demanded can then be identified by a point on the plane. A locus of points defines a linear or curvilinear relationship, which is the demand curve.

Demand curves may also be described by a mathematical expression defining the curve (a demand function). The particular form of a demand function is that the quantity demanded of some commodity is a function of the price of that commodity, $q = f(p)$. The linear demand function $q = 10 - 2p$ is shown.

LINEAR DEMAND CURVE

One important characteristic of a demand relationship expressed in functional form is that quantities demanded may be predicted for prices that have not been observed in the construction of the relationship. In the previous example, even if price had never been observed to be \$2, a predication that the quantity demanded would be 6 units per time period at that price could be made. Although, for pedagogic purposes, linear demand curves are most often used in economic examples, demand functions may be used to describe hyperbolic and other curvilinear demand curves when the data so indicate.

—Robert L. Brite

See also Firm Demand Curve.

DEMAND DEPOSITS, or CHECKING ACCOUNTS, liabilities of depository institutions that are owed to their customers and payable on demand whenever customers write checks on their accounts. Demand deposits were once the sole province of commercial banks, but are now available from thrift institutions (savings and loan associations, mutual savings banks, and credit unions).

Money market funds also allow account holders to write a limited number of checks. Interest-bearing checking accounts are commonly referred to as NOW accounts, the acronym given to the Negotiable Order of Withdrawal accounts first offered by mutual savings banks in the Northeast. Demand deposits account for most of the narrowly defined money supply, M1.

See also Money Supply; Multiple Expansion of the Money Supply; Time Deposits.

DEMAND FOR CAPITAL, a derived demand, like the demand for the other factors of production. That means that the demand for capital is derived from the demand for the final goods and services that capital helps produce. Like all other factors, the demand for capital is derived from the profit-maximizing decision of the firm. When everything else is held constant, if the expected return from the purchase of a piece of capital equipment is greater than the cost of that piece of capital, then the profit-maximizing firm will buy that additional piece of capital. The price of capital is equal to the interest rate.

Economists talk about the expected return on capital because capital equipment lasts for several years and helps produce output for several years. Much of the return on capital is going to be in the future; if the capital purchased is a building, the return may occur 20 or 30 years in the future. It is necessary therefore to predict what the price of the final product will be and what the price of other inputs will be in the future in order to determine the expected rate of return on capital. In addition, the rate of return on capital is subject to diminishing marginal productivity. In other words, if all other factors of production are held constant and the amount of capital is increased, a point will be reached where one additional unit of capital results in a smaller increase in total output than the last additional unit. At the profit-maximizing point, the firm will buy capital up to the point where the expected return of the last unit of capital purchased is equal to the cost of that last unit.

—Timothy P. Ryan

See also Capital.

DEMAND FOR LABOR is derived, as is the demand for other factors of production, from the demand for consumer goods and services. The price of labor (wages) relative to the other factors determines how much labor will be used to fill a given demand for goods and services. Thus, on an overall level, high wages and low interest have encouraged the U.S. employer to substitute capital equipment for workers, while low wages and high interest in certain underdeveloped countries have encouraged the use of human power.

Marginal Productivity Theory. Perhaps the most widely accepted statement explaining the demand for labor is the marginal productivity theory. Given a market, or other fixed wage rate, and assuming that all markets involved are competitive and the other factors of production are fixed in quantity, the employer settles on a level of operation at which the marginal revenue product of labor is equal to the wage rate.

The first point to observe is that the average output varies as the number of workers changes. As more workers are added the average may rise in the early stages, but at some point it must fall. Another way to say this is that the amount added to total output by the last worker hired changes. This amount, called marginal physical product of labor, multiplied by the price at which the output sells is called the marginal revenue product (MRP) of labor, and this MRP and the wage rate determine the number of workers the employer hires. Thus, if the MRP exceeds the wage rate the employer continues to hire additional workers. If the wage rate exceeds the MRP the employer must decrease the work force.

Raising Wages. It is often said that any successful attempt to raise wages by governmental action or by union activity can result only in unemployment. That is because if the wage rate is increased by restricting supply or by minimum wage legislation, and if the MRP is not increased, then the employer must bring the two factors, wages and MRP, back into equality by reducing the number of workers and thus increasing the marginal physical product. The only other way to raise wages without unemployment would be to raise prices (drop the competitive assumption) or to raise the marginal physical product through better management practices or worker improvement.

—William D. Wagoner

See also Labor Market.

DEMAND FOR MONEY. In its most common usage, the demand for money refers to a desire to hold "liquid" assets; it is a liquidity preference. Demand for money is also used to mean the desire for cash rather than the equivalent in demand deposits. In this sense an increased demand for money results in a cash drain from the banking system and reduces the ability of commercial banks to produce a multiple expansion of the money supply.

See also Multiple Expansion of the Money Supply.

DEMAND LOANS. *See* Call Loans.

DEMAND-PULL INFLATION, or Buyers' Inflation, occurs when aggregate demand is greater than the full-employment capacity output of the economy; an inflationary gap exists, and the only way aggregate supply can increase is through rising prices. Even in the absence of active monetary and fiscal policies to reduce aggregate demand, a demand-pull inflation must eventually come to an end if the money supply is not increased. As prices rise, more of the money supply must be used for transactions, making less money available for lending at existing interest rates. Interest rates will therefore increase, causing investment demand and aggregate demand to fall off. However, as long as the money supply increases, the inflation can continue, because the same rising product prices that reduce the purchasing power of the dollar increase the money incomes of the workers and owners. The rising money incomes fuel the next round of inflation.

DEMAND SCHEDULE, a table recording the number of units of a commodity demanded per unit of time at various money prices.

The values in this schedule are the result of empirical observation during various time periods. For example, during the first time period when the price of this commodity was $8 per unit, 2 units were purchased. During a subsequent time period, when the price was $4 per unit, 6 units of the commodity were purchased. The presentation of numerical demand data in this tabular form is one of the methods by which economic relationships are qualified. This particular method of quantification transmits demand

DEMAND SCHEDULE	
Units demanded	**Price (in dollars)**
2	$8
4	$6
6	$4
8	$2
10	$1

data in such a way that pricing and output decisions by firms may be made without necessarily relying upon other more intricate methods to quantify the price-quantity relationship.

DEMAND SHIFT, alteration of an entire demand function (as differentiated from movement along a given demand curve when the number of units of a commodity purchased changes in response to a change in its price, called a change in quantity demand). When a specific demand function is identified, certain parameters are held constant: taste, income, expectations of future price changes, and the prices of related commodities. However, in the real world these determinants of demand do change. Consumers come to desire certain products more or less in response to changes in their incomes, personal tastes, or

expectations about inflation or deflation. The response of consumption patterns resulting from these changes causes entire demand functions to change.

DEMAND-SHIFT INFLATION. *See* Sectoral Inflation.

DEMAND THEORY, a plausible explanation of the manner in which purchasers of commodities respond to price changes. It is an empirical fact that consumers purchase more of a good or service at a low price than at a high price. The various demand theories attempt to discover why consumers behave in such a manner.

Assumptions. In order to explain purchasing behavior, it must be assumed that individuals are rational and that they undertake their apparently uncoordinated economic activities in an attempt to achieve a

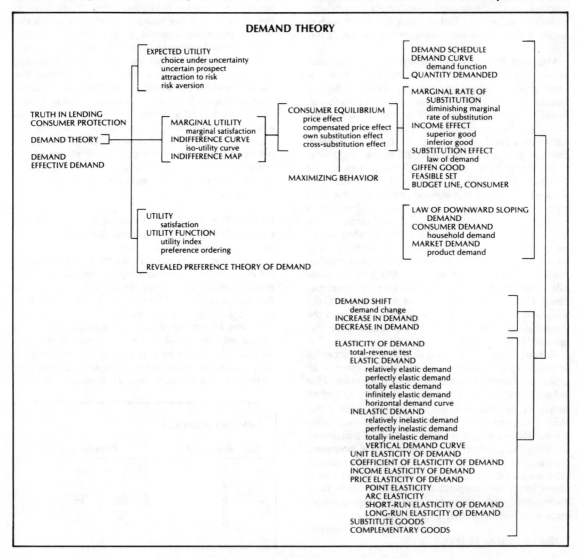

maximum level of satisfaction. This attempt is subject to various constraints: a person cannot effectively pursue an unfettered hedonistic existence in a world where goods, services, resources, and incomes are limited. The principal constraints affecting an individual's demand behavior are income, taste and preference functions, expectations about future price changes, and the market prices of all goods. However, at least in the short run, the principal factor influencing the amount purchased of a given commodity is its price.

Conclusions. One reason consumers buy more of a good at lower prices than at higher ones lies in their willingness and ability to purchase. Another key to demand behavior is the psychological proclivity to prefer more of the things one has few of and not so many more of the things that one has in abundance: additional units of a good provide smaller additions to total satisfaction than previous units consumed (the law of diminishing marginal utility). So, in order for a consumer to be willing to purchase more of a good, its price must fall. In combination with this willingness to purchase must go the ability to purchase (the real income effect of a price change). If the price of a commodity does fall, a constant level of money expenditure allows the purchaser to obtain more of the good in question: the purchaser's real income has increased. The net result of this analysis is to provide a logical system to explain the behavior of consumers in allocating their money incomes between competing uses in which they are interested.

—Robert L. Brite

DEMOCRATIC (LIBERAL) SOCIALISM, an economic system that combines state ownership of at least some of the means of production and a set of democratic political institutions. Significant economic freedom to the consumer is afforded by permitting both consumer choice and some degree of consumer sovereignty.

Democratic socialism is envisioned as coming about by evolutionary processes, chiefly through the ballot box. Its principal goals are less income disparity (by reduction of private property) and more stable economic growth and employment (by a smoother investment stream).

DEMONSTRATION EFFECT (or Rising Expectations) refers to the effect of the desires and expectations of people, particularly in less developed or poor nations, who have become aware of their poverty and the higher standards of the more developed, wealthy nations. Because of the advances in transport and communications, the horizons of these people are no longer limited to their own society. They observe better conditions in other economies and demand the same for themselves, notwithstanding the inability of the economy and society, without extra economic

assistance, to satisfy those desires. This effect is also referred to as the phenomenon of rising expectations.

DEPLETION, reduction in the value of natural resources due to the extraction of natural wealth, such as gas, oil, timber, or minerals.

DEPOSITS. *See* Balance Sheet, Bank; Demand Deposits; Monetary Control Act of 1980; Time Deposits.

DEPRECIATION, reduction in value, quality, and usefulness of a fixed asset (plant or equipment) because of physical deterioration, destruction, or obsolescence resulting from technological development. The annual amount of depreciation equals the original purchase price less the estimated salvage value divided by the estimated useful life of the fixed asset (straight-line or installment method depreciation). Other methods of calculating depreciation are the diminishing-value method, in which more depreciation is taken at the beginning, when the greatest loss is assumed to occur, and the production method, in which depreciation is charged in proportion to actual use.

DEPRECIATION, CURRENCY. A currency is depreciated when it undergoes a loss of purchasing power, either domestically or internationally. Domestic depreciation is usually related to inflationary increases in prices; international depreciation is reflected in a rise in the rates of exchange on foreign currencies. In the U.S. exchange market, an increased demand for a given foreign currency relative to its supply drives up the rate on that currency while that country's rate on the dollar falls. Hence, in terms of the other currency, the dollar is worth less, and if the same amount of imports from that country continues it will necessitate larger dollar payments. Conversely, it will cost the other country less to import from the United States.

See also Devaluation; Exchange Rates.

DEPRESSION. *See* Business Cycles, Phases.

DEREGULATION, an expression used to denote a philosophy of reducing governmental constraints on business behavior. Advocates of deregulation urge repeal of laws restricting business behavior (such as mergers) or mandating certain activities (such as price and safety rules), relaxation of administrative requirements, and abolition of governmental regulatory bodies. While the concept of deregulation is not new, this concept was not politically popular until the late 1970s. One of the first major federal attempts to reduce governmental regulation was the Airline Deregulation Act of 1978, which led to the discontinuance of the Civil Aeronautics Board in 1984.

Deregulatory efforts have also been evident in the ground transportation industry, where the Interstate

Commerce Commission has greatly reduced barriers to entry into trucking. The banking and financial community has seen deregulation through the passage of the Monetary Decontrol Act of 1980, which removed or relaxed interest rate restrictions on deposits and which allowed nonbanks to provide banking-type services, and also through a trend by state governments to allow multiregional banking. The communications industry experienced a reduction in governmental barriers to obtaining broadcasting licenses and reduced requirements for public-information programming and restrictions on commercial minutes allowed during broadcasts. Entry into the long-distance communications field is another by-product of the atmosphere of deregulation. Restrictions on petroleum prices have similarly been relaxed.

Proponents of deregulation claim that it leads to more efficient markets and hence enhances consumer welfare. Critics argue that deregulation has created severe hardships on particular groups (the poor, persons living in smaller cities, etc.), and that government protection is necessary to correct for market inefficiencies and to provide equality.

—*Michael S. Johnson*

See also Consumer Protection; Regulation.

DERIVED DEMAND. *See* Factor Demand.

DEVALUATION, a reduction in the gold content of a currency valued in terms of gold. In 1934 and 1972 the United States devalued by raising the dollar price of an ounce of gold from $20.67 to $35.00 in the first instance and to $38.00 in the latter. A major purpose of these moves was to help the balance of payments by increasing the purchasing power of foreigners vis-à-vis the dollar and increasing the dollar cost of imports. Under International Monetary Fund rules all countries except the United States can devalue in terms of the dollar by establishing new parities.

If a country runs a persistent deficit in its balance of payments and meets this deficit by losing international reserves, there is a clear indication that (1) the country's currency is overvalued relative to its international status, or (2) its trading partners have undervalued currencies. To correct this situation, the deficit country can devalue, or the surplus countries can appreciate. Historically, the burden has usually rested on the deficit country. As a solution, devaluation is preferable to inducing a domestic recession; but countries are hesitant to devalue formally, because devaluation generally creates speculative pressures that could necessitate another devaluation.

—*John R. Matthews, Jr.*

See also Appreciation; Depreciation; Exchange Rate; Undervaluation.

DEVELOPING NATIONS, an expression adopted by the United Nations to refer to less developed countries with poverty-level incomes per capita. Most such countries are located in Africa, Asia, and Latin America and are characterized by illiteracy, disguised unemployment, overpopulation, and reliance on a few export items, generally raw materials. Their economies are predominantly agricultural, although some have well-developed handicrafts.

Economic Growth. In the drive for economic growth, developing nations try to stimulate and encourage private and public capital investments, institute educational and vocational training programs, increase productivity, and, in general, raise their standards of living. In most undeveloped countries, economic development begins with a high degree of government planning and a large amount of foreign technical and financial aid. The International Bank for Reconstruction and Development (World Bank) provides loans and grants to finance basic development projects such as dams, communications and transport facilities, and a variety of health and educational programs.

UNESCO (the United Nations Educational, Scientific, and Cultural Organization), the United States, the U.S.S.R., and several other countries maintain a number of technical assistance programs. They are specifically designed to accelerate the pace of industrial development and therefore help to achieve economic independence and make the most effective use of a country's human and material resources.

See also Less Developed Countries; States of Growth; Underdevelopment.

DICTATORSHIP OF THE PROLETARIAT, a political and economic transition period between capitalism and communism, during which the state, acting on behalf of the proletariat, oppresses and eventually destroys the capitalist class and its institutions. The means of production are no longer in private hands, even though the technology and the organization of production remain very similar to those under capitalism. The workers' pay is similar to that under capitalism. The workers' pay is determined by their contributions to production; those who do not work are not paid. A communist society evolves out of the socialistic dictatorship of the proletariat.

DIMINISHING MARGINAL PHYSICAL PRODUCTIVITY. As more and more units of a factor are used in the productive process, other inputs being held constant, eventually the resulting increments of product (marginal product of the factor) will fall, according to the law of diminishing marginal returns. In the early stages of production, marginal product may rise, however, due to specialization advantages. The point at which total product ceases to increase at an increasing rate and starts to increase at a decreasing rate (inflection point) is the point of diminishing returns. The diminishing marginal product schedule is the basis for downward-sloping factor demand curves.

DIMINISHING MARGINAL UTILITY. *See* Demand Theory.

DIMINISHING RETURNS. *See* Law of Diminishing Returns.

DIRECT INVESTMENT, a term used in international economics for the purchase of land and its natural resources, such as plantations or mines, and the purchase or construction of income-producing real capital, such as oil well rigs or factories in foreign countries. Direct investment results in the ownership and management of land and capital by nationals of one country in another. Direct investment contrasts with portfolio investment, which occurs when nationals of one country buy shares in foreign businesses owned and managed by nationals of another country.

DIRTY FLOAT, results from the intervention of monetary authorities in the foreign exchange market. The supply and demand for foreign exchange determine the foreign exchange rate. The simplest competitive foreign exchange market is the floating exchange-rate system without government intervention or intervention by central bankers. The major countries have been on something close to this system since 1971. The spot (or forward) price of foreign currency is determined by the interaction of supply and demand for that currency. The market clears itself through the price mechanism.

The float from the 1970s has been a "dirty" float due to intervention by various governments. Foreign governments (Japan, for instance) buy dollars to keep the price of the dollar high in order to maintain high prices for imports from the United States. The effect is the same as a tariff on imports to Japan and as a subsidy for Japanese exports.

DISCOUNTED VALUE, the amount that a borrower receives today in exchange for the promise to pay some greater amount at some specified time in the future. Most short-term bonds are sold at a discount. The formula for calculating the discounted value (called P) for a bond that has a future value of FV and an interest rate of i and has n days to maturity is:

$$P = [FV/(1 + i)] (365/n).$$

The process of discounting is exactly the same as is used in calculating the present value of a future amount. Discounting is also used in benefit-cost analysis and cost-effectiveness studies.

DISCOUNT RATE, the interest charged by federal reserve banks on loans to domestic banks and depository institutions and U.S. branches of foreign banks. Prior to 1978, only member banks could obtain loans. In 1978, foreign banks with U.S. branches were extended borrowing privileges. The Depository Institu-

tions Deregulation and Monetary Control Act of 1980 extended borrowing privileges to non-member banks and to non-bank depository institutions. These loans are sometimes referred to as being made through a "discount window."

The discount rate is established by each of the twelve federal reserve banks subject to "review and determination" by the Board of Governors of the federal reserve system. An increase in the discount rate makes borrowing more expensive, thereby discouraging such loans, keeping bank reserves low, and reducing the ability of the banking system to create a multiple expansion of the money supply. A reduction in the discount rate has the opposite effect, thereby encouraging an expansion of the money supply.

See also Free Reserves.

DISCRIMINATION, ECONOMIC, occurs in a market where individuals face terms of trade that are determined by personal characteristics that do not appear to be directly relevant to the transaction. Most concern has centered on differential treatment by race, ethnic group, or sex. The primary focus has been on the labor market and housing market, with research motivated, in large part, by controversy over the role of government in maintaining or eliminating observed differentials.

The modern development of systematic models of economic discrimination began with the publication of Gary Becker's *The Economics of Discrimination* (1957). Becker's treatment took market discrimination to be the result of the personal tastes of the participants. Earnings differentials and discrimination in housing and other markets stem from attempts by owners, workers, and customers to avoid contact or interaction with certain groups. Employers, for instance, may maximize their utility by hiring workers from one ethnic group rather than another, even if it means reduced profits due to higher costs. If such employers dominate the market, the wages of the second ethnic group will have to be adjusted downward if any of them are to be hired. The difference between this adjusted wage and the higher wage of the preferred group measures the pecuniary value of the employer's preference.

It is widely argued that, in the long run, competition will drive out discriminating employers. In a competitive market, any market differential translates into a pecuniary cost the discriminating employer must pay.

Earnings for women have historically been appreciably lower than those for men. The enactment of laws in the 1960s and 1970s has had little effect on the overall distribution of wages by sex. This difference may be due to market discrimination, to institutional discrimination, to measurable pre-market factors such as education or other training, to a household division of labor, or to other unmeasured differences between men and women.

DISECONOMIES OF SCALE occur when average costs rise as output increases. The long-run average cost (LRAC) curve initially falls as output rises, but then slopes upward as output rises further. At the point when this occurs, reducing the scale of operations is efficient because it allows production at lower average costs.

Diseconomies of scale occur because the law of diminishing returns applies in the long run in several ways. It is impossible for a firm to vary all the technological influences on production proportionately and simultaneously, and even large and powerful firms cannot precisely control laws and regulations that influence the cost of production. Production is also influenced by the weather and other natural phenomena, as well as by the laws of physics (gravity) and chemistry, which are not subject to adjustment. Although improvements in technology may increase productivity, technology is assumed to be constant except in the very long run. Managerial control also deteriorates as firms get larger, adding more layers to a hierarchical organization. At some point a threshold is reached where adding a new manager fails to increase marginal revenue, and beyond that point, additions to managerial staff increase long-run average costs. In addition, in large organizations, it is difficult to maintain an atmosphere of personal loyalty or loyalty to the firm as compared with smaller, more intimate work situations, and productivity suffers.

DISGUISED UNEMPLOYMENT refers to a situation that occurs when a decrease in aggregate demand, or in the case of less developed nations, no demand, leads to the withdrawal of labor into occupations with little or no marginal productivity. In other words, resources are not employed most effectively, and labor is underemployed. In rural areas and less developed countries where agriculture is predominant, there is a high rate of disguised unemployment because there is little for the people to do during the off-season. Such people do not appear in the unemployment statistics because they are not seeking work.

See also Underemployment.

DISINFLATION is a slowing of the rate of inflation. If the inflation rate drops from 7% to 5% per year, disinflation has occurred. After inflation escalated during the 1970s, tighter monetary policies than had been followed in over a decade were principally responsible for inflation and interest rates drifting down after 1982.

A significant reduction in the rate of inflation— disinflation—such as occurred in the early 1980s, causes problems for both businesses and consumers. Many people who had expected inflation to continue through the 1980s invested heavily in real estate and other inflation "hedges." With disinflation, they found themselves deeply in debt at high real rates of interest.

Investors had learned to expect that inflation would reduce the real value of future mortgage payments, and when inflation rates declined, they suffered huge losses. Real estate foreclosures reached record highs by the mid-1980s. Farmers and the rural banks from which they borrowed were especially hard hit. Land values had skyrocketed, and farmers were encouraged to borrow against this asset to purchase production-enhancing capital equipment. When both farm incomes and land values plummeted, many faced bankruptcy.

Disinflation affects businesses in several ways. Because disinflation makes it impossible to raise prices, firms must find other ways to boost sales and profits. Increased productivity and new products become relatively more important. New products typically have a higher profit rate and improve a firm's market penetration efforts. The emphasis on productivity encourages firms to cut labor costs and increase worker productivity. More investment is channeled toward productivity-enhancing plant and equipment and less toward expanding capacity. Investment tends to be financed internally as firms attempt to limit their debt burden. Lastly, the acquisition binges some firms undertake during inflationary periods are reversed when firms begin to sell off subsidiaries in an effort to consolidate debt.

DISINVESTMENT, or NEGATIVE INVESTMENT. Net disinvestment occurs when gross investment in fixed capital and in additions to inventories is less than the capital used up during the year. Because there cannot be fewer than no purchases of investment goods, gross investment can never be negative, so disinvestment always refers to net disinvestment. In accounting terms, disinvestment occurs when gross investment is less than depreciation.

DISPOSABLE PERSONAL INCOME, or DISPOSABLE INCOME (DI), the total dollar amount individuals have available for personal consumption and personal savings after taxes and other noncommercial fees have been paid to government. DI may also be determined by adding the total amount of personal consumption, net savings, consumer interest payments, and personal transfer payments to foreigners. In the United States since World War II, disposable income has grown more rapidly than most other economic indicators. An important reflector of consumption expenditures, DI is frequently used to measure changes in the national standard of living, after adjustments have been made for changes in population and for inflation.

See also Consumption; Flow of Income; Personal Income.

DISSAVING, spending more than one's income on consumption. Households can dissave by spending previously saved or inherited money, borrowing, or begging. The economy as a whole could dissave no more than the amount of depreciation, if income is thought of as NNP; dissaving is not possible if income is thought of as GNP.

DISSOLUTION, DIVESTITURE, DIVORCEMENT, remedy-penalty provisions a federal court may invoke upon conviction of a firm for antitrust laws violations, especially monopolization. There is a technical distinction among the terms, though it is being blurred by the growing use of "dissolution," the most general term, to cover all three actions. Dissolution refers to the breaking up of a firm into separate units, however those individual units were obtained by the firm (internal growth or merger). Divestiture requires the firm to dispose of specific properties or securities, which give it control or undue influence over another firm. Divorcement refers to the breaking off of a merger-acquired unit of the convicted firm.

See also Antitrust Policy; Sherman Antitrust Act; United States v. Standard Oil Company of New Jersey.

DISTRIBUTION QUESTION. *See* Market Mechanism.

DISTRICT BANKS. *See* Federal Reserve Banks.

DIVERSIFICATION, the process in which a business firm increases the variety of products it produces and sells, either by introducing new products into the same product line or market, or by going into new product lines or markets. The firm can diversify either by branching out with existing production processes or by merging with other producers into a conglomerate. Diversification permits the firm to soften geographic or cyclical demand declines in one product by deriving revenue from one or more other products.

See also Conglomerate.

DIVIDENDS, earnings distributed to stockholders. Corporations secure capital funds by issuing bonds on which they pay interest—bondholders are creditors. They also issue stock on which they pay dividends—stockholders are owners of a corporation.

Stock has no maturity date, as do bonds, but dividends are not paid unless there are sufficient earnings. In a given year the board of directors decides whether dividends are to be paid, and even then all earnings after taxes are not paid out. Many wealthy stockholders prefer that dividends not be paid in a given year for tax reasons. Undistributed profits (retained earnings) are important sources of internal financing for many corporations, and such retention is reflected in higher values of common stock shares.

See also Corporate Earnings.

DIVISION OF LABOR means that the work associated with producing something is divided up among several workers, so that each worker becomes very fast and efficient at his or her particular task. There are gains in efficiency because "practice makes perfect," but also because labor is allocated to activities where it has a comparative advantage, where it is most productive. People, like countries, have differing natural endowments, and thus are better at some things than others.

There is also a "social division of labor," whereby different professions and kinds of work are divided among the members of a society. The "manufacturing division of labor" divides production activity among firms in an industry and partitions activities within plants. The notion of a division of labor has also been applied to households and is called "the sexual division of labor." Adam Smith believed the division of labor was the principal factor in achieving economic progress.

DUMPING occurs when a nation sells export products in foreign countries more cheaply than the same products are sold domestically. Dumping may be the result of discriminatory pricing: taking advantage of the differing amounts consumers in different submarkets are willing to pay for the same item. Consumers at home may be more willing to pay for a product than consumers abroad; hence the price differential. Predatory dumping occurs when a country prices its exports so low that competitors are driven out of the market. Predatory dumping is aimed at creating a worldwide monopoly for a product. Another form of dumping occurs when governments subsidize exports in order to create jobs at home.

Critics of food aid, for example, maintain that giving surplus U.S. farm products to less developed countries has the same effect as predatory dumping: it drives local farmers out of business, since no one can compete when the competition is selling at a zero price. These critics maintain that food aid should be offered with great caution, since eliminating the indigenous farmers will actually *create* hunger and dependency on aid and/or imports. While making the rest of the world dependent on U.S. wheat may alleviate the U.S. farm surplus and help American farmers, it does so only at the cost of disrupting local farm economies and reducing the ability of less developed countries to be food self-sufficient.

Another form of dumping is continuing to sell on the world market products, especially chemicals and pharmaceuticals, which have been banned for sale to the domestic market. DDT is the most notorious example.

DYNAMIC EQUILIBRIUM, equilibrium in which a time dimension is included. Normal equilibrium is the equilibrium of a system at one point in time; this is referred to as static equilibrium. Dynamic equilibrium looks at what happens to the system over time, allowing such factors as normal growth, inflation, and the like to be included in the analysis.

ECONOMETRICS, a subdiscipline of economics which describes the ways in which statistics and modeling can be combined to qualify economic relationships. Econometrics is more than the application of statistical techniques to economic data. Econometrics implies that an economic model is being quantified and tested.

Regression analysis is the most important tool of econometrics. Most economic models contain at least one proposed functional relationship, and regression analysis is a statistical technique used to estimate functional relationships between variables.

There are two major outputs of econometric analysis. First, a quantified model is produced which can be used for forecasting. Second, in the process of quantifying the model the theoretical foundations of the model are statistically tested. This process of submitting theoretical models to empirical tests using econometrics is basic to the way most modern economic research is carried out.

The set of econometric tools available to economists is continually expanding. Initiallly, economists relied on basic regression techniques developed by statisticians but, as the models being considered grew in size and complexity, many new techniques were developed by economists. Chief among these new developments are simultaneous-equation regression techniques, which allow an economist to quantify a model with many interdependent functional relationships. Both the complexity of econometrics and its importance to modern economics have made knowledge of econometrics very important in the education of economists. Anyone seeking training in economics will find courses in econometrics required for an advanced degree.

See also Model, Econometric; Statistics.

ECONOMIC ACTIVITY, AGGREGATE MEASURES OF. *See* National Income Measurement.

ECONOMIC EFFICIENCY, in the broadest sense, the absence of waste. If a given commodity can be produced by two available techniques, the technique requiring fewer resources per unit of output is the more efficient.

At a more refined level of economic analysis efficiency is defined as absence of waste in terms of the satisfactions people derive from consuming goods and services. If by some rearrangement of economic factors it is possible to increase the well-being of one or more persons without diminishing the well-being of any other, it would be wasteful or inefficient not to make the rearrangement.

This concept of economic efficiency is usually attributed to the Italian economist Vilfredo Pareto and referred to as Pareto optimality. The term optimality as used in this context is a bit unfortunate, since "optimum" implies the "best," whereas in economic situations there are generally a multiplicity of positions in which it is not possible to improve one person's lot without diminishing the well-being of someone else. Pareto optimality is unable to make any distinction between such positions; all are equally efficient.

—*Clarence C. Morrison*
See also Efficiency; Efficient Resource Allocation; Marginal-Cost Pricing; Pareto Optimum.

ECONOMIC FLUCTUATIONS. *See* Business Cycles.

ECONOMIC GOALS, or Economic Objectives, part of the national aspirations that deal with economic issues. The most widely, though not universally, accepted economic goals of most free societies are: (1) full employment, reasonable employment opportunities available to everyone desiring work, (2) a reasonable degree of economic freedom, (3) economic security in old age, (4) control of the harmful, wide, cyclical swings in price levels, inflation and deflation, (5) production in accordance with consumer demands, (6) an equitable distribution of the national income among various segments of society, and (7) a rising standard of living for all members of society, the goal of an increase in the country's output of goods and services.

It should be noted that some of these economic goals are complementary. For example, economic security and equitable income distribution are aided when full employment is achieved. Some goals, however, tend to be in conflict. For example, many excellent economists feel that full employment and price stability are incompatible goals. In view of the fact that any society's resources and energies are limited, and due to the fact that some economic goals are mutually exclusive, society via its government must assign priorities to the achievement of economic goals.

—*Algin B. King*
See also Economic Problems.

ECONOMIC PROBLEMS arise because of unlimited human wants and limited material resources. There are various problems, such as what to produce and which wants to satisfy. A corollary problem in economics is how to produce goods and services once decisions have been made as to what to produce.

Five basic economic problem areas confronting every society are: (1) allocation of percentages of total production to each basic type or class of goods and services; (2) allocation of goods and services to various segments of the society; (3) methods of production; (4) degree and efficiency of utilization of the country's resources; and (5) maintenance of the economy's capacity to produce goods.

See also Economic Goals.

ECONOMIC PROFITS, the amount of total revenue that remains after a firm has paid both explicit and implicit wages, rent, and interest costs as well as a normal profit. Often referred to as pure profits, economic profits can be either positive gains or negative losses. If no economic profits, either positive or negative, exist, the firm is said to have normal profits, the minimum amount of revenue required to sustain a production activity.

Several theories are set forth by economists as to why economic profits might occur. First, entrepreneurs bear certain risks when they undertake a business venture. These risks are uninsurable and stem from both cyclical and structural changes in the economy. Economic profits can then be thought of in part as a reward for the assumption of these risks. A second explanation is related to the possibility of attaining monopoly power. Where firms are able to restrict entry and establish monopoly power, they can restrict output and influence price in such a way as to earn profits. The expectations of economic profits are incentives that encourage investment.

—*William D. Wagoner*

See also Profits.

ECONOMIC RENT, any payment to an owner of a productive resource in the long-run period in excess of the minimum payment necessary to keep the resource in its current use. To keep a resource in its current use, a resource owner must receive a minimum return equal to the return available in the best alternative use. Rents are payments in excess of opportunity costs. The nature of economic rents is revealed more clearly by arithmetic example than by words.

Example. Assume that the resource is land, that there are four grades of land, and, to simplify the illustration, that the land has only one use, growing corn. Further assume that once corn is produced, it sells for $4.00 per bushel. The tabulation shows the total cost, total output (q), total revenue (p × q), and rent on 50-acre tracts of various grades of land.

Equal expenditure of $5000 on each grade of land yields varying outputs due to the natural productivity of the different grades. Grade 1 land yields corn valued at $8000 but with a real social cost of $5000. The land itself has zero real cost because it has no alternative use. Rent is the difference between the real cost of the corn and value of the corn produced on the land, $3000. This rent will accrue to the owner of the Grade 1 land. Grade 2 land, being somewhat less productive than Grade 1, receives a lesser rent. Grade 3 is just productive enough so that total revenue is sufficient to cover all cost but not so great as to provide the owner of Grade 3 an economic rent.

If the price of corn were to rise above $4.00 per bushel, rent would accrue to the owners of Grade 3 land. Grade 4 land is not sufficiently productive when corn is priced at $4.00 per bushel to permit the cost of producing 1000 bushels to be covered by revenues from the sale of corn. Not only does rent not occur on Grade 4 land; a rational producer would not spend $5000 to produce corn worth $4000. Either a smaller expenditure would be made on Grade 4 or no expenditure at all.

Elasticity. When a resource is assumed to have no alternative use as in the example above, the resource will have a perfectly inelastic (vertical) supply curve.

ECONOMIC RENT

	Grade of Land			
	#1	#2	#3	#4
Total Cost	$5000	$5000	$5000	$5000
Total Output (q)	2000 bu.	1500 bu.	1250 bu.	1000 bu.
Total Revenue (p x q)	$8000	$6000	$5000	$4000
Economic Rent	$3000	$1000	0	—

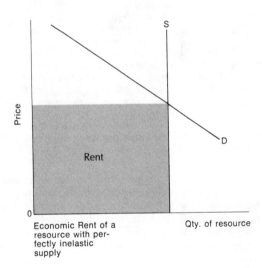

Economic Rent of a resource with perfectly inelastic supply

Economic Rent of a resource with less than perfectly inelastic supply

WINNERS OF THE NOBEL PRIZE FOR ECONOMICS

1970   Paul A. Samuelson (United States) for his efforts to raise the level of scientific analysis in economic theory.

1971   Simon S. Kuznets (United States) for developments in national income accounting that permit quantitative analysis of the economic growth of nations.

1972   Kenneth J. Arrow (United States) and John R. Hicks (Great Britain) for pioneering work in equilibrium theory and welfare theory.

1973   Wassily Leontief (United States) for development of the "input-output" technique of economic analysis for studying specific economic interdependencies.

1974   Friedrich von Hayek (Great Britain) and Gunnar Myrdal (Sweden) for developments in economic thought, particularly on the interdependence of social and economic phenomena.

1975   Tjaling C. Koopmans (United States) and Leonid V. Kantrovich (Soviet Union) for work in economic planning.

1976   Milton Friedman (United States) for influence on monetary policy as a means of controlling the level of economic activity.

1977   James E. Meade (Great Britain) and Bertil Ohlin (Sweden) for developments in the study of international trade.

1978   Herbert A. Simon (United States) for research in structure and decision-making in economic organizations.

1979   Theodore Schultz (United States) and Arthur Lewis (Great Britain) for work in the field of developmental economics.

1980   Lawrence R. Klein (United States) for developments and applications in the use of econometric models in the study of business cycles.

1981   James Tobin (United States) for his creation of the "portfolio selection theory" of investment.

1982   George J. Stigler (United States) for his half century of research on the working of industry and the role of government regulation in the economy.

1983   Gerard Debreu (United States) for his work on how prices in a free market economy work to balance what producers supply and consumers demand so that an equilibrium can be reached.

1984   Sir Richard Stone (Great Britain) for his pioneering work in devising national income accounts.

1985   Franco Modigliani (United States) for his analyses of financial markets and the relationship of a company's financial structure to the value of its stock.

1986   James M. Buchanan (United States) for his work in public choice theory.

1987   Robert M. Solow (United States) for his contributions to growth theory.

1988   Maurice Allais (France) for his work in the field of market theory.

1989   Trygve Haavelmo (Norway) for his contributions to the field of econometrics.

Such a supply curve represents the classical assumption concerning economic rent. Resources with perfectly elastic (horizontal) supply curves cannot receive rents. Resources with positively sloping supply curves may receive rents if payments to the resource in the current use exceed the value of the resources in the best alternative use.   —*John F. Formby*

See also Rent.

ECONOMIC SYSTEMS.

The study of economic systems is now established as a field within the discipline of economics. The world during the twentieth century has lost much of the uniformity of its economic structure. The domination of most of the world's territory and all of its commerce, as practiced by the capitalist countries of the nineteenth century, represents now only one of many possible alternative systems. The event that most shattered the previous economic order was the 1917 rise to power of the Bolsheviks in Russia. The existence of the U.S.S.R. destroyed the illusion that only capitalist markets could answer the basic economic questions. Economists are attempting to develop and apply tools of analysis to all economic systems hoping to gain insight into the workings of social economics.

Basic Economic Questions. A social economy attempts to obtain its economic goals within the restrictions imposed by scarcity of resources. The economy must be organized to answer these questions:

1. What is to be produced? What particular mix of goods and services best meets the needs and wants of the economy—both public and private sectors?

2. How is it to be produced? Given the state of technology, natural resources, and factor endowments, how can production be organized so as to maximize output?

3. For whom are the goods and services to be provided, and what set of distribution rules is acceptable within the system?

Types of Systems

The economic institutions of a country are influenced by history (economic, social, and cultural), ideology, natural resources and factor endowments, and political structure. These factors are fused together in time to establish an economic system.

The multitude of economic systems is almost as great as the number of countries. The spectrum ranges from the theoretical models of perfect competition, with its heavy emphasis on individualism, to the pure

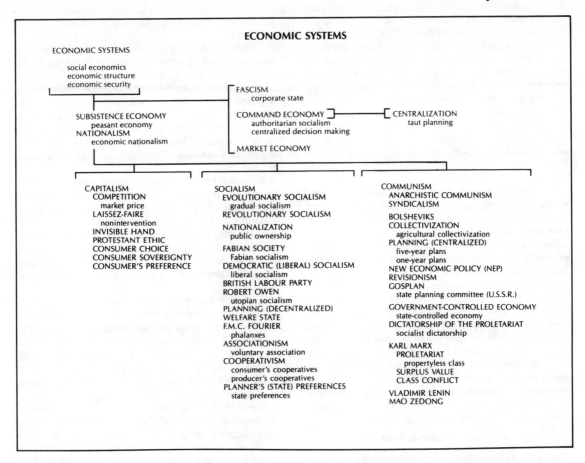

ECONOMIC SYSTEMS

ECONOMIC SYSTEMS
- social economics
- economic structure
- economic security

FASCISM
- corporate state

SUBSISTENCE ECONOMY
- peasant economy
NATIONALISM
- economic nationalism

COMMAND ECONOMY
- authoritarian socialism
- centralized decision making

CENTRALIZATION
- taut planning

MARKET ECONOMY

CAPITALISM
- COMPETITION
  - market price
- LAISSEZ-FAIRE
  - nonintervention
- INVISIBLE HAND
- PROTESTANT ETHIC
- CONSUMER CHOICE
- CONSUMER SOVEREIGNTY
- CONSUMER'S PREFERENCE

SOCIALISM
- EVOLUTIONARY SOCIALISM
  - gradual socialism
- REVOLUTIONARY SOCIALISM
- NATIONALIZATION
  - public ownership
- FABIAN SOCIETY
  - Fabian socialism
- DEMOCRATIC (LIBERAL) SOCIALISM
  - liberal socialism
- BRITISH LABOUR PARTY
- ROBERT OWEN
  - utopian socialism
- PLANNING (DECENTRALIZED)
- WELFARE STATE
- F.M.C. FOURIER
  - phalanxes
- ASSOCIATIONISM
  - voluntary association
- COOPERATIVISM
  - consumer's cooperatives
  - producer's cooperatives
- PLANNER'S (STATE) PREFERENCES
  - state preferences

COMMUNISM
- ANARCHISTIC COMMUNISM
- SYNDICALISM
- BOLSHEVIKS
- COLLECTIVIZATION
  - agricultural collectivization
- PLANNING (CENTRALIZED)
  - five-year plans
  - one-year plans
- NEW ECONOMIC POLICY (NEP)
- REVISIONISM
- GOSPLAN
  - state planning committee (U.S.S.R.)
- GOVERNMENT-CONTROLLED ECONOMY
  - state-controlled economy
- DICTATORSHIP OF THE PROLETARIAT
  - socialist dictatorship
- KARL MARX
  - PROLETARIAT
    - propertyless class
  - SURPLUS VALUE
  - CLASS CONFLICT
- VLADIMIR LENIN
- MAO ZEDONG

authoritarian systems of socialism with its state orientation. A third model is the competitive socialist model, which attempts to merge the positive features of competitive markets and socialist precepts. None of these models describes any particular country, but they help to analyze economic systems.

Free-Enterprise and Command Systems. Categorization of an economic system should focus on two characteristics—ownership of the means of production and control over the means of production. For example, in the free-enterprise market-system practiced in the United States, individuals own most of the means of production. The citizen enjoys freedom of consumer choice and job choice. The firm is free to dictate its output and its technique of production, of which the consumer is said to be sovereign within the system. The state does exercise some control through its taxation policy and restrictions on output (such as illegalizing certain production on the grounds that it is either harmful to health or contrary to the people's moral and social conscience).

The antithesis of private enterprise is the command system, in which the government's economic plan dictates enterprise activities, determines the pace and direction of growth, and, in so doing, restricts the output of consumer goods. Even after perestroika, in the U.S.S.R., the state owns and controls the means of production. The Soviet citizen does have consumer choice and general freedom of job choice, but the state preferences dominate the system.

The economies of eastern Europe, China, and other communist states approximate the organization of the U.S.S.R. with some deviations for special circumstances. In 1989 and 1990, revolutionary changes in many of the Eastern Bloc countries shifted their economies toward a more free-market orientation.

Mixed Systems. The categories between the private-enterprise systems (U.S. capitalism) and the authoritarian socialism (U.S.S.R. command economy) are described as "mixed systems." These systems have both private and state ownership of property, and private and state control of the economic processes. Some countries with a high degree of private ownership, such as Sweden, exert strong central influence on the economy through macroeconomic policies and welfare objectives. A private enterprise authoritarian system (fascism), would best describe the German economy under Adolf Hitler.

Along the spectrum, there is a significant group of countries with a strong tradition of private property and individual freedom that for various reasons have nationalized selected industries. The nationalized industries normally function as private corporations in the markets, but their ultimate responsibility is to the state rather than the private stockholder. Planning either does not exist or exists only as targeted aggregate goals of output, employment, prices, and growth. Britain and France are good examples of this category.

The socialist market system is an experiment Yugoslavia is currently making. This system rests on state ownership of means of industrial production, while control resides with the workers themselves. The firms behave as independent entities with only a broad economic plan. Yugoslavia is attempting to decentralize decision-making with a prominent role for the marketplace in directing resources.

Most of the developing countries of Africa, Asia, and South America have been strongly influenced by their former relationships with the colonial powers. Since World War II, these countries have been searching for their own paths to growth and development, and economists find it difficult to categorize them as particular systems. In fact, economists have become increasingly aware that the tools of economic analysis appropriate for industrialized states may be only partially adequate for the developing world.

Evaluating Economic Systems

In order to evaluate an economic system it is necessary to establish a set of criteria. The criteria below are broad in scope but helpful in analyzing a country's performance.

Economic Wealth and Rate of Growth. The wealth of a country reflects its past economic performance. Gross national product (GNP) tells how product and economy are in one year, while GNP per capita relates how much each individual would receive if output were distributed equally to all citizens in the country.

The leadership of most nations has attempted to design economic policies in order to promote economic growth. A rising GNP per capita increases the economic alternatives available to a country. It has the potential of raising the standard of living and enhancing the political and economic power of the state.

Stability. Economic stability is a criterion of great concern to economic policymakers of any system. Their objective is to promote growth without generating wide and frequent cyclical movements in employment, output, and the price level. A critical question is whether the fluctuations are inherent in the system. If so, policies should be designed to neutralize the problem. Some disequilibrium in a growing system is necessary. Change frequently causes instability, and

the magnitude and consequences of instability require evaluation.

Efficiency. An economy is said to be efficient if it has maximized its output by utilizing its inputs to the most effective way possible to achieve the objectives of the system. Then it cannot increase the output of any one product without reducing the output of another. The efficieny criterion is difficult to apply, since the production capabilities of a system are continuously changing. Thus, an economy must constantly adjust its economic allocations to achieve efficient operation.

Security. How well an economic system provides for security is a critical measure of the well-being of its population. People are concerned about security— security of a job, security from the burden of medical bills, security from lack of adequate income during a period of disability or old age, and security for the family at death. Too much security, however, may have detrimental effects on productivity and motivation.

Economic Freedom. This criterion helps to analyze (1) the extent to which the individual consumer and the firm or enterprise are free to make basic economic decisions, and (2) the influence each has on resource allocation. Such freedoms are freedom of consumer choice, freedom of job choice, freedom of firms to make their basic allocation and production decisions, and consumer sovereignty.

Equality. A system can be evaluated by the extent of economic and social discrimination based on sex, race, or nationality. Discrimination may take such forms as different wage levels for the same job, or using a criterion other than personal capabilities for filling a position.

Application of Criteria. Any analysis of economic systems requires certain cautions. First, theoretical models must be compared with theoretical models, and functioning economies with other existing systems. Second, a set of evaluation criteria will require a value framework for judgements. For instance, if personal freedom is considered a basic right, then within this value framework authoritarian systems would seem to be inferior to more liberal systems. Third, countries should be evaluated within the context of their own set of objectives. If growth is the goal of a society, then to say it does not achieve static equilibrium is to make an observation but not a pertinent evaluation.
                                                    —*Francis W. Rushing*

ECONOMIES OF SCALE. Economies or diseconomies of scale refer to the effects on unit costs of a firm as it increases its scale or plant size over the long run. Economies of scale imply decreasing unit costs as plant size increases; diseconomies imply increasing unit costs concomitant to increases in plant size.

Economies of scale may be reaped due to increased scope given to specialization and division of labor.

Small plant size often requires that one person handle several jobs; time is lost in changing jobs, tools, and so on.

Technological factors may account for lower unit costs as scale increases. Larger machines which increase output by some multiple of smaller machines do not ordinarily require proportional increases in space or in labor to operate. Qualitative as well as quantitative changes occur with increased plant size. Advanced technology often requires large output before it is economically feasible.

Financial advantages can also be reaped with increased size. Unit costs will correspondingly fall. Discounts are often given to large buyers of resources, and the comparatively large firms with high sales volumes have greater access to cheaper credit markets.

Diseconomies are alleged to arise as the firm expands its scale of operations to extremely large sizes. Presumably these are mostly managerial problems. More and more red tape becomes necessary; control and coordination problems become much more important. More and more decisions have to be delegated to others, and informational gaps may well arise. In a sense, this problem may be viewed as the inability of the management system to increase along with the scale of operations. These diseconomies may eventually offset and even surpass the advantages, or economies, referred to above. When diseconomies offset economies, the net result will be increased unit costs.

—*Robert L. Brite*

EFFECTIVE DEMAND. In analyzing a consumer's demand for goods and services, his or her income is typically taken as given. The consumer is then assumed to decide the composition and level of expenditures to maximize utility subject to his or her budget constraint. However, in a world where all markets, including the labor market, are always in equilibrium, the consumer can be viewed as also choosing the amount of hours he or she will work, or conversely the hours of leisure he or she wishes to consume; at the same time, the consumer is making decisions on consumption and savings.

To realize this consumption and savings plan, the consumer must be able to realize leisure-labor choices. If forced to consume more leisure than he or she desires (involuntary unemployment), the consumer will be unable to finance consumption and savings. Hence a distinction needs to be made between consumer demand when all markets clear and consumer demand when some markets may not clear (involuntary unemployment). The former is called national demand, the latter, effective demand.

—*Gerald A. Whitney*

EFFICIENCY, in an economic sense, refers to how effectively the scarce resources of an economy are

allocated to meet society's needs and desires. An economist defines an efficient allocation of resources as one in which there is no way for one person to become better off without making someone else worse off. Efficiency can be broken down into efficiency in distribution and efficiency in production. *Efficiency in distribution* requires that all trades that can make both parties simultaneously better off are carried out. *Efficiency in production* requires that all factors of production are used in their most productive capacity. Efficiency in production is assured if all firms are producing at the point where price equals marginal cost, as competitive firms must do to maximize profits.

See also Economic Efficiency.

EFFICIENT RESOURCE ALLOCATION, allocation that satisfies the criterion of Pareto optimality (any situation in which it is impossible to make one individual better off without making someone else worse off).

Competition. Intermediate and advanced economic theories construct a model representing an entire economy and demonstrate in the context of this model that Pareto optimality requires that firms be operated competitively, pricing output so that its unit cost to customers is equal to the price of any productive factor divided by its marginal physical product. The marginal product of a factor is the increase in output that results from employing an additional unit of that factor while holding all other factors constant.

If market price for the output of the firm is set equal to marginal cost, the consuming public has direct and efficient access to the productive process. With such access, it is reasonable to assume that individual consumers will allocate their incomes in a manner most

Due to economies of scale, electricity is often more efficiently provided by one utility. The utility is then considered a natural monopoly and is subject to regulation of a public utility commission.

satisfactory to themselves and, thus, eliminate the possibility of making someone better off without making someone else worse off. Where all markets are competitive (where firms price at market cost), the market allocation of resources is Pareto optimal.

Monopoly. The foregoing explains the classical indictment of monopolistic market structures. Although one would expect monopolistic firms to be internally efficient, their prices place an economic barrier between consumers and the productive process. Frequently it is argued that in some cases monopolies operate at a more efficient scale than do competitors, and, therefore, it is not certain that monopolistic elements always result in higher prices; but even where this possibility exists, economic theory indicates that there is some possible reorganization, involving marginal cost pricing, that would move toward a Pareto optimum. This conclusion is the basis of the argument that natural monopolies should be nationalized and directed to price at marginal cost.

—*Clarence C. Morrison*

See also Economic Efficiency; Marginal Cost Pricing; Pareto Optimum.

ELASTIC DEMAND. A typical demand curve will contain the total spectrum of elasticities. That is, a downward sloping demand curve will have an elastic range, a point of unitary elasticity, and an inelastic range. If, however, prices tend to stay within a limited range, it is possible to identify the demand as relatively elastic. For example, if the ordinary range of prices for some good is between P_1 and P_2, and if the percentage change in quantity demanded between those two prices is always greater than the percentage change in price, then the demand curve is said to be elastic over the relevant range of price changes.

The demand curves for some specific commodities can be horizontal at a specific price, implying that an infinite number of units of the commodity will be demanded at the going price, and that sellers cannot increase sales by lowering the price. Furthermore, if sellers attempt to raise the price of the commodity, no units will be sold. This type of demand curve characterizes a market with perfect competition where a large number of perfect substitutes are available for the product in question. Such a demand curve is said to be perfectly or infinitely elastic.

ELASTICITY OF DEMAND. The law of demand states that quantity demanded decreases (increases) as price increases (decreases). The slope of the demand curve indicates by how many units quantity demanded will change in response to a change in price. However, in comparing responsiveness to price changes across commodities, there is a units problem. The concept of elasticity is introduced as a meaningful way, free of units of measurements, to compare responsiveness of quantity changes to price changes.

Elasticity of demand measures the proportionate change in quantity demanded relative to the proportionate change in price. If quantity demanded changes more, proportionately, than price, the demand function is said to be elastic over the range in question. Conversely, if proportionately large price changes result in less than proportionate changes in quantity demanded, the demand function is said to be inelastic. Typically, demand curves display varying ranges of elasticity. For example, a downward-sloping linear demand curve will be relatively elastic at high-price, low-quantity combinations and the degree of elasticity will decline as lower-price, higher-quantity combinations are attained.

Coefficient of Elasticity. It is useful to identify the various ranges of elasticity of demand by making reference to a coefficient of elasticity, which is computed by dividing the percentage change in quantity demanded by the causal percentage change in price. The resulting coefficient will have a negative algebraic sign, which reflects the negative relationship between price and quantity demanded. It is the absolute value of the coefficient, however, which is of importance in identifying the degree of elasticity possessed by the demand function over a particular range. If the absolute value of the coefficient is greater than 1, demand is elastic. If the absolute value of the coefficient is less than 1, demand is inelastic. If the coefficient is equal to 1, demand is unitary elasticity.

Total Revenue. The effect on total revenue of a price change can be predicted if the elasticity of demand is known over the relevant range. Total revenue changes in the same direction as price if demand is inelastic and in the opposite direction of price if demand is elastic. Thus, an increase in the price of an item that has an inelastic demand will increase total revenue to producers. An increase in the price of a good with an elastic demand will decrease total revenue. Price changes leave total revenue unchanged if demand is unitary elastic.

—*Robert L. Brite*

ELASTICITY OF SUPPLY, a unit-free measure of the responsiveness of quantity supplied by producers to a change in the price of their product. Elasticity of supply is analogous to the concept of elasticity of demand. The elasticity of supply depends crucially upon the length of the period under consideration. The shorter the period of time given to producers to respond to a price change, the less elastic supply will be. For example, for a given eight-hour period, the supply of fresh seafood will be highly inelastic. Over a one-week period, we would expect supply to be slightly more elastic as fishermen increase their efforts and bring more fish to market.

ELASTIC SUPPLY. The supply of a product is said to be elastic, over some small price range, when the computed coefficient of elasticity is greater than 1.

Theoretically all coefficients greater than 1, up to positive infinity, would be described as elastic. Of course, the greater the coefficient the more elastic is supply. The implication is that over given price ranges and for certain commodities some firms (or industries) are better able to react to price changes; rising costs due to diminishing returns do not immediately appear. It would be safe to say that manufacturing goods are characterized by greater elasticity of supply than are agricultural commodities.

EMERGENCY STRIKES, work stoppages that are especially harmful to the public interest. Most strikes impose an inconvenience on consumers and sometimes they cause serious economic damage. But economic harm alone does not create an emergency. Rather, if a strike seriously jeopardizes the public safety and well-being, an emergency situation results, and the strike becomes an "emergency strike."

Examples. Emergency strikes in the public sector may occur, for example, by refusals to work by firefighters, police personnel, sanitation workers, or nurses; and in the private sector by food and fuel delivery workers. But strikes by school teachers or auto and steel workers generally would not constitute emergencies.

See also Mediation.

EMPLOYEE COMPENSATION, all present and deferred remuneration an employee is eligible to receive from his or her employer. It is the sum of straight wages and fringe benefits, such as bonuses, stock options, pension plans, life and unemployment insurance, discounts on merchandise, and profit-sharing plans.

EMPLOYEE STOCK OWNERSHIP PLAN (ESOP), a type of employee pension plan. The operation of an ESOP is as follows: A company sets up the legal structure of the ESOP and negotiates a large loan from a bank to the ESOP, which in turn loans the money to the company in return for the company's stock. The ESOP now holds the stock in trust for the employees. The ESOP has to repay the bank loan and does so out of payments by the company. For tax purposes, the company can deduct fully its payments to the ESOP as "deferred labor compensation." The bank has to pay taxes on only 50% of the interest income it receives on its loan to the ESOP. As a result, the bank is usually willing to offer financing to ESOPs at substantially reduced rates of interest. As the loan is paid off, shares in the ESOP are vested in (allocated to) the employee accounts. The employees acquire direct ownership of the shares only when they retire or otherwise leave the firm. While they are still working, the shares are voted by trustees for "the sole benefit of the employees," normally according to the recommendations of management rather than those of the workers themselves.

The originator of the ESOP concept was Louis O. Kelso, a San Francisco lawyer, who in 1976 wrote about establishing "universal capitalism" by turning 80 million workers into shareholders of their companies. During the mid-1970s, Sen. Russell Long of the Senate Finance Committee was able to secure significant tax concessions subsidizing the concept, thus paving the way to large-scale implementation. By 1985, it was estimated that 60 buyouts of investor-owned corporations had saved 50,000 jobs.

EMPLOYMENT, as related to the labor force, describes the condition of people working in exchange for monetary payment. There are several categories of employment. *Full employment* exists if somewhere in the neighborhood of 93-96% of the labor force is employed. This usually indicates a prosperous economic condition where jobs are available to almost anyone seeking work. This difference between the full employment rate and 100% is sometimes referred to as the *natural rate of unemployment.* This is unemployment that is caused by employees being between jobs and other frictional problems, as well as by the inability of certain individuals to find work even in prosperous times. In the state of the economy in which there is less than full employment, there are people actively seeking work, but jobs for them are unavailable. The proportion of these people in the labor force who are unable to find work represents the unemployment rate.

A third type of employment, known as *underemployment,* represents the condition in which workers, although employed, are not used to their full capacity. This is also known as disguised unemployment. Examples of this category of employment are often found in agriculture, where more people than necessary are working an amount of land. This usually represents an inefficiency problem.

It has been the goal of the United States since the Employment Act of 1946 to work toward achieving full employment of labor, and policies have been directed toward this end.   *—William D. Wagoner*

See also Full Employment; Labor Mobility; Unemployment of Labor.

ENDOGENOUS THEORY OF BUSINESS CYCLES. *See* Internal Theory of Business Cycles.

ENTREPRENEUR, one whose role is to see the opportunity to make a profit from a new product, new process, or unexploited raw material and then take the organizational risks to promote the opportunity by bringing together the requisite raw materials, manpower, and capital. The entrepreneur's specialty is innovation, not management.

See also Profit System; Risk.

ENTRY, the relative ease with which firms can enter a

particular market. Free entry is a characteristic of purely competitive markets and implies an ease of entry that is not blocked by any major barriers. Unlike the purely competitive markets, oligopolistic and monopolistic markets usually have one or more major barriers that make entry into the industry difficult or impossible. These are of two main types: natural barriers and artificial barriers.

Natural barriers are usually characteristic of certain monopolistic industries. Built into the nature of the industry, they give one firm a natural advantage over other firms. For example, the exclusive rights to resources are a major advantage of the utility companies and form a natural barrier. A second natural barrier is the need for an amount of capital so large that profits could not be obtained. To enter competitively into the automotive industry would be almost impossible because of the large amount of capital, manpower, and knowledge needed.

Artificial barriers include patent and licensing laws, the pricing policies of existing firms that have the ability to undersell new firms, and product differentiation of existing firms that make "off-brands" difficult to market.   *— William D. Wagoner*

See also Barriers to Entry; Free Entry.

ENVIRONMENTAL PROTECTION AGENCY (EPA),

a department within the executive branch charged with enforcing the nation's laws relating to the improvement and maintenance of a good environment. The EPA was created as an agency by an act of Congress in 1970, and President Bush proposed its elevation to cabinet rank in 1990. Among the main duties of the EPA are the enforcement of the Clean Air Act, the Water Pollution Control Act, and the administration of the toxic waste "Superfund" cleanup effort.

Pollution and the use of scarce resources such as clean air and water are classic examples of a market failure known as "externality." It is argued that since no one has clear rights to the air or to the use of water from a river, there is a tendency to treat these resources as if they are free. This lack of property rights (or the "right" of everyone to the resource's use) means that such resources will be used more than is efficient. This externality argument is the main economic rationale for the existence of the EPA.

EQUAL EMPLOYMENT OPPORTUNITY COMMISSION (EEOC),

federal agency established by Title VII of the Civil Rights Act in 1964. Empowered to mediate complaints, to encourage lawsuits by private parties and by the attorney general's office, and to sue employers in its own name (since 1972), the commission is the enforcement arm of the act. The EEOC, with five members, has offices in the major cities and is charged with assuring that hiring and promotion are based on merit, not on race or sex.

The success, or lack of success, of the EEOC is difficult to measure. The legal process is long, and the employee is placed in a difficult position during the years it takes to complete a lawsuit. As with any new program, directions had to be selected, and some women's organizations have been distressed at the EEOC decision to stress race rather than sex.

EQUALIZING WAGE DIFFERENTIALS are those wages paid to individuals to compensate for the non-money differences among jobs. For example, if two workers perform the same duties at the same plant, one working the day shift, the second the night shift, the one on night shift is usually given a wage differential to compensate for the inconvenience of night work. Wage differentials are also used to induce people to work at less attractive or more dangerous occupations.

EQUAL PAY, the same rate of pay for the same job, other facts (such as seniority) being equal. As early as 1942 the National War Labor Board accepted the principle that male and female employees in comparable jobs, performing equally well, should be paid equally. The Equal Pay Act of 1963, supported by Title VII of the Civil Rights Act of 1964, requires, among other things, that employees who "do equal work on jobs, the performance of which requires equal skill, effort, and responsibility, and which are performed under similar working conditions" shall be paid equally. The Equal Employment Opportunity Commission enforces this provision.

In spite of the law, the period since 1965 has seen only small improvement in the ratio of female to male incomes. While various factors account for some of the difference, a portion can be explained only as discrimination. Solution of the problem is made difficult to achieve because so many females work in occupations in which the jobs are nearly all filled by females.

See also Comparable Pay.

EQUATION OF EXCHANGE, a mathematical statement of the fact that the market value of goods sold is equal to the amount of money paid for them, normally written $PQ = MV$, where, in terms of income, P is (roughly) the retail price level, Q is the physical quantity of goods sold to ultimate users (mostly consumers), M is the money supply, and V is the velocity of circulation of money, or the number of times during a year that money changes hands between one income recipient and another. In this form PQ is approximately the same as the monetary value of goods produced, that is, national income. The equation is useful in examining broad trends within the economy, for if any factor of the equation changes, some other factor must also change. If people hoard more (reducing V), then unless the money supply rises, either fewer goods will be sold (Q falls) or prices drop.

Quantity Theory of Money. The quantity theory of

money, developed by Irving Fisher, says that normally both V and Q remain constant, so that a rise in the money supply will cause an exactly proportional increase in the price level, and is the sole cause of inflation. Historical statistics show that the assumption is false. Transactions (and production) have risen continually over time, while velocity has varied unevenly, so that the relation between money and prices is not simple. Nevertheless, the importance of the money supply as one basic factor in price changes is implied in the equation of exchange itself and is accepted by most economists. Modern quantity theorists, led by Milton Friedman, are inclined to say that the money supply is the most important factor in inflation; this group, known as the monetarists, believes that strict control of the quantity of money is the most important policy action needed to stabilize the economy.   — *Walter W. Haines*

EQUILIBRIUM, a state of balance or rest. In order to give the concept a more formal definition, it is convenient to introduce the idea of a system. A system may be thought of as, or described by, a set of *variables* (that is, entities capable of variation), and a set of *forces* acting on the variables, thereby causing them to assume certain values (positions). If the forces that act on each variable are exactly balanced, so that no variable will change its value (position), then the system is said to be in equilibrium.

In economics, equilibrium positions occur in three levels of economic analysis—analysis of individual decisionmakers, market analysis, and analysis of an entire economic system.

Individual Analysis. A typical problem of a firm is to purchase various inputs (factors of production),

price up, and vice versa. A graphical representation of a competitive market is shown in which the curve D is the market demand function, showing the quantities that buyers are willing to buy at different prices. The curve S is the market supply function, showing the quantities that sellers are willing to supply. If the market price is p_1, quantity demanded (x_2) exceeds quantity supplied (x_1), and, therefore, the existence of transform them into one or more outputs (products), and sell these outputs on the market to maximize profit. When the firm chooses levels of inputs and outputs that yield a maximum profit, the firm is in a state of equilibrium; so long as environmental conditions remain the same, the firm has no reason for changing its plan of action. Analogously, individual consumers are in equilibrium when they allocate their income among the available commodities to attain the highest level of satisfaction from their purchases.

Market Analysis is concerned with the determination of market price (if the market is competitive) and quantity exchanged. Under competitive conditions the market price reacts to the forces of supply and demand; an excess of demand over supply drives the excess demand ($x_2 - x_1$) will push the price up. Such a situation is referred to as disequilibrium. Similarly, at prices above p there exists an excess of supply over demand (a negative excess demand), resulting in disequilibrium. When the market price is p, excess demand is 0, which means that the forces of supply and demand are evenly balanced: the price p and the quantity x represent an equilibrium position.

General Analysis. An entire economic system may be represented by a set of markets, one market for each product. Since in the analysis of such a system the concept of equilibrium occupies a central position, it is referred to as general equilibrium analysis. In such a system, an equilibrium occurs when all the constitu-

---

EQUILIBRIUM: TOPIC GUIDE

Equilibrium applies to virtually all economic units in the economy, to the relationships among them, and to the economy as a whole. Building upward from the individual role-players in the economy to the economy as a whole—all viewed in the microeconomic framework—consult CONSUMER EQUILIBRIUM, EQUILIBRIUM OF THE FIRM, and EQUILIBRIUM OF THE INDUSTRY. Then, in regard to the interplay of buyers and sellers, see MARKET EQUILIBRIUM, EQUILIBRIUM PRICE, and EQUILIBRIUM QUANTITY.

For an understanding of macroeconomic equilibrium, see the major article on NATIONAL INCOME DETERMINATION; and in relation to international trade, see BALANCE OF PAYMENTS.

The Subject Maps accompanying the articles on DEMAND THEORY, MARKET SYSTEM, and THEORY OF THE FIRM are also useful in clarifying the interrelationships among the various economic units.

EQUILIBRIUM

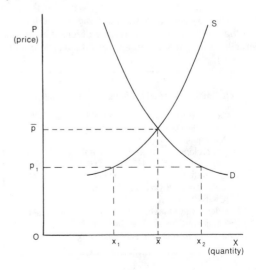

ent markets attain an equilibrium position simultaneously.   —*Josef Hadar*

EQUILIBRIUM LEVEL OF INCOME. *See* National Income Determination.

EQUILIBRIUM OF THE FIRM. In microeconomics, equilibrium of the firm occurs at a point where the firm is maximizing its profits.

Static Equilibrium. Generally in the formal study of economics it is the concept of static equilibrium that is first encountered. Static analysis deals with states of rest relative to the passage of time, while dynamic analysis deals with nonstationary time paths. In static analysis the only significant role that time plays is in furnishing a basis for measurement. Inputs and outputs are thought of as flows which are measured in terms of number of units of input or output per basic unit of time: one speaks of the hourly, daily, or weekly output of a machine or process. If a machine used by the firm is powered by an internal-combustion gasoline engine, then gasoline is one of the inputs of the firm. Similarly, sales can be measured in terms of units of output sold per unit of time. Static equilibrium of the firm involves balancing all of the flows of this type so that profit, measured as a flow, is a maximum.

Short Run v. Long Run. Frequently, input flows are the direct consequence of having access to stocks of objects that are physically durable. A machine shop owning a drill press would have its services (a flow) during a given time period, but the drill press itself would not be used up during that period. The distinction between the long run and short run hinges on durability, but in the theory of the firm the distinction is in terms of economic durability (or variability) rather than physical durability. Although a drill press might have a physical durability of 10 years, a firm does not necessarily commit itself to 10 years of drill press services when it purchases the machine (as long as there is a market for used drill presses). Further, an alternative to owning the machine might be to lease it, and the same machine would have different economic durabilities for different lease terms: if leasable on a 6-

month basis, it is less durable from an economic point of view (furnishes a more variable factor of production) than when leasable only on an annual basis.

Static short-run analysis of the firm assumes that, within the span of the basic time period, the factors in one set are variable and the factors in a second set are not. The cost of the variable factors (variable cost) is found by simply multiplying their respective market prices by the number of units employed. The cost of the nonvariable (fixed) factors (fixed cost) must also be stated in terms of the basic time period and may be thought of as the depreciation on those factors and the interest that the firm could have obtained on the funds tied up in them. Long-run analysis assumes that the maximal number of factors are variable (as they are from the entrepreneur's viewpoint whenever he considers varying the scale of his operation) and does not explicitly account for any fixed cost. Although this analytical scheme implicitly suggests that there are only two economic durabilities when, in fact, there are many, it serves well as a first approximation.

Dynamic Equilibrium. Dynamic analysis deals with time paths, and the firm is in dynamic equilibrium when it is on the time path that the entrepreneur finds most profitable in terms of his or her conception of what the future holds. One case of dynamic equilibrium corresponds to static equilibrium: where the entrepreneur has stationary expectations with respect to the "givens" in the model, the static equilibrium continues through time, generating stationary time paths.   —*Clarence C. Morrison*

EQUILIBRIUM OF THE FIRM, LONG-RUN, the situation that would maximize the firm's profit with all inputs in the production process variable.
See also Equilibrium of the Firm.

EQUILIBRIUM OF THE FIRM, SHORT-RUN. In the short run, the firm adjusts those inputs which are variable so as to maximize profit. This involves equating short-run marginal cost and short-run marginal revenue, since if they are unequal it is possible to increase revenue more than cost by either increasing or decreasing output.
See also Equilibrium of the Firm.

EQUILIBRIUM OF THE INDUSTRY. Equilibrium may be defined as a situation in which there is no tendency to move. Therefore, equilibrium of an industry occurs when the conditions within it are such that no firm, either already in the industry or outside it and potentially an entrant, sees any reason to alter existing arrangements. Thus, equilibrium of an industry can occur only when certain conditions are met, and these conditions are more easily considered in the pure competition case.

Allowing enough time for firms to make basic alterations in plant size, build new plants, or leave the

---

EQUILIBRIUM OF THE FIRM: TOPIC GUIDE

Closely related to the concept of EQUILIBRIUM OF THE FIRM is the article on PROFIT MAXIMIZATION. Equilibrium of the firm applies both to the short and long run; accordingly, see the articles on EQUILIBRIUM OF THE FIRM, SHORT-RUN and EQUILIBRIUM OF THE FIRM, LONG-RUN. Closely related to the latter of these concepts is EQUILIBRIUM OF THE INDUSTRY. For the broader context in which this concept appears, see the major article on THEORY OF THE FIRM as well as the Subject Map accompanying that article.

industry, or for new firms to enter the industry (the long-run period), the conditions under which no one would decide to change the present scale and scope of operations must satisfy the conditions of both short- and long-run equilibrium.

The long-run conditions for equilibrium in the industry exist when only normal profits are being earned by the individual firms. Thus, the price charged by the firms must be just equal to the long-run average cost of production. A price above or below this would create either greater than normal or less than normal profits, and would encourage firms to enter or exit the industry. If this condition of price equality with long-run average costs is met, then one requirement of industry equilibrium is achieved.

However, even if this condition is met, one or more firms already in the industry may find it profitable to change the level of production by more or less intensive utilization of existing plant and equipment. Therefore, the second condition for industry equilibrium is that each firm in the industry should be operating at its equilibrium output. This level of output occurs when, for each plant, marginal cost equals marginal revenue, the profit maximization position. When this condition exists in the short run, and the long-run conditions are met, then long-run average cost equals short-run marginal cost and short-run marginal revenue.

When the individual firms and industry are operating under equilibrium conditions, then, for the moment, equilibrium of the industry exists. This condition, assuming it can ever develop, is a brief one, for changes in technology, in demand, or in other areas, can and will upset it. The safest statement is that a tendency toward this equilibrium is always present in competitive industry.   —*William D. Wagoner*

See also Equilibrium of the Firm.

EQUILIBRIUM PRICE, or MARKET PRICE, the price at which the quantity of a good offered by the producer is exactly equal to the quantity of a good that will be demanded by the consumer for a particular period of time. This equilibrium price represents a compromise of the producer and the consumer. The producer would like to achieve as high a price as possible for his good to maximize his profit. The consumer would like to pay as low a price as possible for the good to allow the purchase of other consumer goods.

If the price were above equilibrium, the producers would produce a larger quantity of the good than consumers would be willing to accept at that price, glutting the market and forcing prices down. If the price were below equilibrium, consumers would attempt to purchase a larger quantity of the goods than were being produced at that price, bidding the price up. Of course, this price movement assumes that there is no government control of prices. If there are price controls of any kind, there is always the possibility of a

black-market bypassing the normal market channels.
See also Market Equilibrium.

EQUILIBRIUM QUANTITY, the quantity of a good that the producers are willing to supply and the consumers are willing to purchase at a given price. In equilibrium, the quantity supplied is equal to the quantity demanded. This situation will occur at only one market price. At higher prices the quantity that producers are willing to supply will exceed the quantity demanded, and at lower prices the quantity that producers are willing to supply will be smaller than the quantity demanded. Thus, only at the equilibrium price is the equilibrium quantity achieved.

EQUITY, as a term, has several connotations, the most common being ownership in part or in whole of a firm. An example of equity is common stock issued by a corporation to secure capital. Equity carries with it risks of ownership, that is, possible gains or losses. The term equity is also used to describe the capital structure of a firm, for example, equity capital (from stock issues) as opposed to debt capital (from bond issues). In corporate financial evaluation equity is defined as the net value of a business derived by subtracting all liens and/or charges against it from its total value.

In welfare economics, equity is used to describe fairness, a method of judging the performance of a firm or the effect of a particular type of market structure on the consumer. Under certain market structures, such as a monopoly, the fairness criteria are not fulfilled, and the consumer may be exploited by the single producer.

See also Common Stock; Stock.

ESCAPE PERIOD. *See* Maintenance of Membership.

ESSAY ON POPULATION (1798). In a reply to the unbounded optimism of Godwin and Condorcet, Thomas Malthus challenged their belief in human perfectibility. He then postulated that (1) food is necessary, and (2) sexual passion will not diminish. Based upon these postulates, Malthus concluded that "the power of population is indefinitely greater than the power in the earth to produce subsistence for man," because population grows at a geometric rate, while food increases only at an arithmetic rate. When population presses against food supplies, the checks of vice, misery, and a higher death rate will prevent further population growth.

While the prediction of the first edition of the *Essay* was quite pessimistic, later editions, beginning with the second in 1803, added a fourth check—moral restraint—which allows man a further means of checking population growth in addition to vice, misery, and death.

See also Malthus, Thomas.

EURODOLLARS, deposits denominated in dollars held in banks and/or financial institutions outside the United States. Though held mostly in England and Western Europe, they can be held anywhere. There is a ready market in these holdings with demand and supply establishing interest rates conducive to regular investment as well as speculation. The use of the dollar as a "vehicle currency" in international transactions was an important factor in the creation of the Eurodollar.

See also Balance of Payments; Foreign Investment.

EUROPEAN ECONOMIC COMMUNITY (EEC), or Common Market. In a free-trade area, restrictions on the free movement of goods and services among members are eliminated, but each country retains its own restrictive devices with the rest of the world. In a customs union all restrictions are removed between members, and a common external tariff (CET) is established on goods entering the union from outside. A common market is the next higher degree of economic integration beyond the customs union; in addition to free trade among members and a CET, national restrictions on the movement of labor and capital among members are removed.

The EEC was established by the Treaty of Rome (1957) and was more or less an extension of the European Coal and Steel Community, created in 1953. The EEC's membership is composed of West Germany, France, Italy, Belgium, the Netherlands, Luxembourg, Great Britain, Ireland, Denmark and Greece, with Spain and Portugal gaining membership in 1986. In addition to the provisions indicated above, the Treaty of Rome provided for: (1) prohibition of cartels and similar restrictive devices (unless they enhanced goals of the Community), (2) common agricultural policy, (3) two investment funds to channel capital from advanced to less developed regions in Europe and associated overseas territories, and (4) a social fund to help relieve economic injuries to workers resulting from movement toward integration. Present plans call for the creation of a single, barrier-free market among the 12 member nations by 1992.

—*John R. Matthews, Jr.*

See also Customs Unions and Free-Trade Areas.

EUROPEAN RECOVERY PROGRAM. *See* Marshall Plan.

EVOLUTIONARY SOCIALISM, the idea of socialism via gradual change rather than revolution. Most socialists agreed that capitalism had to be replaced; the evolutionaries believed that government could be an instrument of reform to reorganize society. A leading spokesman for gradualism was Eduard Bernstein of Germany (1850-1932), who called for a revision of Marxian theories, because many had proved incorrect and because the Marxian revolution was impracticable. The revolutionary approach was adopted in other countries, its supporters favoring such measures as increasing government control of business, gradual expansion of national and municipal ownership of productive enterprises, use of taxation to reduce inequality, and extension of free social services.

See also Nationalization; Fabian Society; Revisionism; Revolutionary Socialism.

EXCESS BURDEN, a term used in connection with the economics of taxation. All taxes, except a "head tax" (a fixed-dollar tax imposed on all individuals), impose economic costs on society in excess of the amount of the tax collected. This amount is the excess burden of the tax, and it arises because the tax itself distorts the allocation of resources away from their optimal use. A tax drives a wedge between the true price or cost (opportunity cost) of the taxed activity, and the cost or price that is *perceived* by businesses and individuals. As a result, decisionmakers tend to reallocate their resources away from the taxed activity in an effort to avoid the tax. These other activities will be less valuable to society at the margin than are the taxed activities.

This concept can be illustrated with the help of a simple graph. Suppose MC is the marginal cost (and hence, in a competitive economy, both the opportunity cost and the supply curve) of automobile tires. The demand curve, $D = MB$, represents the marginal benefits to consumers of additional automobile tires. The market will tend toward equilibrium at point E, and this is an efficient allocation of resources toward the production of automobile tires. Now suppose a tax of $p - p^1$ per tire is imposed on producers of tires. This causes the supply curve to shift to S^1. The tax causes consumers to reduce their purchases of tires from Q to Q^1, and the loss in utility to tire consumers is shown by the area PP^1BE (this is a loss of consumer surplus). The government receives tax revenues equal

EXCESS BURDEN

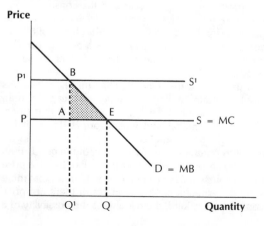

to the area PP¹BA. This amount may be a loss to tire buyers, but it is not a social cost, as it can be used for other productive activities. The shaded area ABE, however, is irretrievably lost because of the tax. This is the excess burden. Theoretically, the excess burden of a tax will be greater the more elastic the demand or the more elastic the supply of the taxed good.

Practical examples of excess burden include: the location of retail shopping centers into low-tax political jurisdictions, when other locations otherwise would be preferable; reduced work effort and reduced savings as a result of personal income taxes; and poorer maintenance of inner-city housing units as a result of property taxes.

See also Consumer Surplus.

EXCESS CAPACITY refers to that scale of plant over and above that needed to produce enough goods to meet aggregate market demand. Often referred to as redundant capacity, excess capacity adds to the costs of production while adding nothing to the value of the product. For example, if a firm invests money in a plant capable of producing 1,000 units when only 500 units of the item are demanded, it is said to have excess capacity. If the firm had invested only enough money for a plant large enough to produce 500 units, the plant would be fully utilized and production costs would be less (equipment that has become obsolete due to technological innovations is not considered to be excess capacity).

Excess capacity has a high incidence in the manufacturing industries, very often reflecting the seasonal nature of products. In addition, manufacturing industries, especially those producing durable goods, are greatly affected by fluctuations in the business cycle. Therefore, these industries are considered to have "cyclical excess capacity."

It is very difficult for industries, as well as individual firms, to determine just how much capacity will be needed at any specific time, because the demand for products in most industries is influenced by fluctuations in the economy. For example, from 1946 to 1956, the steel industry operated at nearly 100% utilization of capacity. In 1956, however, a minor business recession lowered utilization in that industry to less than 60%.   — *William D. Wagoner*

EXCESS DEMAND for a commodity occurs when its price is below the equilibrium. The equilibrium price clears the market by equating supply and demand. When the good's price is less than equilibrium, consumers demand a larger quantity of the good than producers are willing to supply, creating a shortage. Consumers will bid up the price to equilibrium. If there is government interference, a black market may result.

EXCESS PROFITS, in an economic sense, the term is synonymous with economic profits.

Normal profits are implicit returns sufficient to prevent owners from withdrawing capital from the industry. They are called opportunity costs by the economist and are, therefore, included in the average total unit cost of the producer. Should products command a price higher than this unit cost, excess profits appear. These are signals for new firms to enter, whereupon the increased supply tends to reduce market price (production costs may also rise) until the excess profits—economic profits—are eliminated. If there are barriers to entry, such as occur in monopolistic markets, excess profits can remain.

See also Monopoly; Opportunity Cost; Profit System.

EXCESS RESERVES. *See* Multiple Expansion of the Money Supply.

EXCESS SUPPLY of a commodity occurs when its price is above the equilibrium. The equilibrium price is defined as the price that clears the market by making supply equal demand. If the price of the good exceeds equilibrium, producers will tend to supply a quantity in excess of the amount demanded by consumers, creating an excess supply. From this price there will be an automatic tendency for the price to decline as producers' inventories build up.

EXCHANGE RATE, the domestic price of a unit of foreign currency. This price is set by demand and supply and is derived from the demand and supply of goods and services. Claims of foreigners on the United States give rise to demand for exchange in the country; U.S. claims on foreigners give rise to supply. If demand exceeds supply, the exchange rate rises; if supply increases with no change in demand the rate falls. It is in equilibrium when there is no pressure to change. The overall situation in a nation's balance of payments determines whether or not the rate will change. The rate can be manipulated, and such manipulation, or lack of it, has given rise to several exchange rate systems.

Freely Fluctuating Rates vary with demand and supply without limits. Adjustment is automatic; a rising rate makes imports more costly and increases exports (a rise in English pounds in the United States means a decline in the pound rate on dollars, and U.S. goods are cheaper). If the rate change is one of a series in the same direction, there will be destabilizing operations.

Fixed Rates, such as the pure gold standard, move over a narrow range, with the upper and lower points known. Adjustment is automatic, but unlike the freely fluctuating system, the fixed rate places the burden on the domestic economy rather than the balance of payments.

Exchange Control Rates are set by the government, which has direct control over both demand and supply. A multiple rate system is often concomitant with rates being set in line with a specific government program.

Flexible Rates allow the market to set rates within prescribed limits, with government intervention when those limits are reached. Exchange is supplied when demand would drive the rate too high; exchange is purchased when supply would push the rate too low. This system allows for automatic adjustment but relieves the domestic economy of the burden. It was used by the International Monetary Fund (IMF) up until 1971 in that each member agreed to peg its currency, within limits, to the dollar. Resources for pegging could be obtained when necessary from IMF. Problems arose when a nation had to intervene on only one side of the peg and a new official rate had to be established.

Emerging Rate Regimes are the results of the failure to reach agreement on reform of the international monetary system started during the 1960s. Problems and deficiencies in the IMF system led to its collapse in 1971 and nations simply let exchange rates float. The Jamaica Agreement (1976) and subsequent amendments to the IMF were attempts to formalize and regulate exchange arrangements then in existence. Under this system, nations can use any exchange rate arrangement they wish; floating rates are authorized, but an individual nation may peg if it elects to do so. No nation is to manipulate its exchange rate for its own advantage and should consult with others about its intervention in foreign exchange markets. Much flexibility is granted in the holding of reserves and adjustments to balance of payments disturbances. In this context the IMF gives guidelines for national behavior, provides for consultation, and conducts surveillance over the exchange rate practices. The Jamaica agreement also provided for the demonetization of gold and the establishment of Special Drawing Rights (SDR) as the international unit of account and principal reserve asset.

The dollar was the world's undisputed key currency until the mid-1960s. Then its exchange value relative to most other currencies declined slowly until 1978, reversed direction until 1985, then again began to weaken. This pattern is due partly to the increasing rate of inflation in the United States in the 1970s and the decreasing inflation rate in the 1980s. When domestic prices increase faster than foreign prices, Americans buy more foreign imports, thus increasing the supply of dollars abroad. The increased supply lowers the exchange rate—the price of dollars. When inflation decreased, domestic products began to seem more attractive and foreign imports relatively more expensive, so dollars stayed at home. The supply of dollars abroad decreased, and the exchange rate rose.

—John R. Matthews

See also Devaluation; Gold Standard; International Trade Theory.

EXCISE TAX, a type of sales tax which is narrow-based, that is, applied to one commodity or a few. In addition to providing revenue, excise taxes may be imposed on "luxury" goods, for the purpose of income redistribution, or on "undesirable" commodities, such as liquor and tobacco, to discourage consumption. The tax is likely to be borne by the consumer of the taxed product.

EXCLUSIVE DEALERSHIP, an agreement in which a producer of a line of products stipulates that a retailer may sell those products only if he does not handle the products of a rival producer. Such agreements, clearly anticompetitive in their limitation of a rival's opportunity to sell, are prohibited by the Clayton Act (Section 3) where their effect tends to lessen competition substantially.

EXIT, of a firm from an industry usually occurs when a firm makes an economic loss. If a firm is earning less than normal profits in an industry, it will withdraw its capital from that industry. In industries with large capital investment, a firm may put up with these short-run losses for a long period of time before exiting from the industry.

EXOGENOUS THEORY OF BUSINESS CYCLES. *See* External Theory of Business Cycles.

EXPANSION. *See* Business Cycles, Phases.

EXPECTED UTILITY, or CHOICE UNDER UNCERTAINTY. Choice under certainty means that the outcome of a particular choice is known in advance. For example, in the standard theory of consumer behavior, the consumer chooses a bundle of commodities, and he or she knows exactly how much of the various commodities is in each bundle before making his or her choice. Choice under uncertainty, on the other hand, is a situation in which the outcome of a particular choice is not known in advance. Often the nature of the uncertainty can be specified in probabilistic terms. In such circumstances for each possible choice the consumer knows the complete set of all potential outcomes, and to each potential outcome he or she can attach the probability of its occurrence. Thus, with each possible choice there is associated an uncertain prospect, or probability distribution. One important aspect of the theory of choice under uncertainty is the determination of the decisionmaker's preference ordering for uncertain prospects.

Two Payoffs. The problem is illustrated for choices whose outcomes are monetary payoffs. The simplest uncertain prospect is one that has only two possible payoffs, say x_1 and x_2. If, for example, the probability of x_1 is $1/3$, and that of x_2 is $2/3$, then the mean of this probability distribution, also called the expected payoff, and denoted by $\bar{x}$, is given by the weighted average $\bar{x} = {}^{1}/_{3}x_1 + {}^{2}/_{3}x_2$. The two payoffs and the expected payoff are marked on the horizontal axis in Figure 1. The expected payoff divides the interval between the two payoffs into two segments whose lengths are proportional to the two probabilities:

$$\frac{\bar{x} - x_1}{x_2 - \bar{x}} = \frac{2/3}{1/3} = 2$$

Also shown on the diagram is the decisionmaker's total utility curve (utility function), which assigns a utility to every possible payoff x.

Under conditions of uncertainty the actual outcome is not known in advance, and the consumer has no way of knowing with certainty which level of utility he or she will attain when choosing a particular uncertain prospect. However, it is possible to compute the expected utility of any uncertain prospect, which for the above example is defined as the weighted average $U_3 = {}^{2}/_{3}u_2$. Expected utility can be thought of as the utility level that the decisionmaker would attain on the average if he or she chose the same prospect time after time. The value of expected utility u_3 can be found on the vertical axis at a point two-thirds the distance from u_1 to u_2. It can also be located by drawing a horizontal line from point C to the vertical axis.

Expected utility is the criterion for ordering uncertain prospects. For any two uncertain prospects, the prospect with the higher expected utility is preferred. Thus, in the theory of choice under uncertainty, expected utility plays the same role as the utility index in choice under certainty. A choice between two uncertain prospects is illustrated in Figure 2, which in part reproduces the conditions of Figure 1. A second uncertain prospect is introduced with the same payoffs as the first one, but in which the probability of the payoff x_1 is greater than $^{1}/_{3}$. Consequently, the expected payoff of the second uncertain prospect, denoted by x_4, is less than $\bar{x}_3$. Therefore, the expected utility $\bar{u}_4$ of the second uncertain prospect is also less than that of the first prospect; the first prospect is preferred to the second one.

Another example is illustrated in Figure 3, which involves two uncertain prospects A and B. The payoffs of prospect A are x_2 and x_3, and its expected payoff is $\bar{x}_A$; prospect B offers payoffs x_1 and x_3, and its expected payoff is $\bar{x}_B$. Because $\bar{u}_A > \bar{u}_B$, prospect A is preferred. Unlike in Figure 2, the expected payoff of the preferred prospect is smaller than the expected payoff of the other prospect. Thus, to determine preference between uncertain prospects, it is in general not enough to compare the expected payoffs of the prospects under consideration.

Risk Aversion. Decisionmakers operating under uncertainty often exhibit a type of behavior known as risk aversion. By definition, a person is averse to risk if he or she prefers a sure prospect of, say, x dollars, to

EXPECTED UTILITY

Figure 1

Figure 2

Figure 3

Figure 4

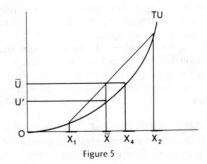

Figure 5

an uncertain prospect whose expected payoff is x dollars. If the individual's utility function is concave, then he or she is a risk averter, as illustrated in Figure 4. The uncertain prospect under consideration consists of two payoffs x_1 and x_2, and its expected payoff is $\bar{x}$. If the individual is asked to choose between $\bar{x}$ dollars for sure and the above uncertain prospect, he or she will choose the sure prospect, because the utility u' of the sure prospect is higher than the expected utility $\bar{u}$ of the uncertain prospect.

If the individual is offered a choice between x_3 dollars for sure and the uncertain prospect represented in Figure 4, he or she will be indifferent between the two choices—both have the same level of utility. The payoff x_3 is therefore referred to as the certainty-equivalent of the above uncertain prospect. If the sure prospect that is offered as an alternative to the uncertain prospect is less than x_3, then the individual will choose the uncertain prospect. The quantity $\bar{x} - x_3$ is called the insurance premium, or risk premium, of the uncertain prospect. This premium may be interpreted in either one of two ways: (1) it may be thought of as the maximum amount of dollars the individual is willing to forgo in order not to be exposed to risk; (2) it may also be thought of as the minimum premium the individual has to be paid to expose him- or herself to risk by switching from the sure prospect to the uncertain prospect. A typical manifestation of risk aversion is the purchase of insurance.

Attraction to Risk is the opposite of risk aversion. By definition, an individual is attracted to risk if he prefers an uncertain prospect with an expected payoff of x dollars to x dollars with certainty. Attraction to risk occurs when the utility function is convex, as in Figure 5. As before, the uncertain prospect is specified by the payoffs x_1 and x_2, the expected payoff being $\bar{x}$. Because the expected utility $\bar{u}$ of the uncertain prospect is higher than the utility u' of the sure payoff $\bar{x}$, the individual prefers the uncertain prospect. If instead of being offered $\bar{x}$ dollars for sure, the individual is offered x_4 dollars for sure, then he or she is indifferent between the sure prospect and the uncertain prospect. Thus, x_4 is the certainty-equivalent of the uncertain prospect. If the sure prospect exceeds x_4, the individual prefers the sure prospect to the uncertain prospect. It is to be noted that the risk premium $\bar{x} - x_4$ is negative. Rather than demanding insurance, a person who is attracted to risk is willing to pay a certain amount to be exposed to risk. In the above example the amount $x_4 - \bar{x}$ is the maximum amount the individual is willing to forgo to assume the risk associated with the uncertain prospect. A typical manifestation of attraction to risk is participation in games of chance.

—*Josef Hadar*

EXPLOSIVE EQUILIBRIUM, a situation in which any disturbance from a point of equilibrium will not result in a return to an equilibrium. Thus, once a disturbance occurs, there will not be a convergence to a new equilibrium. This is contrasted to a *converging equilibrium*.

See also Converging Equilibrium.

EXPORT-IMPORT BANK. The Eximbank was established in 1934 as a District of Columbia banking agency; in 1945 it was reincorporated as an independent government agency. It extends credits to foreign purchasers of U.S. goods and so aids the export segment of the economy. Its loans are "tied" in that the proceeds must be spent in the lending country. In addition, the Eximbank provides guarantees against credit and political risks. Though most of its operations are related to financing U.S. exports, it also extends long-term development loans in maturities from 8 to 20 years. Many such loans have been made to countries in Latin America, and the Eximbank is considered a source of development finance. When these loans are used to finance basic industrial and public utilities projects, U.S. exports of heavy machinery and equipment are benefited. Loans have also been made to less developed countries with balance of payments difficulties, to enable them to maintain their level of U.S. imports. The Eximbank provides little technical assistance to developing nations; its basic interest is the promotion of U.S. exports.

EXPORTS, the credit item in the balance of trade, and a major credit item in the current account in a nation's balance of payments. Exports of goods and services include all the credit items in the current account. The capital account in the balance of pay-

Jet engines are loaded aboard a cargo plane for export to Bordeaux, France.

ments includes both short- and long-term capital exports, which unlike merchandise exports, are debits. When a nation exports merchandise, there is an impact on the domestic economy: the immediate result is an increase in incomes to exporters and a concomitant fall in the supply of goods and services. Therefore, exports have an expansionary impact in the economy of the exporting nation.

The gross national product is composed of personal consumption, domestic investment, government purchase, and net exports. The last component is the difference between gross exports and imports and the reason for recording it on the net basis is to preclude double-counting—the other components include imports as well as domestic goods. Hence any change in net exports has the domestic income multiplier applied to it and is most important in the determination of the foreign trade multiplier. Combined exports and imports for the United States have never exceeded 10% of GNP. Other countries, such as Great Britain, have to trade to live. Less developed nations are constantly trying to develop an export base as a means of obtaining foreign exchange to purchase imports necessary for development.

—*John R. Matthews, Jr.*
See also Balance of Payments; Balance of Trade; Visible Goods and Services.

EXTERNAL COSTS, those costs of the production process, such as water and air pollution, that are not borne by the producing unit and, therefore, are not taken into account by that unit in making its economic decisions. Under pressure from environmental groups and others, government has recently begun to force

Air pollution represents an external cost of production. Government may require firms to internalize these costs through abatement requirements.

producers to internalize a number of costs that were previously externalities. For example, laws passed in some localities requiring deposits on all beverage containers require consumers and bottlers, rather than the local government, to bear the cost of container disposal.

See also Bad, Economic; Externalities; Internal Costs.

EXTERNAL DEBT, the condition where the borrowing unit (the government) acquires money from some lending unit or units outside of the nation itself. There is therefore an outside or external claim against American productive resources and against the income and output which these resources can create. Such borrowing actually transfers real goods and services from the debtor nation to the creditor nation at the time the debt (or interest on the debt) is repaid.

See also Internal Debt.

EXTERNALITIES, also called spillover effects, neighborhood effects, or external costs or benefits. An externality is said to exist when the decisions of the producers or consumers of a good or service impose *direct* costs or benefits on persons or firms other than the decisionmaker. Externalities can be positive (external benefits), such as the benefits provided to owners of neighboring houses when a fire department extinguishes a blaze at a particular house, or when the inoculation of a child reduces the likelihood of others catching a serious disease. Externalities may also be negative (external costs), for example, the dumping of toxic substances into a river as a result of agricultural runoff, or the increased probability of a violent crime in a neighborhood when a house is abandoned and neglected by its owner.

Positive externalities may lead to an inefficient underallocation of resources toward the activity, because the buyer or the seller of the product has no method of charging the aided third parties for the benefits they receive. The market price of the good will be greater than the opportunity cost of consuming extra units of the good, and the marginal benefits to society of additional use will exceed the marginal benefits to the decisionmaker. Ways to solve this problem include schemes to subsidize the private demand for the good, or to subsidize the production of the good, either by offering direct subsidies to producers, by incentives, or by directly providing the good by the government itself.

Negative externalities may lead to an inefficient overallocation of resources to this activity, because the private market price does not reflect the additional costs imposed on others. Hence, consumers will buy more than the socially optimal amount, or producers will produce an excessive amount of the good, as the marginal cost to society of the good's use will be greater than the perceived marginal cost facing the decisionmaker. Policy solutions include taxing the commodity, setting standards for the maximum use of a detrimental product or input, and fines or criminal sanctions against those who use too much of the good.

This situation can best be illustrated with a simple example. Suppose the marginal costs and benefits of producing petrochemicals is given in the graph by the curves marked $S = MC_p$ and $D = MB_p$, respectively. In a competitive market, these represent the demand and supply of the good. The private market will be in equilibrium at point A, representing Q_m units of the good, at a price of P_m. However, suppose the production of the good creates additional costs that are not considered by the firm when deciding how much to produce (such as increased cancer risks facing citizens of communities located downstream from the factories). Suppose these external costs are given by the curve labeled MCe, for marginal external costs. In this situation, the true cost to society of expanding output by an additional unit is really the sum of the private costs (raw materials, labor, etc.) and the external costs (cancer risk). This is shown by the curve MC_s, for marginal social costs. If there are no external benefits from the use of the product (users of gasoline receive benefits as already shown in curve $D = MB_p$), then the marginal social benefits will be the same as the marginal private benefits, and $MB_s = MB_p$. The "optimal" position is at point B, with an amount Q_o, and an efficient price of the good of P_o. Because the good is underpriced relative to its true social costs, too much of the good is consumed ($Q_p > Q_o$).

By moving from quantity Q_p to Q_o, society would experience a reduction in benefits due to the forgone petrochemicals equal to the area Q_oBAQ_p. However, society would gain by not experiencing costs equal to area Q_oBCQ_p. By moving from the market solution to the optimal solution, society could gain an amount equal to the area ABC. One way to do this is to impose a tax on the product equal to BD dollars per unit. If such a tax were imposed, the market would be in equilibrium at quantity Q_o, with consumers facing a perceived price of P_o (at point B), and producers receiving a perceived after-tax price shown by point D.

A tax as suggested above would "internalize" the externality, by making decisionmakers consider all the costs implied by the use or production of the good. However, solving the externality problem may require information that governments simply do not possess. Other analysts suggest that if the definition of property rights could be more clearly established, many externality problems would be self-correcting. For example, if the downstream citizens had a clearly defined right to clean water, they could legally force the firm either to stop dumping toxic wastes into the river or to make payment for the damages done to them. Alternatively, if the firm had a clear right to use water as it sees fit, it may be in the best interests of both the downstream

people and the firm for the citizens to pay the firm not to pollute. Either circumstance lessens the inefficiency involved, although the two scenarios do imply very different equity outcomes.

—*Michael S. Johnson*
See also Benefit-Cost Analysis; Infrastructure.

EXTERNAL (or EXOGENOUS) THEORY OF BUSINESS CYCLES assumes that fluctuations in economic activity are caused by factors outside the economic system. External explanations include, for example, wars and revolutions; politics; even sunspot cycles, a now disused nineteenth century theory. Other external factors include the rates of immigration and population growth, discovery of new resources, and scientific and technological innovations. An innovation, for example, encourages business to invest in the same or similar technology. Exogenous theories, because they seem to indicate that business cycles are neither predictable nor controllable, generally lack favor among economists.

See also Business Cycles, Theories.

FABIAN SOCIETY, a British organization committed to the gradual improvement of society in every legal and ethical way. Founded in 1884, it was named after a Roman general who fought his enemies in a variety of ways without going into battle. The Fabians actively supported labor unions, public education, and the consumer cooperative movement, and were politically involved with social and economic reforms. Initial leaders in this form of evolutionary socialism were George Bernard Shaw and Sidney and Beatrice Webb.

See also British Labour Party; Evolutionary Socialism; Nationalization.

FACT-FINDING, a form of third-party intervention into collective bargaining impasses. In public interest disputes, fact-finding by a government-designated board may cut through the bluff and exaggerated claims of a bargaining position. Supporters of the procedure hope that the public interest generated by the publication of the report of a fact-finding commission will provide an incentive for the bargainers to come together.

As a technique for providing pressure to end a strike, though, the process has not proved to be significant because the public interest generated is usually minor. Therefore, the cost to the bargainers of not heeding the recommendations is small.

— William D. Wagoner
See also Collective Bargaining; Emergency Strikes.

FACTOR COMPLEMENTARITY. Two factors are complementary if increased usage of one raises the marginal physical product of the other.
See also Joint Demand.

FACTOR DEMAND, the demand for a factor of production. Factor demand differs somewhat from the demand for a commodity, which reflects the satisfaction or utility that consumers receive.

Factors and Commodities. When businessmen demand a factor, they do so because the input can produce commodities that ultimately generate revenues to the firm by sales to households. Therefore, indirectly, factors are desired for the satisfactions they produce: factor demand is a derived (indirect) demand. Another difference between commodity and factor demands is that the commodities are purchased outright (by a consumer); factors are hired as a service to be used for a period of time (by businesses). However, the demand for a factor parallels the value theory of commodities; in the final analysis, supply and demand per unit of time determine the market prices of factors.

Demand Schedules. Because the demand for a factor of production depends on that factor's ability to produce goods and services, ultimately the demand schedule of an input reflects the input's productivity according to the law of diminishing returns. It can be demonstrated that in a barter economy the demand curve for a variable factor is the same as that factor's marginal product curve. If, say, the going rate for a factor is 10 bushels of wheat per year in a barter economy, input buyers will hire up to the point where the factor's marginal (extra) product equals 10 bushels. Units of a factor that have marginal product less than 10 bushels will not voluntarily be hired. This result can easily be generalized to a money economy: an input will be hired up to the point where its cost (market price) equals its marginal revenue product (marginal physical product times commodity selling price, under pure competition). A firm will not voluntarily hire an input if it produces goods worth less than the firm has to pay for the input itself. Advanced treatments indicate that a factor's marginal product schedule (physical

or value) is, in fact, the factor demand schedule only when the factor is the only variable input. If several factors may be varied, then their respective demand schedules can be theoretically derived, but they are somewhat more complicated. *—Robert L. Brite*

FACTOR EARNINGS, payments made to the factors of production for their use as inputs. The four factors of production are land, labor, entrepreneurship, and capital.
See also Factor Payments.

FACTOR EMPLOYMENT, the usage of any of the four factors of production—land, labor, capital, and entrepreneurship. The employment of land refers to its use either as a primary productive unit, as in agriculture, or as a secondary means of production, such as the groundwork for the construction of a building. The employment of labor refers to the hiring of workers in the labor force for productive purposes. Capital employment is the use of durable items, such as machinery, tools, and buildings, that are used as inputs in the production process.
See also Factors of Production.

FACTOR INCOMES, that proportion of total payments to factors of production which go to any one factor. They include wages, rent, interest, and profit as payments to labor, land, capital, and entrepreneurial ability, respectively. The distribution of income among factors (the functional distribution of income) isolates the income paid to the various factors rather than payments received by those who supply the factor. A factor supplier may supply several factors, such as his own labor, land he owns, and so forth. His income is the sum of the income he receives from each source. Thus, measuring the total income of individuals tells nothing about the amount of income generated by each factor. Economists feel it is important to know both the distribution of income among individuals and among factors of production.
See also Circular Flow of Income; Factor Payments.

FACTOR MARKETS, the markets for land, labor, capital, and entrepreneurship. A market is a closely interrelated group of buyers and sellers. In the factor markets the buyers and sellers are all concerned with a specific input of production. The buyers, which are usually individual firms, purchase the inputs for production from the sellers for a price, usually determined by the intersection of market supply and market demand curves.

The market for land is based upon three major items, its availability, desirability, and cost of use (rent). If both the buyer and the seller of land agree on a price, land is then used as an input to production.

The labor market consists of individual firms (purchasers of labor) and members of the labor force

FACTOR MARKETS

(sellers of labor). The price of labor (wages) is determined by the supply of and demand for each type of labor. There are many types of labor, depending upon such attributes as skill, training, and experience levels.

The capital market is mainly the market for capital funds that can be used for investment. Capital is the accumulation of durable goods used in the production process, such as machinery, tools, and buildings. The main determinant of the allocation of funds in the capital market is the interest rate. The interest rate is the price paid for the use of money. The sellers in the capital market are normally investors, and usually they will invest where they expect to get the highest rate of interest.   — *William D. Wagoner*

See also Factors of Production; Market Mechanism.

FACTOR MOBILITY refers to the relative freedom with which the factors of production are able to move among alternative uses. These factors are land, labor, capital, and entrepreneurship.

Factors are mobile to the extent that they are free of restraint. For this reason, factor mobility is greatest in purely competitive market structures because, in monopolistic market structures, such things as large investments and few firms inhibit free movement of

production factors. For example, if a man is trained to install telephones, he may not be free to take his knowledge to another telephone company without relocating. Hence, factor mobility is restrained.

FACTOR PAYMENTS, the compensating money flows in exchange for the use of factors of production. Rent, interest, and wages and salaries are usually included as payments for the use in production of land, capital, and labor, respectively. Thus, the use of factors of production generates income flows in the form of factor payments. In capitalistic economic systems, the allocation of the factors of production among competing uses, and the resulting income flows, are accomplished through the system of markets and prices.

FACTOR PRICES in a competitive market structure are determined by the supply and demand conditions existing in the market, as are the prices of other commodities. Thus, if the labor supply curve shifts to the right, showing an increase in supply, then the price of labor (wages) falls, and the quantity demanded subsequently increases. Other shifts in market conditions, shown by movements of the demand or supply curves, would cause other wage and quantity changes, depending upon the direction of the particular shift.

FACTOR PRODUCTIVITY, the ability of a factor to produce goods and services of value to consumers. The productivity of a factor underlies the demand for it by businesses. A factor's productivity is measured both in terms of physical product and in terms of value of physical product. For example, the productivity of an additional hour of labor can be measured in terms of the number of units of output it generates and also in terms of the dollar value of the output generated. The former measures the marginal physical product of labor, while the latter measures the value of marginal physical product.

The physical productivity of a factor is a purely technological phenomenon. As such, a factor's physical productivity (in terms of the various physical product schedules of an input) depends on: (1) the state of the arts (technology), (2) the amounts of other factors used in the productive process (increases in one factor will lead to increased productivity for other factors), and (3) the law of diminishing returns.

The value productivity schedule also depends on the above three considerations. In addition, marginal value schedules are determined by the market price of the commodity produced. The market price reflects the value that society places on the commodity. If consumer preferences change in favor of this commodity, prices will rise, and the value productivity schedules will increase. If tastes change against this commodity, prices will fall, and the value productivity schedules will shift backward, essentially a reduction in the demand for that factor. Thus, the price of a factor depends on the selling price of the commodities it produces.

The price of other factors of production will affect marginal value. If the price of labor rises, then to the extent that the other inputs can substitute for labor in the productive process, the demand for the other factors will rise. Similarly, a reduction in the price of capital will lead to a reduction in the demand for labor and other competing inputs.

FACTOR PROPORTIONS. Factors can be used in variable proportions if factor substitution is possible. Thus a given quantity of output can be produced in several ways by changing factor proportions. On the other hand, if substitution is not possible, factors must be used always in the same fixed proportions to produce a given level of output. Fixed proportions imply that there is only one technically efficient way to produce a given quantity of output. While fixed proportions may fit the layman's notion of production, few examples actually exist.

See also Factor Substitution.

FACTOR SERVICES, the financial services of a person or institution (a factor in this context) who lends a business money on the security of its inventory or accounts receivable. Factor services are typically utilized in industries, such as textiles, so fragmented that the individual businesses are of insufficient size and stature to obtain loans on their own credit.

**FACTORS OF PRODUCTION:
TOPIC GUIDE**

For the general role of factors of production in a market economy, see the article on the *CIRCULAR FLOW OF INCOME. Details of this role are to be found in the articles on *FACTOR MARKETS, FACTOR DEMAND, FACTOR PRICES, and FACTOR PAYMENTS. For still more specifics, see the articles on *LABOR MARKET, LABOR FORCE, LABOR SUPPLY, and DEMAND FOR CAPITAL. For the specific forms of factor incomes, see *WAGES, RENT, DIVIDENDS, and INTEREST.

The articles preceded by an asterisk (*) above are each accompanied by a Subject Map which further illuminates the interrelationship of the various Factors of Production to other articles in the encyclopedic dictionary.

FACTORS OF PRODUCTION, the inputs that a firm uses to produce units of output. The amounts of each input needed for a specified output vary with the product, the production technique, and the degree of substitutability of the inputs. There are four major factors of production: land, labor, capital, and entrepreneurship (management). The higher the degree of substitutability of these inputs is, the cheaper will be the factor costs of the firm, because as the price of one factor rises, the firm can substitute an input with a lower price.

Land, as a factor of production, refers to any land used for purposes of producing an output. Land is a primary factor when it is cultivated or used for grazing in the agricultural industry. Land is a secondary factor when it is used, for example, as the ground on which a building is built. Rent is payment for the use of land.

Labor, as a factor for production, is usually calculated on the basis of man-hours, the number of hours of actual labor needed. The inputs of labor are employed by hiring qualified workers from the labor force, which is made up of individuals who are willing and able to work. The factor payment to labor is in the form of wages and salaries.

Capital, as an input, is the accumulation of wealth that is invested in durable items for the purposes of production. Capital often takes the form of machinery, tools, and buildings that are made to last a certain period of time. The factor payment for the use of capital is in the form of interest.

— *William D. Wagoner*

See also Entrepreneur; Factors of Production Topic Guide; Profit System; Risk.

FACTOR SUBSTITUTION. Much of what is interesting in the economics of production depends on factor substitutability. In most production processes, some factor substitution is possible. Thus firms have a choice as to what input combinations will be used to produce a given quantity of output. Graphically these choices are shown by an isoquant.

Since firms are assumed to minimize costs, factor substitution implies that the amount of a given factor that will be used depends on its price and on the prices of the other factors as well. The elasticity of substitution, which measures the ability of businesses to alter factor ratios in response to factor price changes, ultimately determines factor shares (the distribution of factor payments between labor and capital). If wage rates rise and capital cannot be readily substituted for labor, labor's share of income (factor payments) will rise.

FACTOR SUPPLY, a functional relationship that specifies the determinants of the conditions under which varying amounts of a factor will voluntarily be offered. The factors usually analyzed in elementary economic studies are labor and land.

Some of the potential determinants of the supply of labor, in general, include wage rates, population, and work-ethic notions of the society. Potential determinants of the supply of labor to an industry include relative working conditions and ease of mobility into the industry. Mobility may be restricted by natural requirements (intelligence, skill, strength), transportation costs, or union restrictions.

Land is a special case; the supply of land is generally considered to be in constant supply. Some extreme methods may increase or decrease land, but existing land prices preclude most of them. The uses to which land can be put may be highly responsive to price.

FACTOR SUPPLY CURVE, a two-dimensional graphical representation of the conditions under which various quantities of a factor will be offered per unit of time. Factor price is usually plotted on the vertical axis against quantity supplied. Changes in other determinants of quantity shift the supply curve. In the case of land, for example, if group notions change to more highly prized leisure, a reduction in supply will occur and the supply curve of labor will shift backward to the left. Normally, except for land, factor supply curves are positively sloped; higher prices are required before additional quantities of a factor will be offered.

FAIR LABOR STANDARDS ACT (FLSA) (1938), also known as the Wage and Hour Law or the Minimum Wage Law, an important part of the wide-ranging economic reform legislation of the 1930s. The original act set a minimum wage of $.25 per hour in covered employments and provided for time-and-a-half pay for hours beyond 44 per week. Stair-step increases in the minimum wage to $.40 were provided for, and the regular work week was scaled down to 40 hours. In 1991, the minimum wage became $4.25 per hour.

Numerous amendments to the FLSA have expanded its coverage, dramatically raised the minimum wage level, specified overtime pay for hours beyond 8 per day as well as beyond 40 per week, and added the "equal pay" and several other protections against sex discrimination in employment. The expanding coverage of the federal law now comprises almost 80% of all workers in the private sector. For the rest, state minimum wage laws may apply, but a relatively small percentage of the labor force is protected by them, and fewer still are actually affected. Nevertheless, the importance of this act is still hotly debated.

— *Leonard G. Shifrin*

FAIRNESS. *See* Equity.

FAIR RETURN ON FAIR VALUE, the general standard established by the U.S. Supreme Court in *Smyth v. Ames* (1898) to be used in determining rates in a regulated industry. To substitute an administrative device for the impersonal market mechanism, some standard (guideline) has to be determined for regulatory commissions. The Supreme Court established this standard because rates too low would confiscate property without due process in violation of the 5th and 14th Amendments; rates too high would be "unjust" and "unreasonable." Hence a utility is constitutionally guaranteed the right to recover its operating expenses plus an opportunity to earn a fair return on a fair value. Interpretation of what is "fair" is obviously judgmental.

See also Hope Natural Gas Case (1944); Smyth v. Ames (1898).

FAIR-TRADE LAWS, state laws that permitted manufacturers of brand-name products and retailers to enter into contracts that set the price at which the product was to be sold by the retailer. Since these were state laws, they were not applicable to firms engaging in interstate commerce, where such contracts were considered to be a violation of Section 1 of the Sherman Antitrust Act, which prohibits actions in restraint of trade. However, concern about falling prices and failing businesses during the Great Depression led Congress to pass the Miller-Tydings Act (1937), which enabled firms to enter into such contracts whenever they sold in a state with a fair-trade law. Most states soon thereafter passed such laws.

The economic advantages of fair-trade laws are uncertain at best. In 1977, Congress repealed the Miller-Tydings Act, and vertical price fixing again became illegal.

See also McGuire-Keogh Act; Miller-Tydings Act.

FAMILY PLANNING. *See* Population Growth.

FAMILY SUPPORT ACT (1988), the first major revision to "welfare"—Aid to Families with Dependent Children (AFDC)—since 1935. AFDC served about 11 million people, or 3.8 million families, in 1989. The act toughened procedures for collecting child support from absent parents and required all states to extend income support benefits to two-parent families. In return for income support, parents had to participate in state-run Job Opportunities and Basic Skills Programs (JOBS). Belief that work is the solution to poverty underlay the legislation. The difficulty faced by low-income workers was that the federal poverty level for a family of four was considerably above what a minimum wage worker could earn in a 40-hour work week. The Senate Budget Committee reported in 1989 that over one-third of all workers earned less than the poverty-level income.

See also Poverty; Public Assistance; Aid to Families with Dependent Children; Manpower Policy.

FARM BUREAU FEDERATION, AMERICAN (AFBF) began in one county in 1911 and became a national federation in 1920. By 1980 AFBF had about 3,000,000 members, most of America's farmers, and was the largest of the several national farm organizations. AFBF actively works for agricultural policy it favors. Until about 1950 it usually supported government farm programs; since then it has emphasized individual freedom and free markets and has generally sought to reduce the role of government in agriculture. Numerous affiliates engage in the cooperative purchase of farm supplies and in providing various kinds of insurance. The American Agricultural Marketing Association organizes bargaining associations of farmers to negotiate terms of sale with buyers.

FASCISM, an authoritarian, free-enterprise system with private ownership of the means of production, essentially the same income distribution as in private enterprise, and ostensibly the same economic freedoms. Economic ideas implied in the system are: (1) the state alone has the right to determine what the national interests, defined by the totalitarian leader, require; (2) conflicting interests of all economic participants, including the state, are unified in the corporation, operating under public control; (3) strikes and lockouts are forbidden; and (4) experts take precedence over politicians. This corporate state substitutes class collaboration for class conflict. It is controlled capitalism within the framework of a self-acknowledged totalitarian state and generally occurs in advanced industrial societies. The best-known examples of fascism have been Italy under Mussolini and Germany under Hitler.

See also Centralization; Nationalism.

FEASIBLE SET, the set of choices available to a decisionmaker. In consumer theory it represents the set of all commodity bundles whose cost is equal to or less than the consumer's income.

See also Consumer Equilibrium.

FEATHERBEDDING, the enforcement by a union of work rules or practices that management deems inefficient and obsolete but that the union considers important to the workers' job security and to the union itself. The Taft-Hartley Act expressly prohibited one form of featherbedding, forcing an employer to pay for services that are not performed. Another legal precedent discouraging featherbedding is an NLRB decision that prohibited "[work the employer] . . . does not want, does not need, and is not willing to accept."

Other forms of featherbedding include preserving older methods despite technological change, keeping unneeded workers on the job, and imposing limits on the amount of work permissible per employee.

—William D. Wagoner

FEDERAL ANTI-INJUNCTION ACT. *See* Norris-LaGuardia Act (1932).

FEDERAL AVIATION ADMINISTRATION (FAA), formerly the Federal Aviation Agency, a regulatory commission created by the Federal Aviation Act of 1958. It was transferred to the Department of Transportation in 1967. The FAA is principally a rule-making and operating group as distinct from a regulatory commission. It has physical control of the U.S. airways and operates and manages the nation's air space. Safety, airway control, research and development, and airport improvements are some of the major functions.

See also Civil Aeronautics Board.

FEDERAL BUDGET. The federal government spent over $1.142 trillion in 1989, or over $4,590 for every man, woman, and child residing in the United States. The 1991 federal budget is $1.233 trillion ($1,233,000,000,000.00). This sum is over one-quarter of the Gross National Product. Not all of this large sum represents government purchases of goods and services. In fact, only about one-third of this amount is spent to purchase goods and services (mainly national defense). The rest of the budget represents transfer payments: Social Security, grants-in-aid to state and local governments, income support programs, loans to various persons and organizations,

FEDERAL BUDGET PROCESS IN THE EXECUTIVE BRANCH

and interest on the national debt.

Some expenditures are financed by earmarked taxes and channeled through special trust funds. The most important are Social Security benefits and federal highway expenditures. The remainder, about 75% of the total, is financed through general revenues and appropriated for specific uses by Congress.

Budget Process. The federal budget process encompasses program planning and operation by the executive branch, appropriation of funds by Congress, evaluation by both branches, and audit by the General Accounting Office (GAO), which reports to Congress. It is thus an integral and continuous part of the operation of the federal government.

The budgeting process in the executive branch centers on preparation of the executive budget presented to Congress by the president each January. It contains detailed spending proposals for all departments and agencies for the upcoming fiscal year.

In January, preparation of the budget for the fiscal year beginning some 18 months later begins. Within each department or agency the individual subunits begin to plan their programs and expenditure needs in accordance with guidelines from the Office of Management and Budget (OMB), an agency in the Executive Office that represents the president on budgetary matters. By May, the initial recommendations are collected and reviewed by the department for initial review by OMB during July and August. Economic forecasts for the next fiscal year (still nearly 12 months away) are provided to assess the total fiscal impact of the budget on the economy.

The president examines the OMB recommendations and issues guidelines to all departments for preparation of final requests due in September. The final OMB review occurs in October and November, at which time departments may present appeals for changes to the OMB or even to the president.

During November and December the president receives the recommendations of the OMB along with updated economic forecasts and gives final approval to the budget document that goes to Congress in January.

Appropriations. In Congress, program proposals are examined by congressional committees. Hearings are held, representatives of executive departments and other interested parties testify, and eventually the various executive programs are authorized, usually after congressional alteration. Before programs can be funded, however, Congress must also appropriate the money. Appropriations for specific programs are made after hearings and examination, most of which is handled by subcommittees of the House and Senate appropriations committees.

About 15 appropriations bills pass Congress each year. The president, lacking item-veto power, must accept the whole package contained in each bill—or veto the whole thing—even if he dislikes parts of it. Appropriations for ongoing programs are often made for more than one year, so that in any given fiscal year sizable appropriations are carried over from past years.   —*Charles W. Meyer*

See also Fiscal Federalism; Public Finance.

FEDERAL DEPOSIT INSURANCE CORPORATION (FDIC), an agency wholly owned by the United States government, whose primary function is to insure the depositors of commercial banks and savings banks. Each participant bank pays to the FDIC an annual premium of $1/12$ of 1 percent of its total deposits, in exchange for which the FDIC insures each deposit up to a maximum of $100,000 against loss due to failure of the bank. The FDIC also supervises banks to help prevent failures and assists in the liquidation of banks that do fail.

See also Bank Failure; Resolution Trust Corporation.

FEDERAL FUNDS MARKET, a privately owned network that enables banks to borrow or lend large amounts of money for very short periods. Such borrowing may become necessary if banks suddenly lose more deposits than their reserves can cover. When only a few banks are short of reserves, those banks might borrow funds from institutions that have excess reserves available. Such borrowing has become common through the federal funds market. This mechanism allows banks with inadequate reserves to replenish their reserves and honor all their demand deposit liabilities.

FEDERAL OPEN MARKET COMMITTEE. *See* Federal Reserve System.

FEDERAL RESERVE ACT (1913) created the Federal Reserve System, originally passed in response to the succession of financial crises in the United States, culminating in the crisis of 1907, which almost paralyzed the financial markets of the country. The act was the second attempt to unify the banking system of the country, the first having been the National Bank Act (1863). The Federal Reserve Act provided for the first time a national check-clearing system, a source of credit for the banking system, a flexible currency in the form of Federal Reserve notes, and central control over a large part of the banking system. The act failed, however, to provide a completely unified system, because many state banks decided not to participate.
See also Federal Reserve System.

FEDERAL RESERVE BANKS, the operating arms of the Federal Reserve System, which is the central bank of the United States. There are 12 Federal Reserve banks, each serving a Federal Reserve district. Although each bank is a separate corporation, the policy of the 12 is closely coordinated through the Board of Governors of the Federal Reserve System in Washington. The Federal Reserve banks act as bankers' banks, serving the needs of district member banks and carrying out the monetary policy of the Federal Reserve System.

FEDERAL RESERVE NOTES are issued by the 12 district Federal Reserve banks, are printed by the U.S. Bureau of Printing and Engraving, and constitute almost the entire amount of paper currency in the country. They are currently issued in denominations of $1, $5, $10, $20, $50, and $100; larger denominations of up to $10,000, formerly used, are no longer being printed. The notes are backed by United States government securities held by the Federal Reserve banks.
See also Money; Money Supply.

FEDERAL OPEN MARKET COMMITTEE. *See* Federal Reserve System.

FEDERAL RESERVE SYSTEM, a coordinated group of financial agencies that, at its highest level, acts as the central bank of the United States, issuing paper currency, supervising the commercial banks of the country, and implementing monetary policy. The Federal Reserve Act established the system (1914) and its structure has been extensively modified since, particularly by the Banking Acts (1933, 1935). As presently constituted, the system is composed of three levels: the member banks, the Federal Reserve banks and branches, and the Board of Governors. The organizational structure and functions are shown in the figure.

Member Banks. It was hoped in the beginning that all commercial banks would join the system, so that it would be a single unified association covering the whole commercial banking structure. All national banks are required to join, but state banks have the option of joining, and most have decided not to. Thus, of the 13,800 commercial banks in the United States, only 5,700 are members, of which 4,600 are national banks and 1,100 are state banks. These banks, however, account for 83% of the commercial banking business of the country, indicating that it is the small banks that have not joined, being unable to meet the minimum capital requirements of membership.

Member banks have the right to hold deposits in the Federal Reserve bank of their district, to borrow from it when appropriate, to use federal reserve facilities for check clearing and transfer of funds, to receive information and advice, and to elect directors of the district Federal Reserve bank. Members' obligations include purchase of stock of their Federal Reserve bank, maintenance of legal reserves in an amount prescribed by the Board of Governors, compliance with the regulations of the system, and subjection to examination and general supervision by the federal reserve authorities.

Federal Reserve Banks. Unlike any other central bank in the world, the Federal Reserve includes 12 nominally separate regional banks, each responsible for a specific federal reserve district. These banks (identified by the number of their respective districts) are located in: (1) Boston, Mass., (2) New York, N.Y., (3) Philadelphia, Pa., (4) Cleveland, Ohio, (5) Richmond, Va., (6) Atlanta, Ga., (7) Chicago, Ill., (8) St. Louis, Mo., (9) Minneapolis, Minn., (10) Kansas City, Mo., (11) Dallas, Tex., and (12) San Francisco, Calif. In the larger territories there are branches in addition to the head office of the bank, each branch serving a part of the larger district. The total number of branches is 24.

Each Federal Reserve bank is a legal corporation whose stock is owned exclusively by the member banks of the district in an amount equal to 6% of the individual member's capital and surplus, although only one-half of this amount has been paid in. This stock ownership gives members the right to elect six of the

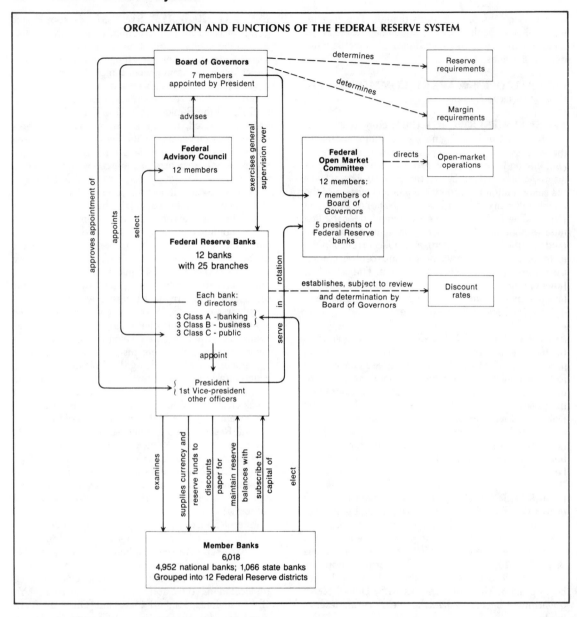

ORGANIZATION AND FUNCTIONS OF THE FEDERAL RESERVE SYSTEM

nine directors of their Federal Reserve bank. The other three directors are appointed by the Board of Governors, which is analogous to a corporate board of directors. Although the Federal Reserve banks are separate institutions, owned and controlled by the member banks of their district and responsive to local needs, the 12 banks are coordinated in terms of national policy. Since their founding, the predominance of this overall coordination has increased markedly.

Each Federal Reserve bank operates a banking business for its customers, primarily member banks, in much the way that an ordinary bank deals with an ordinary depositor. The banking activities of the system are indicated in the aggregate balance sheet of the 12 Federal Reserve banks added together.

Assets. The Federal Reserve banks hold cash and can also create Federal Reserve notes to meet the needs of their depositors. The banks also hold the international monetary reserves of the United States in the form of gold certificates (representing the actual gold stored in Fort Knox) as well as special drawing rights, a form of international money created by the International Monetary Fund.

The Federal Reserve banks make loans to member banks in temporary need of funds to meet their reserve requirements. Usually these loans are for periods not to exceed 15 days. Reserve banks buy bank acceptances, partly to put money into the market and partly to encourage the use of these instruments. The Federal Reserve banks buy obligations of various federal agencies to provide a market that will make such obligations more attractive to prospective buyers. The banks' major lending activity, however, is through the open market purchase and sale of large quantities of government securities, primarily for the purpose of implementing monetary policy.

Liabilities. The Federal Reserve banks accept deposits, primarily from members, but also from certain nonmembers for whom they have agreed to act as clearing agents, from the federal government, and from foreign central banks and governmental institutions. Because these banks hold deposits for the majority of commercial banks in the country, the Federal Reserve provides a very effective clearing mechanism by which checks that are deposited in a bank other than the one on which they are drawn can be presented for payment. The bank in which the check is deposited merely deposits it in turn in its Federal Reserve bank account, thus receiving a deposit credit and increasing its reserves. The Federal Reserve then charges the account of the bank on which the check was drawn, which loses reserves at the same time that it deducts the amount of the check from the account of the depositor who wrote it. When checks must go from one Federal Reserve bank to another, the transfer of funds between them is handled by similar deposit entries in the gold certificate account held by all Federal Reserve banks in the Interdistrict Settlement Fund in Washington. Because the Federal Reserve banks hold deposits of the federal government, all government checks are written on these accounts,

and so the system clears the vast number of federal checks directly on its own books.

Like central banks throughout the world, the Federal Reserve is a bank of issue, distributing the major portion of the nation's currency in the form of Federal Reserve notes, which are fundamentally promissory notes of the banks that issue them. Thus, they appear as liabilities in the same way that deposits do. The quantity of these notes in circulation is determined by the desire of the public to hold cash: the notes are paid out only when requested by a member bank, which obtains them by writing a check against its reserve account.

Float. The two least readily understandable items on the balance sheet are "cash items in process of collection" and "deferred availability cash items." These entries arise from the check-clearing process and are of little individual significance; for the most part they offset each other. The difference between them (float) is a form of loan by the Federal Reserve banks to their members, representing credit to these banks for checks that the Federal Reserve banks have not yet collected.

Profit. The Federal Reserve banks make a substantial profit from their operations, primarily through the receipt of interest from government securities held. A small portion of this profit is plowed back into surplus, an equivalent amount is paid to member banks in the form of a dividend on the stock they hold, and the remainder, the greater part by far, is paid to the U.S. Treasury.

Control Functions. Among the control responsibilities of the individual Federal Reserve bank, the most important is its right to change the discount rate charged on loans to members, but even this responsibility is subject to "review and determination" by the Board of Governors. The Federal Reserve banks also select the 12 members of the Federal Advisory Coun-

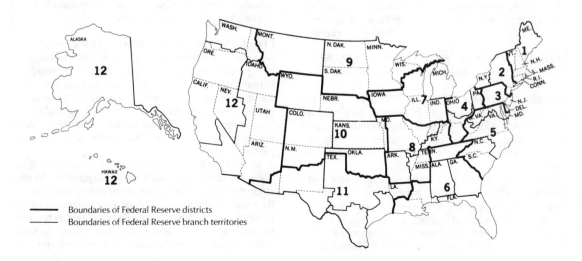

Boundaries of Federal Reserve districts
Boundaries of Federal Reserve branch territories

cil, a group of bankers that makes suggestions to the Board of Governors.

Board of Governors. At the top of the system stands the Board of Governors of the Federal Reserve System, a group of seven members appointed by the president of the United states for 14-year terms, not subject to reappointment. The Board of Governors (at first called the *Federal Reserve Board*) was originally thought of as a rather weak coordinating agency for the 12 district banks. Over time it has been given more and more power until, on paper at least, the board is the center of power, and the Federal Reserve banks are the operating arms of the system, carrying out the directives of the board.

In reality, however, the center for major policy decisions is the Federal Open Market Committee. This committee consists of the seven governors plus five presidents of Federal Reserve banks. The president of the Federal Reserve Bank of New York is a permanent member, and the other presidents serve in rotation. In practice all 12 presidents normally attend the meetings of the committee, usually held every three weeks, and participate in the discussions, although only the five official members can vote.

Legally the only significant function of the Open Market Committee is to determine at what time and in what amounts the system shall engage in open-market operations to carry out monetary policy. The Board of Governors has the sole responsibility for setting reserve requirements, and the individual Federal Reserve banks establish discount rates. Because both the board and the banks are represented on the Open Market Committee, and because it is desirable that the various activities of the system be coordinated, it is hardly surprising that they are all discussed by the committee, which makes recommendations to both the board and the banks with respect to policies generally agreed to by the committee as a whole. It is unusual for either the board or the banks to ignore the advice of the committee, which has thus become the real center of authority of the Federal Reserve System.

—*Walter W. Haines*

FEDERAL SAVINGS AND LOAN INSURANCE CORPORATION. *See* Financial Intermediaries.

FEDERAL TRADE COMMISSION (FTC) shares responsibility for enforcement of antitrust and related laws with the Antitrust Division, Department of Justice. Headed by a five-person governing body, it includes a nationwide network of staff and local agencies.

The FTC's function to counter deceptive acts and practices and anticompetitive behavior by businesses is carried out in research and investigation of specific industries, publication of findings, prosecution of violators, and promotion of voluntary compliance with the laws, especially the Clayton and Federal Trade Com-

mission Acts. To provide a preventive ingredient in administration of these laws, the commission renders advisory opinions on the legality of proposed business practices; writes advisory trade-practice rules (indicating specific practices which violate laws administered by the commission); and develops trade regulation rules which are binding on entire industries.

—*Thomas O. Depperschmidt*

See also Antitrust Division, Department of Justice; Antitrust Policy.

FEDERAL TRADE COMMISSION v. CEMENT INSTITUTE (1948), one of the Federal Trade Commission's several major challenges to basing-point pricing. The FTC charged (1) that identical pricing of cement by producers as a group lessened competition and constituted an unfair trade practice under Section 5 of the FTC Act, and (2) that the phantom freight and freight absorption entailed by the cement basing-point system constitutes price discrimination, violating Section 2 of the Clayton Act.

FIAT MONEY, paper currency that is issued under government decree without any metallic or other valuable backing and is not convertible into anything with intrinsic value. When first issued, United States notes were fiat money.

FINAL GOODS, those goods purchased for final use and not for resale or further processing. It is the sum of the value of these final goods that is used in the determination of the national income accounts. Intermediate goods are not included, because to do so would mean double counting and an overstatement of gross national products. Double counting would occur because the purchase price of the final good includes the purchased price of any intermediate goods utilized plus processing and distribution charges. Thus, if both final goods and intermediate goods were counted, the national income accounts would be exaggerated.

See also Goods; Intermediate Goods.

FINAL OFFER ARBITRATION. This form of interest arbitration has been suggested as a way to keep the two parties from taking a nonrealistic approach to bargaining because they feel the arbitrator will "split the difference." In this procedure, when an impasse has been reached, the sides put forth their final offers. The arbitrator selects one or the other but cannot modify the terms. The situation is all or nothing for the parties.

Several studies have suggested that unions' offers are more often accepted than managements'. In one study the union offers were accepted in two-thirds of the cases. While there is no certain explanation of this result, it may be that the unions have tried in the past to bluff more often and have now moved to more realistic positions in impasses. The best-known use is perhaps that between professional baseball players and management, and here the players' offers have been most often accepted.

FINAL OUTPUT. Output flows to four sectors of the economy: consumers, government, business, and the rest of the world. Purchases of output by consumers almost by definition represent purchase of final output; such purchases are made for the gratification of the purchaser. Government and the rest of the world appear much in the same way: there is no attempt at resale for economic gain, and such purchases can be treated as sale of final output.

Some expenditures of business, such as the purchase of plant and equipment or increases in inventory, can be characterized as purchase of final output, because the commodities will remain within the firm and are not intended for resale at a profit. Other business expenditures do not involve final goods. The flour purchased by a baker is intended to be part of the commodity that the baker sells to obtain revenues. The flour is a purchase of an intermediate good, rather than the purchase of a final good. The distinction between intermediate and final output purchases of business firms is not unambiguous. The necessity of distinguishing between the two types of purchases arises because the inclusion of intermediate output as final output will grossly overstate—in effect, double count—the magnitude of goods and services produced. —*Frank J. Bonello*

FINANCE PAPER. *See* Commercial Paper.

FINANCIAL INTERMEDIARIES, institutions that assemble the funds of one group of persons (savers) to lend to a second group (borrowers) at interest covering the cost of operation. Although savers could lend directly to borrowers, as when a person finances a mortgage for his or her neighbor, borrowers and lenders generally find it more convenient to use intermediaries because they (1) constitute a visible market readily accessible to all, (2) minimize risk, partly by superior knowledge, but primarily by portfolio diversification as a result of their larger size, and (3) accommodate the desires of savers—who frequently want to invest small sums for short periods—with those of borrowers—who are likely to want larger and longer loans. Thus, consumers may each put $10 in a savings bank, knowing that they can get it out when they want it, and the bank can accumulate these small sums in order to make a $60,000 mortgage loan for 20 years.

The major difference between thrift institutions and commercial banks used to be that the banks offered checking accounts while thrifts could not. However, a major revision of the banking laws in 1980 made it possible for thrift institutions to offer accounts that are almost identical to checking accounts.

Savings Banks are mutual institutions operated solely in the interest of their depositors by trustees who are closely supervised by state authorities. Savings banks exist in only 18 states, primarily in the northeast, but in the areas where the banks operate, their frequently higher interest rates attract more time deposits than do commercial banks. Savings banks lend primarily on mortgages on homes, apartments, and business buildings but also hold small amounts of government and corporate securities. When commercial banks lend funds entrusted to them in the form of time deposits, the banks are acting just like savings banks.

Savings and Loan Associations are found throughout the United States, though they are smaller in the aggregate than savings banks. They may be chartered by federal or state governments, and many associations are insured by the Federal Savings and Loan Insurance Corporation (FSLIC), which is similar to the FDIC. Unlike savings banks, they do not normally accept deposits but sell stock to customers in any fractional amount desired, entering the amount in a passbook much as if it were a deposit. When a customer (since the customer buys stock, the customer is actually an owner) wants to withdraw money, the customer sells the stock back to the association at par. These associations lend almost exclusively to members on home mortgages but also hold a small amount of government securities as liquid assets. Federal associations and those state associations insured by FSLIC are supervised by the Office of Thrift Supervision, created as part of the federal government's bail-out plan when the thrift industry suffered massive losses resulting from bad real estate loans and widespread fraud and mismanagememt.

Credit Unions may also be either federally or state chartered, but they are limited to operating among an already established group, such as a labor union, church, or lodge. They also obtain their funds by sale of stock in fractional amounts and make loans only to members, usually on a short-term installment basis. Most credit unions are members of the Credit Union National Association, which is an affiliate of the Cooperative League of the United States of America.

Life Insurance Companies are financial intermediaries, because they must set aside a substantial part of their premiums to meet future claims. These legal reserves represent the cash value of each policy, which accumulates over its lifetime and which belongs to the policyholder, who can borrow against it or withdraw it at any time by lapsing the policy. Life insurance companies invest heavily in mortgages but also hold large quantities of government and corporate bonds. Even property insurance companies (fire, automobile, and so on) are intermediaries, because they also build up large cash reserves from their premiums. These companies' primary investments are in corporate stocks and bonds.

Pension Funds are a large and rapidly growing source of investment money, as they accumulate and hold regular contributions from employers and employees until disbursement is due. Pension funds may be operated by life insurance companies, federal, state, or local governments, corporations, or labor unions. The largest pension fund in the United States is the old age and survivors' insurance fund of the Social Security system. Commercial banks and, to a lesser extent, individuals act as trustees for pension funds and for trusts set up by individuals in living trust agreements or wills. The aggregate size of such trust funds is very large.

Other Savings Institutions. Mutual funds and the similar closed-end investment companies sell their own stock to the general public and use the funds thus obtained to buy stocks or bonds of other corporations. Other institutions that channel savings into the financial markets include charitable foundations and even such nonprofit institutions as colleges, which have endowment funds to invest.

Finance Companies. Personal (consumer) finance companies obtain funds from the issue of stock and by fairly continuous borrowing from commercial banks or from the capital market through the sale of commercial paper. They make installment loans to individuals to enable them to purchase household goods. Sales finance companies obtain their funds in much the same way but specialize in financing the sale of merchandise, primarily automobiles, either from the manufacturer to the dealer (in which case the dealer is the borrower) or from the dealer to the consumer.

Governmental Credit Agencies obtain funds either from general tax revenues or from the issue of their own bonds. These agencies include the Banks for Cooperatives, Federal Land Banks, Commodity Credit Corporation, Urban Renewal Administration, Federal National Mortgage Association, Veterans Administration, Small Business Administration, and Export-Import Bank of Washington. The intent of all of these agencies is to provide funds to particular groups of borrowers on better terms than in the general market.

Service Agencies are not strictly intermediaries, because they do not actually borrow or lend. Several agencies facilitate the transfer of funds by providing facilities or services to intermediaries. The stock market provides a place where buyers and sellers of stocks can meet (stockbrokers handle the actual transactions); investment banks (not really banks at all) underwrite (guarantee) and sell new issues of stocks and bonds; mortgage companies process mortgages for institutional lenders; commercial paper houses find buyers for open market commercial paper; and acceptance dealers provide a market for bank acceptances, a form of bank obligation used primarily in financing international trade.

Intermediation, the function of a financial intermediary, interposes one step between the borrower and lender of funds. To meet its costs, the intermediary introduces a spread between the interest the borrower pays and the interest the lender receives. When lenders feel that they can do without the services or the fees of the intervening institution, funds are removed from intermediaries to be invested directly. Such disintermediation occurs, for instance, when savers withdraw money from savings banks to buy government securities.   —*Walter W. Haines*

FINE-TUNING. The government fine-tunes the economy to make it function as smoothly as possible by adjusting both monetary and fiscal policies to offset even minor fluctuations in economic activity. While the Federal Reserve can alter the money supply almost daily through its open market operations, the long delay from the time fiscal policy is conceived until the time it is implemented makes discretionary fine-tuning by means of fiscal policy alone virtually impossible. Other mechanisms, such as tax rate adjustments, must also be used to counter inflationary pressures or rising unemployment.

The argument for fine-tuning is a controversial one. An ambitious policy designed to keep the economy always at the full-employment level may actually be destabilizing. There is some question as to whether the monetary and fiscal authorities should create policy at their own discretion or in accordance with some preannounced rule. One example of a preannounced rule is the constant growth rule: no matter what happens to the economy, the money supply will grow at a constant rate, say 4%. Another example would be a rule to increase the money supply by 2% for every 1% increase in the unemployment rate above 5%.

FIRM, a business concern usually involved in production. It may be a sole proprietorship, a partnership, or a corporation, and may produce one or more products. Usually, however, only one product or one type product is produced, for example, cars or steel.

A firm often belongs to a specific industry (General Motors belongs to the automotive industry). In addition, a firm very often consists of more than one plant, the physical facility where work is done.

See also Industry; Plant.

FIRM DEMAND CURVE. A firm's demand curve represents the quantities of the firm output that consumers wish to buy at various specified prices (not to be confused with the curve representing the quantities the firm wishes to sell—its supply curve). In the absence of price discrimination the firm's demand curve is also its average revenue curve.

FIRMS, CLASSIFICATION OF. *See* Theory of the Firm.

FIRM SUPPLY CURVE, a relationship between the price a firm receives for its product and the quantity it will voluntarily offer for sale. Since firms are assumed to maximize profits and since perfectly competitive firms maximize profits by producing where price equals marginal cost, the supply curve of a perfectly competitive firm is that segment of its marginal cost curve that is above its average variable cost curve. If a firm cannot receive a price that covers its variable costs, it will not produce at all. Since marginal cost curves are upward-sloping, the firm's supply curve is necessarily upward-sloping.

FISCAL FEDERALISM, the economic relationship between the various governmental units within the nation. The structure of government has both a vertical dimension—national, state, and local—and also a horizontal dimension—the interaction among different local governments, for example. There are currently just under 80,000 distinct governmental units in the United States. There is great variety in the types of services and the means of financing these services throughout the nation; there is, however, a general pattern to the fiscal structure. For example, national defense is provided strictly by the federal government, and most income maintenance programs (Social Security, AFCD, SSI) are funded mainly by the national government. State governments are the dominant

FISCAL FEDERALISM
The Federal System
(Types of Government and Numbers of Units)

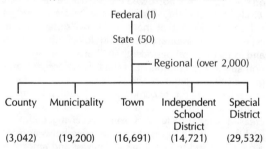

funders of public education, although much of the funding is channeled to local school districts for primary and secondary education. Highway construction is predominantly a state government activity, in which much of highway maintenance is performed by local governments.

One crucial aspect of fiscal federalism that has become increasingly important is the vast system of intergovernmental grants. In 1989, the federal government transferred over $121 billion dollars in aid to state and local governments. The largest category was for welfare-related programs. In this case, the federal grants are matched by the states, then the money is usually directly spent by the state government. Another major component of federal aid (over $30

billion) is General Revenue Sharing. This is a program of direct aid to state and local governments, based on a complex formula developed by Congress. States and localities receive proportionately more funding if their population base is relatively large, if a large proportion of people reside in urban areas, if their population is relatively poor, and if the state or locality has above-average taxes. Much of the money goes directly to cities, by-passing the state government altogether.

In the Reagan administration the trend toward increasing reliance on intergovernmental aid as a revenue source for state and local governments was reversed. Several aid programs were discontinued, and most others were scaled back. Still other special-purpose (categorical) grants were consolidated into a smaller number of "block grants." These block grants give the receiving government more flexibility in determining how the money can be spent.

In addition to federal grants, most state governments also operate large-scale grants programs. The largest category of state grants is for education. The reason for the grants is to "equalize" the ability of poorer school districts to provide education on a par with wealthier localities. Much of the impetus for these equalizing grants came about because of a series of court cases in individual states that mandated more equality in educational spending.

—*Michael S. Johnson*
See also Public Finance.

FISCAL POLICY, the use of the federal budget-making process with the intention to influence the level of economic activity in a predetermined way. In the simplest models, fiscal policy consists of changes in government spending and/or taxes in an effort to expand or contract aggregate demand with the predicted expansion or contraction of the equilibrium national income. *Contractionary fiscal policy* calls for a decrease in government spending and/or an increase in taxes (either the tax base or the tax rate). *Expansionary fiscal policy* calls for an increase in government spending and/or a decrease in taxes. In these simple models, expansionary fiscal policy is used to "cure" excessive unemployment of economic resources, and contractionary fiscal policy is used as a tool to fight inflation.

More sophisticated discussions of the effects of fiscal policy consider the effects of changes in government spending and taxes on interest rates, prices, and the level of real output and income. These considerations include the problem of "crowding out" as well as the differing effects of how a federal budget deficit is financed. Also, there is considerable discussion concerning the combined effects of monetary and fiscal policy.

Many economists continue to support the view that fiscal policy should be used in conjunction with a compatible monetary policy to stabilize the economy.

That is the practice of discretionary changes in aggregate demand to counter the undesirable effects of the business cycle. Other economists, the strict monetarists, believe that fiscal policy is more likely to be procyclical than countercyclical. They support the policy of a fixed rate of growth of the money supply and a balanced federal budget.   —*Philip W. Jeffress*

FISHER, IRVING (1867-1947), mathematical economist and early developer of econometrics, best known for his work with the quantity theory of money. His *The Purchasing Power of Money* (1911) presented the now famous equation of exchange MV = PT, where M = quantity of money; V = velocity of circulation; P = average price level; and T = total number of transactions. This quantity theory of money, given the assumption of a constant velocity, indicates the importance of the money stock in the determination of prices and the level of economic activity.

In addition, Fisher felt that business cycles were not inherent in the economic system but were the result of monetary instability. His solution was a system of 100% reserves, whereby banks would no longer be able to create or destroy money, thus eliminating a large source of monetary instability.

FITZGERALD ACT. *See* Apprenticeship.

FIVE-YEAR PLAN. *See* Planning (Centralized).

FIXED COST OF PRODUCTION. *See* Total Fixed Cost of Production.

FIXED COST PER UNIT. *See* Average Fixed Cost of Production.

FLOAT. *See* Federal Reserve System.

FLOW OF INCOME. *See* Circular Flow of Income.

FOOD FOR PEACE. *See* Public Law 480.

FORCED SAVING, a decreased consumption because of inflation's reduction of real incomes. Forced saving occurs during full employment in inflation, when business or governments bid resources away from production of consumption goods, leaving fewer, higher priced consumer goods. Compulsory saving requires people to lend to the government, as the British did through the tax collecting system during World War II.

FOREIGN AID, government-to-government transfers of resources, capital, and technology for development, usually from advanced to less-advanced nations. It is a relatively recent phenomenon, such transfers traditionally having been handled by private investors. The goals of governmental aid range from

thinly disguised bribery—to insure the friendship of potentially unfriendly nations—to the realization that world stability depends in part on the stability and growth of the "Third World," to, occasionally, humanitarianism. Bilateral (direct government-to-government) aid serves the first of these goals while multilateral aid (channeled through such international organizations as the United Nations) is designed to serve the last two. Bilateral aid is by far the largest component of the total.

Aid implies a transfer of resources leading to a balance-of-trade deficit in the recipient country. This deficit allows the importation of either investment goods to promote growth directly, or consumption goods and raw materials with which to finance domestic saving and domestic production of investment goods.

Yet, aid may not lead to investment and growth if imports are simply used to generate increased consumption rather than savings and investment. The fear of such squandering of aid has led most donors to prefer project aid—tied either to specific investment projects such as dams and steel mills or to specific products such as food stuffs and industrial raw materials. Most recipients, however, prefer program aid, a grant or loan of foreign exchange, to ease the balance of payments and domestic budget deficits, as this can be spent more flexibly to meet the recipient's needs and desires.

Aid Controls. Fear of aid misuse has also led donor countries to prefer lending rather than granting funds, on the theory that borrowed money will be used more wisely and profitably. But loans can be considered as aid only to the extent that they were "softer" (made on more concessionary terms with lower interest rates and longer pay-off periods) than "hard" loans made at non-subsidized commercial terms. Development programs seldom generate the profits expected of them, and repayment has become a serious burden for many countries. Furthermore, the flow of aid has not increased substantially, and some receiving countries find their net aid inflow (the difference between new aid inflows and the outflows of interest and amortization of old loans) dwindling.

Finally, balance of payments deficits in donor countries have inspired the tying of aid to purchases in the donor country, so increased aid is balanced by increased exports. The price of goods purchased from the donor country is often higher than the prices available elsewhere in the world, and the value of tied-aid is consequently reduced.

Aid Goals. A United Nations conference set as a goal the transfer of 1% of the gross national product of advanced nations to less developed countries (LDCs) in the form of aid. There is a limit, however, to the rate at which LDCs can absorb money, and the shortage of managerial, planning and entrepreneurial resources endemic to most LDCs places a limit on the amount of money that any LDC government can manage effectively. Since most reach their absorption limit quite rapidly, increasing attention has been paid to technical assistance—the training of managers and civil servants in modern techniques, the development of new techniques of planning and development administration, and the development of new production technologies more amenable to the LDC environment—in order to improve the absorptive capacity of LDCs.

—*Charles Staelin*

See also Less Developed Countries.

FOREIGN ASSISTANCE ACT OF 1948. *See* Marshall Plan.

FOREIGN INVESTMENT is accomplished through movements of capital between countries. At a given moment the net position of a country can be ascertained that will reflect the total value of its outstanding investments abroad and of outstanding foreign investments made in it. Foreign assets are matched against liabilities to foreigners. If foreign assets exceed obligations, the country is a net international creditor; in the opposite case it is a net debtor. This *balance of international indebtedness* reflects the net results of past transactions on a country's capital position; the balance of payments shows international transaction over a given period of time. If a country is a net creditor on long-term capital account but a net debtor on short-term account (lending long and borrowing short) the liquidity position in its balance of payments will come under strong pressure.

See also Balance of Payments; Capital Account; Capital Movement.

45° LINE, also aggregate supply curve or Z curve; a line that bisects the right angle at the origin of a graph or diagram of the relationship of consumption, investment, government spending, and net exports to aggregate income. Along the line (aggregate), income equals the sum (aggregate) of its components (C, I, G, X—M).

FOURIER, FRANÇOIS MARIE CHARLES (1772-1837), an eccentric utopian socialist who early in his working career was ordered to destroy a stack of goods in order to maintain its market price. He concluded that a better system could be devised than the wastefulness of a free-market economy. His objective was the harmonious development of human nature, free from restrictions imposed by law and convention.

To attain this, Fourier projected and planned in minute detail communities, called phalanxes, that were to operate on a cooperative basis. After abundant subsistence had been provided, the output of the phalanx was to be divided into 12 shares; 5 to labor, 4 to capital, and 3 to the managers (talent reward). Machinery would keep work to a minimum. Fourier's

appeal for financing by capitalists was unheeded, but many phalanxes were organized by his followers. The best known in the United States was Brook Farm, near Boston.

See also Associationism; Cooperativism; Owen, Robert.

FRACTILE. *See* Central Tendency.

FRACTIONAL RESERVES typify the basic principle by which commercial banks create money. The reserves (cash or its equivalent) held by a commercial bank are less than (that is, a fraction of) its demand deposits. If a bank had to maintain 100% reserves, it could not lend money and, hence, could not increase the money supply. By keeping only a fraction of the total, the bank can lend the rest and expand the money supply. If the bank did not have to keep any reserves at all, it could expand the money supply without limit.

See also Monetary Policy; Reserve Requirement.

FREE ENTERPRISE, commonly, a microeconomic concept referring to a business firm privately owned and operated for a profit motive. In the free-enterprise system most of the goods and services are provided by the private sector. The free-enterprise firm is one of the basic units of the economic system, along with the other basic units, such as household, government, and labor union. The majority of goods and services consumed in the United States are produced and distributed by over 7 million private firms.

See also Capitalism.

FREE ENTRY means that a firm is free to enter a market or industry because there are no major barriers that would prohibit entry. Free entry is a characteristic of pure and perfectly competitive markets. Industries that are purely competitive usually have a large number of small firms, making it easy for an individual firm to begin operation without larger and more powerful firms forcing it to close.

Free entry is much more difficult in oligopolistic and monopolistic markets where large investments are needed, and older, more established firms have control of the market.

See also Barriers to Entry; Entry.

FREE GOODS are the few desirable things that are not scarce. You can breathe all the air you want at the current level of pollution free of cost. A free good is one for which supply exceeds demand when the price is zero.

FREE MARKET PRICES, prices established in the market without intervention by government, as distinguished from prices established or at least directly influenced by government price supports or production controls. Although price support has been the principal form of farm market intervention by government, price ceilings are also exceptions to free market prices.

The Food Security Act of 1985 was designed to restore U.S. competitiveness by reducing price support levels over time. During the Uruguay round of the General Agreement on Tariffs and Trade (GATT) negotiations (completed in 1990), U.S. trading partners agreed to achieve a substantial, progressive reduction in agricultural support and protection to correct and prevent distortions in world agricultural markets.

See also Price-Support Programs.

FREE RESERVES are excess reserves of commercial banks minus borrowings at the federal reserve banks. They therefore indicate what excess reserves would be if banks repaid the reserves that they had borrowed, and they represent the basic potential of the banking system to create money.

If free reserves are negative, that is, if borrowings exceed excess reserves, they are called *net borrowed reserves*. Under these conditions the banking system is under pressure to reduce the money supply.

See also Discount Rate; Multiple Expansion of the Money Supply.

FREE RIDER, an employee who refuses to join a union (and pay dues) but who enjoys the employment benefits secured by the union. A union is required by law to represent fairly all employees in the bargaining union, as determined by the National Labor Relations Board (NLRB). For this reason and others, unions want every employee to be a dues-paying member of the organization. When the closed shop was outlawed, unions turned to the union shop as the best way to ensure 100% membership. When a number of states passed right-to-work laws permitted by the Taft-Hartley Act of 1947, the free-rider problem was greatly intensified. The "scab" and the free rider rank high on unions' list of undesirables.

FREE-RIDER PROBLEM is a situation that arises because nonpayers either cannot be excluded from the benefits of a good, or else the government chooses not to exclude nonpayers from the benefits of a good. The free-rider problem implies that markets will not be able to uncover consumers' true preferences for an item, but, unfortunately, political mechanisms may also fail to do so. As a result, pure public goods may be provided in inefficient amounts.

See also Pure Public Good.

FREE-TRADE AREAS. *See* Customs Unions and Free-Trade Areas.

FREQUENCY DISTRIBUTION, a way of organizing observations to show the number of times a certain result or class of results was observed. It may be presented as a table, a bar graph (histogram), or a line graph (frequency polygon). Dividing the frequency of a class by the total number of observations yields the relative frequency distribution. By the law of large numbers, the relative frequency distribution is an approximation of the probability distribution.

See also Probability; Probability Distribution.

FRICTIONAL UNEMPLOYMENT is the loss of work that occurs from time lost changing jobs. No matter what the economic situation, from full employment to depression, there will always be frictional unemployment because there will always be mobility. People change jobs for such reasons as better opportunity, health, or family problems, and very often this involves relocation which is time-consuming. In addition, workers who have been fired or laid off must usually spend time finding new jobs. The fortunate thing about frictional unemployment is that it usually is temporary.

See also Unemployment of Labor.

FRIEDMAN, MILTON (1912-   ). A member of the Chicago school in the tradition of Irving Fisher and Frank Knight, Milton Friedman is among the most controversial and prolific contemporary economists. His support of the quantity theory of money and the position that monetary rather than fiscal policy is the most effective means of controlling the level of economic activity have caused economists to reevaluate their positions and stimulated one of the most important discussions of modern economics. In addition, Friedman has been an outspoken critic of the Federal Reserve System and its monetary policy.

His book, *A Monetary History of the United States 1867-1960* (1963), written with Anna Schwartz, is one of the most important modern works in monetary economics. Friedman has also made significant contributions to the theory of consumption, the methodology of economics, and price theory. *A Theory of the Consumption Function* (1957) presents Friedman's hypothesis that the difference found by Simon Kuznets between long- and short-term consumption behavior can be explained by the division of income into permanent and transitory elements.

In *Essays in Positive Economics* (1953), Friedman suggests that to operate effectively, economics must analyze and present alternative policies free of any normative judgments. He also discusses the Marshallian demand curve and makes a case for free exchange rates. Finally, Friedman's *Capitalism and Freedom* (1962) presents his suggestions for changing many current governmental programs and minimizing the role of government in the economy. His suggestions include a negative income tax, changing public education, and many more. For his many contributions to economics, Friedman was awarded the Nobel Prize in economics in 1976.   — *Clyde A. Haulman*

FRINGE BENEFITS, a labor cost to employers for payment to labor beyond regular wages and salary. Fringes usually include: time off with pay (holidays, vacations, sick leave); deferred payments (retirement pensions, supplemental unemployment benefits); and various types of insurance benefits (life, hospitalization, medical care).

To be classified as a fringe, the benefit must be paid for by the employer but not for something required by law, such as the employer's share of the Social Security tax, the payroll tax to finance unemployment insurance, or the provision of workmen's compensation insurance. Fringes may be required of the employer in the collective bargaining contract or be provided voluntarily.

FRISCH, RAGNAR (1895-1973), Norwegian economist who shared with Jan Tinbergen the first Nobel Prize in economics in 1969 for their work in developing the science of econometrics. From 1931 to 1965 he was professor of economics at the University of Oslo, where he was a founder of the Econometric Society and editor of the journal *Econometrica*.

FULL-COST PRICING, a pricing policy used in some imperfectly competitive market structures. Under this type of pricing policy, a profit rate is usually predetermined by the firm. Price is then set equal to the average cost of the product plus the established profit rate.

Also sometimes referred to as cost-plus pricing, full-cost pricing is often used in those industries that compete for government contracts.

Under certain circumstances when full-cost pricing is used, price is set equal to average cost, allowing only for normal profits.

FULL EMPLOYMENT. The availability of employment opportunities for all workers has been a fundamental objective of the United States since the Employment Act of 1946. Full employment is sometimes said to have been reached when at least 96% of the labor force is employed. Recently economists have accepted as full employment an unemployment rate of 5 or 6%. The reason that 100% employment is not necessary is that there will always be some *frictional unemployment* due to mobility of the labor force, technological changes, growth, and some *hard-core unemployment* of those unable to find jobs in the best of times. Much of frictional unemployment is temporary and does not represent a serious problem.

See also Frictional Unemployment; Hard-Core Unemployment; Labor Mobility.

FULL EMPLOYMENT AND BALANCED GROWTH (HUMPHREY-HAWKINS) ACT (1978), augments the Employment Act of 1946. The Employment Act of 1946 established the Council of Economic Advisers and provided the basic guide to national economic policy until 1978. It gave national priority to the dual goal of full employment with price stability.

The Humphrey-Hawkins Act identifies several specific economic priorities and objectives, directs the president to establish goals and objectives based on those priorities, and creates procedures to improve coordination and development of economic policy by the president, Congress, and the Federal Reserve System.

Section 206 provides the president with standby public employment powers. The jobs provided must be productive and in the lower range of skills and pay, and must not draw workers from the private sector into public employment projects. The administration must identify and target areas of high unemployment, and focus on the victims of structural unemployment, those whose skills are absent or who have skills that have become obsolete. Critics of the act say that it creates a disincentive to invest in the private sector and that it lessens the efficiency of the marketplace.

FULL-EMPLOYMENT EQUILIBRIUM, or "natural level" of employment, the level of national income at which there would be no involuntary unemployment in the long run. It does not mean that there is no unemployment, but rather that only voluntary unemployment exists due to labor mobility and the job search process. Also, the full-employment equilibrium is that level of aggregate national income at which there will be no change in the inflation rate.

Up to the full-employment level of income, employment increases (decreases) in direct proportion to the level of income (employment is a result of, or a function of, income). At and above the full-employment level of income, employment cannot increase further because the labor force is fully employed.

Full-employment equilibrium is important for two reasons: (1) it is the highest level of GNP obtainable without inflation or changes in productive capacity. (2) It is the most desirable level of income, because the economy is producing as much as it can without inflation, and there is no unemployment other than frictional and structural unemployment. The full-employment level of income is seldom an equilibrium level of income. Aggregate demand may be too high or too low to result in an equilibrium income that is also the full-employment income.   — *Anne Mayhew*

See also Frictional Unemployment; Production Possibility Frontier; Structural Unemployment; Underemployment of Productive Capacity.

FUNCTION, a relationship or correspondence between variables such that each value of one is associated with a single value of the other. In $y = f(x)$, to be read "y equals f of x," the function $f(x)$ states a rule by which values of x are transformed or mapped into values of y. The result is a set of ordered pairs of values of x and y, which can be graphed on the rectangular coordinate system. Because the value of y depends on the chosen value of x, y is called the dependent variable and x the independent variable.

There are several standard operations or rules by which x is transformed into y. Some are: constant functions ($y = 7$); linear functions ($y = a + bx$); quadratic functions ($y = a + bx + cx^2$). Other common functional forms are rational functions (formed by taking ratios), such as $y = a/x$, and transcendental functions, such as the exponential ($y = e^x$), logarithmic ($y = \log x$), and trigonometric ($y = \sin x$). Finally, a single dependent variable can be a function of several independent variables: $y = g(x_1, x_2)$. The function g is then a set of ordered triples (x_1, x_2, y) in three-dimensional space. —*Carlisle E. Moody*

See also Variable.

FUNCTIONAL DEPENDENCE. *See* Functional Relationship.

FUNCTIONAL DISTRIBUTION of income in the United States is distribution according to the resource classes into which resources are divided: (1) compensation of employees; (2) business and professional proprietors' income; (3) farm proprietors' income; (4) rental income; (5) interest; and (6) corporate profits.

See also Factor Incomes.

FUNCTIONAL FINANCE is a budgetary principle that calls on the government to determine appropriate fiscal measures according to the way these measures function, disregarding the balancing of the budget. Promotion of the macroeconomic goals of low unemployment, stable prices, and growth are the primary concerns of functional finance. This principle rejects the balanced budget or any other established budget policy; it is more concerned with aggregate economic performance and economic growth objectives. It has its base in Keynesian economic theory.

FUNCTIONAL RELATIONSHIP, an association between a dependent and one or more independent variables. For one variable it is written in the general form $y = f(x)$. A statement of functional dependence is a statement of causality, an assumptin that x determines y. In some cases the function can be inverted to yield $x = f^1(y)$ so that y becomes the independent variable. The notion of causality remains, but the direction is reversed. Some common functional relationships in economics are the consumption function $C = f(Y)$, where C is consumption and Y is dispos-

able income, and the demand function $Q = f(P)$, where Q is quantity demanded and P is price.

See also Function; Variable.

FUTURE MARKETS, organized markets in which a trader can buy a contract that requires him to take delivery of some quantity of a commodity, currency, bond, or stock at some date in the future at some specified future price. As an example, a trader may sign a contract to buy one million bushels of wheat at $2.00 a bushel in 3 months' time. If the price of wheat in 3 months is less than $2.00, the buyer has lost; if, however, the price of wheat is above $2.00, the buyer has gained. The seller of the contract has assured herself that she will receive $2.00 a bushel for her wheat, but she does not benefit if the price goes up. The buyer could lose a great deal if the price goes down but could also gain a great deal if the price goes up.

The sale and purchase of futures contracts are one way that people in business manage risk. There are organized futures markets for many agricultural commodities; metals, such as gold and silver; stocks; bonds, called financial futures; and foreign currencies, called currencies futures.

See also Commodity Markets.

GAINS FROM TRADE. Trade confers net gains to the participants, gains that consist of improvements in human welfare that are not available in the absence of trade. Since natural resources such as petroleum and diamonds are distributed unevenly over the globe, many products are not available without trade. These include agricultural products such as bananas, cocoa, coffee, and sugar.

Nations gain from trade even when domestic production is possible because trade enables specialization, reduces opportunity costs, and increases economic efficiency. Comparative advantage says that mutually beneficial trade can always take place between two countries whose pre-trade cost and price structures differ.

Trade stimulates economic growth and development through the spread of new technologies, and technological advances tend to feed on one another. Higher levels of national production and income stimulate saving and investment in new technology and in research and development, so the process is self-reinforcing.

Trade also increases the interdependencies of the world. The increases in welfare that result from trade will be sacrificed if trade relations are broken due to war or other hostilities. Thus trade creates an incentive to maintain an atmosphere of international cooperation.

If the gains from trade lead to the maximization of human welfare, why is free trade the exception rather than the rule? Governments justify import barriers to protect infant industries until they become mature enough to compete in the world market, to prevent the loss of jobs to foreign competition, to protect industries vital to the national defense, or to reduce vulnerability to fluctuations in world prices that might result from overspecialization in one or two export products.

Most economists argue that the gains from trade are relatively larger for small countries, but others find evidence of a net transfer of wealth from less developed countries (LDCs) to the industrialized world widening rather than narrowing the gap between rich and poor. Within countries, the benefits from trade may accrue to a minority elite, leaving the welfare of the majority unaffected, or even negatively affected when scarce resources are diverted from production for domestic consumption to production for export. Small countries that rely heavily on trade are more vulnerable to fluctuations in the business cycles of larger countries, fluctuations over which they have no control.

It is possible that trade stimulates research and development in new technologies only in relatively mature economies, because the export products of LDCs are usually low-technology agricultural or natural resource products.

A trade-oriented development strategy may create technological dependence, because the trends of technological change are determined by the world's technological leaders. Producers of exports must follow exogenously determined patterns of taste if they cater to a foreign market. Often export products are those appropriate for high-income countries, rather than the low-income domestic population of most LDCs. Poor consumers tend to adopt lopsided consumption patterns, spending limited incomes on inappropriate luxuries rather than on goods to meet their basic needs.

Even where appropriate technology has proven viable in international markets, its viability is short-lived unless continuous technological change maintains its competitiveness, because it is competing with advanced technologies that are changing all the time. Market pressures push appropriate technologies in the very directions they were designed to avoid: increasing scale, specialization, and capital intensity.

Import substitution has been suggested to reduce overdependence on trade. But some economists argue that import substitution merely shifts the production site of industrial luxury goods to the LDCs, exacerbating lopsided consumption and siphoning off savings that could be invested in production facilities for products more suited to the tastes and preferences of the local market. —*Susan Hunt*

GALBRAITH, JOHN KENNETH (1908-   ), professor of economics at Harvard. He served as ambassador to India and was chairman of the Americans for Democratic Action. Galbraith is best known for three

John Kenneth Galbraith, professor of economics at Harvard.

books, which have all created substantial controversy. His *American Capitalism: The Concept of Countervailing Power* (1956) suggested that the existence of large producers in some industries generated the development of large buyers and large unions to counteract their power. *The Affluent Society* (1958) attacked the conventional wisdom of traditional economics and suggested that the development of a large and active public sector is necessary if America is to solve its problems.

Finally, *The New Industrial State* (1967) suggested that the businessman discussed by traditional economic theory has been replaced by a technostructure of specialists because of the complexities of modern economic organizations. The evolutionary approach of Galbraith's work places him as a descendant of the institutionalists, and while many economists do not completely accept his views, he has raised important questions and challenged many aspects of modern economics. Included among Galbraith's other publications in the field are *Economics and the Public Purpose* (1973) and *The Age of Uncertainty* (1977).

—*Clyde A. Haulman*

GANDHIAN ECONOMICS. Gandhi developed an economics that combined ethics with economics in order to maximize the welfare of all. His system was committed to the pursuit of truth (dharma) rather than self-interest (artha). This puts Gandhian economics at odds with Western economics, which is founded on the principle that as individuals act in their own self-interest, they will produce maximal social utility.

Gandhi sought not only material sufficiency, but dignity and socially and morally meaningful work for all, especially the less privileged. His economics was founded on the idea that employers should exhaust the local labor supply before searching for more distant workers, even at the expense of productivity. Workers should sacrifice utility for loyalty and be reluctant to leave local employers for more attractive jobs elsewhere. The supposed gains to be made from violating these principles (lower commodity prices, higher quality, better wages) would be more than offset by the community decay that would result from the pursuit of individual advantage. He aimed to enrich and stabilize the traditional economic life of the villages by promoting labor-intensive technologies. The pursuit of "progress" would only demoralize the many, making them helpless dependents of the rich and expert few.

See also Appropriate Technology.

GENERAL ACCOUNTING OFFICE (GAO). *See* Federal Budget.

GENERAL AGREEMENT ON TARIFFS AND TRADE (GATT), an organization composed of most countries outside the Communist world and including all the important industrial and trading countries of the West. Since 1947, tariff negotiations involving all members of GATT have been held periodically. Their basis is the most-favored-nation principle: any tariff reduction (called a tariff concession) that one member grants to another must be extended on an equal basis to all other members. The most important negotiations in the GATT series were those conducted in 1962-1967, and called the Kennedy Round. The basis for United States participation was the Trade Expansion Act (1962), giving President Kennedy the authority to reduce any United States tariff by up to 50% of its existing level. In fact, the Kennedy Round resulted in decreases in tariffs averaging about 35% among GATT members.

GENERAL THEORY OF EMPLOYMENT, INTEREST, AND MONEY (1936), by John Maynard Keynes, stands with Adam Smith's *The Wealth of Nations* as a milestone in the development of economics. In his work Keynes emphasized the importance of full employment and stable prices as the goal of public policy and constructed a system using many analytical tools which he developed to indicate the means of obtaining such a goal.

Keynes' contribution in the *General Theory* can be divided into three parts. (1) Keynes considered the relationship between saving and investment, concluded that the two must be equal in equilibrium, and analyzed the forces which create a macroeconomic equilibrium. (2) The consumption function with its propensities was analyzed, and the multiplier relationship was made an integral part of the system. (3) The investment function as determined by the marginal-efficiency-of-capital schedule was discussed and included as an important element of the system. The theoretical developments presented in the *General Theory* provided the basis for much of modern macroeconomic theory.   —*Clyde Haulman*

See also Keynes, John Maynard.

GEOMETRIC MEAN. *See* Central Tendency.

GIFFEN GOOD, a good of which more (less) is demanded as its price rises (falls). A Giffen good is necessarily an inferior good. However, all inferior goods are not Giffen goods.

See also Consumer Equilibrium; Price Effects.

GIVEBACKS. Sometimes called "concession bargaining," giveback bargaining refers to unions being forced to give up, in periods of high unemployment, benefits obtained in earlier agreements. In the recession years of 1982 and 1983 unions gave up cost-of-living adjustments (COLAs), time off with pay, wages, and other benefits. Sometimes profit sharing, stock options, and management participation have been granted in exchange for these cuts. Two-tiered wage schedules are the most recent type of givebacks.

See also Two-Tier Wage Rates.

GLUT. *See* Excess Supply.

GNP DEFLATOR, officially called the Gross National Product Implicit Price Deflator, measures changes in the overall price level of all final purchase of goods and services in all sectors of the economy. It is calculated by combining several indexes, including components of the Producer Price Index and the Consumer Price Index, into one index and applying this index to GNP in current dollars to get a GNP figure in constant dollars, using a base year.

See also Price Indexes.

GOLD, long preferred as a basic form of money because it was desirable but scarce (hence, valuable), easily transported, divisible into small units, and rather widely available. Used as early as ancient Greece, gold replaced silver in the nineteenth century as the most popular form of coin. Today gold coin no longer circulates in any country. Although gold bullion (bars) is still used to settle balances between countries in international trade, it will probably soon no longer be used even for that purpose.

See also Gold Standard; International Monetary Fund.

GOLD CERTIFICATES, paper bills issued by the government as a receipt for an equal quantity of gold held in its vaults. The certificates were first issued by the United States in 1866 to save wear on gold coins and became the most important type of currency between 1910-1920. The certificates were recalled in 1933. They are now held by the Federal Reserve banks as nominal title to the gold stock in Fort Knox, but it is illegal for a private citizen to use the certificates as money.

The Treasury is a large owner of gold and buys and sells at a fixed price when transactions are permitted. The Treasury maintains deposit balances at Federal Reserve banks and draws on these accounts to pay for gold imports. These checks are deposited in commercial banks and clear through Federal Reserve banks via increasing commercial bank deposits and decreasing Treasury deposits. The Treasury can restore these balances by issuing gold certificates to the reserve banks, whose assets of gold certificates increase as Treasury deposits rise. If no certificates are issued, the import is "free gold." The reverse of the above occurs with a gold export. Prior to 1968 a certain percentage of gold certificates were required as backing for U.S. currency.

See also Gold Standard.

GOLDEN AGE OF AGRICULTURE, a nostalgic term for the five years 1910-1914, a favorable period for farming, which more or less by accident became the base period for parity price calculations. The period followed two decades of gradual inflation, the closing of the frontier, and slow improvement in the relation of farm product prices to other prices. Technological advances that were soon to start a long-term decline in the number of farms and farmers had not yet appeared. Farm people were one-third of the population and politically powerful. But rural health and educational services were poor, much farm work was sheer drudgery, and the per capita purchasing power of farm people probably was not more than one-third that of 1970.

See also Parity Prices.

GOLD-EXCHANGE STANDARD. *See* International Monetary System.

GOLD MARKET. *See* Two-Tier Gold System.

GOLD STANDARD, a monetary system under which a country (1) defines its currency as a given weight of gold; (2) provides a mechanism by which anyone can exchange any form of domestic currency and gold at the official value; and (3) does not interfere with domestic or international movements of gold. Britain was the first nation to adopt the gold standard (1821), and the last countries in the world to abandon the system did so in 1936. Although the gold standard still has its advocates, it is unlikely to be revived. The "discipline" of the gold standard, which its advocates cite as its most appealing feature, actually led to its abandonment.

Given that the world money supply is fixed in the short run due to a fixed supply of gold, a nation's money supply depends upon its trade balance with other nations. Consider David Hume's famous specie-flow analysis. When a country has a favorable balance of trade, gold flows in to pay for the excess of exports over imports, and the gold inflow expands the domestic money supply, which drives up prices and incomes. The price increases make exports more costly to foreigners and exports drop; the income increase brings in more imports for two reasons: there is increased purchasing power, and foreign goods are relatively cheaper. In addition, interest rates fall in the country gaining gold and rise in the nation losing gold, causing capital to flow to the latter. Although these automatic results provide the discipline to ensure that the trade balance will be restored and the rate of exchange will fluctuate little, the cost of external stability is drastic domestic fluctuation in prices, incomes, interest rates, and other major economic variables.

See also Exchange Rate.

GOMPERS, SAMUEL (1850-1924), London-born American labor leader who believed in the policy of conservatism in labor unions, was an advocate of autonomous craft unions, and vehemently opposed the more militant characteristics of the Knights of Labor and the Industrial Workers of the World.

After only four years of elementary school, Gompers became an apprentice to a cigar maker. Then, in 1863, he sailed with his family to New York City and became a member of the Cigar Makers International Union. He aided in the development of Local 144 of the union and was elected president in 1874, but he was ousted seven years later by socialist opponents.

Gompers helped to found the Federation of Organized Trades and Labor Unions and was a leader in the movement to organize a national federation of labor unions. In 1886 the American Federation of Labor (AFL) was formed and Gompers became its president. He held this position (with the exception of one year when he lost to a socialist) until his death in 1924, when he was succeeded by William Green.

During World War I, President Wilson appointed Gompers as a member of the Advisory Commission to the Council of National Defense. In 1919, at the Versailles Peace Treaty, he served as Chairman of the Commission of International Labor Legislation.

GOODS are the tangible products of the economic system that possess the ability to satisfy human wants or desires. Because the term can be applied in so many different ways, economists attempt to classify goods in several manners.

Durable or Nondurable. At one level goods are classified as either durable or nondurable. A durable commodity provides use to its purchaser over extended periods of time or performs a particular function repeatedly. An automobile is a durable good and an orange is a nondurable good. The distinction between durable and nondurable is not always precise. Clothing is classified as a nondurable good, although it may provide use for as long as an automobile.

Consumer or Producer. At another level, goods are classified as consumer or producer. A consumer good is a commodity purchased by an economic unit for its personal gratification; a commodity purchased by an economic unit for economic gain is a producer good. Because producing and consuming units are distinguished on the basis of their motivation, the classification depends on the motivation of the purchaser of a particular good. An automobile purchased by an individual for his own pleasure is a consumer good, but it is a producer good if purchased for use by his firm. The categories are often combined: consumer durables, consumer nondurables, producer durables, and producer nondurables.

Final or Intermediate. Another means of classifying goods involves their position in the production process. If the good is purchased for final use so that no further processing is to be done, or so that the good is not to be resold, it is called a final good. If, however, further processing of the good is needed before it reaches its final form, or if it is being purchased for resale purposes, it is called an intermediate good.

Necessities or Luxuries. Economists also classify goods by whether they are necessities or luxuries. In addition, the income elasticity of demand is used to indicate whether goods are inferior, normal, or superior. If, as income increases, consumers purchase proportionally less of a good, it is considered inferior. When income increases and consumers purchase proportionally more of the good, it is considered superior. If the proportion of income spent on a good remains the same as income changes, that good is considered a normal good.

Problems. While placing goods within these various classifications can be quite useful, some problems arise. Goods considered luxuries 50 years ago may be necessities today. A final good in some situations may require further processing in others. Thus, economists must be careful when classifying goods and should be prepared to change the classification when the situation dictates.

—*Clyde A. Haulman and Frank J. Bonello*
See also Real Flow; Services.

GOODS AND SERVICES refers to tangible and intangible commodities capable of satisfying human wants. Goods are the tangible commodities and include, for example, cars, food, and clothing. The intangibles, such as catering, chauffeuring, and banking, are called services.

See also Goods; Services.

Tractors such as these are examples of durable goods. An economic system must determine how many goods of each kind to produce.

GOSPLAN, the state planning committee of the Soviet Union, responsible for designing, disseminating, administering, and evaluating the economic plans based on the directives given to it by the government's council of ministers.

See also Planning (Centralized).

GOVERNMENT-CONTROLLED ECONOMY, a system in which the state controls economic activity. Economics may be evaluated in terms of the degree of preference given the consumer in relation to that given the state. In a laissez-faire economy there is consumer's preference only, and in a dictatorship model of communism, state preference only; between are varying degrees of government control and influence.

In mixed economies of regulated capitalism, there is influence but no control except during crisis. In market socialism, as in Yugoslavia, there is control, but consumer preferences exert influence. In centrally-planned command economies, as in the U.S.S.R. and China, state preferences have priority. In these latter examples and in fascism, the government owns and/or controls productive factors and centrally plans their use to meet state preferences.

See also Centralization; Command Economy; Fascism.

GOVERNMENT CREDIT AGENCIES. *See* Financial Intermediaries.

GOVERNMENT SECURITIES, promissory notes issued by the government to those sources from whom it borrows money. In this country the term, often shortened to "governments," normally refers to obligations of the federal government. State and local governments (cities, school districts, and so on) also issue bonds, tax anticipation notes, and other forms of debt, usually termed municipals.

Government Debt and Deficit. When the government spends more than it receives in taxes, the difference (government deficit) must be financed by borrowing. When taxes exceed expenditures, the surplus may be used to repay part of the debt. Deficits are very common during wars, when expenses rise rapidly and taxpayers are unwilling to bear the cost. Deficits may also be deliberately incurred as a matter of fiscal policy to raise national income and employment, but surpluses, whose function is to restrain inflation, are harder to achieve, primarily for political reasons: elected officials are more likely to want to cut taxes than to raise them and to increase expenditures than to reduce them.

Types. The kinds of securities that the federal government issues to finance its deficits come in a wide variety of forms. Perhaps the best known securities are *savings bonds,* sold only to individuals and nonprofit organizations on a discount basis. In 1985, a series EE savings bond with a face value of $50 could be purchased for $25 and redeemed 8 years later for the full face value. If savings bonds are held beyond maturity, interest continues to accumulate and is added on to the maturity value. These bonds cannot be sold, but they may be redeemed through any bank. The other nonmarketable securities, as well as convertible bonds, are special issues sold to rather limited groups of investors under special conditions and frequently on a one-time basis. These securities are not normally available to the general public.

Marketable securities cannot be redeemed prior to maturity, but they may be sold to anyone at a price agreeable to both parties. The minimum denomination is $1,000; more frequently the securities are sold in amounts of $25,000 to $1,000,000.

Treasury bills are short-term marketable securities most commonly with a maturity of 91 days, but sometimes of 182 days or a year. Treasury bills (T-bills) are sold every week at auction. Bids are accepted from the highest downward until the sum of the accepted bids equals the amount the government wishes to sell. Treasury bills bear no interest. A yield is earned because the bills are issued at a discount from their face value and are redeemed at full face value at maturity. Treasury bills are liquid assets and are held in sizable quantities by commercial banks as secondary reserves.

Government notes are intermediate-term securities with maturities of 1 to 10 years. Traditionally, notes bear a stated rate of interest, which is paid semiannually. Notes are sold at auction like Treasury bills.

Government bonds are long-term securities, with maturities of more than 10 years, usually around 20 years. These certificates also bear a fixed rate of interest, payable every 6 months on presentation of the appropriate coupon, which is attached to the bond. Marketable bonds are a rather small part of the total debt.

At one time the government also issued *certificates of indebtedness,* short-term securities with maturities of about a year, frequently issued to fall due on tax dates. These securities have now been replaced by the longer issues of Treasury bills.

Ownership of the Debt. Government securities are owned by individuals and almost all types of organizations. Government agencies themselves hold substantial sums of government securities, primarily in the form of special issues that are not available to the public, but also including some marketable issues. The biggest official holder is the Social Security Trust Fund, and other trust accounts similarly invest their available funds in governments.

The Federal Reserve banks are another semi-governmental group that holds large amounts of these securities, purchased in the open market (not directly from the Treasury) to expand the money supply and help stimulate the economy. More than half of the Federal Reserve holdings are short-term securities, maturing within 1 year.

Commercial banks themselves hold large quantities of government securities of various maturities, thus providing not only income but also liquidity, because they can be sold at any time in an active market and with a minimum of risk. Other financial institutions hold them for similar reasons, as do ordinary corporations when they have excess funds to invest.

Individuals hold more securities than either the Federal Reserve banks or the commercial banks, primarily in savings bonds and other long-term bonds. The large holdings of foreigners and international institutions are primarily the result of the recent dollar glut. Foreigners have acquired large quantities of dollars, which earn interest on government securities.

—Walter W. Haines

GOVERNMENT SPENDING, expenditures by government at federal, state, and local levels on services and currently produced goods. Transfer payments, such as interest on national debt or unemployment insurance, are listed as expenditures in government budgets as they are usually presented. But in the theory of national income determination, government spending does not include transfer payments because they are not demands upon productive capacity requiring the employment of labor, production of goods, and consequent payment of incomes, although transfer payments will affect the disposable incomes of households and, thus, consumption spending.

GRADUAL SOCIALISM. *See* Evolutionary Socialism.

GRANGE, NATIONAL. The Grange began in 1867 as the Patrons of Husbandry and was a vigorous part of the populist movement opposing trusts, railroads, and hard money policies in the latter part of that century. At present, the Grange is strongest in a bloc of states east and north from Ohio and on the West Coast. It apparently ranks second in size among general farm organizations but is much smaller than the American Farm Bureau Federation.

GREEN REVOLUTION, refers to the hoped-for increases in agricultural production in developing countries to be brought about through the introduction of Western technology and chemical fertilizers. Following promising results in the 1970s, the program came to be widely considered a failure as it created dislocation, greater centralization of agriculture, environmental degradation, reliance on foreign markets and products, and disruption of traditional agriculture.

See also Appropriate Technology; Buddhist Economics; Schumacher, E. F.

GRESHAM'S LAW states that "bad money drives out good." Sir Thomas Gresham was a sixteenth-century financial adviser to Queen Elizabeth I of England. He noticed that when coins were debased—when the percentage of base metals relative to gold and silver was increased—older and relatively purer coins disappeared from circulation. People will spend coins that contain less valuable metal than their face value and save or hoard coins that contain metal of a value closer to their face value.

GRIEVANCE ARBITRATION is very often the final step in the grievance procedure. If a worker's grievance cannot be settled through the normal procedure, both union and management may agree to submit the matter to an outside neutral party, an arbitrator, for settlement. The arbitrator's power is confined to the specified agreements of either the collective bargaining contract or the contract between the arbitrator and the parties involved. The arbitrator's decision is usually abided by unless she exceeds her authority, or is found guilty of fraud, misconduct, or unfairness.

Arbitration, being more flexible and less expensive than court proceedings, is usually preferred by both labor and management. Arbitrators are usually chosen from the American Arbitration Association, the Federal Mediation and Conciliation Service, or an agency of the federal, state, or city government.

GRIEVANCE PROCEDURE, a provision in the collective bargaining contract or company rules that is used to settle disputes without the use of a strike when issues arise concerning problems of interpretation of the contract or implementation of certain clauses. The grievance procedure provides the means whereby a worker with a complaint or problem involving management is assigned a representative who is responsible for protecting the rights of the worker as well as for bringing the grievance to the attention of manage-

ment. Typically, there are three or four steps in the procedure with grievance arbitration, using an outside arbitrator, as the final step. This allows a communication channel between labor and management, and protects the worker from having to go through the supervisor with whom he has a grievance in order to make his complaint known.

GROSS INVESTMENT, or GROSS PRIVATE DOMESTIC INVESTMENT, a comprehensive measure of all nongovernmental spending for new buildings, machinery, vehicles, and inventories. Gross investment, a major component of GNP, tends to fluctuate from year to year depending on whether the private sector of the economy expects economic expansion or contraction.

GROSS NATIONAL PRODUCT (GNP), the sum of the values of all goods and final services produced in any given year. Final services, such as a barber's or a lawyer's, are included explicitly as part of GNP. Services of workers who help produce products need not be explicitly included, because the value of their services is already counted as part of the goods that they help to produce. GNP is composed of three broad types of goods: (1) private consumer goods; (2) private investment goods, including producers' buildings, machines, and materials; and (3) government goods, such as national defense and education.

GROSS NATIONAL PRODUCT

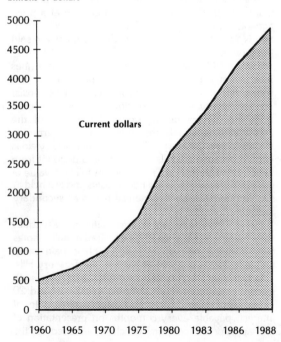

Billions of dollars

Computation. The expenditures approach measures the expenditures on consumer, investment, and government goods. The total of these three expenditures is not quite GNP, because it measures production rather than expenditures. For example, some goods (imports) are purchased by Americans but are produced by foreigners. Other goods (exports) are produced by Americans but are not purchased by them. GNP is, therefore, the sum of expenditures plus net exports (exports minus imports).

The income approach computes GNP by measuring the stream of income derived from the production of the total product. For each dollar of product produced, the producers have certain expenses: wages, rent, interest, indirect business taxes, and depreciation charges. Profits are what is left after expenses. GNP is the sum of the values of the products produced by all producers, or expenses plus profits.

Significance. Because GNP measures a nation's total product, it is, in some sense, a measure of the nation's economic well-being during any given year. Furthermore, comparisons of a country's GNP over the years measure the national rate of economic growth. International comparisons of economic growth may also be made by comparing GNP trends for various nations. Because the output of a nation at any given moment varies closely with its level of employment, GNP statistics may be used to throw light on employment levels and trends. A group of related concepts, such as net national product, national income, and disposable income, are also very useful for many analytical purposes. Recently there has been some criticism because GNP does not take account of "bads" (that is, environmental pollution and resource exhaustion) in addition to the production of goods.   —*Allan B. Mandelstamm*

See also National Income Measurement; Net National Product.

GROSS PRIVATE DOMESTIC INVESTMENT. *See* Gross Investment; National Income Determination.

GROUP PROFIT MAXIMIZATION. *See* Joint Profit Maximization.

GROWTH, in a macroeconomic sense, indicates the increase in the Gross National Product in a country that occurs over time. There are several ways in which a country can grow. First, labor power can be improved through education and training, which aids both the quantity and the quality of production. Second, improvements in productive techniques allow for greater output with given quantities of resources. In addition, the accumulation of capital is an investment into the production possibilities for future consumption and growth. Lastly, the price mechanism plays an important part in growth by channeling resources into alternate uses.

GUARANTEED ANNUAL WAGE, an assurance by an employer to his employees of a certain amount of wages for a certain number of weeks of work (usually 40 or more) in a year. Therefore, any employee forced to work fewer hours or weeks is still guaranteed a certain amount of money. The amount of money and number of weeks guaranteed are determined through the collective bargaining process.

Collective bargaining for guaranteed wages began in the 1890s with the wallpaper industry. It was slowly negotiated in several other industries, but it died with the Depression of the 1930s. In the 1950s, the United Automobile Workers (UAW) sought to bargain with Ford Motor Company for a guaranteed wage. Although the UAW did not succeed in getting the guarantee, they did get the alternative of supplemental unemployment benefits.

Since the 1950s, however, management resistance to guaranteed wages has increased, and the movement seems to have been slowed. The current trend is not in terms of a management guarantee of wages, but of a guaranteed income, which is administered by the government.

HANSEN, ALVIN HARVEY (1887-1975), best known for his interpretations of Keynes's *General Theory* and his efforts to gain general acceptance of Keynes's theory in the United States. Expanding and refining various elements of the Keynesian system, Hansen's work provided the foundation for a generation of American economists.

Hansen's most original contribution was his discussion of the problem of secular stagnation in a mature economy. While he has been greatly criticized for his position that only governmental action could stop the drift of a free-enterprise system toward stagnation, Hansen's discussions opened the consideration of a population growth and resource availability in the economic growth process.

See also Secular Stagnation.

HARD-CORE UNEMPLOYMENT, a term used to describe the unemployment problem of a certain group of workers who, due to problems of an emotional, physical, or mental nature are unable to secure employment even when jobs are available. These people are usually handicapped by such problems as a lack of sufficient education or skill, an emotional inability to handle a job, or a physical disability. Often the hard-core unemployed are from poor socioeconomic backgrounds and are members of minority groups. Special provisions were made for the hard-core unemployed in the Manpower Development and Training Act of 1962, to help train or retrain this group so that their employment opportunities may increase.

See also Employment; Unemployment of Labor.

HAYEK, FRIEDRICH VON (1899-   ), has made

important contributions, in the tradition of the Austrian school, to the history of economic thought, the theory of business cycles, and capital theory. Most significant are (1) the overinvestment hypothesis of the cause of downturns in economic activity during the business cycle; and (2) the introduction of a production period to the theory of capital.

Hayek's later career has been characterized by an adherence to laissez-faire and the belief that the impersonal nature of the market is preferable to any form of governmental intervention. In *The Road to Serfdom* (1944), Hayek also attacked growing statism on the political grounds that totalitarianism was the inevitable outcome. For his many contributions, Hayek was awarded the 1974 Nobel Prize in economics.

See also Overinvestment Theory of Business Cycles.

HICKS, JOHN R. (1904-1989), one of the most important contributors to modern microeconomic theory. In *Value and Capital* (1939), Hicks attempted to reconstruct demand theory based upon indifference curves. While many of his developments did not fundamentally alter the theory, his emphasis upon the general equilibrium analysis of Leon Walras and Vilfredo Pareto, and upon its extension to capital and interest, has seriously challenged Marshall's partial-equilibrium analysis. In addition, the concepts of complementarity and substitution were developed by Hicks.

Hicks's *Theory of Wages* (1932) was a refined statement of a marginal-productivity theory, and his "Mr. Keynes and the 'Classics'" (1937) was one of the earliest attempts to reconcile the work of Keynes with the Neoclassical system. For his many contributions Hicks was awarded the 1972 Nobel Prize in economics.

HIGH MASS CONSUMPTION. *See* Stages of Growth.

HISTORICAL CONSUMPTION FUNCTION. *See* Consumption, Time Series.

HISTORICAL SCHOOL. Beginning with the works of Friedrich List and Wilhelm Roscher in the middle of the nineteenth century, the Historical school continued until the early part of the twentieth century making important changes in the study of economics. The most significant aspect of the school was its evolutionary approach: that economics as an area of study must be considered in conjunction with other social phenomena.

The school was generally critical of the abstract, deductive methods of classical economists and marginalists, feeling that inductive studies of society dealing with a mass of information were a more fruitful approach. This difference led to the famous methodo-

logical debate between historicist Gustav Schmoller and marginalist Carl Menger. The outcome of the debate is the generally held position that economists must consider both methods, accumulating information and developing methods to analyze the information.

See also Sombart, Werner; Weber, Max.

HISTORIC COST. *See* Original Cost.

HOLDING COMPANY, a single firm which owns other companies for the express purpose of exercising control over their management. A holding company is usually formed when the managers of several firms find it more advantageous to cooperate closely with each other without giving up each firm's individual identity. The holding company will then control all of the companies. Holding companies are especially important in the banking industry. The reason for this historically was to get around many banking regulations—such as unit banking, restrictions against out-of-country branching, and restrictions on providing non-banking services.

HOPE NATURAL GAS CASE (1944), case in which the Supreme Court abandoned its previous efforts to review specific formulas for determining fair return on fair value, such as original cost or reproduction cost, and adopted the "end result doctrine." The Court promised to henceforth concern itself only where the end result of regulation failed to cause the firm to (1) operate successfully; (2) maintain financial integrity; (3) attract capital; or (4) compensate investors for risks assumed. Regulatory commissions were to ascertain if these standards were met, with potential Court review, hence restoring much commission latitude.

See also Fair Return on Fair Value; Original Cost; Rate Base; Smyth v. Ames (1898).

HORIZONTAL MERGER, a combination of firms on the same plane or level of competition, that is, firms producing and selling in the same market. A horizontal merger has more direct adverse effect on competition than other forms (conglomerate, vertical), since it immediately reduces the number of independent producers of similar or identical products.

See also Celler-Kefauver Act; Clayton Act; Conglomerate; Merger.

HOURS OF WORK has been a major concern in the past. As far back as 1840, efforts were made to limit the number of hours that women and children could be allowed to work. In 1989, the average work week in manufacturing was 41.0 hours, but in the early 1900s wage earners averaged from 54 to 60 hours a week. In the early 1930s, state governments began to enact protective labor legislation in regard to working hours, and in 1938 Congress passed the Fair Labor

Standards Act which established the 40-hour work week. From this emerged the concept of overtime pay.

HOUSEHOLD, a statistical concept that refers to a living unit functioning as an economic unit. It can consist of a single person living alone, a married couple, or a complete family, but whatever its composition, each such unit will have a source of income and responsibility for its disposal. Thus, the concept can be used to measure, estimate, or predict the quantitative economic consequences of such disposal. For example, the number of households can be of value in predicting the scope of the market for a new consumer durable good. The estimated net increase in the number of households (household formation) enables the economist to forecast the demand for new housing, schools, and health facilities, as well as the sales potential for existing consumer goods, among other things.

U.S. HOUSEHOLDS
(IN MILLIONS)

HOUSEHOLD DEMAND. *See* Consumer Demand.

HUMAN CAPITAL refers to the expenditures that improve the individual in the system in order to increase his or her worth to the society. For the advanced economies of the Western world, the expenditure is normally in the form of educational programs designed to prepare one for employment.

Generally, the greater the investment in human capital made by society, the more wealthy the society. The simple relationship between educational expenditures and per capita incomes is strikingly clear. One study has suggested that this investment is growing much more rapidly than investment in physical capital in the United States.

The less developed nations face their most troublesome problems in this area. The human resource, in both the educational and physical aspects, is often unsuited for work in a fast moving industrial job. Yet, capital to develop this important resource is often difficult to find: steel mills are easier to find, or finance, than schools.

HUMAN RESOURCES. The resources available to a society that may be used to further the goals of that society include the size and the abilities of its population. While natural resources are valuable and necessary, more and more attention has been given to the quality and quantity of the human resource. For this reason, both the developed and the less developed nations of the world are concerned with the development of the human resource factor in economic growth.

HUMAN RESOURCES: TOPIC GUIDE

For concepts closely related to that of human resources, see the articles on HUMAN CAPITAL and LABOR SUPPLY. To pursue some of the problems bearing on the human factor of production, consult the articles on UNEMPLOYMENT OF LABOR, and STRUCTURAL, TECHNOLOGICAL, and HARD-CORE UNEMPLOYMENT. Some of the programs for developing human resources are described in MANPOWER POLICY.

The relationships of these and other articles pertaining to human resources may be seen in the Subject Map accompanying the article on LABOR MARKET.

A number of studies have shown the value of investment in human resources, and most point up clearly the return to be gained from such an expenditure. One study indicates that a nation poor in natural resources but rich in human ones can develop, while none poor in human resources but rich in natural resources have done so. Japan, perhaps the classic case in point, has become an advanced, industrial, wealthy nation by extensive development of its human resources. Lacking most of the natural resources many other wealthy nations take for granted, Japan has given a great deal of attention to its human resources and has earned its position among the advanced nations.   —*William D. Wagoner*

HYPERINFLATION, or RUNAWAY INFLATION, a

condition in which prices rise faster and faster: people rush to get rid of money before it buys even less. Eventually, the system can break down entirely, with people resorting to barter. Classic examples are Germany in 1920-1923 and Hungary in 1946. More recently, Brazil's inflation rate rose in the late 1980s until it exceeded 2,000 percent per year. In 1990, a new government instituted severe austerity measures and restricted access to money, bringing inflation under control but threatening massive unemployment.

HYPOTHESIS, a stated belief concerning a statistical population; for example, that mean family incomes are different in Philadelphia and in Atlanta. Statistical inference can be used to test such an hypothesis to determine whether any observed difference is reasonably attributable to chance.

The testing procedure begins with a null hypothesis and an alternative hypothesis. For example, the null hypothesis is that the true mean incomes are equal and the alternative is that they are not equal. When we reject the null hypothesis we accept the alternative.

See also Inference; Significance; Population, Statistical.

IMPERFECT COMPETITION occurs in those markets that are characterized by barriers that affect the free flow of goods and services found in pure and perfectly competitive markets. The most important barriers are barriers to entry of new firms into the industry. There are essentially three types of imperfectly competitive markets: monopolistic competition, oligopoly, and monopoly.

Under monopolostic competition there are only a few things that impede pure competition. The main difference is that product differentiation occurs. By means of advertising and variations in the quality and design of a product, a seller can persuade buyers that products essentially the same in nature are really very different. This occurs often in the food processing and clothing industries.

Oligopoly refers to a market with only a few sellers, where the actions of one firm almost always affect all other firms in the industry. Thus, because there is a certain amount of interdependence among the sellers, oligopolitic industries have a direct influence on price. Informal collusion, although illegal, sometimes occurs in industries of this nature.

The purely monopolistic market consists of only one firm that has supreme control over the product and, therefore, the selling price.

All of these imperfectly competitive markets lack one or more of the conditions of a purely competitive market: product homogeneity, smallness of individual firms in relationship to the market, freedom of exit from and entry into the market, and mobility of both resources and goods and services to move among alternative uses. If any of these conditions is not met, there is imperfection in the market, and the pricing mechanism then relies on other means than simple supply and demand.   *—William D. Wagoner*

See also Perfect Competition.

IMPLICIT COSTS. *See* Imputed Costs.

IMPLICIT RENT. Economic rent is rather difficult to identify in practice. The payment to a resource may be labeled as wages, profits, or interest, and yet some portions of the payment may be in excess of the minimum necessary return to keep the resource in the current use in the long run and, hence, be an economic rent. Implicit economic rent is the portion of wages, profits, and interest which is, in fact, an economic rent, even though it is not so designated. Almost all economic rent is implicit rent.

The future rents of physical capital and land may be capitalized in the marketplace so that current values of these assets reflect future expected implicit rents.

—John P. Formby

IMPORTS, debit items in the balance of payments of a nation. Imports are deducted from exports to give a favorable or unfavorable balance of trade. Imports of goods and services include all debit items in the current account. Unlike other imports, capital imports, both short- and long-term, are credits in the balance of payments.

When a nation imports from abroad, domestic income earned from adding to the supply of domestic goods is spent on goods manufactured in another country and the supply of domestic goods available for purchase is increased. These effects act as contractive forces on the domestic economy: imports have the same effect as savings; both are treated as leakages in the domestic and foreign trade multipliers. Increases in income call forth increased savings and increased imports, depending on the marginal propensity to save and the marginal propensity to import: national income growth is dampened as part of any increase is siphoned off from the income stream. Imports are

At food or other specialty shops, consumers can choose among imports from dozens of countries.

easy to understand as leakages, because the value added by manufacture (increase in GNP) accrues to the exporting country; imports can be an effective anti-inflationary measure.

Trade patterns among countries, especially import and export consideration, are readily available in published statistics. World trade data show imports exceeding exports, exports being recorded FOB (free on board at port in the exporting country) and imports being recorded CIF (cost, insurance, and freight paid by importers and due upon arrival in the importing country). Insurance and freight are important elements of income to the nations providing them ("invisible" services on its balance of payments). The United Nations and the International Monetary Fund are important sources of information on world trade.
—*John R. Matthews, Jr.*

See also Balance of Payments; Balance of Trade; Exports; Visible Goods and Services.

IMPUTED COSTS, or IMPLICIT COSTS refer to payments for internally owned factors of production. Payments to factors external to the firm, such as wages to laborers or rent to landowners, are explicit costs. Economists maintain that both kinds of cost are important. If an owner of a business fails to consider her own time and effort, or that she is forgoing interest on the money originally invested, she is neglecting imputed (implicit) wages and interest, respectively. These must, in the long run, be considered if the business is to make a rational decision regarding continued operation.

INCENTIVE PAY is a form of wage payment related not to the amount of time worked but to the amount of output produced by a worker. This type of pay is common in the apparel and textile industries. Piecework, where a worker is paid for each piece of work done, is a principal type of incentive pay. A second type is the group incentive plan where bonus payments are given to individual groups for special accomplishments. This is sometimes done on a plant-wide basis to keep competition alive. In sales, the incentive payment is usually in the form of commission.

INCOME EFFECT, the change in demand for a commodity as a result of a change in the consumer's income. If the income effect is positive, the respective good is said to be superior or normal; if the effect is negative, the good is said to be inferior.
See also Consumer Equilibrium; Giffen Good.

INCOME ELASTICITY OF DEMAND, the responsiveness in the quantity demanded of a product to the income changes of the purchasers, measured by a coefficient that is calculated by dividing the percentage change in quantity demanded by the percentage change in income. The commodity in question may be classified as either income elastic or income inelastic according to the value of the coefficient. Income elasticity coefficients for normal goods will be positive, indicating that as income rises, the quantity demanded rises. However, some income elasticities are negative, which indicates that the quantity demanded moves in a different direction from income changes. Commodities with negative income elasticities of demand are called inferior goods.

INCOME MAINTENANCE. During the Great Depression there were no government programs to help people maintain some form of income. Therefore, legislation of the 1930s was aimed at helping essentially four groups of people to maintain an income. These groups were the aged, the unemployed, the disabled, and the children of poor families (non-farm).

The most important legislation for these groups was the Social Security Act of 1935. Its compulsory Old Age, Survivors, and Disability Insurance (OASDI) provides income to retired or disabled workers and to the survivors of a deceased worker. In addition, the worker receives an income (unemployment compensation) if he loses his job through no fault of his own.

Relief or income maintenance funds are provided through programs sponsored by federal, state, and local governments. In addition to government insurance programs such as OASDI, many welfare programs assist the poor, such as Aid to Families with Dependent Children.

INCOME OF UNINCORPORATED BUSINESS is income from individual proprietorships and partnerships—farmers and other self-employed individuals and professionals. A good deal of their income is return for land, labor, and capital they provide for their own business, but national statisticians treat it as profit.
See also Profit System.

INCOME REDISTRIBUTION. In a pure market economy with no taxes or transfer payments, the income of each household would be wholly from earnings of factors of production. Thus, distribution of income would be determined by the distribution among households of owned income-producing property and labor skills. Households with insufficient factor endowments would have to rely on private charity or face starvation. Society may choose to guarantee a socially determined minimal standard of living for all households through money transfers (public assistance and social insurance) or transfers in kind (food, free medical care, and subsidized low-income housing).

Since roughly 30% of U.S. income is collected as taxes, the tax structure can be designed to alter considerably the distribution of income. By adopting progressive taxation, the percentage of income paid in taxes will rise as income rises. High-income households will thus bear a disproportionate share of the tax burden, and the relative gap between families with high and low income will be less after taxes than before.

Income Redistribution Caused by Inflation occurs because inflation changes the real income, or purchasing power, of individuals. For example, people with fixed incomes, such as pensioners, are penalized by inflation because they cannot buy as many goods and services as before inflation began. Inflation benefits debtors at the expense of creditors, lessening the power of the money paid back from its value when borrowed. Inflation also lessens the value of savings.

—*Charles W. Meyer*

See also Public Assistance; Taxation.

INCOMES POLICY: TOPIC GUIDE

For aspects of economic stabilization closely related to incomes policy, consult the articles on WAGE-PRICE GUIDEPOSTS and WAGE-PRICE CONTROLS. For the broad context in which an incomes policy becomes relevant, see the articles on INFLATION and STABILIZATION POLICY.

The student will also find it useful to consult the Subject Map accompanying the article on PRICE LEVEL for other entries related to Incomes Policy.

INCOMES POLICY, any policy that has an effect on real income, the purchasing power of individuals' money incomes. For example, if a man makes $8.00 an hour and can buy a loaf of bread for $.80, he has a purchasing power of 10 loaves of bread for every hour he works. If, however, the price of bread rises to $1.00 a loaf and there is no increase in salary, his real income has decreased to only 8 loaves of bread an hour.

Real income is essentially a function of the money wages and the general price level. A change in either direction of one of these factors, without a corresponding change in the second factor, changes real income. Therefore, policies that affect wages or prices are incomes policies. Two incomes policies that have been used on the national level to help curb inflationary pressures have been wage-price guideposts and wage-price controls.

Wage-price guideposts are voluntary guidelines for changes in wages and prices. There are no penalties for violation. The first national guideposts were set up in 1962 during the Kennedy administration and proved to be very effective. In 1969 and 1970, with inflationary pressures beginning to mount, new wage-price guidelines were established under President Nixon. However, these guideposts did not meet with the same success as the earlier ones, and in August 1971 Nixon announced a 90-day freeze, which held all wages and prices constant in the hope of relieving some of the pressures of inflation.

—*William D. Wagoner*

INCOME TAX. *See* Corporate Income Tax; Personal Income Tax; Taxation; Taxes.

INCREASE IN DEMAND, the shifting outward and to the right on the Cartesian plane of a demand curve. A given demand function is constructed under ceteris-paribus conditions. However, when demand functions are examined over time, it becomes apparent that the determinants (income, tastes, prices of related commodities, expectations) of the position of a given demand curve do not, in fact, remain constant; techniques for deriving subsequent demand functions are necessary.

For example, for normal goods an increase in consumer income will cause demand to increase: a new demand function will be defined with larger amounts of the commodity being purchased at every existing price. If a product becomes more fashionable, there will be an increase in demand. If the price of a substitute good rises, the demand for X will increase. If the price of a complementary good falls, the demand for X will increase. Finally, if purchasers anticipate future increases in the price of a commodity, then they tend to increase their current purchases, causing the demand to increase.

See also Consumer Demand; Decrease in Demand; Demand Curve.

INCREASE IN SUPPLY means that quantity supplied will be greater at every price than it was previous to the change in circumstances. Graphically, the supply curve shifts outward to the right. If a technological change occurs for a firm, then conceivably the marginal product of labor will not be higher for every man. Given constant wage rates, marginal cost will now be lower at every output. Hence the marginal cost curve (supply) falls; costs of production have been lowered. Due to the decreased marginal costs the firm will willingly, and profitably, offer a given output at a lower price than it would have previously.

INCREASING-COST INDUSTRY, one in which expanded resource usage leads to increases in resource prices. Either the resources used by this industry are specialized or this industry is extremely large relative to others. An increase in the demand for the product will, in the short run, cause prices to rise, and individual firms will increase output and receive excess profits. Entry will bid resource prices up for old as well as new firms. The industry cost curves will rise; entry will cease when all firms have a minimum average cost equal to the new price. The supply schedule for this industry will therefore be positively sloped.

INDEX NUMBER, a percentage or ratio of two observations, the denominator being the base item in a cross section or the base period in a time series. The observations could be prices, quantities, or values. If average annual earnings in manufacturing are $22,023 and $32,065 for 1980 and 1987, then the 1987 index of manufacturing earnings with base 1980 (100) is $32,065/$22,023 x 100 - 146. Thus, one can tell at a glance that average earnings rose 46% from 1980 to 1987.

Some commonly used index numbers are the Consumer Price Index and the Index of Industrial Production. These are composite indexes, made up of a variety of objects. The Consumer Price Index, for example, summarizes the price movements in approximately 400 items. To construct a composite index we must decide what items to include and measure their relative importance. A weakness of such index numbers is their inability to allow for quality changes.

INDEX OF LEADING ECONOMIC INDICATORS, an index that includes 12 economic variables that have been found to have a historical tendency to precede the turning points of the level of Gross National Product. The index is a composite of those 12 indicators.

INDICATIVE PLANNING is a French attempt to coordinate the economic activities of various sectors of their economy so that specific shortages, surpluses, and bottlenecks can be avoided. Leaders of government, industry, and labor unions meet regularly to exchange information and negotiate targets for industrial production. Planning expanded under the presidency of François Mitterand, who was elected in 1981. Although indicative planning worked fairly well from the mid-1950s until the mid-1970s, the French economy faltered in the early 1980s, and France shifted to a somewhat greater reliance on markets in the mid-1980s, while denationalizing some major enterprises.

INDICATORS are statistical time series, or groups of series, used by economists to predict future economic activity. Although there are multitudinous time series covering most components of the economic system, most indicators may be categorized as coincident, lagging, or leading.

Leading indicators are indispensable to economic forecasts and public and business decisions. However, during expansion, they tend to turn downward several months before a true peak has been reached, while in a recession, leading indicators tend to turn upward a month or two before the aggregate economy. *Lagging indicators* show probable movement of certain economic components and tend to be slightly more predictable. *Coincident indicators* generally move in agreement with the aggregate economy and are useful approximations of the present state of the economy. In order to obtain a reasonably complete picture of the stage of the business cycle, one must compare the three types of indicators.

INDICES are series of statistical observations used as measurements of specific economic activities. In the United States the majority of indices are published, monthly or quarterly, by the U.S. Department of Commerce. The function of these indices is to measure the current levels of inflation, unemployment, investment, consumption, and output.

Among the most widely used and discussed indices are the Industrial Production Index, the Producer Price Index, and the Consumer Price Index. Other important indices are New Business Starts, Construction Contract Awards, and Department Store Sales. Specifically, the Industrial Production Index is a monthly measurement of total physical output based on manufacturing, mining, and the utilities industries. The Producer Price Index is a monthly measurement of price changes for a representative group of 2,000 commodities from agriculture and industry. The Department Store Sales Index is a monthly measurement of sales volume and indicates the consumer's extreme sensitivity to changes in the general business situation.

In addition to indices for major economic activities, there are indices for individual items, product classes, industries, and industrial groups.

INDIFFERENCE CURVE, or ISO-UTILITY CURVE, the locus of points in the commodity space representing bundles with equal utility. Any two points on the curve represent bundles between which the consumer is indifferent. An indifference curve has a negative slope.

INDIFFERENCE MAP, a diagram containing several indifference curves for bundles with various amounts of commodities X and Y. Indifference curves are negatively sloped, and they do not intersect or touch one another. The farther an indifference curve is from the origin of the map, the higher is its level of utility; thus $U_3 > U_2 > U_1$. The convexity of the indifference curves shows the principle of diminishing marginal rate of substitution.

INDIRECT DEMAND. *See* Factor Demand.

INDUCED INVESTMENT, investment that occurs because demand is expected to exceed current productive capacity. High current levels of demand will not induce investment unless they are expected to continue for long enough to make the investment profitable; conversely, expectations of higher future demand will induce investment even when current levels of demand are low. Thus, induced investment depends more on belief than on actuality.

See also Autonomous Investment.

INDUSTRIAL DEVELOPMENT BOND (IDB), debt instrument issued by state or local governments or government agencies. IDBs are used as incentives for the location of firms and the creation of jobs.

INDUSTRIAL MOBILITY OF LABOR. *See* Labor Mobility.

INDUSTRIAL POLICY. The stagflation of the 1970s was interpreted by many to be an indication of profound structural change in the U.S. economy, which appeared to be moving away from traditional basic industries (steel, automobiles, manufacturing) toward a service economy. Productivity growth was only one-third the rate it had been in previous decades, and real wages in the 1970s actually declined. A national industrial policy, or reindustrialization, was called for to counteract these changes by means of government support of targeted industries. Resources would be directed toward industries where productivity was the highest, linkages to the rest of the economy were high, and future competitiveness was important. It was also argued that industries supported by foreign governments should also be supported by the United States.

Proponents of a national industrial policy want a coherent set of long-run policies to promote economic growth and the international competitiveness of U.S. industries. Opponents maintain that free markets will provide the necessary investment mix in various industries and that a national industrial policy will only misallocate resources to politically powerful, heavily unionized industries.

INDUSTRIAL PRODUCTION INDEX, a monthly measurement of physical output, compiled and published by the Board of Governors of the Federal Reserve System. The Index covers approximately 35% of total U.S. output and includes a representative group of over 200 products from manufacturing, mining, and public utility industries. This index, which fluctuates more widely than most other measures of economic activity, expresses current output as a percentage of annual production levels during the 1967 base period.

See also Business Cycles, Measurement; Indices.

INDUSTRIAL UNION. Because of the mass production technology of American industry, it has often become necessary to break down what were formerly highly skilled operations into somewhat minute tasks. Workers therefore often develop expertise in tasks that, although important in a particular industry, may be useless in other industries. For this reason, these workers often organize on an industry-wide basis for bargaining purposes.

Because industrial unions often have the power to literally shut down an industry's operations, they usually are very powerful in negotiations over wages and other benefits. Two examples of powerful industrial unions are the United Automobile Workers and the International Brotherhood of Teamsters.

INDUSTRY, in price theory, the term most often used to identify a certain segment of productive enterprise, such as the steel industry or the aluminum industry. Individual business firms that produce the same or

**INDUSTRY
DISTRIBUTION OF BUSINESS FIRMS: 1986**

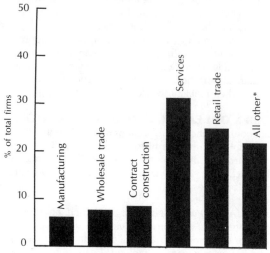

*Includes transportation, finance, insurance, agricultural services, and mining.

similar products are grouped under the collective heading of an industry.

See also Firm; Plant.

INDUSTRY SUPPLY. *See* Market Supply.

INDUSTRY-WIDE BARGAINING occurs when a union represents the bulk of the workers in a particular industry and bargains simultaneously with all of the employers. There are few examples of complete (national) industry-wide bargaining, although multi-employer bargaining is common and there are many cases of "industry-wide" bargaining for a particular geographic sector.

Employers may prefer industry-wide bargaining because it reduces the possibility of competitive disadvantage resulting from dissimilar individual contracts. Unions may like it because it leads to wage uniformity among workers in different firms and possibly to higher settlements by "taking the wage out of competition."

See also Multi-Employer Bargaining.

INELASTIC DEMAND. Demand for a downward-sloping linear demand curve is said to be relatively inelastic if within the ordinary range of price changes the percentage change in quantity demanded is less than the percentage change in price.

Demand curves for some isolated commodities may display characteristics that differ from the typical demand curve. A demand curve for a commodity may intersect the quantity axis at some positive quantity demanded and proceed to rise from that quantity with an infinite slope. That is, the demand curve will appear vertical, implying that a given quantity of the good will be demanded regardless of price. An example of a vertical demand curve is an essential medication, such as insulin, required to sustain life regardless of the price. No substitute is available for a good with a perfectly vertical demand curve. The elasticity implication for this class of demand curves is that any percentage change in price will evoke no percentage change in quantity demanded. This demand curve is hence said to be perfectly, or totally, inelastic.

—Robert L. Brite

See also Demand Curve; Elastic Demand; Elasticity of Demand.

INELASTIC SUPPLY. The supply of a product is said to be inelastic, over some small price range, when the computed coefficient of elasticity is less than 1. Theoretically all coefficients less than 1, down to negative infinity, would be described as inelastic. Of course, the smaller the coefficient the less elastic is supply. The implication of the term is that over given price ranges for certain commodities the firms in question (or the industries) are better able to react to price changes due to changes in demand. Certain characteristics of the firm or industry imply that an increase in output will cause significant diminishing returns and marginal cost will rise rapidly.

INFANT INDUSTRY. If an industry has large potential economies of scale, prices and costs are much higher when the industry is small than they will be later, if growth can occur. Hence, latecomers to the industry may need tariff protection in the early stages of growth until they can compete with established foreign rivals.

INFERENCE, in statistics, refers to the process of estimating the true population values on the basis of experimental or sample values. To find the mean income of nonwhite families living in Boston, for example, we could poll every such family and compute the mean income. This could be expensive or simply impossible. Alternatively, we could select a sample of a few such families and from the sample mean infer the population mean income.

See also Population, Statistical; Sampling.

INFERIOR GOOD. *See* Income Effect.

INFINITE ELASTICITY. *See* Perfect Elasticity.

INFLATION, a continuously rising general price level, resulting in a loss of the purchasing power of money.

Redistributive Effects. The problem of inflation lies in its redistribution of income and wealth. For example, people such as pensioners and salaried employees, whose incomes are fixed in money terms, will be worse off than workers whose wages keep pace with inflation. Also, inflation redistributes income from creditors to debtors as debts are repaid in dollars whose purchasing power has declined. Because the elderly depend most heavily on monetary assets, savings, and pensions for income, there is a redistribution from the old to the young in inflation. Further, because real estate prices tend to rise with the general price level, there is a redistribution of income from renters to homeowners, from the poor to the less poor.

The Record. During the nineteenth century and even up to World War II, periods of inflation alternated with periods of deflation, lending support to the observation that prices were stable in the long run.

INFLATION: TOPIC GUIDE

Inflation is a major concept related to many other terms and concepts in macroeconomics. For the closest of these, see PRICE LEVEL, BUSINESS CYCLES, and BUSINESS CYCLES, PHASES. For some of those aspects of inflation most relevant to the present time, see PHILLIPS CURVE and SECTORAL INFLATION. For methods of dealing with inflation, see STABILIZATION POLICY, MONETARY POLICY, and INCOMES POLICY.

The Subject Maps accompanying the articles on BUSINESS CYCLES, FEDERAL BUDGET, MONEY, and PRICE LEVEL show many other articles touching on inflation.

However, since World War II, prices have been rising continuously in almost every country.

Causes and Cures. Inflation is caused by aggregate demand, which is greater than aggregate supply at full employment output (demand-pull inflation), or by what have come to be called supply shocks (cost-push inflation). The excess demand at full employment output sets off higher prices and output in the short run, followed by further pressures on prices because of price expectations that adjust to actual prices. Any attempt by policy-making authorities to maintain output above the full employment, or natural, rate can be successful only at the expense of building in higher rates of inflation. As the adjustment process takes place, prices will continue to rise until the long-run equilibrium is reached at the same full employment level of output. Inflation that has come to be expected can be "cured" only by a reduction in aggregate demand that will lead to a period in which output is below the full employment level.

UNEMPLOYMENT AND INFLATION RATES: 1948-1989

UNEMPLOYMENT RATE

INFLATION RATE

Percent

Percent

Supply-shock inflation is the result of some phenomenon such as the poor agricultural harvest of 1973 (a temporary shock) or the quadrupling of energy prices following the OPEC oil embargo, also in 1973. A supply shock will be followed by rising prices unless authorities reduce aggregate demand and allow the full effects of the decrease in aggregate supply to be felt in lower output and employment. An attempt by authorities to maintain the same level of output following a severe supply shock will result in inflation.

—*Carlisle E. Moody, Jr.*

INFLATIONARY GAP, the amount by which in-

tended investment, intended consumption, intended government expenditure, or any combination thereof must decrease to achieve full employment at stable prices. For example, if the full-employment stable-price level of income is $900 and the marginal propensity to consume is .75 (and, therefore, the multiplier is 4), and if at that level households spend $700, investment demand is $40, and government demand is $180—all totaling $920—there will be an inflationary gap of $5. That is, a first-stage reduction of $5 in any component of aggregate demand will lead, because of the multiplier, to a fall in income of $20 to the full-employment stable-price income of $900.

Similarly, the deflationary gap is the amount by which intended investment, intended consumption, intended government expenditure, or any combination thereof would have to increase to achieve full employment at stable prices. In the example above, the deflationary gap would be $10, if the full-employment income were $960, rather than $900.

— Walter C. Neale

See also Aggregate Demand; Marginal Propensity to Consume; Multiplier; National Income Determination.

INFRASTRUCTURE can refer to a broad range of enterprises, with perhaps two general characteristics: (1) the goods or services they produce augment the productivity of other industries; and (2) they are usually undertaken by public bodies.

Some infrastructure industries are virtually required for other production to take place; roads, railroads, electricity, water, and sewage supply are prime examples. Others, particularly the service industries, such as public health, urban transportation, education, and even housing, merely contribute to the productivity of other industries, often through an increase in the productivity of labor. The crucial role played by infrastructure in allowing other industries to operate has placed them high in developmental investment priorities. Yet the role played by infrastructure is passive, not formative: they allow other industries to exist but they do not bring them into existence.

Role of Public Bodies. Infrastructure falls normally under the responsibility of public bodies for two major reasons. The first is the existence of externalities. Often, a private firm could not afford to make all consumers pay the full value of the services consumed.

The second is the existence of economies of scale and the indivisibility of large projects, such as hydroelectric dams, where the minimum efficient size of a private firm is so large that it invites monopolies, and government regulation or ownership is thus required.

— Charles Staelin

See also Externalities; Economies of Scale.

INJECTION refers to an expenditure that has a positive effect on aggregate demand and on the equilibrium level of national income. It is the opposite of a "leakage" in the circular flow of income. Injections may take the form of increases in autonomous consumption, investment, government spending, or imports, which represent spending by foreigners. An injection stimulates the multiplier process to lead to an expanded change in the equilibrium level of national income.

INJUNCTION, LABOR. Opposed bitterly by labor, the injunction is a legal technique developed in equity courts to provide relief against continuing injury where recovery in the form of monetary damages does not suffice. If it can be proved that "irreparable damage" might occur to the requesting party unless certain acts of the defendant are stopped, an order can be issued by a judge enjoining continuation of the acts. A refusal to comply by the defending party may result in fines or imprisonment.

In the past, in cases of a union strike against management, an injunction could tie union hands while leaving employers free to discharge union members and otherwise act to destroy union organization before the union could be heard in court. Often before the court date the employer could defeat the union. Such injunctions were effectively outlawed by the Norris-La Guardia Act in 1932.

IN-KIND TRANSFERS are welfare payments made in the form of food stamps, housing subsidies, Medicaid, or educational grants rather than cash.

INNOVATION THEORY OF BUSINESS CYCLES states that scientific and technological inventions and new methods of production have a significant impact on the level of economic activity. Although external to the economic system, innovation is vital to economic growth and provides the incentive that business needs to invest in research and products in the hope of reducing costs and increasing profits. Major innovations—for example, railroads, electric power, the transistor, and nuclear power—have been observed to provide important stimulants to economic activity, causing significant increases in investment which, in turn, result in cyclical upswings.

INPUT, a concept associated with the production process. Certain factors, such as raw materials, semimanufactured goods, labor skills, and machine capability, are fed at one end into the production system, and some product emerges at the other end. The most common classifications of inputs are land, labor, and capital. Land inputs include all primary products, such as land, iron ore, or crude oil. Labor inputs encompass all human services, such as an individual's manual skills, or a person's knowledge of proper market action. Inputs of capital include all man-made aids to production, for example, a fork-lift truck or a drill press. In complex production there may be hundreds of specific inputs entering into the output of a product, such as an automobile.

INPUT-OUTPUT MODELS represent an attempt to quantify and isolate the important intersectoral flows of the economic system. Influenced by the work of François Quesnay and the general equilibrium analysis of Leon Walras, Wassily Leontief constructed a basic input-output model. Leontief divided the economy into various industries and considered the outputs, or production, and the inputs, or consumption, of each industry. Sectors such as households, government, and foreign trade were considered to be industries with their own inputs and outputs. For example, the inputs to the household sector consist of final goods and services obtained from other industries, and the outputs of this sector consist of labor and capital.

Closed Model. Leontief's basic, or closed, model assumed that all outputs of sectors became inputs of other industries. Thus, no final demand exists. Also the model assumes fixed techniques of production. This means that a fixed relationship exists between the inputs and outputs of industries so that if inputs are varied, output will vary accordingly.

Open Model. A more general, or open, input-output model divides the economy into two parts. The first part includes all industries that are functionally related in that they purchase from and sell to each other various intermediate goods and services. The second part of the open model includes the sectors where the industries sell their final goods and services and where those industries obtain their primary inputs, or factors of production. The open model thus allows economists to isolate the relationships among producers in the first part of the model and to view the relationship between producers and those who supply resources and purchase the final output (household, governments, and the rest of the world). Like the closed model, the open model also assumes fixed production techniques.

Uses. For economic planners the information and relationships demonstrated by the models are important. For satisfying a given or planned level of demand, the necessary inputs can be isolated. Also the models can be quite useful for regional planning where the region may have different techniques of production or consumption behavior than the nation as a whole. However, input-output models can only be used in industrial nations; their assumption of fixed production techniques ignores technological change, and the mass of data needed to prepare the model may be difficult to obtain.   —*Clyde A. Haulman*

INSTALLMENT CREDIT CONTROLS (consumer credit controls) prescribe the minimum down payment and the maximum repayment period on installment loans to consumers in order to reduce the amount of borrowing by consumers. These controls were established by the Board of Governors of the Federal Reserve System under the War Powers Act (1941) and the Defense Production Act (1950) and published as Regulation W. They were discontinued in 1952.

INSTITUTIONALISM. One of America's early original contributions to economic thought, the institutional school studied the economy as a whole with the emphasis upon institutions and their role in the economic system. The inductive methodology of institutionalism was adopted from the historical school but

was generally more liberal and democratic. The institutionalists were also concerned with income and wealth distribution and considered that disequilibrium was the normal state of the economy rather than the equilibrium conditions discussed by neoclassical theory.

Major early figures of the school were Thorstein Veblen, first of the institutionalists, and Wesley Mitchell, instrumental in the founding of the National Bureau of Economic Research and in the use of inductive statistical studies. While much of institutionalism has been incorporated into the mainstream of economics, modern economists, such as Gunnar Myrdal and John Kenneth Galbraith, are in many ways descendants of Veblen.

See also Historical School.

INTENDED INVESTMENT. *See* Investment Schedule; Marginal Efficiency of Capital.

INTERDEPENDENCE, OLIGOPOLISTIC. Because in oligopoly market structures there are only a few firms selling, the actions of each firm affect every other firm in the industry, resulting in oligopolistic interdependence. Therefore, if one firm decides to lower its price below the established market price, all other firms may lower their price in order to retain their share of the market. This also holds true in regard to output. If, for example, in the automotive industry, one firm decides to offer air-conditioning as a standard feature, other firms must also offer this feature to remain competitive. Because of this interdependence, a certain amount of collusion usually exists in these markets.

INTERDEPENDENCE OF ECONOMIC BEHAVIOR. Modern market economies have developed because societies have found that there are advantages from the division of labor, and that if the society is to benefit from advancing technology, the economic system must maximize the division of labor. Thus, most economic systems have evolved to the point where there are a multitude of economic units all involved in one or more aspects of production, distribution, or consumption. Although the various economic units in the system do not always appear to be related, all economic activity affects all other activity in some manner. For example, every consumer purchase of goods affects the demand for these goods, which in turn affects, in however small a manner, the industry's or firm's decision of how much to produce and, thus, the decision on the amount of inputs to purchase. All economic decisions have similar impacts.

Eighteenth Century. The realization that the economic system is composed of individual units, that these units can be grouped into sectors, and that all economic units and sectors are interdependent is the framework for the various theories and hypotheses that are central to the study of economics. The interdependence of economic behavior was first recognized by the French physiocrats in the middle of the eighteenth century. François Quesnay's *Tableau Économique,* a three-sector economic flow model, was the culmination of early thought on the interdependence of economic activity and a forerunner of the modern circular flow model. The classical statement of economic interdependence was Say's law, which, in its simplest terms, states that in supplying goods and services, the economy also creates demands for this output.

Nineteenth and Twentieth Centuries. The most important manifestation of the interdependence concept in economic theory, however, appeared in the late nineteenth century with the work of Leon Walras and Vilfredo Pareto concerning general equilibrium analysis of the economic system. This analysis attempted to consider the situation in which all units in the economic system are in simultaneous equilibrium and the adjustments necessary to reach this state. Although much consideration has been given to general equilibrium theory, the complexities of modern economies do not lend themselves to empirical general equilibrium analysis. Input-output models have come closest to such analysis. The realization, however, that such interdependence exists and the attempt to take into account those relationships known to exist greatly improves the validity of economic analysis. —*Clyde A. Haulman*

See also Circular Flow in Income; Input-Output Models.

INTERDISTRICT SETTLEMENT FUND. *See* Federal Reserve System.

INTEREST, the payment for the use of money. In national income accounts, interest is income for the lender and is a cost for the borrower. In order for firms or individuals to accumulate enough resources to purchase capital goods, some current consumption must be forgone. If the purchaser forgoes the consumption, this is called equity financing. If someone forgoes the consumption and the purchaser borrows, this is called debt financing. In debt financing, the borrower must pay the lender something to induce him to forgo this consumption. This payment is called interest.

There are basically two reasons why interest is paid for the use of money. The first is due to the "time value" of money. This argument states that people prefer to consume now as opposed to later. Thus, in order to induce people to put off consumption, you must pay them. Secondly, interest is paid to offset risk. There are two kinds of risks involved in making a loan. The first is the risk that the value of the money lent will be less in the future than it is now due to inflation. Thus, part of the interest paid on any loan is an

expected inflation premium. The second kind of risk is default risk. On any loan, there is always the possibility that the borrower may not be able to pay off the loan; in other words, he may default on the loan. The higher the probability that the borrower will default, the higher the interest rate.

Interest is a very important concept in economics. In macroeconomics, interest is considered the opportunity cost of holding cash balances in the Keynesian model. Interest is also important in the other Keynesian motives for holding money; namely, the precautionary and speculative motives. Interest also allows us to compare the future worth of something to its present worth. This process is called discounting.

—*Timothy P. Ryan*

See also Demand for Capital; Interest Rates; Interest Rate Structures; Time Preference.

INTEREST RATE CEILINGS are established by the Board of Governors of the Federal Reserve System to limit the interest rate that may be paid by commercial banks on demand deposits and time deposits. No interest is permitted on demand deposits. The ceiling on time deposits is changed from time to time and varies according to the form of the deposit and its maturity. These ceilings are published as Regulation Q.

INTEREST RATES, the price paid for the use of money. Because the use takes place over time, interest must be expressed as a rate per unit of time, customarily one year. Thus, if a borrower pays $1 in interest for the use of $100 for one month, the interest charge is 1% per month, but the interest rate is 12% per year. If she pays $12 interest in advance (a discount rather than a loan), she actually has the use of only $88; although the discount rate is 12%, the interest rate is $^{12}/_{88}$, or 13.6%. Furthermore, if she repays the $100 in monthly installments of $8.33, she does not have the use of $88 for a year, but only for 1 month, then

---

INTEREST RATES: TOPIC GUIDE

To examine other aspects of the meaning and function of interest rates in their microeconomic capacity, see the articles on INTEREST and INTEREST RATE STRUCTURE. For an understanding of interest rates as payments to providers of capital, consult the articles on TIME PREFERENCE and RISK.

The major macroeconomic facets of interest rates are explained inb the article on MONETARY POLICY. Closely related concepts are described in PRIME RATE, DISCOUNT RATE, and OPEN MARKET OPERATIONS.

The Subject Map accompanying MONEY displays the interrelated articles on interest rates.

$79.67 for the next month, and so on. The true interest rate in this case is more than twice the nominal rate of 12%.

Structure. There is no single interest rate at a given time, but rather a large variety of rates for different types of loans and securities. Generally speaking, interest rates are higher for long-term loans than for short-term, for small loans than for large, for risky loans than for safe, and for specialized loans than for standard market instruments. Thus, the interest rate on Treasury bills may be 8% and the charge for a $100 personal finance-company loan may be 18%.

Determination. An interest rate is purely the price of credit. Like all prices, interest rates are determined by the supply and demand for credit. The supply of credit depends, to a very large extent, on the supply of money. Therefore, interest rates, unlike many prices, are largely determined by the actions of the federal government. Interest rates have historically been a target of monetary policy by the Federal Reserve since the availability of credit is so important to the health and growth of the macroeconomy. The government is also a very large demander of credit through federal borrowing and therefore also has a large impact on the demand for credit. Not that the government totally determines interest rates; there is a very large private demand for credit, and the supply of credit, for the most part, comes from the privately-owned financial institutions of the country.   —*Timothy P. Ryan*

INTEREST RATE STRUCTURE, rates existing in different types of income-earning assets at a given time. Influencing this structure are credit risk, administrative and credit investigation costs, tax treatment, and differences in maturity. This maturity aspect alone could explain different yields even if the other factors were the same for all types of securities. It is from the maturity structure that yield curves are derived: Curve (1) indicates that the longer the term to maturity, the higher the interest rate will be. The reason for this is that lenders and borrowers believe that interest rates

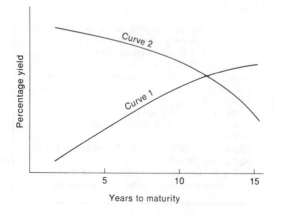

are going to go up in the future. If this is the case, lenders will not lend for a long period of time at current interest rates because their alternative is to lend for a short period, say one year, at current interest rates and then make a new loan next year at the higher interest rates. Thus, borrowers must pay higher interest rates now for a long-term loan to induce lenders to make long-term loans. Curve (2) indicates that lenders and borrowers expect interest rates to fall. Now borrowers do not want to get tied into a long-term loan at current interest rates. Thus, lenders must offer lower rates on long-term loans to induce borrowers to commit.

See also Interest; Interest Rates.

INTERLOCKING DIRECTORATE, business practice in which a member of the corporate board of directors of one firm is a member of at least one other firm. While many forms of "interlocks" exist, only one form is prohibited, that where the director sits on boards of firms of a certain size in direct competition with each other. This prohibition, in the Clayton Act (Section 8), is based on the concern that an interlocking directorate among competitors would facilitate price and output limitation agreements and other anticompetitive actions. Even this limited prohibition is not effective, however, since officers other than directors may serve on a competitor's board, and indirect interlocks are legal (as when directors of two competitors serve together on a third firm's board).

See also Antitrust Policy; Clayton Act.

INTERMEDIATE GOODS, those goods that have not completed the manufacturing process, that are being purchased for modification before final use, or that are being purchased for resale. Many intrasectoral transactions involve intermediate goods. For example, when General Motors purchases a truck engine from Detroit Diesel, the engine will be changed little, if at all. However, it is not a final good, because GM will combine the engine with other parts to make a truck to be sold as a final good. The engine, while complete at the point of sale from Detroit Diesel to GM, is an intermediate step in the production of the final good—a truck.

See also Final Goods; Goods.

INTERNAL COSTS, those costs of the production process that are borne by the producing unit and, therefore, must be taken into account by that unit in making its economic decisions. Businesses have been forced by society to internalize a number of costs that were previously externalities, such as water and air pollution.

See also External Costs.

INTERNAL DEBT, a situation where the borrowing unit (the national government) acquires funds from within its domestic economy. If the gross federal debt of the United States were financed totally by the sale of securities to American governmental agencies, financial institutions, businesses, and individuals, the debt would be purely an internal debt. No claims against the borrowing unit would arise from outside the country. All interest and debt repayment would involve transfers from the nation as a whole (taxpayers) to those who hold the debt within the same nation.

See also External Debt.

INTERNAL (or Endogenous) THEORY OF BUSINESS CYCLES acknowledges that certain external factors influence economic activity, but contends that the major cause of business cycles is attributable to factors or forces within the economic system. Among the endogenous theories are profit-motive (psychological), monetary, overinvestment, and underconsumption. Some internal theories suggest that mechanisms within the system will naturally generate economic cycles so that, predictably, every expansion will be followed by recession, contraction, and renewed expansion. Psychologically, this type of self-generation can be attributed to waves of optimism and pessimism in response to political, social, and economic occurrences which induce businesses to invest and expand, or cut back and save.

See also Business Cycle, Theories.

INTERNATIONAL BANK FOR RECONSTRUCTION AND DEVELOPMENT (IBRD), or World Bank, came into being in 1944 as a specialized agency of the United Nations. Its central activity consists in making loans to less developed member countries. The funds used by the bank are raised largely through bond issues in private capital markets. No loans can be made unless there is reasonable assurance that the borrower can repay and meet service charges. Also, the funds must be used for specific approved projects.

Thus, the World Bank is guided by banking criteria and countries not meeting these criteria do not have access to its facilities. To help overcome these limitations the International Development Associates (IDA) was formed to provide soft loans to less developed countries (terms more favorable than World Bank and with longer periods). The International Finance Corporation, which together with the IBRD and IDA form the World Bank Group, was formed to further economic development in less developed member countries by investing directly in private enterprises in association with private investors.

See also International Monetary Fund.

INTERNATIONAL BROTHERHOOD OF TEAMSTERS (IBT), labor union chartered by the AFL in 1899 as the Team Drivers International Union, which organized the drivers of horse-pulled vehicles. The

present name was adopted in 1903. In 1957, during Senate corruption investigations, James Hoffa became president of the Teamsters, and the AFL-CIO voted to expel the union. The IBT expanded its jurisdiction and became the largest union in the United States, representing truck drivers, retail salespeople, police officers, and clerical workers. The Teamsters union applied for readmission to the AFL-CIO in 1987 but remained under the supervision of government-appointed trustees. It was readmitted to the AFL-CIO in 1989.

INTERNATIONAL MONETARY FUND (IMF), also called simply the Fund, functions as the regulator of foreign exchange rates and as a source of international liquidity. Each member country, upon joining the IMF, receives a quota (its IMF quota) based on its economic size. (Thus, the United States has by far the largest quota.) A country is required to deposit one quarter of its quota in gold and the remainder in its domestic currency with the IMF. These deposits constitute the country's quota subscription. In return, the country has the opportunity to borrow any foreign currency from the Fund.

Provisions. The loan is in reality a purchase-and-resale agreement in which the borrowing country sells its own currency to the Fund for the desired foreign exchange, agreeing to reverse the transaction in three to five years. There is an interest cost (called a service charge).

A country has an unconditional right to borrow until the IMF holds domestic currency equal to 100% of its quota (that is, the 75% it deposits and the 25% it exchanges for other currencies). The amount of foreign exchange it can borrow unconditionally is called its gold tranche, and is equal to 25% of its quota. Beyond the gold tranche a country has the privilege, not the right, of borrowing four successive credit tranches, each equal to 25% of its quota. The credit tranches may be borrowed only at the discretion of the Fund. They are borrowed reserves, as distinct from the country's gold tranche and its holding of gold and dollars, all of which are owned reserves. When the IMF holdings of a country's domestic currency reaches 200% of its quota—that is, the country has borrowed its gold tranches and its four credit tranches—the country has reached the limit of its borrowing power.

SDRs. At discrete intervals international liquidity is increased by increasing countries' quotas with the IMF, with the increased quotas again in proportion to a country's current economic size. Moreover, in 1967 the members of the IMF agreed to establish a new form of international reserves, called *Special Drawing Rights (SDRs)*. Each country receives an SDR allocation (SDR balances) in proportion to its IMF quota.

A country may use its SDRs to purchase another country's currency, thus acquiring foreign exchange, in which case the first country's SDR balances are reduced and those of the second country are increased by the amount of the transaction. SDRs are owned reserves in the sense that they may be used fully without permission of the IMF. However, they resemble borrowed reserves because of the existence of a reconstitution provision: a country must retain at least 30% of its SDR allocation unused as a daily average over the base period.

During the 1980s, the Third World debt crisis drew considerable public attention to IMF policies. Interest rates on the debtor countries' variable rate commercial loans rose sharply as central banks in various countries tightened money supplies to tame accelerating inflation. The steep increase in the value of the dollar raised the effective cost of both the debtors' dollar imports and of payments on dollar-denominated debt. Although the rise in the dollar strengthened the competitiveness of many exports, plummeting world prices for many of the debtors' primary export commodities more than offset this increase. Debt service payments to the International Bank for Reconstruction and Development (IBRD) grew at an average of 24% per year from 1980 to 1987, and several countries suspended debt-servicing payments.

In 1988, first Japan and then France made new proposals for commercial bank debt relief for middle-income countries undergoing adjustment programs. In March 1989, the United States put forward the Brady Plan, by which debt reduction would take place on a case-by-case basis in voluntary agreements between the debtor countries and their creditor banks. For the first time in the management of the international debt problem, an explicit commitment of public resources to support a debt reduction process was allowed. World Bank resources would come out of its recent $75 million capital increase. The IMF would use existing resources, although the plan promised to study an increase. Countries with balance-of-payments surpluses would be asked to contribute to the plan's financing. The Brady Plan also involves a delinking of the disbursements of IMF programs from the management of private banks' balance sheets. This would reverse a policy in place since 1982, by which IMF programs have generally been contingent on a country's attaining prior agreement with its banks to close the financing gap through a combination of debt relief and new money.   —*Lawrence H. Officer*

See also Exchange Rates; Multinational Trade Agreements.

INTERNATIONAL MONETARY SYSTEM, the framework within which balance-of-payments deficits and surpluses are settled between countries. *International liquidity* (also called international reserves, reserve assets, reserve holdings, or simply reserves) are assets held by governments for the purpose of financ-

INTERNATIONAL TRADE
(continued)

MULTINATIONAL TRADE AGREEMENTS
international trade organization

GENERAL AGREEMENT ON TARIFFS AND TRADE
Kennedy Round
Trade Expansion Act
most-favored nation
RECIPROCAL TRADE AGREEMENTS ACT
INTERNATIONAL MONETARY FUND
BRETTON WOODS
INTERNATIONAL BANK FOR RECONSTRUCTION AND DEVELOPMENT
World Bank
EXPORT-IMPORT BANK
TRIFFEN PLAN
CUSTOMS UNIONS AND FREE-TRADE AREAS
EUROPEAN ECONOMIC COMMUNITY
CAPITAL MOVEMENT
FOREIGN INVESTMENT

BALANCE OF PAYMENTS

DOLLAR SHORTAGE
dollar scarcity
DOLLAR GLUT
CHRONIC DEFICIT
RUN ON THE DOLLAR

BALANCE OF TRADE
VISIBLE GOODS AND SERVICES
INVISIBLE GOODS AND SERVICES
EXPORTS
IMPORTS

CAPITAL ACCOUNT
CAPITAL MOVEMENT
GOLD MOVEMENT
FOREIGN INVESTMENT

STAGES OF A COUNTRY'S BALANCE OF PAYMENTS

TARIFFS
BEGGAR-THY-NEIGHBOR POLICY

TRADE BARRIERS
trade restrictions

QUOTAS
import quotas
PERIL POINT
INFANT INDUSTRY

ing balance-of-payments deficits, in which case their reserve holdings increase. The international monetary system of the nineteenth century was the gold standard, in which gold was the only reserve asset. The present international monetary system is known as the *gold-exchange standard,* because both gold and foreign exchange (the so-called hard currencies, chief among which is the dollar) are used as reserve assets. Thus, the dollar is a reserve currency, and the United States is a reserve-currency (or key-currency) country.

INTERNATIONAL TRADE ORGANIZATION. *See* Multinational Trade Agreements.

INTERNATIONAL TRADE THEORY explains why nations trade. David Ricardo and John Stuart Mill are associated with the classical theory of international trade; Alfred Marshall and Frank Taussig were later neoclassicals; prominent names in the modern theory are Heckscher and Ohlin. International trade is based on the law of comparative advantage: each nation should produce those goods and services that its resource endowment and technology indicate it can

produce better and cheaper than other nations; it then trades these products for goods and services that it finds more costly to produce. Prices differ, therefore, between countries, but behind absolute prices lie differences in relative prices based on the pretrade situation.

In pretrade isolation each country has a production-possibility frontier embodying its full potential with all resources fully employed. At full employment the real cost to the economy of more of a good is the value of other goods not produced as a result (opportunity cost). If these opportunity costs for a given good differ between countries, relative cost and price comparisons may be made. These pretrade relative differences are translated into absolute differences via rates of exchange—domestic price of a unit of foreign currency. Exchange rates determine exports and imports; each country exports products with lower comparative costs before trade and imports products whose comparative costs are higher. Trade is beneficial when the opportunity cost of importing is lower than the opportunity cost of producing: the production-possibility frontier is pushed outward.

—*John R. Matthews, Jr.*

See also Comparative Advantage; Exchange Rate; Terms of Trade.

INTERNATIONAL UNIONS. *See* National Unions.

INTERSTATE COMMERCE COMMISSION (ICC), one of the first regulatory commissions, established by Congress in 1887. In the early years, the ICC was concerned with regulating railroad rates and ensuring continuity of service to small communities, although much of its regulatory power was weakened by court decisions. Later, the ICC also began to regulate interstate trucking, inland water transport, and other transportation firms.

ICC regulation has been accused of perpetuating inefficient firms and high costs, rather than the opposite. The ICC served as an effective barrier of entry to firms, which had to receive certification before they could operate, and it also served as a legal means for carriers to set prices. As a result of this policy concern, much of the deregulatory fervor of recent years has centered on the Interstate Commerce Commission, and many of its rules have been relaxed. For example, the Staggers Act of 1980 relaxed regulation of contracts between rail carriers and shippers, and the Bus Regulatory Reform Act of 1982 forced the ICC to issue operating certificates to any bus carrier that met insurance and safety requirements. Many more rules and procedures have been relaxed by the ICC itself.

See also Deregulation.

INTERVENTION CURRENCY, the currency with which member governments of the International Monetary Fund (IMF) intervene in foreign-exchange markets. A country will accumulate dollars (buy dollars) when its exchange rate is at the lower support point and lose dollars (sell dollars) when its exchange rate is at the upper support point. Until August 1971 governments could replenish dollar holdings by selling gold to the United States. Alternatively, governments could increase gold holdings by selling dollars to (buying gold from) the United States. Either transaction involves changing the country's *reserve-asset composition:* the ratio of dollar holdings to gold in its reserves, or, in general, the ratio of any one reserve asset (gold or dollar holdings) to the country's total reserves.

INVENTORY ACCUMULATION, the voluntary or involuntary buildup of goods when production is running ahead of consumption. Accumulation also occurs when merchants, particularly in the economic upswing, overestimate their needs in acquiring stock in an attempt to accommodate anticipated sales.

See also Inventory Investment.

INVENTORY DECUMULATION, the reduction of business inventories. It can occur when consumption exceeds production or, by design, during downswings when businesses want to divest themselves of inventory.

INVENTORY INVESTMENT, the market value of all raw materials, supplies, and finished goods purchased by manufacturers, wholesalers, retailers, and farmers. The rate of inventory investment depends on technological innovation, anticipated economic expansion, and the state of the economy, as measured by the quantity of money, credit, and interest rates.

In years of upswing, businesses seek to build their stocks to accommodate a rise in sales. Conversely, in a downswing, businesses cut back production, reduce inventory, and lay off workers, all of which are ultimately registered in a geometric drop in Net National Product. Waves of optimism and pessimism in the business and financial communities, usually generated by political policies and activities, also cause fluctuation in inventory investment.

To attenuate cyclical fluctuation in inventory accumulation and decumulation, most businesses have short- and long-term investment plans for purchases of new plant and equipment.

INVESTMENT: TOPIC GUIDE

For an explanation of the macroeconomic significance of investment, see the major articles on NATIONAL INCOME DETERMINATION and BUSINESS CYCLES, THEORIES. Other macroeconomic facets of investment are found in the articles on INJECTION, MARGINAL EFFICIENCY OF CAPITAL, and INTEREST. And for more narrowly defined terms, see DIRECT INVESTMENT, AUTONOMOUS INVESTMENT, INDUCED INVESTMENT, and INVENTORY INVESTMENT.

The Subject Map accompanying the article on NATIONAL INCOME shows the interrelationships of these and other investment concepts.

INVESTMENT, in national income accounting and development economics, spending by businesses on currently produced capital goods (I); and in finance, the purchase of stocks, bonds, and other titles to property.

The Income Stream. Investment is spending that contributes to the income stream when that spending is on currently produced goods. When spending is for titles to property rights (real or intangible), it does not contribute to the aggregate demand for goods and services. When spending is for previously produced goods, it makes no demands upon productive capacity—the demand for already produced goods does not require production and, hence, causes no income payments to be made to the factors of production. It is only when new goods are demanded that factors must be employed and paid.

Terminology. In physical terms, capital goods themselves are thought of as fixed capital and as inventory. Fixed capital includes all structures, machinery, or equipment used in further production of goods and services for sale. Capital goods are determined by virtue of this criterion of further production for sale and not by virtue of their physical characteristics.

Governments, of course, purchase capital goods to be used in producing other goods and services and often sell the products, but because the reasons for and processes of political decisions to buy these goods are different from the profit motive of businesses, government purchases of capital goods are classified as government expenditure (G). By definition, in national income theory and national income accounting only businesses invest.

Inventories—materials awaiting processing or products awaiting sale—are the real (as opposed to monetary or financial) working capital of firms. An increase in total inventories is a net investment, because the increase requires suppliers to hire additional labor to provide materials; a decrease is a negative investment, because suppliers of materials, supplying less, will lay off workers. When inventories remain constant, they neither increase nor decrease the stock of goods; the materials supplied and used in production are accounted for as products in the final goods produced. If inventories are maintained at the same level, there is no change from year to year in spending.

Theoretical Structures. In national income theory, spending is divided into the categories of consumption (C), investment (I), government (G), and net exports (F), because the motive for each is different. Investment, which occurs when profits are anticipated and finance is available, has a leading role in the theory of income determination, because I fluctuates more rapidly than C, G, or F. Investment spending is volatile, because expectations about profitability change more quickly than do consumers' standards and tastes, government policy, or the reasons why Americans buy from foreigners (imports: M) and why foreigners buy from Americans (exports: X). Furthermore, it is far more difficult for policy and administration to change expectations of profitability than it is for them to affect disposable income or government spending; and the monetary authorities can limit or encourage investment in ways that cannot be applied to consumption and government spending.

In the study of economic developments, investment is defined in the same way, but its role in theories of development is different. In these theories investment is the addition to the stock of capital in the country and is often symbolized by $\triangle k$ (for change in capital). The importance of investment in these theories is that over time the additions to capital stock increase the productive capacity of the country. In the poorer countries the problem is frequently not that aggregate demand is too low to employ the whole labor force; rather, there is not enough equipment for the labor force to use. The focus is on capacity rather than on demand. —*Walter C. Neale*

See also Actual Investment; Aggregate Demand; Autonomous Investment; Induced Investment; Investment Schedule; National Income Determination.

INVESTMENT SCHEDULE, a schedule of the amounts that would be spent on investment (capital) goods at each possible level of income (most realistically GNP in this case). When the relation of investment to income is plotted on a graph or expressed as an algebraic equation it is called the *investment function*. The schedule of that portion of investment which is autonomous would show only one amount whatever the level of income; on a graph it would plot as a horizontal line (investment plotted on vertical axis, income on horizontal axis). The schedule of *induced investment* will show greater investment at higher incomes, an upward sloping function, most likely showing 0 or negative net investment at low incomes. The total investment schedule, the sum of the two, will show higher investment at higher incomes and be upward sloping.

The investment schedule is also the schedule of *planned investment*. Planned investment, also called *intended investment*, is the amount that businesses expect to invest, based on anticipated GNP. The planned investment schedules are based upon the expectation of profits from buying and using the investment goods. —*Walter C. Neale*

See also Autonomous Investment; Induced Investment; Investment; Marginal Efficiency of Capital.

INVISIBLE GOODS AND SERVICES. All items in the current account of a balance of payments other than merchandise exports and imports are classified as invisibles. These include services which cannot be seen or touched, such as freight handling, insurance, tourist expenditures, and interest on investments abroad (or due foreign investors).

INVISIBLE HAND, theory that individuals free to pursue their own self-interests will automatically promote the interests of society, as if by an "invisible hand." The concept, first advanced by Adam Smith in the *Wealth of Nations* (1776), of the market as an "invisible hand" that channeled individual selfish actions into socially useful activities supported a doctrine of laissez-faire in which the primary function of government would be to support and encourage profit making. According to Smith, a purely competitive market—characterized by small and numerous economic units, homogeneous products, market knowledge, and mobility—would be a safeguard against misuse of economic self-interest.

See also Competition; Laissez-Faire; Market Economy; Profit System.

INVOLUNTARY INVESTMENT. *See* Disinvestment.

IRON LAW OF WAGES, an outgrowth of the thinking of the classical economists, especially Thomas Malthus and David Ricardo, in the early 19th century. As a wage theory the Iron Law of Wages states that a rise in real income of a worker is self-defeating because, as income rises, family size begins to increase substantially and thus the number of workers eventually increases. This increase in population will cause food prices to rise so that the initial increase in real wages is canceled out by the increase in food prices.

ISOCOST LINES. If labor is plotted on the vertical axis and capital on the horizontal axis, then for any given money outlay by the firm, an isocost curve can be constructed showing all the combinations of labor and capital that can be purchased at prevailing factor prices. The slope of the isocost line is negative, and its magnitude is equal to the ratio of the price of capital to the price of labor, that is: $\triangle L/\triangle K = -P_K/P_L$. A family of isocost lines shows the total cost of every possible factor combination.

ISOPRODUCT CURVE, or ISOQUANT, the locus of points in the input space representing the varying combinations of inputs that can produce a given output of some commodity, Isoquant analysis assumes that inputs can substitute for each other in the productive process: hence, a given output quantity can be produced in several ways, for example, by using much labor and little capital, and much capital and little labor.

Ideally the curve will be continuous, implying that the same output can be produced by making very small substitutions, and that many combinations of inputs are able to produce a given output quantity. A family of isoproduct curves may be plotted with two factors on the respective axes. Higher isoquants represent larger outputs. Isoquants slope downward and do not intersect.

See also Production Function.

ISO-UTILITY CURVE. *See* Indifference Curve.

JEVONS, WILLIAM STANLEY (1835-1882). English economist who, with Carl Menger and Leon Walras, laid the foundation for development of neoclassical economics and developed an important element of modern microeconomic theory. Building upon the base of Bentham utilitarianism, Jevons combined the marginal concept with utility, using a mathematical approach. He then applied the marginal utility concept thus developed to individual consumer decisions, constructing a theory of value which provided the basis of modern demand theory. This analysis was also extended to considerations of exchange. In addition, Jevons made significant advances in the use of index numbers and is also remembered for his hypothesis that business cycles were the result of sunspots.

JOINT DEMAND. Factors are not very productive unless they cooperate with other factors. Labor, by itself, can produce only negligible output. This fact is the origin of the endless quarrels by owners of factors as to which factor is the most important in the productive process. More important, the necessarily joint demand for factors of production sets the stage for an important economic riddle: if land, labor, and capital jointly produce a given output, how can one measure the individual contributions? This important question, which is related to the distribution-of-income problem, is answered by long-run marginal productivity theory.

JOINT PROFIT MAXIMIZATION, a method of determining a market price of an industry by adjusting all output and prices to that point which will produce the largest aggregate of profit to all firms combined. Joint profit maximization is most often found in oligopolistic market structures because there are only a few sellers in these industries and, therefore, collaboration is relatively easy. When all firms in an industry join in this type of price determination, the industry is able to achieve much the same effect as a monopolistic industry.

JOURNAL ENTRY. *See* Balance Sheet.

JURISDICTION, UNION. Each union claims a group or groups of employees and asserts its claim as the only union to organize these workers. Thus, the jurisdiction of the Teamsters, as the union views it, includes at least 20 different groups of workers in a number of occupations. Often other unions claim the same workers, and a jurisdictional dispute, that is, a conflict between two or more unions, occurs.

JURISDICTIONAL DISPUTES, conflicts between unions as to which one shall represent a certain group of workers. Such disputes were common in the period of organizing rivalry between unions of the Congress of Industrial Organizations (CIO) and the American Federation of Labor (AFL) before the two federations merged in 1955. CIO unions were mainly industrial, with jurisdictions defined by industry boundaries, while AFL unions generally defined their jurisdictions by skill or craft boundaries. Overlap and hence competition and conflict resulted.

As unions evolved into more loosely-defined heterogeneous organizations, the boundaries became blurred, but the quest for growth continues to generate jurisdictional disputes. These now tend to be settled within the labor movement or by the National Labor Relations Board, rather than through overt actions.

KENNEDY ROUND. *See* General Agreement on Tariffs and Trade.

KEY BARGAIN, agreement that sets an industry precedent. Unions that engage in multi-employer bargaining often negotiate first with the most prominent firm in the industry, and the features of that bargain in relation to wage increases, work rules, pensions, and other matters tend to become those the union seeks to establish in contracts with other firms. The contract that sets the pattern is the "key contract" and is the result of the "key bargain."

See also Collective Bargaining.

KEYNES, JOHN MAYNARD (1883-1946). The best known and one of the most important figures in economics, English monetary expert Keynes was responsible for the development of much of the framework of modern macroeconomic theory. A prolific writer, Keynes published a number of books, each of which had important impact. His *Economic Consequences of the Peace* (1919) eloquently presented the controversial view that the problems after World War I could be attributed to the peace settlement, not to those who had caused the war. *A Tract on Monetary Reform* (1923) and *The Economic Consequences of Mr. Churchill* (1925) were also policy-oriented works. The first suggested that the gold standard which had existed prior to World War I was no longer workable; the second attacked the restoration of the gold standard by Winston Churchill as Chancellor of the Exchequer.

Keynes's most important work on economic theory appeared later in his career. The two-volume *A Treatise on Money* (1930) was a complete treatment of monetary theory and policy. In these volumes Keynes made important contributions to (1) the theory of the demand for money and other financial assets; (2) the analysis of the relationship between saving and investment; and (3) the theory of the return on capital. In *The General Theory of Employment, Interest, and Money* (1936), Keynes refined many of the concepts developed in his *Treatise on Money* and presented a theory of macroeconomics which has become known as the Keynesian system. While the initial reaction to the *General Theory* was unfavorable and, while economists now agree that the system has many problems, Keynes did change the direction of economics to the extent that most economists agree that "today we are all Keynesians."   *—Clyde A. Haulman*

KINDLEBERGER, CHARLES POOR (1910-   ), American economist and expert on international trade. A graduate of the University of Pennsylvania (1932), he received his Ph.D. from Columbia (1937). His publications include *Economic Growth in France and Britain, 1851-1950* (1964), *International Economics* (1953-1968, editions), *Power and Money: The Politics of International Economics and the Economics of International Politics* (1970), and *The World in Depression 1929-1939* (1973). He was professor of economics at MIT (1948-1976).

KINKED DEMAND CURVE, an analytical approach using certain assumptions to explain price rigidity in oligopolistic markets. The assumptions are, first, that the industry is mature and has certain established prices. Second, if one firm attempts to lower prices, all other firms will follow in order to retain their share of the market. Third, the demand curve assumes that firms will not follow a price rise. Therefore, the kinked demand curve shows that if a firm prices above an established price it will lose its share of the market, and if it prices below the established price, since each firm will follow, it will merely retain its share of the market, but at a lower revenue.

KIRKLAND, LANE (1922-   ), U.S. labor leader who succeeded George Meany as president of the AFL-CIO in 1979. He had previously served as Meany's executive assistant and from 1969 as secretary-treasurer of the AFL-CIO. Kirkland was an adviser to President Carter on personnel selection and was also a member of President Reagan's Productivity Council, although he resigned in 1981 because he disagreed with the administration's stand on the air traffic controllers' strike. In 1989, when the Teamsters Union was readmitted to the AFL-CIO, Kirkland was elected to a sixth term as president.

KLEIN, LAWRENCE ROBERT (1920-   ), American economist instrumental in the development of models for forecasting economic trends. A graduate of the University of California (1942), with a Ph.D. from the Massachusetts Institute of Technology (1944), Klein became professor of economics and finance at the University of Pennsylvania, where he has taught since 1958. His teaching, research, and application of economic forecasting models earned him the 1980 Nobel Prize in economics.

KNIGHTS OF LABOR, formed in 1869, represented the first serious attempt to organize labor on a national basis in the United States. It was conceived as a coalition of a large number of local unions and labor organizations. The organization, unlike the later trade unions, tended toward the system of industrial unionism, trying to organize all workers in an industry regardless of skill. Also, it concerned itself with demands for a fundamental reform of the economic structure.

The Knights reached their peak in 1886 after a strike on the Wabash, Missouri-Kansas-Texas, and Missouri Pacific railroads forced Jay Gould, the financier who controlled these railroads, to grant recognition. From 100,000 the previous year, membership rose to 700,000. Its decline, however, was as rapid as its ascent. The loss of several strikes and the separation of skilled men into a rival organization turned the tide. In 1893 membership was down to 75,000, and the organization was dissolved in 1913.

KONDRATIEFF CYCLES are economic fluctuations, named for the Russian economist N.D. Kondratieff, which last from 50 to 60 years. Each cycle consists of a series of long waves in prices, production, and trade. Kondratieff suggested that such changes as technological innovation, new markets, and war and revolution—rather than random occurrences—were the most important factors affecting these variables.

KOOPMANS, TJALLING CHARLES (1910-   ), Dutch-born economist, noted for his contributions to the development of mathematical methods of economic analysis. He received an M.A. (1933) from the University of Utrecht, and a Ph.D. (1936) from the University of Leiden. His publications include *Statistical Inference in Dynamic Economic Models* (1950, editor), *Activity Analysis of Production and Allocation* (1951, editor), and *Three Essays on the State of Economic Science* (1957). Director of Yale's Cowles Foundation for Research in Economics from 1961-1967, he has been a professor of economics at Yale since 1955. For his many contributions Koopmans was awarded the 1975 Nobel Prize in economics.

KURTOSIS is a measure of how peaked or pointed a distribution is. The fourth moment about the mean measures kurtosis, but the concept is seldom used.

KUZNETS, SIMON SMITH (1901-   ), a Russian-born American economist, considered the father of the current national income accounting system. Working in the National Bureau of Economic Research, Kuznets studied the problem of measuring the level of aggregate economic activity and its composition. His *National Income and Its Composition 1919-1938* (1941) presented estimates of national income for the United States. However, while Kuznets had developed the concept of national income during the 1930s, it was not until after World War II that an effort was made to construct a systematic framework of national income accounts with Kuznets' earlier work providing the foundation. Kuznets has also estimated national income in the United States for the last half of the nineteenth century in his book *National Produce Since 1869* (1946).

In that book, Kuznets also estimated consumption functions. He found that the long-term relationship between income and consumption was proportional, rather than the nonproportional relationship found in short-term functions and used in the Keynesian system. This finding, further supported by Goldsmith, has led to numerous attempts to reconcile the contradiction between long- and short-term consumption

behavior including Friedman's permanent-income hypothesis and the life-cycle hypothesis.

Finally, in his *Modern Economic Development* (1966), Kuznets discussed the growth process and isolated the major sources of economic growth. His other publications include *Economic Growth of Nations* (1971) and *Population, Capital, and Growth* (1973). For his efforts, Kuznets was awarded the Nobel Prize in Economics (1971).   —*Clyde A. Haulman*

KUZNETS CYCLES, economic fluctuations which average from 15 to 25 years. They were identified in 1930, and named for Simon Kuznets, who suggested these cyclical variations were associated closely with immigration and natural rates of population growth, railroad building, capital imports, and the growth rate of the money supply.

See also Business Cycles.

LABOR, as a factor input, involves demand and supply relationships. Early economists believed wage rates were determined exclusively by labor's productivity (demand), but modern economists recognize the importance of supply, too. Modern derivations of labor supply make use of indifference curves; an individual decides the optimal trade between leisure and income for various wage rates. Some individuals may work less as wage rates rise, but it is generally agreed that group supply is upward sloping; if labor purchasers are to attract greater quantities, there must be higher wage rates.

It is proper to visualize supply and demand operating in many labor markets, rather than just one. Thus, different labor skills would lead in equilibrium to different wage rates even if there were no unnatural barriers to entry across industries. Moreover, even for a given quality of labor, wage rates may in equilibrium vary across occupations due to different working conditions (equalizing differences). The demand for labor, of course, is a function of its productivity. The interaction of supply and demand for labor in more or less segmented markets accounts for wage differentials.   —*Robert L. Brite*

LABOR FORCE, all members of the working-age population who are either employed or seeking or awaiting employment. The size of the labor force is one of the three main dimensions of the aggregate supply of labor to the market sector of the economy. (The length of the average workweek and the average intensity of work are the other two.)

The labor force consists of the employed and the unemployed. According to the current official definitions in the United States, the employed are persons aged 16 and over who worked for pay or profit or worked in a family business or on a family farm during the preceding week, plus those who were absent from their jobs because of illness, vacations, labor disputes,

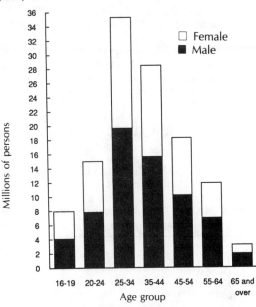

LABOR FORCE: TOPIC GUIDE

For additional articles closely related to the labor force, see LABOR SUPPLY and HUMAN RESOURCES. The relationship between the labor force and the population as a whole is discussed in LABOR FORCE PARTICIPATION RATE. For the role of the labor force relative to the demand for labor, see the article on LABOR MARKET. Definitions of the two components of the labor force are presented in the articles on EMPLOYMENT and UNEMPLOYMENT. And for the extent and patterns of unionism in the labor force, see LABOR MOVEMENT.

These and other interrelated concepts are displayed on the Subject Maps accompanying the articles on LABOR MARKET, LABOR MOVEMENT, and WAGES.

---

bad weather, or personal reasons. The unemployed are persons aged 16 or over who looked for work during the last four weeks, or who were on layoff from their present jobs and waiting to be recalled, or who were waiting to start a new job within 30 days. Persons in the armed forces are also counted in the labor force but not in the civilian labor force. Persons 16 and over not in the labor force include those who have retired or who are unable to work, inmates of institutions, the voluntarily idle, many seasonal workers during their "off season," many housewives, house husbands, students, and persons who would like to have a job but are not looking for one because they believe that no work in their line is available. The latter group is often called the "hidden unemployed."

Size. The size of the labor force depends on the size of the working population and the percentage of this population that is in the labor force. The labor force is subject to seasonal variations and tends to be somewhat larger, other things being equal, when unemployment is low than when it is high.

Comprehensive labor force statistics in the United States are gathered each month by the Bureau of the Census from a scientifically selected sample of about 47,000 households in all parts of the country. The most closely-watched statistic is the seasonally-adjusted overall unemployment rate (the percentage of the civilian labor force that is unemployed), which is an important measure of the health of the economy and a key guide to economic policy.

Current labor force statistics are presented monthly by the U.S. Department of Labor in *Employment and Earnings.* Labor force developments in the preceding year are analyzed in the annual *Manpower Report of the President.* Special reports on the labor force appear in the *Monthly Labor Review,* also published by the Department of Labor.   — *T. Aldrich Finegan*

See also Labor Force Participation Rate; Labor Supply.

LABOR FORCE PARTICIPATION RATES
PERCENT OF TOTAL POPULATION IN THE LABOR FORCE (1987)

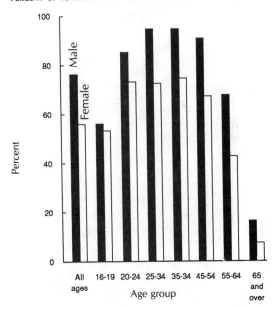

LABOR FORCE PARTICIPATION RATE (LFPR), the percentage of a population group that was in the labor force during a specified period of time. These rates vary across countries and across groups within countries; they have also changed markedly over time.

In 1987, the average LFPR for the total noninstitutional population aged 16 and over in the United States was 65.6%. But these were rates for selected groups: men aged 25 to 34, 94.6%; men 18 to 19, 68%; married women 45 to 64, 52%; and men 65 and over 16.3%.

From 1970 to 1987, the overall LFPR in the United States increased from 60.4% to 65.6%. The rate for married women more than doubled from 1960 to 1987, while the rate for elderly men (65 and over) fell by almost one half.

LABOR-MANAGEMENT RELATIONS. *See* Collective Bargaining.

LABOR-MANAGEMENT RELATIONS ACT OF 1947. *See* Taft-Hartley Act (1947).

LABOR MARKET, hypothetical meeting place for employers who need workers and employees who

need jobs. The market is as broad as the two groups involved decide to make it.

Most universities have agencies that assist graduates in finding jobs. Such an agency, if it does its assignment well, should list openings in the various occupations from all over the country. None could carry all possible job listings, but a typical placement office might list openings for engineers, say, in 20 states, with employers representing all areas of industry and government. Students in Maine, California, or South Dakota may learn of and apply for the same job, and two roommates in any of these states may accept positions thousands of miles apart. Thus the market in this case is national, or even international, and exists in many places.

At the same time, the labor market for some occupations may be very narrow and well-defined. Employers and employees in the market may decide to operate through some type of hiring hall, and both may meet there on a regular basis to make arrangements for employment. On some docks, for example, a market in the more normal sense of the word seems to exist, with workers and employers physically meeting to settle on jobs. A worker needing a job shows up to offer his services, and employers needing men send representatives to this employment area. There, in noise and confusion, the market works.

These represent two extreme market conditions, one narrow and one broad. Each, in its own way, works to bring employer and employee together. Most people operate in some in-between situation, where the market may be the city or even the state. The limits of the market determine for the individual what jobs may be available, and how much competition there will be for them.

Limitations. In a "tight" labor market the employer may broaden his or her market, and you may see ads in the newspaper that a firm from another state is hiring carpenters to move to its place of operation. In a market where jobs are hard to find, the employee may attempt to look in areas she normally would not consider, and thus expand her market.

In some situations the market is limited by formal or informal regulations of one or more types. Some cities, for some positions, hire only from the city population, and anyone outside is not considered. Some states, for some occupations, require a state license to be eligible for jobs, and sometimes a person can be licensed only by attending a school within that state. A public school teacher, for example, usually is "certified" by the state, and often, except in temporary situations, one who is uncertified is unemployable. In other situations, customs have grown up in a market limiting employment to individuals with certain ethnic, racial, or sexual qualifications.

Generally, the individuals who must sell their labor services know the characteristics of the market in which they operate, and can find employment. The dock worker may view with amazement the paperwork associated with the college graduate's job search; so may the student view the practices on the dock. Yet, both are markets, and both, however imperfectly, work.   — *William D. Wagoner*

See also Labor Force; Labor Supply.

LABOR MOBILITY. The freedom to move from job to job has always been a normal and important characteristic of the American worker. The United States has the most mobile labor force in the world. Labor mobility has always gone along with the American dream that, regardless of a person's origin, that person can move up the ladder of success; that anyone who works hard can improve his or her job, prestige, and income. For this reason, it is no surprise that few people hold only one job during their lifetimes. Rather, it is common to change not only jobs, but industries and locations as well.

Three major types of labor mobility common to the United States are occupational, geographical, and industrial.

Occupational Mobility is the most common. This simply means that a worker moves from one job to another, either with the same or another employer. Although there are numerous reasons why workers change jobs, usually the move involves an upward mobility; that is, a change that improves the worker in some way (better income, more responsibility, etc.). The logic behind this is that the economic and social costs involved with changing jobs usually means that only improvement will attract the worker to a new position.

Geographical Mobility involves relocation, either within a county, or from one county or state to another. Every year in the United States, about eight-and-one-half million people move across state lines and twice as many more move across county lines. If the people who move within counties are taken into consideration, mobility of Americans involves about 1 in every 6 people. Historically, geographic mobility has been the farm-to-city migration or European immigration. However, it now entails also the newer city-to-suburb move.

Industrial Mobility is the movement from one industry to another. Usually, to distinguish this from occupational mobility, this implies staying with the same type of job or trade but changing the industry, such as a machinist who moved from the automotive industry to the steel or plastics industry.

LABOR MOVEMENT may be viewed as consisting of those actions taken by groups of workers in a society to improve their economic or social position, or the economic or social position of their children. Generally, in the United States these actions have been directed at improving the economic position of the wage earner. The worker has apparently accepted the political, economic, and social system of the country, and the main thrust of the labor movement has been to provide a better life style for the individual. Only a small portion of the American movement has been devoted to an overthrow of the system.

Beginnings. The beginnings of the U.S. labor movement are, perhaps, lost forever. Almost any date from the arrival of the *Mayflower* may be cited as the first evidence of organized action by workers. Certainly, the movement was observable during the colonial period, and by the time of the Revolution, strikes had occurred. Toward the end of the century, organizations of workers on a planned permanent basis were created. These early unions were generally found among the better-trained workers—the shoemakers, printers, carpenters, and tailors. Their demands, phrased in the polite language of the day, were for better pay, shorter hours, and a right to the jobs for members of the organization.

LABOR MOVEMENT

LABOR MOVEMENT

AFL-CIO
AMERICAN FEDERATION OF LABOR
CONGRESS OF INDUSTRIAL
    ORGANIZATIONS
KNIGHTS OF LABOR
UNITED AUTO WORKERS
INTERNATIONAL BROTHERHOOD
    OF TEAMSTERS

NATIONAL UNIONS
    international unions
LOCAL UNION
CRAFT UNION
INDUSTRIAL UNION
COMPANY UNION

BUSINESS AGENT
BUSINESS UNIONISM
UNION CONVENTION
UNION CONSTITUTION

TRUSTEESHIP
JURISDICTION, UNION
INJUNCTION, LABOR
YELLOW-DOG CONTRACT
UNION LABEL
STEWARD

SENIORITY
BOYCOTT

COMMONS, JOHN
DEBS, EUGENE VICTOR
GOMPERS, SAMUEL
HOFFA, JAMES
LEWIS, JOHN L.
MEANY, GEORGE
REUTHER, WALTER
WOODCOCK, LEONARD

COLLECTIVE BARGAINING
BILATERAL BARGAINING
FEATHERBEDDING
FRINGE BENEFITS
KEY BARGAIN
UNION SECURITY
RECOGNITION
INDUSTRY-WIDE BARGAINING
MULTI-EMPLOYER BARGAINING
CLOSED SHOP
OPEN SHOP
UNION SHOP
AGENCY SHOP
MAINTENANCE OF MEMBERSHIP
BARGAINING UNIT

MEDIATION
    third-party intervention
ARBITRATION
CONCILIATION
FACT-FINDING

STRIKE
    LOCKOUTS
    WILDCAT STRIKES
    EMERGENCY STRIKES
    WORK STOPPAGE
    PUBLIC INTEREST DISPUTES
    STRIKE NOTICE
    STRIKE BENEFITS
    JURISDICTIONAL DISPUTES

REFUSAL TO BARGAIN
UNFAIR LABOR PRACTICES

PICKETING

LABOR LAW
    RAILWAY LABOR ACT (1926)
        National Mediation Board
    NORRIS-LA GUARDIA ACT (1932)
        Federal Anti-Injunction Act
    SOCIAL SECURITY ACT (1935)
        retirement pensions
    WAGNER ACT (1935)
        National Labor Relations Act
    NATIONAL LABOR RELATIONS BOARD
    FAIR LABOR STANDARDS ACT (1938)
        Wages and Hours Law
        Minimum Wage Law
    TAFT-HARTLEY ACT (1947)
        Labor-Management Relations Act
    LANDRUM-GRIFFIN ACT (1959)
        Labor-Management Reporting
            and Disclosures Act

The employers responded with court actions, and the courts, bringing English common law to the cases, found the unions guilty of criminal conspiracy. From 1806 to 1842, any group(s) of workers acting in concert to improve their condition of employment could well face fines or other punishment. The years were not totally wasted, however, for in several states the movement, continuing to fight for the legal right to exist, secured through political action full public education, some relaxation of the imprisonment-for-debt laws, and other gains as citizens, including the right to vote for some improvements. After the court restricted the use of the criminal-conspiracy doctrine in 1842, organization continued.

Experiments. In the middle 1800s a number of experiments were tried. The unions were trying to organize on a larger scale, and the national union concept arose. The first of these failed, and others were attempted, but the national concept was not really successful until late in the century. The movement turned to other methods of attaining goals, and several attempts were made to improve the position of the worker through communal societies, producer and consumer cooperatives, and opening of public lands to settlement. None worked, and the movement turned again to economic action.

In 1866 the National Labor Union (NLU) was organized as a combination of labor groups, farmer organizations, suffragettes, and other reform movements. Described by one writer as labor leaders without members, farmers without land, and women without husbands, the NLU turned to the 8-hour day as a goal. After some success, it turned to monetary reform and cooperatives. The unions withdrew, and the movement failed.

As the NLU was declining, the Knights of Labor (1869) was organized. The Knights turned to reform as well as economic action and admitted as members everyone except a few specified groups on an occupational basis. After 1879 the organization grew rapidly. Riding on a few successful strikes, membership rose to over one-half million. Its decline was soon to follow, perhaps speeded by strike losses. However, the most important cause of its failure was its organizational framework. It took in too many members too fast, with few common interests and no common philosophy. The trade unions could not accept the reform philosophy, and the division of interests broke the back of the movement.

The American Federation of Labor (AFL). The most valuable contribution of those two organizations was negative—they showed what *not* to do in the labor movement. Samuel Gompers learned the lesson well and in 1886, when he formed the American Federation of Labor, these negative contributions were very visible. Thus, the AFL was created as an economic union, not as a reform body. Based on the philosophy that unions are for skilled workers, that every skilled worker should be in a union with others of his or her trade, that power should rest in the locals and the nationals, that the job of the union is to secure for its members better conditions for employment, that the union is a responsible organization that will honor its contracts, and that the proper role of the union is to bargain with employers, the AFL grew slowly and solidly.

The AFL was attacked from both sides. On the right the employers fought this rising union structure and, in many ways, were successful. On the left the Industrial Workers of the World (IWW) cursed the conservatism of the AFL. Perhaps the only really radical movement in U.S. labor history, the IWW apparently opposed the AFL almost as much as it did the employer or the system.

These attacks may have resulted in some reduction in the growth rate, but the AFL continued to grow until 1920, when it had about four million members. In the 1920s the organized labor movement actually lost membership in a period of prosperity. By 1930 almost two million members of labor unions had been removed from the rolls. The loss continued until the Depression of the 1930s. However, in this decade, legislation was passed making union organization easier.

The Wagner Act. One of the most important gains for labor was the Wagner Act (1935), which granted workers the right to be members of labor organizations and which placed a duty on the employer to bargain. If the employees wanted a union, the employer could not oppose them.

Perhaps the most important result of the Wagner Act was the effect it had on those employees who were ignored by the AFL—the industrial workers. Under the rights granted by the act, workers in steel, automobiles, and other mass-production industries showed an interest in organization. A group of AFL leaders formed the Committee for Industrial Organization. The committee was opposed by the AFL, and in 1938 the committee's unions were expelled from the federation and a new labor group, the Congress of Industrial Organization (CIO), was created. These two rival organizations dominated the labor movement until 1955, when they finally united.

Another result of the Wagner Act was a rapid growth in union membership. From 1935 to 1945, membership grew from more than three million to more than 14 million. Although some of the increase was due to the increased employment resulting from World War II, much of the growth came from the easy requirements for organization under the act.

Postwar Problems. By the end of the war the favorable treatment of labor was attacked, and Congress again turned its attention to the movement. In 1947 the Taft-Hartley Act placed restrictions on the union. Still the most important piece of labor legislation, the act proscribed a series of unfair labor practices for unions, abolished the closed shop, made state right-to-work laws legal, and set forth a procedure for national emergency strikes. Passed over President Truman's veto, the law was bitterly resented by labor leaders.

In the 1950s the progress of the labor movement

Union leaders George Meany and Walter Reuther hold aloft a single gavel as a symbol of 1955 AFL-CIO merger.

slowed down, and membership grew very slowly. As a percentage of the labor force, membership actually declined. The major unorganized groups in the country remained unorganized—the Southern worker, the female worker, the white-collar worker, and the employees of small firms. It seemed as though these groups were rejecting the unions, and nothing the unions did seemed to improve the situation.

Also during the 1950s, Congress again looked at the labor movement and did not like what it saw. Some unions seemed corrupt, seemed to be involved with organized crime, and did not appear to be furthering the interests of their members. Congress, in the Labor-Management Reporting and Disclosure Act (1959), attempted to resolve some of these problems.

This law, popularly known as the Landrum-Griffin Act, represented a major attempt to correct some of the flaws, as Congress viewed them, in labor union practices. Financial practices, elections, officers, constitutions, member rights, and more came under the law, and the unions were required to be more responsive to the membership. The union movement was relatively stable from 1950 to 1980 but declined as a percentage of the total labor force in the 1980s. A major problem facing union organizers is the growing importance of white-collar workers, who tend to be antiunion.

President Kennedy issued an executive order in 1962 granting federal Civil Service employees the right to organize. Strikes and wage negotiations were prohibited, but unions now negotiate federal policies governing promotions, discharges, transfers, or leaves of absence. Striking federal air traffic controllers were fired by President Reagan in 1981.

Outlook. The problems the unions faced may have been related to the changing value system in the society, to the revolt on civil rights, and, later, to the attitudes on the Vietnam War and on pollution. It has been suggested that what future success the movement may have will be related to its ability to change. If it cannot adapt to the needs of the younger worker, the white collar worker, the minority worker, or the female employee, it may continue to fade.

— *William D. Wagoner*

See also Collective Bargaining; Strike; Unfair Labor Practices; articles on individual labor unions and acts of labor legislation.

LABOR SAVING, the decrease in the share of labor relative to the share of capital. Applied to a business or industry, labor saving is achieved through innovation or by a plan. When an electronics manufacturer substitutes printed circuits for conventional circuitry, she or he is reducing the amount of labor previously necessary for assembly of conventional models. Steady increases in wage rates have induced many employers to introduce laborsaving devices in order to reduce

their overall costs and maintain reasonable profit margins in relatively inelastic markets.

See also Capital Saving.

LABOR SUPPLY is the amount of labor available to a society, expressed as a fraction of the population size or the percentage of the population that is in the labor force. The labor force in the United States includes those who are at work or who are looking for work. The groups included in the labor force vary among countries, and this variation alters the labor supply among the populations of the world. A society may exclude from its work force children below a certain age, it may encourage older people to retire, it may exclude or discourage females from entering the labor force, or it may take other actions to affect the number of its people who can work.

At a point in time in a particular society, given the possible labor force size, the supply of labor may be related to the wage rate. The exact relationship is not always clear. One firm can get more employees by raising wages, but a wage increase may actually decrease the number of individuals in the total market. An increase in the wages of parents may send more children to school for more years. On the other hand, a wage decrease may force individuals who are now out of the market into the market to maintain family income. The supply curve may bend backwards at some point.

Over a number of years, the supply of labor would seem more flexible. Given a rising wage level the labor force may well increase in 20 years, the time necessary to bring children to maturity. The short run seems to be inelastic, however, and the major cause of changes in labor supply may be the number of hours the individual is willing to work. — *William D. Wagoner*

See also Labor Force.

LABOR SUPPLY CURVE, a graphic representation of the labor supply and the wage rate at a certain point in time. The supply curve is upward sloping due to the generally positive relationship between wages and available workers. That is, as wage rates rise, more labor enters the market; as wages decrease, fewer hours of labor are offered.

LABOR THEORY OF VALUE, the theory that the value of a good is determined by the amount of labor necessary to produce that good. Suggested by numerous pre-classical economists as one of several alternative value theories, it emerged in the late classical period as the central value theory of economics. Karl Marx based his economic analysis upon the labor theory of value, and its use led to the position that labor was exploited, because the owners of capital obtained a return (profit) for which they had no claim.

The labor theory of value, however, lacked generality because it could not explain value in situations where little or no labor was used. This theory was eventually replaced by the marginalists' analysis in which scarcity and utility determine the value of a good.

See also Das Kapital.

LABOR UNIONS. *See* Labor Movement.

LABOUR PARTY. *See* British Labour Party.

LAFFER CURVE, a relationship between marginal tax rates and the level of tax revenue. The Laffer Curve is named for its inventor, economist Arthur Laffer. The Laffer Curve depicts the fact that, initially, increases in marginal tax rates are associated with increases in tax revenues but, eventually, increases in marginal tax rates will be associated with decreased tax revenues. The inverse relationship between marginal tax rates and tax revenues which eventually occurs is caused by the fact that marginal tax rate increases will discourage production sufficiently to decrease tax revenues.

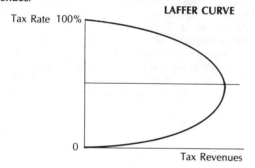

LAFFER CURVE

Tax Rate 100%

0

Tax Revenues

One conclusion that follows from this is that there is some marginal tax rate associated with maximum tax revenue. A few economists, including Laffer, argue that tax rates are above this marginal rate associated with maximum revenue. Therefore, they support cuts in marginal tax rates and argue that these cuts will actually raise tax revenues because they stimulate production. This concept was utilized as one of the main justifications for the tax cuts enacted in 1981 as the Tax Reform Act of 1981. Much debate continues as to "where on the Laffer Curve" the economy is today.

LAGGING INDICATOR, an economic measurement or time series of one aggregate of the economy which follows or trails a change in total economic activity. Lagging indicators include the value of manufacturing or trade inventory, labor cost per unit of output, and bank rates on short-term loans.

LAISSEZ-FAIRE ("let them do"), a concept of non-intervention by government developed by the eighteenth-century French physiocrats in reaction against

mercantilism, and incorporated into classical economic writings by Adam Smith and others. They believed the market mechanism in a free-enterprise competitive economy coordinates production and distributes income in a self-adjusting manner which tends toward full employment without government intervention.

The intervention advocated by those who propose a laissez-faire approach is minimal. The government must act to protect private property and private contracts so that the market mechanism can function properly. In addition, the government must provide for national defense and for those goods that the market fails to provide; these are called "public goods." The problem in this advocacy is that it is not clear from theoretical grounds where the line should be drawn. In other words, those who advocate the laissez-faire system cannot separate the legitimate from the illegitimate government interventions into the market system.

LAND, generally considered to be a factor fixed in supply by nature. Graphically the supply of land will be parallel to the vertical axis. Regardless of price, the same quantity will be offered for productive use. Higher prices are impotent to induce greater quantities of land: lower prices will not lead to withdrawal from markets, because owners prefer something to nothing. This interesting result implies that the price of land is determined by the demand for the commodities it is used to produce; hence, the prices of commodities are not determined by the price of land. This latter point is true when one's viewpoint is society as a whole. An individual or industry that uses land must pay for its service and include rent as a long-run cost factor; fixed factors viewed this way are commodity price determiners.

LAND REFORM, normally, the redistribution of agricultural land from landlords to peasants, primarily to transfer income from the rich to the poor, but hopefully to increase agricultural productivity as well. Occasionally, as in India, attempts have been made to consolidate splintered land holdings to raise productivity through economies of scale.

Where land is transferred from absentee landlords to peasants, the cultivator's security of ownership is apt to induce him to improve the land and his farming techniques and thus increase output. The fragmentation of large, well-run plantation-type holdings into small plots, however, is likely to lower output unless cooperatives can be formed to replace the equipment, working capital, and expertise, both managerial and agronomic, formerly provided by the old landowners.

See also Economies of Scale.

LANDRUM-GRIFFIN ACT (1959), also known as the Labor-Management Reporting and Disclosure

Act. Its passage resulted from (1) disclosures, during Congressional hearings in the late 1950s, of corruption and lack of internal democracy in unions; (2) continued feelings that union power and practices needed further curbs; and (3) dissatisfaction with certain features of the existing laws. The act covers several different areas: democratic reforms in union operations; restrictions on Communist party members and persons convicted of certain felonies in regard to holding union offices; and amendments clarifying and strengthening provisions of the Taft-Hartley Act (1947). It also makes picketing under certain circumstances an unfair labor practice by unions and has provisions on the eligibility of striking workers to vote in representation elections.

The Landrum-Griffin Act has a decided anti-union tone. Like the Taft-Hartley Act, it makes the basic assumption that neither unions and employees nor unions and their own members are synonymous, then spells out limitations on unions in regard to their relationships with employers, members, and the public.

—*Leonard G. Shifrin*

See also Taft-Hartley Act.

LAW OF DEMAND. *See* Substitution Effect.

LAW OF DIMINISHING RETURNS, a property of a production process which states that when one input is given successive increments, all other inputs being held constant, then a point will be reached beyond which the increments in output will diminish. Geometrically, diminishing returns to an input occur in a range in which the total product curve of that input is concave.

See also Production Function.

LAW OF DOWNWARD-SLOPING DEMAND, an overwhelming fact that more of a given commodity is purchased at lower prices than at higher prices. Furthermore, the major causative factor in changing the quantity purchased of a good is a change in its price. The theory of downward-sloping demand achieved its transformation into law by the weight of overwhelming empirical evidence. The behavioral aspects in the theory of demand need not even be explored for the law of demand to be accredited. It is a statistical fact that the price of a commodity is inversely related to the quantity of the commodity demanded.

LAW OF LARGE NUMBERS. *See* Probability.

LAW OF SUPPLY AND DEMAND states that, other things being equal, price and demand vary inversely (the law of demand), and price and supply vary directly (the law of supply). The demand curve shows the relationship between price and quantity, and the supply curve relates price and supply.

A change in demand will also occur if there is a

LAW OF SUPPLY AND DEMAND: TOPIC GUIDE

The law of supply and demand is an inclusive concept, related to virtually all other concepts in the broad area of the MARKET SYSTEM; other articles covering many of the same points are ALLOCATION, MARKET EQUILIBRIUM, and MARKET MECHANISM. To see that economic questions can be answered by societal mechanisms not structured around the law of supply and demand, consult the articles on SOCIALISM, COMMAND ECONOMY, and COMMUNISM.

The Subject Map accompanying MARKET SYSTEM displays many of these and other relationships.

change in the price of related goods or a change in consumer tastes and preferences. Such a change in demand will shift the entire demand curve to the right or to the left. The quantity of a good supplied also varies with changes in the cost of production, due to changes in technology, changes in the wage rate, or numerous other reasons. Such a change in supply will shift the entire supply curve to the right or to the left. Although there are exceptions to the law of supply and demand, these exceptions are few, and the basic laws cover most circumstances. Together, supply and demand curves can be used to determine market equilibria.

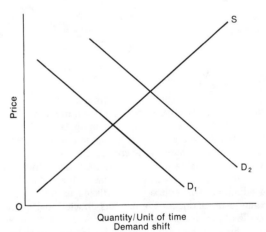

Demand shift

LAYOFF, a term used when employees lose their jobs not for cause, but due to a necessary cutback in the number of workers needed by a company. In keeping with seniority rights, when a layoff becomes necessary, the last person hired by the company is the first person to be laid off.

LEADING INDICATOR, an economic measurement or time series of one aggregate of economic activity which precedes a change in total economic activity. Leading indicators include new durable goods orders, average weekly state unemployment insurance claims, and new building permits.

See also Business Cycles, Measurement; Coincident Indicator; Lagging Indicator.

LEAKAGE. *See* Multiple Expansion of the Money Supply.

LEAST-COST FACTOR COMBINATION. If labor is plotted on the vertical axis and capital is plotted on the horizontal axis, then a family of isoquants can be derived for some commodity, given the level of technology. These downward-sloping, nonintersecting isoquants have the property that the absolute value of the slope decreases as one moves down an isoquant. The absolute value of the slope is equal to the ratio of the marginal product of capital to labor. The level of output associated with an isoquant depends upon its position. The higher the isoquant (further from the origin) the greater the level of output associated with it.

Isocost lines may be plotted on the same coordinate system discussed above. The absolute value of the slope of these lines is equal to the ratio of the price of capital to the price of labor. The level of expenditure associated with each isocost line is determined by its position. The lower the isocost line (closer to the origin), the less is the associated level of expenditures required to purchase the input combinations on the line. It is easily shown that to minimize costs the firm must choose that input combination associated with the lowest isocost line that touches the isoquant representing the chosen level of output. This occurs at a point of tangency between the isocost curve and the isoquant. Because slopes are equal at tangency points, the ratio of the marginal product of capital to labor equals the ratio of the price of capital to the price of labor at the least-cost factor combination.

—Gerald A. Whitney

See also Isocost Lines; Isoproduct Curve.

LEAST SQUARES. *See* Curve Fitting.

LEGAL TENDER, any form of money that the law requires a creditor to accept in payment of debt. All currency in the United States is legal tender, but checks are not.

See also Currency; Money.

LENIN, VLADIMIR ILICH (1870-1924), Russian Communist leader. Lenin became a revolutionary at 17, with his brother's execution for plotting to assassinate the tsar, and his own arrest and expulsion from the University of Kazan. He obtained a law degree in 1891, was exiled to Siberia from 1896 to 1899 for revolutionary activities, and went to Switzerland in 1901 to help found a Marxist newspaper. Thereafter, many travels, mostly involuntary, marked the inter-

twining of his life with that of the Russian Revolution. He organized the Bolsheviks in 1903 (from London), and the Communist party started publishing *Pravda* ("Truth") in 1912. Lenin's classic study, *Imperialism, the Highest Stage of Capitalism,* was published in 1916.

Economic Thought. The growth of finance capitalism and large business assets at home caused capitalists to look abroad, delaying the fulfillment of Marx's predictions. But Lenin, deeming imperialism the last stage of capitalism, indicated that imperialists would face two forces—domestic proletariat and colonial proletariat abroad—in inevitably violent confrontation. Russia, although not industrialized, was the first country to experience revolution, explained Lenin, because it was the weakest link in the imperialistic chain.

—John R. Matthews, Jr.

See also Bolsheviks; Class Conflict; Marx, Karl; Proletariat.

LEONTIEF, WASSILY (1906-   ). The concept of mutual interdependence among economic sectors dates back to François Quesnay and the *Tableau Économique*. While the theoretical concept was extended by Leon Walras and Vilfredo Pareto, it was not until Wassily Leontief developed the input-output table that an effective means of handling the empirical data of general equilibrium was available. Leontief's *The Structure of American Economy, 1919-1929* (1941) presented the first input-output table, which isolated flows of goods and services between various economic sectors and measured the inputs and outputs of each sector. Thus, the table allows an economist to view the source of the inputs in any given sector and the uses of that sector's output.

LESS DEVELOPED COUNTRIES (LDC), nations, primarily in Africa, Asia, and Latin America, characterized by poverty income levels, little or no savings, high rates of population growth, labor forces primarily employed in agriculture, extensive underemployment, illiteracy, and reliance on a few export items. They are also known as underdeveloped, or low-income countries. The governments of most such countries are either controlled or influenced by a small, wealthy elite, religious leaders, or tribal chieftains.

Less developed countries, as designated by the United Nations, include Indonesia, India, Kenya, Syria, Brazil, Turkey, and Ecuador. These countries try to develop their economies through UN-initiated technical cooperation and assistance programs and various bilateral financial and technical aid programs.

See also Developing Nations; International Bank for Reconstruction and Development (World Bank); Underdevelopment.

LESSENING OF COMPETITION. *See* Substantial Lessening of Competition.

LEVERAGE, a concept used to describe the effect of an increase in sales or the price on a firm's profits. There are two kinds of leverage: operating leverage and financial leverage. *Operating leverage* looks at the ratio of fixed costs for a firm. The firm with the higher fixed costs has a larger break-even point, but will experience a larger increase in profits when sales rise above this break-even point. Operating leverage is measured by the percentage change in operating income (profits) divided by the percentage change in sales.

Financial leverage is defined as the proportion of the firm's assets that have been raised by borrowing, as opposed to equity financing. The financial leverage ratio is equal to the ratio of the firm's total debt to its total assets. A firm is said to be highly leveraged if this ratio is high. In times of increasing sales and prices, such as might occur during inflation, a high financial leverage ratio is desirable because most debt involves fixed interest payments and an increase in sales will result in a magnified effect on stockholders' returns.
— *Timothy P. Ryan*

LEWIS, JOHN LLEWELLYN (1880-1969). The son of an Iowa coal miner, Lewis climbed to prominence as head of the United Mine Workers (UMW). In 1909, AFL President Samuel Gompers appointed him legislative agent for the United Mine Workers, and in 1911 he became an AFL organizer. He became UMW president in 1920.

John L. Lewis, head of the United Mine Workers (1920-1960).

In 1935, in an effort to sponsor industrial unions, Lewis led the Committee for Industrial Organization within the AFL. In 1938 he became president of the Congress of Industrial Organizations outside the AFL. Lewis remained UMW head until he retired in 1960.

In 1947 Lewis became the subject of a nationwide controversy when he was fined $10,000 by a federal court because of his defiance of a restraining order issued under the Taft-Hartley Act directing the miners to end a strike. Lewis directed the miners back to work but became a bitter foe of the Taft-Hartley Act.

In 1964 Lewis received the U.S. Presidential Medal of Honor.

LIBERAL SOCIALISM. *See* Democratic Socialism.

LIMIT PRICING is a strategy employed by oligopolists by which they set a profitable price that is low enough to discourage potential entrants into their industry. Limit pricing depends on high fixed costs that confer substantial economies of scale, so small firms are at a distinct cost disadvantage relative to large firms. Thus, by setting a price below the short-run profit-maximizing price, existing firms can make it unprofitable for new firms to enter the industry, while they themselves continue to earn economic profits.

LIMITED LIABILITY is the legal condition that exists when individuals purchase the stocks of a corporation. They are thus assured that their losses can only amount to the purchased price of the stocks. They are not held responsible for any debts or other liabilities of the corporation.

The purpose of limited liability is chiefly the promotion of capital accumulation for industrial endeavors. When investors are assured that their involvement in a corporation is limited to the amount of their investment, more people are willing to buy stocks. Thus, large firms can gather huge amounts of capital with a minimum of risk for their stockholders.

See also Corporation.

LIQUID ASSETS are assets that can be turned into cash rapidly and with little loss of value. Liquidity is relative. Money is 100% liquid. Near money is almost as liquid as cash. Government securities, and to an even greater extent corporate bonds and stocks, have a ready market but fluctuating values and hence, are much less liquid than cash. Commodities, such as houses, are not liquid at all.

See also Liquidity Preference; Portfolio Balancing.

LIQUIDITY PREFERENCE is the desire to hold money (currency and demand deposits) rather than equivalent amounts of higher-interest-earning assets, such as bonds or stocks. Currency and demand deposits can be used at any time to buy goods, but earning assets (other than interest-bearing demand deposits) must be sold before the proceeds can be spent. Such a sale may take time or yield less than the book value of the assets, or both. There are three primary motives for holding money balances.

Transactions demand is the desire to have money readily available to meet regular or anticipated day-to-day purchases. The need to have cash for this purpose arises from the fact that income is usually sporadic (weekly or monthly) and payments are continual. Transactions demand depends primarily on the level of income.

Precautionary demand is the desire to have emergency funds to meet unexpected expenditures, whether as a result of accident, emergency, or unusual opportunities. Precautionary demand depends primarily on the amount of wealth.

Speculative demand is the desire to hold money because of the expectation that it will rise in value or that prices will fall. The expected decline may refer to goods (a falling price level) or to securities (a rising interest rate). If prices are expected to rise, speculative demand disappears or becomes negative, which implies borrowing. Speculative demand depends primarily on interest rates.

—Gerald A. Whitney

See also Bond Yields.

LOANABLE FUNDS, money available for lending. There are two sources of loanable funds: savers and commercial banks. Savers include individual consumers, corporations (which save both by depreciation allowances and reinvested earnings), and governments, which save when they have a surplus of tax receipts over expenditures. Savings become loanable funds only if they are actually offered on the market and not hoarded. Savers may make their funds available directly to borrowers or through financial intermediaries. Commercial banks simply create the money they lend and, hence, are limited in the loanable funds they can provide by their reserve requirement.

See also Demand Deposits; Loans and Discounts; Monetary Policy.

LOANS AND DISCOUNTS. A loan is money lent by one person or institution to another, usually for a specified period of time and at a given rate of interest. A discount is a loan on which the interest is deducted in advance. Thus, with an ordinary loan of $1000 for 3 months at an interest rate of 6%, the borrower would receive $1000 and repay $1015 (6% of $1000 being $60 a year, or $15 for one-quarter of a year. On a discount of the same terms the $15 would be deducted in advance, so that the borrower would get $985 and repay $1000. When merchandise is bought on credit, the transaction is sometimes also referred to as a loan of the value of the goods by the merchant to the customer.

LOCAL UNION, the smallest element in the union structure. Employees at particular plants or in particular regions will be members of a local union, which is in turn under the jurisdiction of a national union. The national union itself may be affiliated with an even larger umbrella group such as the AFL-CIO or the Teamsters. Rank and file decisions are made in regular meetings of the local union, and this is where local issues are resolved.

LOCKOUTS, the management counterpart of strikes. To enforce its bargaining position, to show firmness, or to put pressure on the workers and the union, management may refuse to continue production without a labor contract, even if the union is willing to do so.

Although the resulting work interruption is the employer's doing, not the union's, it is as permissible a tactic in the bargaining of a new contract as a strike and is part of the strategy and maneuvering brought into play at the bargaining table.

See also Strike.

LOGARITHMIC FUNCTIONS. *See* Function.

LONG RUN, a period of time long enough for all the factors of production to be variable. It is not so long, however, that the basic technology in use can be changed. In the long run, labor and raw materials are variable, and capital equipment may be increased or decreased, but decisions on the future of the operation must be made under the assumption of fixed technology. Within any long-run period there will be a number of short-run periods in which labor is the variable factor of production, with plant size and capital equipment fixed. Under the assumption of fixed plant size, the output or capacity utilization of that plant may be varied.

See also Short Run.

LONG RUN: TOPIC GUIDE

An understanding of the economic meaning of the long run is aided by also consulting the article on the SHORT RUN. Other articles that relate to or help define this concept are EQUILIBRIUM OF THE INDUSTRY; EQUILIBRIUM OF THE FIRM, LONG-RUN; LONG-RUN AVERAGE COST CURVE; and LONG-RUN MARKET EQUILIBRIUM. For a specific difference between the short and long run, consult the article on TOTAL FIXED COST.

The Subject Maps accompanying the articles on SUPPLY and THEORY OF THE FIRM show the interrelationships of these and other concepts.

LONG-RUN AVERAGE COST CURVE, the "envelope" of all the short-run curves for the firm. Production always takes place in the short run, and along short-run curves. The long run may be viewed as a planning horizon for the firm; it decides on the best way to combine inputs to produce the most profitable output. The long-run average cost curve indicates the minimum cost possible (by varying all inputs, including firm size) to produce any given output.

The actual long-run average cost curve depends, in the final analysis, on the extent of economies and diseconomies that accompany increases in the scale of the firm. Assume initially that the firm experiences some economies of scale due to specialization possibilities, technology, or financial matters. This means that as firm size expands, the minimum cost points on the new short-run cost curves (corresponding to the larger-sized plants) will be to the right and *below* the minimum cost points of the old short-run cost curves. Hence the long-run average cost curve will initially fall as output is increased. Eventually it would be expected that economies of scale would be exhausted. When this happens, the long-run average cost curve will be flat. When diseconomies of scale emerge, the long-run average cost curve will rise, reflecting the fact that the short-run average cost curves associated with larger-scale operations have minimum points to the right and *above* the old short-run average cost curves. Hence over the entire range of output, the firm's long-run average cost curve will be U-shaped.

—Robert L. Brite

LONG-RUN COST AND SUPPLY. In the long run, which really is a planning horizon, the firm has the option of varying *all* inputs to produce the most profitable output. The long-run cost curve for the firm depends on the extent of its economies (reduction in unit costs as firm size increases due to specialization, technological, and financial advantages) and diseconomies (increases in unit costs as firm size increases, due to increased management problems). Another crucial curve is the effect on resource prices as the firm size increases.

The shape of the long-run average cost curve of the firm tends to affect the long-run supply curve of the industry. In addition, one must consider the effect on resource prices as the industry expands. This latter consideration depends largely on whether the industry in question is a relatively large buyer of the resources used. The supply curve of the industry shows the conditions under which the firms in a given industry will voluntarily produce different outputs. Of course, another consideration with industry supply must be the entry and exit of firms in response to abnormal and subnormal profits.

Persisting decreasing costs due to economies will lead to the breakdown of competition and the industry supply schedule will be difficult to establish. Normally some economies will appear as a firm expands, then some diseconomies will arise; the long-run average cost curve will be U-shaped. If resource prices remain constant throughout, then the industry supply sched-

ule will be a horizontal line at the minimum average cost, parallel to the X axis. If resource prices rise as the industry expands, average cost will tend to rise for the old as well as the newly entered firms. Before the industry will voluntarily increase output, therefore, price must rise; the supply schedule will be upward sloping.

—Robert L. Brite

See also Economies of Scale.

LONG-RUN ELASTICITY OF DEMAND measures the responsiveness of consumer purchases initiated by price changes over a time period sufficiently long that changes in the shape and position of the demand curve for the good in question can occur. This change in shape and position of demand curves occurs because of changing incomes, tastes, expectations, and prices of related goods. Evidence tends to support the claim that the elasticity of demand for a good increases in the long run, primarily because of the increasing number of available substitute goods.

LONG-RUN ELASTICITY OF SUPPLY refers to a firm's or industry's ability to react to demand changes in the long run, in which capital is also a variable factor of production, so that the firm has the option of increasing plant size and equipment. Assuming the industry is relatively small so that expansion will not dramatically increase input prices, the firm can take on more labor and capital simultaneously, thereby offsetting diminishing returns and increasing costs somewhat. We would expect, therefore, that long-run elasticity of supply should be considerably greater than short-run elasticity. Changes in demand are reflected mostly in *price* changes in the short run, mostly in *output* changes in the long run.

See also Elasticity of Supply.

LONG-RUN INDUSTRY SUPPLY. The long-run supply curve for an industry shows the relationship between industry output and price when the industry is in long-run equilibrium. An industry can be in long-run equilibrium only when existing firms are earning a normal rate of return at the prevailing price and are operating at the minimum of their long-run average cost curves. This condition ensures that existing firms have no incentive to expand and new firms have no incentive to enter the industry.

Now consider what happens when there is an increase in demand for the industry's product. Initially, price rises and firms increase output along their marginal cost curves. Firms in the industry are now earning economic profits; new firms are attracted to the industry, and market price falls. For long-run equilibrium to be restored, market price must fall until no firm is capable of earning economic profits. But this occurs only when price has fallen back to its initial level and firms are once again producing at the minimum of their long-run average cost curves. Hence, the industry has responded to an increase in demand by simply increasing supply (each firm is producing the same output as before but now there are more firms in the industry). Therefore, the long-run industry supply curve is horizontal.

An implicit assumption in the analysis above is that industry expansion has no effect on the individual firm's long-run average cost curves. If industry expansion increases factor prices, this assumption will not be valid; the firm's long-run average cost curve will shift up as industry output expands. In this case the response to an increase in demand for the industry's product will initially be the same as described above; existing firms will increase their output and new firms will be attracted by economic profits. However, entry of the new firms will not drive price back to its initial level. Prices will fall to a level that will allow firms to earn a normal profit when producing at the minimum of their (higher) long-run average cost curve. The new equilibrium price will hence be higher than the old, reflecting the increased factor costs. The long-run supply curve for the industry will slope upward.

—*Gerald A. Whitney*

LONG-RUN PHILLIPS CURVE. Those who subscribe to the natural rate hypothesis suggest that the Phillips curve is vertical at the natural rate of real GNP. That means that the trade-off implied by the short-run Phillips curve applies (as the name implies) only in the short run. This suggests also that the Phillips curve is unstable in the long run.

See also Natural Rate Hypothesis; Phillips Curve.

LONG-TERM CAPITAL MOVEMENT. *See* Capital Account.

LOOSE-KNIT ASSOCIATIONS. *See* Trade Association.

LORENZ CURVE, a device for representing the

distribution of income among groups. The cumulated percent of the population is shown on the horizontal axis, the cumulated percent of income on the vertical axis. If all members of the population had equal incomes, then the first 20% of the population would account for 20% of the income, and so on. The curve would lie along the diagonal AC. If the first 20% received less than 20% of the income, the curve would lie below the diagonal. As the inequality of income distribution increases, the Lorenz curve is bowed further away from the diagonal.

LOSS MINIMIZATION is a special case of profit maximization, where the maximum profit is negative. If the firm can generate revenue in excess of its variable cost, it will pay the firm to continue operation until such time as it can free itself of its fixed obligations—even if there is no way to show a positive profit. If an unprofitable firm were to cease operation prior to this time, it would incur a loss equal to the full amount of its fixed cost. If the firm can cover variable cost, it will minimize its loss by maximizing its negative profit.

See also Profit Maximization.

LOW INCOME COUNTRIES. *See* Less Developed Countries.

McGUIRE-KEOGH ACT (1952) reestablishes the validity of the "nonsigners" clause in fair-trade contracts executed by firms selling goods in interstate commerce. The Miller-Tydings Act of 1937 permitted individual states to pass resale price-maintenance (or fair-trade) legislation, under which firms selling in these states could contract with retailers to set a minimum resale price and be exempt from prosecution under the antitrust laws.

A significant feature of these contracts was the nonsigners clause, by which any retailer selling the product in a state could be bound by the provisions of a resale-price-maintenance contract executed with any other seller in the state.

In the *Schwegmann v. Calvert Corp.* decision (1951) the Supreme Court rendered the nonsigners clause invalid, holding that it was not a part of the Miller-Tydings Act. Thus, only those contracts voluntarily entered into would be binding on a retailer. The McGuire-Keogh Act in effect reverses the *Schwegmann* decision and established as law the validity of the nonsigners clause.

Both the McGuire-Keogh and the Miller-Tydings Acts were repealed in 1977, making resale price maintenance illegal.   —*Thomas O. Depperschmidt*

See also Fair-Trade Laws; Miller-Tydings Act.

MACHLUP, FRITZ (1902-1983), a specialist in international economics, one of the first to consider the international trade aspects of the Keynesian multiplier.

Machlup's *International Trade and the National Income Multiplier* (1943) used a period analysis to consider the impact of trade upon the multiplier process. Much of the current knowledge of foreign trade multipliers is the result of Machlup's work. In addition, Machlup provided an excellent discussion of foreign exchange in his article "The Theory of Foreign Exchanges." Machlup has also been an important figure in analyzing various plans for reforming the international exchange system. His other publications include *Education and Economic Growth* (1970), *International Monetary Systems* (1975), and *A History of Thought on Economic Integration* (1977).

MACROECONOMICS, a study of economics using a total or aggregate approach. Such economic factors as total output of goods and services, total income, total employment, and average level of prices are analyzed. For example, the study of the aggregate expenditure patterns of all consumers or the total output of all firms is a macroeconomic approach. Out of this aggregate approach have developed what are commonly referred to as macroeconomic theory, Keynesian economics (after the British economist John Maynard Keynes), or national income theory.

Concepts. The more important concepts employed in macroeconomics are gross national product, net national product, national income, total savings, total investment, total personal consumption expenditures, government purchases of goods and services, total employment, the multiplier, transfer payments, and balance of payments. Macroeconomic theory has developed a system of national accounts in which the relationship of the aggregate or macrovariables is established and analyzed.

Concerns. Macroeconomics concerns itself with the effects of changing one macrovariable on another variable and on the economy of the country. Such analyses are helpful to federal, state, and local governments in formulating sound fiscal and monetary policies, and in developing other legislation to meet national economic goals. An example of fiscal policy is the employment of the rediscount rate to affect interest rate levels. Another example of government action was the imposition of direct price and wage controls in 1971 to help curb inflation. Another major area of concern in macroanalysis is the determination of the flow of income. In an effort to get a better insight into the workings of an advanced industrial economic system, macroeconomics theorists have developed a basic theoretical structure or model that depicts a circular flow of income.   — *Algin B. King*

MAINTENANCE OF MEMBERSHIP, provisions in collectively bargained contracts that require those union workers to remain so, although nonmembers may not be required to join. It is one of the less frequently used union security arrangements. Fre-

quently an "escape period" is provided, during which workers may terminate their union membership. If they do not, they must remain members until another escape period occurs.

MALTHUS, THOMAS ROBERT (1766-1834). Best known for the theory of population in his *Essay on Population* (1798), the Reverend Malthus of England also made significant contributions to classical economics in his *Principles of Political Economy* (1820) and in his correspondence with David Ricardo.

The most significant economic doctrine which Malthus developed was his contention that it was possible to have a general overproduction (or underconsumption) of goods. While Malthus introduced this concept, most of his contemporary economists, particularly Ricardo, argued against the possibility, and it was not until the Keynesian development a century later that such a consideration again entered the mainstream of economic thought. Malthus also made important contributions to the theories of rent, wages, and the returns to capital.

See also Essay on Population.

MANPOWER POLICY. Although there has always been considerable emphasis on the development, training, and efficient use of manpower resources, it was not until the 1960s that the United States developed a major national manpower policy.

In 1962, Congress passed the Manpower Development and Training Act (MDTA), providing nearly $15 million annually for programs to retrain the unemployed. Originally, the act only provided for the retraining of mature, experienced, family heads who had been displaced by technological and economic changes. However, amendments later provided for the training of youth, also provided for in the Vocational Education Act of 1963.

In 1965, the Higher Education Act provided special federal funds to higher education, and the Elementary and Secondary Education Act provided federal assistance for schools in poverty-stricken areas. In that same year, two acts were passed for concentrated redevelopment of depressed areas. These were the Public Works and Economic Development Act and the Appalachian Regional Development Act.

Many types of programs went into effect in the 1960s. The institutional training programs included Job Corps, the Concentrated Employment Program (CEP), and the Work Incentive Program. On-the-job training programs included JOBS, Public Service Careers, and Job Optional. Programs dealing with work experience and work support were the Neighborhood Youth Corps, In-School and Summer programs, Out-of-School programs, Operation Mainstream, and Foster Grandparents.

The Comprehensive Employment and Training Act (CETA) consolidated existing manpower programs in

1973. The Job Training Partnership Act (JTPA) of 1982 succeeded CETA and recruited the private sector to help train workers. The Work Incentive Program (WIN) for welfare recipients was authorized in 1967 and was superseded by the JOBS (Job Opportunities and Basic Skills) state-run programs, part of the Family Support Act of 1988.

The positive effects of these programs have been modest. Little headway was made in providing the hard-core unemployed with marketable skills. Earnings gains usually came from working additional hours rather than from higher wages. At its height, CETA reached at most 5% of the unemployed and 10% of the working poor. Manpower funding was radically diminished during the Reagan administration. In 1988, funding for JTPA was 70% less than CETA's funding in 1980 and funding for WIN had decreased to one-third of its 1980 level. — *William D. Wagoner*

MAO ZEDONG (1893-1976), Communist leader of China, who helped found the Chinese Communist party in 1921. In 1926 he staged an unsuccessful peasant revolt and in 1931 established a short-lived "soviet republic." Emerging as the leader of Chinese communism, Mao became both party chairman and chief of state when the Communists took over in 1949, but resigned the latter position in 1959.

Peasant-emphasis and nationalism are China's posture. When the Communist movement originally led by urban industrial workers was crushed, Mao drew support for his guerrilla movement from the peasantry, indicating that revolutionary possibilities are far better in poor agricultural countries. Mao also believed that capitalists of developed, industrialized nations are exploiting the peasants in the underdeveloped world more than the traditional industrial proletariat.

— *John R. Matthews, Jr.*

See also Nationalism; Revisionism; Revolutionary Socialism.

MARGINAL ANALYSIS, an analytical technique frequently used in economics in which small increments in quantities are examined. As an illustration, assume the total cost of producing 10 units of product is $100, and the total cost of producing 11 units of product is $132. From the total cost data we may easily compute the average costs by dividing the total costs by the number of units of product. Thus, the average costs for 10 and 11 units would be $10 ($100 ÷ 10 units) and $12 ($132 ÷ 11 units), respectively. The marginal cost of the eleventh unit is $32, that is, the total cost of producing 11 units ($132) minus the total cost of producing 10 units ($100). The preceding is merely illustrative of marginal analysis. Economists use many other marginal concepts in addition to the concept of marginal cost.

Marginal Utility. The first widely accepted application of marginal analysis came in the 1860s when

---

MARGINAL ANALYSIS: TOPIC GUIDE

Marginal analysis can be applied usefully to many aspects of economic behavior. For its application to consumer behavior, see the articles on CONSUMER EQUILIBRIUM and MARGINAL UTILITY; in regard to the theory of the firm, see PROFIT MAXIMIZATION and LEAST COST FACTOR COMBINATION. For application of marginal analysis in a macroeconomic frame of reference, see MARGINAL EFFICIENCY OF CAPITAL and CONSUMPTION FUNCTION.

---

marginal utility became an important tool for economists. Prior to this time, Adam Smith, in his famous book *An Inquiry into the Nature and Causes of the Wealth of Nations* (1776), had noted that diamonds sold for a high price even though they were less useful than water, which had a very low price. Smith failed to solve this paradox of value, but in 1862 the English economist Stanley Jevons explained that the price of a good is not determined by the total satisfaction (or total utility) obtained from the good. Rather, the good's marginal utility (the additional satisfaction obtained from a small increment of the good) determines its value. The total satisfaction we gain from water is greater than that received from diamonds. On the other hand, one drop of water added to the universe would produce virtually no additional satisfaction (marginal utility) because of the large quantity of water already existing. A small increment of diamonds, however, would give more marginal utility because of their greater relative scarcity; so, their price is greater.

At about the same time that Jevons was writing in England, three influential Austrian economists, Carl Menger, Friedrich von Wieser, and Eugen von Böhm-Bawerk, and the famous French economist Leon Walras were utilizing marginal analysis. By the mid-1880s the new methodology had swept the economics profession.

Equilibrium. The neoclassical school of economics (1880-1940), with its British leader, Alfred Marshall, used the law of diminishing marginal utility to explain the slope of the demand curve for almost all individual goods. Within a given period of time, if a person receives more and more and more units of one particular good, the marginal utility of each new unit of the good would decline; for example, the tenth suit of clothes received in one year's time adds less utility than the first. Because of this law, each person could be induced to buy additional suits only if the price were lowered: it follows that the lower the price, the more suits buyers would stand ready to buy. Marshall and the other neoclassical economists used this analysis, together with a new treatment of supply, to demonstrate the determination of the equilibrium price and the equilibrium quantity traded for each commodity. Much of this analysis remains as part of current economic theory.

Resource Allocation. Modern economics also uses marginal utility as a tool in teaching proper resource allocation. A resource is properly allocated when the marginal utility derived from it in each of its uses is equal. In other words, so long as there is greater marginal product from a resource when it is producing product A rather than product B, the resource should be transferred from B to A, but as more of A is produced, its marginal utility declines, and as less of B is produced, its marginal utility increases. There is less and less additional satisfaction from resources transferred to A and more and more satisfaction lost from resources taken from B. So long as the gain exceeds the loss, the transfer should continue, but eventually the marginal utility of labor when used to produce A will equal the marginal utility of labor when used to produce B. At that point the transfer should stop.

The same type of marginal analysis can be applied to many specific resource allocation decisions, such as whether to devote more resources to public goods, like dams, or private goods, like refrigerators. Cost-benefit analysis helps make allocation decisions on the basis of the marginal returns versus the marginal costs. Economists also analyze the behavior of the business firm by assuming that it will decide to produce a unit of product only so long as its marginal revenue (that is, the additional revenue to be received as a result of the production and sale of the unit of product) is greater than its marginal cost.

In 1936 the distinguished economist John Maynard Keynes introduced several new marginal concepts, among which were the marginal propensity to consume and the marginal propensity to save. These concepts refer to the percentages of an increment of income utilized for additional consumption and additional savings, respectively. If, for example, the government reduces taxes to stimulate demand for goods, the extent of the increase will depend on the values of the marginal propensities to consume and save. Among the marginal concepts used as part of the analytical framework of economics are marginal efficiency of capital, marginal product, marginal revenue product, and marginal rate of substitution. All of these concepts focus attention on additional units in analyzing important economic questions.

—Allan B. Mandelstamm

See also Consumption Function; Equilibrium; Marginal Cost; Marginal Revenue; Marginal Utility.

MARGINAL COST measures the rate at which total cost changes as output is varied; it can be thought of as the difference in total cost between producing or not producing an additional unit of output.

See also Average Cost; Total Cost.

MARGINAL COST OF PRODUCTION (MC), the increment in total cost (TC) resulting from a small increase in output. For a discrete increase in output X, MC is defined as $\triangle TC/\triangle X$ (or $\triangle TVC/\triangle X$), with $\triangle$ signifying "change in." If the TC function is differentiable, then MC is defined as the derivative of TC.

See also Cost Function.

MARGINAL-COST PRICING, a particular concept of economic efficiency. A rigorous development of this concept involves complex mathematics, but an intuitive idea of what is involved is easy to grasp if one reasons by analogy. An efficient firm maximizes its profit by equating marginal revenue and marginal cost: it expands output as long as additional units of output add more to revenue than to cost. If society could define social benefit and social cost, an efficient society would maximize benefit by equating marginal social benefit and marginal social cost. Where exchange is voluntary, many economists find it persuasive to take market price as measuring marginal social benefits, and accordingly advocate pricing goods and services.

—Clarence C. Morrison

MARGINAL EFFICIENCY OF CAPITAL (MEC) or Marginal Efficiency of Investment (MEI), a term used in both micro- and macroeconomics. In microeconomics, the marginal efficiency of capital (or investment) is defined as the increase in output (or the rate of return) that results from an increase in the capital stock (or an increase in investment), holding everything else constant.

In the narrowest, least realistic sense, MEC would be the value of the output added annually by the capital without the use of any other additional inputs (in which case there would be no deductions: one would divide the value of the additional output per year by the cost of the equipment to compute the rate of return). In this case one would have the exact conditions for the application of the law of diminishing returns: one input (the new capital equipment) increasing, while all other inputs remain constant. One would therefore expect that increasing investments would be accompanied by smaller rates of return: the MEC curve would slope down to the right, as a demand curve. Since the reason for investment is profits, and since the rate of return measures them, MEC is the demand for capital.

In a more realistic world one would expect possible investments to have different expected rates of return, so that if only a few investments were undertaken, they would be the most profitable ones, and that if more investments were undertaken, they would have lower rates of return. For this reason, too, one would expect the MEC curve to slope downward, even if the full requirements for the law of diminishing returns were not met, and more of other inputs were used.

Capital Supply and Demand. In Keynes's original treatment the quantity of investment that would occur equates MEC with the rate of interest, the intersection of the demand and supply curves for capital. The supply of and demand for money result in an interest rate; equating MEC with the interest rate results in a specific amount of investment spending; investment and consumption spending result in a specific level of income and employment.

Realistically, the rate of interest is not the operative limit to investment. Most businesses expect the investments they plan to make to have a rate of return appreciably higher than the rate of interest. In addition, bankers and other suppliers of capital want a margin or cushion for error. A realistic MEC demand curve would, then, be the expected value added by the investment project less all additional input costs other than the costs of the capital, and a realistic supply curve would be what bankers were persuaded was safe to lend.   — *Walter C. Neale*

MARGINALISM. The extension of the marginal principle to all areas of economic theory must stand as one of the most significant developments in economic theory. The idea that economic decisions generally are made in terms of a little more of this or a little less of that, rather than in all-or-nothing terms, made possible the fruition of the theory of market in Alfred Marshall's curves of supply and demand. The acceptance of the marginal principle allowed the concept of equilibria, and introduced the possibility of expanding economic theory through the use of differential calculus. The development of marginalism is unusual in that the concept was developed simultaneously but independently by William Jevons, Carl Menger, and Leon Walras.

See also Jevons, William Stanley; Menger, Carl; Neoclassical Economics; Walras, Leon.

MARGINAL PHYSICAL PRODUCTIVITY, or MARGINAL PRODUCT, of a factor is the extra output obtained by using one more unit of that factor, other factors of production being held constant. The marginal product of a factor can be calculated by taking the slope (first partial derivative) of the total produce curve, if it is differentiable.

MARGINAL PRODUCTIVITY OF LABOR. *See* Wage Theories.

MARGINAL PROPENSITY TO CONSUME (MPC). *See* Consumption Function.

MARGINAL PROPENSITY TO IMPORT, the proportion of an increase in income that will be spent on imports. Imports are leakages from the income stream, because the payments go to foreigners and, therefore, do not maintain domestic money incomes.

MARGINAL PROPENSITY TO SAVE (MPS), the ratio of the change in saving resulting from a change in income to the change in income, 1.00 minus the marginal propensity to consume. Either MPS or MPC can be used to compute the multiplier, which tells the ultimate effect of a change in spending on national income.

See also Consumption Function; Marginal Propensity to Consume; National Income Determinations.

MARGINAL RATE OF SUBSTITUTION, the rate at which one good can be substituted for another good while keeping the level of utility constant. Geometrically, the rate is the slope of the isoquant. Diminishing marginal rate of substitution accounts for the convexity of the indifference curve and the negative slope of the demand curve.

See also Indifference Curves; Utility Function.

MARGINAL RATE OF TECHNICAL SUBSTITUTION, the rate at which one input must be substituted for another so as to keep the level of output constant. Geometrically, it is the slope of an isoquant.

See also Production Function.

MARGINAL REVENUE is the rate at which total revenue varies as sales quantity varies and can be thought of as the difference in revenue between selling an additional unit and not selling that unit.

MARGINAL REVENUE PRODUCT OF LABOR. *See* Demand for Labor.

MARGINAL TAX RATE, the incremental tax burden due to an incremental change in the tax base. It is the amount of tax that would have to be paid if the tax base were increased by a dollar, or the amount of tax savings if the tax base were reduced by a dollar. If a tax is progressive, then the marginal tax rate rises as the tax base increases. If a tax is regressive, then marginal tax rates fall as the tax base increases. For proportional taxes, the marginal tax rate does not change. When examining behavior of individuals and firms in response to taxes, it is the marginal tax rate that is the most relevant factor.

See also Personal Income Tax; Taxation; Tax Rates.

MARGINAL UTILITY, the rate of increase in utility due to a small increase in the amount of one commodity. If the utility function is differentiable, the marginal utility of X is defined as the first partial derivative of the utility function with respect to X.

MARGIN REQUIREMENTS, government restrictions concerning the maximum proportion of a purchase of stock that can be borrowed from a financial institution, with the stock pledged as collateral. For example, if the margin requirement is 50%, the investor can have a maximum of 50% of the current market value of the stock in borrowed funds.

Assume an investor wants to buy 1,000 shares of XYZ Corporation at $50 a share. This purchase will cost $50,000; the investor is allowed to borrow up to $25,000 from a bank or other financial institution, using the stock as collateral. The real problem occurs when the price of the stock decreases. If the stock price decreases to $40 a share, the investor now has $25,000 of borrowed funds on stock worth only $40,000; in other words, he has 62.5% of the value of the stock in borrowed funds, which is above the margin requirement. He will then receive a *margin call*, and he must either repay $5,000 of the loan or sell the stock and pay off the entire loan. If he sells all or part of the stock to cover the margin call, he will realize a capital loss.

MARKET ANALYSIS. *See* Equilibrium.

MARKET CLEARING occurs when the market price of a commodity is such that the quantity demanded by consumers equals the quantity supplied by producers. The market will not clear at any other price.

MARKET CONCENTRATION, the control of a large proportion of total sales by a small absolute number of firms in an industry. For example, of total sales in the soaps and detergents industry in 1982, 60% of these sales were controlled by the 4 largest firms in the industry. Given that there were 642 firms in that industry in 1982, it can be said that the soaps and detergent industry has a high degree of market concentration.

Concentration of control of U.S. business corporations seems to be very heavy. The very large corporations are relatively few in number but they control a high majority of all corporate assets. For example, in 1975, about 1% of the number of U.S. corporations controlled over 75% of all corporate assets. In addition, 95% of the number of all corporations controlled only 10% of all corporate assets.

Because a few large corporations control the bulk of employment, sales, and assets, competition is lessened. In addition, each very large corporation can centralize within its management a considerable amount of economic power. In spite of the growing concern over market concentration, statistics indicate that concentration of control by a relatively few giant corporations has actually declined somewhat since the early 1930s.   —*William D. Wagoner*

See also Concentration Ratio.

MARKET DEMAND for a product is represented by a schedule showing the various amounts of the good demanded at the various possible prices. These market demand curves are the functions facing the firms producing for sale in a particular market. Markets will absorb additional output only at lower prices, and

higher prices paid will result from restricted quantities of output. The law of demand applies to markets. The market demand curve is constructed by horizontally summing the demand curves of all individuals constituting the market. The resulting demand curve shows that the market will absorb only the aggregate quantity of goods that all individuals will demand at various prices.

MARKET ECONOMY, one in which the basic questions of what, how, and for whom goods shall be produced are answered by market forces in a system of interrelated markets involving exchange of large quantities of goods and services. Markets are defined in terms of time, area, and types of product. Prices are set by demand and supply of buyers and sellers, respectively.

In the diagram, PE is the equilibrium price and QE the equilibrium quantity; the market is cleared. This

MARKET SUPPLY AND DEMAND

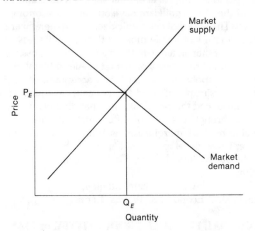

tendency to automatic adjustment of consumers' preferences, reflected in demand, and producers' costs, reflected in supply, is the result of a competitive market in which (1) factors of production are privately owned; and (2) production is carried out through the initiative of private enterprise. Resources are allocated via prices, as consumers and producers aim toward maximizing their economic gains with no restrictions on their capacity to participate. This allocative function can be modified by governments or by the exercise of monopoly powers in markets where competition does not prevail. —*John R. Matthews, Jr.*

See also Allocation; Command Economy; Competition; Evolutionary Socialism; Invisible Hand; Laissez Faire; Market Clearing.

MARKET EQUILIBRIUM is determined through supply and demand. The demand curve for a commodity represents the various quantities that the consumer would purchase at various prices. The supply curve for a commodity represents the various quantities that producers would be willing to supply at various market prices.

Theory. The individual quantity that is demanded is, of course, dependent upon the market price, the income of the consumer, the price of related goods, complements and substitutes, and consumer taste and preferences. A change in any one of these variables would cause a change in the amount of the good demanded. The supply curve is dependent upon the price of the commodity and the cost of producing that commodity. Together the supply and the demand curves determine the equilibrium price and quantity. Equilibrium avoids excess supply and excess demand.

The schedule shows equilibrium at market price where the quantity supplied is exactly equal to the quantity demanded: consumers are willing to purchase exactly the amount that producers are willing to produce. This price is the market equilibrium price. At higher prices the producers would like to supply a

MARKET EQUILIBRIUM

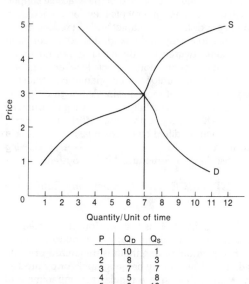

P	Q_D	Q_S
1	10	1
2	8	3
3	7	7
4	5	8
5	3	12

larger quantity than consumers are willing to purchase, and at lower prices the consumers would like to purchase a larger quantity than producers are willing to supply. Graphically, the intersection of the supply and demand curves is at market price $3 and equilibrium quantity 7 units per unit of time as shown.

Significance. If price is above equilibrium and there is excess supply, the inventory of producers tends to build up and the producers will lower price toward the equilibrium to clear their inventories. If price is below the equilibrium, then consumers will demand a larger quantity of the good than is being produced and will bid up the market price toward the equilibrium. Once this market equilibrium is established, there is no

tendency to move away from it unless there is a disturbance in either the market's supply or demand curves.   —*Robert L. Brite*

See also Market Structure.

MARKET FAILURE. Ideally, competitive markets allocate production and consumption so that marginal social benefit and marginal social cost are equal. When this equality fails to hold, it is said that "markets fail." Some market solutions may be inefficient or inequitable. In cases of market failure, the government may intervene to provide a socially optimal allocation of economic pluses and to minimize economic minuses. Market failures may be categorized as problems of allocation, distribution, or stabilization. Antitrust laws, public utility regulation, and legislation to control environmental pollution are attempts by government to rectify allocative market failure. Distributive market failures are rectified by means of government taxes and transfers. Fiscal and monetary policy to even out fluctuations in the business cycle are remedies for stabilization market failure.

MARKETING ORDERS, AGRICULTURAL, are economic regulations, enforced by federal or state governments and intended to benefit producers, that apply to all sales of particular farm commodities in specified areas. Almost all milk produced under sanitation conditions that make it eligible for consumption in fresh form is sold under orders regulating large metropolitan markets or areas containing smaller cities. All such orders establish minimum prices to be paid to producers for milk actually sold for fresh consumption (Class I) and for extra milk diverted to manufacturing uses (Class II). Some state orders also establish minimum wholesale and retail prices.

Numerous marketing orders for particular fruits and vegetables, mostly for fresh consumption, are also in effect in California, Florida, and elsewhere. Among the provisions sometimes included in such orders are minimum standards for quality and size, requirements for diverting products to processing uses under some conditions, rate-of-shipment regulations, and assessment of producers to provide funds for research or advertising.

See also Price-Support Programs.

MARKET MECHANISM, the way in which the market system provides the necessary information to enable supply and demand to work to determine prices and output in any particular market. Through the market mechanism the diverse desires of millions of consumers are made known to businesses, and the millions of economic decisions and actions of buyers and sellers are coordinated. The market mechanism is often referred to as the invisible hand regulating the everyday economic processes and activities in a market economy. In a market system the market mecha-

MARKET MECHANISM IN OPERATION FOR 12-INCH BLACK AND WHITE PORTABLE TELEVISIONS			
$ Prices	Quantity Demanded Millions Per Quarter	Quantity Supplied Millions Per Quarter	Pressures on Prices
$ 105.	2.3	4.8	Declining
$ 99.	3.2	3.2	Equilibrium State
$ 85.	4.5	1.9	Increasing

nism is the key instrument that enables the system to solve the three basic economic problems confronting any society: what economic goods to produce, how to produce them, and how to distribute the economic goods to the members of society.

There are four basic components of the market mechanism which enable consumers to signal effectively to businesses that they wish more beef and less chicken, or more furniture and less clothing, X type car, Y type television set, etc. These four components are: (1) demands of consumers translated into demand schedules for each type or class of goods; (2) available supply as furnished by businesses at a given time, usually referred to as a supply schedule for each type or class of goods; (3) price, which serves as a linking and coordinating device; and (4) competition, a component ensuring that proper efforts are made by businesses to supply goods and services in forms desired by the public, in proper quantities and at times when consumers want them.

Supply and Demand Schedules. A demand schedule is an aggregate of consumer demand for any brand or class of products at a given price or at several price levels. A supply schedule is an aggregate of the amounts of any given brand or class of products that producers are willing to supply at given price levels.

Price and Competition. In a money economy everyone receives money for what he sells and in turn purchases what he wants with money. If consumers want more of a good than is currently being offered, in the process of bidding against each other, they will cause the price to rise and, thereby, induce producers to produce more. Conversely, if supply exceeds demand, competition will force prices down, and producers will not produce as much of the good as before. Thus, supply and demand will gradually move to an equilibrium state through the mechanisms of price and competition.

Equilibrium State. As a result of the operation of the market mechanism, there evolves a state of equilibrium in which the amount of a product demanded by consumers and the amount supplied by producers are equal. The interactions of the four components bring supply and demand together at a given price. The equilibrium state is shown for 12-inch portable televisions. For this particular type of television set supply and demand are at equilibrium at a price of $99 and a volume of 3.2 million sets. The market

mechanism works in an impersonal but effective way to supply consumers with what they want and are capable of purchasing.

Imperfections. The components of the market mechanism can operate in the manner discussed only under the conditions of perfect competition. Actions and effects are often modified under other market conditions, such as oligopoly, monopolistic competition, and monopoly. For example, under oligopoly the normal downward pull on prices of excess supply may not be fully realized, because there are so few suppliers involved that they control most of the available supply: through gentlemen's agreements they can immediately withhold goods from the market and not reduce prices in response to a drop in demand. It is not uncommon to find some degree of administered pricing under oligopoly market conditions especially where one or a few powerful labor unions or companies constrain the effects of the market mechanism. Although only partially effective in successfully coordinating consumers' demands with supply in the most efficient economic manner when modified by reality, it is, nevertheless, a powerful force.   —*Algin B. King*

See also Market Structure; Market System.

MARKET PRICE. See Competition; Equilibrium Price.

MARKET SHARING is the division of a market or sales territory by agreement among producers so that price competition among them is minimized or eliminated. This division may be geographic or by product class. Market sharing is a regular accompaniment of price-fixing plans, since agreements not to compete leave pricing to the one producer with "selling rights" in that area. Market sharing is inherently *(per se)* illegal under the Sherman Antitrust Act.

See also Collusion; Restraint of Trade.

MARKET STRUCTURE. There are a number of different market structures in any economy. They range from pure competition to pure monopoly. In between the two extremes lie oligopoly and monopolistic competition.

An assumption of pure competition is that the industry contains many firms producing a homogeneous product. There is free entry and exit of these firms from the industry and a situation where no one firm can affect the market price. That is, any one firm is so small relative to the total market that its increasing or decreasing output cannot influence the market price.

On the other extreme there is monopoly, an industry of only one firm. This firm obviously controls the industry's output and has a number of advantages. A monopolistic firm will normally produce a smaller output and charge a higher market price than a number of firms (pure competition) producing the same total industry output.

MARKET STRUCTURE: TOPIC GUIDE

For the various characteristics that determine market structure, see PRODUCT DIFFERENTIATION and MARKET CONCENTRATION. To follow up on the various types of market structure, see PERFECT COMPETITION, IMPERFECT COMPETITION, MONOPOLISTIC COMPETITION, OLIGOPOLY, MONOPOLY, MONOPSONY, and BILATERAL MONOPOLY. And for a view of some of the underlying factors that influence the characteristics of markets, see ENTRY, BARRIERS TO ENTRY, and ECONOMIES OF SCALE.

The Subject Maps accompanying MARKET SYSTEM and THEORY OF THE FIRM show these and other interrelationships.

Between the two extremes there is oligopoly, an industry of only a few firms. It is closer to pure monopoly than it is to pure competition. The other type of industry is monopolistic, or imperfect, competition, where several firms produce a similar output. The major difference between monopolistic competition and pure competition is that under monopolistic competition there is product differentiation: all firms in the industry are not producing identical products. Under monopolistic competition there is free entry and exit whereas under either monopoly or oligopoly, entry is difficult. —*Robert L. Brite*

See also Competition; Monopolistic Competition; Monopoly; Oligopoly.

MARKET SUPPLY. The market (or industry) supply curve is a relationship between the price of a product and the quantity voluntarily supplied by all firms in the industry producing the product. As such it shows the total amounts that will be forthcoming at various prices, per unit of time.

Graphically (unless expansion of industry output drives up input prices) the market supply curve is the horizontal sum of all the individual firm supply curves (the quantity supplied is on the horizontal axis). This schedule will have the important property ascribed to an individual firm's supply schedule: it will be upward-sloping. The interaction of the market supply schedule and the market demand schedule determines the price of a good.

MARKET SYSTEM, an economic system that relies predominately on a market mechanism to determine allocation of scarce resources, production techniques, pricing, distribution of goods and services to members of society, and so on. Under a market system, economic activity is highly organized via a system of markets, through which buyers and sellers interact. Common synonyms for a market system often used in the literature are "price system," "free-enterprise system," and "capitalism."

The Invisible Hand of the Market. Because they have virtually unlimited economic wants, consumers must choose how to spend their incomes. Consumers' decisions are translated into a demand schedule communicated to businesses in the market places. In developing supply schedules, the business decision-maker tries to supply goods and services demanded by consumers in quantities that will maximize firm profits. Consumers are relatively assured that their demands as to type and quantity of goods and services will be met through the market mechanism of competition. Firms that produce what consumers want are patronized, and vice versa. Business firms compete for consumer dollar votes and will shift economic resources, such as labor and capital, to synchronize production choices with consumer choices. To a substantial degree the market economy similarly governs how resources are to be allocated among specific industries and how resources will be combined to maximize profits efficiently. Technological innovation is encouraged to achieve competitive advantage.

The Distribution of Goods and Services in a market system is based on the consumer's ability to pay the equilibrium price for any particular good or service. Ability to pay is a function of current income, accumulation of wealth, or both. Income and wealth distribution under the market system is impersonal, being predicated on the premium placed by society on the skills and talents each individual has to contribute to society. Inequalities of income distribution among individuals or households is common in a market system. The distribution is not based upon needs.

Imperfections. The market system's major controlling mechanism, competition, weakens over time, leading to great concentrations of economic power in a few hands, finally stifling the system's virtues of innovation, responsiveness to consumer wants, and ease of market entry. Over time the concentration of wealth in a relatively small segment of society can be excessive, and, thus, the system fails to provide a desirable allocation of economic goods to a large part of society. Furthermore, the price system is incapable of registering social or collective wants satisfactorily. Critics contend that some goods and services, such as education, highways, and national defense, cannot be economically purchased in household-unit demand but can only be consumed economically on a collective basis. Finally, there are failures to adjust rapidly to drastic changes desired by society, such as a shift from peace to war.

America's Economy could be characterized as a modified market economy. Three important modifications can be cited. First, in some major product and resource markets a few giant firms dominate, thus modifying the pure market-economy model. Second, the giant and powerful labor unions frequently distort the type of market mechanism discussed in the model. Third, the role of government is much more active and

significant in the United States than is envisioned in a pure capitalistic system.   —*Algin B. King*

MARK-UP INFLATION, a version of cost-push inflation where firms are assumed to set price by applying a markup over average cost. A cost-push inflation could occur without a wage push if some firms increased their markups.

MARK-UP PRICING refers to the pricing policy of a business firm in regard to the rate of profit that it establishes. Mark-up pricing usually entails a certain percentage increase over the cost of the item. For example, if the mark-up pricing policy of a firm is

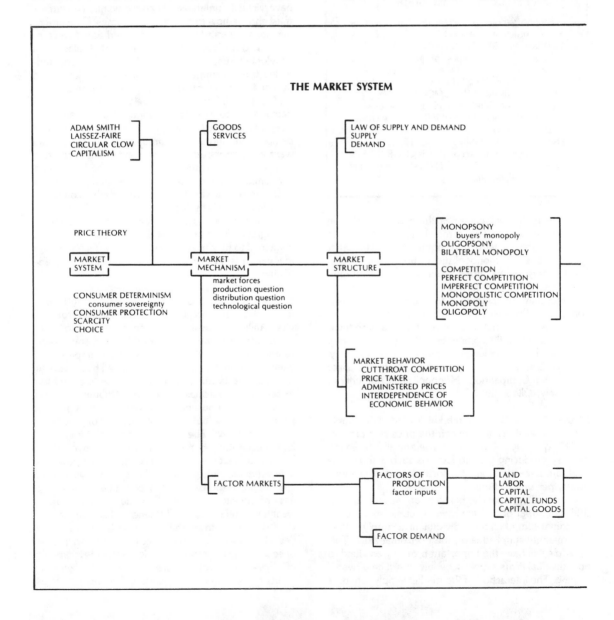

THE MARKET SYSTEM

40%, any item that costs the firm $1 will be priced at $1.40, or 40% more than cost. Mark-up pricing is used most frequently in noncompetitive market structures where some individual control over price is present. In purely competitive industries, mark-up pricing is seldom used because prices are usually set by the market.

MARSHALL, ALFRED (1842-1924). The most important and influential of the neoclassical economists, Marshall stands with Adam Smith, David Ricardo, and John Maynard Keynes as one of the greatest of modern economists. His *Principles of Economics* (1890) was a synthesis of classical and marginalist economics.

Demand, according to Marshall, is based upon diminishing marginal utility and the balancing of marginal utilities among goods, whereas supply is determined by the cost of production. Both are schedules or curves, and it is the interaction of the desires of consumers and the willingness of producers which determines the market price or economic value of goods. Marshall's discussions of elasticity, his concept of the short run, with its variable and fixed cost, and his long-run concept were other important additions to economic theory.

The use of the concept of the representative firm, increasing and decreasing long-run cost, internal and external economies of scale, and a marginal-productivity theory of distribution characterized Marshall's

THE MARKET SYSTEM
continued

EQUILIBRIUM PRICE
market price

RATIONING
ALLOCATION
CONSUMER SURPLUS
CONSUMER WELFARE
consumer satisfaction

GENERAL EQUILIBRIUM
PARTIAL EQUILIBRIUM

DYNAMIC EQUILIBRIUM
CONVERGING EQUILIBRIUM
STABLE EQUILIBRIUM
unstable equilibrium
EXPLOSIVE EQUILIBRIUM

EFFICIENCY
EQUITY
GROWTH

MARKET EQUILIBRIUM

market performance

SHORT RUN
LONG RUN
VERY LONG RUN

WELFARE ECONOMICS
PARETO OPTIMUM

EQUILIBRIUM QUANTITY

MARKET CLEARING
EXCESS SUPPLY
oversupply
glut
overproduction
EXCESS DEMAND
undersupply
shortage
UNDERPRODUCTION

FACTOR EMPLOYMENT

WAGES
RENT
SALARIES

FACTOR PAYMENTS
FACTOR EARNINGS

FACTOR PRICES

DIVIDENDS
INTEREST
PROFITS

ECONOMIC RENT
pure rent
QUASI RENT

economics. These, combined with Marshall's use of partial equilibrium analysis and the ceteris paribus assumption, provided a complete treatment of microeconomic theory, some elements of which are the foundation of economics as it exists today.

See also Theory of the Firm.

MARSHALL PLAN, a foreign-aid program intended to rebuild the European economy after World War II. Also known as the European Recovery Program, it was passed as the Foreign Assistance Act of 1948.

Aims and Results. For his role in its development, Secretary of State George C. Marshall received the 1953 Nobel Peace Prize. The program arose from the desire of the United States to (1) reestablish the commercial ties from which both the United States and Europe had long profited; and (2) contain the spreading influence of communism and the U.S.S.R., which had been aided by the post-war economic and political demoralization of most European nations.

Between April 1948 and June 1951, when the Marshall Plan was superseded by the Mutual Security Program, approximately $12 billion in grants and loans were made available for European recovery by the United States, much of it used for the purchase of U.S. exports by European nations.

MARX, KARL (1818-1883), the founder, with Friedrich Engels (1820-1895), of "scientific" socialism and leader of the revolutionary movement to overturn

Karl Marx, nineteenth-century German philosopher and writer, advocate of revolutionary socialism.

capitalism. Born in Prussia, Marx studied at universities in Bonn, Berlin, and Jena, receiving a doctorate in philosophy at 23. With university positions closed to him because of his radicalism, he turned to journalism. Expelled from Germany for his writings, he went to Paris, studied French socialism and English political economy, served as a New York *Tribune* correspondent, and met Engels. Expelled from France and Belgium, he finally settled in London. Much of his life was spent in poverty and ill health, causing him at times to borrow funds at exorbitant interest rates and to accept financial support from Engels.

In 1848, Marx and Engels wrote the *Communist Manifesto* as a call to revolution. It contains the concept of the dialectical process—thesis, antithesis, and synthesis—of the philosopher Hegel and an economic interpretation of history in which Marx saw each stage containing the seeds of its own destruction. Feudalism (thesis) had been destroyed by capitalists (antithesis), and capitalism had its antithesis in the proletariat. As thesis and antithesis struggle, there emerges a synthesis that becomes the thesis for the subsequent stage until the final synthesis of communism, when all classes but the proletariat have been eliminated. Marx's thoughts were further developed in *Das Kapital,* the first volume of which was published by Marx in 1867; the second and third, by Engels after Marx's death.

Marxian Economics. The economics of Marx employ the labor theory of value, assuming that goods exchange on the basis of labor of average skill and intensity using modern means of production and producing commodities that are in demand. The exchange value of labor itself is determined by the labor time needed to produce the means of subsistence for laborers. The difference between the wage paid and the revenue from the product is surplus value, or profit, which the capitalist keeps for himself. The value of the commodity thus consists of constant capital (depreciation and raw materials), variable capital (labor), and surplus value. Only labor produces surplus value, but with technological advances more constant capital is used with less surplus value resulting. Increased use of machinery makes some labor superfluous, creating a reserve army of unemployed with downward pressure on wages, which reduces the consuming power of the masses even though productive potential in the economy has risen. However, with greater unemployment, profits increase, more capital is accumulated, and more labor is demanded.

Therefore, periodic crises are inherent in the capitalistic system. In each crisis real wages and the standard of living fall; the proletariat grows. The existing property relations imply antagonistic conditions of distribution, leading to inadequate demand relative to production. Therefore, the seeds of social revolution are a part of the capitalistic system, and socialism will emerge to fill the void resulting from capitalism's demise.   —*John R. Matthews, Jr.*

See also Economic Systems; Revolutionary Socialism.

MATURE CREDITOR. *See* Stages of a Country's Balance of Payments.

MAXIMIZING BEHAVIOR, a basic assumption in economics that individuals will maximize their total satisfaction subject to certain external and internal constraints. The principal external factors influencing maximizing behavior are the incomes of the individuals and the price of the goods they purchase. Internal constraints include their preference functions and their expectations concerning future price changes.

The rational consumer takes all of these constraints into consideration when she determines her expenditure pattern for all goods and services that she purchases. Assuming that an individual's purchases can be sequentially separated, her first purchase will yield her the greatest amount of satisfaction per dollar's worth of expenditure. She will continue to purchase additional units of the most important item (the item that yields the greatest satisfaction per dollar) until the increase in satisfaction yielded by one more unit of the given item per dollar is less than the increase in satisfaction she would achieve if she transferred the dollar to buy another good. The rational economic person will pursue, by her or his expenditure pattern, the goal of achieving the greatest possible total satisfaction within the income price structure.

This goal of maximization of total satisfaction is reached whenever the consumer has optimally allocated income among all of the goods and services, and the income budget is exhausted. The consumer may, of course, save from her income, but the act of saving in itself yields some measure of satisfaction. The consumer has maximized satisfaction when the consumer cannot achieve any increase in satisfaction by spending one dollar less on any good or one dollar more on any other good. Maximization of satisfaction occurs whenever the marginal utility per dollar's worth or expenditure is the same for each good or service purchased.

The assumption of maximizing behavior does not rule out altruism. It simply implies that individuals derive some satisfaction from their generosity to others.   —*Robert L. Brite*

MEAN. *See* Central Tendency.

MEANY, GEORGE (1894-1980), was born in New York City, educated in the public school system, served a brief apprenticeship and became a journeyman plumber in 1915. Seven years later, he was elected business representative of Plumber's Union Local 463, and in 1934 he was elected president of the New York State Federation of Labor.

AFL-CIO's George Meany was among labor leaders who met with President Nixon to discuss what steps would follow Nixon's 90-day wage-price freeze.

In 1940, he began working for the American Federation of Labor, acting as treasurer. During World War II he was a member of the National War Labor Board. In 1952, after the death of William Green, Meany was elected president of the AFL. In 1957 he served as U.S. delegate to the United Nations.

In 1955, after the American Federation of Labor merged with the Congress of Industrial Organizations, forming the AFL-CIO, Meany was chosen to be its president, a position he held until 1979.

MEASURES OF ECONOMIC ACTIVITY. *See* National Income Measurement.

MEDIAN. *See* Central Tendency.

MEDIATION is an important and often effective form of third-party intervention in the bargaining process, particularly in an "emergency strike" situation. Unlike an arbitrator, who renders a decision after hearing labor's and management's positions, the mediator endeavors mainly to keep the bargaining from breaking down and to seek paths to an agreement. By clarifying the issues, defining and containing areas of disagreement, offering suggestions, and serving as an intermediary, the mediator can contribute substantially to a settlement.

See also Collective Bargaining; Conciliation; Emergency Strike.

MEDICAID, a federally subsidized, state-administered program to pay for medical and hospital costs of low-income families. Recipients of public assistance qualify automatically, and other low-income families may be eligible for at least partial coverage.

See also Medicare; Public Assistance.

MEDICARE, a federal medical program that pays a substantial portion of the hospital costs of those over age 65. Although Medicare is funded through the payroll tax as part of the Social Security program, there is no restriction on eligibility: age is the sole criterion. In 1989, there were approximately 32 million recipients of Medicare, with an anticipated cost to the government in 1990 of $94.2 billion. Because of concerns about the future solvency of the program, and because of general concerns about waste, Congress made major changes in the Medicare program as part of the Social Security Amendment of 1983. The new rules set maximum reimbursement rates for specific procedures, as determined by regional cost trends. In addition, for hospitals to be eligible for Medicare reimbursements, they must become members of a "Peer Review Organization" whose job is to ensure efficient hospital administration. In 1989, Congress moved to regulate the amounts physicians are reimbursed under Medicare. Nevertheless, Medicare's trust fund was projected to run out by the late 1990s unless something was changed.

See also Social Insurance; Social Security.

MEDIUM OF EXCHANGE. *See* Money.

MEMBER BANK, a commercial bank that has accepted membership in the Federal Reserve System. All national banks must join, and state banks may join if they wish and if they can fulfill the requirements of membership, including a minimum amount of capital. All member banks must be insured by the Federal Deposit Insurance Corporation. Only 40% of commercial banks have joined the system, but they conduct 80% of the banking business. Those member banks located in some 50 of the largest financial centers (reserve city banks) are subject to somewhat higher reserve requirements than other banks (country banks). At one time, banks in the financial districts of New York City and Chicago were classified separately as central reserve city banks, but this class has been absorbed into the reserve city designation.

MENGER, CARL (1840-1921), a leading Austrian economic theorist, chiefly notable as the originator of the Austrian school's explanation of economic phenomena. Menger's principal work is *Foundations of Political Economy* (1871), a study in which he demonstrated, through the use of very basic terminology and illustrations, how the utility principle connects use-value with scarcity. Further, he stressed the role marginal utility plays in determining economic value.

The 1870s revolution in the theory of value used to explain income and price formulation was in large part stimulated by Menger's development in this area, along with similar developments by Jevons and Walras. Menger subsequently employed the marginal-utility principle in studies of money and its value. The chief distinction between Menger and the other marginalists lies in his approach, which was outside the utilitarian tradition. For him, economic man, rather than pursuing maximization of pleasure, seeks to satisfy his needs by the most efficient means.

See also Marginalism.

MERCANTILISM. As Western civilization emerged from the Middle Ages and economic activity shifted from the feudal community to a system of merchant capitalism, economic thought developed its first meaningful doctrines. These doctrines existed in many countries at many different times from as early as the sixteenth century to as late as the middle of the eighteenth century. However, whether we consider English mercantilism with writers such as Munn, French mercantilism under Colbert, or the later German cameralists, several common themes appear.

The most distinguishing feature of mercantilism was its view of a nation's wealth in terms of its treasury of gold and silver. The earliest manifestations of this view were the bullionist policies of a nation's participating in international trade only if the transaction increased the nation's wealth, that is, its holdings of precious metals. As trade increased, this position was modified to consider the overall balance-of-payments aspect of a transaction. Thus, gold could leave a country if by doing so more gold eventually came into the country.

The mercantilist view of wealth and the emphasis upon international trade led to a number of policies which, it was felt, would promote trade and increase the nation's wealth. Policies such as (1) extensive colonization and the exploitation of the colonies' raw materials; (2) strong government participation in the economy, including establishing trade monopolies; and (3) strong nationalism were all developed and supported by mercantilist thought.

Later mercantilist thinkers, such as Sir William Petty, David Hume, and Richard Cantillon (some would regard them as being transitional between mercantilism and the Physiocrats) anticipated many of the doctrines which would appear in later works and were surprisingly modern in many of their concepts.

—Clyde A. Haulman

See also Balance of Payments; Balance of Trade; International Trade Theory.

MERGER, a contractual joining of the assets of one hitherto independent business firm with another. Since the merged firms become one business entity, the merger is the surest method of providing identity of interests among firms (as compared to various forms of intercorporate stockholding, community of interests, overt or tacit agreements). Mergers are undertaken for a variety of reasons: diversification of product line, credit availability, acquisition of managerial talent, or acquisition of patents or research capabilities. But the ultimate reason is financial gain to one

TYPES OF MERGERS

Examples:
Horizontal merger:
    If Shoe producers A and B merge.
Vertical merger:
    If Shoe producer B merges with Leather goods producer E ("backward integration") and/or Retail shoe store F ("forward integration").
Conglomerate merger:
    If Shoe producer B merges with Typewriter producer C and/or Motion picture producer D.

or both of the merging firms.

From the point of view of economic structure, mergers fall into one of three categories: (1) horizontal, combining firms on the same plane or level of competition; (2) vertical, combining firms at different stages of a productive process; and (3) a conglomerate, combining firms in dissimilar product lines.

Mergers are accomplished through one of two methods (and sometimes both). In stock acquisition, the acquiring firm secures controlling interest of voting stock in another firm and then votes absorption of that firm into the acquiring firm. In asset acquisition, the acquiring firm directly purchases the assets of another firm. (Often acquisition of some voting stock is preliminary to asset acquisition.)

Mergers which may tend to lessen competition substantially have been prohibited since the Clayton Act of 1914. It barred mergers by stock acquisition only, however; not until the 1950 Celler-Kefauver Act was a similar prohibition placed on asset acquisition.
            —*Thomas O. Depperschmidt*
    See also Conglomerate; Horizontal Merger; Vertical Merger.

MERIT GOODS (BADS) result when intellectually or morally elite groups override individual preferences. For example, welfare programs often provide in-kind goods rather than cash because they suspect that the preferences of the poor are inappropriate. Welfare recipients may spend money intended for healthy food for their children on alcohol or cigarettes. Similarly, primary education is compulsory because there are parents who may prefer to have their children work for them at home, or might not care enough to make sure they attend school voluntarily. Restrictions on how adult magazines can be displayed, or the Surgeon General's warning on cigarette advertisements that smoking may cause cancer are sanctions against merit bads.

The rationale behind merit goods is especially elitist in that welfare givers perceive welfare recipients to be inherently incompetent. The poor are seen to be poor either through their own fault or because they are stupid, not because they lack income or because allocation may be inequitable or inefficient. Sanctions against merit bads may be equally elitist, assuming consumers to be gullible and easily misled by advertising. Or they may result from a fairly realistic assessment of information asymmetries: suppliers know more about their products than consumers and tend to keep negative information to themselves.

MICROECONOMICS, the study of the individual business firm—what it is; how it works; how it allocates various resources inputs; how it prices goods and services; how it reacts to competitive pressures; and the various types of competitive environments and their ramifications on it. A second major focus of microeconomics deals with an analysis of individual or single-family consumption behavior, particularly as it relates to demand schedules, allocation of income in consumption, and effects of price variation on demand and on product substitution. Among the more important concepts in microeconomics analysis are demand and supply schedules, price elasticity, variable costs, fixed costs, marginal utility, marginal costs, short-run analysis, long-run analysis, equilibrium condition, marginal revenue, total revenue, and profit maximization.

Analytic Tools. To better understand firm behavior, the economist uses analytical concepts of general types of market conditions: pure competition, monopoly, monopolistic competition, and oligopoly. For example, the firm will price its products and services at the point that will maximize profits if it is operating under monopoly market conditions, but if it is operating under conditions of pure competition, pricing will be set by the market forces of supply and demand. In microeconomic analysis dealing with the individual consumer or family unit, such concepts as individual demand schedules, diminishing marginal utility, shift in the demand curve, elastic demand, inelastic demand, unit elasticity, and supply curves are useful.

Analytic Goals. The purpose of the analytical and conceptual tools is to enable the business firm to determine what to produce (the types of goods and services the consumer wants), how to best combine

John Stuart Mill, philosopher and classical economist.

scarce economic resources (land, labor, and capital) to minimize costs and economic waste and thus maximize the efficiency of economic processes of an individual firm in meeting the economic needs of the consumer and society.   —*Algin B. King*

MILL, JOHN STUART (1806-1873), political philosopher and last of the important classical economists. His *Principles of Political Economy* (1848) stands as the ultimate statement of the classical system.

Mill's most important contribution to economics was in his extension of international trade theory. Based upon Ricardo's concept of comparative advantage, Mill completed the system by using the concept of reciprocal demand to determine the exact terms of trade. In doing this, he also became aware of the concept of demand elasticity and developed one of the few analytical arguments favoring tariffs.

Beyond Natural Law. Mill's work also contains a number of other important economic concepts. In his *Principles*, Mill makes a distinction between production, which he felt was governed by natural laws beyond man's control, and distribution, which he felt was in part institutionally determined. While he failed to see that the two processes are also interrelated, the freeing of distribution from the bonds of natural law

provided a challenge to existing economic theory which became the basis for many future developments.

The Wages Fund. Mill's wage theory replacing Ricardo's subsistence theory was the basic wages-fund doctrine: that wages are determined by the number of workers and a predetermined portion of capital set aside to pay the workers—a wages fund. While this theory was used extensively before the development of the marginal-productivity theory of wages, it is basically incorrect because there is no set amount of capital which must go to labor.

Based upon a falling rate of profit, Mill felt that the accumulation of capital would eventually stop and a stationary state would result. The stationary state, however, would not be reached in the near future, and if population were checked, it could be a state free from the problems and pressures of increasing production.

Finally, Mill made no contribution to value theory because he felt that "the theory of the subject is complete."   —*Clyde A. Haulman*
    See also Classical Economics; International Trade.

MILLER-TYDINGS ACT (1937), the first national legislation enabling firms selling in interstate commerce to engage legally in so-called "fair-trade" pricing, which is the establishment of a minimum resale price for a nationally branded product by contract between manufacturer and retailer. The act was enabling legislation: if individual states passed fair-trade laws, firms selling into those states would be exempt from prosecution under the Sherman Act for price fixing and under the FTC Act for unfair trade practices when they entered into the resale price-maintenance contracts.

An important feature of these contracts was the "nonsigners" clause, whereby retail firms selling the branded product were bound by a contract executed by any other seller of the same product in that state not to sell the product below the price minimum set in that contract. The nonsigners clause was rendered invalid in the case of *Schwegmann Brothers v. Calvert Corp.* (1951) but was reestablished as law by the McGuire-Keogh Act of 1952.

The Miller-Tydings Act, along with the McGuire-Keogh Act, was repealed by Congress in 1977. Since that time, resale price maintenance schemes have been illegal.   —*Thomas O. Depperschmidt*
    See also Fair-Trade Laws; McGuire-Keogh Act.

MINIMUM WAGE LAW. See Fair Labor Standards Act (1938).

MINIMUM WAGES. In an effort to keep people out of poverty, minimum wage laws have been enacted on both the federal and state levels (40 states now have such laws). The federal government, after several laws involving minimum wages in particular industries had been enacted, eventually passed a comprehensive wage law, the Fair Labor Standards Act, in 1938. At that time, minimum wages were set at $.25 per hour; this figure increased over the years to keep up with the increasing cost of living. In 1981, the minimum wage was raised to $3.35 per hour, and to $4.25 in 1991.

The law covers most workers in the United States (about 84% of nonsupervisory positions are covered), but still exempts several types, including proprietors and other self-employed persons, outside salesmen, apprentices, handicapped persons, domestic servants, and most employees in agriculture, forestry, and fisheries.

MISES, LUDWIG VON (1881-1973), an advocate of political individualism, who continued the tradition of the Austrian school to the extreme. Much of Mises's work was directed toward criticizing economic socialism, which he felt was unworkable because it contains no effective pricing system. In addition, Mises believed that any governmental intervention in the economic system placed the system in danger. His dogmatic and unyielding position placed him on the conservative perimeter of economics.

MIXED ECONOMY, an economic system with some characteristics of socialism. The political-economic spectrum may be characterized as follows: At one end of the spectrum is laissez-faire capitalism—a system in which almost all economic means are privately owned and almost all economic processes are market-determined. At the other end of the spectrum is socialism, a system in which almost all the means of production

A hydroelectric dam is an example of the type of goods produced by government in mixed economies like the United States.

are owned and controlled by government. Somewhere between these extremes lies the mixed economy. The primary reasons for the emergence of the so-called mixed economy are: (1) social goals have been given higher priorities by society through democratic governmental processes; and (2) the private sector did not want to provide certain goods or services.

In a mixed economy the private sector produces many of society's goods and services, but a significant amount of goods and services are under direct government ownership. An example of a mixed economy would be that of the United Kingdom. Many of its basic industries, such as transportation, steel, and coal, are owned or operated by government, but a large portion of goods and services are still produced by private enterprise. In the United States' economy, the current peacetime economic output mixture is approximately 80% private and 20% government.
—Algin B. King

MODE. *See* Central Tendency.

MODEL, ECONOMETRIC. Econometric models are empirical statements of economic theory. Rather than merely being content with abstract *a priori* reasoning,

---

MODEL, ECONOMETRIC: TOPIC GUIDE

To compare econometric models of the economy with other types, see the articles on INPUT-OUTPUT MODELS, NATIONAL INCOME DETERMINATION, and CIRCULAR FLOW OF INCOME, as well as the Subject Map accompanying this last article.

---

econometric models place the relationships that such reasoning indicates exist in mathematical form and, using a host of analytical techniques, attempt to measure or estimate these various economic relationships. Econometric models combine economic theory with the reality of economic events, providing a means of validating economic theories and isolating exact relationships.

The information needed to create econometric models may be difficult or impossible to obtain. Often, detailed information on a wide range of economic variables is needed. While much of these data are supplied by governments and other institutions, some must be generated by economists to fit a particular need.

Some econometric models are essentially microeconomic, concerned with measuring economic relationships that influence individual units in the economy. Estimating supply and demand relationships, measuring the degree of industrial concentration, and explaining individual consumer behavior are examples of microeconometric models. Macroeconometric models, on the other hand, are concerned with estimating aggregate economic relationships. Models of various sectors of the economy, growth models, and large models of the entire economy are examples. Both macro- and microeconometric models use data that comes from the actual performance of the economy rather than from controlled experiments.

— *Clyde A. Haulman*

See also Econometrics; Model, Economic.

MODEL, ECONOMIC, a construct embodying a particular economic theory. The core of a model is a set of *assumptions* concerning the factors, or variables, that are believed to be relevant to the phenomenon, and the relationships between these factors. From the assumptions of a model, one deduces certain conclusions in the form of statements, or *hypotheses*, about various aspects of the phenomenon. These derived hypotheses constitute the essence of the theory embodied in the model. Thus, a model may be thought of as a medium for the construction of a theory.

A theoretical model may be stated in the form of a set of mathematical equations or specifications, and often may be depicted graphically. Sometimes a model is represented as a three-dimensional physical construct, like models of a molecule.

Economic models are found on all levels of analysis and in most branches of economics, such as the theory of the firm, consumer behavior, market or industry analysis, regional analysis, general equilibrium analysis, and economic relations among nations. Economic phenomena being manifestations of the actions of decisionmakers, the assumptions incorporated in economic models can usually be identified as assumptions about the *environment* in which the decisionmaker operates, or assumptions about the *objectives* (or goals) of the decisionmaker.

An example of an economic model of a competitive firm is shown in the figure. The ATC (average total cost) curve shows the unit cost of production, and the shape of this curve embodies certain assumptions

**ECONOMIC MODEL:
COMPETITIVE FIRM**

about the technological environment of the firm. The MC (marginal cost) curve is derived from the ATC curve and shows the increments to total cost of small increases in output. The AR (average revenue) line represents the economic environment of the firm, indicating that it can sell any amount of its product at the current market price p_1. The assumption about the firm's objective is that it wants to maximize total profit in each period of time. Then, according to the model, the firm will produce x_1 units of its product in each period (the output at which MC = AR). One of the hypotheses generated by the model is that when the market price rises, the firm will increase its production. As may be seen in the diagram, if the market price rises to p_2, the firm increases output to x_2.

— *Josef Hadar*

MODEL OF THE FIRM. *See* Theory of the Firm.

MODIGLIANNI, FRANCO (1918-   ), Italian-born economist who has achieved recognition for his contributions to the understanding of macroeconomic policy and his work on the Federal Reserve-MIT econometric model. He received doctoral degrees from the University of Rome (1939) and The New School for Social Research (1944). His publications include *National Incomes and International Trade* (1953), *Planning, Production, Inventories and Work Forces* (1960), *The Role of Anticipations and Plans in Economic Behavior and Their Use in Economic Analysis and Forecasting* (1961), and *New Mortgage Designs for Stable Housing in an Inflationary Environment* (1975). Modigliani became professor of economics and finance at MIT in 1964, and was awarded the Nobel Prize for economics in 1985.

MOMENTS, of a probability distribution, are a set of parameters which summarize or describe that distribution. Some important moments are the mean and variance, which measure central tendency and dispersion. Higher moments measure skewness and kurtosis.

See also Central Tendency; Kurtosis; Skewness.

MONETARISM, a school of economic thought that focuses on the importance of the effects of changes in the money supply on the aggregate economy. Monetarism is closely linked to the tradition at the University of Chicago, particularly with the work of Milton Friedman. The basic analytical device of monetarists is the equation of $PQ = MV$, and most monetarists espouse some form of the quantity theory of money.

In many ways monetarism has grown as a reaction to the macroeconomics of Keynes and the active pursuit of stabilization policies advocated by Keynes and his followers. Monetarist positions include a belief in the limited effectiveness of fiscal policy. Fiscal expansion is said to be ineffective because private borrowers will be crowded out of lending markets by the government borrowing that finances the fiscal expansion. While monetarists believe fiscal policy is ineffective, they feel that money-supply changes can be very effective. However, the typical monetarist does not advocate active countercyclical monetary policy because monetary policy, while effective, is unpredictable. Rather, following Milton Friedman, monetarists advocate a monetary rule—a provision for a constant rate of change for the money supply.

The followers of monetarism share many views with neoclassical economists, particularly a great faith in the market mechanism. They trace most of the fluctuations in the aggregate economy to inappropriate policy and thus counsel a limited role for macroeconomic policy.   —*Robert B. Archibald*

See also Equation of Exchange; Friedman, Milton; Stabilization Policy.

MONETARY AUTHORITY, CENTRAL, the agency or group of agencies whose function is to implement monetary policy through the control of the money supply or other monetary aggregates or indicators. This may be done directly through the issue of currency or indirectly through such market influences as interest rates or the conditions under which loans may be made by commercial banks (thus affecting the volume of demand deposits) or financial intermediaries (thus influencing the wider financial markets). In most countries the central bank is the primary monetary authority, frequently in conjunction with the national treasury and, sometimes, with the help of other agencies, such as an exchange stabilization fund. In all cases a parliament or congress establishes the rules under which these agencies work and, hence, holds the ultimate authority over monetary matters.

MONETARY POLICY, all activities of the federal government intended to produce changes in the money supply, the availability of loanable funds, or the level of interest rates to influence general economic activity. Monetary policy is one of the two major forms

of governmental action designed to stabilize the economy; the other major action—*fiscal policy*—covers measures concerned with governmental receipts, expenditures, and debt management. The objective of both these policies is to provide countercyclical forces to reduce the severity of business cycles by stimulating the economy in a depression and calming it during inflation.

Some forms of monetary policy have been used for this purpose for at least 100 years, but they have become increasingly significant as the economy has become more complex. The financial panic of 1907 led to the Federal Reserve Act, and the Great Depression of the 1930s forced a substantial strengthening of controls to prevent a repetition of the catastrophe.

Objectives. In terms of its countercyclical policy, the objectives of the Federal Reserve System are normally stated as full employment and a stable price level. Two additional objectives are economic growth and external stability of the value of the dollar. With the adoption of floating exchange rates in the 1970s, this latter goal has not been pursued as strongly as it once was.

Tight Money and Easy Money. Monetary policy affects real output by making it easier or harder for businesses to obtain loans to expand facilities or to make other investments. Under a tight monetary policy, loans are made more difficult to obtain by restricting the money supply, thereby forcing interest rates up. Under an easy monetary policy, the money supply is allowed to increase substantially, lowering interest rates and generally making loans more attainable. The effect of monetary policy on prices is summarized by the equation of exchange. Given that the velocity at which money circulates is stable (at least in the short run), an increase in the growth rate of money, particularly if the economy is near full employment, will lead to an increase in inflation. A decrease in money growth will moderate inflation.

Control of Monetary Policy. The board of governors of the Federal Reserve System is primarily responsible for the conduct of monetary policy. However, other government agencies may affect

Controlling monetary policy is an important function of the Federal Reserve System. This bank in Boston is one of 12 regional FED branches dealing with financial institutions in their territory.

money market conditions by their actions. The U.S. Treasury affects interest rates by the form and timing of its borrowing from the public, although Congress determines the ultimate amount of borrowing by its tax and expenditure policy. At this point monetary and fiscal policy overlap and may conflict. When the government is operating at a substantial deficit and must borrow large sums of money, it is impossible to produce tight money conditions without driving interest rates extremely high, denying funds to legitimate borrowers.

Instruments of the Federal Reserve Policy. The central bank has ultimate control over the money supply, and if Congress allows the bank sufficient independence, it can use this control to influence greatly the pace of economic activity. The tools that it has to work with are numerous.

Quantitative Controls, which directly affect the amount of excess reserves, include open market operations, the most important and flexible tool, used almost continuously; changes in the discount rate; and changes in reserve requirements. The latter is used quite infrequently because of its relatively drastic effects.

Qualitative Controls influence the size or maturity of specific kinds of loans to discourage such loans more than others. These controls make use of margin requirements, specifying the maximum amount that can be borrowed for the purchase of securities; installment credit controls and mortgage lending controls to restrict the volume of loans made to consumers, used during past war periods but not now in effect; and interest rate ceilings, regulating the amount of interest that banks can pay on deposits. Most interest rate ceilings were phased out by the Banking Act of 1980, however.

Moral Suasion is designed to obtain voluntary compliance with monetary objectives, and includes bank examination and visitation, publicity, and voluntary credit restraint.

Operation. The primary method that the Fed (as the central bank is often called) uses to achieve its objectives is adjusting the amount of reserves in the banking system through open market operations. Reserves are sometimes referred to as base money. Given a stable money multiplier, the base money ultimately determines the quantity of money available. The Fed uses two operating targets to guide weekly open market operations: free reserves, and, the federal funds rate (the interest banks charge for loans to each other). The former has a direct bearing on money growth, whereas the latter gives a good indication of the effect of policy on interest rates.

Effectiveness. It would seem a simple matter to conduct contracyclical monetary policy. During economic downturns, the Fed should use open market operations to increase the money supply and lower interest rates. During periods of inflationary expan-

sion, open market operations should be used to slow or stop money growth and to raise interest rates. But in practice there may be lags, various lengths of time between the implementation of a particular policy and its effect on the economy. Some economists argue that the time between implementation of a particular policy and its effect on the economy is long and variable. Hence, it is argued that the Fed often promotes or increases fluctuations in the business cycles by practicing contracyclical monetary policy. This occurs, for example, when easy monetary policy that is adopted during a recession takes hold after the recession has passed, and expansion is already underway. These economists have urged the Fed to adopt a simple money growth rule that is consistent with the long-term rate of growth in real income and to abandon its contracyclical policies.

Another problem is that the Fed, as may be expected, has been willing to pursue easy money policies and hesitant to pursue tight money policies that lead to high interest rates. The Fed's job has also been made more difficult by large deficits that effectively have made it choose between tight money or very high real interest rates. Prior to 1979, the Fed almost always opted to moderate increases in the interest rate.

Many economists blame the Fed's preoccupation with interest rates for the high levels of inflation and unemployment experienced in the 1970s. The presence of both double-digit inflation and high unemployment is a relatively new phenomenon. It is argued that the Fed may have contributed to this by pursuing policies that made inflation the norm. This led consumers, businesses, banks, and labor to anticipate inflation and to adjust their plans accordingly. Banks factored in inflation while making loans to businesses and consumers. Nominal interest rates rose, reflecting built-in premiums for anticipated inflation. The Fed's response to moderate the rise in interest rates further fueled inflation.

A Shift in Operating Policy. In October 1979, the Fed, determined to control inflation, announced that it would pay closer attention to the effects its policies were having on excess reserves and less attention to the effects on the federal funds rates. In essence the Fed announced its determination to control money growth and its willingness to "take the heat" for the resulting high interest rates. By 1984, the Fed had substantially reduced inflation and had begun to ease up on the money supply. By 1986, interest rates had dropped 5 to 6 percentage points.

Since 1979, the Fed had announced targets and annual growth ranges for M1, but in 1987 it announced neither. Evidently the short-run relationship between various monetary aggregates had begun to break down in the mid-1970s and was further distorted by a combination of financial deregulation, disinflation, and possible other factors during the

1980s. The Fed consequently adopted a more varied monetary policy.　　—*Gerald A. Whitney*

See also Equation of Exchange; Fiscal Policy; Open Market Operations.

MONETARY THEORY OF BUSINESS CYCLES.

Some economists attribute fluctuations in economic activity to the expansion and contraction of money, credit, and interest rates. The quantity of money and the rate of interest are dependent on the decisions of monetary authorities, such as central banks in European countries or the U.S. Federal Reserve Board. The nonmonetarist view is that the rate of interest and the level of income (or wealth), determined both by the authorities and by demand conditions, influence the level of investment, which, through the multiplier, determines aggregate income. Thus, when interest

rates and credit conditions are favorable, they encourage business to borrow (invest and spend).

In a downswing, banks usually restrict credit by making less money available and increasing interest rates, because they are beginning to deplete their reserves and additional funds are not being extended. On the whole, contraction of the quantity of money is an internal factor influenced significantly by external forces that contribute to the cyclical process.

On the other hand, monetarists believe that business cycles, to a great degree, are the result of ill-advised discretionary monetary and fiscal policies. They suggest that the demand for money is relatively constant, thus placing greater emphasis on the real money supply as a determinant of aggregate demand. The monetarist policy prescription for smoothing the business cycle is to have monetary authorities follow a

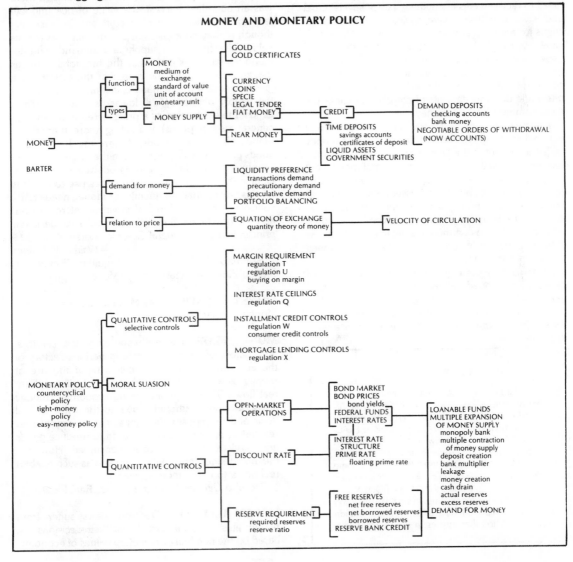

"rule" (a constant rate of growth for the real money supply) rather than their own discretion in the determination of the money supply and interest rates.

—Philip W. Jeffress

See also Business Cycles, Theories; External Theory of Business Cycles; Internal Theory of Business Cycles.

MONEY, anything that is accepted as a means of payment at a given time and place. There is no single medium that universally serves as money. In primitive societies, money consisted of such valuable commodities as cattle, shells, or beads. The American colonists used wampum, tobacco, and beaver skins. More commonly, nations have concentrated on gold and silver coin. Indeed, prior to the Civil War the United States government issued no money except coins and refused to receive taxes in anything except specie. Gold and silver certificates were basically warehouse receipts for an equal amount of specie in the Treasury's vault. As people became accustomed to the use of paper, they cared little about the backing, and other forms of paper currency became common. More recently, the extensive use of checks for payment of bills has made demand deposits of commercial banks the most common form of money.

The creation of money is traditionally a function of national sovereignty. The yen, for instance, is money in Japan but not in the United States. In international transactions, gold has been the traditional money, but today it is being replaced by special drawing rights (SDRs), a form of bank credit issued by the International Monetary Fund. Thus, in international as in domestic trade, money is rapidly becoming a ledger entry rather than a commodity even in token form. As long as people will accept it, the form that money takes is not important.

Medium of Exchange. Money as a medium of exchange developed naturally as a result of the disadvantages of barter as a means of trade. Barter requires that one must want what the other person has and have what he wants in equal value. Only in a well-developed money economy, where money wages can be spent for the hundreds of different products that workers want, is it possible to develop the specialization of labor that lies at the heart of economic efficiency and high productivity. Money that can be spent anywhere provides freedom of choice of goods, freedom of choice of jobs, as well as freedom of movement.

The Monetary Unit of a country is its standard of value or unit of account. If a business has $10,000 in assets, the things it owns have that much value in terms of the monetary unit. In the United States the monetary unit is the dollar.

In the days of commodity money, when rice was money for instance, its value depended on supply and demand—how much rice there was in comparison with the community's desire for rice. That is, if there was an abundant harvest, the value of rice (money) fell, and the rice-price of everything else rose. Although money no longer has any quantity desired, its value still depends on supply and demand. The demand for money is essentially the sum total of things that money will buy; the output of the country in a given period. If the demand is given, any increase in the supply of money will lower its value, which is almost the same thing as a price increase. Inflation (a general rise in prices) is nothing more than much money chasing few goods. If there are 100 units of goods produced in a period when the available money supply is $100, the price of goods will be $1 each. Double the money supply, and prices rise to $2. It is for this reason that the quantity of money needs to be controlled by some form of government regulation, and in the United States this control is undertaken principally by the Federal Reserve System.

—Walter W. Haines

See also Banking System; Liquidity Preference; Money Flow; Monetary Policy; Money Supply.

MONEY CREATION. *See* Multiple Expansion of the Money Supply.

MONEY FLOW. The exchange of goods, services, and factors of production among various sectors of the economy would be difficult without the use of money as a medium of exchange to facilitate these real flows. Thus, in money-using economies, money flows develop in amounts equal to the value of real flows and in opposite directions. The money has no real value, in that it cannot be used to produce goods and services and it cannot be consumed. However, the money does represent a claim and as such enables real flows to occur more efficiently.

See also Circular Flow of Income; Real Flow.

MONEY ILLUSION. Decisionmakers suffer from money illusion to the extent that their decisions are based on the nominal or monetary values of economic

---

MONEY: TOPIC GUIDE

For further information on the money supply, see the articles on DEMAND DEPOSITS, NEAR MONEY, and MONEY SUPPLY. To see the theoretical basis behind the money supply, consult FRACTIONAL RESERVE. For views of the monetary and financial systems as a whole, refer to BANKING SYSTEM and FINANCIAL INTERMEDIARIES; some additional macroeconomic aspects are discussed in MONEY FLOW and MONETARY POLICY.

The Subject Maps accompanying this article and the article on BANKING SYSTEM show the relation of MONEY to other articles in the Encyclopedia.

variables rather than on the real values of the variables. Viewing wages based on the dollar figure rather than its purchasing power is an example of this illusion.

MONEY MARKET FUNDS, mutual funds that invest in short-term debt of businesses and government agencies. These funds have high yields and are very liquid; checks may be written on most. The growth of these funds since 1978 has been remarkable. This rapid growth can be attributed to their safety and, in the late 1970s, to high interest rates that reached 10% above the yields available through bank accounts at commercial banks or savings and loans. The Banking Act of 1980 phased out the interest rate ceilings that prevented banks and thrift institutions from effectively competing with money market funds for deposits. Even though the yields on money market deposit accounts at these institutions are about three-quarters of a percentage point below those for money market funds, they have the advantage of being federally insured. Their safety made money market accounts very attractive after the stock market crash of October 1987.

MONEY MARKET MUTUAL FUNDS. *See* Mutual Funds.

MONEY SUPPLY. At the present time there are four measures of the money supply used by the board of governors of the Federal Reserve System. M1 is the narrowest definition and is often referred to as transactions balances. The broadest in scope is L, which includes assets such as U.S. Treasury Bills.

M1: Currency in circulation, plus demand deposits at commercial banks, plus other checkable deposits including NOW accounts and traveler's checks.

M2: M1, plus money market deposit accounts, plus overnight repurchase agreements, money market funds, savings, and small-time deposits at all depository institutions, plus overnight repurchase agreements at banks, plus overnight Eurodollars held by nonbank U.S. depositors in Caribbean branches of U.S. banks, plus balances at money funds (excluding institutions-only funds).

M3: M2, plus large time deposits at all depository institutions, term reserve requirements at banks and savings and loans, plus balances at institutions-only money funds.

L: M3, plus other liquid assets such as term Eurodollars held by nonbank U.S. residents, bankers' acceptances, commercial paper, Treasury bills and other liquid government instruments, and U.S. savings bonds.   *—Gerald A. Whitney*

See also Gold; Monetary Policy; Money; Near Money.

MONEY WAGES are the amount of money received for services rendered, hence, the price paid for labor. Money wages are usually paid an individual in the form of a wage rate per unit of time. They differ from real wages insofar as they do not consider the purchasing power of the money.

MONOPOLISTIC COMPETITION is one of four major markets that characterizes the American economy; the other three being pure competition, oligopoly, and monopoly. Monopolistic competition is

The U.S. Bureau of Printing and Engraving prints over $50 million 24 hours a day, providing the currency to buy goods and services. The supply, however, would quickly run out without bank checks.

characterized by relatively many sellers in a market where the product of each seller is similar in nature, but differentiated in other ways. Examples of monopolistically competitive products are most clothing items, such as shoes and dresses, and various food products, such as frozen foods and canned foods. Because there are many sellers, no one seller has much influence over price and, therefore, must differentiate its product in order to gather a larger share of the market.

Demand Curve. With the exception of product differentiation, monopolistic competition has many of the characteristics of pure competition. There is usually relative ease of entry into a monopolistically competitive market. In addition, resources as well as goods and services in these markets are considerably mobile. And, as mentioned above, each seller has little, if any, influence over price because of the large number of firms in these markets. For these reasons, the demand curve of these markets is relatively elastic; that is, there can only be small variations in price (justified by product differentiation) if a seller wants to remain in the market, because the substitutability of these products is very great.

However, an exact representation of a demand curve for a monopolistically competitive product is very difficult because product differentiation can make similar products quite different. For example, toothpastes and toothpowders are virtually the same things in nature, but different in product. The same is true between fresh milks and powdered milks. Because of these minor distinctions the monopolistically competitive markets can allow for some restriction of output and increase in prices that cannot be allowed for in purely competitive markets. For this reason, marginal revenue is usually less than price, and output is usually short of that point where marginal cost equals price.

Market Structure. In discussing any market structure, a distinction must be made between short run and long run. The short run is that time span in which the firm is unable to change its scale of plant and, also, in which new firms do not have sufficient time to enter the market. For this reason, it is often possible for firms to achieve economic as well as normal profits in the short run. In the long run, however, if entry is not blocked and firms are free to enter and exit the market, there are no economic profits. The reason for this is that the entry of new firms shifts the demand curves faced by individual firms downward and cost curves of the firms upward, causing profits to decrease. New firms will continue to enter the market until the point where all pure profits have been eliminated.

The main advantage of monopolistically competitive markets to the consumer is that he or she is given a wide range of products, styles, and brands from which to choose.   —*William D. Wagoner*

See also Imperfect Competition; Market Structure; Perfect Competition.

MONOPOLISTIC PROFITS refer to those returns to input that are over and above the firm's total costs after a normal profit has been taken out. Monopolistic profits are called economic or pure profits and are found in industries that are less than perfectly competitive. Usually the fewer the number of firms in an industry, the greater the amount of monopolistic profits. For example, monopolistically competitive industries are expected to earn less monopolistic profits than oligopolistic or monopolistic industries.

Purely monopolistic industries are able to earn economic profits because their marginal revenue curve lies below their demand curve. For this reason, a monopoly firm can set its output at that point where marginal costs equal marginal revenue, but instead of setting its price at this point, it can set a higher price because of the position of the demand curve. This higher price results in pure economic profits.

In an oligopolistic industry, an industry with only a few firms, output is again set at that point where marginal costs equal marginal revenue. However, again, the demand curve lies above the marginal revenue curve and a higher price can be set. Because of the unusually kinked demand curve that occurs, caused by the interdependence of the firms in an oligopolistic industry, all firms usually sell at the same price, producing a monopolistic effect. Because economic profits must be shared among the firms in the industry, these profits are usually less for each firm than they would be if the firm were a monopoly.

In monopolistically competitive markets, some, but relatively little, economic profits occur. The reason is because the demand curve is less than perfectly elastic and causes the marginal revenue curve to fall somewhat below it.   —*William D. Wagoner*

See also Monopoly Profits; Profits.

MONOPOLIZING, or MONOPOLIZATION, is the intent or attempt on the part of a business firm or firms to acquire a position of monopoly in a market by damaging or eliminating competitors. To the extent that oligopolists behave as one firm, have similar motives, and take similar actions against rivals, they can also monopolize.

There is an essential difference between monopoly, a type of market structure in economic analysis in which there is but one firm setting price and output for a product, and monopolizing, a legal concept describing the illegal behavior (predatory practices, sales below cost, local price discrimination) of one or more firms designed to damage economic rivals. In law (Sherman Antitrust Act, Section 2) a firm may be a monopoly without having monopolized (if it can show that "monopoly was thrust" upon it); a firm may have monopolized without achieving a monopoly. The act's prohibition clearly is against monopolizing. For while the result (monopoly) threatened by monopolizing is feared, the legal proscription of monopolizing looks to the anticompetitive effects of a monopolizing firm's behavior toward rivals. Thus, interpretation of the Sherman Act has emphasized the acquisition and use of economic power against actual or potential rivals rather than the structure of markets.

— *Thomas O. Depperschmidt*

See also Collusion; Monopoly Thrust Upon a Firm; Oligopoly; Predatory Practices; United States v. Aluminum Company of America; United States v. U.S. Steel Corp.

MONOPOLY, a market structure in which there is only one seller in the industry and there are no perfect substitutes for the product. Thus, the firm has no rivals or competition; a condition that can only persist if entry into the industry is blocked. This is done in several ways. For example, a natural monopoly can exist when the economies of scale are so pronounced that competition is impractical, inconvenient, and unworkable. A second block to entry occurs when the government reserves exclusive rights of production to itself or to firms that it designates by means of a license. A third but less effective bar to entry is the patent right.

Economies of scale are an important factor in monopolies, because most monopolies require huge investments and, to be profitable, the firm's average cost scale must decline over a wide range of output. Public utilities, such as American Telephone and Telegraph, that have high investment costs, are perfect examples of this need for economies of scale. In addition, it can easily be seen that duplication of certain utility lines, such as telephone and gas lines, cannot be profitable.

Monopoly price determination is almost always on a profit maximizing basis, although in special cases the price set is a socially optimum one. A monopoly, like all other market structures, produces output to the point where marginal cost equals marginal revenue. However, instead of charging the price indicated at that point, the monopolist can charge a higher price because of lack of competition.

Regulation. There are two main reasons why some economists feel that monopoly should be minimized. First, in any situation where price is higher than marginal cost there is a misallocation of resources. Second, monopoly tends to lower the incentive for cost reducing technology and for the development of new and better products. Because of the "restraints of trade" that a monopoly imposes on the public, the government has attempted to curtail monopoly power by law. The Sherman Antitrust Act of 1890 and the Clayton Antitrust Act of 1914 make any attempt to monopolize trade a criminal offense against the federal government. The Federal Trade Commission was also set up in 1914 and given the power to investigate unfair business practices and to take legal action if required.

— *William D. Wagoner*

See also Imperfect Competition.

MONOPOLY: TOPIC GUIDE

For further consideration of monopoly as one type of market structure, see the articles on PERFECT COMPETITION, IMPERFECT COMPETITION, OLIGOPOLY, MONOPOLISTIC COMPETITION, and MONOPSONY. One of the numerous factors contributing to monopoly is discussed in BARRIERS TO ENTRY.

For an examination of the legal definition and status of monopoly, consult the relevant statutes and some of their most notable applications. The major statutes are examined in the articles on SHERMAN ANTITRUST ACT, CLAYTON ANTITRUST ACT, and CELLER-KEFAUVER ACT; notable applications are described in UNITED STATES v. ALUMINUM CO. OF AMERICA, UNITED STATES v. STANDARD OIL CO. OF NEW JERSEY, and UNITED STATES v. E.I. DU PONT AND CO. Additional details on legally prohibited and permissable actions are explained in RESTRAINT OF TRADE, PRICE FIXING, MONOPOLIZING, COLLUSION, and MERGER.

An economically and socially defensible type of monopoly is explained in the article on PUBLIC UTILITIES.

The Subject Maps accompanying the articles on ANTITRUST POLICY and REGULATION display the interrelations of these and other articles in the encyclopedic dictionary.

MONOPOLY BANK. *See* Multiple Expansion of the Money Supply.

MONOPOLY PROFITS. There are several types of profit that a firm can reap. Firms in purely competitive industries enjoy what is called normal profits. A monopoly firm also enjoys normal profits, but, in addition, receives economic or pure profits. Normal profits are simply the minimum return to inputs (capital and labor) necessary to maintain a given production level. Therefore, when a firm receives a price that is set at the point where its marginal cost is equal to the marginal revenue, it earns normal profits.

Pure Profits, however, are the returns to a production level over and above all cost—both implicit and explicit—or that amount of revenue left over after all costs have been covered.

A monopoly industry is able to earn pure profits because its marginal revenue curve lies below its demand curve. Therefore, a monopoly sets its output at that point where marginal costs equal marginal revenue; the point at which a competitive firm or industry would also set price. However, because of the placement of the demand curve of a monopolist, he or she is able to charge a higher price and in this way earn pure profits.

The pure profits of a monopolist represent a misallocation of resources, however, and often a certain amount of inefficiency in the industry.

MONOPOLY THRUST UPON A FIRM describes a defense plea to a charge of monopolizing under Section 2 of the Sherman Antitrust Act. It means that a firm, having obtained dominance or monopoly in a market, argues that it achieved its position through normal, benign, and legal business practices, without intent or attempt to monopolize. The plea has legal status, but has not been employed with much success, for the firm using it must be free of virtually all semblance of wrongdoing in its relations with competitors.

See also Antitrust Policy; Monopolizing; Predatory Practices; United States v. Aluminum Co. of America.

MONOPSONY is a market in which there is only one buyer. An example of a monopsony would be a single firm in an industry purchasing the factors of production for that industry. The monopsony is commonly known as a buyers' monopoly. In the labor market the monopsonist is able to pay a wage lower than the value of output produced by the marginal worker (exploitation of labor). A typical monopsony is the telephone industry, where the telephone company is the only employer of telephone operators.

MOONLIGHTING is the taking on of an additional job by workers who are employed at a regular, full-time job. The term originated because these second jobs are very often night jobs. Moonlighting accounts for only about 5% of labor force overtime. The primary reason for moonlighting is financial pressure, with 40% of moonlighters working to meet regular expenses, and 10% working to pay off debts.

MORAL HAZARD, an effect of economic institutions arranged so that individuals have an incentive to maximize consumption at a social cost to others because they do not bear the full cost of their consumption. Health insurance is the usual example. Those who are uninsured and become ill will consume medical services until they feel that the marginal cost of those services equals their marginal benefit. But if an individual has medical insurance, the cost of medical services to that person is much lower, increasing the temptation to consume much more health care than if one paid for it oneself. This creates a moral hazard.

The social cost enters when everyone covered by the same insurance company behaves the same way. The company will then be forced to raise its premiums, to the detriment of everyone.

MORAL SUASION refers to pressure exerted on the banking system or the public by the Federal Reserve System in an attempt to achieve specific objectives of monetary policy, but without compulsion. The most important forms of moral suasion are: (1) suggestions made during bank examination with respect to the volume, kind, or safety of the bank's various loans and investments; (2) discussions with banks under a program of informal visitation for the purpose of explaining Federal Reserve objectives and policies; and (3) publicity directed toward the general public, including information and statistics concerning the present state of the economy, explanations of the nature of Federal Reserve operations and objectives, and admonitions with respect to current policy.

During the Korean War the Federal Reserve encouraged and coordinated voluntary agreements among financial institutions to restrain the inflationary expansion of that period. The program was suspended in 1952 as inflationary pressures eased.

See also Monetary Policy.

MORTGAGE LENDING CONTROLS prescribe the minimum down payment and the maximum repayment period on mortgage loans. Such controls were established by the Board of Governors of the Federal Reserve System under the Defense Production Act of 1950 and published as Regulation X. They were discontinued in 1953.

MOST-FAVORED NATION. *See* General Agreement on Tariffs and Trade.

MOTOR CARRIER ACT (1935), the basic law regulating motor transportation and a portion of the Interstate Commerce Act. It has six basic parts. Carriers are classified as common carriers, contract carriers, private carriers, brokers, and exempt carriers. Entry is controlled by use of certificates of public convenience and necessity and permits by a grandfather clause. Rates are controlled in the same manner as railroad rates are, consolidations and mergers are controlled, and securities and accounts are supervised. Finally, a series of innovational regulatory devices such as exemptions, joint boards, and insurance controls are utilized. It is essentially a modification of railroad regulation imposed on trucks and buses.

See also Interstate Commerce Commission.

MULTI-EMPLOYER BARGAINING occurs when a union representing workers in several or all firms in an industry enters into contract bargaining with a number of employers simultaneously. It is likely to result when either party considers uniform contract provisions desirable and individual bargaining wasteful, difficult, or undesirable. Employers may favor this type of bargaining in an attempt to protect themselves from "whipsaw" tactics (playing one employer against another).

See also Collective Bargaining.

MULTINATIONAL COMPANY, a firm based in one country with operations in one or more additional countries.

Some controversy surrounds the legal status of American-based multinational companies. Proponents argue that they tend to break down trade barriers and promote cooperation among countries. Opponents, especially in labor groups, contend that domestic unemployment is increased, and that these firms enjoy unfair tax advantage over smaller domestic companies and aggravate the balance-of-payments problem.

ስፕራይት
Sprite in Amharic

樂可口可
Coca-Cola in Chinese

كوكا كولا
Coca-Cola in Arabic

達發
Fanta in Chinese

Koka Kola
Coca-Cola in Cyrillic

コカ・コーラ
Coca-Cola in Japanese

КОКА-КОЛА
Coca-Cola in Greek

こーく
Coke in Japanese

A multinational company must often cope with a wide variety of work customs and even languages.

MULTINATIONAL TRADE AGREEMENTS. In a conference at Havana in 1948 a charter for an International Trade Organization (ITO) was approved by representatives of 54 countries. The United States failed to ratify the charter and the ITO never came into existence. However, many provisions of the charter are embodied in the General Agreement on Tariffs and Trade (GATT). Significant characteristics of GATT, based in Geneva, are its general provisions, which constitute a code of commercial policy, and the multilateral approach to negotiations. Among the general provisions of GATT are unconditional most-favored-nation treatment, elimination of quantitative restrictions, and the obligation to negotiate tariff reductions at the request of a member. The 70-odd members have met often since 1948. Between sessions, work is carried on by a Council of Representatives (delegates from participating nations). In addition, major tariff negotiating conferences are held when deemed desirable by a consensus of member countries. There have been six bargaining conferences thus far: 1947, 1949, 1951, 1956, 1962, 1964. Prior to 1964, the United States attended on the basis of the Reciprocal Trade Agreements Act; the Trade Expansion Act of 1962 gave the nation new bargaining areas

and the call for the conference led to the "Kennedy Round." GATT deals with less-developed nations under the aegis of UNCTAD—United National Conference on Trade and Development.

—John R. Matthews, Jr.
See also General Agreement on Tariffs and Trade.

MULTI-PLANT FIRM, a business unit with more than one production facility, or plant. Typically, economic analysis distinguishes between the firm, as the organizational-administrative-financial aspect of a business unit, and the plant, as the physical production unit. Most major, national, goods-producing firms are multi-plant in nature.

MULTIPLE DETERMINATION. *See* Correlation.

MULTIPLE EXPANSION OF THE MONEY SUPPLY, the power of the banking system to increase the money supply through the creation of demand deposits on the basis of a fractional reserve system. While thrift institutions now offer checkable deposits, the overwhelming volume of demand deposits are accounted for by commercial banks. Because demand deposits are a form of money, any increase in such deposits represents an increase in the money supply. Because they are simply liabilities of the bank (or thrift institution) representing the amounts the bank has promised to pay to depositors against their checks, a bank can increase its deposits at any time by crediting a customer's deposit account.

Loans. Banks increase their deposits by accepting cash or checks for the account of the depositor (primary or deposited deposits) and by creating a deposit for a borrower in exchange for his promissory note (derivative or created deposits). Thus they create money whenever they make a loan. The limits to a bank's ability to lend are determined by its reserve requirement compared to the actual reserves held in the form of cash, deposits with a Federal Reserve bank, or other assets normally acceptable as reserves. More precisely, any bank may make loans equal to its excess reserves, which are computed by subtracting required reserves (either legal reserves or the amount of reserves the bank believes that it is necessary to set aside to meet normal withdrawals) from its actual reserves. Thus, if a bank has $100 million in deposit liabilities, $20 million in actual reserves, and a reserve requirement of 18%, its required reserves are $18 million, and its excess reserves are $2 million. The $2 million is the amount of new money the bank can create by making loans.

To take a simpler illustration, if a customer deposits $100 in cash in bank A, and bank A has a reserve requirement of 20%, only $20 must be kept in reserves, and the bank may lend the other $80, or 80% of the original deposit. Normally the borrower does not keep this money on deposit; he borrowed it to pay a bill of some kind. If he writes a check against his account for the full $80 and gives it to his creditor, who deposits it in bank B, bank B now has an additional $80 of deposits and reserves. If this bank also has a reserve requirement of 20%, $16 must be reserved and $64 may be lent. This process can continue through a long chain of banks, as shown in the accompanying table.

Bank Multiplier. If nothing occurs to interrupt the process, the total monetary expansion of the whole banking system is a multiple (in the illustrated case, five) of the initial deposit. That is, total deposits are $500 ($100 by cash and $400 by check), or five times the initial deposit of $100. The total loans made are $400 or five times the initial increase in excess reserves of $80. The bank multiplier is, thus, the reciprocal of the reserve requirement. A high reserve requirement inhibits expansion, and a low reserve requirement encourages expansion.

Leakages. The bank multiplier applied to an initial figure for excess reserves for the banking system shows the maximum possible expansion of the money supply. Leakages are apt to occur to reduce the actual expansion. The most common leakage is a cash drain, which occurs when depositors withdraw their funds in cash. This amount of reserves is lost to the banking system. It is unlikely that banks will lend exactly the amount of their excess reserves, and if business is slow, banks may lend a great deal less than the maximum possible.

Multiple Contraction of the Money Supply. If the monetary authorities were to contract the amount of excess reserves through open-market operations by selling a $100 bond to an individual who pays with a check written on a bank, exactly the reverse of what is described above will occur. The bank on which the check is written will simultaneously have its reserves and deposit liabilities reduced by $100. But assuming that this bank was loaned-up to begin with (had no excess reserves) and that the reserve requirement is 20%, this transaction has left the bank short of reserves. Actual reserves have fallen by $100, but required reserves have fallen by only $20 (−$100 × .2). This leaves the bank $80 short of the reserves it

needs to meet its legal reserve requirement. The bank will have to contract its loans by $80. Ultimately, the money supply will fall by $500. —*Gerald A. Whitney*

MULTIPLIER: TOPIC GUIDE

The basic theoretical concept underlying the multiplier is explained in the article on the CIRCULAR FLOW OF INCOME. The significance of the multiplier is shown in the articles on the INFLATIONARY GAP and NATIONAL INCOME DETERMINATION (especially those parts dealing with changes in the level of national income).

MULTIPLIER, the ratio of the ultimate increase in income caused by an original increase in spending to that original increase; or the process by which the original increase in spending gives rise to the ultimate increase in income. In early expositions of national income determination the original change was in increase (or decrease) in investment, partly to show that the fluctuations in national income could occur quite independently of government policy, and partly because spending on investment goods is considered the least stable component of aggregate demand and, hence, the most important in accounting for the business cycle. However, the original change in spending can equally well be in consumption (upward or downward shift in the consumption function), in government spending, or in net exports (purchases by foreigners).

The Process. As a process, the multiplier is the sequence of consumption spendings set off by the original increase in spending. The original increase, being new, will add to the incomes of some people, who will spend a portion of their new incomes on consumption, in turn adding to the incomes of other people, who will then spend, and so on. Since the marginal propensity to consume (MPC) is less than 1.00, each stage in the series will be smaller than the previous one, in a declining series. As a ratio, the multiplier equals $1/(1-MPC)$.

	Increase in actual reserves				
	by cash deposit	by deposit of check drawn on preceding bank	Increase in required reserves	Increase in excess reserves	Loans made
Bank A	$100.00		$20.00	$80.00	$80.00
B		$80.00	16.00	64.00	64.00
C		64.00	12.80	51.20	51.20
D		51.20	10.24	40.96	40.96
E		40.96	8.19	32.77	32.77
F		32.77	6.56	26.21	26.21
G		26.21	5.24	20.97	20.97
H		20.97	4.19	16.78	16.78
I		16.78	3.36	13.42	13.42
J		13.42	2.68	10.74	10.74
First 10 banks	$100.00	$346.31	$89.26	$357.05	$357.05
All remaining banks		53.69	10.74	42.95	42.95
Total, all banks	$100.00	$400.00	$100.00	$400.00	$400.00

MAXIMUM POSSIBLE EXPANSION OF THE MONEY SUPPLY ON THE BASIS OF A NEW DEPOSIT OF $100 AND A UNIFORM RESERVE REQUIREMENT OF 20 PERCENT multiplier process while, on the other hand, the increase in taxes sets off a downward multiplier effect by reducing the disposable income of consumers. In the latter, downward process, the first stage is not a reduction in spending, but causes a "second stage" reduction in spending of (MPC) x (change in after-tax income). One can view the balanced budget multiplier either as a full upward multiplier effect minus a tax increase multiplier (the same as a negative tax reduction multiplier), or as a full multiplier of the net effect of increase in government spending minus the decrease in consumption spending. — *Walter C. Neale*

MUNICIPAL TAX-EXEMPT BONDS, debt instruments issued by local governments, or by their agencies. These bonds have traditionally been used to finance major capital construction projects such as public buildings, roads, bridges, and parks. More recently, municipal bonds have been used to promote local economic development, to create jobs, and to provide low-cost mortgages to homebuyers.

Municipal bonds are exempt from federal income taxes and are also exempt from state income taxes in the state of origin. This feature allows local govern-

Tax-Reduction and Transfer-Payment Multipliers. These are one less than the investment, government spending, consumption spending, and net export multipliers, because the first stage (leaving people with larger disposable incomes by not taking from them or giving them more) is not a payment for services rendered, and does not involve tangible spending.

The Balanced Budget Multiplier. This is the point at which all additional government spending on goods and services is exactly balanced by increased tax revenues, is 1.00; because, on the one hand, the additional government spending sets off an upward ments to raise money at a rate that is lower than the private market rate of interest. For example, consider a potential investor who is in the 40% federal income tax bracket. If this person buys a taxable corporate bond that yields a rate of 15%, the investor will receive an after-tax return of 9% (i.e., (1 − tax rate) × 15%). If the investor can buy an equal risk municipal bond that yields only 10%, the municipal bond is the better deal.

Critics of tax exemption argue that it leads to an excessive amount of state and local government, at the expense of useful private economic activity. In particular, the widespread use of municipal bonds to finance home mortgages or to aid in industrial development has become a very controversial topic.

See also Industrial Development Bond.

MUNN v. ILLINOIS (1877), the original Supreme Court decision upholding the legal right of the public to regulate business "affected with the public interest." Using ancient common-law precedents, the Court upheld the public's right to regulation of special categories of business which were "clothed with the public interest."

MUTUAL FUNDS, companies composed of the stocks, bonds, or other financial assets of other companies. People buy stock in the mutual fund, a company that produces nothing but purchases other financial assets. During the 1970s, interest rates increased substantially, giving rise to quite a few new financial instruments and new financial innovations. Mutual funds were one of the leading areas in devising new instruments.

In the wake of the stock market crash of October 1987, many investors shifted to money market funds, which were also popular during the late 1970s. These mutual funds generally purchase only government bonds, commercial paper of large corporations, and large certificates of deposit from commercial banks, the latter making up the greater part of the funds' portfolios. These money market mutual funds use the interest that they earn on these bonds to pay dividends to their stockholders. These dividends can be considered to be interest, and during the late 1970s and early 1980s these interest payments were as high as 20%. Many of these money market mutual funds began to allow stockholders in the fund to write negotiable orders of withdrawal (NOWs) on the balance held in their accounts. Thus, the money market mutual funds became known as "non-bank" banks. To allow commercial banks to compete with these non-bank banks, the federal government allowed banks to offer money market mutual fund accounts that were similar to the money market mutual funds. "Do-gooder funds," funds that specialize in socially conscious investing, were a new development of the 1980s, yielding returns comparable to ordinary funds. — *Timothy P. Ryan*

MYRDAL, GUNNAR (1898-1987). An outstanding Swedish economist and social thinker, Myrdal made important contributions to economic theory in the areas of economic development, international trade, and macroeconomic theory and policy and addressed questions such as the use of the scientific method and the racial problem in the United States.

Myrdal is probably best known for his study of the race problem in *The American Dilemma* (1944). However, his early work on the saving-investment relationship and his discussions of the problems of development are more important from an economic standpoint.

He felt that the gains to less developed nations that international trade theory predicts will result from trade with developed countries do not really exist. In addition, Myrdal felt that the gap between the rich nations and the poor nations is widening and traditional economic policies are unable to cope with the problem. The governments of less developed coun-

tries, therefore, must play a larger role in the implementation of economic planning to promote progress. These plans should include a more equitable distribution of income, the volume and distribution among sectors of investment, and the control of foreign trade. Myrdal took this stand on the role of government in less developed countries because he felt that such countries function in an institutional framework that operates against their interest. For his many contributions, Myrdal was awarded the 1974 Nobel Prize in economics.
— *Clyde A. Haulman*

NATIONAL ASSOCIATION OF SECURITIES DEALERS. *See* Stock Market.

NATIONAL BANK, a commercial bank that chooses to obtain a charter from the federal government under the National Bank Act (1863) as amended, particularly by the Federal Reserve Act (1913). National banks are chartered by the Comptroller of the Currency and are under the Comptroller's supervision and that of the Federal Reserve System, of which they must be members, and that of the Federal Deposit Insurance Corporation, which they are required to join. Subject primarily to federal law, they are also subject to the law of the state in which they operate, and they cannot carry on a public banking business in more than one state. Although only one-third of the commercial banks in the United States are national banks, they hold two-thirds of the deposits.

NATIONAL DEBT, INTEREST. In order to carry a national debt, a nation must pay interest, which is the price of borrowing money. Interest payments on the national debt depend upon the size of the outstanding debt and the market rate of interest on federal securities. The actual interest rate on comparable securities influences the interest rate the government must pay to borrow money. Tax revenues finance the interest payments. Keeping these payments low reduces the amount of tax revenues needed. But during recessionary periods, this can cause instability in the economy. Higher interest rates and the growth of the federal debt have caused interest payments to increase in recent years.

NATIONAL EMERGENCY STRIKE, work stoppages that are especially harmful to the public interest. If the president feels that a strike jeopardizes the public interest, he or she may appoint an emergency fact-finding board. While the board is supposed to have the fullest authority over the facts, it is forbidden by the Taft-Hartley Act from making specific recommendations for a settlement.

After receiving the panel's report, the president may request an 80-day injunction that requires the parties to bargain during this period. If no agreement is reached in the first 60 days, a public report is issued,

and the NLRB goes directly to the membership to see if an agreement may be reached. If no decision is reached at the end of the 80 days, the union is free to strike. Examples of national emergency strikes might include strikes by police or firemen, but most likely would not include strikes by auto workers.
— *William D. Wagoner*

NATIONAL HEALTH INSURANCE. Many countries operate some form of comprehensive program of compulsory health insurance that provides coverage for all residents. Programs may be financed by special taxes earmarked for the purpose, funded from general tax revenues, or a combination of the above. Personnel in the health services industry (including physicians) may be employees of the government or may be in private practice and receive partial or total reimbursement of fees. Patients may be free to choose their physicians or may be assigned them by a government agency. The plan may cover in part or in full the cost of dental service, drugs, and devices such as eyeglasses, crutches, and wheelchairs. A national health insurance program, even if comprehensive, need not preclude continuance of private practice for clientele willing to pay.

See also Social Insurance.

NATIONAL INCOME may refer either to a specific accounting measure or to a general concept of the total value of goods and services produced in an economy during a particular period, such as a year.

As a specific measure, national income is defined as Net National Product (that is, Gross National Product less depreciation) minus indirect business taxes, and is a measure of the total cost of factors of production used in the production of the NNP, or of total incomes earned in producing the GNP. Indirect business taxes are part of the price or total value of output but are not payments to a factor of production.

As a general concept and as commonly used in the theory of national income determination, however, the term refers either to a gross or net value of an economy's output, or expenditures for that output. National income (or "Y," its usual symbol) is thus defined as the sum of C (consumption) + I (investment) + G (government expenditure for goods and services) + (X − M) or net exports. In the theory of national income determination this definition is sufficient.

Specific Measures. For calculating a country's national product or income, a number of specific measures and procedures known as national income accounts and accounting have been developed. National income does *not* refer to the total wealth of a country. The total wealth would include the value of all the capital, land, and natural resources, and every other material thing of value.
— *Anne Mayhew*

See also Capital; Gross National Product; National Income Measurement.

NATIONAL INCOME AND PRODUCT ACCOUNTS, a generic term used in national accounting, refers to a series of statistical statements of aggregate national output or income, published regularly, usually monthly or quarterly, by the U.S. Department of Commerce. These statistics are used by economists in every sector—business, industry, and government—to determine the present level of productivity, and as a base from which to forecast future economic growth and expansion.

The economic measurements, indices, and components used to determine national income were developed by the National Bureau of Economic Research, which began its studies in this area during the 1920s and 1930s. The Congress directed the preparation of national income accounts in 1932, and a few years later the Department of Commerce began issuing its regular statistical statements. The monthly personal income series was initiated in the late 1930s. During World War II, the development of the Gross National Product (GNP) series was accelerated because of its value in planning the war effort and in instituting controls.

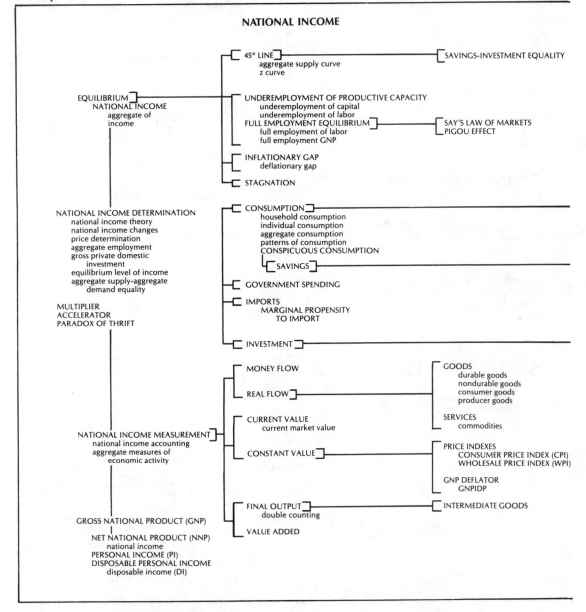

During the postwar period, the accounts were extended beyond the original scope of measuring the size and composition of national output. Today, they include not only the GNP and personal income series, but Net National Product and disposable income series, as well as the following individual indices: consolidated business income and products accounts, construction contract award data, gross savings and investment accounts, import and export statistics, and a variety of other data such as consolidated government receipts and expenditures, and new business starts and business failures.

This statistical information is augmented regularly by the Department of Commerce breakdown of national income by industry, listing the income in terms of dollars and as a percentage of the country's total output.

The diversity of the data that contribute to the make-up of national income and product accounts, when combined into a unified statistical statement, provides a picture of the total volume of production of goods and services over a specific period.

See also Business Cycles, Measurement.

NATIONAL INCOME DETERMINATION (National Income Theory). According to modern, or Keynesian,

NATIONAL INCOME
continued

theory, national income, the value of an economy's output during a year, is determined by a country's productive capacity *and* the demand for that output. Pre-Keynesian economics emphasized the productive capacity, or ability to supply output, as the determinant of the level of national income. The ability of an economy to produce goods and services limits the level of real national income, but within this limit it is the level of total (aggregate) demand for currently produced goods and services that determines how much will be produced.

Aggregate Demand. Total, or aggregate, demand is divided into four categories: (1) the demand of households for consumption goods and services, or consumption (C); (2) the demand of businesses for capital goods, or investment (I); (3) the demand of governments for goods and services, government expenditure (G); and (4) the net foreign demand for goods and services (exports minus imports: X – M, or F). So, aggregate demand and, therefore, national income (Y) are equal to C + I + G + F. Aggregate demand is divided into these four categories because the reasons for spending are different in all four cases.

Households spend to keep the family alive and happy. In national income theory it is assumed (fairly accurately) that consumption is determined by households' disposable income. If one ignores taxes and transfer payments and that part of national income retained by businesses as depreciation allowances and retained earnings, consumption may be said to be a function of national income. Savings, that part of disposable income not spent on consumption, is, therefore, also a function of income.

Business firms spend to earn profits from investment. Investment demand is assumed to consist of two parts: (1) autonomous investment demand, which is not determined by the current level of income; and (2) induced investment, which does vary with the level of income. In national income theory, investment is frequently called gross private domestic investment because (1) it is the total expenditure for goods currently produced in the country that is of concern, and whether those goods are purchased to replace equipment or to add to the stock of capital goods is not important in determining the level of total demand; and (2) although governments buy capital goods, these public expenditures are included in government expenditures.

Governments spend to carry out public policies of all kinds, ranging from economic stabilization to defense to public education. Government demand for goods and services is assumed to be autonomous, not related to or determined by the level of income, except insofar as countercyclical policy is a response to the level of income and employment.

Foreign Goods. These are purchased by households, businesses, and governments when they prefer foreign goods or find them cheaper, and foreigners purchase American goods for the same reasons. United States imports wll increase as income increases, and the demand in other countries for goods and services produced in the United States will increase as income increases in those countries. Of course, the demand for imports and exports depends upon a number of things other than income, such as relative prices and tariff policies. In national income theory, it is assumed that these other factors do not change—and if they do change, the results can be expressed as a change in the marginal propensity to import. So, imports are a function of income, and exports are autonomous.

Net exports—exports minus imports—are added to total demand, because spending by foreigners on American goods (American exports: X) is demand for goods and services currently produced by Americans, and the imported components (American imports: M) of C, I, and G are not demand for American production and employment, but for foreign production and employment. Imports are, therefore, along with savings and taxes, leakages from the income stream. If exports exceed imports, the foreign balance (X – M) is positive, which is to say foreign trade adds to the demand for goods and services produced during the year. If imports exceed exports, the foreign balance is negative, which is to say the the net effect of foreign trade has been to reduce the demand for goods and services produced during the year.

Since imports and exports are a fairly small percentage of GNP in the United States, the foreign balance is often ignored and the economy is assumed, in order to make the analysis simpler, to be a "closed economy"—an economy with no foreign trade.

Equality of Aggregate Supply and Aggregate Demand. National income is determined by the total demand for goods and services: Y = C + I + G + F. Of course, during any period of time national output is also the total value of goods and services produced during that period, and the question arises as to what happens if this dollar quantity is not equal to the dollar amount of aggregate demand. Because the decisions about how much to produce during any period of time are made independently of the decisions about how much to purchase, the producers (businesses) may be unable to sell all they had planned to, or may be able to sell more than they had planned.

Businesses produce what they hope to sell plus what they want to add to inventories. If households, governments, foreigners, and other businesses do not want to purchase as much as a firm produces, the firm will find itself with more inventories than it wants to hold. Since inventories are part of investment, if businesses as a whole produce more than they can sell, total actual investment will exceed total planned investment. Thus actual aggregate demand, which may include some unintended demand by businesses in excess of what they planned to demand, will equal aggregate supply, even though planned aggregate demand did not equal planned aggregate supply.

National Income Changes. If businesses are producing more than is being demanded, they will cut production and so buy or hire fewer inputs. Both aggregate supply and the incomes paid to produce it will fall. As households receive less income, they will spend less, and incomes will fall still further. The total amount by which income falls depends on how much households' demand decreases as income decreases (the multiplier). Incomes will continue to fall until the total (aggregate) planned spending by households, businesses, governments, and foreigners equals the value of the amount being produced. The income at which this equality exists is the *equilibrium level of income.*

At the equilibrium level of income, planned investment plus planned government expenditures plus exports will equal savings plus taxes plus imports. All of the output supplied and not consumed by households will be demanded by businesses, governments, or foreigners. If planned total demand is greater than planned aggregate supply, aggregate supply will rise to the point where the amount that households, businesses, governments, and foreigners want to buy is equalled by the amount being supplied. National income will rise as businesses expand output, to satisfy demand for goods and services, and consequently purchase more inputs— which will become increases in household income and lead to further increases in consumption. As in the previous case of declining income, the amount by which income will rise depends on the marginal propensity to consume.

National income will also change as a result of changes in any component of aggregate demand. If businesses decide to increase investment, national income will rise by the amount of the increase in investment plus the amount by which consumption will increase as a result of the change in income. Thus, income will eventually rise by the amount of the initial change in income (the change in investment) times the multiplier. If households decide to save more and consume less, aggregate demand and national income will fall. National income will also change if government demand for goods and services changes or if net foreign demand changes. Of course, if businesses increase investment and governments decrease their expenditure for goods and services by the same amount there will be no net change in aggregate demand, and national income will not change.

Reality of Constant Changes. In reality, businesses and households do not make plans for a year and then wait to alter them. Production plans and spending plans are altered as often as households and firms see that significant changes have occurred in the economic conditions they face. And, in reality, the full effects of any one change in aggregate demand are not fully worked out before another change is made.

This means that we do not achieve an equilibrium level of income nor can we say that any particular level is an equilibrium level. What we can say is that a particular level is too high or low for equilibrium, meaning that given the plans of households, businesses, governments, and foreigners to purchase goods and services, income will rise or fall.

Graphic Analysis. The determination of national income and changes in national income are frequently explained by use of a graph.

The 45° line, used to represent aggregate supply, shows the dollar amount that will be supplied at the levels of income measured on the horizontal axis. For each level of income the associated aggregate demand is measured on the vertical axis: first C, then I added to it, then G added to that, then F to all of them, giving the aggregate demand curve. The equilibrium level of income—the level at which planned aggregate supply is equal to planned aggregate demand—will be that level at which the aggregate demand curve intersects the aggregate supply curve. The slope of the consumption curve is the marginal propensity to consume and shows how much consumption will change as income changes. If income increases from Y_o to Y_e, consumption will increase by the amount measured by the distance AB and the marginal propensity to consume— $\triangle/\triangle Y$ — is AB/ $(Y_e - Y_o)$. As drawn here, investment, government spending, and net exports

NATIONAL INCOME

are assumed to be independent of income: they are the same at all the levels of income shown on the horizontal axis. This means that the C, C + I, C + I + G, and C + I + G + F lines are parallel. In using this diagram, F is usually ignored and aggregate demand is C + I + G. The difference between the level of consumption at any level of income and the aggregate supply curve represents savings plus taxes: that part of income, or total supply, that is not consumed. For any level of income to be the equilibrium level, governments, businesses, and foreigners must plan to take this amount of the total output.

National Income, Employment, and the Price Level. In more recent and sophisticated models of national income determination, prices are not assumed to remain constant as the level of national income changes. Also, the relationship between the level of income and employment is recognized in such a way that the problems of inflation and unemployment can be analyzed more clearly than is possible with the more basic models.

Aggregate demand is a downward-sloping function of the level of spending and the money supply. Thus, the quantity of aggregate demand is expected to be greater the lower the price level. Aggregate supply is viewed as an upward-sloping function with respect to the price level, in the short run, but vertical at the "natural rate" of income (and employment) in the long run. The short-run aggregate supply curve is expected to shift as workers' expectations regarding the price level adjust to actual changes in the price level. The speed and nature of the adjustment depends on assumptions of *adaptive* or *rational* expectations, and whether markets are expected to clear in the short run.

The recent developments in national income theory provide a clearer explanation for inflation, inflationary cycles, stagflation, and the concurrent problems of inflation and unemployment.

See also National Income.

NATIONAL INCOME EQUILIBRIUM, the level of aggregate national income at which aggregate demand is just equal to aggregate supply. This is the level of income from which there would be no built-in tendency to change, because the quantity of goods and services purchased is just equal to the quantity of goods and services currently produced and sold. Thus, another criterion for the determination of equilibrium national income is that there be no net change in inventories, since it is the change in inventories that signals producers (sellers) to change the level of output.

If current production is greater than current demand, inventories will begin to accumulate. Inventories will be depleted if current spending is greater than current production.

NATIONAL INCOME MEASUREMENT. The Department of Commerce undertakes the difficult task of estimating national income data. These data take the form of national income accounts, which represent measurements of various aspects of aggregate economic activity. Through its efforts, the Department of Commerce hopes to provide some understanding of the nature and level of current economic activity, the basic structure of the economy, and the nature and extent of changes taking place within the economy over time.

The National Income Accounts. These are estimates and, as such, lack the precision of hard count enumerations, which are physically difficult and financially prohibitive. The estimates are generated in dif-

---

> **NATIONAL INCOME MEASUREMENT: TOPIC GUIDE**
>
> A fuller analysis of the way aggregate economic activity is measured is presented in the article on NATIONAL INCOME AND PRODUCT ACCOUNTS. Some of the more commonly used measures are discussed in GROSS NATIONAL PRODUCT, PERSONAL INCOME, CONSUMPTION, and INVESTMENT. A full discussion of all facets of national income can be found in the article on NATIONAL INCOME DETERMINATION. The interrelationships of these and other articles are displayed on the NATIONAL INCOME Subject Map.

ferent ways, including sample surveys and trend projections, but care is taken to ensure that the estimating techniques are statistically sound.

GNP. Although there are many national income accounts, the gross national product or expenditure account seems to have the widest currency. GNP may be defined in various ways: two definitions employed by the Department of Commerce are (1) "GNP is the market value of the output of goods and services produced by the nation's economy, before the deduction of depreciation charges and other allowances for business and institutional consumption of durable capital goods," and (2) "GNP comprises the purchase of goods and services by consumers and government, gross private domestic investment and exports."

These two definitions emphasize different facets of GNP. The first highlights the meaning of "gross" in the term GNP: market value of goods and services produced before the deduction of items that represent a reduction in the productive capability of the economy. The second indicates the four sectors that purchase the goods and services produced. The four sectors and the official title of their purchases are: consumers (personal consumption expenditures), government (government purchases of goods and services), business (gross private domestic investment), and the rest of the world (net export of goods and services).

Analysis. Aside from the definiton of the term, there are several important characteristics of GNP. First, GNP is the broadest of the national income accounts. Second, GNP is a flow variable and, thus, must be expressed in terms of a time dimension, say, for a quarter or a year. Third, because GNP is a market value concept—the sum of quantities of various goods and services multiplied by their respective prices—it may change without a change in the quantities of goods and services produced by the economy. Fourth, GNP is a crude measure of the economic well-being of the country; a better measure would be GNP adjusted for price and population changes.

—Frank J. Bonello

See also Gross National Product; National Income and Product Accounts.

NATIONAL INCOME THEORY. *See* National Income Determination.

NATIONAL INDUSTRIAL RECOVERY ACT (NIRA) (1933). A major part of the New Deal program of the 1930s was directed to general business recovery from the Great Depression. While economists of the traditional school were counseling a cautious recovery program (balance the budget, limit government intervention in the private economy), the Roosevelt administration undertook more aggressive measures. The National Industrial Recovery Act (NIRA) was based on the belief that the general business depression was traceable to two principal causes: disorderliness of markets leading to excessive price competition, and insufficiency of consumer demand.

The NIRA sought to accomplish price stabilization by allowing agreements among firms of an industry on most aspects of business practice, including output and price. By limiting price competition leading to lower prices, the squeeze on profits would be reduced. Under the aegis of government, nearly 900 industry codes containing these and other agreements were written. Cooperating firms were allowed to display the "Blue Eagle," the symbol of the National Recovery Administration.

Stimulation of consumer demand was to be accomplished indirectly by setting minimum wages and by permitting laborers to organize and bargain collectively through their own trade unions. This legislation (Section 7) marked the first positive recognition and encouragement by the national government of workers' rights to organize into unions. The higher wages (thus purchasing power) accompanying unionization were expected to boost consumer demand. At the same time, prices would be stabilized through the code provisions (hopefully, price increases to cover the wage increases would be deferred), leading to more sales, more employment, and eventually economic recovery.

The effect of the program was to suspend the antitrust laws regarding restraint of trade. In 1935, the Supreme Court rendered the NIRA unconstitutional in *Schechter Brothers v. United States,* on the grounds that (1) violations charged were mostly of a local nature, had only an indirect effect on interstate commerce, and hence were outside the power of Congress to regulate, and (2) Congress had delegated powers to the president excessively.

— *Thomas O. Depperschmidt*
See also Competition; Sherman Antitrust Act.

NATIONALISM, intense loyalty and devotion to the national state, expressing itself in such varied ideological forms as democracy, fascism, or communism. Each form is conditioned by social structure, intellectual traditions, cultural history, and geographic location. Economic nationalism is usually directed toward self-sufficiency for a group or area, with industrialization as a goal, and is often coupled with fear or envy of other nations. The mercantilists were extremely nationalistic, as are the less-developed countries today, with Communist China a prime example.

See also Mercantilism.

NATIONALIZATION, the process of achieving public ownership in desired areas of the economy. At a minimum it covers industries such as coal, electricity, gas, transportation, iron and steel, with some control over central banking. Under socialism, nationalization tends to be complete; in countries such as the United Kingdom, France, and Italy there are varying degrees, with compensation implied when there is a change from private to public ownership.

See also British Labour Party; Fabian Society.

NATIONAL LABOR RELATIONS ACT. *See* Wagner Act.

NATIONAL LABOR RELATIONS BOARD (NLRB), independent regulatory agency empowered under the Wagner Act (1935), the Taft-Hartley Act (1947), and the Landrum-Griffin Act (1959). The NLRB is made up of five members appointed by the president for five years and a general counsel appointed for four years. The board performs quasi-judicial and quasi-legislative functions aimed at preventing and remedying unfair labor practices by employers or by union organizations and at protecting fair union representation. In disputes over recognition, it supervises secret-ballot union elections. The general counsel brings cases and complaints before the board for a ruling, and most are settled by voluntary action.

The board maintains 31 regional and several subregional offices. The NLRB has been crucial in formulating and altering national labor policy since the 1930s. It is the single agency most responsible for ending violent labor/management confrontations. A strong pro-labor reputation earned by the NLRB for its early and forceful action guaranteeing employees' rights to strike and to organize has been mitigated by forceful NLRB application of subsequent legal strictures on the unions.

NATIONAL LABOR UNION. *See* Labor Movement; National Unions.

NATIONAL MEDIATION BOARD. *See* Railway Labor Act (1926).

NATIONAL UNIONS. Approximately 200 unions in the United States are national or international organizations. "National" suggests that the union has members in several states, while "international" normally means one or more locals in Canada. The national or international union may have fewer than 100 members, or more than one million.

As an organization, the national union stands between the locals and the federations, and usually includes members from a specific work group. For example, the Steelworkers' Union includes almost all blue-collar employees of the steel industry, and the Carpenters organize individuals who work as carpenters in any industry. The AFL-CIO, the largest of the federations, is an organization of national unions.

NATURAL GAS. *See* Hope Natural Gas Case (1944); Natural Gas Pipeline Case (1942); Phillips Case (1954).

NATURAL GAS PIPELINE CASE (1942), decision in which the Supreme Court began abandoning its traditional role of reviewing the procedure by which fair return on fair value was calculated, and became concerned with the overall effect of regulation rather than the procedure or formula. The Court specifically indicated that it would not be bound to a given formula for rate-making purposes and also established the concept of a "zone of reasonableness" for "fair return" rather than a specific numerical figure.
See also Regulated Industries.

NATURAL MONOPOLY, an industry in which the economies of scale are particularly pronounced and in which competition is impractical and almost unworkable, because of the natural barriers to entry, the high financial investment needed, and the fact that market demand is not large enough to support several of these large firms.

The best examples of natural monopoly are the public utilities industries, including the electric and gas companies, the transportation services such as railroads, and the water supply and communication facilities. To duplicate telephone lines or man-made water facilities would be unfeasible. Thus, these industries are sanctioned monopolies due to natural causes.

Natural monopolies are usually given rather exclusive franchises by the government, which usually reserves the right to regulate these monopolies to prevent abuses or restraints of trade. Even more so than most other types of monopolies, natural monopolies have heavy fixed cost and, therefore, have decreasing cost of production.

A natural monopoly can also be established by obtaining exclusive rights to, or ownership of, raw materials. For example, the United States retained its monopoly position in the aluminum industry for many years by controlling the basic sources of bauxite.
— *William D. Wagoner*

NATURAL RATE HYPOTHESIS, the hypothesis that there is a long-run level of real gross national product (GNP) that exists independent of the inflation rate. This suggests that factors that are built into the economy determine this so-called natural rate. It is assumed that any level of GNP other than the natural rate will be associated either with an acceleration or a deceleration of the inflation rate.

NATURAL RATE OF UNEMPLOYMENT, the difference between full employment and 100% employment. This definition of unemployment follows the general rate hypothesis. It suggests that there is some built-in tendency in the economy such that some rate of unemployment can be expected to exist at which inflation will not be expected to accelerate or decelerate. Job search and mismatch theories are used to explain the natural rate of unemployment.
See also Employment.

NEAR MONEY, earning assets that can be converted quickly and inexpensively into currency or demand deposits. That is, near monies are highly liquid assets such as deposits in savings accounts, money market deposit accounts, money market funds, and overnight repurchase agreements. Less liquid assets such as Treasury bills, commercial paper, and banker's acceptances are also sometimes referred to as near monies.
See also Liquidity Preference; Money Supply.

NEGATIVE INCOME TAX (NIT), an income maintenance scheme that would provide a guaranteed minimum income for eligible families with no other income and a supplement for families with incomes below a predetermined level. A variety of plans have been proposed, but all contain the same basic elements. They include the basic allowance (B), which varies with family size and provides a guaranteed minimum; the marginal rate (t) at which B is reduced as income from other sources (Y) rises; and break-even income (Yb), above which NIT transfers cease.

Total payment (P) is determined by the formula $P = B - tY$ and break-even income is reached when $Y = B/t$. To illustrate, if $B = \$2,000$, $t = 0.5$, and family income, Y, is $2,000, the family will receive a supplement of $1,000. NIT supplements will cease if family income exceeds $4,000.
See also Income Tax; Public Assistance; Social Dividend.

NEGATIVE INVESTMENT. *See* Disinvestment.

NEOCLASSICAL ECONOMICS. Criticism of the classical economic system by Marx and others generated attempts by those favorable to the classical school to eliminate some of the more important errors. The development of marginalism in the 1860s and 1870s provided the basis for restructuring the classical system with the emphasis upon the theory of individual units and their decision-making process. While the neoclassical school is generally considered to have reached a peak by World War I, the bulk of present-day microeconomic theory can be traced directly to developments of this school. In addition, important developments in interest theory and some aspects of macroeconomic theory have been made by economists following neoclassical traditions.

See also Marginalism.

NET BORROWED RESERVES. *See* Free Reserves.

NET CAPITAL FORMATION. *See* Net Investment.

NET INVESTMENT, or NET CAPITAL FORMATION, the amount of net private domestic spending by business, industry, and agriculture for new capital goods and net increases in inventory. Net investment occurs only when additional real capital is created and is equal to gross private domestic investment less depreciation, the capital consumption allowance. An important component of Net National Product, net investment tends to remain relatively stable. As a whole, it is influenced by autonomous elements, such as new population, new territory, innovations, and other growth elements, rather than anticipated returns and economic expansion.

See also Net National Product.

NET NATIONAL PRODUCT (NNP), the dollar value of all goods and services produced by an economy in a given year. NNP includes net production of all goods and services available for current consumption and, thus, reflects personal consumption expenditures, government purchases, and net exports.

Computation. In the flow-of-product approach to national accounting, NNP may be computed by adding all personal consumption expenditures, net private investments, and all government purchases. The same result can be obtained by first calculating GNP and then deducting capital depreciation (CCA), which is the approach utilized by most governments.

From the flow-of-income or cost approach, NNP is the total of wages and salaries, interest, rents, corporate profits, income from unincorporated businesses, and indirect business taxes. Another way of looking at NNP is through the value-added approach. By carefully calculating the value added to a good at each stage of production, and subtracting expenditures or intermediate goods, the value of the final product is derived. Therefore, the sum of all final products from which wages, rent, interest, and profits have been deducted equals NNP.

Significance. NNP is often used interchangeably with GNP, as they differ little more than a twelfth. NNP is also used as a point of departure for figuring national income, personal income, and disposable personal income. It should be noted that the calcula-

tions for NNP do not allow for inflation and deflation. Therefore, to compare one year's NNP to another's requires multiplication by an official price index number. The result, NNP expressed in constant dollars, is called real NNP.

See also Gross National Product.

NET PRODUCTIVITY OF CAPITAL, the net return from capital investment. Capital equipment is expected to provide an income stream over its useful life by producing a saleable output. After allowing for depreciation, capital has a net productivity that can be expressed as a yearly rate.

See also Capital Equipment; Marginal Efficiency of Capital.

NEW CREDITOR. *See* Stages of a Country's Balance of Payments.

NEW ECONOMIC POLICY (NEP), instituted in the U.S.S.R. by Lenin in 1921 in an attempt to speed the country's recovery from World War I and the Civil War and to reestablish popular support for the Communist Party, particularly among the peasants. The NEP restored a high degree of capitalism in agriculture and the trade sectors, while the state controlled heavy industry, transportation, the credit system, and international trade. It was terminated with the introduction of the First Five-Year Plan in 1928.

NEW INDUSTRIAL STATE (1967), by John Kenneth Galbraith, concentrates on the private sector of the American economy, examining how industry has obtained power and how this power is corrupting the U.S. economy.

Galbraith's theme is that industry has reached such an influential level in American society that it now concentrates on using this influence to further increase its power. This has occurred because the influence of unions has declined, the dramatic increase in college education has made the white-collar worker more dependent upon industry for employment, and the use of advertising to influence demand has increased significantly.

With the power that industry possesses, it has developed systematic plans for the future. The complexities of the plans and problems of successfully completing them have led to the development of a technostructure which has replaced the entrepreneur. Because industries are led by the technostructure, the profit-maximizing goal which is the center of conventional economic theory is no longer applicable. Thus traditional economic analysis is no longer valid for contemporary American industry.

In order to correct the situation, Galbraith suggests, many reforms must take place, the most important being to reduce the prevalent U.S. belief that anything the market does is good. This will involve not only

breaking down the now powerful private sector but also building up a new more powerful public sector.
—Clyde A. Haulman

NONCOMPETING GROUPS, a term that originated in the nineteenth century to distinguish between different categories of labor that are not in direct competition with one another. The theory is that because noncompeting groups are only partial, not perfect, substitutes for each other, wage differentials are justified.

For example, an engineer may be a highly skilled and well-trained individual. However, he cannot compete for a job that requires the skills of a heart surgeon. Thus, engineers and heart surgeons belong to noncompeting groups.

NON-EQUALIZING WAGE DIFFERENTIALS are differences in money wages that have no real basis for existence. Unlike equalizing wage differentials which compensate for differences among jobs, non-equalizing wage differentials are the result of imperfections in the labor market. Such things as unions, monopolies, and lack of perfect knowledge of the market all add to the uneven wage distribution of workers.

NONINTERVENTION. *See* Laissez-Faire.

NON-PRICE COMPETITION, a means of attracting a larger part of the market for a product without changing price. The main form of non-price competition is called product differentiation, and is carried out by advertising and by variations in the quality and design of the product.
See also Product Differentiation.

NONRATIONAL WAGE DIFFERENTIALS are those based on illogical reasons such as historical accidents, unessential peculiarities of places and practices, and on the relative skill of different groups in gaining wage increases. For example, members of powerful unions, because of their tremendous bargaining power, very often make much more money than members of the same trade who do not belong to a union. In addition, women and minority groups often receive lower salaries than their white male counterparts.

NONSIGNERS CLAUSE. *See* Miller-Tydings Act.

NORMAL PROFITS, in microeconomics, a measure of the opportunity cost of capital. Normal profits are the average level of accounting profits that firms in the economy are earning. This is used to measure the opportunity cost of capital because any investor should be able to earn these normal or average profits by investing in other companies. If the investor invests in his or her own company, then he or she is giving up

this normal return; thus it is a measure of the opportunity cost of capital. If a firm is earning just normal profits, then the firm is earning no economic or pure profits.

In a perfectly or purely competitive market in the long run, the only profits that individual firms can achieve are normal profits. Any firm entering the market that cannot achieve normal profits is forced to leave the industry because it would be operating at a loss. Therefore, it can be said that a firm must earn normal profits in order to remain in the competitive market. *See also* Profits.

NORMATIVE ECONOMICS is based on value judgments and addresses questions of *what should be?* Normative issues are frequently issues of equity or fairness. Advocating that wealth should be redistributed from rich to poor is a normative judgment because it implies that the benefits to be gained by the poor would outweigh those lost by the rich.

NORRIS-LA GUARDIA ACT (1932), also known as the Federal Anti-Injunction Act, the first of numerous laws passed by the federal government during the 1930s directly favorable to organized labor and collective bargaining. It contains a turning-point declaration of public policy in support of workers' freedom to unionize and bargain collectively, free of employer interference. To promote this freedom, and to maintain the government's neutral role in labor-management relations, the act severely restricted the availability to management of one of its most potent anti-labor weapons, the injunction granted by federal courts. No comparable legal devices had been available to labor. *—Leonard G. Schifrin*
See also Injunction, Labor; Yellow-Dog Contract.

NOW ACCOUNTS, interest-bearing checking accounts. NOW (for *Negotiable Order of Withdrawal*) accounts were first offered by mutual savings banks in the Northeast. The Banking Act of 1980 gave commercial banks and thrift institutions the right to offer interest-bearing checking accounts.
See also Demand Deposits.

NUCLEAR REGULATORY COMMISSION (NRC), a federal agency created in 1975 to regulate and license nuclear power facilities. The NRC conducts inspections of existing facilities, oversees construction of new nuclear power plants, and must approve new proposals. The NRC replaced the Atomic Energy Commission.

OCCAM'S RAZOR is a rule which states that the simplest workable theory is also the best. The best model or theory is the one that explains or predicts the way the world operates in the simplest manner possible.

OCCUPATIONAL SAFETY AND HEALTH ADMINISTRATION (OSHA), a federal agency established by act of Congress in 1970. OSHA is tasked with developing standards of workplace safety, issuing regulations to protect workers, and enforcing these laws, regulations, and standards. OSHA is empowered to inspect workplaces and to issue citations and fines for noncompliance.

OSHA has been a source of controversy ever since its creation. Studies have shown that the cost of compliance with workplace standards is very high, leading critics from industry and business to claim that the program is a waste of taxpayers' money and also a source of higher prices for products. The solution to this problem would be (in part) for OSHA to make an effort to pay more attention to the economic consequences of its actions.

Others have argued that OSHA has done too little to enforce adequately the standards it has itself set, that it needs to broaden enforcement activities, and that it needs to be more forceful in issuing citations for noncompliance. These critics point to the continuing high rate of worker injuries and to the size of the agency's budget as evidence of the need to do more. One aspect of occupational safety and health that is receiving increased attention is the possible long-term effects of workplace conditions in chemical-related occupations and worksites. — *Michael S. Johnson*

OFFICE OF MANAGEMENT AND BUDGET (OMB). *See* Federal Budget.

OFFICE OF PRICE ADMINISTRATION. *See* Wage-Price Control.

OKUN, ARTHUR MELVIN (1928-1980), American macroeconomist. He received his A.B. (1949) and Ph.D. (1956) from Columbia. His publications include *The Battle Against Unemployment* (1965, editor), and *The Political Economy of Prosperity* (1970). He was a contributor of articles on economic forecasting, potential output, and fiscal and monetary policy in professional journals. Okun served on the Council of Economic Advisers (1964-1969), was a member of the advisory committee of the Bureau of the Census, a senior fellow at the Brookings Institution in Washington, and was on the faculty at Yale (1952-1967).

OLD AGE ASSISTANCE, a federally subsidized categorical public assistance program for indigent persons over 65. It is administered by state and local welfare agencies. Beneficiaries include the declining number of indigent elderly not included in the Social Security program and, in some cases, Social Security recipients whose benefits fall short of state-designated minimum standards.

See also Public Assistance.

OLIGOPOLY, a market that consists of relatively few sellers. Because there are only a small number of firms in the market, the actions of each individual firm usually affect all the other firms in the industry and the sellers are interdependent.

The firms in oligopolistic markets usually have similar products that are distinguished from one another only by means of product differentiation, a non-price mechanism used to increase the firm's share of the market by differentiating its product from that of the other firms. The two major means of product differentiation are advertising and variations in the quality and design of the product.

An oligopolistic market, of which the automotive industry is a prime example, is faced with what is known as kinked demand curve. This demand curve is an analytical tool used in explaining why oligopolists have fairly rigid prices. The kinked demand curve assumes that, first, if one firm lowers its prices below the existing market price, all other firms in the industry will follow in order to keep their relative shares of the market.

Second, it assumes that firms will not follow a price rise. Using these assumptions, it is easy to see why oligopolistic firms tend to stay with the established market price. If a firm raises its price, it prices itself out of the market and, if a firm lowers its price, it tends to keep the same share of the market, but at a lower income.

Oligopolistic markets often relied on collusion to set the established price. However, collusion is now illegal and not usually practiced openly.

— *William D. Wagoner*

OLIGOPOLY: TOPIC GUIDE

To view oligopolistic industries or markets in relation to other types, see the articles on MONOPOLY, MONOPOLISTIC COMPETITION, PERFECT COMPETITION, and OLIGOPSONY. Closely related to the concept of oligopoly is MARKET CONCENTRATION, as measured in CONCENTRATION RATIO.

For an important concept in theory of oligopolistic behavior, see KINKED DEMAND CURVE. And for some aspects of oligopolistic pricing and market behavior, see CARTEL, CONSCIOUS PARALLELISM, PRICE LEADERSHIP, and QUALITY COMPETITION. Three of the numerous factors that contribute to the existence of oligopoly are explained in ECONOMIES OF SCALE, BARRIERS TO ENTRY, and MERGER.

The Subject Maps accompanying the articles on ANTITRUST POLICY and THEORY OF THE FIRM display the interrelationships of these concepts.

See also Interdependence, Oligopolistic; Kinked Demand Curve; Product Differentiation.

OLIGOPSONY, a market in which a few buyers dominate the market. In a wage oligopsony the buyer is able to avoid paying a wage rate equal to the value of the output of the marginal worker. In the American automobile and steel industries there are only a few firms purchasing labor input.

OMB. *See* Federal Budget.

100% RESERVES, the name of a proposal that would require each commercial bank to hold in reserves every cent of its demand deposits so that it could pay to its depositors instantly the total amount owed them. Such a proposal would make it impossible for banks to create money through fractional reserves, by which loans of commercial banks produce multiple expansion of the money supply.

See also Monetary Policy; Money Supply; Reserve Requirement.

ONE-YEAR PLAN. *See* Planning (Centralized).

OPEN MARKET COMMITTEE. *See* Federal Reserve System.

OPEN-MARKET OPERATIONS, the purchase or sale of government securities (or sometimes other securities) by the Federal Reserve banks to implement monetary policy. Buying such securities puts money into the economy, stimulates business, and tends to reduce unemployment. Selling securities removes money from the economy and reduces the pressure toward inflation.

The decision as to how many securities shall be bought or sold is made by the Federal Open Market Committee of the Federal Reserve System. The actual purchase or sale is carried out by the Federal Reserve Bank of New York as agent for all 12 Federal Reserve banks. The Federal Reserve buys from (or sells to) government-bond houses, some 20 private corporations that specialize in creating a market for govern-

ment securities (bills, notes, and bonds) by standing ready to buy and sell them at all times.

The figure illustrates a purchase of securities. The Federal Reserve finds which government-bond house will sell at the lowest price, orders the bond, and pays the bond house by means of a cashier's check drawn on itself. When the bond house deposits this check in its commercial bank, it has more money (demand deposits) than it had before (and fewer earning assets). Then the bank deposits the check in its account with the Federal Reserve bank and increases its reserves.

The effects of the purchase are (1) to increase the money supply in the hands of the public (so far represented by the bond house) and (2) to increase the reserves of commercial banks so that they are thereby permitted to launch a multiple expansion of the money supply. The bond house, finding its inventory of securities reduced, will try to replenish it by offering a higher price for such securities. This rise in bond prices is a fall in bond yields, lowering interest rates.   —*Walter W. Haines*

See also Monetary Policy; Quantitative Controls.

OPEN SHOP, a situation in which the employer is free to hire without considering applicants' status as members of a union and in which the workers are under no compulsion to join a union as a condition of job retention. The open shop thus affords no security to the union, which must seek out the workers and recruit them on a voluntary basis.

See also Closed Shop.

OPPORTUNITY COST, or ALTERNATIVE COST, the value of the benefit that is given up to produce one economic good as opposed to another.

The concept of opportunity cost is crucial to all economic activity, because all resources are limited. Steel used to produce girders cannot be used to produce locomotives; labor services used to produce shoes cannot be used to build houses. Therefore, in

**OPEN MARKET OPERATIONS/
TRANSACTIONS INVOLVED IN
FEDERAL RESERVE PURCHASE OF
GOVERNMENT SECURITIES**

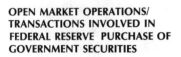

Final result
Federal Reserve Bank:
    Owns more government securities (assets)
    Owes more deposits (liabilities) to commercial banks
Commercial Bank:
    Owns more reserves (assets)
    Owes more deposits (liabilities) to general public
Government-Bond House:
    No change (has sold securities to Federal Reserve
    and replaced them by purchases from the public)
General Public:
    Owns fewer government securities (assets)
    Owns more money in the form of bank deposits (assets)

OPPORTUNITY COST: TOPIC GUIDE

Additional concepts related to the principle of opportunity cost are discussed in the article on NORMAL PROFITS. The basic idea of opportunity costs derives from the fact of SCARCITY and the necessity of CHOICE. Consult these articles for an understanding of these relationships. For one application of the opportunity cost concept, see the article on PRODUCTION POSSIBILITY FRONTIER.

---

order to ascertain the cost of choosing one alternative use of a given set of limited resources rather than another, the economist uses the opportunity cost concept. He measures the "real" cost of doing business by its opportunity cost, not by its explicit, or outlay, cost. The real cost of producing nails, for example, is the value of another product, say rails, that might have been produced from the same amount of resources.

In utilizing the opportunity cost concept, however, it is not sufficient simply to compare the values of different products that can be produced by utilizing a given set of resources in more or less the same manner. To illustrate, assume that a man has a farm and has invested his life savings in land and equipment, with all of which he grows alfalfa. The opportunity cost of such economic activity might be the difference between the value of alfalfa and the value of some other crop that he could also produce. He could have put his self-owned, self-employed resources to entirely different uses, however. By using his resources as he has, he has forgone the opportunities of (1) lending his savings and receiving interest on that investment, (2) renting his land and receiving income therefrom, and (3) working for someone else for wages. If the total return from such alternative uses of his resources were greater than the return from the production of any crop that he might grow, it is that return that is the measure of the opportunity cost to him of growing alfalfa.

Although opportunity cost is the true measure of the cost of one use of a given set of resources as compared with any other use, the most rational use is that which produces the greatest return. Therefore, the economically relevant opportunity cost of a given activity is the value of the benefit that would have been produced by the most rational alternative use of the resources concerned.   *—Josef Hadar*

OPPORTUNITY COST OF CAPITAL, a term used in microeconomics to measure the cost of investing your own capital in your business. If you did not invest your capital in your own firm, you would have been able to invest this capital in the stock or bond market. Thus, the average or normal return on the stock or bond market is the measure of the opportunity cost of capital. This average return is referred to as "normal profits."

ORIGINAL COST, one way to determine the fair value of a regulated firm. The procedure is to calculate the original cost of the physical plant used (and usefulness to the public), less accumulated depreciation, plus additions and betterments. Sometimes called historic cost, book cost, or actual cost.

OUTER COUNTRIES. *See* International Monetary System.

OUTPUT, the goods and services that emerge as a result of the production process. Output is viewed in either a micro (a single firm) context or a macro (an entire economy) context. Output is one of the most significant variables in the production process. In economic analysis of the firm, comparisons between levels of inputs and resulting levels of outputs are the basis for measurement of profit and productivity; different levels of output for a firm will directly affect its unit costs of producing a product. Aggregate output is an important device to compare the growth rates of a nation's economy and to determine a nation's relative state of health, its general productivity level, its output per man hour, and so on.

See also Input.

OUTPUT EXPANSION PATH, the locus of all the points of tangency between a family of isoquants and a series of budget lines. It defines the long-run total cost curve for a firm; the firm purchases *all* inputs in the least cost combinations so as to minimize total cost. The long-run average cost envelope curve can also be derived from the output expansion path. Each point on the curve is a paired combination of total cost and quantity produced. Dividing total cost by output defines average cost for that given output.

OUTPUT RATIO. *See* Capital/Output Ratio.

OVERINVESTMENT THEORY OF BUSINESS CYCLES attributes cyclical downswings or recessions to too much rather than too little investment. This internal theory holds that business overinvests to meet anticipated rises in demand and then sharply curtails such investment if, and when, it realized that such enthusiasm was unwarranted. This type of investment behavior is said to be one of the primary forces responsible for initiation of cyclical activity within the economy.

See also Business Cycles, Theories; Internal Theory.

OVERPRODUCTION. *See* Excess Supply.

OVER-THE-COUNTER MARKETS. *See* Stock Market.

OVERVALUATION. *See* Devaluation.

OWEN, ROBERT (1771-1858), most famous of the founders, in about 1800, of utopian socialism. His basic premise was that human nature is molded by environment and that the way to produce better people is to produce better conditions. To prove this Owen converted the New Lanark Mills into a model community and, in the process, developed the largest and best spinning mills in Scotland while making a profit. Reforms included a minimum work age, shorter work day, high wages, social insurance, abolition of fines and punishments, free schools, comfortable housing, and recreational facilities.

Owen believed his "villages of cooperation" would bring producers and consumers together and hence eliminate the competitive system and capitalism. The New Harmony Venture (Indiana, 1825) failed; the Rochdale Pioneers (England, 1844), however, was highly successful.

See also Associationism; Cooperativism; Evolutionary Socialism.

OWN SUBSTITUTION EFFECT. *See* Consumer Equilibrium.

PAID HOLIDAYS, days for which employees receive wages but do not work or, if required to work, receive extra pay or compensatory time off at a later date. Besides national holidays such as Christmas and New Year's Day, there are holidays limited to certain regions, states, or individual companies. The average number of paid holidays in the United States annually is 11.

PANIC. *See* Business Cycles.

PARADOX OF THRIFT, the apparent contradiction that as households try to save more, they may find that they are only saving the same amount out of a smaller total income, or even saving less than they were originally. The explanation of the paradox is that a decrease in consumption, which is the obverse of an increase in savings, causes income to fall by the amount of the decrease in consumption times the multiplier. A new equilibrium level of income will be reached only when income has fallen to that level where saving is again equal to investment. If investment does not decrease as income decreases, income will fall to that point where the same amount is being saved out of the new smaller level of income as was previously being saved out of the larger income. If investment decreases as income decreases, income will fall to a point where both savings and investment are smaller than they were previously.

PARAMETERS, or PARAMETRIC CONSTANTS, are the constants written in a general equation, for instance a and b in the equation $y = a + bx$. Changing a parameter generates a whole family of curves.

PARAMETER

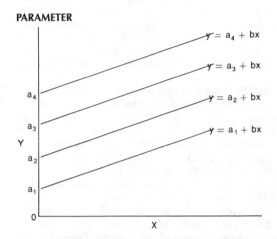

PARAMETRIC CONSTANT. *See* Parameters.

PARETO, VILFREDO (1848-1923), Italian economist and socialist who, like Walras, made extensive application of mathematical analysis to economic problems, in particular, expanding the concept of general equilibrium and its implications. In continuing the Walrasian mathematical approach to political economy, Pareto introduced concrete matter, made distinction between abstract reasoning and empirical inquiry, and employed not only competitive but also monopolistic and collectivist assumptions in examining and analyzing economic systems.

Pareto also paved the way for the changeover from utility analysis to indifference curve analysis by stripping the indifference curve principle of its utility content, making it instead an ostensibly empirical observation about combinations of goods equally acceptable to the consumer. In this, Pareto followed Edgeworth's interpretation of the utility of a good as a function not of the quantity of that one good but of the quantities of all goods under the control of the individual.　　　　　　　　　　　　*—Clyde A. Haulman*

See also Indifference Curve; Pareto Optimum.

PARETO OPTIMUM, a situation in which no action can be taken to benefit some members of society without hurting someone else. Any social action that benefits some members of society without hurting anyone is desirable. The Italian economist, Vilfredo Pareto (18481923) pointed out, however, that if a social action hurts some persons while helping others, one cannot clearly say that it is desirable, since it is impossible to compare the damage to some people with the benefit to other people. A point of Pareto optimality is sometimes referred to as a point of economic efficiency.

There are, of course, a large number of situations that are Pareto optimal. Unfortunately, the criterion provides no basis for choosing among the situations; for example, a transfer of goods or income from a rich man to a poor man could not be evaluated. All that can be said is that if a society is not at a Pareto optimum, at least one other situation is better, in that some individuals would benefit at no one's expense.

PARITY PRICES represent an effort to define fair prices for farm products. The method now in use traces back to the early 1920s, when there was an intuitive appeal in saying that a fair price for a farm product was one that had changed from the pre-war level exactly as much as had an index of prices paid by farmers. The idea was retained as time passed and was written into the Agricultural Adjustment Act of 1933 as the parity price formula.

Farm prices collectively are at parity when the index of prices received by farmers, on a 1910-1914 base, is the same as the index of prices paid by farmers (called the Parity Index), also on a 1910-1914 base. The parity ratio is computed by dividing the first index by the second and multiplying by 100.

Until 1950, parity prices of most individual farm commodities were computed simply by multiplying the 1910-1914 average farm price of the product by the parity index and dividing by 100. Now the parity price for an individual commodity is computed by (1) dividing the average farm price during the most recent 10 years by the average index of prices received by farmers (1910-1914 base) during the same 10 years and (2) multiplying by the current value of the parity index (1910-1914 base). The revised method has the effect of increasing the parity prices of those commodities that have been high-priced in relation to other farm commodities during the past 10 years and of reducing parity prices of commodities that have been relatively low-priced.

The proposition that parity prices are fair prices is hard to support, especially today. A principal reason is that techniques of agricultural production have been revolutionized since 1910-1914. In tacit recognition of the lack of realism of parity prices, legislation aims at different percentages of parity for different products.
— *George E. Brandow*

See also Golden Age of Agriculture; Price-Support Programs.

PARITY PRICING. *See* Price Floor.

PARTIAL CORRELATION. *See* Correlation.

PARTNERSHIP, the result of an agreement between two or more people to own and operate a business together. Each individual assumes full personal liability for the debts of the joint endeavor. A partnership can be a verbal agreement between two individuals or a very detailed legal entity.

Partnerships are a common practice and are very often most successful among professional people, such as doctors, lawyers, and accountants. Advantages include the ability to share both facilities and staff as well as the opportunity to share knowledge and consultation.

However, when there is a clash of opinion, decision-making is often difficult. In addition, the individual owners of the partnership, unlike the corporation, are personally responsible for any debts or other legal matters incurred by the partnership. If one individual takes action under the partnership's name, the other partners are legally responsible.

See also Corporation; Proprietorship.

PASSIVE BENEFICIARY OF MONOPOLY. *See* Monopoly Thrust Upon a Firm.

PATENT, a form of property right giving an inventor of a new product, design, or process (or the owner of the patent, if sold) the sole legal right to use, not use, or dispose of the invention. Patents in the United States are issued for a period of 17 years by the U.S. Patent Office, with renewal possible after significant modification of the original design.

A patent has importance in economic analysis and antitrust policy because it provides a monopoly to the owner. Especially troublesome is the extension of such inherent monopoly power to pricing and output policies of the patent-holding firm or a licensee. Patent rights might also be misused (1) as the basis for tying contracts; (2) in the hoarding or monopolization of patents by one firm; and (3) in cross-licensing and patent pools, which tend to reserve technology to a few dominant firms in an industry.

See also Antitrust Policy; Monopolizing; Restraint of Trade.

PATTERN BARGAINING, attempt by a union, in bargaining with various firms in an industry, to attain with each a set of terms comparable to those established in a key bargain. To the extent that comparable terms are achieved, an industry-wide pattern or similarity results. Deviations from the pattern often occur, largely due to economic differences among the firms.

See also Key Bargain.

PEAK OF PROSPERITY. *See* Business Cycles, Phases.

PEASANT ECONOMY. *See* Subsistence Economy.

PEGGED EXCHANGE RATE. *See* Exchange Rate.

PENSIONS, periodical allowances to workers, or their spouses or children, received from the time of retirement. The first major legislation dealing with pensions was the Social Security Act of 1935, which provided a worker with an income upon retirement after age 65. (This has since been changed, however, to allow payment of retirement benefits if the employee retires before age 65.) However, Social Security payments could not keep up with the cost-of-living; and as a result, many private pension plans have come into existence. The Employee Retirement Income Security Act (ERISA) made private pensions more secure. In order to reduce this problem, the Social Security system has been changed to include an automatic cost-of-living adjustment clause, or COLA.

The development of the bargained pension dates from the early 1900s but did not get any major attention until 1946, when John L. Lewis won a health and welfare fund for coal miners. After that, major pension plans were added in steel companies and in the automotive industry. By 1986, 75% of the labor force was covered by industrial pension plans. Social Security is by far the largest pension plan, covering approximately 92.5% of the U.S. labor force.

There are two major types of pension plans, contributory and non-contributory. In contributory plans, the employee usually pays the greater share of the costs; in non-contributory plans the employer pays the cost. In addition, there are non-funded plans, under which the employer pays the cost of the pension as it is incurred. The type of plan, benefits paid and received, and eligibility for retirement are almost always agreed upon through a collective process.

PER CAPITA REAL INCOME, individual personal income, mostly wages, stated in noninflationary monetary units. It is calculated by dividing net national income, adjusted to eliminate the effect of inflation or deflation, by population. It represents a national average.

It does not reflect the unequal distribution of income that exists to some degree in most countries due, among other things, to regional differences in the mix of industries and between industry and agriculture, or the fact that higher wage levels are more prevalent in large cities than in small towns and rural areas.

PERCENTILE. *See* Central Tendency.

PERESTROIKA, Soviet term for economic reform or "restructuring." Perestroika was the first priority of Soviet President Mikhail Gorbachev. As important as social liberalization and democratization are in themselves, they can also be regarded as facilitators of the goal of economic revitalization.

A critical aspect of Gorbachev's strategy was his investment program, designed to modernize the industrial sector quickly. The bulk of investment was to go toward reconstructing and reequipping existing plants, rather than building new ones. Thus, investment in machinery and equipment was to rise sharply at the expense of investment in plant buildings and structures. The plans called for nearly doubling the retirement rates of old machines and the replacement of over one-third of the total capital stock by 1990.

An increased slice of the investment pie was to go to the energy-producing sector, and the chemical industry was to get a 50% increase. The agro-industrial sector was to remain unchanged, as were other industries and the social infrastructure. The planned upsurge of growth was to be attained by an increase in the efficiency with which labor and capital were used. Gorbachev's strategy called for major improvements in efficiency in the economy's use of energy and raw materials. Along with savings in all resources, the strategy demanded large gains in technical quality and a radical upgrading in modernity of design.

One aspect of this restructuring aimed at altering the thinking of workers and managers, to transform them into disciplined employees who take personal responsibility for the quantity and quality of the product and who innovatively seek ways to produce more and better products with fewer resources. This aspect of *perestroika* is often described as mobilizing the human factor.

A second aspect of restructuring revolved around the perceived need to alter the basic parameters of the so-called economic mechanism; i.e., economic organization and incentives. Gorbachev therefore called for radical economic reforms. These reforms fell into three categories: the reorganization of bureaucracies, the revision of working arrangements affecting individual firms, and miscellaneous other changes. According to both Western and Soviet official measures, economic growth has thus far improved only modestly as a result of *perestroika*.

PERFECT COMPETITION suggests a purely competitive market with the addition of the condition that all economic units of the market have perfect knowledge of all relevant facts. For example, if one seller has a price different from existing market price, all buyers will know of this price and purchase accordingly. Under this assumption, no one would sell above or below the market price.

In addition to perfect knowledge of the market, there are four other conditions that must be met in order for a market to be perfectly competitive.

First, there must be product homogeneity. This means that the product sold by each individual seller in the market is identical to that same product sold by all other sellers. This condition must be met in pure competition so that product differentiation cannot play a part in the decisions of buyers.

A second condition of perfect competition is that each individual seller has such a small share of the

---

PERFECT COMPETITION: TOPIC GUIDE

For comparison and contrast between perfect competition and other types of markets, begin with the article on MARKET STRUCTURE, which sets forth the characteristics by which markets are classed as to structural "type." To compare perfect competition with others of these types, consult the articles on IMPERFECT COMPETITION, MONOPOLISTIC COMPETITION, OLIGOPOLY, MONOPOLY, MONOPSONY, and OLIGOPSONY.

For the historical roots of the concept, and some of its present policy implications, see LAISSEZ-FAIRE, PARETO OPTIMUM, FREE ENTERPRISE, CAPITALISM, and CLASSICAL ECONOMICS.

The Subject Map accompanying the article on MARKET SYSTEM displays the relationships of these and many other concepts.

---

entire market that he or she cannot influence price. In addition, there must be many buyers so that no one buyer can influence price.

Third, there can be no artificial restraints that would influence price. In this way, prices can freely fluctuate with changing conditions in the market. This implies no government price fixing or other administered prices, such as union wages.

The final condition of pure competition is that of mobility. Firms must be free to enter and exit the market and resources must be free to move among alternative uses.

When these conditions are met there is a market where only one price, the market price, prevails in the long run. There are, however, some fluctuations in the short run. Although there may be no perfectly competitive markets, the concept of one is valuable when discussing the less-than-perfect models more relevant to the real world.   — *William D. Wagoner*

See also Imperfect Competition.

PERFECT ELASTICITY, or INFINITE ELASTICITY

of supply is a theoretical, polar extreme of elasticity coefficients. The coefficient approaches positive infinity in the limit; an infinitely small change in price elicits an infinitely large output response.

When discussing perfect or infinite elasticity, one usually is referring to the long-run supply schedule for some relatively small industry characterized by perfect competition. This supply schedule would be parallel to the horizontal axis. An increase in the demand for the product will result in no change in price; the total response to the demand would appear as a quantity change.

PERFECT INELASTICITY, or TOTAL INELASTICITY

of supply is a theoretical, polar extreme of the set of elasticity coefficients. In the limit the elasticity coefficient approaches zero; very large changes in

price lead to infinitely small changes in quantity supplied. Normally one is involved in the very short run when discussing perfectly inelastic supply. This supply curve would be parallel to the vertical Y axis.

In the theoretical case of perfect inelasticity of supply, an increase in demand will theoretically lead to no change in quantity supplied; the total response would be a price change. Price is said to be demand-determined.

See also Inelastic Demand.

PERIL POINT. In tariff-reducing negotiations, a country will consult with interests likely to be affected by potential cuts. Out of these consultations emerges an idea of a point beyond which tariff cuts will imperil domestic industries. This peril point sets the floor for tariff cutting in bargaining for reciprocal cuts from other nations.

See also Reciprocal Trade Agreements Act; Tariffs.

PERMANENT INCOME HYPOTHESIS, attributed to Milton Freidman, suggests that consumption is a function of what income earners consider to be their "permanent income" rather than their actual income in any particular year. This hypothesis is based on the idea that consumers will divide their income into that which is considered permanent and that which is transitory. For spending decisions, only income that is permanent is considered.

This hypothesis is used to explain why in the long run (time series) consumption is proportional to disposable income, while in the short run (cross-section) consumption falls as a proportion to income as the level of income increases. Also, the hypothesis suggests that one-time tax cuts or surcharges will be ineffective as a means by which the level of consumption, and therefore national income, can be changed.

PERSONAL INCOME (PI), the aggregate amount of current income received by all individuals in a given year. This figure includes all wages and salaries; unincorporated business and nonprofit institutional income; rental income; dividends and interest; transfer payments from government and business, such as Social Security benefits, pensions, and unemployment insurance; and nonmonetary income, such as the estimated value of food consumed on farms and the estimated value of homes occupied by their owners.

Personal income is usually derived from the National Income (NI) because of the difficulty in estimating such components of PI as nonmonetary income and unincorporated business income. Undistributed profits and direct corporate taxes are deducted from NI, and transfer payments are added to the remaining figure to arrive at PI. Transfer payments are not a part of NI because they do not reflect any current production.

Personal income is often used interchangeably with

disposable income as an indication of standard of living or individual spending because PI is the actual amount people have to spend, save, and pay taxes.

See also Disposable Personal Income; Transfer Payments.

PERSONAL INCOME TAX, a tax on income from wages, rents, dividends, and interest. The personal income tax is the largest single source of revenue for the federal government, constituting almost 50% of federal revenues. The tax is a major revenue source to many states and a few local governments as well.

The income tax is a *progressive* tax in that the percentage of income devoted to the tax increases as one's income rises. This is because the tax is based on a graduated rate schedule; increments of income may move a taxpayer into a higher tax bracket.

The tax code is very complex and has many special features designed to achieve different public policy goals. For example, prior to 1985, a household could reduce its tax burden by making energy-saving improvements to a house or apartment. Payment of interest on a home mortgage is deductible from the tax, which serves as an incentive for people to be homeowners. Charitable contributions also reduce one's tax burden. However, the plethora of special exceptions, credits, and deductions means that the rate at which the remaining tax base is taxed must be increased in order to generate a given amount of revenue.

The Tax Reform Act of 1986 replaced the 11 tax brackets under the old system (ranging from 11% to 50%) with two brackets—15% and 28%. The 15% bracket and the personal exemption are phased out for high-income returns, resulting in an implicit 33% tax rate for a broad income range. Preferential treatment for all long-term capital gains was dropped, as were miscellaneous itemized deductions less than 2% of adjusted gross income, state and local sales taxes, nonmortgage interest payments, and IRA contribu-

tions for high-income individuals with employer-provided pension plans. Tax shelters were made less attractive.

The bill was not intended to be a tax cut. Rather, it aimed to assure people that others in similar circumstances paid similar taxes (horizontal equity) and that people with high incomes pay their "fair share" (vertical equity). It was also intended to simplify personal bookkeeping.

The income tax has been the center of a great deal of research and debate. One issue is whether or not the tax creates harmful distortions in the economy. It has been alleged that high rates of taxation cause people to reduce their creative, income-generating activity, cause many to spend a great deal of energy and resources toward avoiding the tax, and reduce the level of savings within the economy. If these allegations are true, then the income tax can be a severe retardant of economic growth. These concerns were part of the reasoning behind the Tax Reduction Act of 1981, which cut tax brackets significantly and "indexed" tax rates so that tax burdens would not rise faster than inflation (a phenomenon known as "bracket creep"). —*Michael S. Johnson*

See also Corporate Income Tax; Laffer Curve; Marginal Tax Rate; Taxation.

PERSONAL INVESTMENT, individual spending of disposable personal income for consumer durable goods, new securities and bonds, and other potentially profitable ventures. Personal savings are not a part of personal investment.

The rate of personal investment depends on such noneconomic elements as technology, politics, and expectations and, thus, is extremely variable.

PERSONAL SAVINGS, the amount of disposable personal income not spent on consumption. Personal savings is influenced by the size of family income and future expectations. As the amount of disposable

PERSONAL INCOME TAXES 1989

	SINGLE TAXPAYER		MARRIED FILING JOINT RETURN	
Taxable Income[1]	Dollar Amount of Tax	Average Tax Rate[2]	Dollar Amount of Tax	Average Tax Rate[2]
$ 0	$ 0	n/a	$ 0	n/a
2,000	298	15%	298	15%
4,000	596	15%	596	15%
6,000	896	15%	896	15%
8,000	1,196	15%	1,196	15%
10,000	1,496	15%	1,496	15%
20,000	3,182	16%	2,996	15%
30,000	5,982	20%	4,496	15%
40,000	8,782	22%	7,170	18%
50,000	11,835	24%	9,970	20%
75,000	18,411	25%	16,977	23%
100,000	28,344	28%	25,234	25%
200,000	56,560	28%	56,060	28%

1 Income after adjustments for exemptions and surplus deductions.

2 Tax as a percentage of taxable income.

income increases, the marginal propensity to save usually increases. On the other hand, there is less motivation to accumulate savings when anticipated future income appears stable, regardless of its size.

See also Saving.

PERSONAL TAXES, federal, state, and local levies on personal income to finance governmental expenditures and to redistribute income. These direct taxes include income, property, estate (inheritance), and gift taxes. Indirect taxes, levied on goods and services, are not considered personal.

See also Taxes.

PHALANXES. *See* Fourier, François Marie Charles.

PHANTOM FREIGHT. In a system of basing-point pricing, the price of a commodity is made the same at various delivery points by adding the averaged freight charge to the base price (that prevailing at the production city). Those products sold at delivery points nearer the basing-point therefore carry a higher freight rate than actual freight costs would be. The difference is called "phantom freight" and is borne by the buyer.

See also FTC v. Cement Institute.

PHILLIPS CASE (1954), key decision in which the Supreme Court concluded that the Federal Power Commission (FPC) has "jurisdiction over the rates of all [sales for resale] . . . of natural gas in interstate commerce . . . whether occurring before, during, or after transmission by an interstate pipeline company." The decision negated part of the Natural Gas Act of 1938, which provided for FPC regulation of the interstate transmission of natural gas and its sale for resale and specifically exempted the production and gathering of gas from FPC control. As a result of this decision, the FPC expanded the scope of its activities to include the regulation of the prices of natural gas producers.

See also Regulated Industries; Regulation; Regulatory Commissions.

PHILLIPS CURVE, the statistical relationship between the rate of change of money wage rates and the level of unemployment, first described by British economist A.W. Phillips. A generalized Phillips curve is shown. The shape of the curve corresponds to what one may expect from simple economic theory. As demand for any commodity increases, its price rises, and vice versa. Thus, if unemployment is low, any increased demand for labor will result in rising wage rates. If unemployment is high, wages will rise less rapidly and may even fall.

The original Phillips curve related the rate of wage increase to the level of unemployment. A similar relationship can be derived between increases in the general price level and unemployment. For example,

PHILLIPS CURVE

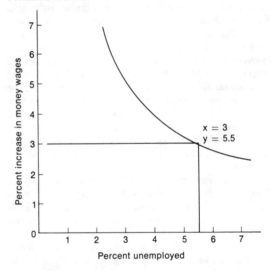

suppose productivity (output per worker) is growing at 3% per year. According to the figure, if unemployment is 5.5%, then wages will rise by 3%. However, because productivity is also up by 3% there is no increase in labor costs to the firm and, therefore, no pressure on prices. Policies that encourage rapid productivity growth, labor mobility and the acquisition of skills can shift the Phillips curve to the left and mitigate the terms of the trade between inflation and unemployment.

A major controversy during the 1960s and 1970s centered around the stability of the Phillips curve. One group of economists and a generation of textbooks said that the Phillips curve represented a long-run trade-off between inflation and unemployment. Another group said that the Phillips curve was stable only in the short run. Those economists suggested that the long-run "Phillips curve" is vertical at the natural, or full employment, level of output. That is, shifts in the short-run Phillips curve can be expected to occur as

inflation expectations adapt to actual rates of inflation. The series of shifts in the short-run curve depends on the speed with which expected inflation adjusts.
— *Carlisle E. Moody, Jr.*

PHYSICAL PRODUCTIVITY, as distinguished from value productivity, is a purely technological phenomenon. The physical product schedules usually analyzed in economics are total, average, and marginal. These schedules, calculated for the short run, reflect the law of diminishing returns.

The total product schedule defines the maximum output, given the quantities of other factors and the state of the arts, that can be obtained by varying a given factor of production. As labor increases, over broad limits, total product rises.

The average product schedule is derived by dividing total product by the quantity of the relevant factor used to produce that output. Average product is plotted against factor quantities.

The marginal product schedule is derived by dividing the change in total product by the increment in the factor necessary to effect the change. Marginal product is plotted factor against quantity. — *Robert L. Brite*

PHYSIOCRATS, a group of economic writers influential in France in the middle of the eighteenth century. Led by François Quesnay, they attempted to discover the general or natural laws which direct economic activity and to refute the doctrines of mercantilism. Their abstract reasoning marks the first step toward the development of economics as a discipline. The major contributions of the Physiocrats were (1) the broadening of the concept of wealth, from the mercantilists' treasure to goods produced with nature's aids and (2) the development of the concept of interdependent sectors in the economic system and the importance of intersectoral flows.

See also Quesnay, François; Tableau Économique.

PICKETING, the advertising of a labor dispute on signs carried by people (usually striking employees) walking past the plant gate, store entrance, or work site. The dispute may be over the employer's unwillingness to recognize a union or over new contract terms.

Picketing has long been a controversial activity. Besides advertising the dispute, it encourages customers, other workers, or other unionists to "respect" (not cross) the picket line. Because it threatens or actually imposes economic harm on the employer, courts sympathetic to management, long after legal recognition of unions, continued to prohibit or enjoin picketing. Further opposition was based on the possibly intimidating presence of the picketers, or their potentially violent opposition to strikebreakers crossing their lines and entering the work place.

With the turn to more favorable attitudes toward labor in the 1930s, picketing became legal if it was done peacefully and was not obstructionist, threatening, or used to enforce an illegal demand. The Landrum-Griffen Act (1959) limited the right of unions to picket for recognition and organizational purposes.
— *William D. Wagoner*

See also Strike.

PIECE WORK describes the payment of wages for each unit of work accomplished rather than for each unit of time worked. Since earnings become a function of output, this is an incentive form of pay that provides a direct stimulus to the worker. It is most common in the apparel and textile industries.

PIGOU, ARTHUR CECIL (1877-1959), was the most important neoclassical economist, after Alfred Marshall, and the father of welfare economics, through his book *Economics of Welfare* (1920). Concerned with unemployment and other social problems, Pigou attempted to use money as a measure of the economic welfare of society. He considered the size, distribution and stability of income as measurable welfare criteria and developed a distinction between social and private cost and benefits. The concept of social cost, in particular, has been used extensively in the economic analysis of pollution and other aspects of economic activity.

Pigou also suggested an alternative to the Keynesian argument that the economic system contained no mechanism for restoring full employment after a depression. The "Pigou effect" suggests that as prices and wages decline, the value of money-holding will increase, thus causing an expansion in consumer spending. While the Pigou effect has theoretical validity, it does not appear to be a powerful enough influence to bring an economy out of a depression situation.

PIGOU EFFECT, the effect named after its formulator, A.C. Pigou, an English economist, of falling prices on the real value of liquid assets and, thus, on saving and consumption. As prices fall, the real value (purchasing power equivalent) of financial assets of fixed money value increases. According to Pigou, this causes an increase in consumption (an upward shift in the consumption function) if, as Pigou postulated, the increase in the value of these assets achieves some part of the objectives of the savers. The Pigou effect (of falling prices) reduces fluctuations in consumption and, therefore, in incomes and employment.

PLANNED INVESTMENT. *See* Investment Schedule; Marginal Efficiency of Capital.

PLANNER'S (STATE) PREFERENCES, the particular quantities of goods and services that the planners (central planning board) prefer to have produced over all feasible alternatives. Planner's preferences can be revealed *ex ante* (beforehand) through the announced plan and *ex post facto* (after the fact) through the actual governmental expenditures.

An economy is said to be dominated by planner's preferences when a large portion of resources are directed by the administrative plan rather than by consumer behavior in the free markets (consumer preferences). Most economies have their resource allocation influenced by both consumer's and planner's preferences.

PLANNING (CENTRALIZED). Economic planning is the institution established by the Communist states to achieve their long-term goals of economic growth and development. The Communist party establishes the broad economic objectives for the state and these are incorporated into a five-year plan, whose goals are broken into annual plans that provide the economic units with their operating instructions. The annual plan permits the state to incorporate revisions in its long-term objectives when conditions warrant.

Operation. The first stage of the progress is for Gosplan, the state planning committee, to take the broad objectives of the government and design a tentative plan, with control figures, to achieve these goals. Meanwhile, the ministries and firms are assessing their capabilities and categorizing their needs. The control figures are broken down by the ministries and the enterprise is informed of the level of operation necessary to obtain the economic goals. This is generally accomplished by May. During the next few months the production enterprise negotiates for alterations in the plan to accommodate specific circumstances at the

ECONOMIC ORGANIZATION OF THE SOVIET COMMAND ECONOMY

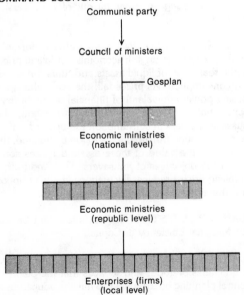

Communist party

Council of ministers

Gosplan

Economic ministries
(national level)

Economic ministries
(republic level)

Enterprises (firms)
(local level)

firm level. These modifications are aggregated as the plan retraces its steps to Gosplan, usually by sometime in October.

Gosplan now has the monumental task of assuring that the plan is consistent and feasible and will accomplish the government's objectives. This is done by a method known as "material balances." The size and complexity of the economic system guarantees that the plan is "balanced" in name only. The priority system is necessary to have flexibility in the program.

Once the plan is as nearly balanced as the system and time will permit, the government approves it, and it is broken down once again. In this manner, the state firms receive their operating instructions for the next year, hopefully before the calendar year begins.
—*Francis W. Rushing*

See also Gosplan.

PLANNING (DECENTRALIZED), a term that covers a wide range of economic systems in which private ownership of productive resources is mixed to a greater or lesser extent with planning and welfare systems. There is actually more economic planning in France, a nominally capitalistic country, than in Marxist countries such as Yugoslavia. Yugoslavia combines the social ownership of productive resources with market determination of prices and output and enterprise management by workers' councils. Most economic activity is conducted by 566 small communes, or self-contained government units. In France, the leaders of government, industry, and labor unions meet regularly to exchange information and negotiate targets for industrial production.

See also Indicative Planning; Centralization; Government-Controlled Economy; Market Economy; Planning (Centralized).

PLANNING FOR GROWTH, the optimal allocation of resources, particularly capital investment, among the various sectors of the economy so as to promote development.

The need for planning springs from several sources. The vital role of government in the typically small less developed country (LDC) economy as an important (if not the most important) employer of labor, a major saver (through taxes) and investor in infrastructure, and the recipient and allocator of foreign aid, gives government the ability and the responsibility to investigate and regulate the impact of its actions on development. Secondly, the often important externalities associated with individual investments in LDC's require that investments be coordinated.

In addition, market imperfections in LDC's lead to incorrect market prices and may lead, possibly, without government planning and intervention, to improper resource allocation by private investors. Social and other goals frequently override optimal economic goals (Pareto optimum), requiring government intervention and planning even in a perfect market system. The tools of planning are many, as are the methods of implementation—from tax/subsidy intervention in the market to direct control through fiat or government ownership (nationalization).   —*Charles Staelin*

See also Allocation; Infrastructure; Less Developed Countries; Nationalization; Subsidy.

PLANT, the smallest whole entity in a firm or industry, that physical facility of a firm where workers are employed. The plant belongs to an individual firm and the firm is usually a part of an industry. There may be only one, or there may be several plants belonging to one firm. A plant may take the form of a factory or any actual building, or it may be any place where operations of the firm take place, such as coal mines, oil fields, or drilling rigs in the ocean.

See also Firm; Industry.

POINT ELASTICITY, the value of price elasticity of demand at a given point on a demand curve. The concept of elasticity of demand, however, implicitly requires that changes in quantity demanded result from changes in prices: technically a demand curve possesses elasticity only between two points. This problem is circumvented whenever estimates of point elasticity are made by allowing price to change only very slightly and recording the resultant change in quantity demanded. When the change in price from a certain value is very small, then the ensuing change in quantity demanded will likely also be small, and the resulting coefficient of elasticity can be said to refer to the elasticity of demand at a given point on the demand curve. Strictly, point elasticity is the reciprocal

of the slope of the curve times the ratio of price to quantity.

POINT FOUR PROGRAM, a U.S. technical assistance program for less-developed countries, first put forward as the fourth point of President Truman's inaugural address of 1949. It envisaged "a bold new program for making the benefits of our scientific advances and industrial progress available for the improvement and growth of underdeveloped areas" and resulted in the Act for International Development of 1950 and the establishment of the Technical Cooperation Administration—forerunner of the present Agency for International Development (AID). Early programs concentrated primarily on technical assistance in such areas as agriculture, education, public health, and transportation and were accompanied by limited financing of related infrastructure.

See also Foreign Aid; Infrastructure.

POLLUTION ABATEMENT PROGRAMS. *See* Bad, Economic.

POPULATION, STATISTICAL. In statistics, population refers to the totality of phenomena under investigation. It is the reference set, the set of all possible observations or outcomes from which we can select samples. Populations can be hypothetical (the results of an infinite number of rolls of a pair of dice) or real (consumption expenditures of Detroit residents), finite (expenditures for pollution control by U.S. cities) or infinite (the income levels of all past, present, or future visitors to Miami Beach).

See also Sampling.

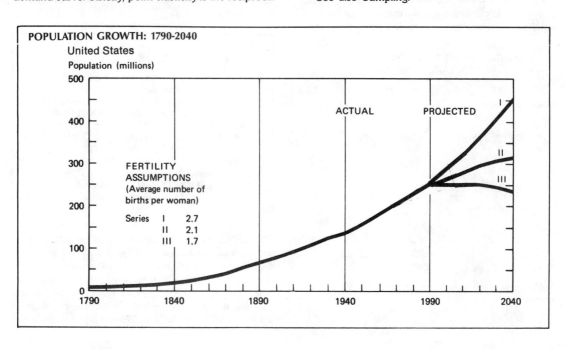

POPULATION GROWTH: 1790-2040
United States
Population (millions)

FERTILITY ASSUMPTIONS
(Average number of births per woman)

Series	I	2.7
	II	2.1
	III	1.7

POPULATION GROWTH, trends of increases and decreases in population and, more broadly, effects of population changes on a nation's economy, ecological equilibrium, and growth trends.

In 1798, Thomas Malthus observed that the population tended to double every 25 years in the American colonies, where resources were abundant, and postulated a universal tendency for population to grow in a geometric progression unless checked by food supply. The means of subsistence, however, increased in an arithmetic progression. Thus, theorized Malthus, growing rates of population result in diminishing return to workers.

According to neo-Malthusian theory, the pressures of overpopulation will be lessened through war, pestilence, and famine. In many less-developed countries, in which overpopulation is common, a high rate of disease and hunger shorten life expectancy. Such countries are working to control their population growth through birth control and family planning programs.

The failure of the "Green Revolution" of the 1970s made it obvious that chemical farming and trade-oriented agriculture increased rather than cured hunger. Currently, the emphasis is on sustainable agriculture and a renewed respect for traditional peasant farming methods to balance populations and their means of subsistence.

Population Trends. In Western Europe and the United States, the net reproduction rate, a measurement of population growth, appears to be declining, although the birth rate in the United States is higher than in most advanced or wealthy nations. This growth rate, however, affects the nation's ecological equilibrium. Ecologists maintain that a child born in the United States is more a burden on the environ-

ment than a child born, for example, in India, because he or she generates more waste, uses more electrical power, and contaminates the air with more toxic gases. Thus, population growth, as well as technological progress, is a major cause of ecological imbalance.

— *Charles Staelin*

See also Malthus, Thomas.

PORTFOLIO, in financial markets, all the stocks, bonds, or other securities held by an individual or corporation for investment purposes. In banking, the term is sometimes stretched to include cash and loans.

See also Balance Sheet, Bank; Portfolio Balancing.

PORTFOLIO BALANCING, the attempt on the part of investors, particularly, to arrange their holdings of monetary assets—including long-term securities, short-term securities, loans, and cash—to earn the maximum income consistent with maintaining the liquidity needed for day-to-day operations. Holding all cash yields no income, but tying up all assets in long-term commitments may lead to bankruptcy if immediate payments exceed the cash on hand.

PORTFOLIO INVESTMENT. See Direct Investment.

POSITIVE ECONOMICS involves scientific predictions about economic relationships. Ideally, positive economics is value-free and studies the nature of the economy and economic relationships, as opposed to normative economics, which makes value judgments about the way things should be. Policies can be evaluated by how well they accomplish goals, but positive economics cannot determine whether any goal is good or bad.

AVERAGE ANNUAL PERCENT CHANGE IN POPULATION 1985-1990

Developed Countries	Percentage rate of growth
Australia	1.2
Canada	0.9
Czechoslovakia	0.2
France	0.4
Israel	1.6
Japan	0.4
Union of Soviet Socialist Republics	0.8
United Kingdom	0.1
United States	0.8
West Germany	−0.2
Less Developed Countries	
Algeria	3.1
Brazil	2.1
Chad	2.5
China (mainland)	1.4
India	2.1
Kenya	4.2
Pakistan	3.5
Peru	2.5
United Arab Emirates	3.3
Venezuela	2.6

POVERTY: TOPIC GUIDE

For measuring poverty, see the article on POVERTY LINE. A wide variety of programs exist to deal with poverty, and are discussed in the articles on AID TO FAMILIES WITH DEPENDENT CHILDREN, INCOME MAINTENANCE, MEDICAID, MINIMUM WAGE, NEGATIVE INCOME TAX, PUBLIC ASSISTANCE, SOCIAL SECURITY, and SUPPLEMENTAL SECURITY INCOME.

The Subject Maps accompanying PUBLIC FINANCE and WAGES display the interrelationships among many of these concepts.

POVERTY LINE, an arbitrary measure of a level of income below which a family is deemed to be unable to achieve a satisfactory standard of living. Poverty data based on the official government definition were first tabulated for 1959. By this definition, the poverty rate fell dramatically in the 1960s, decreasing from 22.4% in 1959 to 12.1% in 1969, while the number of

POVERTY IN THE UNITED STATES, VARIOUS MEASURES

Percentage of Population in Households with Incomes Below the Poverty Line

Year	Market Income[1]	Census Income[2]	Adjusted Income[3]
1965	21.3%	15.6%	12.1%
1968	18.2	12.8	10.1
1972	19.2	11.9	6.2
1976	21.0	11.8	6.7
1980	20.0	13.0	6.1
1987	21.0	13.5	8.5

[1] Adjusted Gross Income (excludes all transfer payments).
[2] Adjusted Gross Income plus all cash transfer payments (Social Security, AFDC, Supplemental Security Income).
[3] Census Income plus the value of in-kind transfers (food stamps, housing subsidies, etc.), also adjusted for underreporting of income, and less taxes.

poor declined from 39.9 million to 24.1 million. Between 1970 and 1977, the size of the poverty population fluctuated between 23.0 and 26.1 million, and the poverty rate ranged from 11.1% to 12.6%. Between 1978 and 1983, the number of poor people increased by 44%, from 24.5 to 35.3 million, and the poverty rate rose from 11.4% to 15.2%. From 1983 to 1988, the number of poor and the poverty rate both declined slightly, but both remain well above 1978 levels.

Half the nation's poor in 1987 were children (40%) or the elderly (10.7%). Historically, the poverty rate for persons 65 years and over has been higher than that for the total population, but in 1983, this relationship was reversed, and the poverty rate for the elderly remained at a record low of about 12% between 1983 and 1987. Although minorities are overrepresented among the poor, two out of every three poor people are white. In 1987, poverty rates were 10.5% for whites, 33.1% for blacks, 28.2% for Hispanics, and 18.3% for persons of other races. In 1988, 61% of poor families were headed by a female.

—*Michael S. Johnson*

This homeless person is among those who live below the official U.S. poverty line.

PRECAUTIONARY DEMAND. *See* Liquidity Preference.

PREDATORY PRACTICES, those actions by a dominant firm in a market having the intent of damaging or eliminating competitors and thereby ensuring monopolistic advantages to the dominant firm. Because of these anti-competitive effects, predatory practices such as local price discrimination, sales below cost, or malicious interference with a competitor's product or business operations have been regularly condemned by federal courts under the antitrust laws.

In economic analysis there is often a thin line between price competition and practices deemed predatory, and the evidence of predatory intent is not often easily detected.

See also Antitrust Policy; Monopolizing; Sherman Antitrust Act.

PREFERENCE, ORDERING. *See* Utility Function.

PREFERRED STOCK, a type of capital stock, is that stock on which dividends must be paid before they are paid on common, or ordinary, stock. It also has preference in the distribution of net assets as well as of a specified amount of the profits. Preferred stock, also called prior stock or preference stock, is often divided into Class A and Class B, where Class A stock has priority over Class B stock. Unlike common stock, preferred stock is not issued by all corporations.

See also Stock.

PRE-MARXIAN SOCIALISM can be conveniently divided into two basic schools of thought: (1) utopian socialism and (2) analytical, or Ricardian, socialism.

Utopian socialist thought, represented by men such as Saint-Simon, F.M.C. Fourier, and Robert Owen, was aware of and critical of the evils of capitalism. However, the Utopians rarely had much beyond a humanitarian basis for their criticism and thus had little influence upon economic thought.

Analytical or Ricardian socialism, however, used existing economic techniques to criticize the classical analysis of capitalism. Writers such as Sismondi, Proudhon, and Hodgskin rejected the optimism and harmony of interest which characterized classical economies. Sismondi, for example, felt that competition and the separation of labor and capitalists would lead to overproduction and crises. These writers provided Marx with many of the ideas central to his criticism of capitalism.

See also Das Kapital; Owen, Robert; Ricardo, David.

PRESENT VALUE, the current value of a single amount or a stream of payments in the future. Because of uncertainty and because people prefer present consumption to future consumption, an amount, or stream, that will occur in the future is worth less than that same amount today. Thus, to arrive at the present value of a future amount or stream of payments, it is necessary to discount. The formula for determining the present value of a future amount is:

$$PV = A/(1 + i)n$$

where: PV = present value,
    A = the future amount,
    i = the interest rate,
    n = the number of years.

The formula for the present value of a stream of future payments is:

$$PV = Aj/(1 + i)j$$

where: PV = present value,
    Aj = the future payment in year j,
    j = the year,
    n = the total number of years,
    i = the interest rate.

See also Discounted Value.

PRICE is the pecuniary consideration that induces the exchange of a unit of that commodity or service between two individuals. Assuming that the exchange involved is voluntary, price may be thought of as a manifestation of a "meeting of minds."

Exchange takes place in markets, and in the typical market a large number of units change hands at a single market price. By analogy, market price can be thought of as representing a meeting of minds for a group of individuals—frequently a large group. An individual purchaser has an implicit schedule of quantities that he or she would purchase at various prices; and, similarly, sellers have schedules of quantities that they would be willing to sell at various prices.

These individual schedules may then be aggregated

PRICE

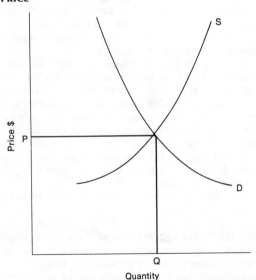

Quantity

to yield market demand and supply schedules which may then be graphed as market demand and supply curves (such as D and S in the figure). Market price is given by the intersection of the demand and supply curves and is that price at which the quantity that demanders wish to buy is just the quantity that suppliers wish to sell. —*Clarence C. Morrison*

See also Demand; Supply.

PRICE CEILING, a government-enforced maximum price for a consumer good; that is, the government passes a law that states that the market price of a good cannot go above some set maximum. Price ceilings are sometimes called price controls. In order to keep consumer prices low, the U.S. government, on several occasions, has instituted ceiling prices. If the market equilibrium price is below this ceiling price, the price ceiling has no effect. If the market equilibrium price is above the ceiling price, then the ceiling price will affect the market. In this case, the price is not allowed to ration the good, and some other method of rationing must be used.

Price ceilings have been used in the United States in several instances in the twentieth century. During World War II, price ceilings were used to restrict domestic demand for many consumer goods so that more resources could be diverted to the war effort. In the years following World War II, many cities, most notably New York City, imposed rent controls—price ceilings on rental units. In 1971, President Richard Nixon imposed wage-price controls on almost all goods and types of labor to control inflation. These price ceilings lasted in one form or another for three years. These price controls were the main cause of the long gas lines that resulted from the first and second Arab oil embargoes of 1973 and 1978.

—*Timothy P. Ryan*

See also Rationing.

PRICE COMPETITION, a means of competing for greater shares of the market. Pure price competition occurs in those market structures where products are homogeneous and cannot compete by product differentiation, such as advertising and variations in design of the product.

A homogeneous product is a product (such as nails) that is identical in all firms in the industry that sell it. All products of purely competitive markets are homogeneous. In purely competitive markets, price competition is the only means of competition available.

In other market structures, such as monopolistically competitive industries, price competition also occurs, often in the form of price wars. Price wars begin when one firm in the industry lowers its price below the prevailing market price. In order to retain their share of the market, all other firms in the industry must lower their prices. This type of price competition is sometimes found among gasoline companies.

PRICE DETERMINATION. *See* National Income Determination.

PRICE DISCRIMINATION occurs when a firm sells a product to two different buyers at different prices where all other material aspects of the sales are the same. Some forms of price discrimination are routine and legal: different electric power rates to residential and industrial users; higher adult than children's theater ticket prices. Other forms are illegal where the effect is to lessen competition substantially either at the seller's (Clayton Act, Section 2) or buyer's (Robinson-Patman Act) level of competition. The principal thrust of the prohibition is against the mass distributor who, through his ability to absorb losses in other parts of his market, may price products lower in a locality where competition is especially vigorous, thereby damaging the local (often smaller) competitor.

Economic analysis of price discrimination suggests that much of the legal concern is over a nonissue. In fact, many have suggested that present laws forbidding price discrimination do more harm than good, by preventing active competition among sellers. Objections to the practice must be made on equity grounds, as there is very little problem with the practice in terms of efficiency.

See also Antitrust Policy; Clayton Act; United States v. New York Great A & P Company.

PRICE EFFECT. *See* Consumer Equilibrium.

PRICE ELASTICITY OF DEMAND. According to the law of demand, the quantity of a product demanded is inversely related to its price. This concept of demand defines the nature of the relationship between price and quantity demanded. The responsiveness, or price elasticity of demand, is calculated by dividing the percentage change in quantity demanded by the percentage change in the price of a commodity.

PRICE FIXING is agreement (conspiracy) among several or all firms in an industry to set prices jointly to yield a profit greater than would result if price competition prevailed. Price fixing is challenged in antitrust law because it eliminates business firm efficiencies flowing from the pressure of price competition. Federal courts have consistently ruled that overt price-fixing agreements (cartels, bidding rings), being restraints of trade forbidden under Section 1 of the Sherman Act, are *per se* illegal, as are output-limitation agreements (market sharing, quotas) in support of price fixing.

An alternate method of securing the same end as overt price fixing is conscious parallelism of action, or tacit compliance in the price set by a competitor. The pricing agreement is difficult to prosecute, however, because of the absence of clear intent.

See also Collusion; Conscious Parallelism; Conspiracy Doctrine; Market Sharing; Restraint of Trade; Trade Association.

PRICE FLOOR, a government-enforced minimum price for a good or service. The government passes a law that states that the price for a certain good cannot go below a certain amount. Unlike price ceilings, which are designed to keep prices low to protect the consumer, price floors are designed to keep prices high to help producers. There are basically two kinds of price floors in the United States: minimum wage laws, which attempt to keep wages high, and price supports for agricultural products, which attempt to keep prices up for farmers. Although minimum wages do keep wages up for some low-paying jobs, it has been acknowledged that they contribute to higher unemployment in the low-skilled, poorly-educated segment of the labor force, mostly teenagers.

Farm price supports have existed in the United States for many years and have been applied to numerous kinds of agricultural products. For agricultural goods, the price floor is set at the parity price, which is calculated by a formula that attempts to keep farm prices, in real terms, at historical levels. If the actual equilibrium price is above the parity price, the price floor has no effect. If, however, the equilibrium price is below the parity price, then the government agrees to support the price by agreeing to purchase any surplus that the farmers cannot sell to the market.

—*Timothy P. Ryan*

PRICE INDEXES, indicators of the general level of prices, and attempts to average price changes of individual goods and services into a composite that will reflect the net effect of all the price changes upon the general level of prices.

The Consumer Price Index (CPI) is the index most frequently quoted in reference to the price level. CPI is a statistical measure of changes in the prices of commodities that are deemed essential to maintain a standard of living for an urban working-class family unit. Each item is given a weight equal to its importance in the family budget, as determined from consumer spending patterns in the early 1960s. CPI is compiled by the Bureau of Labor Statistics of the Department of Labor and is often referred to as the cost-of-living index. This cost-of-living index is sometimes used to compute pay increases in labor-management contracts.

The Producer Price Index (PPI) is a statistical composite of price changes in the primary markets based on large lot sales of selected commodities in primary markets. It is particularly useful in determining long-run trends. Because CPI and PPI do not measure and weigh the same commodities, they do not necessarily move in the same direction.

The Gross National Product Implicit Price Deflator measures changes in the average price of final goods and services by combining several other indexes and applying them to GNP in current dollars to derive GNP in constant dollars relative to a base period.

— William D. Wagoner

PRICE LEADERSHIP refers to the situation in which one or more firms act as a leader in setting a price that other firms in the industry follow. The firm that becomes the leader in price setting is usually the firm with the lowest cost. Due to low cost, a lower price can be charged the consumer. As a result, the other firms in the industry, in order to capture any part of the market, must charge the same price as the price leader.

A second way in which price leadership occurs is in oligopolistic situations, where there are only a few firms in the industry. In this case, the firm that sets the price is very often the largest or dominant firm.

PRICE LEVEL, the average level of money prices, a general indicator of the state of the economy.

Measurement. The price level is usually measured by a price index, which relates current prices to prices of a base period in the past and indicates periods of inflation and deflation. The Consumer Price Index measures changes in the power of the dollar to purchase typical items in a consumer's budget. The Producer Price Index measures shifts in the primary markets by examining large commercial transactions. The Gross National Product Implicit Price Deflator measures movements in the average price of final goods and services included in GNP.

Changes. Inflation is a general rise in the prices of goods and services. Unless money incomes rise at the same rate as prices, inflation causes real income of individuals to fall, because the amount of goods and services they can buy with a given money income

decreases. When the purchasing power of consumers decreases, their total welfare is decreased. On the other hand, deflation is a fall in the general level of prices. Deflation gives fixed amounts of income more purchasing power. Therefore, deflation improves the welfare of individuals if their money income does not fall with prices.

Theories of Inflation. The demand-pull theory of inflation states that inflation occurs because there is excess demand in the economy; fiscal and monetary policy can often be used to correct this type of inflation. The cost-push theory is that resource prices rise because of such costs as labor unions' wage victories, and that these higher resource prices inflate the prices of finished goods; price guideposts and freezes are sometimes used to correct this type of inflation. The structural imbalance (sectoral) theory states that a large and rapid shift in the makeup of demand can cause a sharp increase in the prices of those sectors where demand has increased; because of factor immobility and price reluctance to fall, price increases in the new higher demand sectors are not offset by decreases in the other sectors.

Remedies. Because major changes in the general level of prices indicate upsets in the economic system, the United States has set the stabilization of prices as one of the national economic objectives. When costs get out of control, the government sometimes takes action to stabilize them. Two methods used are price guideposts and price freezes, essentially voluntary guidelines for management to follow. In 1971, when price guideposts proved ineffective, President Nixon enforced a 90-day freeze on prices.

Significance. Because prices act as allocators of economic goods, they are the mechanism that determines what goods are to be produced in an economy, who is to produce them, and how they are to be distributed. In this sense, therefore, prices act as the basic force in a capitalistic economy.

—William D. Wagoner

PRICE SUPPORT. *See* Price Floor.

PRICE-SUPPORT PROGRAMS are governmental means of assisting farm income by putting floors under prices received by farmers. A program usually involves both holding a commodity price at or above a certain level and dealing with the resulting imbalance between production and consumption. Virtually all countries have agricultural price- or income-support programs of some kind.

The usual device for supporting prices of crops in the United States is the nonrecourse loan. The means of supporting the price of milk for manufacturing purposes is even simpler: the government merely stands ready to buy cheese, butter, and dry nonfat milk at prices that will return a desired price to farmers for the milk used for such products.

In the absence of support, the price of a farm commodity moves to a point where the amount removed from the market by private buyers equals the amount supplied to the market. When support prices are above market-clearing prices—as they usually are intended to be—the amount demanded falls short of the amount supplied. The unmarketable surplus must somehow be dealt with by the government. The usual first step is for the government to acquire the surplus and store it if the commodity is or can be made storable. In order to avoid endless accumulation of surpluses, however, it may (1) give the commodities to the poor or to a special outlet like the School Lunch Program, (2) give the commodities to poor countries, (3) sell them in commercial markets abroad by means of export subsidies, and (4) control production so that no surpluses are produced.

A sustainable price-support program for an exported crop may include government commodity loans to maintain a floor price, storage of any unmarketable surpluses, export subsidies to permit sales abroad, prohibitions on imports of the commodity, and production control to keep farmers from growing more than can be utilized. Such programs can be costly to the government and may conflict with international trade policy.

Origin and Use. Price-support programs in the United States have evolved over the years. They began in a tentative way with the Farm Board of 1929 and became firmly established in 1933 after years of extreme depression. Following World War II, the principal source of economic pressure on farmers was rapid technological advance, which increased production, depressed farm prices relative to other prices, and greatly reduced the farm population. Programs have been directed mainly to the principal field crops—feed grains, wheat, cotton, tobacco, rice, pea-

nuts, and sugar beet and cane. Dairy products have been almost continually supported, but meat animals and poultry products have had only occasional and comparatively unimportant support.

Under the Agricultural Acts of 1965 and 1970, market prices of feed grains, wheat, and cotton were supported at comparatively low levels, at or near world trade prices. Production was restricted by acreage controls. Payments offered to farmers to induce them to comply with acreage controls substantially augmented incomes, especially of cotton and wheat growers. Tobacco, rice and peanuts had high-level supports and were under compulsory acreage controls.

—George E. Brandow

See also Commodity Loans; Crop Restrictions; Marketing Orders, Agricultural; Parity Prices.

PRICE TAKER, a firm in a purely competitive market structure that has no individual control over price and "takes" the price that is set by the market in order to gain a share in the market. This is possible because purely competitive markets have homogeneous products. Because these firms have no voice in pricing their products, they must adjust their output in order to cover any expenses that are incurred.

Price takers are not found in noncompetitive market structures, because any deviation from pure competition allows a firm to have some control over price because of the ability to differentiate products.

PRICE THEORY, a branch of economics that analyzes how prices for individual goods are determined and how firms in various types of industries will maximize profits under stipulated conditions. It also examines the social consequences of these profit-maximizing decisions. Price theory is, thus, greatly concerned with resource allocation decisions.

Labor Value and Marginal Utility. The ancient and medieval writers attempted to lay down moral rules for the conduct of sellers when they set prices. Aristotle and Thomas Aquinas argued that a just price should be charged by all sellers. Although many scholars in the late Middle Ages and during the Renaissance endeavored to determine why goods had value, Adam Smith in his *Inquiry into the Nature and Causes of the Wealth of Nations* (1776) still had no firm answer. He posed the famous paradox of value: why is it that diamonds, which are not extremely useful, have a relatively high market value, whereas water, which is extremely useful, has a comparatively low market value? Although Smith could not solve this conundrum, he hinted that prices of goods will tend to equal their costs of production.

David Ricardo (1772-1823) argued that the relative quantities of labor required to produce commodities determined their relative prices. This became known as the labor theory of value. On closer examination of this theory, however, Ricardo himself recognized that it held only when labor was the only scarce input. Ultimately Ricardo concluded that the prices of reproducible goods will in the long run tend to equal their costs of production. Nonreproducible goods, such as works of art, are not included in the Ricardian analysis. If in the short run the price of a good is greater than its cost of production (including a normal profit to the producer), more of the product will be produced, the supply of the good will increase, and the price will fall until it equals the cost of production. The reverse will occur if the short-run price of a good is less than the cost of production. Ricardo's theory therefore emphasizes supply as the primary determinant of long-run price tendencies. In arriving at these conclusions, Ricardo assumes that pure competition exists. Even Karl Marx's dogmatic labor theory of value has no validity except under conditions where labor is the only factor of production.

Starting in 1862 with a paper by the Englishman Stanley Jevons, a group of economists, including Carl Menger, Friedrich Von Wieser, Eugen Von Böhm-Bawerk, and Leon Walras, uncovered the importance of marginal analysis in analyzing prices. Returning to Smith's paradox of value, they argued that the total utility or total satisfaction received from a good does not determine its market value. Rather, the market value is determined by the marginal utility or additional satisfaction received from a small increment of the good. Because water is plentiful, a very small addition to its total quantity would not add much total satisfaction. In other words, the marginal utility of water is low, so its price is low even though the total utility is high. The reverse is true for diamonds. In this way the marginalists emphasized the marginal utility of the good to the buyer (and the demand side of the market) in the determination of short-run prices.

The Neoclassical School. It remained for the turn-of-the-century English economist Alfred Marshall and his co-workers to synthesize the cost-of-production and marginal-utility analyses. This synthesis constitutes the core of modern price theory. At any given moment a buyer of a particular good will normally receive more marginal utility from the first unit of a good than from the second, and will receive still less marginal utility from the third unit. Thus, additional units must be sold at progressively lower prices. The lower the price for a given good is, the more of it buyers will stand ready to buy. One can, therefore, formulate a demand schedule of various possible prices and the corresponding quantities of the good that buyers will stand ready to purchase.

Similarly, under usual conditions, the price varies directly with the quantity of the good that sellers will stand ready to sell. A supply schedule can then be formulated to show the various price-quantity combinations. In most cases there is one price at which the quantity that buyers wish to buy equals the quantity that sellers stand ready to sell. This price-quantity point will prevail in the marketplace providing there are many informed potential buyers and sellers, and a uniform good is being offered by all sellers.

The demand and supply schedules demonstrated the determination of the day-to-day market prices of goods under competitive conditions. Marshall, Edgeworth, and the other members of the neoclassical school then went on to show, in a manner similar to Ricardo, that the long-run price would tend to equal costs of production under competitive conditions. Ricardian theories were, thus, synthesized with marginal analysis to form a theory of short-and-long-run prices involving demand and supply.

Modern Price Theory. Although Marshallian analysis still constitutes the core of modern price theory, the analysis emphasized conditions of pure competition and touched only lightly on cases when only a few sellers prevailed in the marketplace or when similar products were differentiated in the minds of potential buyers by advertising or other factors. The American economist Edward Chamberlin did much to plug these gaps during the 1930s. His analysis of the spectrum between pure competition and pure monopoly is incorporated, with refinements, into modern price theory. Chamberlin shows that pure competition allocates resources most efficiently, with least cost, and with the lowest price to the consumer in the long run. Monopoly will usually result in relatively high prices, less efficient production, and improper resource allocation. Such an analysis forms the intellectual underpinning for antitrust legislation. The social conclusions, however, have been challenged by Joseph Schumpeter, who argued that large firms are socially desirable, because they hold out the possibility of high profits. The hope of attaining such profits would encourage persons to innovate, yielding long-term economic growth.

Modern price theory includes many additional tools and topics. Indifference curve analysis is used to demonstrate consumer and producer equilibria, various production functions are examined in detail, and numerous concepts of elasticity are utilized for many analytical purposes. The most common of the elasticity concepts, price elasticity of demand, measures the response of potential buyers to a change in the price of a product. Similarly, income elasticity of demand measures the response of potential buyers to a change in their incomes. Recently game theory and linear and non-linear programming have been employed to give fresh insights into many related problems. In addition, price theory has been utilized to cover wider areas of the economy, thereby presaging a possible merger with its sister, macroeconomic analysis, in which broad economic variables, such as the overall price level and employment rates, are analyzed. The tools of price theory have also been utilized widely to analyze the market for labor, land, and capital. Price theory has figured prominently in many of the allied fields of

economics, such as agricultural economics.
—Allan B. Mandelstamm

PRIME RATE, the interest rate that large commercial banks charge their very best customers for commercial and industrial loans. Beginning in the 1930s this rate was published and changed only infrequently—not more than once or twice a year. In 1972, however, after two years of frequent change, some banks adopted a *floating prime rate,* adjusted weekly to changes in the interest rate on Treasury bills or other sensitive market rates. There is some feeling that a published prime rate is misleading and should be abandoned.

PRIOR STOCK. *See* Preferred Stock.

PRIVATE COSTS. Normally there exists close correspondence between private and social costs, the latter being a measure of what society must forego for some commodity. Institutionally, market economies require firms to pay resource owners for inputs. The firm produces up to the point where marginal private benefit (price received) equals marginal private cost (marginal cost). However, if a firm avoids private costs by polluting, it will impose costs on society. Equilibrium for the firm (equating of price and marginal cost) now implies that marginal social costs are greater than marginal social benefit (price). Market price will be too low and output too large. Since self-interest will not maximize group welfare, external intervention may be required.

PRIVATE INVESTMENT. *See* Gross Investment.

PRIVATE PROPERTY, a legal right of a person, natural or corporate, to own and control an economic good within the limits imposed by law. For example, a person in a Western democracy organized on capitalistic or mixed lines may own and hold legal title to a home, a business, a rental property, and so on, and put such economic goods to personal use.

PROBABILITY, an underlying concept of statistics. There is some disagreement among statisticians as to its meaning. There are two basic approaches to a definition of probability. The *frequency definition* denotes probability as a relative frequency or ratio between the number of times an outcome occurs and the total number of occurrences. The theory rests on the law of large numbers which states that the probability of an event is its relative frequency as the number of observations increases indefinitely.

An alternative is the *Bayesian approach* which defines probability as a subjective, or personal, value. This value is determined by each individual on the basis of his or her belief in the likelihood of an occurrence, and is modified by experience. The fre-

quency definition is most common, but the Bayesian approach is gaining favor.

See also Frequency Distribution; Probability Distribution; Statistics.

PROBABILITY DISTRIBUTION, a function giving the probabilities corresponding to values of a random variable. Commonly used probability distributions include the normal and binomial distributions. The normal distribution is the most widely used because almost any distribution can be closely approximated by a normal curve if the number of observations is large enough.

See also Frequency Distribution.

PRODUCER GOODS, buildings and equipment, excluding raw materials, necessary for production of consumer products.

See also Goods.

PRODUCER PRICE INDEX (PPI) has replaced the Wholesale Price Index (WPI) as the most important monthly measure of prices at the wholesale level. The PPI is really three price indexes, one for producer finished goods, one for intermediate products, and one for crude commodities. The PPI usually refers to the finished goods index, but the Bureau of Labor Statistics includes all three indexes in its monthly releases.

The prices collected for the PPI are the same prices that were collected for the WPI. The PPI, which does not combine price for goods in various stages of processing, is considered by most economists as a major advance over the all-commodities WPI.

PRODUCT DEMAND. *See* Market Demand.

PRODUCT DIFFERENTIATION, a device used by business firms to distinguish their product from products of other firms in the same industry. Product differentiation is a form of non-price competition found chiefly in oligopolistic and monopolistically competitive markets. Oligopolistic markets usually have such few firms that price competition is very

Even virtually identical products may be differentiated by brand name, packaging, or design.

harmful; monopolistically competitive markets have products so similar that price competition is ineffective. Product differentiation usually takes the form of either advertising or variations in the design and quality of the product.

Often, by advertising, even products that are identical in nature can be differentiated by the use of brand names. For example, aspirin tablets must all conform to certain specifications and are all equally effective. However, through successful advertising, some brands are able to outsell others. The second form of product differentiation, variations in quality and design of a product, occurs, for example, in the automotive industry, where companies innovate to achieve a greater share of the market. Chrome, metallic paints, and fastbacks tend to differentiate otherwise identical body frames.

See also Non-Price Competition; Promotional Competition.

PRODUCT HOMOGENEITY implies that all products in a particular market are identical in nature. A condition of pure and perfectly competitive markets, it indicates that each seller in the market has the exact same product as every other seller in that market. When products are homogeneous in nature, such as milk, wheat, and other agricultural products, buyers cannot differentiate and, therefore, will buy at the lowest price.

When product homogeneity exists in markets that are not purely competitive, product differentiation can be used to distinguish one product from another. For example, although all aspirins are identical in nature, certain brand names have been able to gain a large share of the market.

PRODUCTION. Utility in economic literature means the capacity to satisfy wants. Production is the creation of utility in material things or the rendering of services for markets. A market is made up of actual or potential buyers and sellers engaged in transactions related in time, location, and types of products. It is the supply side of markets that production theory analyzes. The basic decision-making unit in the productive process is the firm; the basic producing unit is the plant.

Productive activities can be placed in three categories. Production involved with agriculture, raw materials, extractive industries, and other natural resources is primary. Secondary activities are manufacturing and all forms of fabrication involved with changing the form of materials to make them have more utility. Tertiary activities involve production in the service industries. The more highly developed an economy, the greater is its proportion of total production involved with tertiary activities.

See also Opportunity Cost; Production Possibility Frontier.

PRODUCTION FUNCTION. The act of production may be thought of as a process that transforms inputs (factors) into an output (good or service). The production function is a technically determined relationship (a schedule or a mathematical equation) between inputs and output. A production function is technically efficient; it shows the maximum output obtainable with a specified amount of inputs. Since a firm cannot vary the quantities of some inputs, such as machinery and structures except in the long run, a distinction is made between production in the short run and long-run production. For a production process with two inputs, labor and machines, the short-run production function is illustrated graphically in Figure 1. Output X is measured on the vertical axis and the input labor hours are measured on the horizontal axis. The curve labeled TP(M) is called the total product curve and the notation in parentheses indicates that the position of the TP curve depends on the amount of the fixed input M, machine hours.

Marginal Product. The TP curve of L shows the quantities of product X that can be produced with various amounts of input L, and some fixed amount of input M. The TP curve has a positive slope, which indicates that when the amount of one input is increased, the amount of the output increases as well. For a small increment in an input, the resulting increment in output is called the *marginal product* of the input. For a sufficiently small increase in an input, the marginal product is measured by the slope of the TP curve. Thus, the slope of the TP curve in Figure 1 measures the marginal product of L.

Starting from a very small amount of L, and increasing L up to the point L_1, the curvature of the TP curve shows that the amount of X increases at an increasing rate; that is, in that range the marginal product of L increases. Increasing L beyond L_1 causes X to increase at a decreasing rate; that is, beyond L_1 the marginal product of L decreases. Thus, at levels of L beyond L_1 the production function is said to exhibit *diminishing returns* with respect to input L. The curvature of the TP curve implies, therefore, that the marginal product (MP) of L attains its maximum at L_1 (the point of inflection of the TP curve), so that the MP curve has the general shape shown in Figure 2.

Average Product. Another concept of productivity is that of *average product* (AP). It is defined as total product divided by the total amount of one of the inputs used. For example, the AP of labor is defined as X/L, where both X and L are coordinates of some point on the TP curve of L. Geometrically, the AP can be represented by the slope of a ray from the origin to the appropriate point on the TP curve. At the L_2 in Figure 1, the AP of L is equal to the slope of the ray OR shown in that diagram. Since the ray OR is tangent to the TP curve at L_2, the AP attains its maximum at that point. Thus, like the MP curve, the AP curve has the shape of an inverted bowl, and it intersects the MP

PRODUCTION FUNCTION

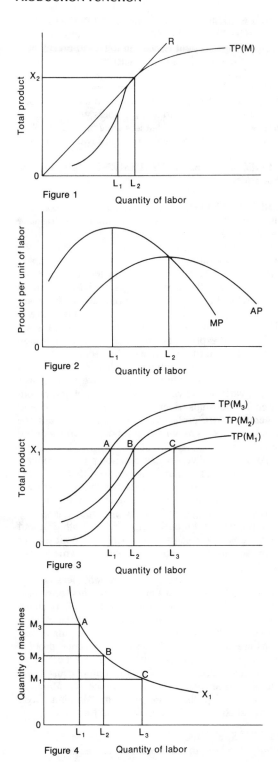

Figure 1 Quantity of labor

Figure 2 Quantity of labor

Figure 3 Quantity of labor

Figure 4 Quantity of labor

curve at the point at which the latter curve has its maximum, as shown in Figure 2.

Isoquants. If the amount of input M is changed, the TP curve of L shifts. From the assumption that all marginal products are positive, it follows that if the amount of M is increased, the TP curve of L shifts up. Figure 3 illustrates three TP curves for three levels of M, M_3 M_2 M_1. Among other things, the diagram shows that any particular level of output can be produced with several different input combinations; for example, the combinations L_1, M_3 (point A); L_2, M_2 (point B); or L_3, M_1 (point C). The points A, B, and C can be mapped into the input plane as shown in Figure 4. The other points on that curve are obtained in a similar fashion. In other words, the curve in Figure 4 is the result of mapping all the points on the horizontal line at X_1 in Figure 3 into the input plane. Any point on the curve in Figure 4 represents an input combination which yields X_1 units of product X. Such a curve is called an *isoquant* (isoproduct curve). Since all marginal products are positive, an isoquant has a negative slope. Thus, if output is to be held constant, increasing (decreasing) one input requires a decrease (increase) in another input. The slope of the isoquant measures the rate at which one input must be substituted for another so as to keep the output constant, and is referred to as the *marginal rate of technical substitution*. When an isoquant is convex to the origin, as the one in Figure 4, its slope becomes flatter as the amount of L is increased. This property is known as *diminishing marginal rate of technical substitution*.

One can draw an isoquant for any arbitrary level of output. Several isoquants drawn on one diagram constitute an *isoquant map*. No two isoquants can touch one another. For any two isoquants, the one farther from the origin represents a higher level of output. —*Josef Hadar*

PRODUCTION POSSIBILITY FRONTIER, frequently used by economists to explain the costs to the economy of producing more of one good in terms of the resultant lost quantities of other goods. Price theory, growth theory and international trade theory employ this tool. At each moment in time a nation has given techniques of production and given quantities and types of basic resources (land, labor, capital, and enterprise). It might be possible to produce, say, 30 million units of good A, provided all resources were devoted to its production. The nation, however, may also produce some of good B by transferring some resources out of the production of A into the production of B. In this case, less than 30 million units of A could be produced, because not all of the nation's resources would be left to produce A. Perhaps 5 million units of B could be produced, with 29 million units of A. Further transfers of resources from A to B might yield 10, 15, 20, and 25 million units of B, with 26, 21, 12, and 0 million units of A respectively. The combinations of A and B are summarized in the production possibility table.

The Production Possibility Curve, or production possibility frontier, is a graph of this table, such as curve LM.

The graph depicts the various combinations of A and B that the nation can produce under conditions of full employment. A combination of A and B inside the curve, such as at point X, is produced with less than full employment of available resources and yields less of both A and B. With full employment it is impossible to produce more of B without producing less of A, as shown by the curve's negative slope. A point beyond the curve, such as Z, is unattainable with present techniques and resources, though such a combination of A and B may be attained in the future, as resources grow and techniques improve.

Cost Analysis. The production possibility frontier is bulged outward because of the presence of increasing costs. As the economy produces more and more of B, the cost of B, in terms of A lost, increases. Increasing costs occur because the first resources to be transferred from A to B tend to be those resources most capable of producing B and least capable of producing A. As more of B is produced, however, resources must be transferred that are less and less capable of producing B relative to A. As a result, more and more of A is lost for each increment of B. *—Allan B. Mandelstamm*

PRODUCTION POSSIBILITY TABLE

Units of A (millions)	30	29	26	21	12	0
Units of B (millions)	0	5	10	15	20	25

PRODUCTION POSSIBILITY CURVE

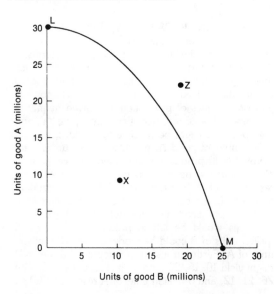

PRODUCTION QUESTION. *See* Market Mechanism.

PROFESSIONAL AIR TRAFFIC CONTROLLERS ASSOCIATION (PATCO), union best known for its support for President Reagan in the 1980 presidential election and for the strike against the government in 1982. Faced with an impasse in bargaining, the union called an illegal strike. President Reagan turned the full power of the government against the union leadership and members. Striking members were fired and not rehired, and several leaders were fined and jailed. The union went into bankruptcy and was decertified.

PROFIT-AND-LOSS STATEMENT. *See* Income Statement.

PROFIT MAXIMIZATION. In economic theory it is assumed that the primary goal of the firm is to make profit and that a firm is in equilibrium when its profits are maximized. Firms secure profits by selling goods and services (output) for more than it costs to employ factors of production input. When the market structure in which the firm operates and the technical relationship between inputs and outputs are specified, maximizing profit implies a particular input pattern. This pattern can be described in two equivalent ways.

The more explicit description of profit maximization is directly in terms of inputs. The technical relation between inputs and outputs is called the production function. If we specify this function we specify how output varies as we vary inputs; with input and output price relationships given, we specify how cost and revenue, hence profit, vary with inputs. We assume that the firm opts for whatever input pattern yields the largest profit.

As an alternative, we can describe profit maximization in terms of output. If we assume that the firm's goal is to maximize profit, it follows that the firm will seek to minimize the cost of whatever output it produces. Minimizing cost for a given output will specify an input pattern for each output. Thus, both cost and revenue can be calculated in terms of output. In this approach, the firm chooses that output that maximizes profit.

The two approaches are equivalent because the profit maximizing input pattern in the first approach also implies a particular output and the profit maximizing output in the second approach also implies a particular input pattern. Equivalent equilibrium conditions are also implied. The marginal revenue product for each factor must equal the marginal cost of its employment and marginal cost of output must equal marginal revenue.   *—Clarence C. Morrison*

See also Equilibrium of the Firm; Marginal Cost; Marginal Revenue; Total Cost; Total Revenue.

PROFITS, a prime mover of a capitalistic economy, influencing both the allocation of resources (by channeling capital funds into alternative uses) and their level of utilization. Because entrepreneurs expect profits, profits can be said to act as a stimulator of output.

Accounting profits are defined as the difference between the income of a business and the expenses of the business in a given period, usually a year. Profits are calculated on an income statement of a business, and all expenses, including non-cash items such as depreciation, are recorded. Profits can be either positive (gains) or negative (losses). Economists also define profits as the difference between income and costs. However, when economists talk of costs, they mean opportunity costs. Opportunity costs include both explicit costs and implicit costs incurred by the firm. So while an accountant may determine that a firm has made a profit when income exceeds the costs recorded on the firm's income statement, an economist may find that the same firm has actually made no economic profit or has even sustained economic losses.

An example will serve to illustrate the difference between accounting profits and economic profits. Consider an owner-manager who receives profits but no salary. This owner worked 10-hour days, six days a week during a year. Assume that the same hours worked elsewhere would have earned the owner $30,000. Further, if the resources tied up in the firm's physical plant had been invested elsewhere, a return of $20,000 would have been earned during the year. The firm's income during the year was $100,000. Explicit costs (such as employees' wages, utilities, raw materials, etc.) were $50,000. According to the firm's income statement, a profit of $50,000 was earned. However, an economist would subtract from the figure the opportunity costs of the owner-manager's time and capital investment ($30,000 + $20,000 = $50,000) and conclude that the firm broke even.

Normal Profits. In the example above, the owner of the firm will continue in business since he or she is earning the same rate of return that he or she could earn elsewhere. In this case, economists would say that the firm is earning a normal return or a normal profit. If the firm were earning less than a normal rate of return, it would eventually leave the industry, as resource owners pursue profits elsewhere.

Pure or Economic Profits. The discussion above reveals that economists consider a normal profit to be part of a firm's costs, specifically the cost of retaining the talents and resources of the owner-manager. A pure or economic profit then is earned only when a firm earns in excess of a normal return. Of course, economic profits would attract others to the industry. In the absence of barriers to entry, we would not expect economic profits to persist in the long run; the entry of new firms will shift the supply curve out and lower prices.

— *Gerald A. Whitney*

PROFITS: TOPIC GUIDE

For a full understanding of the role of profits in our economic system, see the articles MARKET SYSTEM and PROFIT SYSTEM. A bit more specifically, perhaps, the economic function of profits is shown in ALLOCATION.

The significance of profits to the individual firm is described in the articles on EQUILIBRIUM OF THE FIRM, THEORY OF THE FIRM, and PROFIT MAXIMIZATION. Narrower but important aspects of profits can be found in NORMAL PROFITS, MONOPOLISTIC PROFITS, and ACCOUNTING PROFITS.

The Subject Map accompanying THEORY OF THE FIRM displays many of these related concepts.

PROFIT SHARING, a means used by employers to give employees a greater incentive to work, calls for distribution to workers of a share in the profits of a company after all ordinary expenses have been met. The usual form of this plan is either the periodic payment of cash to a worker or payments into a trust fund earmarked for employee benefits.

There are several problems with profit sharing as an incentive program. The major one is that profits do not always correlate with production; therefore, if there is an increase in production but profits are reduced for some reason, profit-sharing may very easily become a counterincentive.

PROFIT SYSTEM, another name for the free enterprise, or capitalistic market, system for allocating and distributing scarce resources.

Economists define two kinds of profits: accounting profits and economic profits. *Accounting profits* are defined as the difference between a firm's total revenue, the dollar value of sales, and total explicit costs. *Economic profits* are defined as the difference between total revenue and total costs, which include explicit and implicit costs. Implicit costs are the opportunity cost of any owner-used resource, such as the owner's time or the owner's capital. In a corporate form of enterprise, implicit costs are usually the opportunity cost of capital. These economic profits are also called pure profits.

Competitive Market. In a competitive market in equilibrium, all firms will realize the same return, which is the amount necessary to keep resources committed to that industry. Returns beyond this will cause additional firms to enter to participate in the excess. Any return below this will cause resources to be withdrawn because of economic losses. Economists consider normal returns a cost, and economic profits emerge when returns exceed that amount. In long-run equilibrium under competitive conditions, the entry or withdrawal of firms assures the elimination of economic profits and losses. Their presence in any type of market implies either short-run disequilibrium or monopoly conditions that prevent free entry and exit of firms.

Thus, in the long run, profits in a competitive market are competed away. Long-run profits can exist only in a market where one or more firms have monopoly power or where one competitive firm has a unique resource. This last kind of profit is called economic rent.

Profit Sources. Karl Marx was virtually the first economist to have an explicit profit theory; his surplus value was profit, and its rate was the rate of exploitation. To economist J.A. Schumpeter, profits came with the emergence of the entrepreneur as a reward to enterprise and innovation including the concomitant financial risks. Professor Frank Knight believed that all true profit is linked with uncertainty and that abnormal returns are necessary to induce entrepreneurs to undertake uncertain ventures. Goods involving uncertainty and uninsurable risks must be priced to cover wages, interest, etc., and "profits."

As indicated, profits can arise from monopoly behavior. People with unusual talents and owners of particularly fertile or strategically located land get higher than normal returns as a result of natural scarcity; these cannot be competed away. In addition, there are "contrived scarcities" arising from behavior of firms in less than purely competitive markets, and profits derived from them will not be competed away because of market imperfections.

The profit system in socialist and communist countries is either nonexistent or used sparingly as a motivating device to spur output but never to allocate resources.   —*John R. Matthews, Jr.*

See also Demand for Capital; Entrepreneur; Excess Profits; Risk; Surplus Value; Uncertainty.

PROGRESSIVE TAX, a tax whose rate increases as the base of the tax grows larger. Income is generally used as the tax base in the United States. A progressive tax on income would mean that taxes paid as a percentage of income would increase as income increases. The marginal rate is greater than the average rate as the tax base increases. The federal income tax is the best example of a progressive tax in the United States.

See also Regressive Tax; Taxation.

PROLETARIAT, a large, propertyless, working class dependent on their own labor, or its sale, for their existence. The rise of capitalism created conditions that separated workers from the land and the materials with which they worked. This, according to Marx, created only two mutually hostile classes, and dictatorship of the proletariat would ultimately supplant that of the capitalistic bourgeoisie.

See also Marx, Karl; Revolutionary Socialism.

PROMOTIONAL COMPETITION, a form of non-price competition in which firms in an industry compete with each other through advertising and other promotional media. Promotional competition is very common in monopolistically competitive market structures where all firms in the industry produce essentially the same type of product but try to differentiate by clever advertising campaigns. One form of promotional competition, common in the toothpaste industry, the aspirin industry, and the soap power industry, is the use of brand names as a means of gathering a greater share of the market. By convincing the public to associate "quality" with its brand, a company can make it difficult for off-brands to enter the market.

PROPENSITY TO CONSUME. *See* Consumption Function.

PROPENSITY TO SAVE, the idea that the amount that households save depends on their disposable income and their expectations of future wealth, incomes, and uses for their savings. When the idea is expressed as an exact relationship, it is called a savings function or savings schedule. The propensity to save, the savings function, and the savings schedule are the obverse of the propensity to consume, the consumption function and the consumption schedule, because savings plus consumption always, by definition, uses up all disposable income.

See also Consumption Function.

PROPERTYLESS CLASS. *See* Proletariat.

PROPERTY TAX, a tax on the value of property. The most common type of property tax is the real property tax, which is a tax on land and the structures thereon. Personal property taxes (such as a tax on a firm's inventories, or on a household's clothing and furniture) are also fairly common. The property tax has historically been the mainstay of local government financing. Its relative importance has lessened in recent years, as local governments have received larger amounts of revenues in the form of grants from state and federal government. In 1985, 18.3% of state and local government revenues came from property taxes, 11.9% from personal income taxes, 3.1% from corporate profit taxes, 21.0% from sales taxes, 27.3% from other taxes, and 18.4% from federal grants.

The property tax is often unpopular, partly because some believe that property wealth is a poor indicator of both the ability to pay local taxes and the benefits received from local government and partly because the tax is perceived by many as being unfairly administered. The lack of uniform treatment of all property owners in determining tax liability is due in some cases to poorly trained assessors, infrequent updating of assessments, and possible political motivations to alter property valuations. This equity issue has led several states to oversee closely the property assessment activities of local governments.

One of the biggest economic debates about property taxes centers on who actually bears the burden of the tax. The "old view" was that the tax was paid by homeowners and the consumers of products produced by taxed businesses (such as renters); the "new view" suggests that the tax will be effectively paid by all owners of capital within the economy, both taxed and nontaxed. Neither side has prevailed in convincing the other, and the debate continues.

—*Michael S. Johnson*

See also Taxation; Tax Incidence.

PROPORTIONAL SUBSTANTIALITY. *See* Quantitative Substantiality.

PROPORTIONAL TAX, a tax whose *rate* remains constant as the tax base grows larger. With income as the tax base, taxes paid as a percentage of income do not change as income increases. The marginal rate is equal to the average rate. A tax on income at a 20% rate, regardless of the amount of income, is an example of a proportional tax.

PROPRIETORSHIP refers to a single private owner of a business enterprise, and represents the most usual

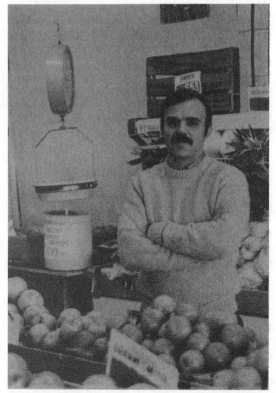

Single proprietorships are often small businesses like the corner grocery store or fruit market.

type of legal organization in business. However, these businesses usually are small, and the total output of all proprietorships represents only a small portion of the total national output.

See also Corporation; Partnership.

PROSPERITY. *See* Business Cycles, Phases.

PROTESTANT ETHIC. Max Weber observed in *The Protestant Ethic and the Spirit of Capitalism* (1904-1905) that, historically, business and economic leaders, skilled labor and trained personnel, and owners of capital in centers of capitalist development were overwhelmingly Protestant. He found the explanation in the Calvinistic doctrine of predestination, in which man is either saved or condemned eternally by God. Hard work could allay anxiety in this regard, and individual economic success could be construed as a sign of election for ultimate redemption. The income from hard work was not to be used for self-indulgence, so the righteous individual lived frugally with savings accumulating as sources of investment funds.

PSYCHOLOGICAL THEORY OF BUSINESS CYCLES states that the reactions of people, waves of optimistic and pessimistic expectations, initiate fluctuations in economic activity. The influence of such external forces as politics and social events, prospects for war or peace, and changing consumer taste, as well as internal economic activity, such as anticipated returns on investment and profit expectations, triggers psychologically based decisions which result in changes in investment and spending. All of these reactions and decisions contribute to the psychological attitude of business, and hence to the level of business activity, a major force contributing to cyclical changes in the economic system.

See also Business Cycles, Theories.

PUBLIC ASSISTANCE, government program created to improve the welfare of poor families by providing them with financial assistance and other services. Sometimes referred to as "welfare" or "relief," the program is administered by local offices operated by state or local governments.

A family or individual in need must apply to the welfare agency for admission to the program. Recipients must pass a "means" test, which restricts eligibility to those with incomes and property below certain levels. Applicants may be required to accept additional conditions in order to qualify for assistance. For example, the family head may be required to accept work or job training if it is available unless this is precluded by poor health or household responsibilities. The family may also be required to subscribe to standards of morality and lifestyle demanded by the agency.

Cost and Benefits. Benefits are generally tailored to

the needs of the individual family. Each state welfare agency prescribes a budget for families of different size that is supposed to provide for minimum necessities. A family with no other source of income will presumably receive a monthly payment equal to the estimated cost of the minimum budget, although in many states low appropriations force payments to fall below the state's own minimum. If family earnings exceed a minimum, benefits are reduced. Agencies are allowed to make additional payments to families with special needs.

In the United States, the cost of public assistance is split among federal, state, and local governments. The federal government absorbs about half the cost through matching funds. Only the categorical programs for families with dependent children, the elderly, the needy blind, and the totally disabled receive federal funds. General assistance for other needy persons, including many working poor, is financed fully from state and local sources.

Although there is some federal control over the categorical programs, there are great interstate differences in benefits and eligibility requirements. For example, maximum payments to a family of three under the AFDC program (Aid to Families with Dependent Children) ranged from $96 in Mississippi to $492 in Vermont in 1980. Even within states nonuniformity is generated by lax administrative control and the social work philosophy, which leaves a great deal to the discretion of the social worker.

See also Aid to Families with Dependent Children; Medicaid; Negative Income Tax; Old-Age Assistance; Social Dividend; Social Insurance.

PUBLIC CHOICE, the study of nonmarket decision-making. Public choice, one of the fastest growing areas of economic analysis, utilizes the theoretical tools and approaches of economics and applies them to the behavior of individuals as voters and to the behavior of governments and bureaucrats. There is both a positive and a normative aspect to public choice. The positive approach consists of examining and predicting outcomes within the political process. For example, the probability of individuals voting in a particular election might be seen as depending upon the perceived closeness of the election, the direct monetary stake the person has in one outcome or the other, the person's membership in a group or organization, and the costs the person must incur in order to vote (time, transportation, information-gathering).

The normative approach consists of analyzing alternative voting procedures or organizational structures to see if some are more efficient than others. For example, which form of representation, individual districts or at-large seats, is more likely to provide a true measure of the desires of the electorate in a community? Public choice represents an important intersection of economics and political science.

PUBLIC EMPLOYMENT SERVICE. The Wagner-Peyser Act (1933) as amended by the Social Security Act of 1935 provided federal matching funds for states to establish employment services, with the primary goals of (1) administering the work test for unemployment insurance claimants and (2) providing employers with qualified workers. Recently, a third goal, to give priority to the employment problems of the disadvantaged, was added. In the 1960s, the public employment service underwent drastic changes because of the new emphasis on manpower programs, which opened up numerous agencies concerned with the problems of unemployment.

PUBLIC EXPENDITURES. *See* Federal Budget.

PUBLIC FINANCE, the study of the use of the budgetary process for carrying out the allocative, redistributive, and stabilization functions of the modern state. The fiscal instruments available to governments for carrying out these functions are the taxing, spending, and borrowing powers. Each of these instruments may have an impact upon the three functional objectives depending upon their theoretical incidence and economic effects.

The allocative function is concerned with the way a nation's resources are used, whether for the production of "guns or butter"; the redistributive function is concerned with changing the market-determined distribution of income so that it conforms to some predetermined notion of equality; the stabilization function is concerned with assuring a nation's growth with a minimum of unemployment or inflation.

All levels of government carry out public financial activities, though usually the central government has at its command more resources and more powerful control over the tools necessary for carrying out fiscal objectives. In federal countries such as the United States, intergovernmental fiscal relations, particularly subsidies and transfers, are an integral component of the study of public finance.   —*Irving J. Goffman*

PUBLIC GOOD. *See* Pure Public Good.

PUBLIC INTEREST DISPUTES, strikes that may jeopardize the national health and safety, such as strikes of police or fire departments, sometimes called "emergency-strikes." In order to protect the public in these situations, the emergency strike provisions of federal and state laws may be invoked. The Taft-Hartley Act provides for public action in these disputes.

See also Emergency Strike; Strike; Taft-Hartley Act (1947).

PUBLIC LAW (P.L.) 480, enacted in 1954 and later called Food for Peace or Food for Freedom, established procedures for sale of surplus farm products by

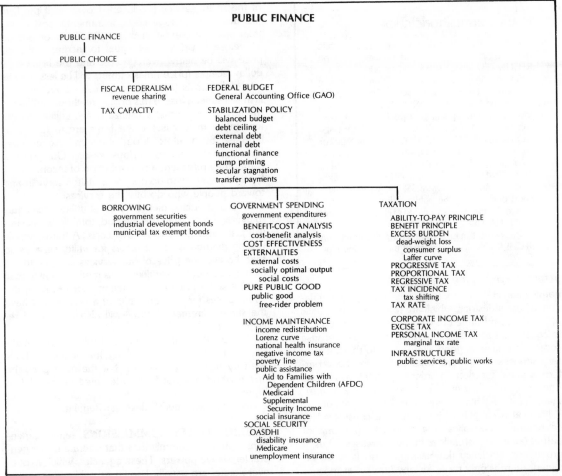

PUBLIC FINANCE

PUBLIC FINANCE
|
PUBLIC CHOICE

FISCAL FEDERALISM   FEDERAL BUDGET
   revenue sharing   General Accounting Office (GAO)

TAX CAPACITY   STABILIZATION POLICY
         balanced budget
         debt ceiling
         external debt
         internal debt
         functional finance
         pump priming
         secular stagnation
         transfer payments

BORROWING   GOVERNMENT SPENDING   TAXATION
  government securities   government expenditures   ABILITY-TO-PAY PRINCIPLE
  industrial development bonds   BENEFIT-COST ANALYSIS   BENEFIT PRINCIPLE
  municipal tax exempt bonds   cost-benefit analysis   EXCESS BURDEN
       COST EFFECTIVENESS   dead-weight loss
       EXTERNALITIES   consumer surplus
       external costs   Laffer curve
       socially optimal output   PROGRESSIVE TAX
       social costs   PROPORTIONAL TAX
       PURE PUBLIC GOOD   REGRESSIVE TAX
       public good   TAX INCIDENCE
       free-rider problem   tax shifting
            TAX RATE

       INCOME MAINTENANCE   CORPORATE INCOME TAX
       income redistribution   EXCISE TAX
       Lorenz curve   PERSONAL INCOME TAX
       national health insurance   marginal tax rate
       negative income tax   INFRASTRUCTURE
       poverty line   public services, public works
       public assistance
         Aid to Families with
           Dependent Children (AFDC)
         Medicaid
         Supplemental
           Security Income
       social insurance
       SOCIAL SECURITY
       OASDHI
       disability insurance
       Medicare
       unemployment insurance

the United States to poor, less-developed countries under terms highly favorable to buyers. Sales for local currencies of recipient countries, convertible to dollars only in limited amounts, have accounted for most P.L. 480 shipments, but outright donations in emergencies and for special purposes have also been used. Shipment of foods not in surplus was authorized in 1966. Expenditures under the program gradually increased to $1.6 billion in 1965. The amendment in 1966 required a gradual shift from sales for foreign currencies to dollar sales with long-term credit at low interest. These less favorable terms, together with the Green Revolution in some parts of the less-developed world, reduced P.L. 480 shipments after the mid-1960s.

See also Green Revolution.

PUBLIC OWNERSHIP. *See* Nationalization.

PUBLIC SECTOR UNIONS, unions that represent employees in public service occupations, whose employers are generally local or state governments.

In 1962, President Kennedy issued an executive order granting federal civil service employees the right to organize. Since the mid-1970s, public sector unions have grown faster than those in the private sector. The public employee unions differ from those in the private sector only in the employer and in the tactics, and many private sector unions have members in public employment. Unions of educators, police, and firefighters are now common.

Public sector workers and their unions do not have the protections granted by the National Labor Relations Act and cannot use the services of the NLRB. They are covered by a series of state labor laws and, at the federal level, by the Civil Service Reform Act of 1978 and other legislation. Over 50% of federal employees are covered by collective bargaining agreements, and almost 40% at the state and local levels are covered. The largest public employee union is the National Education Association, with over 1.6 million members.

PUBLIC SERVICES. *See* Infrastructure.

PUBLIC UTILITIES: TOPIC GUIDE

Further information closely related to the public utility concept can be found in the article on REGULATED INDUSTRIES, and for additional material on a major economic condition underlying the public utility industries, see ECONOMIES OF SCALE and NATURAL MONOPOLY. To see what is involved in the regulation of public utilities, consult REGULATION, REGULATORY COMMISSIONS, and PUBLIC UTILITY COMMISSIONS. For some specific aspects and methods of public utility regulation, refer to CERTIFICATE OF PUBLIC CONVENIENCE AND NECESSITY and INTERSTATE COMMERCE COMMISSION. Two landmark court decisions in the public utility area are discussed in the articles on SMYTH v. AMES and HOPE NATURAL GAS CASE.

The Subject map accompanying the article on REGULATION displays many of those relationships.

PUBLIC UTILITIES, industries with certain economic characteristics that are subject to public regulation. These industries, which are referred to as "public utilities," are presumed to offer indispensable services to consumers and to be natural monopolies. Because consumers have no good alternatives to these necessary services, the natural monopolists, in effect, perform a public function. In order to prevent these firms from exploiting their monopoly positions, the government substitutes public regulation for competition.

Natural Monopolies. Industries are considered to be natural monopolies when the cost per unit of output (average cost) falls as output increases. Thus, if production efficiency (low average cost) is to be attained, there is only room for one firm or, at most, a few firms to carry on business in a given market. Consequently, competition cannot be depended on to keep prices low.

Another reason given for regulation of such industries is that price competition could become destructive. When a firm has declining average costs, it has an incentive to cut its price so as to increase its sales. If all of the industry's firms end up in a price-cutting war, price could fall below per unit costs and drive some firms out of business. The reduction of industry productive capacity may be undesirable to society if the service produced is essential to consumers. In some cases, however, it may be that this fear of "destructive competition" is exaggerated and has led to unnecessary restrictions on healthy competition.

Price Setting. In regulating public utilities, regulatory agencies are primarily concerned with controlling prices. Various methods have been considered for setting utility prices.

First, many economists have maintained that society will benefit most if price is set equal to the incremental cost (that is, marginal cost) of the last unit of the utility service produced. However, if the firm has declining average costs, incremental cost is less than average cost at each possible level of output. Therefore, if price is set equal to incremental cost, price will be below average cost and the firm's total dollar receipts (price times output) will be less than its total dollar costs (average cost times output) and the firm will suffer a loss. If this pricing method is followed, the government must subsidize public utilities by the amount of their losses if the firms are to remain in business. Such subsidies out of general tax revenues have been criticized for various reasons. One criticism is that they represent a redistribution of income away from taxpayers who do not use a utility's services and toward people who do buy the services.

A second pricing method is to set utility price equal to average cost. With this method, total dollar receipts will just cover the utility's total costs. A third possible pricing method is to set prices for utility services so that the average price of the services is equal to the average cost of the services. This method, which may involve some price discrimination—for example, different prices for different units of a service that have the same incremental cost—will also allow total receipts to cover total costs.

Of these three, the second and third pricing methods come closest to describing the actual methods used by regulatory agencies. For the most part, the first method has not been attempted in the United States.   —*Joseph Jadlow*

See also Regulated Industries; Regulation.

PUBLIC UTILITY COMMISSIONS, semi-independent regulatory commissions that operate under general legislative powers. These agencies, which exist in every state, are usually known as public utility commissions, public service commissions, railroad commissions, or corporation commissions. Most of these state commissions have jurisdiction over motor carriers, railroads, and gas, water, electric, and telephone service. They usually have the authority to regulate rates and the quantity and the quality of services. The members of state commissions are appointed by the governor in many states and are elected by the people in others. Most state commissions suffer from such problems as technically incompetent, low-salaried commissioners, and inadequate budgets and staffs.

See also Regulatory Commissions.

PUBLIC UTILITY ENTRY, control by a regulatory commission of entry into a regulated industry. Ordinarily, a firm entering such an industry must first obtain approval from the commission in the form of a certificate of public convenience and necessity. By restricting entry, it is thought that destructive competition may be avoided so that public utilities have financial stability and provide continued service.

See also Certificates of Public Convenience and Necessity; Public Utilities; Regulated Industries.

PUBLIC UTILITY PRICE, the rate charged per unit of use of a public utility's service. Control of such rates is the heart of public utility regulation. A regulatory commission tries to keep a public utility's rates from being unreasonably high but high enough for the utility to attract capital from investors.
See also Public Utilities; Rate Level.

PUBLIC UTILITY SERVICE, the quantity, quality, and conditions of service supplied by a public utility, usually controlled by a regulatory commission. Control of utility prices has little meaning unless the quality of service offered at regulated prices is also controlled.
See also Regulation.

PUBLIC WORKS. *See* Infrastructure.

PUMP PRIMING, term widely used in the early 1930s to refer to the policy resulting from the belief that the Depression was a reflection of a lack of confidence on the part of the business sector. It was felt that if the government would institute some spending programs, employment would increase, followed by an increase in consumer spending, which would then restore confidence in the economy and hence result in increased private investment. What the economy needed, adherents argued, was a "shot in the arm" to get things moving again. If, indeed, a one-time discretionary set of expenditures does build up sufficient confidence, the desired result might very well be generated. For many reasons, economic and political, the "pump priming" activities of the early 1930s did not generate sufficient confidence on the part of private investors.

PURCHASES, the value of goods and services acquired by individuals and businesses during a given period. Changes in the rate of purchases are useful indicators of changes of aggregate individual decisions allocating disposable income between consumption and savings.

PURCHASING POWER. *See* Price Level.

PURE COMPETITION. *See* Perfect Competition.

PURE PROFITS. *See* Economic Profits.

PURE PUBLIC GOOD, a good or service that is collectively consumed. A pure public good is one that is characterized by being both nonrival and nonexcludable. This represents the theoretical extreme from what could be called a "pure private good," which is both rival and excludable. These concepts can best be understood by way of example. An apple is a pure private good. It is *rival* in that consumption of the apple by person A means the apple cannot be consumed by person B. The more of the good consumed by one party, the less that is available for others. The apple is also *excludable* in that it is simple to prevent person B from consuming apples if he is unwilling to pay for the privilege. A free-market system based on voluntary exchange and private ownership will efficiently allocate resources toward the production of apples. People reveal their desire for apples by their willingness to pay the price the market sets.

Now consider the case of a lighthouse that a shipping company might build. The lighthouse is largely *nonrival* in that use of the services of the lighthouse by one ship in the harbor does not diminish the benefits available to another ship at the same time—they can jointly consume the good. Also, the lighthouse is *nonexcludable* in that it is hard to prevent others from consuming the benefits even if they did not contribute toward the cost of building the lighthouse. Other examples include national defense services and insect control. Markets will fail to provide adequately such services, as there is no market means to determine how much of the good each person is willing to pay for. Such goods may have to be financed via coercion (taxes) if they are to be provided. This preference revelation problem is called the free-rider problem.

A good is not necessarily a pure public good just because it is provided by a government. However, most of the products that governments provide have some element of publicness to them. For example, parks and limited access highways have a large degree of nonrivalness, yet they are excludable (entrance fees and tolls can be charged and enforced). Many goods that government provides are excludable by social choice, not by nature of the product.

—Michael S. Johnson
See also Externalities; Free-Rider Problem; Merit Goods; Public Finance.

PURE RENT. *See* Economic Rent.

QUALITATIVE CONTROLS are restrictions placed by the Federal Reserve System on particular types of loans by commercial banks or financial intermediaries in order to implement the goals of monetary policy. While quantitative controls restrict (or encourage) changes in the total money supply, qualitative controls have the effect of channeling a given total of loans away from particular types of financing.

Margin requirements restrict the amount of money that can be borrowed to purchase stock. *Installment credit controls* regulate the amount that can be borrowed for the purchase of consumer goods, while *mortgage lending controls* limit the amount that can be borrowed for the purchase of residential housing. The dangers of diversion of funds into consumer markets are greatest during periods of war when resources generally are scarce, and controls over these purchases have been limited to war periods.

A different form of qualitative control prescribes *interest rate ceilings* that may be paid by *commercial banks*. These controls are intended primarily to prevent banks from entering into competitive races to pay higher rates than they can safely afford in order to attract funds away from other institutions. Although the Federal Reserve System normally has control only over member banks, its powers to supervise qualitative controls extend to practically all lenders.

—*Walter W. Haines*

See also Monetary Policy; Quantitative Controls.

QUALITY COMPETITION, a form of non-price competition in which individual firms in an industry attempt to gather the largest possible share of the market by improving the quality of their products. A form of product differentiation, it is found most often in oligopolistic and monopolistically competitive market structures.

Quality competition has advantages for the consumer, because constant research on the products placed on the market results in a greater variety of styles and types from which the consumer can select. However, these industries, because of the intense non-price competition, tend to be the least efficient.

See also Product Differentiation.

QUANTITATIVE CONTROLS of the Federal Reserve System, instruments of monetary policy that directly affect the quantity of money in circulation. The three major quantitative controls are changes in reserve requirements, changes in the discount rate, and open-market operations. All such controls influence the multiple expansion of the money supply through their effect on excess reserves. Any action that reduces actual reserves or increases required reserves has the effect of reducing excess reserves, putting downward pressure on the money supply by reducing demand deposits of depository institutions.

The effect of changes in reserve requirements is direct and obvious, immediately affecting excess reserves and the bank multiplier. A 1% change in reserve requirements on just demand deposits produces a $2 billion change in excess reserves, which is frequently too large to do what is required. Such changes, therefore, have been infrequent.

A change in discount rates alters the cost of acquiring additional reserves by borrowing from the Federal Reserve banks and, hence, tends to affect actual reserves. In practice, however, banks have been encouraged to reduce their borrowings to the absolute minimum, and changes in the discount rate have little practical effect. They do, however, signal the thinking of the central bank, thus influencing the banks psychologically or morally.

Open-market operations are by far the most important tool of monetary policy. Aside from affecting the money supply directly, they change the actual reserves of the commercial banks, as well as influencing interest rates on government securities. Open-market dealings can be carried out in any volume over any time period, and they can be reversed instantly if necessary.   —*Walter W. Haines*

See also Discount Rate; Open-Market Operations; Qualitative Controls; Reserve Requirement.

QUANTITATIVE SUBSTANTIALITY. In interpretation of the Clayton Act, it must be determined if firms engaging in practices prohibited by that act tend to lessen competition substantially. Until recent years, the rule of "proportional substantiality," or percent of the market affected by the practice, was emphasized. Now attention is shifting to the rule of "quantitative substantiality," or the absolute dollar volume of trade affected irrespective of the percent of the market involved.

See also Substantial Lessening of Competition.

QUANTITY DEMANDED, the number of units of a commodity that are or would be purchased per time period at a specific price. Quantities of a commodity purchased change from one time period to another but the change is called a change in quantity demanded only if the different purchase level is caused by a price change. Changes in quantities demanded occur from movements along a given demand curve in response to price changes and not from changes in tastes, prices of related goods, or expectational changes. Parametric changes of the latter sort cause entire demand functions to change, and the result is called a change in demand and not a change in quantity demanded.

QUANTITY SUPPLIED is, technically speaking, merely a point on the supply curve. At any given price, quantity supplied can be found at the perpendicular from the curve to the X axis. The often-missed, but essential, distinction is that supply and demand are schedules, not points.

Since supply is a schedule of intentions, then a change in supply implies a new functional relationship between price and quantity supplied. At any given price, quantity supplied will be different. Or putting it in a more meaningful context, since one of the variables previously held constant has now varied, then before a *given* quantity will be voluntarily supplied by a producer, price must be higher or lower (depending on the circumstances).

Contrasted with this is a change in quantity supplied which can result (holding supply, the schedule, constant) only from a change in price. Given the supply schedule, a change in price can occur only due to a change in the demand schedule. Geometrically, a change in supply is represented by a shift upward or forward from the original schedule; a change in quantity supplied is a movement along the original supply schedule. 　　　　　　　　*—Robert L. Brite*

QUANTITY THEORY OF MONEY. *See* Equation of Exchange.

QUASI RENT, the payment in the short run to the owners of a resource above that which is necessary to keep that resource employed in its current use. In the purely competitive model, this quasi rent is equal to the excess profits due to the existence of a unique factor of production, either a human or a material factor of production. In the long run, this quasi rent will disappear because the opportunity cost of the resource will increase and this excess profit will disappear.

It has recently been acknowledged that the government can create economic rent for firms by imposing barriers to entry for other firms and the like. If this is the case, then firms will try to get the government to take these kinds of actions on their behalf. This is called *rent-seeking theory*. Rent seeking was first discussed in economics by George Stigler, who received the Nobel Prize in economics primarily for this work.

QUESNAY, FRANÇOIS (1694-1774), the leader and most important thinker among the Physiocrats. The personal physician to Louis XV, Quesnay first wrote on medicine and philosophy, then turned to economics late in his career, making contributions in a number of areas.

The role of a natural order was central to Quesnay's system, with the natural order being determined according to the principle of economic individualism: in working for himself or herself, every individual would be working in the best interest of the society. This concept became the central theme in the works of Adam Smith and other classical economists. However, Quesnay's most significant contribution was the *Tableau Économique* (1758), the first macroeconomic circular flow model.

See also Invisible Hand; Physiocrats; Physiocrats; Tableau Économique.

QUOTAS. Import quotas set limits, in physical or value terms, on the amount of a good that can be received into a country during a given time. The limits may be on a country or global basis. A "tariff quota" does not set a fixed limit on imports but sets the amount beyond which higher duties apply. A licensing system is usually necessary in the administration of quotas and, unless the licenses are auctioned off, windfall profits can accrue to fortunate applicants. From the standpoint of the country using them, quotas have advantages over tariffs: they are a more certain

and precise instrument of control and they can be changed by administrative decree.

See also Tariffs; Trade Barriers.

RAILWAY LABOR ACT (1926), legislation that tried to promote labor and management organization, so that the collective bargaining of new contract interpretation disputes would promote labor-management harmony and, hence, uninterrupted railway service. It was the outgrowth of the government's regulation of railroads, and its intention was that free collective bargaining, protected by law, be an essential feature of the rail industry's operation. Air carriers are also covered by this law.

Provisions. Among its most significant features was its specification of ways in which peaceful settlements of contract disputes were to be reached when private collective bargaining failed. Alternative methods of dispute resolution were (1) mediation of disputes in contract interpretation over pay, work rules, and working conditions by the Railroad Adjustment Board, a new agency set up by the act or, if the dispute was over new contract terms, by the National Mediation Board; (2) voluntary arbitration; and (3) action by Congress following the report of a presidentially-appointed fact-finding board. 　　　　　　*—Leonard G. Shifrin*

RANDOM NUMBERS. A useful aid in selecting a random sample is a table of random numbers, numbers printed in random fashion. By numbering items in the population and selecting those items whose numbers occur in the random number table, we can be assured of a random sample.

See also Sampling.

RATE BASE, term describing the measured value of the capital of a public utility. The regulated firm is allowed to earn profits (revenues in excess of operating costs) equal to the rate base times the policy-determined fair rate of return. Determination of the rate base is a major factor in the determination of the rates that the utility can charge its customers. Most regulatory bodies determine the rate base through some combination of the original cost of a firm's capital stock and the cost of replacing the capital stock.

See also Rate Level; Regulation.

RATE LEVEL, the general level of rates (prices) of a regulated company. The primary concern of regulatory commissions is to control rate levels so as to prevent regulated firms from exploiting their monopoly position by setting unreasonably high prices, restricting output, or receiving excessive profits.

See also Public Utility Price; Regulation.

RATE OF RETURN, the earnings of a regulated company as a percentage of its rate base (the value of the property it uses to provide its services). Earnings are calculated by deducting current operating costs and depreciation from the firm's revenues for the relevant time period. Usually, regulatory commissions attempt to establish a rate of return that prevents firms from receiving unregulated monopoly profits but still allows them to attract new capital.

See also Rate Base; Regulation.

RATE OF SUBSTITUTION. *See* Marginal Rate of Substitution.

RATIONAL EXPECTATIONS refers to an assumption about expectations behavior which is used by some economists. Many dynamic economic models depend in large part on assumptions about how economic agents form forecasts of the future levels of important variables. Traditionally, economists assumed that expectations are formed by looking at past values of the variables in question. Advocates of rational expectations argue that this type of modeling of expectations is naive. The assumption of rational expectations is the assumption that people form their expectations based upon the appropriate economic model. This appropriate economic model most times includes much more than past values of the variable in question.

The major results of the application of rational expectations have focused on macroeconomics. Rational expectations models have been developed which show that both fiscal and monetary policy are completely ineffective. The modelers argue that if expectations are formed rationally, the consequences of the policy will be anticipated and economic agents will act in such a way that the impacts of the policy are voided. Much of the research in macroeconomics is focusing on discussions of the validity of models based on rational expectations assumptions.

RATIONAL IGNORANCE, the decision by an economic agent that the cost of obtaining information outweighs the consequences of ignorance. Information is costly, and it takes a certain amount of time and effort, and often money, to become an informed consumer. Information for decision-making is therefore sought only as long as the benefits expected from acquiring more information exceed the costs of acquiring it. Beyond that point, consumers rationally choose to be ignorant. Thus, private decision-making is inevitably flawed because economic agents choose to be somewhat rationally ignorant. *Consumer Reports* and similar consumer information services have emerged to help consumers obtain information more efficiently.

RATIONAL WAGE DIFFERENTIALS, often referred to as equalizing wage differentials, are wage differentials given to workers in order to compensate for non-monetary differences in jobs, such as unpleas-

ant tasks, inconvenience, or danger. Differentials are usually paid, for example, to those workers who are employed on graveyard shifts, who work more than six days without an off-day, and who work overtime. In addition, jobs involving an element of danger, such as parachutist or skin diver, carry wage differentials of a rational nature.

See also Wage Differentials.

RATIONING, in an economic system, the method by which scarce resources can be allocated between competing uses. Because of scarcity, there are not enough goods and services to satisfy the needs and wants of all the people; thus, these scarce goods must be rationed.

There are basically two ways that rationing may be accomplished in an economic system. The first, and by far the most important, is the rationing effect of prices in the market. For example, if a shortage develops in the market for a particular commodity desired by consumers, and consumers refuse to pay the higher prices and shift purchases into other products, factors are freed from the industry characterized by the shortage. So, goods are automatically rationed.

However, at times rationing through the price mechanism seems too harsh. For example, the shortage may involve a necessity, and citizens would suffer greatly if unable to purchase it. In this situation, the government may use price ceilings to keep the market price from getting too high. If price ceilings are instituted, the price cannot be used to ration the good fully. In most cases of price ceilings, the rationing device is "first come, first served." This usually results in long lines, and those who cannot wait do not get the good.

Other methods of rationing are black markets (the good is sold illegally at the higher price), coupon rationing (the government issues coupons or tickets that a buyer must have to purchase the good), discrimination in selling (firms sell only to their friends or regular customers or do not sell to certain groups, such as minorities), and tied sales (firms require that you buy a non-controlled good at a higher price with the purchase of the price-controlled good. In the gas crisis, some firms were requiring customers to buy a quart of oil at $10 with the purchase of gasoline).

— *Timothy P. Ryan*

See also Scarcity.

REAL FLOW involves the physical movement of goods and services and/or the use of factors of production. Goods and services flow from producers, usually business firms and government, to purchasers, including consumers, or other business firms. Factors of production flow to producers in exchange for factor payments. Since money is used as a means of exchange, there are money flows to compensate for the real flows of goods, services, and factors of production.

See also Circular Flow of Income; Money Flow.

REAL INCOME. *See* Price Level.

REAL PROPERTY is land and any asset permanently attached to it, including buildings and trees and any asset that occurs naturally under the surface of it, including petroleum, sand, minerals, and so forth. A house is real property and is distinguished legally from chattels or personal property.

In an economic system in which real property is predominantly privately owned, there are necessarily restrictions on the owners' rights with respect to the property. Property rights are governed by law and are protected by the Constitution.

The supply of land and the resources that occur naturally under the surface of land are fixed in absolute quantity. While it is possible to find substitutes for these real property resources, we cannot generally augment their quantities. As population and income grow, the demand for real property resources tends to rise. Rising prices may lead to economic rents and increasing wealth for the owners. —*John P. Formby*

See also Rent.

REAL WAGES, the amount of goods and services that can be purchased with the money received for labor rendered, the purchasing power of nominal (money) wages. A common expression for the real wage is (nominal wages/price level) with the price level at a certain time set to be one (1).

Because real wages represent the cost of living, they can change without the nominal wage changing. In the rapid price increases of the late 1970s and early 1980s, the real wage fell for most employees even though nominal wages increased during that period.

RECALL, the term used when employees who have previously been laid off by a company are called back to work. In keeping with seniority rights, the last person laid off is usually the first person to be recalled.

RECESSION. *See* Business Cycles, Phases.

RECIPROCAL DEALING. *See* Conglomerate.

RECIPROCAL TRADE AGREEMENTS ACT. The Hawley-Smoot Tariff (1930) raised U.S. tariffs to the highest levels in history. The Reciprocal Trade Agreements Act (1934) gave the president the power to negotiate treaties with foreign countries to reduce tariff barriers on a reciprocal basis by as much as 50%. Later, the base for the 50% limit was tariffs prevailing on January 1, 1945. Before the General Agreement on Tariffs and Trade (1947) the United States had negotiated trade agreements with 29 countries. U.S.

tariffs were reduced by more than 75% between 1934 and the final expiration of the Reciprocal Trade Agreements Act in 1962. The act had been renewed 11 times over that span of years and the last renewals had included weakening amendments related to escape clauses, peril-point provisions, and national security clauses.

See also Multinational Trade Agreements.

RECOGNITION, employer acceptance of a union as the bargaining agent for a group of workers. Usually, the union must prove it is the choice of the majority of workers in the bargaining unit by winning an election conducted by the National Labor Relations Board (NLRB). By law, the employer must recognize and bargain with a union certified by the NLRB as the representative of the workers.

See also Bargaining Unit.

RECOVERY. *See* Business Cycles, Phases.

REDUNDANT CAPACITY. *See* Excess Capacity.

REFUSAL TO BARGAIN, failure by a negotiating party to bargain in good faith with the other. Either's refusal to bargain is a violation of federal labor law and is thus an unfair labor practice with potentially serious consequences for the offending party.

REGRESSION. *See* Curve Fitting.

REGRESSIVE TAX, a tax whose rate decreases as the tax base increases. With income used as the tax base, taxes paid *as a percentage of income* will decrease as income increases. This means that the marginal rate is less than the average rate as the tax base increases. The sales tax is an example of a regressive tax because the same tax rate causes people with lower incomes to pay a relatively larger percentage of their incomes.

See also Progressive Tax; Taxation.

REGULATED INDUSTRIES, as designated by Congress and state legislatures certain industries, regulated by semi-independent commissions. Among the industries subject to public regulation are the transportation, power transmission, communications, and atomic energy industries. Because many of these industries are natural monopolies that provide customers with essential services for which no good substitutes exist, the prices and the quality of their services are regulated so as to ensure that consumers can obtain desired amounts at reasonable prices.

Regulatory Agencies. The interstate transmission and sale for resale of electricity and natural gas is regulated by the Federal Energy Regulatory Commission. These products, which are sold by natural monopolists, are essential to consumers and there are few good substitutes for them. The Commission also regulates the prices of natural gas producers. This control does not seem justified because there are thousands of competing producers; moreover, ceilings imposed on producers' prices seem to have resulted in a shortage of natural gas.

The railroad, motor carrier, water carrier, and oil pipeline industries are regulated by the Interstate Commerce Commission. Although public regulation may at one time have been necessary in most of these industries, its usefulness has been questioned increasingly in recent years as competition has grown among different transportation modes. For similar reasons, doubts about the desirability of economic regulation of commercial air transportation by the Civil Aeronautics Board led to that agency's elimination at the end of 1984. There has been extensive "deregulation" of the airline and motor-carrier industries, and some in the railroad industry as well.

The Federal Communications Commission regulates broadcasting (radio and television) and interstate telephone and telegraph services. Telephone and telegraph services are regulated because they are essential to consumers and are produced by natural monopolists. Broadcasting is regulated because of the limited space available on the radio spectrum. Some people argue, however, that there is little economic justification for FCC regulation of broadcasting and that the limited air space could be allocated by allowing broadcast licenses to be bought and sold in the market like other property rights.   —*Joseph Jadlow*

See also Civil Aeronautics Board; Interstate Commerce Commission; Public Utilities.

REGULATION, the social control of regulated industries. The three basic devices are regulation of entry, regulation of price, and regulation of service. These three are interrelated, and it is necessary to utilize all three in order for regulation to be even minimally effective.

Entry. Entry is controlled by use of certificates of public convenience and necessity, franchises, licenses and permits. One firm, or a limited number, is allowed to operate in a given service territory with the explicit idea that the public will be better served by one large supplier than by many smaller competing firms. Also, since regulated industries use public streets, highways, and thoroughfares, the public will be inconvenienced less by one firm than by many. In return for this monopoly privilege, the firm must serve all comers and assume other "common law" and common carrier obligations.

Price. In order that the supplier firm does not exploit its monopolistic position, prices must be controlled. Discrimination in price and service must be avoided. Likewise, it has been deemed to be in the public interest that the supplier firm be economically sound and able to serve. Hence the *rate level* must be such that the firm earn a fair return on a fair value.

Service. Finally, the service offered is controlled in some ways because (1) there is a natural tendency of a monopolistic supplier firm to maximize its return by lowering service levels under regulated prices, and (2) there is a need to impose some level of service capability as a substitute for the natural action of the market mechanism under competition. Service competition regulation takes many forms, such as levels of

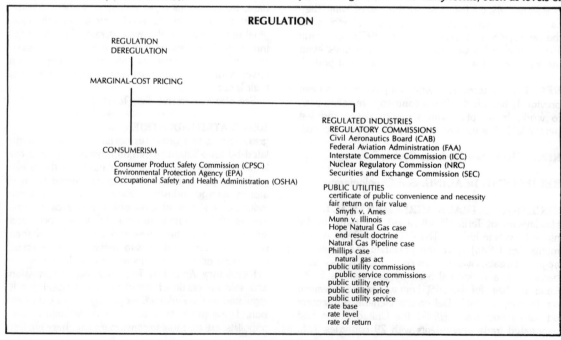

REGULATION

REGULATION
DEREGULATION

MARGINAL-COST PRICING

CONSUMERISM
    Consumer Product Safety Commission (CPSC)
    Environmental Protection Agency (EPA)
    Occupational Safety and Health Administration (OSHA)

REGULATED INDUSTRIES
    REGULATORY COMMISSIONS
    Civil Aeronautics Board (CAB)
    Federal Aviation Administration (FAA)
    Interstate Commerce Commission (ICC)
    Nuclear Regulatory Commission (NRC)
    Securities and Exchange Commission (SEC)

PUBLIC UTILITIES
    certificate of public convenience and necessity
    fair return on fair value
      Smyth v. Ames
    Munn v. Illinois
    Hope Natural Gas case
      end result doctrine
    Natural Gas Pipeline case
    Phillips case
      natural gas act
    public utility commissions
      public service commissions
    public utility entry
    public utility price
    public utility service
    rate base
    rate level
    rate of return

safety, frequency, and routes in transportation and reliability, minimum physical attributes of service, and obligation to serve all customers in utilities.

During the late 1960s and early 1970s, there was a significant trend toward regulation of the marketplace in general, not just of firms that have monopoly powers. This nontraditional regulation was characterized by the creation of the Environmental Protection Agency, the Occupational Safety and Health Administration, and the Consumer Product Safety Commission. More recently, there has been a marked trend toward "deregulation," or a removal of regulatory constraints on businesses. Both trends represent significant departures from the past regulatory pattern.
— *Martin T. Farris*

See also Public Utilities.

REGULATION Q. *See* Interest Rate Ceiling.

REGULATION T. *See* Margin Requirement.

REGULATION U. *See* Margin Requirement.

REGULATION W. *See* Installment Credit Controls.

REGULATION X. *See* Mortgage Lending Controls.

REGULATORY COMMISSIONS, semi-independent agencies that control industries by public regulation. Such a commission usually consists of three to seven members who are appointed or elected for five- to seven-year overlapping terms. Ordinarily, the law requires that a political party have no more than a one-man majority of commission members, that a commissioner be discharged only for neglect of duty, and that a commission be independent of the executive branch of government but subject to judicial review.

It was once assumed that independent regulatory commissions would be composed of experts, that they would be free from political pressures, that overlapping terms would ensure continuity and consistency of decisions, that their procedures would be flexible, and that they would act quickly. Instead, politicians have tended to be appointed or elected to commissions, commission decisions have often been inconsistent, procedures have become rigidly institutionalized and slow, and pressure from the government and industry have influenced commission decisions. It has been recommended that regulatory efficiency and accountability would be improved if certain commissions were replaced by single administrators. — *Joseph Jadlow*
See also Public Utility Commissions.

RELATIVE FACTOR PRICES, the ratio of input prices, play an important role in profit maximization for the entrepreneur. The firm must choose a combination of inputs, out of the manifold possibilities, that minimizes the cost of producing a given output. To do so, the firm must take into consideration relative factor prices and factor substitutability. Relative factor prices and the respective quantities of the factors in an economy determine the distribution of income. The supply of the respective factors, interacting mutually with the demand for these factors, determines relative factor prices.

RENT has a number of distinct meanings in economics.

Rent is a payment to the owners of real property, such as land, housing, commercial space or some other durable good for use of the real property. Rental payments in this sense are made not only for the use of land but also for physical capital, including interest and depreciation on the capital, and possibly even for janitorial service, protection service, and repair service. It is this concept of rent that is most common in everyday usage. However, from the point of view of economic analysis, this concept of rent is not very useful. The payment of rent for use of land alone—excluding any physical capital on the land—is the return to the resource "land" in the same sense as wages and salaries are the return to the resource "labor."

Rent in the National Income and Product Accounts is denoted as rental income of persons and is one of four major sources of national income. The rental income of persons consists of net rents of non-farm persons, the imputed value of net rental income from owner-occupied housing, and net rents of farm realty. Property taxes, depreciation, interest, and maintenance expenses are deducted from gross rent to arrive at net rent. Rental income of business firms is not included as rent in the National Income and Product Accounts, but rather as profits. It should be clear that the net rental income of persons really represents the profits accruing to individuals from their rental activities.

Economic Rent is any payment in the long-run period to an owner of a resource (factor of production) that is not necessary to keep the resource in its current use. The resource may either be a property resource or a human resource. The payment necessary to keep a resource in its current use is the opportunity cost of the resource, that is, the value of the resource in the best alternative use. The opportunity cost is the real social cost of the resource. Economic rent, or pure rent, as it is occasionally designated, is a payment in excess of the real cost of the resource and constitutes a socially unnecessary payment that could be, if identifiable, taxed away with no change in the allocation of resources. Even if it is not a social cost, rent will be reckoned as a private cost by the person (or firm) paying it. To the recipient, rent is a source of income.

Classical Land Rent is the payment to the owner of

land which has only one use. The opportunity cost of such land is zero. In classical economics land was defined as "the indestructible powers and qualities of the soil." It was assumed implicitly by David Ricardo, one of the greatest of the classical economists and an important contributor to rent theory, that such land had only one use. Any payment to the owner of land is, thus, an economic rent. Ricardo and other economists failed to realize that the owners of resources other than land may receive economic rents and that land, like other resources, has more than one use.

—*John P. Formby*

See also Economic Rent; Implicit Rent; Quasi Rent; Real Property.

REPURCHASE AGREEMENTS, or Repos, transactions in which a borrower sells securities to a lender with an agreement to buy back the securities at a specified time at a specified rate. Repurchase agreements are usually of short duration. Overnight repurchase agreements are especially attractive to private and public enterprises as a way of earning interest on cash balances with minimal risk of being caught short of operating funds.

RESALE PRICE MAINTENANCE, the setting by the supplier of the prices that a customer firm may charge for a particular product purchased from the supplier. This is essentially vertical price fixing and is often called retail price maintenance. For example, a cosmetics manufacturer could insist that a retailer charge the manufacturer's list price to its customers, thus precluding the product from being sold at a discount by price-cutting retailers.

Largely as an effort to stem the trend toward large-scale high volume retailing and to preserve the importance of "mom and pop" stores, Congress passed several pieces of legislation that promoted (and in some cases forced) the practice of resale price maintenance. Most notable were the Miller-Tydings Act (1937) and the McGuire-Keogh Act (1952). These acts have been accused of maintaining competitors at the expense of competition. In a major policy reversal, Congress repealed both acts in 1977, making vertical price fixing illegal. There is still debate among experts as to whether or not resale price maintenance is a desirable or a detrimental business practice.

See also Fair-Trade Laws; McGuire-Keogh Act; Miller-Tydings Act.

RESEARCH AND DEVELOPMENT, usually a branch or part of a firm devoted to improving existing products and developing new ones. Research and development programs are seldom found in purely competitive market structures, but are quite common in imperfectly competitive market structures, such as monopolistically competitive, oligopolistic, and monopolistic industries.

Because imperfectly competitive market structures often use nonprice competition to gather shares of the markets, it is essential that firms constantly make improvements in their products in order to remain competitive with each other. This is especially impor-

Research and development is essential for success in the construction of any product, such as these missiles being built at a Lockheed plant.

tant in monopolistically competitive markets where product differentiation plays a major role in distinguishing products of one firm from those of others in the industry. Also, in oligopolistic markets where there are only a few firms, a firm that did not improve its product could easily be forced out of the market.

See also Product Differentiation.

RESERVE-ASSET COMPOSITION. *See* Intervention Currency.

RESERVE BANK CREDIT is the amount of money provided by the Federal Reserve banks to the banking system as a result of their loans and purchases of securities.

See also Discount Rate; Federal Reserve System; Open-Market Operations.

RESERVE CITY BANK. *See* Member Bank.

RESERVE CURRENCY. *See* International Monetary System.

RESERVE REQUIREMENT, or LEGAL RESERVES, the minimum amount of reserves that a bank must maintain, stated as a percentage of its deposit liabilities. If a bank has $100 million in deposits and a 16% reserve requirement, it must hold $16 million in reserves. Although a few states set requirements for savings banks, reserves are normally applicable only to commercial banks. Reserve requirements for member banks of the Federal Reserve System are established by its Board of Governors within limits set by Congress. The Monetary Control Act of 1980 expanded the Federal Reserve's control of reserves to non-member banks and also to thrift institutions with a phase-in of new required reserve percentages to be in operation by September 1987. Against time deposits the range is 3% for time deposits of 18 months' maturity or less and 10% for time deposits of longer maturity. Against demand deposits the range is 3% for each bank's first $28.9 million and 12% for higher amounts.

Legal reserves for member banks consist only of vault cash and deposits with the Federal Reserve banks. The legal reserve ratios for non-member state banks, determined by state law, are frequently similar in amount to requirements of the Federal Reserve but may include deposits in other commercial banks. In foreign countries various forms of securities may be counted as part of legal reserves.

Changing reserve requirements can be a strong instrument of monetary policy: the multiple expansion of the money supply depends on banks having excess reserves over the legal requirement. Thus, raising reserve requirements reduces excess reserves and the bank multiplier, putting downward pressure on the money supply; lowering requirements has exactly the opposite effect. In practice changes of reserve requirements have been rather rare, because as a monetary tool they are considered overly blunt, causing more extensive swings in the money supply than is usually desired. — *Walter W. Haines*

RESERVES, currency or certain other liquid assets retained by a bank as a fund that can be used to meet the demands of depositors who wish to withdraw cash from their accounts. Reserves may be stated as a dollar amount or, more commonly, as a percentage of the bank's deposit liabilities, the reserve ratio.

Form of Reserves. The particular form that reserves may take varies according to circumstances and often is defined by law. Vault cash is the only thing that can be paid out on the spot and, thus, is the basic form of reserves, but deposits in other banks are becoming increasingly important as a form of reserve. When a bank maintains a deposit account in another bank (referred to by the depositing bank as "due from banks"), it can speedily withdraw cash from this account to meet the demands of its own customers. In the United States most large banks hold such deposits in the Federal Reserve bank of which they are members, but they may also maintain deposits in other ordinary banks, and smaller banks invariably hold such accounts. When a bank maintains a deposit account in another bank, both banks are referred to as correspondents of each other. Serving also for clear-

ing checks between banks, correspondent balances are more useful, though a little less readily available, than vault cash.

Other assets that are highly liquid may be readily sold to obtain cash if needed, and these assets are frequently called secondary reserves, because they can be called upon when primary reserves are exhausted. Secondary reserves earn interest for the bank. Secondary reserves may include Treasury bills or other government securities, bank acceptances, or call loans.

Size of Reserves. Because primary reserves do not earn interest, a bank likes to keep them as low as possible, but maintaining too low a level invites bank failures if depositors ask for cash in unexpectedly large amounts. In the absence of legal requirements, each bank must decide for itself what level is safe by weighing past experience with the current practices of the business community. The more readily that checks are accepted as money, the lower the reserve ratio may safely be. In the earliest days of banking, 100% reserves were kept, but as checks became more and more common, the reserve ratio fell to its present level, below 20%.

Today most countries establish reserve requirements by law, specifying how much a bank must keep in reserves. Because these reserves must be on hand at all times, they cannot be used to pay depositors and no longer, therefore, serve as a fund available to meet withdrawals. — *Walter W. Haines*

See also Reserve Requirement.

RESOLUTION TRUST CORPORATION (RTC), organization created in 1989 as a part of President Bush's plan to bail out and restructure insolvent savings and loan institutions. RTC is a private corporation charged with taking control of more than 300 insolvent S&Ls. The mission of the RTC is to determine if those S&Ls should be closed or sold. A second agency, the Resolution Funding Corporation, will issue $50 billion in 30-year bonds that the RTC will use to pay off the indebtedness of the S&Ls. The RTC board includes the Secretary of the Treasury, the chairman of the Federal Reserve Board, and other prominent government officials.

RESOURCE MOBILITY refers to the relative freedom with which resources are able to move among alternative uses. Ideally, when all restraints are removed, resources—chiefly land, labor, capital, and entrepreneurship—should be able to move to the situation that offers the best opportunity or is the most profitable. Workers, for example, should be free to enter and exit jobs as better opportunities arise, and capital should be used in the most profitable ventures.

However, certain economic restraints hinder resource mobility. Among the major restraints is the lack of perfect knowledge of the market. Thus, workers and investors may not even know about opportunities that exist. A second restraint results from monopoly and monopsony structures that control such things as employment and natural resources. Other restraints include government intervention, geography and political policies.

See also Labor Mobility.

RESOURCE RIGHTS, the right to own and use certain scarce resources, usually the type that are fixed in terms of known available quantities. Examples are land, certain minerals, and fresh water. Confronted with conditions of unlimited human economic wants and nationally determined goals (a certain economic growth rate, national defense, etc.) and that of the fixed character of certain natural resources, a society must determine the rules dealing with ownership and utilization of scarce resources.

In the free-market society, resource rights are based on a variety of rules: (1) the concept of private ownership of property, (2) licensing by a government agency providing rights to a firm to mine or to take a natural resource, and (3) setting of quotas on the amount of the resource that may be taken in a given time period. The reasons for restrictions include the public's need for certain resources for present and future use and the need to maintain a livable environment.

Resource rights may also have an international dimension. When scarce resources are owned by foreign capital, a government may decide to confiscate such resources for national purposes.

RESOURCES, the inputs with which products are produced. Economists distinguish four basic resources: land, labor, enterprise, and capital. *Land* refers to all natural resources. *Labor* is usually defined to include the productive contribution of all human beings, with the exception of the entrepreneur. *Enterprise* is the contribution of the entrepreneur, who initiates productive activity, takes risks, and makes important production decisions. *Capital* includes all producers, buildings, machines, and tools and some materials.

Resources are usually scarce, not available in unlimited quantities relative to the demand for them. They must, therefore, be paid some return. Specifically, land, labor, enterprise, and capital receive rent, wages, profits, and interest, respectively. All other resources are combinations of the four basic resources. Aluminum, for example, comes from land and is worked on by labor, capital, and enterprise before emerging as a widely used input.

RESTRAINT OF TRADE, collusive action by a business firm or firms to control or eliminate competition or to prevent the emergence of new competitors. The effect sought is the enhancement of price and thereby the profits of the agreeing firms. The specific practices used range from tight-knit combinations such as cartels and bidding rings to basing-point systems, trade associations, and conscious parallelism of action. Enhancement of price is also facilitated by indirect methods such as market sharing, quotas, and other forms of territorial allocation whereby the downward price pressure exerted by direct competition is avoided.

Contracts, combinations, and conspiracies in restraint of trade are prohibited in the Sherman Antitrust Act (along with monopolization). The keys to enforcement of this prohibition are (1) the availability to government prosecutors of evidence of agreement among nominal competitors and (2) the nature of the agreement. Certain practices are considered illegal *per se* where evidence indicates overt agreement to fix prices or share markets. Such violations are not defensible on the grounds that either the action or the result was "reasonable." Where evidence of agreement is less certain, such as in price-reporting plans of trade associations, courts must consider how seriously competition was affected adversely. Similarly, difficult interpretation attends the practice of "conscious parallelism" where the effect of price fixing is achieved oftentimes without any overt agreement among competitors.

The prohibitions on restraint of trade and monopolization state in law the society's conviction (1) that price competition, as the impersonal and automatic regulator of activity in a market economy, is most satisfactory and efficient, and (2) that artificial barriers to the operation of competition should be condemned.   —*Thomas O. Depperschmidt*

See also Antitrust Policy; Collusion; Conscious Parallelism; Market Sharing; Price Fixing; Trade Associations.

RESTRICTED ENTRY. *See* Public Utility Entry.

RESTRICTION OF NUMBERS, a term used to describe the policy of certain labor groups that try to limit the number of workers in that group. Certain trade unions, in order to keep the price of their labor high, restrict the number of workers that can enter the union.

RESTRICTION OF OUTPUT, a method used chiefly in oligopolistic or monopolistic market structures to keep prices high. When an industry has complete control over the production of an item, it may be advantageous for that industry to restrict output in such a way that individuals are willing to pay higher prices to obtain the product.

RETAIL PRICE MAINTENANCE. *See* Resale Price Maintenance.

RETAINED EARNINGS OR UNDISTRIBUTED

PROFITS, a business' income after taxes and dividends have been paid. Retained earnings serve as an internal source of funds for business expansion and allow a company to finance its growth without diluting stockholders' equity or increasing fixed-interest obligations.

RETURNS TO SCALE, a term used to describe how output responds to changes in inputs in the long run when the scale (amount of capital) of the plant can also be changed. There are three possible outcomes: (1) output may increase at a rate proportionate to the increase in all inputs. This result is called constant returns to scale; (2) output may increase at a rate that is less than proportionate to the increase in all inputs. This result is called decreasing returns to scale; and (3) output may increase at a rate that is more than proportionate to the increase in all inputs. This result is called increasing returns to scale.

Unlike economies of scale, returns to scale are determined solely by production technology.

See also Economies of Scale.

REUTHER, WALTER PHILIP (1907-1970), American labor leader. Educated at Wayne University, Reuther worked as a tool and die maker for Wheeling Steel until 1927. In 1933, after his discharge from Ford Motor Company for union activism, he went abroad, spending 18 months traveling in Europe and Russia. While in Russia, he worked at the Ford Plant in Gorki. In 1935 Reuther assisted in the founding of the United Automobile Workers. He became UAW vice president in 1942 and was its president from 1946 until his death.

REVEALED PREFERENCE THEORY OF DEMAND, a relatively new theory in microeconomics, that attempts to derive indifference curves based on actual behavior, rather than from a person's stated preferences. The method is behaviorist: observe what people do rather than what they say they do.

Given a person's preference (tastes), money income can be varied experimentally; reaction to these changes can be recorded. Thus, in principle, a person chooses one bundle of goods and services over another either because it is more preferable or because it is affordable while the other is not. If prices are varied so that both bundles cost the same, and the same bundle is chosen, it may be deduced that this bundle is revealed preferred to the other. Advanced texts indicate how, graphically, this procedure can be carried out often enough to eliminate zones of ignorance as to where the indifference curve is located. Recently, revealed preference has provided a basis for testing to see if empirically observed behavior can be rationalized by a well-behaved utility function.

REVENUE SHARING. *See* Fiscal Federalism.

REVISIONISM, an approach to socialism based on the systematic reexamination and correcting of Marx's doctrines. Led by Edward Bernstein (1850-1932) in Germany, who contended that many accepted Marxian theories had proved incorrect, the revisionists believed that socialism would be reached by evolutionary means, consciously reconstructing the social system, not through the breakdown of capitalism as Marx had predicted.

See also Evolutionary Socialism; Fabian Society.

REVOLUTIONARY SOCIALISM implies the necessity of using force to secure desired social changes and attain a socialist society. The doctrine assumes that (1) capitalism involves a constant class war between capitalists and workers; (2) if capitalists have power bestowed upon them via ownership of capital, they will then exploit the workers; (3) government and laws would assist in this exploitation, primarily by enforcing property rights; and (4) the proletariat, therefore, cannot acquire power over the economic system without gaining possession of the political state. The basic work for revolutionary socialism is the *Communist Manifesto* (1848) of Karl Marx and Friedrich Engels.

See also Evolutionary Socialism; Lenin, Vladimir; Marx, Karl.

RICARDIAN SOCIALISM. *See* Pre-Marxian Socialism.

RICARDO, DAVID (1772-1823), considered by some to be the greatest classical economist, was the first major economist to develop a rigorous theoretical model based upon abstract thought and building upon the works of his predecessors. However, Ricardo shifted from the Smithian focus upon development to an emphasis upon distribution; he foresaw economic progress leading not toward a bright future but toward a dim future, with subsistence being the lot of most of the people.

Ricardo's contributions in his *Principles of Economics* (1817) fall into several categories:

Value Theory. While Ricardo had a general cost-of-production theory of value, he was interested in changes in the rate at which exchange between goods occurs. He felt this rate was the result of changes in the relative content of labor embodied in the goods. This assumption served as a foundation for Marx's labor theory of value.

Differential Theory of Rent. Combining the concept of diminishing returns with the principle of intensive and extensive margins, Ricardo developed a theory of the return to land which was in essence a marginal productivity theory.

Wage Theory. Ricardo held a subsistence view of wages based upon the wages fund doctrine.

International Trade. Building upon Smith's discussion of absolute advantage as a basis for international trade, Ricardo developed the concept of comparative advantage.   —*Clyde A. Haulman*

See also Classical Economics.

RIGHT-TO-WORK LAWS. *See* Agency Shop; Union Shop.

RISING EXPECTATIONS. *See* Demonstration Effect.

RISK, the possibility of gain or loss in an investment. As Frank Knight pointed out in *Risk, Uncertainty and Profit* (1921), many kinds of risk can be insured against because previous experience provides sufficient samples for actuarial calculations. The best-known example is the risk of loss from theft or fire. Though unpredictable for a given building, the likelihood of fire loss for a group of buildings is reasonably predictable. By pooling the premiums on a large number of buildings, insurance companies can eliminate risk.

In financial markets, risk is always of primary concern. Much of the innovations in the financial markets that occurred during the decade of the 1970s was concerned with ways to minimize financial risk. Hedging, selling short, and the purchase of certain futures contracts are methods of reducing financial risk.

See also Profit System; Uncertainty.

RISK AVERSION. *See* Expected Utility.

ROBINSON, JOAN (1903-1983), published her *The Economics of Imperfect Competition* (1933) a few months after Edward Chamberlin's *The Theory of Monopolistic Competition* appeared. Both studies covered the same basic material in developing the concept of monopolistic competition. In addition, Robinson considered the problem of the exploitation of labor in her discussion of distribution.

After the appearance of this work, Robinson expanded her studies to include Keynesian theory, international trade, and Marxian economics. Her *Essay on Marxian Economics* (1942) is an excellent critique of Marx's analysis and her *The Accumulation of Capital* (1956) expanded upon her earlier work. Her attention then turned toward the problems of growth and the development of a long-run version of the Keynesian system.

RUNAWAY INFLATION. *See* Hyperinflation.

RUN ON THE DOLLAR occurs when governments hasten to convert their dollars into gold—comparable to a run on a commercial bank—as they see that the United States has less and less gold relative to its dollar liabilities. Alternatively, they fear that the United States might increase the dollar price of gold (as actually occurred in December 1971), thus reducing the gold value of their dollar holdings; or, finally, they fear that

the United States might demonetize gold; that is, abrogate the gold convertibility of official dollars.

SAHLINS, MARSHALL (1930-   ), economic anthropologist noted for his book *Stone Age Economics* (1972), which questions the universality of the first assumption of economics: the assumption of scarcity. Sahlins points out that the majority of the world's people perceive abundance in the world rather than scarcity. This is because custom and tradition set their consumption at a modest level, so that needs and wants are easily satisfied with readily available resources. According to Sahlins, there are two possible roads to affluence: "Wants may be 'easily satisfied' either by producing much or desiring little." Modern industrial society has chosen the former, while most other societies have traditionally chosen the latter.

For Sahlins, scarcity is not a natural fact, like gravity, but rather a product of the market-industrial system. Economics assumes that human wants and desires are infinite and that the means for satisfying them are limited but improvable by means of advancements in technology and productivity. Nevertheless, the "axiom of local nonsatiation," the scarcity axiom, implies that there can never be "enough."

Sahlins points out that if a society begins with a different set of assumptions, it is possible to reach a "bliss point" of perceived plenty. Other cultures have achieved material satisfaction at low levels of consumption by assuming that wants and needs are bounded. Sahlins observes, "We are inclined to think of hunters and gatherers as *poor* because they don't have anything; perhaps better to think of them for that reason as *free.*"

SALARIES. One of the costs of production, salaries are payments made to white-collar workers to compensate for services rendered. Salaries include cash payments as well as in-kind income, which refers to such items as room and board. Wages are payments to factory and manual labor workers. Wages and salaries make up nearly two-thirds of national income and are very often one of the largest costs of a firm.

See also Factor Prices.

SALES TAX is a tax on the value of goods that are exchanged. Although a sales tax can be placed on any level of exchange (manufacturing, sale of inputs, wholesaling, retail sales), a tax on retail sales is by far the most common form of sales tax in the United States. A sales tax can be *general*, that is, imposed on almost all commodities, or it can be *selective*, imposed on a particular good or service. Selective sales taxes are also called specific sales taxes or excise taxes. Examples of selective sales taxes are taxes on cigarettes, gasoline, and motel rooms.

The general sales tax is one of the mainstays of state government finances, and its use as a local government tax source is rapidly growing. Over $113 billion in revenues were collected from this tax in 1985. Its range of usage extended from over 20% of all state and local government revenues in four states (Arizona, Hawaii, Tennessee, Washington) to no state or local sales tax in four other states (Delaware, Montana, New Hampshire, Oregon). Combined state and local general sales tax rates average around 5% of the sales price on an item, but are higher in some localities.

The sales tax is generally thought to be regressive, that is, lower-income households pay a larger percentage of their incomes in sales taxes than do higher-income households (higher-income households do tend to pay more total dollars in tax). This trend is exacerbated by the widespread exemption of the purchase of services from sales taxation; services are disproportionately purchased by higher-income households. In an effort to reduce the regressivity of the tax, 43 states exempt prescription drugs from taxation, and another 27 exempt most food purchases.

While no tax is ever popular, the sales tax is often well accepted by many people. Explanations for this finding include the fact that the tax is relatively painless—it is paid in very small amounts very frequently. Furthermore, the tax is often indirectly paid, with the tax viewed as part of the purchase price of a good. Finally, the tax is paid by virtually everyone, giving taxpayers a sense of tax equity.

—Michael S. Johnson

See also Taxation; Tax Incidence; Turnover Tax; Value-Added Tax.

SAMPLE. Since it is usually impractical or impossible to examine every member of a statistical population, it becomes necessary to examine a chosen set of members—the sample—and make inferences concerning the rest. A sample that contains all the members of a population is called a census. The random sample, in which each possible sample has an equal chance of being chosen, is the basis for statistical inference.

See also Inference; Population, Statistical; Sampling.

SAMPLING refers to the process of selecting for study a limited number of persons from a population in order to make inferences concerning the entire population. Although inference relies on random sampling, there are many sampling procedures that preserve randomness; stratified samples, cluster samples, and others.

The target population is the population whose characteristics we wish to infer; the sampled populations should therefore be identical. If the target population is all residents of Chicago, for example, a random sample from the telephone book will result in a sample population of Chicagoans who have telephones, and inferences based on this sample may not apply to the target population.

See also Inference; Population, Statistical; Sample.

SAMPLING DISTRIBUTION. If we take several random samples and compute the sample mean for each, it is likely that these sample means will not all be equal. The distribution of sample means is called the sampling distribution of means. The mean of the sampling distribution of means is the true population mean.

See also Sample; Sampling.

SAMPLING THEORY. A fundamental concept in statistical inference is the sampling distribution. The central limit theorem states that any sampling distribution of means will approach a normal distribution as the number of sample observations increases. In fact, for samples of 30 observations or more ("large samples") the normal curve is a close approximation of the sampling distribution and can be used for significance tests. For samples less than 30, the normal curve is not as good an approximation and other distributions must be used.

See also Confidence Interval; Hypothesis; Inference; Significance.

SAMUELSON, PAUL ANTHONY (1915-   ), one of the most important American contributors to economics. His early work concerning the interaction of the multiplier and accelerator helped to develop an important area of the Keynesian system. However,

Paul A. Samuelson

Samuelson's most important work is his *Foundations of Economic Analysis* (1947). In this work he used mathematics to support his position that the similarities among economic theories suggest the existence of a more general concept which binds together the various areas of economics. According to Samuelson, this concept was the equilibrium as a maximizing or minimizing situation, and the analyses of the forces around equilibrium and movements away from equilibrium are the main points of economic theory.

Samuelson applied his views to the theory of cost and production, to the theory of consumer demand, and to welfare economics. Of these, his revealed preference theory of consumer behavior is best known. Yet, Samuelson's most important contribution was his development of the concept of economic dynamics.

In addition to his *Foundations*, Samuelson has written numerous articles and books in many areas of economics including macroeconomic theory and policy and international trade. His widely used introductory textbook, *Economics*, has taught a new generation of economists. Also, his famous debate with Milton Friedman concerning the role of fiscal versus monetary policy has helped to bring important economic policy questions into focus.

For his many contributions, Samuelson was awarded the Nobel Prize in Economics (1970).

—*Clyde A. Haulman*

SAVING is dollars of income not spent (withdrawn from the income stream). When households save part of disposable income, they are not demanding the production of goods and services, the employment of labor, and the payment of incomes to the factors of production. When businesses retain earnings, the owners of the businesses do not spend the retained earnings on consumption goods and services. These business savings are considered the equivalent of savings by the owners, who have "left their savings" with the business.

Households frequently save with consumption in mind: for old age, vacations, etc. Households often save by making so-called "investments" (buying stocks or bonds but not capital goods) and may sometimes genuinely invest in capital goods. For instance, a family may save to obtain the purchasing power to start a business.

Firms save because they spend on investment goods and buy property, other firms, and existing goods, none of which are purchases of currently produced goods. A firm may save now to buy capital goods later or to repay old debts that financed past investment spending. Even when a firm is saving as it invests, it is extremely unlikely that the earnings retained will exactly equal the amount spent on new investment goods. Lack of saving by a business does not stop it from investing in new capital goods, be-

---

SAVING: TOPIC GUIDE

For the role of saving in the macroeconomy, see the articles on CIRCULAR FLOW OF INCOME, WITHDRAWALS, and SAVING INVESTMENT EQUALITY. The relationship between income and saving is also discussed in MARGINAL PROPENSITY TO SAVE. Some of the microeconomic aspects of saving are discussed in the articles on FACTOR SUPPLY, LOANABLE FUNDS, INTEREST, and INTEREST RATES.

The Subject Maps accompanying CIRCULAR FLOW OF INCOME and NATIONAL INCOME display additional aspects of saving.

---

cause it can borrow to pay for the new capital goods. It is because it is current investment spending, not past or future spending, that national income theory treats both household and business savings separately from investment spending.

—*Anne Mayhew and Walter C. Neale*
See also Consumption.

SAVINGS ACCOUNTS. *See* Saving; Time Deposits.

SAVINGS AND LOAN ASSOCIATIONS. *See* Financial Intermediaries.

SAVINGS BONDS. *See* Bonds; Government Securities.

SAVINGS FUNCTION. *See* Propensity to Save.

SAVINGS-INVESTMENT EQUALITY. National income determination is frequently explained by using a simple model of an economy in which there is no foreign trade (or in which exports equal imports) and no government expenditures or taxes (or one in which G = taxes). In this case, the equilibrium level of income will be that level at which savings equal investment.

See also National Income Determination: Changes.

SAY'S LAW is named after one of its early formulators, the French economist J.B. Say. Say's Law maintains that supply creates its own demand. Thus, there can be no general oversupply or glut of goods and services, because the total value of goods and services produced will be available for their purchase. It is implied that resources not consumed (released by saving) would be employed by investment expenditure. This law was important in the pre-Keynesian explanation of why, in the absence of interference with market mechanism, overproduction or underconsumption would not occur.

SCARCITY is the most critical economic problem. Scarcity results from the fact that there are not enough

---

SCARCITY: TOPIC GUIDE

Scarcity is a pervasive and central economic phenomenon. For other articles that describe the impact of the fact of economic scarcity, see CHOICE, ALLOCATION, and OPPORTUNITY COST. Analytical concepts that deal with economic decisions in the context of scarcity are presented in MARGINAL ANALYSIS.

---

resources in the world to satisfy all the wants and needs of all the people in the world. Scarcity limits the total output possible from the economy. The economic problem at any point in time, therefore, becomes one of choosing what goods and services to produce, how they should be produced, and who should get them, given the economy's limited means of production. Scarcity, however, does not imply that the amount of resources or state of technology is fixed over time; as the means of production change, corresponding changes in the economy's output occur.

SCATTER DIAGRAM. If we take observations on two variables that we suspect are functionally related and plot each pair of observations as points on graph paper, the result is a group or scatter of points called a scatter diagram. The shape of the scatter may give clues to the actual relationship.

See also Functional Relationship.

SCHECHTER BROS. v. U.S. *See* National Industrial Recovery Act (NIRA).

SCHULTZ, THEODORE WILLIAM (1902-   ), American economist who has achieved recognition for his contributions to agricultural economics and human capital theory. A graduate of South Dakota State College, he received his M.S. (1928) and Ph.D. (1930) from the University of Wisconsin. He became professor of economics at the University of Chicago in 1943. His numerous publications include *The Economic Organization of Agriculture* (1953), *The Economic Value of Education* (1963), *Transforming Traditional Agriculture* (1964), and *Economic Growth and Agriculture* (1968). Schultz has served as a consultant or economic adviser to many organizations and government agencies. He has been director of the National Bureau of Economic Research since 1949, and he was president of the American Economic Association in 1960. For his many contributions, he was awarded the 1979 Nobel Prize in Economics.

SCHUMACHER, E.F. (FRITZ) (1911-1977). Best known for his international best seller *Small Is Beautiful: A Study of Economics as if People Mattered* (1973), E.F. Schumacher was an Oxford-educated economist, journalist, industrial advisor, and inventor

of the concept "appropriate technology."

Schumacher became interested in developing countries after a visit to Burma in 1955 and began to work on the concept of an "intermediate technology" that would increase both output and employment. The technology indigenous to developing countries has a low capital-to-labor ratio and low productivity. Increasing the capital-to-labor ratio increases productivity but contributes nothing to solving problems of unemployment. What is needed is an intermediate technology adapted to the needs of each developing country. Although this idea undoubtedly changed the direction of thought about economic development, it has proven difficult to implement in practice since it runs counter to large-scale multinational enterprise.

While in Burma, Schumacher became a Buddhist (he later converted to Roman Catholicism), and this influenced his attitude toward Western economics. Capitalism enables a higher standard of living through competition and efficiency, but only at the cost of debasing culture. Schumacher's "Buddhist economics" allows culture to shape the goals and policies of economics. He also wrote *A Guide for the Perplexed* (1977) and *Good Work* (1979).

See also Appropriate Technology; Buddhist Economics; Gandhian Economics.

SCHUMPETER, JOSEPH ALOIS (1883-1950), outstanding Austrian-American economist who constructed, in his *Theory of Economic Development* (1912) and *Business Cycles* (1939), an economic theory to explain both the development of capitalism and the existence of business cycles in such a system. Schumpeter's system focuses upon the entrepreneur or businessperson and his or her role of introducing innovations. According to Schumpeter, innovation is any change in supply techniques; invention means nothing until it is applied, thus becoming an innovation.

It is the innovating entrepreneur, seeking profit, whom Schumpeter sees as the key to economic development, which comes from within the system. However, innovations occur in clusters rather than continuously, because one important innovation creates a situation within which other innovations are favored. This results in an economic boom. But the boom brings conditions which work against further innovation. Thus, the very process which creates economic growth also generates the business cycle—a system of creative destruction.

Schumpeter's *Capitalism, Socialism, and Democracy* (1942) suggested that capitalism was beginning to fail because (1) the entrepreneur had become obsolete; (2) the political strata which had protected capitalism had been destroyed; and (3) the institutional framework within which capitalism operated was disappearing.

Finally, Schumpeter's posthumous *History of Eco-*

nomic Analysis (1954) is an outstanding work which presents one of the most detailed, scholarly histories of economics.   —*Clyde A. Haulman*

SCHWEGMANN BROTHERS v. CALVERT CORP.
See McGuire-Keogh Act.

SCIENTIFIC SOCIALISM. To give socialist doctrine and tactics a scientific, rather than utopian, cast, Marx adapted Hegelian philosophy into a "science of human history." Its basic premise is that changes occur in society only as real conditions change mental states. Therefore, only an oppressed class, never a prosperous one satisfied with its condition, would be receptive to new ideas such as socialist reasoning or change.

Historically, change occurs when (1) the oppressed realize their interests and the conditions of their fulfillment while (2) the oppressors have become weak. The proletariat revolution will succeed, but, with no class below it to be oppressed in turn, will be the last. The result is a classless society with antagonisms gone.

See also Class Conflict; Marx, Karl; Revolutionary Socialism.

SEASONAL FLUCTUATIONS are regularly recurring, noncyclical variations in economic activity, particularly evidenced in sales and agricultural employment. Typically, retail sales are high around Easter and Christmas, and agricultural employment peaks during the harvest seasons. In measuring business cycles, seasonal fluctuations are not in themselves important because their effect is averaged out over the entire year.

See also Business Cycles, Types; Short-Term Business Cycles.

SEASONAL UNEMPLOYMENT is unemployment that occurs as the result of changes in the demand for labor due to the changing seasons. For example, summer months and holiday seasons such as Christmas and Easter usually bring increased demand for labor because there is an increased demand for products. Similarly, postsummer and postholiday seasons decrease the demand for products, and thus labor, resulting in seasonal unemployment. Another cause is weather conditions, as when winter months decrease demand for labor in the agricultural sector and in building trades. To deal with this problem in keeping records, unemployment statistics are usually adjusted seasonally to reflect the fluctuating demand.

See also Unemployment of Labor.

SECTION 7. *See* National Industrial Recovery Act (NIRA).

SECTORAL INFLATION, also called demand-shift, structural, or bottleneck inflation, occurs when market imperfections exist in important industries or sectors of the economy, resulting in prices and wages that can easily rise but cannot easily fall. A shift in demand, say, from metal to plastic containers, will cause prices and wages to rise in the chemical industries without an offsetting decline in the metal industry. Moreover, the wage increases in the chemical sector may spill over into other sectors. The result could be inflation even in the face of deficient aggregate demand.

SECULAR STAGNATION. The "stagnationist thesis" was defended strongly during the 1930s as an explanation of the Great Depression. Its leading advocate was Alvin Hansen, who argued that the major problem of that period was a lack of investment opportunities for the savings that were accumulating. The stagnationists believed that the inadequacy of investment opportunities resulted from a long-run decline in the rate of population growth and the apparent reduced rate of technological progress. Both these factors, it was argued, had provided the prime stimuli for investment, and in their absence government expenditure action was called for. This thesis was hotly debated in the late 1930s, but the advent of World War II and the resulting military expenditures rendered it academic.

SECURITIES AND EXCHANGE COMMISSION (SEC) is an independent federal agency that supervises all aspects of the securities industry—including brokers, investment companies, the stock exchanges, and the actions of corporate officials. The SEC, which consists of five members appointed by the president for five-year terms, was established by the Securities Exchange Act of 1934. The main purpose of the commission is to preserve the integrity of the securities industry. Concentrating on prevention of abuses rather than punishment, the SEC relies primarily on self-regulation within the industry. The SEC has long been considered to be the most successful regulatory agency.

SECURITIES MARKET. *See* Stock Market.

SELECTIVE CONTROLS. *See* Qualitative Controls.

SELECTIVE SALES TAX is a tax on the sale of a particular commodity. Such taxes are used by virtually all levels of government. Some selective sales taxes can be viewed as "nuisance" taxes, imposed on items the government may wish to discourage. Examples often cited are taxes on cigarettes, alcohol, and gambling. In reality, the tax is probably imposed on these items because such taxes are effective ways for a government to raise revenues.

There is a large variation in the use of such taxes. The tax on cigarettes, for example, is eight times higher in New Jersey than in the tobacco-producing states. Maine taxes the sale of alcoholic beverages, but the neighboring state of New Hampshire does not. As a result, many Maine residents cross the border to buy alcohol. The wide range of cigarette taxes has led to a serious "bootlegging" problem of cigarettes from low-tax states being sold illegally in high-tax states. Similar variations exist in the rates of gasoline taxes.

See also Sales Tax.

SELF-SUSTAINED GROWTH is a stage of economic growth at which the very processes of production have reached the point of generating increased production. Self-sustained growth usually occurs when an economy's technological and entrepreneurial skills, as well as its foreign trade, have developed to the point where almost anything can be produced at will. At that point, the fertile imaginations of the population generate ever-new products, the ideas for which create their own demand and, thereby, increase investment to support production of the newly invented items.

Self-sustained growth is used in another sense in the case of Less Developed Countries (LDC's) to refer to that point of economic maturity at which the internal economy has developed to such a point that continued growth can be financed out of internally generated funds, without reliance on external infusions of capital and purchasing power.

See also Stages of Growth.

SELLERS INFLATION. *See* Cost-Push Inflation.

SENIORITY. Prior to the development of a shop constitution through collective bargaining, management had the right to exercise its power of hiring and firing in an entirely arbitrary manner. Considerations such as length of service did not always enter into personnel policies and employment practices. Seniority clauses in collective bargaining contracts generally provide that long-service employees in a plant or subdivision thereof shall receive preference in layoffs and rehiring. The seniority system applies also to the determination of the order of promotion of equally qualified workers.

SERVICES. The difference between a good transaction and a service transaction hinges on whether or not a commodity is exchanged. If a commodity—something with physical substance—is exchanged, a commodity or good transaction has taken place; if not, a service transaction has taken place.

Services, considered as final output, are purchased by three sectors of the economy. Services purchased by consumers are broken down by the Department of Commerce into four major categories: household operations, housing, transportation, and other (such items as private higher education, physician services, and lawyer services). Services are also purchased by all levels of government. The major type of service purchased by government is labor services (compensation of employees). Services are also exchanged with the rest of the world and are calculated on a net basis from the international balance of payments. From the sum of such inpayments as receipts of income on United States investments abroad and transportation on United States carriers by foreigners are deducted corresponding out-payments to arrive at the net services portion of net exports of goods and services. The fourth sector, business, does not receive or purchase services in terms of final output.

—*Frank J. Bonello*

See also Final Outputs; Goods; Real Flow.

SHADOW PRICE, the value of a factor of the economy that is lost when it is shifted from its current use to the use being analyzed; that is, its value in its best alternative employment. Shadow price is most often associated with the valuation of unskilled labor.

See also Opportunity Cost.

SHERMAN ANTITRUST ACT (1890), the first piece of national antitrust legislation, designed to encourage and maintain a more competitive economy. With the Interstate Commerce Act of 1887, its passage marked the beginning of the era of government's attempt to affect the nature and performance of the American economy.

The principal thrust of the Sherman Act is found in its first two sections. Section 1 makes it a misdemeanor for business rivals to contract, combine, or conspire in restraint of trade. Section 2 makes it a misdemeanor to monopolize, attempt to monopolize, or combine or conspire to monopolize trade. The act applies to interstate commerce as well as to the District of Columbia, American Territories, and foreign companies doing business in the United States. It provides that a private party injured by the illegal activities proscribed in Sections 1 and 2 may sue for triple damages. It defines as a person a corporation or association.

What restraint of trade and monopolization mean in the Sherman Act, as interpreted by the federal courts, is not the same as what they meant in common law. The common law on monopoly was aimed at privilege, especially at monopolistic grants by the Crown in England. Now monopoly means the power to dominate markets in regard to pricing, market sharing, and exclusion of competitors. The common law on restraint of trade arose out of protection of value in a sales contract, where a seller was allowed by the buyer to set limited conditions on competition. The Sherman Act prohibition focuses on anticompetitive behavior, particularly division of sales territories, joint action on pricing, and exclusion of potential rivals by business competitors.

Principal responsibility for enforcement of the act rests with the Antitrust Division of the Department of Justice.

—*Thomas O. Depperschmidt*

See also Ancillary Agreement; Market Sharing; Monopolizing; Predatory Practices; Price Fixing; Restraint of Trade.

SHIFT IN SUPPLY. *See* Changes in Supply.

SHOP. For articles on various types of shops, *see* Agency Shop; Closed Shop; Open Shop; Union Shop.

SHORTAGE. *See* Excess Demand.

SHORT RUN, a period of time so short that some factors of production cannot be varied. There are two types of factors of production, the fixed and the variable. In the short run the variable factors are labor and raw materials. Capital cannot be varied in the short run and is, therefore, a fixed factor of production. The period defined as the short run will vary considerably depending on the industry under discussion. Short run analysis of a firm is conducted by holding the amount of capital equipment constant and varying the other factors of production. In this way, it is possible to determine the variable costs of production for a given quantity of capital.

SHORT-RUN ELASTICITY OF DEMAND measures the responsiveness of purchasers to price changes during a time period sufficiently small that the determinants of the purchasers' demand cannot change. Assuming incomes, tastes, and prices of other goods to be constant, short-run elasticity measures the responsiveness in quantity demanded that is produced by a change in the price of that commodity. Although short-run elasticities can take either high or low values, the tendency is for the elasticity of demand to be smaller in the short run than in the long run.

SHORT-RUN ELASTICITY OF SUPPLY refers to the ability of a firm or industry to react to price changes in the short run. Since the short run implies a fixed amount of capital, increases or decreases in output will be effected by using existing plant and facilities more or less intensively. Starting from equilibrium, assume an increase in demand, which increases price. The firm can increase output by having labor work overtime, adding another shift, etc. Marginal cost will rise rapidly, and output response will therefore be slight in the short run.

SHORT-RUN EQUILIBRIUM OF THE FIRM. *See* Equilibrium of the Firm, Short-Run.

SHORT-TERM BUSINESS CYCLES are fluctuations in economic activity, particularly prices, production, and employment. The cycles average from two to ten years, in the opinion of Alvin Hansen, or about 40 months, according to Joseph Kitchin, who was the first analyst to study short-term cycles in detail. He contended that such fluctuations were caused by changes in inventory investment and small waves of innovation created by invention of equipment that can be produced quickly.

SHULTZ, GEORGE PRATT (1920-   ), American university dean who has made significant contributions to the study of business. A graduate of Princeton (1942), Schultz received his Ph.D. in industrial economics from MIT (1949). His publications include *Management Organization and the Computer* (1960) and *Strategies for the Displaced Worker* (1966, with Arnold R. Weber). Schultz was senior staff economist of the President's Council of Economic Advisers (1955-1956), and later became staff director of the national labor policy study for the Committee on Economic Development (1961). He became dean of the Graduate School of Business at the University of Chicago in 1962. After serving as President Nixon's first labor secretary and as chairman of the FTC, he was named director of the new Office of Management and Budget in 1970. He became treasury secretary (1972) and, as chairman of the Council on Economic Policy, was one of Nixon's special assistants in the reorganized executive branch. He served as secretary of state during both Reagan administrations.

SHUT-DOWN POINT, the point at which it will be better for the firm to shut down its plant and produce zero output. If the firm shuts down, it will lose an amount equal to its fixed costs. If total revenue is very low, the firm may lose even more by continuing to produce. The shut-down point for a firm is the point at which the price is just equal to average variable costs. Above this price, the firm is covering all of its variable costs and some of its fixed costs, so it should not shut down. Below this price, the firm is covering none of its fixed costs and only part of its variable costs. This firm should shut down.

SIGNIFICANCE, the probability that a given result in sampling could occur entirely by chance. In testing a hypothesis, significance is the risk we are willing to take of erroneously rejecting a null hypothesis that is actually true. This risk can be made as small as necessary.
See also Hypothesis; Population, Statistical.

SILVER CERTIFICATES, paper notes of the U.S. Treasury, fully backed by silver in its vaults at the rate of 371.25 grains (about four-fifths of an ounce) per dollar. First issued in 1878, silver certificates constituted the bulk of $1 bills (and some larger denominations) until 1963, when one-dollar Federal Reserve notes were introduced to replace them. They have now been retired, and the silver that backed them has been disposed of.

See also Money; Money Supply.

SKEWNESS is the amount by which a distribution departs from symmetry. If the distribution has a longer "tail" to the right, it is said to be positively skewed. If the long tail runs to the left, it is negatively skewed.

SKEWNESS

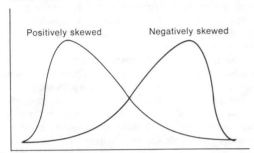

Positively skewed   Negatively skewed

SLIDING PEG. *See* Exchange Rate.

SMALL SAMPLES. *See* Sampling Theory.

SMITH, ADAM (1723-1790). The founder of the classical school of economic thought, and considered by many to be the father of economics, Adam Smith developed the first systematic analysis of economic phenomena. His first work, *The Theory of Moral Sentiments* (1759), was a philosophical discussion of the ethical forces which are necessary for a society to operate.

Smith's most important work, however, was *The Wealth of Nations* (1776). Smith traveled in France and became familiar with the Physiocrats. He combined many of their ideas with his own and those of others to formulate a general theory of economic activity. In Smith's view, the mercantilist policy which had dominated Europe actually worked against economic growth and development. His system, based upon the division of labor, widening markets, and the harmony of self-interest, suggested a limited role for the government with dependence placed upon market forces as the means of solving economic problems.

Smith was generally optimistic and did not see the possibility of economic problems such as unemployment and the business cycle in his system. However, as the first person to bring together in one volume the consideration of all aspects of economic activity, Smith provided the basis for the development of economics as a discipline.   —*Clyde A. Haulman*

See also Classical Economics; Invisible Hand; Mercantilism; Physiocrats; Wealth of Nations, The.

SMYTH v. AMES (1898), a case in which the Su-preme Court set forth criteria by which to judge public utility commission valuations and declared that rates should be set so that the regulated firm receives "a fair return upon . . . the fair value of the property being used by it." Earlier, in an 1877 decision *(Munn v. Illinois),* the Court held that public utility rates fixed by the government are not subject to judicial review. However, that position was reversed in 1886 *(Stone v. Farmer's Loan and Trust Co.),* when the court said that rates fixed under legislative authority are subject to judicial review and may be set aside if they are found to deprive investors of their property without due process of law.

Unfortunately, most of the criteria enumerated by the court in *Smyth v. Ames* for determining fair value were either irrelevant, inconsistent, or illogical. Following this decision, the original cost and reproduction cost of construction became the main items considered by the courts in determining the fair value of public utility property.   —*Joseph Jadlow*

See also Fair Return on Fair Value; Munn v. Illinois.

SOCIAL ACCOUNTING SYSTEMS are designed to give governments and other institutions concerned with the operation of modern economies a factual record of the economy's performance during a specific time period. The most common system is the National Income Account, which measures the value of the total production or output of the economy during a year (GNP) and indicates the various sources and uses of this production. Such systems, however, generally measure only market-oriented production, thus ignoring some of the economy's output, such as the work of housewives and house husbands, and overlooking the environmental costs associated with production.

SOCIAL COSTS, those costs society pays when its resources are used to produce a given quantity of some particular commodity, are clearly related to opportunity costs. The benefit given up must be weighed against the advantage gained. The economic problem that society faces is the "proper" composition of total output. Society is optimizing when it produces a given commodity up to the point where the marginal social benefit is equated to the marginal social cost of producing that last unit. Social costs assume significance mainly when contrasted with private costs; the divergence of private and social costs creates social problems for a free-enterprise economy.

SOCIAL DIVIDEND, a plan for a per capita grant to be paid to everyone regardless of financial well-being. It would provide a guaranteed income for all individuals. The amount could be the same for everyone or higher for adults than for children. Payment is not reduced directly as income rises (in contrast to the negative income tax), but in order to finance the program it would be necessary to raise the taxes of higher income families by more than they receive in grants. Since everyone receives the grant, the stigma associated with being on welfare is eliminated. A major objection to the program is its very high cost, especially if the dividend is to be large enough to replace existing welfare programs.

See also Negative Income Tax; Public Assistance.

SOCIAL INSURANCE, a program designed to give insured citizens and their dependents minimal protection against loss of income owing to the retirement, unemployment, disability, or death of the insured. In some cases, coverage may include medical care. In the United States, social insurance is provided primarily through the Social Security system.

Social insurance is generally compulsory for eligible persons. Under Social Security those eligible include most wage earners (except for employees of the federal government and railroads, who are under similar compulsory federal programs) and most self-employed. The program is funded through a payroll tax levied on employers and employees and on income from self-employment. Because benefits are financed by earmarked payments to a trust fund rather than from general tax revenue, they are regarded as a form of insurance. Benefits are prescribed by law, rather than by contract, as in the case of private insurance, but with the understanding that they are earned through payment of the compulsory tax or "contribution" to the benefit fund. Eligibility is determined by statutory formulas. There is no necessity for recipients to prove that they are in need of help, as in the case of public assistance. Consequently, social insurance is free of the stigma associated with being on public welfare.

Transferring Income. Although payments are a function of previous contributions, a considerable amount of redistribution does take place among participants who include all insured, only a fraction of whom are receiving benefits at any point in time. For example, most persons now receiving retirement benefits under Social Security entered the labor force before they entered the program, which dates to 1935. Some, notably farmers, worked in occupations that came under the program years after it started, and thus typically receive benefits well in excess of their contributions. The program also favors insureds with large numbers of dependents, since they pay no more tax, but they or their survivors are eligible for higher potential payments. Benefit increases voted periodically by Congress, notably the periodic cost-of-living adjustments, increase the redistribution from contributors to beneficiaries. These forms of redistribution are necessary if the goal of providing a minimum level of protection for all participants is to be realized.

All of the components of the OASDHI (Old Age, Survivors, Disability, and Health Insurance), part of the Social Security program, have counterparts in the field of private insurance. Private insurance, often purchased voluntarily to supplement social insurance, is funded on the actuarial principle, which requires that payments by the typical beneficiary plus accumulated interest on premiums equal the expected cost of serving the beneficiary. Social insurance cannot meet this criterion once the principle of redistribution described above is adopted. The OASDHI program is thus better described as a device for transferring income from current contributors—the working population—to current beneficiaries. It is operated on a pay-as-you-go basis with annual receipts approximating annual benefits.

The unemployment compensation program is administered jointly by the Social Security administration and the states. It is financed by a joint federal-state tax on payrolls under rules set within federal guidelines by the individual states. Taxes are higher on firms with high layoff rates, a feature designed to provide a financial incentive for reducing cyclical hiring practices.   —*Charles W. Meyer*

See also Medicare; National Health Insurance; Social Security; Unemployment Insurance.

SOCIALISM, a body of thought from which a set of economic and social objectives are derived. The organization and methods of accomplishing these objectives are varied.

Socialist Aims. Adherents to socialism generally hope to achieve: (1) a reduction in the private ownership of the means of production by a transfer of ownership and general control to the state; (2) more equitable distribution of incomes; (3) a smooth growth path facilitated by a steady flow of funds into investment; (4) economic planning of some level and scope; (5) elimination of "capitalist waste" that results from duplications of output, aborted investments, and luxury goods.

To accomplish these objectives, socialists seek to obtain political power in the state, then to replace the old order with socialist institutions. This can be achieved through an evolutionary process such as success in political elections. The Labour Party in Britain was elected in 1945 with a nationalization program in its platform, as was Salvador Allende in Chile in 1970. By contrast, Fidel Castro came to power in Cuba through the revolutionary process.

Mechanics of Socialism. The socialist world underwent sweeping changes starting in 1989. Until that time they were divided into two principal types: democratic socialist, as in some Scandinavian countries; and authoritarian socialist, as in China, the Soviet Union, and the East European states. In a revolutionary wave, most of the East European nations, as well as Nicaragua, overthrew their political and economic systems beginning in 1989 and moved toward some mixture of market economies and pluralist democracies. The maximization of social welfare remained an important stated aim of these new regimes, but unemployment and other economic dislocations appeared. The Soviet Union was slower to embrace market structures, but shortages and widespread inefficiency and discontent added pressure to move in that direction. Privatization of nationalized enterprises also increased in democratic socialist countries as the greater efficiency of the market was more widely recognized.

SOCIALISTIC DICTATORSHIP. *See* Dictatorship of the Proletariat.

SOCIALLY OPTIMAL OUTPUT. *See* Externalities.

SOCIAL SECURITY, a large-scale federal program of payments to persons for retirement, disability, illness, and the like. The program often is referred to by its acronym, OASDHI, which stands for Old-Age, Survivors, Disability, and Health Insurance. The original Social Security Act, passed in 1935, included old-age and survivors insurance. Disability insurance was added in 1956, and health insurance (Medicare) was added in 1965.

In 1987, there were over 38 million persons receiving benefits from the OASDI portion of the program. Of these, 62% were retirees, 7% were disabled workers, and 19% were survivors, spouses, and dependent children of deceased workers. Another 32 million persons benefited from the Medicare program. All persons over age 65 are automatically eligible for Medicare, but the other programs are subject to various eligibility tests. For example, in order to receive old-age benefits, a person must have worked over 40 quarters in jobs that paid in contributions to finance the program. An eligible worker can retire at age 65 and receive full benefits, or retire slightly earlier at a reduced benefit rate. These age limits are scheduled to be increased in future years. Recipients are subject to an earnings test also, which can reduce benefits for retirees under the age of 70.

Social Security is financed through the use of a payroll tax of over 7.65% of wages paid by the employee, and an additional matching "contribution" (tax) of 7.65% of wages paid by the employer. These monies go into a "trust fund" out of which benefits are paid to current recipients. The trust fund should be expected to accumulate money to ensure that there will be adequate funds to pay current workers when they retire. The program is intended to be self-financing.

Problems and Reforms. Because of its huge size (over $246 billion, excluding Medicare, in 1990), and the large number of people receiving benefits, Social Security is an immensely popular program. This has caused Congress to be very generous in increasing benefits, but rather lax at maintaining adequate reve-

nues to finance the system. During the early 1980s, it became increasingly apparent that the program was headed toward severe financial problems. The trust funds were depleted, and general fund revenues had to be used to maintain the solvency of the program. In a strong show of bipartisan cooperation, Congress passed the Social Security Amendments of 1983, which placed the program upon sound footing again. This act increased the payroll tax, broadened the number of workers who must participate in the program, instituted a tax on benefits for retirees with high incomes, scheduled future increases in the retirement age, and delayed benefit increases that had been previously authorized. These changes successfully converted the 1982 deficit into a surplus of $52 billion by 1989 and assured the program's solvency into the next century. —*Michael S. Johnson*

See also Disability Insurance; Medicare; Social Insurance; Unemployment Insurance.

SOCIAL SECURITY ACT (1935), the basis of extensive U.S. social insurance programs. The current characteristics of the Social Security program largely reflect the numerous and substantial amendments that have been made to the original act. Spurred by the massive unemployment and poverty of the Depression and confronted with the inability of state and local governments to provide assistance on a significant level, the federal government in the early 1930s began to provide several forms of financial assistance to the states to help them aid people.

As the focal point of public policy in this area shifted from the short-run alleviation of poverty to its long-run prevention, the federal government adopted broad-based, compulsory insurance programs against income interruption because of unemployment and old age. The third major element of the law was a public assistance (welfare) program for those remaining in need or not helped by these insurance programs.

Federal Grants. The act provides for a system of federal grants to the states to support their own programs of assistance to the needy, conditional on the programs' compliance with certain federal requirements. Welfare benefits, in the form of income payments and medical care, are provided under programs to benefit the needy aged, dependent children, the blind, and those under the maternal and child welfare program.

Pensions and Compensation. The insurance programs set up in the act were those for old-age retirement pensions and unemployment compensation. The old-age retirement pension program, popularly (but not quite correctly) referred to as "social security," is only one part of the Social Security program and has been expanded to provide income benefits for the retiree's dependents or surviving dependents, benefits for disabled workers, and medical insurance benefits for the aged.

The unemployment compensation benefits are payable to covered, eligible recipients through individual state programs. If these state programs meet certain federal standards, federal grants pay their administrative expenses. The actual financing of benefits comes through payroll taxes levied by the state, most or all of which can be deducted by the employer from his federal payroll tax liability. Thus, in large part, the state unemployment compensation systems are financed by tax money that otherwise would have gone to the federal government.

Social Security taxes have risen steadily, both in terms of the rate of tax and the amount of income subject to tax. The amount the employee is taxed is matched by the employer. Disabled veterans' monthly benefits vary, depending upon the extent of the disability.   — *William D. Wagoner*

SOCIAL VALUE. *See* Externalities.

SOIL BANK, an acreage-control program which offered payments to farmers for removing land entirely from crop production. Most prior programs permitted land taken out of controlled crops to be used for growing other crops. Thus surpluses suppressed in one crop showed up in others.

The Acreage Reserve (1956-1958) took some land out of selected crops on farms of all levels of productivity, one year at a time. The Conservation Reserve (1956-1960) offered payments for removing farms of low productivity entirely from crop production for periods of three to ten years. The chief objection to the Conservation Reserve was that poor land was geographically concentrated and its retirement depressed extensive rural areas. The principle of the Acreage Reserve was used in modified forms in the feed-grain acts of the early 1960s and the Agricultural Acts of 1965 and 1970.

SOMBART, WERNER (1863-1941), German historical economist, whose avid support of Nazism toward the end of his career rested in part upon his explanation of the rise and development of the capitalistic system. He felt that the growth pattern contained three distinct stages: early capitalism, high capitalism, and late capitalism. In the late capitalistic stage, Sombart felt, the decadent tendencies of capitalism would become so entrenched that a new economic organization must arise. He believed that the stage had been reached following World War I and that the Nazi system was its logical replacement.

See also Historical School.

SOREL, GEORGE. *See* Syndicalism.

SPECIALIZATION. International trade leads to a

Cattle are sent from the farm to feedlots where they double in weight to 1,000 pounds or more. This specialization in modern beef production increases the supply and lowers prices to consumers.

wider market and more benefits from the division of labor. Each nation should specialize by applying the law of comparative advantages to its resource endowment. If sufficient quantities of goods can be produced to meet their demand without raising costs, then specialization will be complete among countries. Country A will specialize in X, if that is where its comparative advantage lies, and produce all X demanded by itself and Country B. It will obtain from B its Y since B produces enough for both. If costs rise as outputs increase, specialization will not be complete; trade will be carried to the point where costs are equalized in the countries.

See also Comparative Advantage; International Trade Theory.

$20 gold coin; this specie is no longer in circulation.

SPECIE is coin, usually gold or silver, whose metallic worth is equal to its face value.

See also Money.

SPECIFIC EXCISE TAX, an excise tax whose tax base is defined in terms of the number of units of the commodity purchased, such as federal and state taxes on gallons of gasoline. Because of the difficulties in applying this type of tax to a large number of economic goods, specific excise taxes are generally applied to very few commodities.

SPECULATION is the purchase or sale of title to goods or financial obligations in the expectation that the price will rise or fall. When purchasing, possession of title to the good is sometimes taken immediately. When selling, the contract usually calls for future possession, the seller hoping to fulfill the contract at a lower price in the future. Such speculative investments have no role in national income analysis; in monetary analysis, speculation is not another term for investment as defined in economics.

SPECULATIVE DEMAND. *See* Liquidity Preference.

STABILIZATION POLICY, a policy that has, as its chief goals, the control of runaway prices caused by inflationary pressures and the prevention of chronic or excessive unemployment and stagnant growth. There has been no serious American deflation since the late 1930s. There are three major stabilization strategies: fiscal policy, monetary policy, and incomes policy.

Fiscal Policy, as a stabilizer, is a relatively new weapon against unemployment and inflation, having emerged with the economics of John Maynard Keynes in the 1930s. The government uses taxation as a stabilizer in two ways. First, there are built-in stabilizers that react automatically to any changes in the economy. For example, the progressive income tax guarantees that as a person's income decreases, his or her rate of taxes will also decrease. Another automatic stabilizer is unemployment compensation, which allows laid-off workers to receive an income.

A second form of taxation as a stabilizer is known as discretionary fiscal policy and involves a decision by Congress and the president to change the existing tax structure. For example, in the early 1960s a general decrease in taxes was passed to stimulate spending and ward off a recession. Several years later a 10% surtax was placed on incomes to curb inflationary pressures.

The federal government also uses public expenditures and transfer payments to regulate the economy. These stem from discretionary fiscal policy by the legislature and the president. In depressions, government decisions usually involve large-scale spending to stimulate the economy and aid in the reduction of unemployment. In addition, the government may initi-

ate spending in public works, such as the building of roads, and acts directly as an employer, creating jobs for the unemployed. In the same manner, during inflationary periods, government policy may involve the reduction of public expenditures. When a substantial decrease in government spending occurs, the result is often a halt in rising prices, due to a decrease in general demand. One of the major problems of the use of public expenditures as a stabilizing policy is that there is often a large gap in the time periods between when the programs are initiated and when the effects of the programs occur. Fiscal policy, to be an effective stabilizer, must work with monetary policy in the fight against inflation and unemployment.

Monetary Policy, in some form or another, has been around almost as long as the existence of money. The policy's effectiveness lies in its immediacy of operation. The United States has adopted a monetary policy of which the main objective is to assist the economy in achieving a full-employment, noninflationary level of total output. With this stabilizing objective, the Federal Reserve Act (1913) established the Federal Reserve System. Among its many objectives is the regulation of the money supply to correspond with the needs of the economy. Because the country's commercial banking system has the ability to effectively create additional money through money lending, the need for a central control over the money supply is essential. The Federal Reserve System can control the money supply in three main ways: (1) by regulating the reserve ratio; (2) by changing the discount rate; and (3) by buying and selling securities on the open market. The reserve ratio is a specified percentage of a bank's total deposit liabilities that must be kept in the Federal Reserve bank. By decreasing or increasing the reserve ratio, the Federal Reserve can limit (in inflation) or expand (in deflation) a bank's lending ability and, thus, the money supply.

A second way in which the Federal Reserve can control the money supply is by use of the discount rate. The discount rate is the interest rate at which the Federal Reserve bank lends money to commercial banks. The higher the discount rate, the less willing these banks are to borrow money. An increased discount rate will contract the money supply, and a decreased discount rate will expand the money supply.

The third and most effective way in which the Federal Reserve controls the money supply is by open-market buying and selling of securities. To contract the money supply, the Federal Reserve sells government bonds to commercial banks and the general public, removing money from the public and the banks, therefore further decreasing the money supply. The Federal Reserve usually sells bonds during inflationary periods and buys during deflationary periods.

Discretionary monetary policy includes the use of the tools mentioned above to achieve the desired results with respect to level of output and employment and to the price level. However, monetarists suggest that discretionary policy should be abandoned in favor of a fixed monetary growth rate rule. That is, a policy should be adopted whereby the Federal Reserve (or central bank) should fix the rate of growth of the monetary supply and take steps to make the growth rate constant over time. They suggest that the economy would be more stable with constant growth of the money supply than with the discretionary changes in the monetary growth rates in response to changes in the economic outlook.

Incomes Policy is the third type of stabilization strategy. Incomes policies affect the real income of individuals and usually effect changes in wages and prices. There are essentially two types of incomes policy: guideposts and controls. Wage and price guideposts are voluntary guidelines set up for labor and management to follow to curb inflationary pressures. Because these guideposts are voluntary, there is no penalty for violation. In 1962 President Kennedy set forth the first peacetime guideposts to ward off an impending inflation. These guideposts proved to be very effective for several years. In 1969, however, President Nixon issued another set of guideposts, which were virtually ineffective in curbing unemployment and inflation.

A second incomes policy is wage and price controls, employed three times since 1940. These controls have always been a wartime policy, because the diversion of production from consumer to war goods results in more dollars chasing fewer consumption goods. During World War II, the National War Labor Board (the Wage Board) and the Office of Price Administration aided in the success of keeping both wages and prices stable (1941-1946). During the Korean War, these controls were carried out by the Office of Price Stabilization but proved to be relatively ineffective because they were not strictly enforced (1950-1953).

In 1971 Nixon instituted a 90-day wage and price freeze (Phase I), regulated by the Cost of Living Council and the Price Commission, and enforced by the IRS.

In 1979, President Carter applied voluntary wage and price guidelines that had little effect. During the 1980s, monetary policy was used by the Reagan administration to slow inflation, resulting in the recession of 1982.   — *William D. Wagoner*

See also Incomes Policy; Stabilizers.

STABILIZERS refer to either qualities inherent in the economic system or policies specifically designed to bring stability in price, income, and employment to the economy. Those qualities inherent or built into the system are generally termed automatic stabilizers, whereas those specifically designed to maintain or restore stability are called discretionary stabilizers. All stabilizers operate by affecting the spending-saving

streams either in the public or private sectors or both.

Automatic Stabilizers, or Built-in Stabilizers. These refer to automatic forces inherent in the modern fiscal system, or built into that system, which help to keep the economy stable. Automatic changes in tax receipts are the most significant automatic stabilizers. Because of a heavy reliance on progressive income taxes (both personal and corporate) during a recession, as incomes in the economy decline, the government receives proportionately less tax revenues. This leads to increased availability of funds for personal consumption, which leads to larger production, which in turn pushes incomes upward. Therefore, income fluctuations are moderated automatically. The reverse occurs during an inflation. In this case, tax receipts increase as incomes increase. This, too, moderates income fluctuations.

Unemployment compensation and other welfare transfers also serve as automatic stabilizers. During prosperous years, when employment is high, unemployment compensation reserves grow and exert downward pressure on spending. Conversely, during years of higher unemployment, the reserve funds are used to pay out income, which moderates the decline in income by sustaining a higher level of consumption than would otherwise occur.

Government farm aid programs serve to automatically stabilize prices of farm products. When surpluses exist, the government absorbs them, thereby causing the prices on these products to decline. In the opposite case, when prices begin to rise, the government sells its surpluses, thereby holding the prices down.

Another automatic stabilizer is inherent in our private institutions. The custom of corporations maintaining dividends regardless of short-run changes in their incomes results in an automatic stabilizer. Also, families maintaining a certain standard of living rather than making quick adjustments to income fluctuations results in greater stability.

Discretionary Stabilizers. Stabilization policies that deliberately alter taxes or expenditures for the purpose of achieving full employment and stable price levels are termed discretionary policies. Another primary objective of these policies is to moderate economic fluctuations by stabilizing total spending or demand. This is achieved either by government spending, which compensates for changes in private spending, or by cyclical variations of tax rates.

When unemployment increases and the economy contracts due to a fall in private demand, government spending should rise. When economic expansion and inflation occur, government spending should fall. In other words, the existing economic conditions determine which expenditure policy the government chooses. Expenditure programs such as those initiated during Franklin Roosevelt's New Deal provide employment and increase aggregate demand in the economy. Making transfer payments to individuals is another way government stimulates demand.

Variations in tax rates help governments attain economic stability. A cut in tax rates can help offset an economic recession by encouraging business and consumer expenditures. An increase in the tax rates can have the opposite effect and dampen inflation. A weakness in the case for this policy is that once tax rates are lowered to fight a recession, it may be politically difficult to return them to the higher level after the recession has ended.

—*Irving J. Goffman*

STABLE EQUILIBRIUM, an equilibrium that will be restored if disturbed; the price and quantity of the commodity will tend to return to their equilibrium levels. An unstable equilibrium is one in which the price and quantity will not be restored if disturbed; there will be an explosive divergence of the price away from the equilibrium. In this situation the market price cannot be restored if once disturbed. A stable equilibrium is one from which there is no tendency to move.

STAGES OF A COUNTRY'S BALANCE OF PAYMENTS. The balance of trade is the single most important item in a nation's balance of payments. Merchandise imports and exports represent movements of real consumer goods or real investment goods. When exports exceed imports the trade balance is favorable; the balance is unfavorable when imports exceed exports. These terms pertain only to the technical definition of the trade balance, not to its status in the overall balance of payments. Whether the trade balance is favorable in this greater sense depends on the stage of economic development of the nation.

Young Debtor. Any nation embarking on a program of economic growth must have an unfavorable trade balance. The nation's productive capacities are poorly developed, so that it has little to export, with most goods needed for domestic consumption. Because the lack of capital means high returns, investment is attractive to foreigners. Hence, imports will exceed exports and be financed by capital imports; this is owed by foreigners, and payments of interest and principal will grow.

Mature Debtor. As growth in the economy occurs via domestic savings and continued import of capital, exports can be expected to increase more rapidly than imports, and a favorable balance of trade is achieved. The nation's own foreign investment will begin to grow, but not fast enough to offset interest and principal owed annually to foreigners. The favorable trade balance procures the exchange necessary to pay for this interest and principal.

Young Creditor. As foreign investments continue to grow while foreign debts mature and are paid off, payments of interest and principal by foreigners will exceed amounts paid to them, and the nation be-

comes a net creditor with a continuing favorable balance of trade.

Mature Creditor. The continued buildup of foreign investments brings in larger amounts of interest and principal payments each year. These funds can finance larger imports, and the nation's citizens will consume increased imports. Therefore, the balance of trade must turn unfavorable.

—*John R. Matthews, Jr.*

See also Balance of Payments; Balance of Trade; Capital Account; Capital Movement; Foreign Investment.

STAGES OF GROWTH, the levels of technical, industrial, and agricultural achievement that a society experiences as it develops. The idea that countries and economies develop from lower to higher forms first appeared in the middle of the nineteenth century, and it has taken many forms since then.

Karl Marx proposed six major stages of history: prehistory, primitive culture, feudalism, capitalism, the dictatorship of the proletariat, and communism or socialism. During the last two stages, all basic industries and productive resources would first be nationalized, and gradually, in the absence of capitalistic exploitation, all material wants would be satisfied and the need for government would fade.

There have been many non-Marxist theories of the stages of economic development. Perhaps the best known is by Walt W. Rostow, concerning the stages of transition from a primitive economy to a fully developed, mature industrial economy. According to Rostow's scheme, traditional economies begin to change when agricultural productivity increases, and surpluses allow investment in capital goods and release workers for industry. During "take-off," an increasing rate of savings allows rapid expansion of productive capacity. This is followed by a "drive to maturity," characterized by further growth and culminating in a stage where there is high mass consumption for all members of society and where services become increasingly important.

Implicit in the stages of growth theories is the assumption that less materialistic cultures are inferior to western industrial society. Rostow considered culture a barrier to development.

See also Take-Off; Traditional Economy; Underdevelopment.

STAGFLATION, a term created to describe a situation of simultaneous economic *stag*nation and in*flation*. Stagflation was a frequent problem in many economies in the decade of the 1970s. Economists, after considerable controversy, have come to view stagflation as the result of aggregate supply movements which overwhelm aggregate demand movements. Typically, stagflation occurs when policymakers attempt to use monetary and fiscal policy to combat an inflation problem. The past inflation is built into peoples' expectation patterns, and through a wage-price spiral, the price level is driven up. At least in the short run, contractionary aggregate demand policy has no effect on the momentum of inflation, but it does create unemployment. The result is stagflation—simultaneous high (and sometimes growing) inflation and high, and often growing, unemployment.

STAGNATION, the failure of real output of the economy to grow sufficiently rapidly over a period (longer than a year or two) to provide for full employment. In the 1930s Alvin Hansen of Harvard (and others) argued that the Depression was the result of the disappearance of two of the three main sources of growth during the nineteenth and early twentieth centuries: (1) rapidly increasing population, which meant increased demand for goods and therefore many investment opportunities; and (2) expansion into new territories. The third major source of growth had been, according to Hansen, technological progress (e.g., railroads, automobiles), but Hansen and others doubted that the rate of technological change would be rapid enough in the future to give rise to enough (more) investment spending to offset household saving at the full-employment level of income. Without population growth and territorial expansion to call forth additional investment, technological change would have to be more rapid than it had been in the past to ensure full employment.

In the post-World War II period some have argued that private investment would have been inadequate to ensure full employment, but that high levels of government spending have been responsible for the lack of stagnation since 1945. The argument is essentially the same as Hansen's: in a "mature" economy (such as that of the United States and those of Western Europe) investment opportunities will be insufficient to give rise to the level of private investment necessary to maintain full employment.

—Anne Mayhew

STALIN, JOSEPH (1879-1953), the chief architect of the economy of the Soviet Union. As a reward for his loyalty and activities on behalf of the Communist party before and during the Russian Revolution, Stalin was appointed to the Council of People's Commissars in 1917. In 1922, Lenin named him general secretary of the Communist party, a position that Stalin then used to eliminate Leon Trotsky as his rival to succeed Lenin. By 1927 he had either removed or neutralized his opposition within the Party and established himself as leader of the U.S.S.R.

Economic Policies. Stalin helped design and get approved the First Five Year Plan initiated in 1928. With this plan the Soviet system became a common economy, with rapid industrialization as its principal objective. In order to generate sufficient investment

funds to support this plan, Stalin dramatically collectivized agriculture. During the 1930s the Soviet industrial output grew rapidly, but so did opposition to Stalin's extreme economic methods. During 1935-1937, he purged the Party of his opponents and then ruled in a police state environment.

Stalin's wartime leadership and postwar political maneuvering established the U.S.S.R. as the dominant military, political, and economic power in Eastern Europe. His death in 1953 permitted a relaxation of the stringent political controls, but his economic model has remained principally intact.

—Francis W. Rushing

STANDARD OF LIVING, the scale of consumption, including necessities, comforts, and luxuries, that a nation can achieve with its per capita real income. According to theories of David Ricardo and Thomas Malthus, optimum per capita real income (or an ultimate standard of living) is reached at optimum population, the point past which average output per capita begins to decline.

In the United States, during the period 1890-1990, the standard of living, measured in terms of annual per capita real income, rose steadily, and the average working hours per person declined. Although, on a national average, the standard of living has risen, and the United States is now experiencing the stage of growth known as high-mass consumption, the per capita real income does not reflect the unequal distribution of income among individual households. Thus, to alter income distribution and thereby raise the standard of living among low-income groups, governments are being forced to assume the responsibility for income redistribution.

Redistribution Methods. Redistribution is achieved, in some measure, through a variety of public assistance programs and direct interventions in the market pricing system; for example, through price supports for farmers, minimum wage legislation, and channeling public expenditures. The primary device used to alter the distribution of income among individual households and to raise their standard of living has universally been the progressive income tax, which takes more from those who earn more, and less from low-income households.

See also Income Redistribution; Per Capita Real Income; Stages of Growth.

STANDARD OF VALUE. *See* Money.

STANDARD OIL CASE. *See* United States v. Standard Oil Co. of New Jersey.

STATE BANK, a commercial bank that is chartered by one of the 50 individual states. The bank is subject to the laws of the chartering state and is controlled by the state superintendent of banks or similar official or board. State banks may join the Federal Reserve System if they wish. Two-thirds of the commercial banks in the United States are state-chartered, but these banks hold only one-third of the total volume of deposits.

See also Commercial Bank.

STATE-CONTROLLED ECONOMY. *See* Government-Controlled Economy.

STATE PLANNING COMMITTEE (U.S.S.R.). *See* Gosplan.

STATIC EQUILIBRIUM. *See* Theory of the Firm.

STATIONARY STATE, stage of economic development at which a full-employment economy can be sustained on the basis of consumer expenditures without investment in new plant and equipment. Such a state exists in the traditional economy, but has not been achieved in other stages of growth. Ricardo, Marshall, and Keynes thought a stationary state would be reached when an economy consumed 100% of full-employment income.

STATISTICS, the science concerned primarily with the analysis of empirical data. The word can also refer to the data itself—population counts, tax receipts, import duties—or to the characteristics of a sample, such as the sample mean and standard deviation.

Statistics and the Scientific Method. The primary goal of statistics is to allow the researcher to proceed from knowledge derived from a sample to a statement concerning the entire population from which the sample was taken. This is the process of inference, drawing conclusions concerning the whole on the basis of a careful examination of the parts. It is basically the scientific method.

Statistics in the Social Sciences. Much of social science, including economics, relies heavily on statistical techniques and methods. Because of its ability to separate the effects of systematic variation of a variable from the effects of chance variation, statistics allow the scientific method to be applied to phenomena that cannot be controlled in laboratory conditions. Moreover, statistics allow us to make exact statements of confidence concerning the characteristics of the population on the evidence supplied by the sample.

Hypothesis and Belief. We all formulate beliefs concerning the world on the basis of the evidence supplied by our senses. An important branch of statistics is concerned with the testing of these beliefs, called hypotheses, by confrontation with the facts. Suppose we are interested in reducing the crime rate. If we believe that increased police protection will reduce crime, we can test the hypothesis by hiring more police in some cities while maintaining existing levels in others. Suppose the mean crime rate in those cities

with increased police protection drops by 10% in comparison with the other cities. Can this decrease be attributed to the expenditure on police or could it be merely due to chance? Statistics has the power to answer such questions, questions which can have profound implications for society.

—*Carlisle E. Moody*

See also Population, Statistical.

STEWARD, in labor unions, the lowest member of the union official structure (not always considered a union officer), typically elected to represent the employees in one shop or workplace. A large local may have many shop stewards. The steward's most important job is involved with contract administration at the shop or floor level, and he or she is the one who first takes a worker's case to management. Normally, if the steward and the foreman cannot work out an agreement over a specific management action, the case goes on to the next higher level of both the union and management.

STIGLER, GEORGE JOSEPH (1911-   ). An outstanding authority in the areas of price theory and the history of economic thought, Stigler has educated many young economists through his textbooks *The Theory of Price* (1952) and *Production and Distribution Theories* (1947). A member of the Chicago school, Stigler significantly contributed to many aspects of microeconomic theory.

Stigler's work in the history of economic ideas has been collected in the volume *Essays in the History of Economics* (1965). He assigns "a minor, and even an accidental, role to the economic environment in the development of economic theory since it has become a professional discipline" *(Essays)*. While many economists agree with this position, many feel that environmental forces have shaped economic ideas. Stigler's other publications include *The Citizen and the State* (1975).

STOCK, as used in the financial sense, is a certificate showing ownership in a corporation. When a corporation is formed, stock is issued to individual purchasers. In this way, capital is accumulated. When additional capital is needed, the corporation may issue additional stock.

Capital stock is divided into shares with each share representing proportional ownership in the corporation. Shares of stock, in the form of stock certificates, can usually transfer ownership by endorsement of the current owner. Most stock transactions go through what is known as the stock or securities market, with a broker being used as an intermediary.

Classes. Stock is divided by types into various classes. A popular type is called common or ordinary stock. This is stock that has claim to both the net assets and the profits of the corporation. Some corporations also issue preferred or prior stock. When preferred stock is issued, it has priority over common stock in the claiming of assets and profits. Preferred stock can also be divided into classes, such as Class A and Class B, or first and second preferred stock. These subclasses are called classified stock.

Rights and Limitations. Most stocks have certain rights and privileges as well as special limitations. These rights or limitations are often indicated in the name of the stock. For example, a convertible stock grants the owner the right or option to exchange it for some other type of security. A callable preferred stock gives the corporation that issued the stock the option to buy it back from the stockholder at any time after due notice has been given. And, an assessable stock is subject to an assessment if the corporation's financial affairs deem it necessary. Other stocks of this nature include full-paid or paid-up stock, guaranteed stock, participating preferred stock, and redeemable preferred stock.

Other Characteristics. In addition, other stocks are named for a particular characteristic they contain. For example, on the stock market there are so-called active stocks, stocks bought and sold continuously in heavy volume. A listed stock is one traded on a recognized stock exchange. Barometer stocks are indicators of market conditions. Other stocks that are indicators include clearinghouse stock, handled on the New York Stock Exchange, and curb stock, listed by the American Stock Exchange.

Some stocks carry with them the privilege of stock dividends. Paid in the form of shares of capital stock, these dividends usually do not change the financial condition of the corporation because they simply transfer funds from the undistributed corporate profits account to the capital stock account. Shares of capital stock may or may not carry a par or face value.

— *William D. Wagoner*

See also Common Stock; Equity; Preferred Stock.

STOCK, as a component of bank portfolio. *See* Balance Sheet, Bank.

STOCK MARKET, a group of financial institutions developed in the United States to aid in the distribution of new securities and the buying and selling of existing ones. Also called security exchanges, these institutions are subject to regulation at both the state and federal levels.

Because of the major financial disaster that hit the stock market in 1929, Congress passed the Securities Exchange Act in 1934. This act required all security exchanges to register with the Securities and Exchange Commission (SEC) and subjected them to SEC regulation.

Organized Security Exchanges. These organized exchanges provide a centralized medium of exchange for the buying and selling of listed securities. Sellers

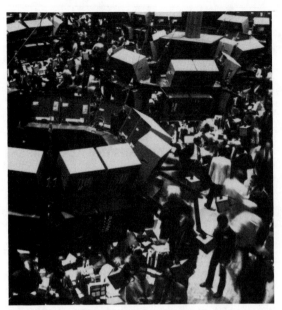

Typical bustling activity at New York Stock Exchange.

attempt to receive the highest price for their securities while buyers attempt to buy at the lowest possible price. When a price is agreed upon, a securities transaction occurs. This is usually facilitated by the aid of a member of the exchange, often referred to as a broker, who receives a fee (commission) for each transaction she or he handles. Brokers often enlist the aid of a securities specialist if they are unable to carry out orders in many different stocks at the same time. Specialists often accept buy and sell orders to be executed at specified prices, or they may aid in decreasing the gap between buying price and selling price.

For a security to be listed on an organized stock exchange, the corporation issuing the security must apply to the exchange and prove that the security satisfies all necessary conditions established by that exchange. These may include a written history of the company; descriptions of the firm's properties, securities, dividend record and policies; and financial statements. The exchange reviews the application and decides whether or not to grant listing. If a company fails to observe the necessary conditions and standards of the exchange, it can be delisted from the exchange.

There are two major organized security exchanges in the United States: the New York Stock Exchange and the American Stock Exchange. Located in New York City, these two exchanges account for nearly 90% of all trading on national exchanges. In addition, there are regional exchanges, such as the Pacific Stock Exchange. On the national exchanges, over 2,500 companies are listed. Twice as many stocks as bonds are listed.

Over-the-Counter Markets. Security transactions take place in over-the-counter security markets as well as in organized security exchanges. In over-the-counter transactions, prices are determined by negotiations between buyers and sellers instead of by centralized bids. In addition, there is considerable diversity in the broker-dealer firms that operate in over-the-counter markets. For example, certain dealer firms tend to specialize in particular types of securities.

Investment Banking. The group of financial institutions known as the investment banking industry is comprised of investment banking firms, commercial banks' underwriting departments, and banker-dealer firms. About 50 investment banking firms handle security offerings in the United States, and together these firms form a highly centralized and efficient mechanism for the distribution of securities.

Government Securities. There are several ways in which the U.S. government securities are distributed. Treasury bills are sold to the highest bidder in the competitive market, while intermediate and long-term securities are sold to all those who are willing to buy them. State and local governments usually distribute their securities by the use of competitive bidding.

Regulation. As noted earlier, security markets are subject to both state and federal legislation. The Securities Act of 1933 was the first federal law requiring issuers of securities to make full disclosures at the time new issues are offered to the public. A year later, the Securities Exchange Act made several provisions regarding the buying and selling of securities, including the registration and regulation of security exchanges, of brokers and dealers, and of all securities. In addition, the submission of financial reports of issues of registered securities, and the submission of reports on transactions in registered securities of officers, directors, and principle security holders was required. Lastly, the board of governors of the Federal Reserve System was given the responsibility to regulate the use of credit in all security transactions.

In 1938, the Maloney Act introduced several amendments to the act of 1934. It provided for the registration of any national securities association with the SEC and established certain standards for these associations. In 1972 the only association registered with the SEC was the National Association of Securities Dealers, Inc. (NASD), established for cooperative regulation of the over-the-counter market. Additional changes in legislation occurred in the mid-1960s. As a result, the SEC imposed comprehensive regulations concerning qualifications, experience, and business practices upon registered broker-dealers who were not members of the registered national association.

In 1966 the New York Stock Exchange adopted rules allowing member firms to execute off-board trading in listed stocks through nonmember firms. In 1966 the SEC, in its report on mutual funds, criticized the size of sales commissions and fees paid for management of the funds' portfolios. In mid-October 1987, the stock market posted a string of large declines, culminating in a one-day plunge of unprecedented magnitude. The stock market had gained more than 40% in value from the beginning of the year until it peaked in August, but by the time it closed on October 16, nearly half that gain was gone. On Monday, October 19, the Dow Jones Industrial Index lost 22.6% in one day. Trading volumes were enormous, and panic threatened to undermine the markets further. The sharp decline was worldwide, progressing from the Tokyo exchange and extending to Europe.

The impact on U.S. economic activity and damages to the financial system were remarkably minor. Several brokerage firms merged or closed, and a number of Wall Street firms announced layoffs. Investors remained nervous, but the Fed's prompt provision of liquidity reassured them. By the year's end, the Dow was back to nearly the previous year's level. A longer-term effect was the loss of foreign equity purchases as a source of financing, but even that seemed to be receding as a cause for concern.

STRIKE, a collective refusal by employees to work. Although unorganized workers may act together and refuse to work, perhaps to gain recognition of their union or to obtain some demand from the employer, strikes are mainly associated with unions and take place in the context of collective bargaining. In a normal year there will be 4,000-5,000 strikes, and over 75% of them will be over wages and hours.

These striking workers are participating in one of the 4,000-5,000 strikes that occur each year. Seventy-five percent of these strikes will be about wages and hours.

Role in Bargaining. As a labor-management contract nears expiration, the two parties begin to bargain over the terms of the new contract, employing various strategies as they argue, make concessions, and work toward a compromise of their differences. Among the strongest pressures each side can exert is that of severing the work relationship until a new contract is agreed upon: management's weapon is the lockout, labor's is the strike.

The threat or possibility of a strike is a factor influencing management's resistance to union demands, whether or not one actually occurs. The threat exists to the extent that the union has previously demonstrated its willingness to strike.

Thus, strikes in a real sense contribute ultimately to settlements. When strikes occur, they impose economic loss on both sides and create an urgency to the bargaining that may hasten a resolution. Also, compromises may appear less unattractive than before, when weighed against losses of profits and wages.

Types of Strikes. Other than contract strikes, there are those called when unions object to management actions during the life of a contract. These strikes are usually in violation of that contract, and, because of their unauthorized nature, are called "wildcat strikes." There are also emergency strikes, public interest disputes, jurisdictional strikes, and the colorful and dramatic "sit-down" strikes of the past.

—Leonard G. Shifrin

See also Emergency Strikes; Lockout; Picketing; Public Interest Disputes; Wildcat Strikes.

STRIKE BENEFITS, payments by a union to its striking members in order to help them to stay off the job, thus maintaining pressure on the employer. While workers are on strike and the employer is experiencing partial or total loss of production and sales, each side is suffering economic loss and is under financial pressure to come to terms. The greater this pressure is on either side, the sooner that side may capitulate to the other's terms, and the further it may be compelled to go in effecting a compromise. To enhance its staying ability, each side has various methods of reducing or offsetting its losses.

Benefit Characteristics. The main method used by the union is to provide strike benefits. Because striking workers are ineligible for unemployment insurance, their unemployment being presumed voluntary, most unions provide payments sufficient to meet essential minimum living expenses. These may be flat-rate, a fixed percentage of regular or base wages, or a variable amount depending on family dependency status or other differences among workers.

Benefits are paid from a strike fund, which is built up in anticipation of need. If the fund becomes depleted during a strike, it frequently is supplemented through special assessments levied on nonstriking members of the union or by contributions or loans from other unions.

—Leonard G. Shifrin

STRIKE NOTICE, notice served on the employer by a union wishing to impose a deadline on the bargaining over a new labor contract. The notice states that as of some specific date, the workers will no longer work without a contract. The strike notice is both an expression to the employer of the seriousness of the union's position and an announcement to the workers that a work stoppage is impending. Under the Railway Labor Act, a strike notice is a legal requirement.

STRUCTURAL DEFICIT results from an expansionary fiscal policy where government spending exceeds the amount of revenue received from taxes when the economy is operating at its capacity. A structural deficit results directly from tax and spending decisions made by Congress and the president. A structural deficit should be distinguished from a cyclical deficit, which results when an economic slump reduces government revenues from taxes but government spending remains unchanged.

STRUCTURAL INFLATION. *See* Sectoral Inflation.

STRUCTURAL UNEMPLOYMENT, unemployment that occurs due to changes in the basic characteristics of an economic structure, such as shifts in industrial location, variations in the rate of population growth, and changes in the type of labor demanded. For example, if a major firm decided to relocate in a different part of the country, many people who (for any reason) could not move with the company would be left structurally unemployed. Likewise, the increased U.S. demand for Japanese automobiles, combined with technological changes in how cars are produced, resulted in major unemployment problems in Detroit in the late 1970s and early 1980s. Other areas of the country hit with structural unemployment include Appalachia and the Ozark Plateau.

See also Unemployment of Labor.

SUBSIDY, a type of financial assistance or a concession having economic value granted by a government to certain producers. The usual purpose of a subsidy is to encourage a producer to undertake or continue a given type of production that, although unprofitable, is considered essential to public welfare, such as steel mills for domestic self-sufficiency or merchant marine shipbuilding for national defense.

SUBSISTENCE ECONOMY, one in which all economic activity occurs outside the market. With households caring for their own economic needs directly, independent of the rest of the community, money and trade are absent. All goods are homemade, and both productivity and consumption are very low. Hunting,

Public subsidies are important elements in the operation of many major urban mass transit systems, such as this modern commuter train that is part of San Francisco's BART system.

fishing, and foraging supplement agriculture. The term subsistence economy is associated with peasant economies, and today's closest approximations are in "underdeveloped" areas.

See also Sahlins, Marshall; Underdevelopment.

SUBSISTENCE THEORY OF WAGES states that wages tend to equal what the worker needs to maintain a bare subsistence level of living. This theory emerged in the early nineteenth century as a result of the writings of two classical economists, David Ricardo and Thomas Malthus.

According to the subsistence theory, when a worker receives a higher wage than he or she needs for mere subsistence, the result will be an increase in the number of children and eventually an increase in the number of workers. As more people become workers, either competition reduces wages paid to workers, or increased demand for food raises the cost of food. In either case, real income is reduced. Therefore, a worker cannot receive a permanent increase in wages. By the twentieth century, this theory had given way to more progressive theories.

See also Wage Theories.

SUBSTANTIAL LESSENING OF COMPETITION.
In determining whether a firm has violated the Clayton Act prohibitions against price discrimination, exclusive dealerships and tying contracts, and mergers, the Federal Trade Commission and federal courts must consider whether the effect of the firm's practices "may be to substantially lessen competition."

Apart from the evidence of a violation, at least three areas of interpretation are called for in litigation under the act. "May be" has come to mean a reasonable probability, not just possibility, of injury to competition. Lessened competition has been found in elimination of rivals or diversion of trade from rivals. (These

effects actually show an impact on competitors rather than competition.)

What is "substantial" has not been determined precisely. For some time prior to World War II, courts emphasized the test of "proportional substantiality," an assessment of the percent of the market affected. No "magic number" as to percent necessary to show violation was announced, however. Since that time, more, but not exclusive, emphasis has been placed on "quantitative substantiality," a test based on the absolute dollar volume of trade, rather than the percent of the market affected.

—*Thomas O. Depperschmidt*
See also Clayton Act; Exclusive Dealership; Merger; Price Discrimination; Quantitative Substantiality; Tying Contract; United States v. New York Great A & P Co.

SUBSTITUTE GOODS, in consumption, goods that are to some extent interchangeable with each other. If the price of one good fell, the demand curves for its substitutes would shift inward toward the origin, increasing a decrease in demand for the substitute goods. Formally, two goods are said to be substitutes if an increase (decrease) in the price of one leads to an increase (decrease) in the demand for the other.

See also Complementary Goods.

SUBSTITUTION EFFECT. For nearly all products or services, an increase in price results in a smaller amount demanded. This is the law of demand: a rise in price causes a fall in the quantity demanded, whereas a decline in price causes an increase in the quantity demanded.

When the price of a product goes down, people can afford to buy more of it, and when the price goes up, they cannot afford to buy as much. This is the income effect on demand.

When the price of a product rises, people tend to buy less of it and buy a less expensive substitute instead. This is the *substitution effect* on demand: replacing a costly item with a less costly one.

See also Consumer Equilibrium.

SUPERIOR GOOD. *See* Income Effect.

SUPPLEMENTAL SECURITY INCOME (SSI), a federal program established in 1972, that provides a guaranteed minimum income for the elderly and the disabled. The SSI program is funded almost entirely by the federal government, and replaced several other programs that were jointly funded by the federal government and state governments, such as Old-Age Assistance, Aid to the Blind, and Aid to the Permanently and Totally Disabled. These latter programs are still funded, but are being slowly phased out. SSI is administered by the Social Security Administration, and paid out over $14.8 billion in benefits in 1987.

Eligibility is determined by a means test—i.e., income must fall below certain minimums, and wealth must also fall below certain limits.

SUPPLEMENTAL UNEMPLOYMENT BENEFITS,

benefits that, under certain conditions, an employee may receive in addition to unemployment compensation. There are two types: the insurance fund and the individual account plan.

Under the insurance fund, a company contributes a certain amount of money to a trust fund established for the benefit of the employees. When an employee becomes unemployed for reasons beyond his or her control, the employee receives unemployment compensation from the fund in addition to that provided by the state.

The individual account plan establishes an account for each employee, to which the company contributes, upon which the employee may draw when he or she leaves the company, retires, becomes ill, or is laid off. Although this is a much broader plan, it is not as popular as the insurance fund.

SUPPLY is a functional relationship between quantity supplied and a host of other variables, the most important of which is usually considered to be price. The supply relationship defines the conditions under which a producer will voluntarily produce and offer for sale differing outputs. It is a flow concept and is therefore defined per unit of time. Variables other than price which are potential determinants of supply are: (1) the price of such inputs as labor and raw materials; (2) the current level of technology in the industry in question; (3) the future price expectations; and (4) the prices of alternative commodities that the firm potentially can produce in the short run. Moreover, if we are concerned with the short run then certain inputs such as land and capital are considered to be fixed.

It is important to note that, unless specified otherwise, demand considerations are ignored. Thus, the supply schedule shows conditions under which outputs will be voluntarily offered; whether they can actually be sold or not is important but not immediately relevant. The fact that supply and demand are considered independent implies that a change in one will not directly lead to a change in the other. This theoretical contrivance is called partial equilibrium analysis.
                                        —*Robert L. Brite*

SUPPLY CURVE, the graphical representation of a supply schedule. It is two-dimensional, showing the relationship between prices and quantities supplied, holding other potentially important variables constant. Because it is a flow concept, the axis should be labeled per unit of time.

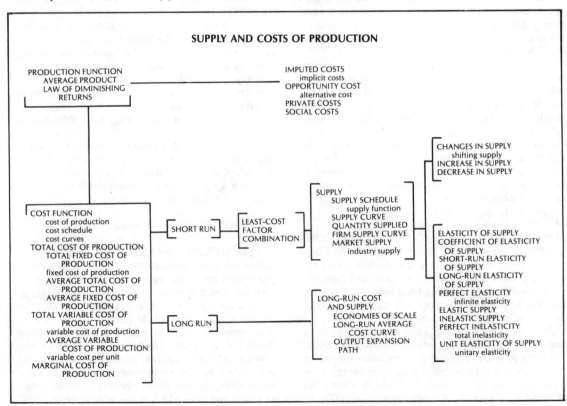

SUPPLY AND COSTS OF PRODUCTION

The supply of food, as with other commodities, is determined by a variety of factors including the level of available technology.

Mathematically it is the convention to put the dependent variable on the Y axis and the independent variable on the X axis. However, following the convention originating with Alfred Marshall (the famous neo-classical Cambridge economist), economists usually plot price on the Y axis and quantity supplied—the dependent variable—on the X axis. Since the Y intercept and the slope change with the labeling of the axis, this is an important consideration and care must

SUPPLY CURVE

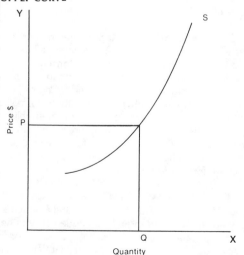

be taken to avoid confusion in the more mathematical treatments of supply schedules.

Since negative prices and outputs are not economically meaningful, the supply schedule will lie entirely in the first quadrant of the coordinate system. To reflect the inverse relationship between price and quantity supplied, the supply schedule should slope upward from left to right. The positive slope reflects the fact that the marginal cost of output rises due to diminishing returns to labor. The firm will voluntarily increase its output per unit of time only if price rises to offset this increased marginal cost of later units of output.

The supply curve can also be viewed as the locus of all points representing potential or possible equilibrium positions for the firm. Since the supply curve defines the outputs voluntarily supplied under differing circumstances (prices) it must simultaneously define the profit maximizing positions for the firm, following the assumption that the producers are attempting to maximize profits.   —*Robert L. Brite*

SUPPLY FUNCTION. *See* Supply Schedule.

SUPPLY SCHEDULE, a two-dimensional relationship often depicted in a table showing the various amounts that a firm will voluntarily offer under differing prices, assuming that all other determinants than price (such as wage rates, technology, expectation) remain constant. This is the famous *ceteris paribus* ("other things being the same") assumption, an extremely useful pedagogical device in economics as well as other scientific disciplines.

Supply schedules show a direct relationship between price and quantity supplied; this is usually referred to as the law of supply. The fact that low prices are associated with small outputs voluntarily offered, and high prices with larger quantities offered, is of paramount importance in economics and is accounted for largely by the law of diminishing returns.

The supply schedule we are concerned with is the short-run relationship between price and quantity supplied. Since land and capital (as well as technology) are considered to be constant in the short run, the firm can only increase output by taking on more labor. Adding more and more quantities of labor to fixed inputs inevitably causes diminishing returns to occur; the marginal product of labor falls, whereupon, assuming constant wage rates, marginal cost of output rises. If wage rates = $1.00/hr., and the marginal product of the last worker equals 10, then the marginal cost of output equals roughly 10 cents. If marginal product falls to 5 cents for the next laborer, the last unit now costs roughly 20 cents. Since later units of output cost more than earlier units, the firm will voluntarily offer larger amounts only if price rises to offset increased marginal cost.   —*Robert L. Brite*

SUPPLY SHOCK, a disturbance to the economy whose first impact is to shift the aggregate supply curve. The macroeconomic story of the 1970s was largely a story of supply shocks. The two major supply shocks during the 1970s were increases, engineered by OPEC, in the price of oil from 1973 to 1974, and again from 1979 to 1980. The first OPEC shock produced a quadrupling of the price of oil between 1971 and 1974, and helped to push the U.S. economy into the 1973-75 recession, until then the worst recession since World War II. The second OPEC price increase further doubled the price of oil, sharply accelerated the inflation rate, led to a tough monetary policy during 1980-81 to fight inflation, and this in turn led to an even deeper recession than the one in 1973-75.

The second oil price shock left the price of oil so high that many new suppliers entered the market. This resulted in the virtual collapse of the OPEC pricing system, dropping the price of oil to 1978 levels. This is an example of a favorable supply shock.

SUPPLY-SIDE ECONOMICS refers to an emphasis on the determinants of aggregate supply in economic modeling. The typical macroeconomic model used to guide policy emphasizes monetary and fiscal policy, determinants of aggregate demand. Economists who focus on supply-side economics argue that, to a large extent, stagnation and inflation in modern economies result from difficulties on the supply side and that these difficulties are ignored by standard theory.

Remedies for stagnation and inflation advocated by supply-side economists involve attempts to increase productivity. There are many provisions of current government policy that supply-side economists see as barriers to productivity. Particular villains are price controls and minimum wages which interfere with efficient allocation in individual markets. Also, governmental environmental and health regulations which impose costs and impede production are opposed by many supply-side economists.

This focus on deregulation has started considerable controversy on many fronts. Nevertheless, the supply-side approach has been successful in focusing attention on one of the costs of regulation that was not well understood when the initial regulations were enacted.

SURPLUS FINANCE. When the government collects more in revenues than it spends, a surplus results. This surplus has contractionary effects on the economy. The way in which this surplus is used can either reinforce or neutralize the contractionary effect. Maximum economic contraction results when the surplus is held idle and not allowed to reenter the private sector. If the surplus is distributed to those who would immediately spend it, the contractionary effect is substantially offset; if it is used to retire government debt that already exists, the degree to which the contraction is offset depends upon who holds the debt that is to be retired, whether they are spenders or savers.

SURPLUS VALUE, the difference between the value of commodities produced by labor and the wage payment to labor. According to Marx, surplus value, the source of capitalist profits, arose because in the average working day, a laborer produced more than enough to provide for his own subsistence.

See also Marx, Karl; Proletariat.

SYNDICALISM, a revolutionary movement that originated in France in the late nineteenth century, with Georges Sorel as one of its intellectual leaders. Deeming class conflict the dominant characteristic in society, syndicalists believed workers must liberate themselves from employers and the state through boycotts, sabotage, mass demonstrations, and strikes. A general strike would overturn the existing system, and industries would be operated by associations of workers to be formed from existing labor unions.

See also Anarchistic Communism; Revolutionary Socialism.

TABLEAU ÉCONOMIQUE, the first macroeconomic model combined with the first analysis of aggregate economic relationships. François Quesnay's *Tableau Économique* (1758) attempted to indicate the flows of goods and money between economic sectors in a competitive economy. Of the three sectors considered—landlords, tenant farmers, and manufacturers-merchants—only the tenant farmers were deemed productive, following the Physiocrats' view that only nature can produce a net product. The *Tableau* then indicates how the net product of the agricultural sector circulates and how it is reproduced from one year to the next. Quesnay's work provided the basis for some aspects of macroeconomics, including national income accounting and the circular flow.

See also Physiocrats; Quesnay, François.

TACIT AGREEMENT, an agreement that is only inferred or implied and is never directly stated. Agreement is usually in the form of silent consent.

Tacit agreements are sometimes found in oligopolistic market structures where firms tend to "agree" on a market price or any other policy without formal or written contracts. For example, if one firm establishes a price for its product, by a tacit agreement all other firms may use this same price for their products. Agreements of this type are often used as substitutes for illegal forms of collusion.

TAFT-HARTLEY ACT (1947), also known as the Labor-Management Relations Act of 1947, amended the Wagner Act of 1935 and also added several new features to federal labor legislation. These changes reflected the one-sidedness of the original Wagner Act in labor's behalf (which in 1935 may well have been justified but by 1947 perhaps no longer was). The great growth of unionism between the mid-1930s and the end of World War II had brought labor to its greatest strength, and equality in collective bargaining now made necessary some restraints on this power, of a sort similar to those imposed on management in the earlier law.

Wagner Act Changes. Section 7 of the Wagner Act protected the right of employees to join unions and bargain collectively. Taft-Hartley added the protection of the workers' right not to join unions. Section 8 of the Wagner Act, which specified the "unfair labor practices" prohibited to employers was left almost unchanged. But Taft-Hartley added protections for both employers and workers by designating unfair labor practices prohibited to labor organizations or their representatives. Taft-Hartley also amended the Wagner Act in regard to the structure and operation of the National Labor Relations Board (NLRB).

New Features. The act required unions to file certain information with the government in order to remain under NLRB protection and set forth a detailed procedure for resolving "national emergency strikes."

In strikes that may seriously affect the national safety and well-being, the president may ask the attorney general to seek an 80-day strike injunction. During the first 60 days, mediation is attempted and a fact-finding board studies the situation. The board then reports to the president, and a "last-offer" vote is conducted among the employees. After 80 days, if no resolution has occurred despite these steps, the strike may resume, and any further action is left to labor and management.

Effect. All in all, the Taft-Hartley Act is a complex and detailed law with several aims. It seeks to reestablish a "balance of power" in labor-management relations, to protect the uninvolved third parties from economic harm resulting from labor disputes, and to protect the public from strikes that seriously affect its safety and well-being.   —*Leonard G. Shifrin*

See also Unfair Labor Practices; Wagner Act.

TAKE-OFF (Spurt), the stage of growth during which the old societal values and resistances to growth are overcome and a modern industrial society emerges. The state is characterized by a surge in technological development, the reinvestment of business profits in new plant and equipment, and an increase in private savings and investment. Western Europe experienced the take-off phase of its development during the late eighteenth and early nineteenth centuries.

TARGET PRICING refers to that policy of a business firm that establishes a designated or target rate of profit to be earned in a certain period of time.

Because of their independent nature, target pricing

policies are usually found in noncompetitive market structures where individual firms have some voice in pricing policies. Target pricing is especially popular in monopolistic industries where price can be set by the individual firm. Purely competitive firms cannot successfully use target pricing because price is usually established by the market.

TARIFFS, taxes placed on imports either by value (ad valorem duty) or per unit of quantity (specific duty). A single-columned tariff schedule has the same rate on a particular good irrespective of the country of origin; a multi-columned tariff discriminates according to the country of origin. The chief purpose of tariffs today is protection of import-competing domestic firms, but the original purpose of American tariffs was revenue.

Effects. The imposition of a duty may affect the price and production of the taxed good in the importing country in several ways. There may be no effect when the duty is placed on a commodity also exported by the country, or when the entire duty is borne by the foreign exporter. The price may rise by the amount of the duty when the commodity taxed is produced abroad at constant costs. Finally, the price may rise by less than the duty. Under increasing cost conditions a duty will cause the foreign and domestic price to differ by an amount equal to the duty, unless the duty is so high as to be prohibitive, but the price rise in the importing country is equal to the duty less the fall in price in the exporting country. This effect is most general. The burden of the duty will always be shifted toward the area of least elasticity: the more elastic the supply is in the exporting country, the higher will be the price increase in the importing country.

Arguments for Tariffs come in many forms. Tariffs improve terms of trade, reduce unemployment, encourage industrialization, further military security, prevent pauperization of labor, keep money at home, effect retaliation, and increase bargaining power. The terms-of-trade argument is valid, if the foreign exporter will bear the burden. The infant-industry argument is rational for any less developed country, which needs a protected market until economies of scale are reached and lower costs allow the country to compete internationally. A problem arises in determining responsive industries and realistic time goals and in avoiding retaliation. Economically, tariffs would equalize costs of production at home and abroad, completely destroying the whole basis for trade. Therefore, most pleas for tariffs are actually pleas for subsidies.   —*John R. Matthews, Jr.*

See also Balance of Trade; Terms of Trade; Trade Barriers.

TAUSSIG, FRANK WILLIAM (1859-1940), presented a body of economic thought very much in the classical tradition and in many respects can be called the American Alfred Marshall. Taussig's most important contributions were in the fields of tariffs and international trade. His *Tariff History of the United States* (1888) was an attempt to integrate theory with empirical data to provide a better understanding of tariff questions. This work provided much of the foundation of his book *International Trade* (1927) in which he combined the theory of international trade and comparative advantage with the effects of monetary credit systems.

Taussig is also an important figure because of his significant role as teacher of an important generation of American economists.

TAUT PLANNING. *See* Centralization.

TAXATION, the collection of revenues for governmental purposes by use of the coercive power of the state. Taxation takes many forms, and has evolved in several different ways over the years.

Taxes by Level of Government. The table below outlines the main sources of tax revenue by each level of government in the United States, as of 1981. The table points out that each type of government tends to rely on particular tax sources instead of all levels of government utilizing the same tax bases. Income taxes are predominantly federal, although state income taxes have increased in importance in recent years. The payroll tax that finances Social Security is strictly a federal tax. State governments are the heaviest users of general sales taxes, and much of the "other tax" category comes from selective excise taxes, such as gasoline, cigarette, and severance taxes. Property taxes are utilized almost exclusively by local levels of government. The federal aid and state aid listed in the table have become major revenue sources in recent years, but do not constitute taxation by the receiving government.

Principles of Taxation. There is no uniform consensus on what constitutes a "good" or "bad" tax, although the definition in political terms often is simply that a good tax is one someone else pays, while a bad tax is one you yourself have to pay. Unfortunately, such a definition is unworkable. A good tax from the

---

TAXATION: TOPIC GUIDE

For a discussion of how taxes affect the economy as a whole, see articles on CIRCULAR FLOW OF INCOME and PUBLIC FINANCE. Details on particular taxes are found in articles throughout this book. See the list with the TAXATION GLOSSARY for more details. Also see the article on FISCAL FEDERALISM for a discussion of intergovernmental revenues.

The Subject Map accompanying the article on PUBLIC FINANCE provides more detail.

FEDERAL REVENUES AND EXPENDITURES (1991)

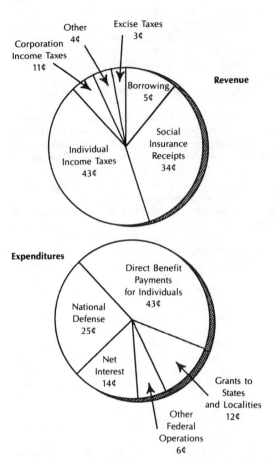

point of view of economics is a tax that is relatively easy to collect, tends to have a minimal impact on the allocation of resources in the economy, and is equitable. None of these concepts is easy to define. The concept of *excess burden* deals with the issue of the allocation of resources and taxes. Taxes that cause massive attempts to avoid them clearly have detrimental consequences in terms of the efficient allocation of resources in society. The personal income tax has received a great deal of attention in recent years as causing wasteful investment in tax shelters merely for the sake of avoiding taxes, and as causing a reduction in work effort and savings. Changes in the tax law to enhance both the efficiency and fairness of the federal tax system occurred through the Tax Reform Act of 1986.

Equity of the tax is hard to measure, but two principles are most often utilized: taxation on the basis of the *ability to pay* the tax; and taxation on the basis of the *benefits received* from the activities the taxes finance. The ability-to-pay principle often is the main one used in political discussions of taxation, although

TAXATION GLOSSARY

See separate listings for the following taxation terms:

Ability-to-Pay Principle
Benefits Principle
Corporate Income Tax
Excise Tax
Marginal Tax Rate
Negative Income Tax
Personal Income Tax
Progressive Tax
Property Tax
Proportional Tax
Proposition 13
Regressive Tax
Sales Tax
Selective Sales Tax
Tax Capacity
Tax Incidence
Tax Rate
Tax Shifting
Turnover Tax
Value-Added Tax

Accelerated Cost Recovery System (ACRS)—a schedule of rates at which investments in capital goods can be deducted from income for tax purposes. For example, under ACRS, a real estate investment made in 1985 could be expensed over an 18-year period. This is "accelerated" in the sense that a building usually has an expected life of much more than this time period.

Ad Valorem Tax—tax that is proportional to the monetary value of the tax base, such as a property tax.

Capital Gains Tax—tax on the net income gained from the sale of an asset, such as stocks or a house.

Credit—reduction in the amount of tax due below the scheduled amount of tax. An example is the credit for child care expenses in the personal income tax.

Custom Duties—tax collected on items imported into a country. Occasionally a tax on exports as well.

Deduction—a reduction in the amount of a tax base subject to tax. For example, personal income taxpayers can either itemize specific deductible amounts such as charitable contributions and excessive medical expenses, or they can deduct a predetermined amount, or standard deduction.

Depreciation Allowance—a reduction in taxable income related to the aging and wearing out of a capital good. Current depreciation rules involve a modified ACRS, introduced through the Tax Reform Act of 1986.

Depletion Allowance—tax preference extended to owners of exhaustible natural resources, such as oil, natural gas, or timber.

Double Taxation—taxing the same tax base twice. For example, the taxation of corporate income without allowing a deduction for dividends paid, then also taxing the dividends paid by the corporation, constitutes double taxation.

Estate Tax—tax on the value of a deceased person's estate.

Excess Profits Tax—tax on profits that are socially deemed to be excessive; usually applied during wartime, but recently imposed on oil profits resulting from the shortages of the mid-1970s.

Exemption—part of the conceptual tax base that is legally removed from being subject to tax. For example, income from interest received from state and local bonds is exempt from the federal income tax. Similarly, land and buildings owned by religious organizations are exempt from local property taxes.

Gift Tax—tax on donated property or income; designed to prevent avoidance of inheritance or estate taxes.

Inheritance Tax—tax on the portion of an estate received by an individual.

Severance Tax—a tax on the removal and sale of a natural resource. Severance taxes are major sources of revenue to resource-rich states such as Alaska, Texas, Louisiana, and Oklahoma.

Single Tax—plan, popularized by Henry George in the 1800s, that would tax away all rents earned from the ownership of land. George argued that such income was unearned and not a rightful gain of the landowner and also that such a tax would raise sufficient revenue to finance government. The latter is certainly no longer true.

Standard Deduction—an amount available to all personal income taxpayers that is not subject to tax.

Tariff—another term for custom duties.

Tax Avoidance—the legal attempt to escape payment of tax; for example, by investing in tax-exempt activities, or by utilizing tax deductions and tax credits.

Tax Evasion—the illegal attempt to escape payment of taxes; for example, by not reporting taxable income to evade the income tax, or by understating sales to escape sales taxes that should be legally paid.

Tax Loophole—an element of the tax law, usually unintentional, that allows for the avoidance of taxes.

Tax Reform—the revision of the tax laws, usually with the intent of closing tax loopholes, making the system simpler, making the tax system fairer, or some combination of all three.

Tax Shelter—an investment that allows for minimization of tax liabilities as an important part of the investment itself.

Use Tax—tax on the initial use, rather than the sale, of an item; normally used to prevent avoidance of a sales tax by purchasing an expensive item in another lower-tax jurisdiction.

Withholding—collection of a tax by the government in anticipation of a future tax liability; for example, federal income taxes are withheld from wages earned throughout the year, although the actual determination of personal income tax liability is not made until after the year has ended.

Zero-Bracket Amount—the same thing as the standard deduction.

many economists stress the need to consider the benefits and the taxes as a package, as implied by the benefits-received criterion. From an equity perspective, a tax is said to be *progressive* if the tax payment rises faster than income (i.e., high-income taxpayers pay a larger percentage of income in tax than do lower-income taxpayers). A tax is *proportional* if the tax burden is the same percentage of income for all incomes. A tax is *regressive* if lower-income taxpayers pay at a higher percentage rate than do higher-income taxpayers. Actual tax payments under a regressive tax may be (and usually are) higher for a higher-income taxpayer, but they represent a smaller percentage of income.

Many taxes are legally paid by businesses and by persons, yet these taxes may not be effectively paid by them in an economic sense. This is known as *tax shifting*. For example, a tax on corporate profits may be paid by the owners of the corporation (its stockholders), but if the tax causes stockholders to shift their investments into other firms, reducing yields available in other investments and raising before-tax yields in the taxed investment, the tax will be effectively shifted to all investors—not just those of the taxed firm. Similarly, if the tax causes wages to fall in the taxed firm, the tax is shifted from the firm to the workers. Alternatively, it is possible that the tax will be passed on to consumers of the firm's products in the form of higher prices. Determination of the ultimate bearer of the burden of a tax is known as *tax incidence* analysis. Tax incidence studies have reached conflicting conclusions with respect to several major taxes. It is generally believed that the sales tax is passed on to customers in the form of higher prices, so that the tax is somewhat regressive (lower-income households spend larger proportions of their income on consumption than do higher-income households). The inci-

dence of the personal income tax is thought to rest with the taxpayer (the tax is not shifted), and is therefore progressive. There is much debate as to the incidence of corporate income taxes and property taxes, however. Studies of the overall federal, state, and local tax structures usually suggest that the overall tax system is approximately proportional.

—*Michael S. Johnson*

TAX CAPACITY, a measure of the ability of governments to raise revenues. Tax capacity is sometimes measured by income per capita, but this is much too simplistic, as the ability of governments to collect revenues from nonresidents of the taxing jurisdiction (called *tax exporting*) varies greatly from state to state or locality to locality. In many grants-in-aid programs, the amount of aid received by a government from another government is inversely related to the tax capacity of the recipient jurisdiction. For example, state aid to local school districts is often greater for districts that have a low level of property wealth per pupil in an effort to equalize at least partially the ability of the various school districts to fund public education.

See also Fiscal Federalism; Taxation.

TAX CAPACITY

(Selected States as of 1980 Census)

State	Capacity*
Alabama	76
Alaska	260
California	117
Delaware	111
Florida	100
Indiana	92
Louisiana	108
Michigan	97
Minnesota	102
Mississippi	69
Nevada	154
New Jersey	105
New York	90
Texas	124
Utah	86
Wyoming	196
U.S. AVERAGE	100

*An index number, measured relative to the U.S. average of all states. For example, a value of 108 means that the state would collect 8% more revenues per capita than the typical state if it imposed all taxes at the average tax rate prevailing throughout all the states.

TAXES, the income of governments. Originally confined almost exclusively to import duties, the incidence and extent of taxation by the United States Government have expanded throughout the country's history as a function both of the increasing demand for

TAXATION

Revenue Trends in the United States, 1986

	LEVEL OF GOVERNMENT		
	Federal	**State**	**Local**
Total Revenues (billions)	$ 847.5	$ 481.2	$ 434.8
Per Capita Revenues	$3,515	$1,988	$1,804
Percentage Distribution by Source:			
Federal Aid	n/a	19.2%	0.9%
State Aid	n/a	n/a	33.8%
Income Taxes (personal and corporate)	48.7%	17.8	2.0
Social Security Tax	40.1	0.0	0.0
Property Taxes	0.0	0.8	24.7
General Sales Taxes	0.0	15.5	3.7
Other Taxes	7.2	13.5	2.7
Charges and Misc.	12.6	13.9	20.3

governmental services and, more recently, of the post-Keynesian emphasis on regulation of the economy through fiscal policy.

Kinds. Taxes are of many types, the most common of which, in addition to income tax, are tariffs (import duties), sales, excise, estate, gift, value-added, and property taxes. The type of tax imposed and its rate depend on a variety of factors, the most prominent being the political acceptability of the tax, the need for revenue, and the ease with which the tax may be collected.

Tariffs are frequently imposed because of a government's desire to bolster its own economy by restricting outside competition. It is a goal that is usually desired by the people and opposed by foreigners. *Estate taxes* are primarily a means of redistribution of wealth. As compared to tariffs, estate taxes are a new development, imposed only since disproportionate wealth has become socially undesirable. *Gift taxes* are a nuisance to both governments and individuals and are subject to easy evasion. They are used only to support estate taxes; without a gift tax, most individuals could avoid estate taxes by arranging to have no estate.

Property taxes, long the mainstay of taxation at the local level, recently have been questioned on constitutional grounds in both state and federal courts. From the viewpoint of local governments, this development is likely to prove unfortunate. Property taxes may be the ideal tax for local governments. The tax is difficult to evade or escape: real estate can be neither concealed nor removed. More important, local governments, because of the nature of their responsibilities, need the tax's stable source of revenue. For the federal government, income taxes are a more satisfactory instrument from which to gain needed revenue than any other tax. The federal income tax began in 1913 with an amendment to the Constitution.

See also Public Finance.

TAX INCIDENCE, the measurement of who pays a tax in an economic sense. The economic incidence of a tax may differ from the legal incidence if the taxed party is able to shift the tax burden to others through higher prices or lower wages. Tax incidence refers to the ultimate bearer of the tax, after all economic responses have been carried out.

See also Taxation.

TAX RATE, the percentage or absolute amount to be applied to the tax base in order to determine the tax liability. The tax base may be income, sales, gallons of gasoline, or any other specified unit. The tax rate can be a percentage of income or of sales, or a specific nominal amount per unit.

TAX SHIFTING is the passing on by one taxpayer to another all or part of the tax payment. This is accomplished through the adjustment of prices and incomes.

As a consequence of a tax, the prices of goods or services sold may increase or the tax may be said to have been shifted forward. Alternately, prices of factors of production (materials, rent on land and buildings, interest on borrowing, and wages to employees) may fall because of the tax. In this case, the tax is said to have been shifted backward. Shifting may also be a combination of forward and backward. In many cases the shifting procedure is minimal, as in the case of the personal income tax. In others, such as the tax on corporate profits, the final resting place (or incidence) is in doubt.

TAX STRUCTURE refers to the *actual* or *effective* rates of taxation paid by individuals or firms, at different levels of income. Specifically, this measures whether the tax system is actually progressive, proportional, or regressive. Although the statutory rates may suggest progression, special treatment (deductions, exemptions, etc.) of certain types of incomes will reduce considerably the actual progressivity.

TECHNICAL COOPERATION ADMINISTRATION. *See* Point Four Program.

TECHNOLOGICAL CHANGE is brought about within a technology by invention, innovation, imitation, improvement, adaptation to local conditions, and development of full-scale plans. Economic demand, physical resources, costs, and profitability are factors determining the effort devoted to, and the magnitude of, technological change.

As a nation's production-possibility frontier is advanced through such change, the interrelated nature of production tends to cause a clustering of inventions and innovations, with a corresponding increase in capital investment, which leads to economic expan-

A nation's production-possibility frontier is advanced through technological change, such as these robots in an automated body shop.

sion. Change that increases the productivity of existing resources, and makes new equipment more productive than old, makes economic growth easier.

See also Technology.

Another example of technological change is the ubiquitous computer.

TECHNOLOGICAL QUESTION. *See* Market Mechanism.

TECHNOLOGICAL UNEMPLOYMENT results when a particular type of labor is displaced either by machines or by a different type of labor. When advances in technology make machinery less expensive to use than manpower, jobs become obsolete. Likewise, if newer and cheaper products or methods of production come about, jobs pertaining to the old products or methods of production may be eliminated. Technological unemployment can involve as few as one or two jobs in an industry (the burglar alarm replacing the watchman), or may involve an entire industry or skill (blacksmiths).

See also Unemployment of Labor.

TECHNOLOGY, a body of skills and knowledge that provides techniques for accomplishing desired goals. A particular technology involves inputs and outputs and the quantitative relations between the amounts of each. If a technology can produce several outputs in variable proportions, production functions can be used to derive an output-possibility curve or "efficiency frontier," summarizing the production choices open to a nation with given resources and technology.

See also Demand for Capital; Technological Change.

TERMS OF TRADE, the ratio at which goods are exchanged internationally, usually measured in terms of export and import prices. In barter terms it refers to the quantity of exports that must be given up to obtain a given quantity of imports. If more exports have to be sent abroad to get the same amount of imports, the terms of trade have turned against the country in question. They have turned favorable when fewer exports will command the same or more imports.

The terms of trade can better or worsen irrespective of the status of the balance of trade, which is the difference between merchandise exports and imports.

See also Barter; Comparative Advantage.

TERM STRUCTURE OF INTEREST RATES, the term to maturity of a loan. The length of time that the loan is outstanding will influence the interest rate paid on the loan. The longer the term to maturity, the higher the interest rate will be. People must be paid more for the use of their money for a longer period of time. A series of short-term loans can, in most cases, be considered a substitute for a long-term loan. Thus, the expectations concerning short-term interest rates can influence the term structure of interest rates.

See also Interest Rate Structure.

THEORY, ECONOMIC. A theory consists of definitions, assumptions, and hypotheses. The purpose of theory is to develop valid generalizations to predict how people, things, and systems will behave under given conditions. Economic theory attempts to explain how and why certain economic processes, such as production, consumption, allocation of scarce resources, determination of prices, levels of employment, and conditions of competition, behave in a given manner. Economic theory also attempts to enable business and government leaders to predict future behavior of general levels of production, employment, demand, and other significant economic processes. There are a variety of specific economic theories, such as the law of supply and demand, the theory of marginal utility, and the theory of price elasticity.

Schools. There are basic schools of economic thought that represent generally accepted sets of empirical and philosophical tenets, the composite of which is commonly referred to as economic theory. These composite economic theories or schools of economic thought are commonly categorized into three groupings: Classical economic theory prevailed from about 1750 to the early 1900s. Neoclassical economic theory, which developed during the last two decades of the nineteenth century, culminating in Alfred Marshall's *Principles of Economics* (1890), dominated economic theory for the first half of the twentieth century. Many of the school's postulates are still considered valid. Keynesian economic theory (national income theory) was initiated by Lord Keynes in *The General Theory of Employment, Interest, and Money* (1936). National income theory has dominated much of advanced economic theory since 1940.

— *Algin B. King*

See also National Income Determination; Neoclassical Economics.

THEORY OF MONOPOLISTIC COMPETITION

(1933), by Edward H. Chamberlin, developed the theory of the firm to include the great area between pure competition and pure monopoly. Chamberlin's work appeared a few months before Joan Robinson's *The Economics of Imperfect Competition,* although both books covered much the same ground.

Chamberlin attempted to combine elements of competition and monopoly in developing the theory of monopolistic competition. Like monopolists, many firms face downward-sloping demand curves for their products; yet, like the competitive situation, most firms operate in industries with freedom of entry and exit. Under these conditions the equilibrium position of the firm is quite different from the competitive or monopolistic situation.

THEORY OF THE FIRM, in microeconomics, the

analysis of the decision-making process of firms. In the theory of the firm, all firms are assumed to maximize profits. In economic theory, a firm is defined as any organizationally separate production unit. At the broadest level of abstraction, the definition of the firm encompasses corporate giants such as General Motors, economically minuscule individual proprietorships as the television repairman with a workbench in his basement, and the person who feeds his or her family and operates a catering service from the same kitchen.

Classification of Firms: By Product Type. Although precise classification by product type is not always possible, a collection of firms that produce and sell the same or closely related products or services is referred to as an industry. Thus we speak of the automobile industry, the television repair industry, and the food service industry.

By Ownership. Legally, firms are classified in terms of their form of ownership. A single proprietorship is a firm that is owned by one individual. A partnership is jointly owned by two or more persons who share the profits and losses of the firm and who are individually liable for the full extent of any financial obligations of the firm. A corporation is also jointly owned, but the corporation is itself an individual in the sight of the law, and if it fails, the owners (stockholders) stand to lose only what they have previously invested.

The Place of the Firm in Economic Theory. The purpose of economic theory is to explain how various economic systems work. We are primarily interested in understanding our own and similar economies. To this end, we borrow an approach from the more exact engineering and natural sciences and construct models that are intended to analogue the essential functional processes and interrelationships of the system we wish to study. (What makes economics a "soft" science relative to the engineering and natural sciences is that in economics we are not able to test our models under controlled laboratory conditions and must settle for testing by less exact statistical techniques.) In the generalized model employed in economics, production units (firms) and consumption units (consumers) comprise the fundamental "atoms" of the model. Analytically there are many similarities as well as differences between firms and consumers. The similarities stem from the assumption of maximizing behavior on the part of both.

Description of the Model of the Firm. As a theoretical abstraction, the firm consists of a number of market relationships and a process which transforms inputs into outputs. This process includes a decision-making unit that coordinates the process.

A firm acquires inputs (factors of production) and sells outputs and thus operates in a variety of markets. Certain factors of production may be owned by the firm and thus incorporated into its productive process without a formal purchase transaction taking place; but it is convenient analytically to pretend that these factors have also been purchased and impute a cost to them equal to their market value. As an example, the single proprietorship owner will usually contribute her or his own labor to the productive process without entering a cost for this labor on the books. Economists include the market value of this labor as a cost to the firm.

The technical relationships between the inputs and outputs for the firms constitute the production function: the maximum amount of a given output that can be obtained from a given set of input quantities and given levels of any other outputs. The economist is not concerned with the engineering aspects of these relationships but simply takes them as being given. The inputs of the productive process can be divided into labor services and the services of inanimate objects such as buildings and machines.

One human component of the firm deserves special mention. Production requires organization, and there can be no effective organization without a decision-making process. The technical name for this function within the firm is "entrepreneurship." Entrepreneurship can be exercised individually or collectively and is not necessarily connected with ownership, although the great entrepreneurs of economic and business history, such as Henry Ford, Sr., both owned and managed the firms that made them famous. In modern corporate structure, however, the entrepreneurial

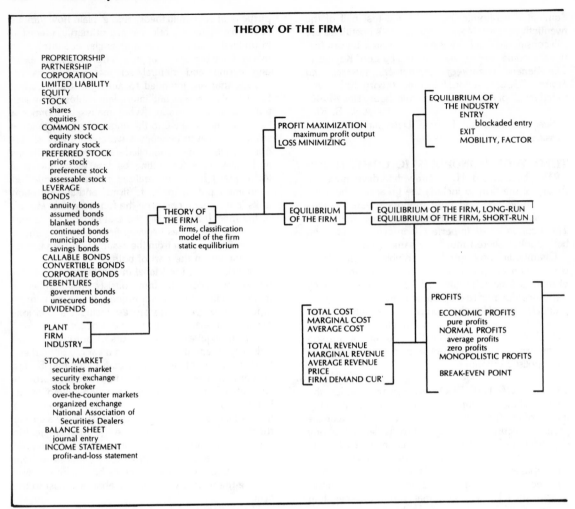

THEORY OF THE FIRM

PROPRIETORSHIP
PARTNERSHIP
CORPORATION
LIMITED LIABILITY
EQUITY
STOCK
  shares
  equities
COMMON STOCK
  equity stock
  ordinary stock
PREFERRED STOCK
  prior stock
  preference stock
  assessable stock
LEVERAGE
BONDS
  annuity bonds
  assumed bonds
  blanket bonds
  continued bonds
  municipal bonds
  savings bonds
CALLABLE BONDS
CONVERTIBLE BONDS
CORPORATE BONDS
DEBENTURES
  government bonds
  unsecured bonds
DIVIDENDS

PLANT
FIRM
INDUSTRY

STOCK MARKET
  securities market
  security exchange
  stock broker
  over-the-counter markets
  organized exchange
  National Association of
    Securities Dealers
BALANCE SHEET
  journal entry
INCOME STATEMENT
  profit-and-loss statement

THEORY OF
THE FIRM
  firms, classification
  model of the firm
  static equilibrium

PROFIT MAXIMIZATION
  maximum profit output
LOSS MINIMIZING

EQUILIBRIUM
OF THE FIRM

EQUILIBRIUM OF
THE INDUSTRY
  ENTRY
    blockaded entry
  EXIT
  MOBILITY, FACTOR

EQUILIBRIUM OF THE FIRM, LONG-RUN
EQUILIBRIUM OF THE FIRM, SHORT-RUN

TOTAL COST
MARGINAL COST
AVERAGE COST

TOTAL REVENUE
MARGINAL REVENUE
AVERAGE REVENUE
PRICE
FIRM DEMAND CUR'

PROFITS

ECONOMIC PROFITS
  pure profits
NORMAL PROFITS
  average profits
  zero profits
MONOPOLISTIC PROFITS

BREAK-EVEN POINT

---

function is often exercised by hired professional managers whose ownership relation to the firm is minimal and somewhat incidentally related to their wages in the form of stock options.

Operation of the Model. We have now described the general nature of the economic model of the firm except for what makes it work. That requires some kind of motive force, which, as a first approximation, we take to be profit-seeking. Profit is defined as the difference between revenue (the proceeds from selling outputs) and costs (derived from explicit and implicit purchase of factors of production). Generally it is assumed that the firm maximizes profit, although in some more refined and specialized models this motive force is modified by other considerations such as sales maximization and other managerial motivations.

Firms make different decisions, depending on the market structure of the industry of which they are a member. In economic theory, we identify four kinds of market structures: perfect competition, monopolistic competition, oligopoly, and pure monopoly. Firms in perfect competition maximize profits by operating at the point where price equals marginal costs and will not make pure profits in the long run. Firms in the other three market structures maximize profits at the point where marginal revenue equals marginal costs and may make pure profits in the long run.

—*Timothy P. Ryan*

See also Monopolistic Competition; Monopoly; Oligopoly; Perfect Competition.

THIRD-PARTY INTERVENTION. See Conciliation; Fact Finding; Mediation.

TIGHT-MONEY POLICY. See Monetary Policy.

TIME DEPOSITS, deposits in a commercial bank or savings bank for which the bank may, or must, require advance notice of withdrawal and for which interest is normally paid. The maximum interest that may be

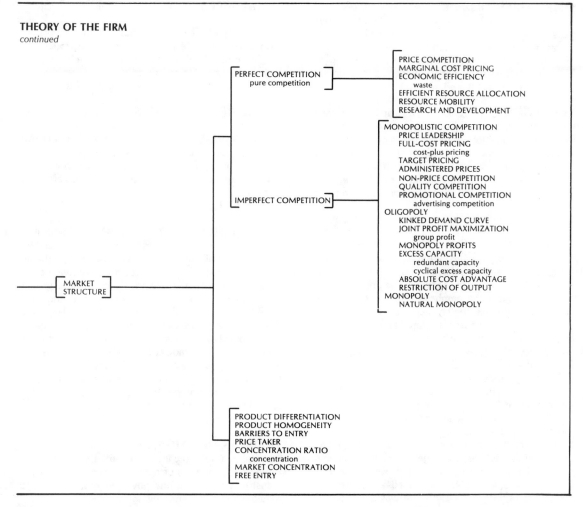

THEORY OF THE FIRM
continued

MARKET STRUCTURE

PERFECT COMPETITION
pure competition

- PRICE COMPETITION
- MARGINAL COST PRICING
- ECONOMIC EFFICIENCY
  waste
- EFFICIENT RESOURCE ALLOCATION
- RESOURCE MOBILITY
- RESEARCH AND DEVELOPMENT

IMPERFECT COMPETITION

- MONOPOLISTIC COMPETITION
- PRICE LEADERSHIP
- FULL-COST PRICING
  cost-plus pricing
- TARGET PRICING
- ADMINISTERED PRICES
- NON-PRICE COMPETITION
- QUALITY COMPETITION
- PROMOTIONAL COMPETITION
  advertising competition
- OLIGOPOLY
- KINKED DEMAND CURVE
- JOINT PROFIT MAXIMIZATION
  group profit
- MONOPOLY PROFITS
- EXCESS CAPACITY
  redundant capacity
  cyclical excess capacity
- ABSOLUTE COST ADVANTAGE
- RESTRICTION OF OUTPUT
- MONOPOLY
  NATURAL MONOPOLY

- PRODUCT DIFFERENTIATION
- PRODUCT HOMOGENEITY
- BARRIERS TO ENTRY
- PRICE TAKER
- CONCENTRATION RATIO
  concentration
- MARKET CONCENTRATION
- FREE ENTRY

paid by member banks on time deposits is set by the Federal Reserve System. For other banks, such limits may be set by state regulation. The Federal Monetary Control Act of 1980 expanded the Federal Reserve bank's authority over all time deposits in national or state banks and in savings and loans. Time deposits are of three kinds:

Savings Deposits are restricted by law to accounts of individuals or nonprofit organizations. The bank may require up to 30 days' notice of withdrawal but in practice never does.

Time Certificates of Deposit may be purchased by anyone, including corporations. The certificates represent a deposit of a specific sum of money for a specified period of time, not less than 30 days, and they cannot be redeemed prior to the date specified. If the certificate is negotiable, it may be sold to someone else. Both savings and commercial banks provide certificates of deposit for small savers, but the great bulk of such deposits are owned by corporations,

frequently in denominations of a million dollars or more.

Time Deposits, Open Account, are primarily corporate deposits made without a specified maturity date. By law they cannot be withdrawn without 30 days' advance notice.   —*Walter W. Haines*

See also Interest Rate Ceiling.

TIME PREFERENCE, a concept that assumes that individuals prefer the present over the future. Although current capital investment will yield more consumer goods at some future time, most people will choose assured present consumption over uncertain future consumption. Therefore, to induce people to abstain from present consumption so that new capital equipment can be manufactured, the increased future consumption (reflected in interest payments) must be enough to overcome their current time preference.

See also Capital Deepening; Demand for Capital; Net Productivity of Capital.

TIME SERIES. Observations of variables taken at various points in time (monthly, quarterly, yearly) generate a time series, which can exhibit trends, cycles, and seasonal and random variation. Analysis of time series is usually concerned with predicting or forecasting future values of the variables in question on the basis of past experience.

TINBERGEN, JAN (1903-   ), Dutch economist who shared the first Nobel Prize in economics with Ragnar Frisch in 1969 for their work in developing the science of econometrics. Professor at the Netherlands School of Economics from 1933, and an adviser to the Dutch government, he was the author of *Shaping the World Economy* (1963) and *Development Planning* (1967).

TOBIN, JAMES (1918-   ), American economist and Nobel laureate who, after early work on consumption and saving behavior, has consistently contributed to macroeconomic theory. The unique aspect of Tobin's work is the emphasis upon asset portfolio choice: He feels that the balance sheet as well as the current account must be considered and uses a micro approach in analyzing the balance sheet. For example, Tobin's work with growth models includes the unique feature of capital asset choice.

Tobin also possesses a distinctive ability to summarize and clarify the existing state of a subject. While much of his technical work has been very mathematical, Tobin is also a political economist who served on the Council of Economic Advisers under President Kennedy. He has maintained a keen interest in many public issues such as the negative income tax and poverty. His publications include *The New Economics One Decade Older* (1974). Tobin has been professor of economics at Yale since 1955. He was awarded the Nobel Prize for economics in 1981.

TOTAL COST is the cost of producing a given output. It is the sum of total fixed cost and total variable cost.

TOTAL COST OF PRODUCTION (TC), the cost of all the inputs used to produce some level of output. It is the sum of all the variable and all the fixed costs; that is, TC = TVC (total variable cost) + TFC (total fixed cost). TC is an increasing function of the level of output.

See also Cost Function.

TOTAL FIXED COST OF PRODUCTION (TFC), the cost of all the inputs which are independent of the level of output, that is, costs which a producer has to pay regardless of whether she or he is producing anything or not. Sometimes these costs are referred to as overhead costs.

See also Cost Function.

TOTAL INELASTICITY. *See* Perfect Inelasticity.

TOTAL REVENUE is the sum of all the receipts of a firm in a given time interval. For a firm producing a single output, total revenue is simply the number of units sold times the selling price.

See also Average Revenue; Marginal Revenue.

TOTAL-REVENUE TEST. *See* Elasticity of Demand.

TOTAL VARIABLE COST OF PRODUCTION (TVC), the cost of all the variable inputs used to produce some level of output. TVC is an increasing function of the level of output; when the level of output is zero, TVC is zero.

See also Cost Function.

TRADE ADJUSTMENT ASSISTANCE, financial assistance or retraining offered to workers who lose their jobs because of foreign competition. Although the net gains from trade are supposed to be positive, economists recognize that there are losers. Some groups suffer a comparative disadvantage when they are forced to compete with foreign producers. Plants shut down, and workers are laid off.

Economists argue that everyone would be better off if there were free trade without such restrictions, but that workers who lose their jobs should be offered trade adjustment assistance. Congress has not provided much funding for this program because it tends to be viewed as welfare for the middle class.

See also Gains From Trade.

TRADE ASSOCIATION, an organization of firms in an industry (ordinarily less tightly knit than a cartel) to promote the interests of member firms, represent the industry to the public and governmental bodies, and regulate industry standards and practices.

From an economic standpoint, the importance of trade associations relates to possibly anticompetitive practices a trade association may encourage. Especially significant are discussions by members relating to price and output, which may be encouraged by "disorderliness of the market," meaning rapid shifts in price by one or more member firms tending to disrupt the established patterns of distribution. Such concern may foster collusive activities to stabilize the market by price fixing or market sharing. In the latter practices, trade associations run afoul of the Sherman Antitrust Act prohibition on restraint of trade.

See also Collusion; Market Sharing; Price Fixing; Restraint of Trade; Sherman Antitrust Act.

TRADE BARRIERS. International trade theory dictates that trade be free based on the law of comparative advantage, but nations have seen fit to incorporate barriers to trade as elements of commercial policy. The most prominent is the tariff. Quotas are also important when definite restrictions on quantities are sought. A host of nontariff (or quota) barriers has also arisen. Customs administrations, or red tape, may provide barriers far more difficult to surmount than formal tariffs. The procedure for setting customs classifications often leads to uncertainty as to the exact amount of duty to be paid. Administration of antidumping laws, whereby imports are alleged to have entered a country at unfair low prices, sets obstacles to exporting—it generally takes an inordinate amount of time to get a decision. National patent and trademark systems are employed by domestic sellers to curb goods originating in other countries. Health and safety rules either block imports or add appreciably to the cost of importing. The same is true of labeling requirements. Buy-at-home campaigns, subsidies, mixing and milling requirements, taxes, import-export licensing, and currency controls also operate as barriers to trade.

See also Balance of Trade; Quotas; Tariffs.

TRADE EXPANSION ACT. See General Agreement on Tariffs and Trade.

TRADE REGULATION RULES. See Federal Trade Commission.

TRADE RESTRICTIONS. See Trade Barriers.

TRADITIONAL ECONOMY, the economy of a traditional society. Economists are beginning to realize that these economies are much more complex and sophisticated than originally thought. Narrowly focusing on yields blinded Western agronomists to the advantages gained by a traditional agriculture that integrated food crops into a multipurpose ecosystem finely tuned to

In a traditional economy, productivity is limited due to a lack of the benefits of modern technology.

the local environment. Analysis of these systems in the aggregate shows many of them to be much more efficient than Western models, especially in terms of net energy produced. The previous economic bias often caused real harm.

See also Stages of Growth.

TRANSACTIONS DEMAND. See Liquidity Preference.

TRANSFER PAYMENTS, expenditures for which no goods or services are exchanged. Governments, federal, state, and local, are the largest distributors of transfer payments, which include welfare payments, Social Security benefits, and unemployment compensation. These payments amount to over 35% of all government expenditures. Some government subsidies, such as farm price supports, are considered transfer payments. Repatriation payments from one

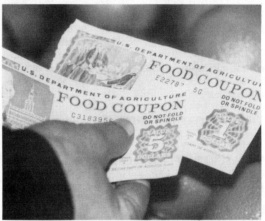

The Food Stamp Program, one of the government's largest transfer payment programs, enables low-income persons to buy more groceries.

country to another are also considered transfer payments, because they involve no output. Business transfer payments, which amount to several billion dollars each year, include payouts under deferred compensation arrangements, gifts, and donations.

Transfer payments, both public and private, essentially redistribute income from the employed to the unemployed, from the urban areas to the farms, and from corporations to individuals. In effect, transfer payments alter private goods production in favor of the recipients of the payments and provide injections into the circular flow of income. Transfer payments by governments also have a stabilizing effect on the economy. During boom years the unemployment reserve funds grow and exert stabilizing pressure to prevent too great spending. Conversely, during slack years reserve funds are used to moderate the decline and sustain consumption. Welfare programs and government subsidies also show an automatic anticyclical type of stabilizing behavior.

TRANSITIONAL UNEMPLOYMENT describes the loss of work that occurs due to the changing of jobs and the relocation of workers. Often referred to as frictional unemployment, this condition is almost always temporary and poses no real threat to the economy. It occurs even during the most prosperous times, for many reasons such as health, relocation, and family pressures. Transitional unemployment often occurs during the interim between school and the acceptance of a first job as well as between jobs.

See also Unemployment of Labor.

TRANSPORATION ACTS. In the twentieth century, Congress has enacted three transportation acts (1920, 1940, and 1958), each essentially an amendment to an original act of 1887. The Transportation Act of 1920 directed the Interstate Commerce Commission (ICC) to maintain railroad rates which would yield efficient carriers a "fair return." The act of 1940 called for "impartial regulation of all modes of transportation" so as to "preserve the inherent advantages of each" and develop "a national transportation system." The act of 1958 directed the ICC not to hold the rates of one mode up to a level so as to protect another mode unless it was necessary to protect inherent advantages or the national defense.

TRANSPORTATION INDUSTRY. *See* Regulated Industries.

TREASURER OF THE UNITED STATES, a presidential appointee whose functions are to receive, hold, and pay out the public monies of the federal

The most widely circulated of U.S. governmental signatures is surely that of the Treasurer.

government. Receipts of the government are paid to the Treasury, and all checks written by the government are drawn against the Treasury account, which is kept in the Federal Reserve banks. The Treasury also supervises the issue and retirement of all United States paper currency.

TREASURY BILLS. *See* Government Securities.

TRENDS IN BUSINESS CYCLES, long-term, noncyclical patterns of economic activity which occur over

the course of many business cycles or period fluctuations. A trend or pattern of activity concerning the Gross National Product can be identified readily by examining its movement over a period of time, say, 100 years. An example of such a trend is the steady growth of the per capita GNP at an average of 2% per annum between 1870 and 1989.

See also Business Cycles, Types.

TRIFFIN, ROBERT (1911-   ), an American economist best known as the author of the Triffin Plan for reforming the system of international payments established after World War II. In his *Gold and the Dollar Crisis* (1960), Triffin correctly analyzed the problem of the gold-exchange standard and its tendency to be extremely vulnerable to crisis. He felt that the system was self-destructive and only a massive reform centering on the role of the International Monetary Fund would correct the situation. Many of Triffin's ideas are elements in the current changes in the system of international payments.

See also Triffin Plan.

TRIFFIN PLAN, reform in the international monetary system calling for the establishment of a world central bank (international bank), or an expanded International Monetary Fund (XIMF), proposed first by Lord Keynes and later elaborated by Robert Triffin. The international bank would operate with countries' central banks exactly as an individual country's central bank operates with the country's commercial banks. All reserves would be held in the form of deposits at the international bank (called *bancor deposits* or *bancor balances*). International liquidity would be created by the bank's making loans to central banks and investing in countries' government securities. The amount and distribution of additional international liquidity would be decided nationally by the international civil servants managing the world bank. The principal problem with this scheme is the requirement that countries give up substantial national sovereignty to the world bank, perhaps a highly desirable but also unlikely prospect.

TRIGONOMETRIC FUNCTIONS. *See* Function.

TRIPLE DAMAGES, also treble damages, are a remedy in antitrust law (Sherman and Clayton Acts) whereby a competitor damaged as a result of proved illegal (anticompetitive) behavior of a defendant may recover from the defendant three times the amount of actual monetary damages sustained.

See also Antitrust Policy.

TROUGH. *See* Business Cycles, Phases.

TRUSTEESHIP, in labor unionism, a control technique under which a national union can assume the decision-making functions of a local union by suspending its autonomy. Now limited by the Labor Management Reporting and Disclosure Act of 1959, trusteeships have sometimes been used illegally to assume control of the subordinate organization.

TRUTH IN LENDING. In 1968 Congress passed the Truth in Lending Bill. This bill was widely hailed as a step forward in consumerism (a movement to protect and preserve rights of consumers). The bill requires full disclosure of the rates on finance charges and other aspects of consumer credit transactions.

TURNOVER TAX, a tax imposed on the monetary value of all transactions. The effective tax base of such a tax is the total value of sales at *all* stages of production. Because some products exchange hands many more times during the production process than do others, a turnover tax has much higher effective rates on some products than on others.

The tax also encourages vertical ownership of several stages of a production process, so that no transaction occurs as the firm passes a product from one stage of production to another. For example, if a paper company sells paper to a publisher for $300, and there is a turnover tax of 1%, then a tax of $3 will be paid. If the publisher then sells books made from the paper for $500, then an additional turnover tax of $5 will be paid, for a total tax of $8. However, if the publisher owns its own paper company and sells the books for $500, the total tax bill would be only $5. The turnover tax is used in Europe and in some Communist bloc nations, but it has been replaced in many other nations by a value-added tax.

See also Value-Added Tax.

TWO-TIER GOLD SYSTEM. In addition to the official gold market, meaning the gold-convertibility of official dollars, there is a private gold market, located principally in London. From 1961 to 1968 the private gold price was stabilized at the official gold price of $35 an ounce. by means of the *gold pool.* Members of the gold pool were the United States and seven other major countries, and together they bought or sold gold to satisfy any excess demand or excess supply of gold at the pegged price. However, the private demand for gold, especially toward the end of the period, was so great that the gold reserves of these countries were greatly reduced; so in March 1968 the gold pool was disbanded and the private gold price was left free to find its own level. The resulting situation—a free private market for gold coupled with a pegged official price of gold—was called the two-tier gold system.

TWO-TIER WAGE RATES, different wages for the same work. Unions and management have agreed to wage programs under which newly-hired employees are paid wages well below the rates paid to employees already on the payroll. One form of concession bargaining, or givebacks, two-tier arrangements have been accepted by unions to avoid wage or benefit reductions for current employees. Many large companies now have such agreements with their unions.

While such programs apparently do not violate equal pay laws as long as the tiers are based solely on seniority, unions seem to fear that employers will try to replace higher-paid old workers with lower-paid new workers. Some evidence also suggests tension between the tiers as newer workers resent their lower pay. Companies facing foreign competition have been particularly interested in two-tiered wage rates as a cost-cutting arrangement.

—*William D. Wagoner*

TYING AGREEMENTS. *See* Tying Contract.

TYING CONTRACT, an agreement between a producer and retailer of a product whereby the retailer, as a condition of acquiring a preferred product for resale, must agree to handle one or more other products of that producer. A variant is "full-line forcing," under which the retailer must handle all products of a producer's line. Tying contracts limit competition by preventing the access of rival producers to a retail market. For example, the retailer may be prevented from carrying a competitor's product available at a lower cost. Or a monopolist may force a tying agreement with several retailers to sustain his or her position against potential competitors. Tying contracts are prohibited, when their effect is to limit competition substantially, under the Clayton Act, Section 3.

See also Clayton Act; Exclusive Dealership.

UNCERTAINTY, one of the most important concerns in economic analysis and economic life. All business and personal decisions are made in the face of uncertainty. Risk, which is the chance that uncertain future events may turn to one's disadvantage, is always a key factor in economic decision-making. Although the future will always be uncertain, the empirical part of economics attempts to use existing data to give economists, businesspeople, and government officials some insights into what can be expected to happen in the future so that some of the uncertainty may be reduced.

See also Profit System, Risk.

UNDERCONSUMPTION THEORY OF BUSINESS CYCLES. This internal theory contends that recessions result from consumption falling behind output as a result of the retention of more income from the amount that might be invested. Underconsumption, therefore, may result from unequal distribution of income, preventing all goods produced from being purchased, or too great a portion of income going into savings, particularly by wealthy or thrifty people. As one major internal force contributing to business cycles, underconsumption acts to lower aggregate demand and causes prices to decline to an unprofitable level.

See also Business Cycles, Theories.

UNDERDEVELOPED COUNTRIES. *See* Developing Nations; Less Developed Countries.

UNDERDEVELOPMENT is a term used by Western economists to compare (usually unfavorably) Third World economies and cultures to their own. The term "development" was borrowed from biology, where in 1839 it was first used to denote a progression from a lower to a higher or more complex type of organism. First applied to nations in 1862, it meant that a nation's later characteristics were potentially present in its earlier societies. The word "primitive" embodied this concept. "Primitive" societies were more or less undeveloped versions of Britain. During the 1930s and 1940s, the term "primitive" was changed to "backward." After World War II, newly independent colonies were called "emergent nations." President Truman's Point Four initiative was the first program intended to "develop" "underdeveloped societies." The later terms "develop*ing* societies" and "less developed countries" (LDCs) are more flattering synonyms.

Understandably, the people referred to by these terms are affronted by them, and various attempts have been made to redefine these nations in a more

About two-thirds of the world's population lives in underdeveloped countries where both human and material resources are underemployed.

favorable light. The term "Third World" was an attempt to define a "third way" independent of both capitalist and communist norms, but in usage it came to be associated with underdevelopment.

Four decades of "development" have succeeded only in widening the gap between rich and poor in many Third World countries. Anthropologists point out that with economic development, tribal nations find it difficult to sustain their traditional ways of adapting. They suffer demographic upheavals, resource depletion, internal inequality and conflict, and increased illness. Such unforeseen results of development, as well as the negative side-effects of the Green Revolution and industrial agriculture (water pollution, depletion of topsoil, degradation of the genetic pool), have led to a new respect for traditional agriculture and modes of subsistence and an emphasis on "sustainable development" that takes ecological and cultural factors into account as well as the aspirations of the people to be "developed."

See also Developing Nations; Less Developed Countries; Stages of Growth; Standard of Living.

UNDEREMPLOYMENT refers to a decrease in demand that leads to the withdrawal of labor into occupations with little or no marginal productivity. In other words, employed resources are not being used most efficiently. In industry, for example, when an employer retains a greater number of workers than required during a decrease in demand in order to have sufficient experienced labor available when demand increases, his or her resources are being underemployed. Although the labor is not actually unemployed, it is underemployed.

UNDEREMPLOYMENT OF PRODUCTIVE CAPACITY, a level of production making less than optimal use of all of the available factors of production. The productive capacity of an economy is the quantity of goods and services that can be produced using all available factors efficiently. Thus, the productive capacity is determined by the size of the labor force and its skills, the amount of capital equipment and its technology, the quantity and quality of land and other natural resources, and the ability of entrepreneurs to organize these other factors of production. The productive capacity of an economy changes as the quantity or quality of inputs changes.

Underemployment of Labor. In national income analysis, underemployment of productive capacity is usually defined as a state in which more than 3% to 4% of the labor force is unemployed. Labor is a basic index, because it is the most basic, evident, and easily measured input to use. Unemployment creates problems for the worker, the worker's family, and society. Furthermore, unemployment of labor is often a strong political pressure against those in Congress and presidents in office. An owner of a factory may be unhappy about having an idle machine, but it does not threaten the livelihood of other households or the political lives of public officials in the same way that unemployment of labor does.

Underemployment of Capital and Natural Resources. Underemployment of productive capacity is sometimes used to describe a state in which plants and equipment are not being fully utilized. When there is underutilization of capacity in steel and most other major industries, there is, almost certainly, general unemployment; but in small industries, or in industries producing goods for which demand is decreasing, or in industries that have expanded their capacity for their own good, underutilization of capacity need not be accompanied by general unemployment of labor, and such underutilization would not be regarded as a serious general problem.

Underemployment as Inefficient Use. Full employment of productive capacity also means that inputs are being used to produce as much as possible. Some economists speak of underemployment of labor as a problem in achieving full use of productive capacity, meaning that some workers are not being as fully or efficiently employed as they might be. In the study of economic development this interpretation is often used, even though it is impossible to measure or estimate with any confidence.   —Anne Mayhew

See also Full Employment.

UNDERGROUND ECONOMY is defined as the income people earn that they fail to report to tax authorities. The waiter who reports only half his tips, the auto repairman who gives a discount to customers who pay cash, or the drug dealer who keeps no records at all are part of the underground economy. Estimates of the size of the underground economy range from 3% of GNP to as high as 20%.

Researchers disagree on the size of the underground economy, but they do agree that it is growing at a rate roughly twice that of the GNP. One reason is that economic growth and the growth of the inflation rate have pushed taxpayers into higher tax brackets, increasing the incentive to cheat. Another reason is the falling probability of an income tax audit—from 3% in the 1960s to about 1.5% today. Also, tax-resistance has become respectable to those who sympathize with movements opposed to certain government policies, such as the Vietnam War.

About 70% of the underground economy consists of income that would be legitimate if reported. The other 30% of untaxed income comes from criminal activities such as prostitution, pornography, loan-sharking and gambling, trafficking in stolen goods, and drug-related activity.

Consequences of growth in the underground economy are higher taxes for those who do report all their income, and underestimation of GNP growth. Labor force participation may also be underestimated. Also,

if poor people participate in the underground economy to a greater extent than middle- or upper-class people, the need for welfare may be overestimated. On the other hand, to the extent that middle- and upper-class self-employed professionals fail to report their incomes, deduct personal items as business expenses, or engage in white-collar crime, income may be less evenly distributed than the figures indicate. However large the underground economy in the United States, it is nevertheless significantly smaller than those of many other countries.

UNDERPRODUCTION occurs when the market price is below the equilibrium price, inducing producers to produce less than consumers are willing to purchase. Overproduction would occur at a price higher than equilibrium, when producers are inclined to produce in excess of demand.

UNDERSUPPLY. *See* Excess Demand.

UNDERVALUATION. A persistent surplus in a nation's balance of payments and a buildup of international reserves reflect an undervalued currency. The rates of exchange prevailing in that country and/or controlled domestic prices make its goods cheaper internationally than they would be if the balance of payments were in equilibrium. Deliberate undervaluation operates to spur exports and dampen imports.

See also Devaluation; Exchange Rates.

UNDISTRIBUTED PROFITS, post-tax earnings retained after dividend payments. Distributed profits constitute taxable income in the year received; if undistributed, the corporation pays the tax on its taxable earnings but the stockholder gets the advantage of capital appreciation while postponing taxes. Undistributed profits are recorded as part of national income but not personal income.

See also Corporate Earnings; Dividends.

UNEMPLOYMENT INSURANCE, or unemployment compensation, temporary income maintenance for workers who become unemployed under the unemployment compensation provisions of the Social Security Act. Recipients receive benefits equal to a fraction of previous wage income (subject to upper limits and, in some states, lower limits). Benefits are financed by federal and state payroll taxes paid by employers.

UNEMPLOYMENT OF LABOR, a term denoting the percentage of people in the labor force who are not working. By definition, those not seeking employment (students, housewives, house husbands, and others) are not in the labor force and thus are not considered unemployed. Usually there is said to be excessive unemployment when less than 94-96% of

UNEMPLOYMENT OF LABOR: TOPIC GUIDE

For the opposite side of the unemployment picture, see the article on FULL EMPLOYMENT. Some of the numerous causes of unemployment are discussed in the articles on CYCLICAL UNEMPLOYMENT, STRUCTURAL UNEMPLOYMENT, and LABOR MOBILITY. For macroeconomic explanations of unemployment, see DEFLATIONARY GAP. The unemployment-inflation dual occurrence is explained in PHILLIPS CURVE.

Macroeconomic policy measures designed to reduce unemployment are explained in the article on STABILIZATION POLICY. Specific methods of reducing unemployment or alleviating its impact are described in the articles on MANPOWER POLICY, RETRAINING, MANPOWER DEVELOPMENT AND TRAINING ACT, PUBLIC EMPLOYMENT SERVICE, and UNEMPLOYMENT INSURANCE.

The Subject Maps accompanying LABOR MARKET and WAGES display these and other relationships.

the labor force is employed. Thus, an unemployment rate of 4-6% may still be considered full employment. The economic cost of unemployment falls both on society as a result of lost output and on the individual as a result of lost income. There are several types of unemployment, including seasonal, frictional, structural, cyclical, and technological.

Seasonal unemployment results from a decrease in the demand for labor due to the changing of the seasons; it is usually found in such fields as agriculture and construction.

Frictional unemployment is the loss of work that occurs when workers change jobs or locations. This is not considered a serious type since it is usually temporary.

Structural unemployment usually results from a major industrial change in a region, causing many people to lose their jobs, as when a major industry either shuts down or relocates.

Cyclical unemployment is the relationship between unemployment and the business cycle: the more prosperous the economy, the lower the unemployment rate. This type of unemployment is most severe because it reflects upon the entire nation and not just a subgroup.

Technological unemployment is the displacement of labor that occurs when new techniques, products, or methods of production make jobs obsolete, or too expensive to maintain. This may be considered a special case of structural unemployment.

There are also several types of unemployment that are particular to certain groups. For example, there is *hard-core unemployment*, which is the unemployment of people with particular disadvantages or problems that keep them from securing employment even during the most prosperous times. Included in this group

are many minority groups, the unskilled and uneducated, as well as the emotionally disturbed.

A second type of discriminatory unemployment is *entry unemployment*, which is the unemployment that results when workers with no experience find that the competition of the more experienced keeps them from securing employment.   —*William D. Wagoner*

Unemployment lines may reflect the fact that the economic goal of full employment has not been attained.

UNFAIR AND DECEPTIVE PRACTICES are those activities of business firms that damage consumers or have an adverse effect on competition. Examples are "bait advertising," deceptive pricing, and misbranding and mislabeling. Under Section 5 of the Original Federal Trade Commission Act, the FTC was authorized to proceed against business practices doing potential or actual damage to competition (a less rigorous test of damage than restraint of trade found in the Sherman Act). With the Wheeler-Lea Act of 1938, the prohibition was extended to include unfair practices outside the normal antitrust category as well as practices unfair to the general consuming public.

See also Antitrust Policy; Deceptive Advertising; Federal Trade Commission; Unfair Methods of Competition; Wheeler-Lea Act.

UNFAIR LABOR PRACTICES, anti-union actions by employers. The 1930s marked a great turning point for organized labor, and no law aided its cause more than the Wagner Act (1935), also known as the National Labor Relations Act, which allowed unions to organize and bargain collectively. It also listed unfair labor practices in which employers were forbidden to engage. No comparable restrictions, however, were placed on unions.

Restrictions on Management. The five unfair labor practices denied to employers were:

1) To interfere with, restrain, or coerce employees in the exercise of their rights to organize and bargain collectively through representatives of their own choosing.

2) To dominate or interfere with the formation or administration of any labor organization or to contribute financial or other support to it.

3) To discriminate against individuals supporting a labor organization with respect to any term or condition of employment.

4) To discharge or otherwise discriminate against an employee because the employee has filed charges or given testimony under the provisions of the Wagner Act.

5) To refuse to bargain collectively with the union representing his or her employees.

Restrictions on Labor. The one-sidedness of the Wagner Act was changed by the Taft-Hartley Act (1947), which retained the prohibition of unfair labor practices to the employers but, among other provisions, added a set of seven labor practices denied to labor. These are:

1) To restrain or coerce workers in exercising their rights to organize.

2) To cause an employer to discriminate against a worker who has been dismissed from union membership for any other reason than nonpayment of dues.

3) To refuse to bargain collectively with an employer.

4) To strike or boycott in order to force the employer to commit acts prohibited by law.

5) To charge excessive initiation fees under a union shop.

6) To force an employer to pay for services that are not performed.

7) To engage in organizational picketing to pressure an employer to recognize a union without a representation election.   — *William D. Wagoner*

See also Landrum-Griffin Act; Taft-Hartley Act; Wagner Act.

UNFAIR METHODS OF COMPETITION are practices designed to damage or eliminate a business firm's competitors illegally. The term is comprehensive, applying to the specific activities prohibited by the Sherman and Clayton Acts as well as the less sharply defined violations of the Federal Trade Commission Act. The prohibition applies to any activity causing a diversion of trade from a competitor other than through normal and legal competition. Though its thrust is on damage to competition or competitors, "unfair and deceptive practices" are also prohibited if the consuming public is damaged. For example, mali-

ciously misrepresenting a competitor's product to weaken its attractiveness to customers (and divert trade to the violator) would be an unfair method of competition. Deceptive pricing, having the effect of increasing the violator's sales, might damage both competition and the consumer, and would be an "unfair or deceptive practice."

The Federal Trade Commission is given authority to prosecute unfair methods of competition in Section 5 of the Federal Trade Commission Act.

— *Thomas O. Depperschmidt*

See also Antitrust Policy; Federal Trade Commission; Unfair and Deceptive Practices.

UNINTENDED INVESTMENT. *See* Disinvestment.

UNION CONSTITUTION, the document containing the rules and regulations of the organization. Typically the constitution begins with a preamble setting forth the broad goals of the union, and then goes on to outline the internal structure. It will include statements on union government, election of officers, powers of elected officials, membership criteria, and many other subjects of interest, including amendment procedure. The Labor-Management Reporting and Disclosure Act of 1959 specified certain contents of the document.

UNION CONVENTION, the supreme authority in the union structure, holding the legislative, judicial, and executive power of the organization. The unions hold conventions at will (every two years on the average), but, under current legislation, elections of officers must take place at least every five years. Each local sends delegates to the convention, and each votes based on the number of dues-paying members. The actual conventions range from a managed exercise in union goodwill to open fights over issues. Perhaps the greatest effect of the convention results from the informal discussion between leaders of various sections of the country. Thus, ideas and methods are spread rapidly throughout the organization.

UNION LABEL, a tag or stamp placed on a commodity to show that it has been made by members of a labor union or that it has been made in a union shop. Its purpose is to promote the use of union-made goods.

UNION SECURITY, the requirements on workers to belong to and support the union that represents them in bargaining. It means, in particular, the type of shop that exists—closed, union, open, agency, or some other type of shop. The union security provisions are stated in the collective bargaining contract and are enforced by the union.

See also Agency Shop; Closed Shop; Open Shop; Union Shop.

UNIONS. *See* Labor Movement.

UNION SHOP, one in which all workers must belong to the union that represents their bargaining unit. The employer may hire whomever she or he chooses, but new workers who do not belong to the union are required to join, usually within 30 days after they begin work. The union shop arrangement is permissible under federal labor law, although the Taft-Hartley Act modifies it somewhat and, more important, permits its prohibition by individual states in "right-to-work" laws.

UNITED AUTOMOBILE WORKERS (UAW), one of the largest unions in the United States, was formed in the early 1930s by merging a number of AFL locals in the automobile industry. It withdrew from the AFL in 1936 and joined the CIO. The new organization effectively used the sitdown strike, and, in spite of a general protest over the technique, secured union recognition at both General Motors and Chrysler. In 1981, the UAW reaffiliated with the AFL-CIO. Total membership is approximately 1,500,000. Despite hard times in the early 1980s, the UAW position is still strong.

UNITED STATES NOTES, or greenbacks, were first issued during the Civil War without any backing at all to finance the fighting. After the war they were given a partial gold backing, and in 1878 Congress fixed the total amount in circulation at $347 million (later reduced to $323 million). That quantity still circulates, all of it in $5 bills. In spite of a 50 percent gold backing, the notes are nevertheless not redeemable in gold.

See also Money; Money Supply.

UNITED STATES v. ALUMINUM CO. OF AMERICA, 148 F. 2d 416 (1945). Alcoa had been the dominant firm in aluminum production, and was the sole domestic manufacturer of virgin ingot in 1937 when the government charged it with monopolizing in violation of the Sherman Act. Judge Learned Hand determined, after considering several alternative definitions, that Alcoa's share of the pertinent market (which excluded secondary aluminum but included Alcoa's primary production for its own use) was 90 percent.

This market share, said the Court, amounted to monopoly. The remaining legal issue was whether the monopoly had been achieved or maintained by means that would indicate illegal monopolization. Judge Hand, in a novel and bold decision, argued that the distinction between the existence and exercise of monopoly power is "purely formal." Alcoa could escape a Sherman Act conviction, he stated, only by showing that monopoly had been thrust upon it, that it was the "passive beneficiary of a monopoly."

Under this extremely stringent standard, Alcoa was found to have monopolized illegally. However innocent its behavior, Judge Hand concluded, it did act purposefully to maintain its market position. This strong presumption against market power which marks the Alcoa decision has not generally been followed in later Sherman Act cases.

—Peter Asch

See also Abuse Theory of Mergers; Monopoly Thrust Upon a Firm; United States v. United States Steel Corp.

UNITED STATES v. AMERICAN TELEPHONE & TELEGRAPH (1982), one of the most far-reaching antitrust cases. The case hinged around AT&T's monopoly in local phone service (which was closely regulated by state governments), as it related to AT&T's sale of long-distance phone service and of telephone-related equipment. The suit was filed by the Department of Justice in 1974, and the case was resolved in 1982 by the signing of a consent decree by the two parties. AT&T agreed to a major dissolution of the company, which now consists mainly of seven independent regional telephone companies and AT&T. AT&T operates long-distance phone services and also manufactures telephone, computer, and other electronic equipment.

The case is important because it reflects the intricacies of regulation of private business within the economy. The government's case (and private Sherman Antitrust Act cases brought by competitors of AT&T) centered around the restriction of access of other long-distance companies to AT&T's local service as a barrier to entry into the long-distance communications market. Control of local service also prevented other equipment manufacturers from selling telephones that could be hooked into the local network.

As a result of the dissolution, there have been major changes in the communications industry, and many more changes are to come. In particular, competition has forced down the prices of long-distance phone calls and the price of telephone equipment. On the other hand, regulation of the old, integrated AT&T (the Bell System) had led to substantial subsidization of local service out of the profits generated from the sales of equipment and long-distance service. The new Bell regional phone companies do not have these sources of profits at their disposal and must therefore raise local service charges to maintain profits. The rise in local charges is economically efficient in the sense that the price of the service now more closely reflects the cost of providing it. However, there are social policy concerns over the ability of low-income households to receive phone service.

UNITED STATES v. AMERICAN TOBACCO CO., 211 U.S. 106 (1911). In a companion case to *Standard Oil,* the original "tobacco trust" was found by the Supreme Court to violate the Sherman Antitrust Act.

The trust, consisting of five major tobacco manufacturers, controlled about 95% of the domestic cigarette industry, and drove numerous competing firms from the market. The Supreme Court held that a dominant market position was not alone sufficient to infer a violation of law. Under the *rule of reason*, the company's intent as evidenced by overt acts was a critical basis for judging legality. The Court found that the record of predatory and ruthless behavior on the part of the tobacco manufacturers supported the claim of Sherman Act violations.

See also United States v. Standard Oil Co. of New Jersey.

UNITED STATES v. E.I. DU PONT AND CO., 353
U.S. 586 (1957). The du Pont Company is a major supplier of auto finishes and fabrics to General Motors, the nation's leading automobile manufacturer. The supplier-customer relationship between these two large companies was complicated by the fact that du Pont held a 23% stock interest in General Motors, an interest acquired several decades earlier. In 1949, the government charged that the original stock acquisition violated Section 7 of the Clayton Antitrust Act by tending to substantially lessen competition. The government's main argument was that du Pont's interest in General Motors had prevented GM from purchasing supplies from du Pont's competitors.

The defendant companies argued that their customer-supplier relationship was based solely on objective business considerations. The Supreme Court, however, noting that du Pont always supplied the bulk of General Motors' fabric and finish requirements, concluded that the original stock acquisition violated Section 7, and ordered du Pont to rid itself of its General Motors holdings.

See also Clayton Antitrust Act.

UNITED STATES v. FIRST NATIONAL CITY
BANK. *See* Bank Merger Acts.

UNITED STATES v. INTERNATIONAL BUSINESS
MACHINES, a major antitrust case initiated by the Justice Department in 1969. The case was finally dropped by the government in 1982 as being "without merit." The government had claimed that IBM, one of the nation's most successful firms, had sought to monopolize the digital computer market. The government pointed to IBM's large market share (over 70% in 1976) and also to its policies of tying sales of its software to sales of computers. IBM claimed the government was trying to penalize it for being efficient, innovative, and successful. The dropping of the case by the government represented a major turning point in government attitude toward business in the United States.

See also United States v. Aluminum Co. of America.

UNITED STATES v. NEW YORK GREAT A & P
CO., 67 F. Supp. 626 (1946), one of the most controversial cases in antitrust litigation. A & P was charged with price discrimination under Section 2 of the Clayton Antitrust Act (as amended by Robinson-Patman, 1936) for selling grocery products in certain localities at prices below those of local competitors. It was able to do so because of concessions that it, as a major purchaser, was able to extract from manufacturers. A consent decree was negotiated, forbidding A & P to price products so as to eliminate competition, and requiring other minor adjustments in A & P business practices.

The result is controversial because of the intent of antitrust policy being served by the consent decree. A & P clearly was engaging in price competition. It attributed the price concessions on its purchases, which permitted its charging lower prices to customers, to the shrewd bargaining of its buyers. However, local competitors, damaged as a result of the price competition, were provided redress in the decree. — *Thomas O. Depperschmidt*

See also Price Discrimination.

UNITED STATES v. PHILADELPHIA NATIONAL
BANK. *See* Bank Merger Acts.

UNITED STATES v. PROVIDENT NATIONAL
BANK. *See* Bank Merger Acts.

UNITED STATES v. STANDARD OIL CO. OF NEW
JERSEY, 221 U.S. 1 (1911), is significant in the development of antitrust policy for two reasons. The breakup of Standard Oil into 11 parts was the first major dissolution ordered under the Sherman Antitrust Act where monopolization was found. And the Supreme Court, despite the judgment against Standard Oil, announced the "rule of reason." Whereas the Sherman Antitrust Act prohibited every contract, combination, or conspiracy in restraint of trade and every attempt to monopolize, the Standard Oil decision showed that the Court would condemn only "unreasonable" restraints and attempts to monopolize. The rule in effect marked a relaxation of governmental prosecution of antitrust law violations. Standard Oil violated the Sherman Antitrust Act not by virtue of its position alone, but because its predatory behavior indicated "the intent to drive others from the field and to exclude them from their right to trade."

See also Monopolizing; Predatory Practices; Restraint of Trade.

UNITED STATES v. U.S. STEEL CORPORATION,
251 U.S. 417 (1920). The government charged U.S. Steel with monopolizing and restraining trade in violation of the Sherman Antitrust Act. The company, which had been formed by consolidation of about 180 separate concerns at the turn of the century, had

accounted for about 50 percent of national iron and steel capacity, although its share had since fallen to about 41 percent.

The Supreme Court, upholding a District Court decision, concluded that U.S. Steel had not monopolized in violation of the Sherman Act. In one of the most famous phrases in modern antitrust, the Court stated: " . . . the law does not make mere size an offense, or the existence of unexerted power an offense. . . ." U.S. Steel thus could not be found to have monopolized by virtue of its market position alone. In addition, the Court could find no "overt acts" in the company's history that would indicate intent to monopolize. The company was therefore acquitted despite a position indicating significant market power. This case provided a clear antitrust precedent for many years: a company does not violate the law simply by growing large; it must also engage in somehow wrongful conduct in the process of achieving its growth. —*Peter Asch*

See also Monopolizing; Sherman Antitrust Act; United States v. Aluminum Co. of America.

UNIT ELASTICITY, or UNITARY ELASTICITY, of supply. The supply of a product is said to be of unitary elasticity, over some small price range, when the computed coefficient of elasticity is equal to 1. Assume that the price of commodity "Z" changes by some small percentage. If the response on the part of the producers of that commodity is such as to increase output by an identical percentage, then the computed coefficient of elasticity will exactly equal 1, and this would be called unitary elasticity. The importance of this concept is that it is a watershed; coefficients greater than 1 are called elastic, coefficients less than 1 are considered inelastic.

UNIT ELASTICITY OF DEMAND. A demand curve is said to possess unitary elasticity of demand if a given percentage change in the price of the commodity in question results in the same percentage change in quantity demanded. The coefficient of elasticity in such a case will be -1. Every downward-sloping demand curve will have at least one point on it with unitary elasticity. For the typical downward-sloping linear demand curve, this point of unitary elasticity will occur at the point on the quantity-demanded axis where the marginal revenue of additional price change equals zero. A special class of demand curves possess unitary elasticity throughout. When these curves are graphed, they always assume the shape of a rectangular hyperbola asymptotic to both axes of the graph.

UNIT OF ACCOUNT. *See* Money.

UNSECURED BONDS. *See* Debentures.

USER CHARGE, a payment made for a good or service provided by a government. Unlike a tax, a user charge is strictly voluntary, and the payment is linked to the consumption of the good being provided. In other words, a user charge is the same thing as a price charged for a privately provided service. Examples include bus fares for mass transit, tuition paid to a public university, a water bill paid to a municipally owned water company, or a fee paid for use of a public park. User charges are increasing in importance as a source of state and local government revenues.

USURY, the charging of interest on borrowed money. Usury is still prohibited by the Muslim religion and was prohibited by Christianity until the late Middle Ages, when some theologians established that it was just to reimburse the lender for the risk involved in lending and for deferring consumption.

Today's usury laws set ceilings on the rate of interest that can be charged. Whenever market interest rates exceed these ceilings, funds are not available for legal borrowing.

UTILITY. Underlying the basic theory of consumer behavior are two fundamental assumptions: (1) when considering any set of commodity bundles, the consumers are always able to rank these bundles in the order of their preferences; (2) when making a choice among the bundles that are within their budgets, the consumer always choose the most preferred bundle. More formally, the first assumption postulates the existence, for each consumer, of a complete *preference ordering,* while the second assumption says in effect that the consumer is a hedonist.

Utility Index. Given the preference ordering of a consumer, it is possible (with an additional assumption of a technical nature) to assign numbers to all commodity bundles in such a way that they reflect the order of the consumer's preferences. The number assigned to a particular bundle is called a *utility index.* It has no intrinsic meaning, and should *not* be interpreted as a measure of the satisfaction which the consumer derives from the respective commodity bundle. The utility index of a commodity bundle assumes a meaning only when compared with that of another bundle, and all that can be inferred from such a comparison is that, for any two bundles, the bundle with the higher utility index is preferred by the consumer to the other bundle.

UTILITY FUNCTION. It may be possible to describe the relationship between the quantities of the various commodities in a particular bundle and the utility index of the bundle by means of a mathematical formula, or function; such a function is called a utility function. Consequently, when a consumer chooses the most preferred bundle, he or she is in fact choosing a bundle for which the utility function attains its

UTILITY FUNCTION

Figure 1   Quantity of X

Figure 2   Quantity of X

maximum value. It is for this reason that theories of consumer behavior are often formulated as a utility maximization problem.

Utility Curves. Figure 1 illustrates a utility function for the case of bundles with two commodities, X and Y. Commodity X is measured on the horizontal axis, and the utility index U on the vertical axis. The curves shown are total utility curves: each curve shows the utility associated with various bundles containing some fixed amounts of commodity Y, and $Y_3 > Y_2 > Y_1$. For example, the curve TU (Y_2) shows the utility of bundles containing Y_2 units of Y and various amounts of X. The fact that each TU curve has a positive slope reflects the assumption of greediness; that is, a consumer always prefers a larger bundle to a smaller one, where a larger bundle is one with more of at least one commodity and no less of any other commodity, compared to the other bundle. Thus, the bundle denoted by B is larger than bundle A, and, therefore, the utility of bundle B is higher than the utility of bundle A. Similarly, bundle C is preferred to bundle A.

The change in the utility index resulting from a small increase in one commodity is called the marginal utility of that commodity. For example, moving along the curve TU (Y_2) in Figure 1 from bundle A toward bundle B causes the utility index to increase. These increases in utility are the marginal utilities of successive increments in X. Geometrically speaking, the marginal utility of X is measured by the slope of the respective TU curve. The greediness assumption says,

in effect, that the marginal utility of every good is positive.

Indifference Curves. A utility function may also be represented by certain curves in the commodity space, the XY plane. For example, mapping the points C, B, and D from Figure 1 into the XY plane yields the three points shown in Figure 2. Because these three bundles have the same level of utility, they are considered to be equally desirable by the consumer. If all the points on the horizontal line going through points C, B, and D in Figure 1 are mapped into Figure 2, one obtains a curve such as that labeled U_2. All commodity bundles represented by points on that curve have the same level of utility: the consumer is indifferent between them. For this reason, such a curve is called an indifference curve, or, isoutility curve.

For any two bundles on an indifference curve, one bundle has more of X and less of Y than the other bundle; in other words, an indifference curve has a negative slope. A movement along the indifference curve in Figure 2 from bundle C to bundle B shows how commodity X is substituted for commodity Y to keep the level of utility constant. The curvature of the indifference curve, that is, the fact that it is convex to the origin, implies that the indifference curve becomes flatter as the amount of X is increased. But the slope of the indifference curve indicates the rate at which commodity Y is reduced for each additional unit of X added. For this reason, the slope of an indifference curve measures the marginal rate of substitution (rate of substitution in consumption) between the commodities in question. If the indifference curve is convex to the origin, as in Figure 2, the marginal rate of substitution decreases as X is increased. This property is known as diminishing marginal rate of substitution. One can draw an indifference curve for any level of utility. A diagram depicting several indifference curves is referred to as an indifference map.

— Josef Hadar

UTOPIAN SOCIALISM. *See* Owen, Robert; Pre-Marxian Socialism.

VALUE ADDED by a firm, approximately equivalent to the difference between its sales and its purchases of intermediate output—ingredients that enter into the fabrication of sold output. The value added by a firm is equivalent to the factor incomes that the firm must pay out. What a firm receives through its sales must be distributed to the firms from which it buys or to the factors it employs. Recognizing this feature yields the conclusion that summing up either the value added or the factor income generated by each firm will yield equivalent dollar magnitudes, equivalent estimates of GNP.

The summation of the value added by each firm is also equivalent to the sum of final output. To make this fact clear, take the cost of a commodity purchased by a consumer. The cost of this item to the consumer will equal the sum of the value added by each firm that participates in the production and distribution of the commodity. Thus, the price of a loaf of bread received by a retailer is partly paid out to factors and to bakers, bakers in turn will distribute its revenues to factors and suppliers, and these suppliers will distribute their proceeds to factors and still other suppliers. Thus, in the calculation of GNP the sales of all firms are not added together, only the value added by each firm. If all sales were added together—taken as final output—many transactions would be counted more than once; total sales far exceeds the sum of factor incomes, the value of final output, or, identically, the sum of the value added by each firm.   —*Frank J. Bonello*

VALUE-ADDED TAX, tax with a base defined as the net "value-added" at each stage of the production process. Value-added is the payment for wages and other factors of production that increase the value of materials and other inputs that a business purchases. It is determined by subtracting the purchase cost of a good from its selling price. Such a tax can be based on sales, with allowances for taxes incorporated in the prices of purchased goods, or it can be based directly on each company's value-added.

This type of tax is in use in several European nations and in at least one state (Michigan) and has recently been the subject of discussion for use in the United States. In other nations, it has usually acted as a substitute for some sales taxes.

VALUE PRODUCTIVITY. *See* Factor Productivity.

VARIABLE, a symbol, denoted by a letter whose numerical magnitude can change. Some common variables in economics are quantity demanded, consumption, price, and profits. Any variable is allowed to assume different values from a given set of numbers, usually positive real numbers in economics. If these values can be arranged so that there are no gaps or holes in the set, however small, then the variable is said to be continuous. Discontinuous or discrete variables take only certain values from the appropriated number set, such as integer (whole number) values. Whether a variable is considered continuous or discrete often depends on the units in which it is measured and the convenience of the researcher.

If one variable (y) is related to another variable (x) in such a way that the value of x determines the value of y, then y is called the dependent variable and x the independent variable. The set of numbers from which the independent variable can assume its values is called the domain of x. The corresponding set of values for the dependent variable is called the range of y.   —*Carlisle E. Moody, Jr.*

VARIABLE COST OF PRODUCTION. *See* Average Fixed Cost of Production.

VARIABLE COST PER UNIT. *See* Average Variable Cost of Production.

VAULT CASH, coin and paper currency held on bank premises to meet the immediate demands of depositors wishing to withdraw cash from their accounts. United States banks keep 2% to 3% of their deposits in vault cash.

VEBLEN, THORSTEIN (1857-1929), founder of the institutionalist school, a pessimistic American critic of society and the economic system. His most important book, *The Theory of the Leisure Class* (1899), approached economics from a broad evolutionary perspective and introduced such terms as leisure class and conspicuous consumption. Veblen felt that the structure of society and the economy could be best viewed as the outcome of a process of natural selection of institutions. However, institutions do not change as rapidly as society, thus creating a continual state of conflict.

In the *Leisure Class* and other works, Veblen attacked marginalist and conventional economics on a number of grounds. He felt that the view of the entrepreneur as a risk-bearer was basically incorrect and that marginalist theory supported the present income and wealth distribution. Veblen wished to replace conventional theory with an exposure of the business system and its effect upon man.

While much was wrong with Veblen's work, it did confront economics with questions and problems which conventional theory had generally ignored until that time.   —Clyde A. Haulman

See also Conspicuous Consumption; Institutionalism.

VELOCITY OF CIRCULATION, the speed with which money changes hands. Transactions velocity is the number of times on the average that each dollar is spent during a given year. Income velocity is the number of times that each dollar becomes income during the year. Income velocity for a nation can be measured by dividing national income by the money supply.

See also Equation Exchange.

VERTICAL DEMAND CURVE, a demand curve that intersects the quantity axis of a rectilinear coordinate system and rises from that intersection point with an infinite slope. The economic implication of a vertical demand curve is that a given quantity of the product in question will be demanded regardless of whatever level the price of that commodity might reach. This type of demand curve displays perfectly inelastic demand: the total expenditure on a commodity and its price will always change in the same direction.

VERTICAL MERGER, a combination of firms at different stages of the production process into one business unit. The result of such a merger is also called "vertical integration." A firm is said to integrate "backward" when, for example, it absorbs a firm supplying to it, "forward" when it acquires another firm to which it supplies, such as a wholesale or retail outlet. The legality of vertical mergers is subject to the same test as other mergers: does its effect tend to lessen competition or create a monopoly?

See also Celler-Kefauver Act; Clayton Act; Merger; Monopoly.

VERY LONG RUN, a period in which all variables are subject to change. Under the assumptions of the short run and the long run, technological change was not possible. In the very long run any technological possibility is open to the firm. The technological improvements implemented within the firm may be either internal or external. Decisions in the very long run must take cognizance of technological change.

See also Long Run.

VISIBLE GOODS AND SERVICES. The current account of a balance of payments is made up of *visible* and *invisible* items. Visible items are physical, tangible goods which can pass through customs and be quantitatively identified and on which a value can be placed. These characteristics make visible items subject to the levying of tariffs or imposition of quotas. Merchandise exports and imports are the visible items in the current account and it is with respect to these that the most reliable quantitative data is obtained. An automobile imported from Germany into the United States is an obvious example of a visible item in the current account. Just as visible would be Europeans traveling in the United States, but tourist expenditures are classified as invisible items by balance of payment criteria.

See also Balance of Payments; Invisible Goods and Services.

WAGE AND HOUR LAW. *See* Fair Labor Standards Act (1938).

WAGE CRITERIA are devices used by both labor and management to aid in the determination of wage rates. Of the several wage criteria used in collective bargaining, cost-of-living and ability-to-pay are the most frequently used today.

The ability-to-pay criterion states that justified cost of living wage increases can only be granted if management is in a position to be able to pay the higher wage rate.

The cost-of-living wage criterion bases its justifica-

tion for higher wages on the rise in the cost of living as reflected in higher prices. To adjust for the loss of real income that may occur with inflation, a bargaining contract may include an escalator clause, specifying a precise relationship between changes in the cost of living and changes in the wage rate. These clauses therefore provide for an "open end" increase in wage rates.

Other wage criteria sometimes used are maintenance of take-home pay despite the reduction of hours worked, and improvement in productivity.

WAGE DIFFERENTIALS, differences in wage rates that occur either for rational or nonrational reasons.

Rational wage differentials, or equalizing wage differentials, are paid to compensate for the nonmoney differences among jobs. A major job difference is risk or danger, as in steeplejacking, skin diving or combat service. Another rational wage differential is extra pay for unpleasant or inconvenient jobs—workers on a graveyard shift usually receive a night differential, generally a certain percentage of their wage rate.

The nonrational or nonequalizing wage differential is based on such illogical reasons as peculiarities of places and practices, historical accidents, and the relative skill of different groups in gaining wage increases. For example, certain union workers earn more than nonunion workers of the same trade, and many minority group workers are paid less than whites.

WAGE FLEXIBILITY means that wages change with changing conditions in the labor market. The degree of flexibility determines the impact on employment of a change in the demand for labor. Assuming flexible wages, and a decrease in demand, a reduction in the wages workers are willing to accept permits employment to hold up rather than decrease. Flexible wages permit the market system to operate, as do flexible prices.

WAGE GUIDEPOSTS. Although wage and price control by government is somewhat acceptable during times of war, in peacetime it is looked upon with disfavor. For this reason, government has experimented with a system of controls known as wage and price guideposts, which indicate to both management and labor the limits of wage and price changes that are compatible with economic stability. Adherence to these guideposts is usually voluntary, with no penalty for violation.

In 1962, when high levels of unemployment existed along with inflation, President Kennedy, through his Council of Economic Advisers, announced a set of voluntary guidelines for wage and price changes. The general guide for noninflationary wage behavior was that the rate of increase in wage rates in each industry be equal to the trend rate of overall productivity

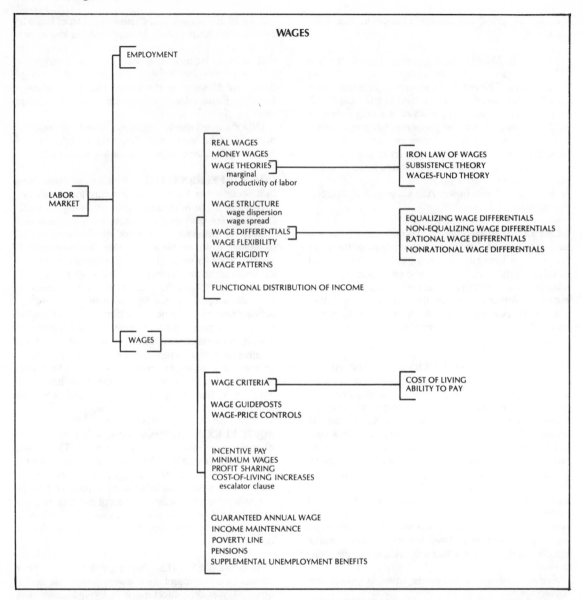

WAGES

EMPLOYMENT

LABOR MARKET

WAGES

REAL WAGES
MONEY WAGES
WAGE THEORIES
   marginal
   productivity of labor

IRON LAW OF WAGES
SUBSISTENCE THEORY
WAGES-FUND THEORY

WAGE STRUCTURE
   wage dispersion
   wage spread
WAGE DIFFERENTIALS
WAGE FLEXIBILITY
WAGE RIGIDITY
WAGE PATTERNS

EQUALIZING WAGE DIFFERENTIALS
NON-EQUALIZING WAGE DIFFERENTIALS
RATIONAL WAGE DIFFERENTIALS
NONRATIONAL WAGE DIFFERENTIALS

FUNCTIONAL DISTRIBUTION OF INCOME

WAGE CRITERIA

COST OF LIVING
ABILITY TO PAY

WAGE GUIDEPOSTS
WAGE-PRICE CONTROLS

INCENTIVE PAY
MINIMUM WAGES
PROFIT SHARING
COST-OF-LIVING INCREASES
   escalator clause

GUARANTEED ANNUAL WAGE
INCOME MAINTENANCE
POVERTY LINE
PENSIONS
SUPPLEMENTAL UNEMPLOYMENT BENEFITS

increase. In addition, the guide for noninflationary price behavior called for price reduction if the industry's rate of productivity increase exceeded the overall rate, and it called for price increases if the industry's rate of production increase was below the overall rate. For the case where the two rates were equal, stable prices should exist.

These guidelines seemed to have been fairly successful from 1962 to 1964. In 1965 and 1966, government used its position as a purchaser, subsidizer, and regulator to influence the use of guideposts in such industries as copper, steel, and aluminum. In 1969 and 1970, with inflationary pressures beginning to mount, interest in wage and price regulations was again revived. New wage and price guideposts were administered under President Nixon. However, guideposts did not seem to be as helpful this time in relieving inflationary pressures, and in 1971 a 90-day wage and price freeze was put into effect.

— *William D. Wagoner*

WAGE LEVEL of a country is a composite of a wide range of different specific wage rates. Usually the higher the demand for labor in relation to the supply of labor, the higher the wage rates will be.

The wage level depends upon several factors, including: (1) the amount of capital a country has available; (2) natural resources; (3) the level of technology; and (4) the extent and nature of education and training of labor. The higher the productivity of labor, the higher the wage level will be. For this reason, the United States ranks highest in wage levels of all countries.

A problem arising from a rising wage level is that, as money wages begin to increase, the supply of labor available also begins to increase and the price level to rise, often causing a decrease in real wages.

WAGE PATTERNS is a term often used in labor economics to show the spread of an idea in collective bargaining across an industry or the economy. Thus, one firm will be the "pattern setter" in an industry, and the other firms may be expected to follow the pattern set. The wage package—that is, the total of the payments made to an employee—can often be traced from firm to firm and from industry to industry, and the pattern can be easily observed.

WAGE-PRICE CONTROL, an incomes policy to curb inflation through mandatory limits on wage-price changes. Wage-price controls have been wartime policies only. For example, during World War II (1941-1946) the National War Labor Board and the Office of Price Administration were set up to stabilize wages and prices. The Office of Price Stabilization effected similar controls during the Korean War (1950-1953). However, because these controls were not strictly enforced, they had relatively little effect.

For nearly two decades after the Korean War, the only incomes policy used was the wage-price guideposts—voluntary guidelines for labor and management. The guideposts proved successful under President Kennedy, but in 1971 President Nixon, having been unable to relieve inflationary pressures through guidelines, resorted to a wage-price freeze for 90 days. The first freeze ever placed on wages and prices during ostensible peacetime, the policy met with great controversy but was moderately successful in curbing excessive inflationary pressures.

See also Incomes Policy.

WAGE-PRICE GUIDEPOSTS, incomes policies used mainly during inflationary periods to stabilize wages and prices through voluntary guidelines for labor and management to follow, preventing real income from decreasing. Unlike wage-price controls, these guideposts carry no penalty for violation.

In 1962, President Kennedy and his Council of Economic Advisers set up some guideposts which proved to be very successful and lasted through 1964. In other instances, the government has been able to use its influence as a purchaser, regulator, and subsidizer to enforce guidelines. In 1969, with unemployment beginning to rise along with inflationary pressure, new interest in wage-price policy arose. President Nixon announced a set of guidelines that

same year. However, they were unsuccessful and in August 1971 were replaced by a wage-price freeze.

See also Incomes Policy.

WAGE-PUSH INFLATION, essentially cost-push inflation where the prime mover has been identified as union wage demands in excess of productivity gains. The increased costs to the firm are passed to the consumer as higher prices.

WAGE RIGIDITY refers to a situation in which, for whatever reason, wages do not respond to the changing conditions in the labor market. Wage rates are difficult to change, particularly in a downward direction, but to the degree that wages are sticky, the market cannot work as it should. For example, a wage level that does not change in the face of a decreased demand for labor can only result in a decrease in the number of people employers can hire. On the other hand, wages that are variable permit the labor market to work efficiently.

WAGES, the price paid for labor, represent a cost to the employer and income for the worker. As income (constituting about 70% of national income), wages include "in-kind" income, such as room and board furnished to the worker by the employer, as well as cash payments. These represent a worker's money wages, as distinguished from his real wages or purchasing power. If prices increase at a faster rate than an individual's money wages, his real wages are decreasing.

Wages are usually stated as a rate on an hourly basis. For example, the minimum wage in the United States in 1991 was $4.25 per hour. Conflict over what the wage rate of workers should be often arises, whereupon wages often have to be decided upon by the collective bargaining process.

In many industries a wage structure is used. A wage structure is a hierarchy of jobs to which wage rates are attached. This is often done by the use of a labor grade, a ranked classification, with each grade having specifications as to the amount of skill, experience, and seniority a worker needs to qualify for that grade. Within each grade there is often a wage spread with a maximum and a minimum rate.

A second way in which wages are paid is by the incentive system. This system pays workers according to the amount of work actually done, so much per piece produced or a commission on goods sold. Two other forms of incentive pay are bonuses and profit sharing.

Wages can help allocate labor to its best alternative use. As wage rates in an industry increase, for example, more and more labor becomes available to that industry. Wages also function in determining the overall volume of employment. Up to a certain level, higher wage rates induce more and more people to enter the labor force.   —*William D. Wagoner*

WAGES-FUND THEORY evolved in the latter part of the eighteenth century and stated that the rate of wages was a function of the ratio between the amount of funds available for paying wages and the amount of workers. Under this theory, wages could only rise if there was an increase in the fund or "capital," or a decrease in the number of workers. This theory was often used to prove that an attempt by workers to raise real wages was futile.

WAGE STRUCTURE is a hierarchy of jobs, ranked in ascending or descending order according to their importance, with wage rates allotted to each job.

For simplicity, jobs are often classified into labor grades with each grade having a wage spread with a minimum and a maximum rate and usually with progressive steps within the grade. The use of this rate range allows management to recognize both seniority and individual merit. Most government jobs use this type of wage structure. A second wage structure method is the concept, pushed by unions, of equal pay for equal work. However, problems often arise in dealing with this type of wage determination because it is often difficult to translate a ranking of jobs into a system of money wages satisfactorily.

Wage structures are set up by management or through the collective bargaining process, and changes in the wage rates within the structure are usually adjusted periodically for increases in the cost of living.

WAGE THEORIES have been in existence almost as long as the science of economics. Although Adam Smith formulated no actual theory of wages, he did set a pattern of thought in regard to minimum levels of pay.

The Iron Law of Wages was one of the first theories of wages. A concept of the classical economists, David Ricardo and Thomas Malthus, it stated that wages tend to equal what the worker needs to maintain a bare subsistence level of living. It further stated that higher wages result in increased population, thus increased demand for food, thus rising food prices, thus a drop in real income.

The Iron Law gave way to a more sophisticated wage fund theory presented by John Stuart Mill in 1848. Mill stated that there is a set wage fund at any given time and that the only way a worker's wages could increase would be by a decrease in the number of workers.

A third major wage theory was the marginal productivity theory, under which the worker is paid a wage rate equal to the marginal output. Another wage fund theory deals with bargaining. This theory states that management and labor will engage in bargaining

to achieve outcomes at which neither party can improve its position except at the expense of the other.   —*William D. Wagoner*

WAGNER ACT (1935), organized labor's greatest single legislative victory, gaining workers the explicit right to organize and bargain collectively and requiring management to recognize these unions and to bargain with them. To promote these ends, the law, also known as the National Labor Relations Act, denied to management certain "unfair labor practices." The National Labor Relations Board was set up to administer the act.

Explicit, bold, and comprehensive in its support of organized labor, much of its content derived from earlier legislation, particularly the Railway Labor Act of 1926 and the short-lived National Industrial Recovery Act (NIRA) of 1933. Passed by Congress within a few weeks of the Supreme Court's decision declaring the NIRA unconstitutional, the Wagner Act resurrected and greatly expanded the protections to labor contained in Section 7(a) of the defunct law.

Bolstering Labor's Power. The act states that "employees shall have the right to self-organization, to form, join, or assist labor organizations, to bargain collectively through representatives of their own choosing, and to engage in concerted activities for the purpose of collective bargaining or other mutual aid or protection." The law protected these rights by prohibiting management from engaging in certain acts, designed as "unfair labor practices," such as refusal to bargain collectively, or interference with or discrimination against workers or unions in their organization, administration, or bargaining.

The constitutionality of the act could not be taken for granted; however, the Supreme Court, in the landmark case *National Labor Relations Board v. Jones and Laughlin Steel Corporation,* upheld the validity of the law. With this decision, the rapid growth of the labor movement, which would bring it quickly to large size and substantial power, was assured.

Counterbalance Needed. But the growth of the labor movement itself made the Wagner Act too limited to serve as the key labor law. It was recognized as totally one-sided, designed to aid unionism and restrict management in labor relations. Certain restrictions on labor were deemed necessary, lest its newly developed power be used without restraint. Limitations on unions in regard to their actions against employers and nonunion employees were therefore added to the Taft-Hartley Act of 1947, and the balance of power between labor and employers, as in 1935, would again move toward equalization.

—*Leonard G. Schifrin*

See also National Industrial Recovery Act; Railway Labor Act; Taft-Hartley Act.

WALRAS, LEON (1834-1910), French economist,

principally known for his authorship of *Elements of Pure Economics* (1874-1877), a classical work in the area of pure economic theory. In addition to including an analysis of value and marginal utility similar to that of Jevons and Menger, this outstanding work was a pioneering effort in applying the tool of mathematical analysis to general economic equilibrium under, in Walras's words, "a regime of perfectly free competition." In other words, it provides a conceptual solution to the problems of price equilibrium, quantities of products, and the productive factors.

In his major attempt to solve the problem of linking the various markets which constitute the economy, Walras developed a system requiring perfect competition, freedom of entry, mobility, and price flexibility. The system's most notable characteristic was Walras's effort to demonstrate, through mathematical analysis, that a perfectly competitive economy would tend to approximate equilibrium positions.

The Walrasian system, being presumed the supreme representation of classical and neoclassical economics, was a prime focus of those who attacked what they saw as a dichotomy between the theories of relative prices and money and the theory of the price level. They argued that in the Walrasian system the price level is indeterminate. With such arguments, the Walrasian system thus provided at least the point of departure for further contributions in the field of economic analysis. —*Clyde A. Haulman*

WASTE. *See* Economic Efficiency.

WEAK ROAD–STRONG ROAD PROBLEM arises because the Interstate Commerce Commission, as a practical necessity, sets uniform rates for whole groups of competing railroads. Under these uniform rates some railroads (strong roads) have more than adequate earnings while others (weak roads) receive insufficient earnings.

Suggested possible solutions to the problem include consolidation of railroads into a few large systems and government ownership and operation of railroads. To the extent that the problem is not dealt with adequately, it is likely that some useful lines will be abandoned.

WEALTH OF NATIONS, THE. Adam Smith's *An Inquiry into the Nature and Causes of the Wealth of Nations* (1776) was the first volume to develop a general theory of economics and apply that theory to the explanation of various aspects of economic life. Two general themes dominate: (1) that the division of labor is the root of much of the economic progress of man; and (2) that harmony of interest guides society, wherein each individual seeking to improve his or her own condition contributes to the betterment of society through these actions. Based upon these concepts, Smith analyzes the workings of the economic system

and suggests the policies which he feels are necessary to promote economic growth and development. In addition, the *Wealth of Nations* is centered on the concept that the wealth of a nation stems from its treasury, as the mercantilists felt, or from its agricultural sector, as the Physiocrats believed.

Smith's work is divided into five books or sections dealing with (1) production; (2) distribution; (3) economic development; (4) economic history; and (5) public finance. The first two are the most important since they consider the theory of value, market price, wage theory, the theory of profit, rent theory, and capital. Smith's statement of several value theories and his inability to deal with rent theory create problems. However, his treatment of important aspects of price theory and his consideration of factors creating different wage rates, in addition to his concept of declining profits, laid the foundation for classical economics. This, combined with his treatment of other economic phenomena, marks the emergence of economics as a discipline and set the stage for later advances in theory. —*Clyde A. Haulman*
See also Classical Economics; Smith, Adam.

WEBB, SIDNEY JAMES (1859-1947), and BEATRICE POTTER (1858-1943). Lord and Lady Passfield were the founders of the London School of Economics (1895). Together with George Bernard Shaw, they were the guiding spirits of the socialist Fabian Society and made important contributions to political and social thought in England during the early part of the twentieth century. Central to Fabian thought was the concept of the inevitability of gradualness in the development of socialism, with a democratic government planning and controlling this development. Their approach to economics emphasized the realities of the situation rather than theoretical, abstract concepts.
See also Fabian Society.

WEBB-POMERENE ACT (1918) exempts joint marketing associations of American firms selling in foreign countries from prosecution under the Sherman Antitrust Act for activities such as market sharing and joint price setting, so long as these association activities are not conducted domestically. About 30 such associations exist.
See also Cartels; Market Sharing; Sherman Antitrust Act.

WEBER, MAX (1864-1920), noted German sociologist and political economist who found his main challenge in the Marxist idea of economic determinism. Weber's *The Protestant Ethic and the Spirit of Capitalism* (1904-1905), a painstakingly complete historical study, was an attempt to demonstrate that, at least in the specific case under examination, religious and ethical ideas held great sway. Weber then developed the question of historical causation into the even broader issue of discovering what element in the spiritual history of Western civilization was responsible for the development of capitalism, particularly as other cultures failed to produce such an economic system.

Weber's most significant contribution is to economic sociology. Stubbornly adhering to Hume's distinction between what is and what ought to be, and maintaining that there must be no value judgements in social science, Weber laid the groundwork for modern social science's characteristic distinction between personal and professional attitudes.

WEIGHTED AVERAGE. *See* Central Tendency.

WELFARE. *See* Public Assistance.

WELFARE ECONOMICS, a branch of economic study concerned with how an economic system attempts to maximize the welfare of its people. In addition, welfare economics studies the principles by which alternative economic objectives can be ranked in terms of social welfare. The study emerged as a separate discipline with the publication of A.C. Pigou's *The Economics of Welfare* (1920).

Included in the theoretical approaches of welfare economics is the goal of optimizing both resources allocation and product distribution. An economic system maximizes welfare when the marginal productivity of social benefits, the marginal utility of private benefits, and the marginal utility of consumers are equal. For example, if products currently being produced for private consumption could be transferred to social consumption to add a greater amount to total welfare, then the existing system would not be maximizing welfare. The optimal position in maximizing welfare is to reach a point where the marginal rate of substitution between any two goods equals the marginal rate of transformation of the two goods in production.

Usually, in the study of welfare economics the socioeconomic goals of the economy are predetermined by factors other than economic analysis, such as legislation or consumer preference. The optimum is achieved when the welfare of the greatest possible number of people is maximized without regard to the profit of an individual or a firm.

—Robert L. Brite
See also Consumer Surplus; Marginal Utility.

WELFARE STATE, an economic system committed to providing security to its population in the areas of minimal incomes, health care, job security, and provisions for old age.

An economic system may be described as a welfare state regardless of its degree of public ownership of the means of production. Sweden has a low percentage of public ownership but a highly developed welfare system. To meets its aims of social welfare, the state may

tax private property owners or direct incomes from state properties.

WHEELER-LEA ACT (1938) amended the Federal Trade Commission Act, Section 5, to prohibit "unfair or deceptive acts or practices" (including misleading and false advertising). It made more explicit the types of "unfair practices" prohibited in the FTC Act and made the test of legality of such practices not the effect on an offender's competitors (or competition generally) but the effect on the general public. The Wheeler-Lea Act is unique in antitrust legislation in providing such direct protection to consumers.

WHIPSAW TACTICS. *See* Multi-Employer Bargaining.

WHITE-COLLAR WORKER. Although not a distinct Bureau of the Census classification, white-collar jobs usually fall under the categories of "sales workers," "clerical and kindred workers," and "professional, technical, and kindred workers." Since World War II, the number of white-collar jobs has grown very rapidly. By 1956 it had surpassed the number of blue-collar jobs and, since that time, white-collar jobs have been increasing at a faster rate than blue-collar jobs. In the mid-1980s, about 67% of all jobs were classified as white-collar jobs.

WHOLESALE PRICE INDEX (WPI), one of the best known of the price indexes, a statistical composite measure of price movements in wholesale, or primary, markets. Using a sample of over 2,200 commodities, WPI bases its price quotations on the level of the first significant commercial transaction of these commodities. These price quotations are usually those of the producers and reflect their large lot sales and not necessarily sales to wholesale dealers or distributors. The commodities and the weights used for WPI are not the same as the Consumer Price Index and, therefore, both indexes need not move in the same direction in the short run. Beginning in 1978, the Bureau of Labor Statistics replaced the WPI with the Producer Price Index (PPI), which uses the same prices.

See also Price Indexes.

WICKSELL, KNUT (1851-1926), Swedish monetary economist who made numerous important contributions to monetary theory and developed some of the concepts which became central elements of the Keynesian system.

Wicksell's monetary theory was directed toward an analysis of aggregate price changes and the role of the interest rate in such changes. Because he felt that prices could not be stable until the bank interest rate equaled the natural rate, governmental and central bank monetary controls over interest rates were considered to be crucial in promoting stability.

While Wicksell felt that the normal state of the economy was one of full employment, he did address the question of the relationship between saving and investment and developed the concept of ex-post and ex-ante saving. However, it was left for Keynes to apply these concepts to the situation in which the economy reached an equilibrium at less than full employment. —*Clyde A. Haulman*

WICKSTEED, PHILLIP H. (1884-1927). A theologian and Dante scholar, Wicksteed contributed to economics as one aspect of his broad intellectual interests. A follower of William Jevons, he made independent contributions to distribution theory and to the study of the relationship between supply and demand.

Wicksteed's *Essay on the Co-ordination of the Laws of Distribution* (1894) considered the distribution of output among the various factors of production based upon the marginal productivity principle. He concluded that output would be totally exhausted if each factor received its marginal production. However, *Common Sense of Political Economy* (1910) was Wicksteed's most important work. In it, he considers all the technical implications of pure marginalism in economic theory.

See also Marginalism.

WIESER, FRIEDRICH VON (1851-1926), Austrian follower of Carl Menger and classmate of Eugen Böhm-Bawerk, noted for his introduction of the term marginal utility to describe the concept developed by his mentor and others. Using this concept, Wieser rejected the labor theory of value and, in *Karl Marx and the Close of His System* (1896), presented one of the leading criticisms of Marxian economics. Wieser also developed the doctrine of opportunity cost. The concept that cost can be viewed in terms of opportunities or alternatives forgone has become an essential element of economic analysis.

See also Marginalism; Opportunity Cost.

WILDCAT STRIKES, unofficial or unauthorized work stoppages by employees, usually over a dispute arising during the life of a contract and involving the interpretation of an issue that is perhaps not covered by the contract. With the maturing of collective bargaining relationships, increased mutual respect of labor and management, and greater reliance on the grievance procedure as a method of resolving disputes under a contract, the frequency and impact of wildcat strikes have diminished.

They are most likely to arise where lingering hostility or militancy between the parties exists, or where the grievance process does not afford an effective means of conflict resolution. This occurs in the construction and longshoring industries and others where jobs are of short duration, and, therefore, the workers believe immediate confrontation is necessary.

See also Strike.

WITHDRAWAL OF LABOR. *See* Disguised Unemployment; Underemployment.

WITHDRAWALS. When money flows are received by various sectors of the economy, all of the income may not be passed on directly to other sectors. That part of income not passed on is a withdrawal from the income stream. One of the most important withdrawals in the economy is saving by the household sector. Any income received by households but not spent for goods and services is considered saving. While household saving is generally the most important withdrawal, a number of others exist. Quite similar to household saving is business saving, or what is generally called retained earnings.

An additional withdrawal from the domestic circular flow of income is expenditures for imports. When households purchase goods and services produced in other countries it means that the households' income flow has been diverted from domestic businesses to foreign businesses. In a two-sector (household and business) circular-flow model, another withdrawal to consider is tax payments to the government. This withdrawal may be injected back into the circular flow through government spending or, if the government merely accumulates the funds, may remain outside the circular flow.

Withdrawals are an important consideration in macroeconomic theory because they reduce the spending stream. This is especially important in the analysis of the multiplier and the macroeconomic adjustment process. —*Clyde A. Haulman*

See also Circular Flow of Income; Saving.

WOODCOCK, LEONARD FREEL (1911-   ), American labor union leader. Born in Rhode Island, Woodcock spent World War I in England. He returned to the United States with his parents, attended Wayne State University in Detroit, and joined the United Automobile Workers (UAW) in the 1930s. He held many positions in the union, and was an International Vice President in 1970 when, on the death of Walter Reuther, he became the union's fourth president. President Carter appointed him ambassador to the People's Republic of China.

WORKER-UNION RELATIONS. *See* Union Security.

WORKING CONDITIONS. Under the Taft-Hartley Act of 1947, labor and management were expected to bargain over wages, hours, and working conditions—which encompass every aspect of an employee's situation on the job. Working conditions relate to the work rules of the individual company regarding such matters as lunch hours, coffee breaks, relief time, smoking and drinking rules, and dress codes. These working conditions may be negotiated through the collective bargaining process if either labor or management is dissatisfied.

Another working condition stressed in collective bargaining is the safety conditions under which an employee must work. Many jobs are dangerous and many safety rules must be obeyed under penalty of law. Other conditions not covered by law have to be bargained for to assure a worker maximum safety.

WORK RULES are a code of conduct included in a collective bargaining contract that employees are expected to follow in order to carry out their duties effectively and safely. Work rules have been the basis of some bitter battles between labor and management. For example, in 1959 the steelworkers went on strike in an effort to maintain their jurisdiction over work rules which could help protect their jobs. Their employers wanted a free hand in introducing and controlling new methods of production. In 1964, General Motors barely escaped a major strike by agreeing to bargain over such things as lunch hours, coffee breaks, and relief time.

WORK STOPPAGE, an interruption in the regular employer-employee work relationship, usually resulting from an impasse in bargaining over a new contract. It may be caused by the union's decision to strike or by management's decision to halt production until an agreement occurs. Thus, the work stoppage is a tactic used by either party to bring pressure on the other. It occasionally occurs while a contract is in force.

See also Strike.

WORLD BANK. *See* International Bank for Reconstruction and Development.

YELLOW-DOG CONTRACT, an agreement between an employer and a worker, whereby, as a condition of employment, the worker agrees not to join a labor union during the time in which he or she is employed. The condition implies that the worker is subject to automatic discharge if the agreement is violated. This practice of discrimination because of union membership is now illegal, having been outlawed by Congress in 1932.

YOUNG/GROWING DEBTOR. *See* Stages of a Country's Balance of Payments.

Z CURVE. *See* 45° Line.

ZERO PROFITS. *See* Normal Profits.